Encyclopedia of
AFRICAN HISTORY AND CULTURE

Encyclopedia of
AFRICAN HISTORY AND CULTURE

VOLUME I

ANCIENT AFRICA

(PREHISTORY TO 500 CE)

Willie F. Page, Ph.D.
Emeritus Professor of Africana Studies,
Brooklyn College

A Learning Source Book

Facts On File, Inc.

Encyclopedia of African History and Culture
Volume 1: Ancient Africa (Prehistory to 500 CE)

A Learning Source Book
Editorial: Brian Ableman, Edward C. Haggerty,
Bertram Knight, Christopher Roberts, Anthony Yearwood
Consultant: Emilyn Brown

Facts On File, Inc.
132 West 31st Street
New York NY 10001

Library of Congress Cataloging-in-Publication Data

Page, Willie F., 1929-
The encyclopedia of African history and culture / Willie F. Page.
p. cm.
"A Learning Source Book"
Includes bibliographical references and index.
Contents: v. 1. Ancient Africa — v. 2. African kingdoms — v. 3. From conquest to colonization.
ISBN 0-8160-4472-4 (alk. paper)
1. Africa — Encyclopedias. I. Facts on File, Inc. II. Title

DT3 .P27 2001
960'.03--dc21

00-063613

Design: Joan Toro, Joseph Mauro III
Illustrations: Pam Faessler
Maps: Dale Williams

Printed in the United States of America

VB 10 9 8 7 6 5 4 3 2 1

This book is printed on acid-free paper.

For my wife, Grace,
and my sons, Ed & Chris

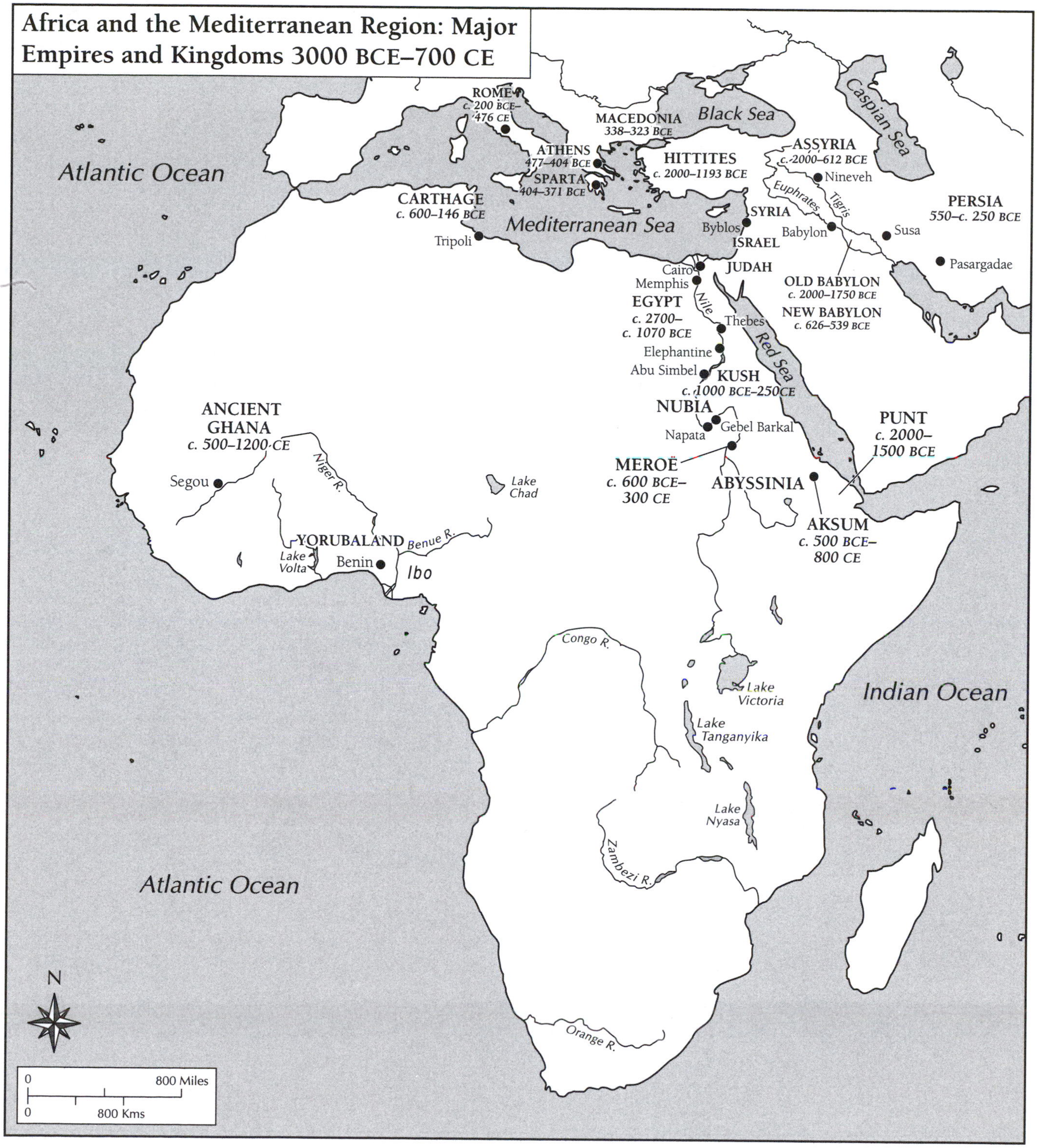
Africa and the Mediterranean Region: Major Empires and Kingdoms 3000 BCE–700 CE
Atlantic Ocean
ROME c. 200 BCE–476 CE
MACEDONIA 338–323 BCE
Black Sea
Caspian Sea
ATHENS 477–404 BCE
SPARTA 404–371 BCE
HITTITES c. 2000–1193 BCE
ASSYRIA c. 2000–612 BCE
Nineveh
Euphrates
Tigris
CARTHAGE c. 600–146 BCE
Mediterranean Sea
SYRIA
Byblos
Babylon
Susa
PERSIA 550–c. 250 BCE
Tripoli
ISRAEL
JUDAH
Pasargadae
Cairo
Memphis
OLD BABYLON c. 2000–1750 BCE
NEW BABYLON c. 626–539 BCE
EGYPT c. 2700–c. 1070 BCE
Nile
Thebes
Red Sea
Elephantine
Abu Simbel
KUSH c. 1000 BCE–250 CE
NUBIA
Gebel Barkal
Napata
PUNT c. 2000–1500 BCE
ANCIENT GHANA c. 500–1200 CE
Niger R.
Segou
Lake Chad
MEROË c. 600 BCE–300 CE
ABYSSINIA
AKSUM c. 500 BCE–800 CE
YORUBALAND
Benue R.
Lake Volta
Benin
Ibo
Congo R.
Lake Victoria
Indian Ocean
Lake Tanganyika
Lake Nyasa
Zambezi R.
Atlantic Ocean
Orange R.
N
0 800 Miles
0 800 Kms

Political Map of Africa in 2001 CE
Atlantic Ocean
MOROCCO
TUNISIA
Mediterranean Sea
Canary Is. (SPAIN)
ALGERIA
LIBYA
EGYPT
WESTERN SAHARA
Red Sea
MAURITANIA
CAPE VERDE
MALI
NIGER
CHAD
SUDAN
ERITREA
SENEGAL
THE GAMBIA
GUINEA-BISSAU
GUINEA
BURKINA FASO
NIGERIA
DJIBOUTI
ETHIOPIA
SIERRA LEONE
IVORY COAST
GHANA
BENIN
LIBERIA
TOGO
CENTRAL AFRICAN REPUBLIC
CAMEROON
SOMALIA
EQUATORIAL GUINEA
SÃO TOMÉ AND PRÍNCIPE
GABON
CONGO
UGANDA
KENYA
RWANDA
DEMOCRATIC REPUBLIC OF THE CONGO
BURUNDI
SEYCHELLES
Cabinda (ANGOLA)
TANZANIA
Indian Ocean
COMOROS
ANGOLA
MALAWI
Atlantic Ocean
ZAMBIA
MOZAMBIQUE
MADAGASCAR
NAMIBIA
ZIMBABWE
MAURITIUS
BOTSWANA
Réunion (FRANCE)
SWAZILAND
N
SOUTH AFRICA
LESOTHO
1
3
2
4
5
1 North Africa
2 East Africa
3 West Africa
4 Central Africa
5 Southern Africa
0
800 Miles
0
800 Kms

Physical Map of Africa in 2001 CE

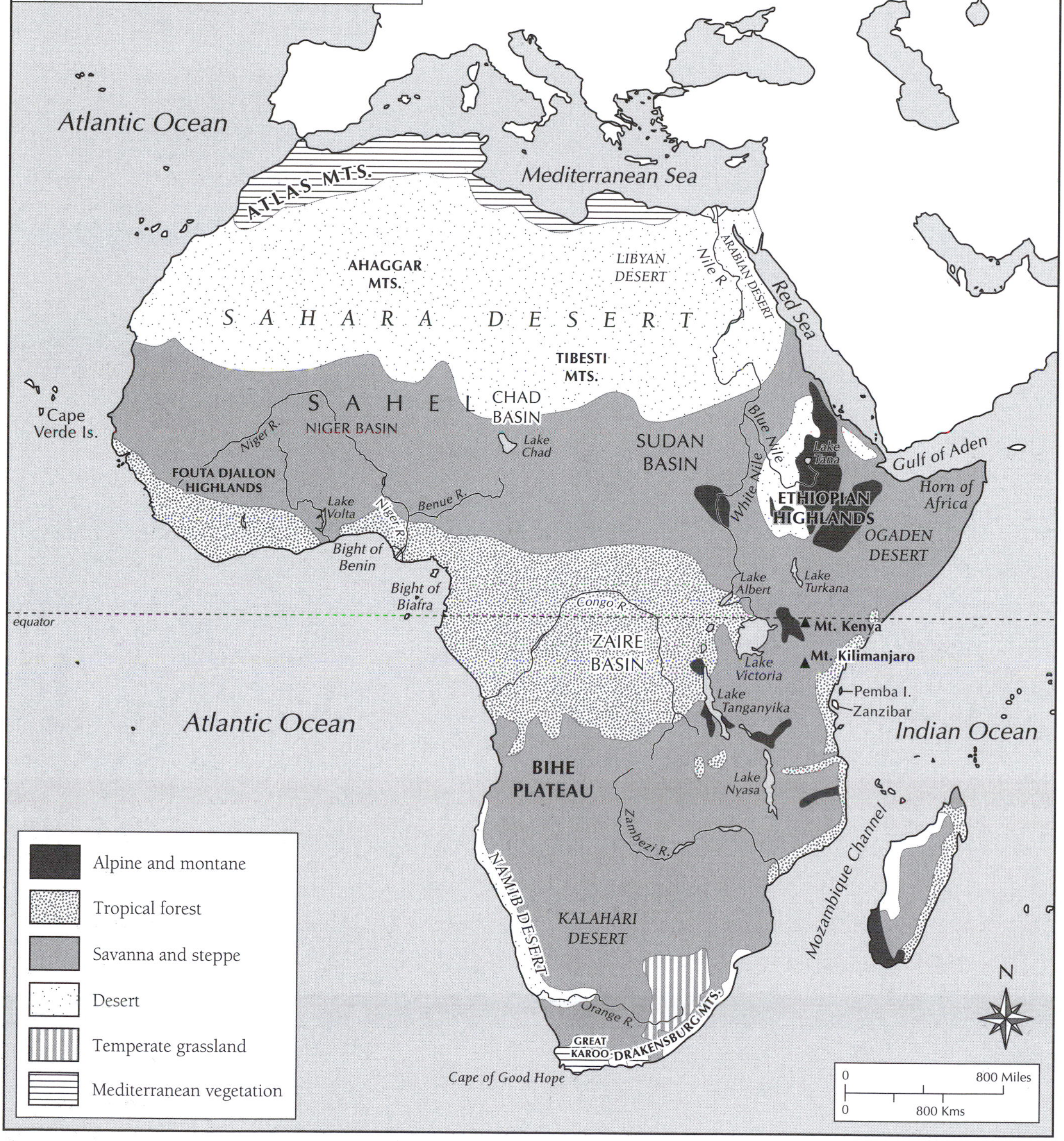

Contents

List of Entries

C

D

E

F

J

K

L

M

N

S

X

Y

Z

List of Images

Photographs and Illustrations

Maps

Introduction

Africa . . . the word conjures up a wealth of mystery and fascination, not just for visitors or other "outsiders," but also for people who live there and know firsthand the vastness of its natural and human riches. To know such a place in its totality is an impossibility; even to comprehend its extremes is a challenge.

Africa, for example, is the world's second-largest continent, occupying 20 percent of the earth's land surface. It contains both the world's longest river, the Nile, and its largest desert. (Technically, of course, Antarctica is the world's largest "desert," but in the conventional view that says that deserts are hot, dry places, nothing compares with Africa's Sahara.) Even the continent's climate and topography are given to great extremes, ranging from hot arid deserts to rain-drenched forests and from below-sea-level depressions to the peaks of Mount Kilamanjaro.

Africa, moreover, is as vast and rich in its people as it is in its geography and natural features. Its population is as diverse as any that could be imagined, with, quite literally, hundreds of ethnic groups and cultures, from the Berbers of North Africa to the Maasai of the plains to the diminutive Mbuti of the forests. No means of livelihood, no religious faith, and no physical type seems to be totally missing in Africa. Africa's history is as vast and rich as everything else about it. The continent is, after all, what many of its inhabitants have called *Alkebulan*, meaning "the mother of humankind." It is in Africa, after all, that our very earliest human ancestors—dating back millions and millions of years—have been identified, which makes Africa the continent with the longest history of all. Africa also has been home to some of our planet's grandest civilizations, from the Egypt of the pharaohs to the gold-rich splendors of medieval Ghana. Africa's cultures are equally grand and enduring, for the continent is home to peoples like the San and the Mbuti, who have continued to live, right into the modern era, virtually unchanged since the dawn of time.

Africa's history also represents, in many ways, a vast mystery; some of it is known, but much of it still awaits unraveling and discovery. For example, how did the Haya, ancient inhabitants of Tanzania, learn to create acceptable-quality steel more than 2,000 years ago? What sparked the massive migration of Bantu-speaking peoples, a population movement that lasted centuries and that transformed the cultural and political landscape of the continent forever? And exactly who were the Egyptians? Were they, as many Afrocentric scholars have argued, black Africans who migrated into the Nile River Valley from elsewhere? Or, as many traditional Egyptologists have maintained, were they a different race—or even mixture of races—altogether?

Riddles like these, however, are not the only reason for the mysteries that mark African history. There is, after all, far less known about Africa's past than about other parts of the world. To some extent this is due to the nature of Africa itself, the vast majority of which has a climate that makes conventional historical and archaeological research difficult, if not impossible. (The Tropics are not kind to aging organic matter.) To an even greater extent, though, this is due to the fact that relatively few African cultures—especially those of sub-Saharan regions—used written languages. This leaves those seeking to learn about Africa's past without the kinds of documents and relics that historians have relied upon so often in their studies of other peoples and cultures. As a result, much of what we know about African history comes to us through oral traditions, which has forced scholars to develop new ways of uncovering the past.

Still, there is a desire—even a need—to discover and unravel Africa's past. For millions of people around the world, in Africa and elsewhere, it is part of a discovery of the traditions and past of themselves, their neighbors, and their ancestors. For others, it is a wish for knowledge. Who can let so vast a part of human life and history go unexplored?

About This Encyclopedia

Obviously, then, writing about African history is a daunting task. However, it also is a task for which there is great need. Much has been written about Africa, but much more needs to be written. This is especially true in regard to volumes like these, which are intended not necessarily for specialists and scholars but for students and general readers who are motivated to find out about the fascinating world of African history.

In line with this understanding of who the readers of these volumes will be, we have structured the encyclopedia chronologically, dividing Africa's history into three major eras. We feel that this division helps make the vastness of African history more manageable—and more easily studied. It also allows students and general readers to go to exactly the volume or volumes they need. Volume I, *Ancient Africa*, deals with Africa up to approximately 450–500 CE (roughly, in terms of classical European history, to the Fall of the Roman Empire). The second volume, *African Kingdoms*, deals with medieval Africa, from the sixth century to the beginning of the sixteenth century CE, which is the period that saw, not only the effects of Islam and the Arab invasions, but also the flowering of some of Africa's greatest and most fascinating indigenous kingdoms. Volume III, *From Conquest to Colonization*, continues Africa's story from the early sixteenth century to the beginning of the nineteenth century, dealing with Africa during the beginnings of European exploration and colonization.

About This Volume

In Volume I, *Ancient Africa*, readers will find everything from information about the earth's earliest hominids to the history and culture of the Egyptians and Nubians to the events that led to the establishment of Roman Africa. These, of course, are the areas for which we have the most historical information, and, as a result, toward which the volume is somewhat skewed. However, readers also will find entries about a wealth of other peoples, places, and events, from the fascinating San and Mbuti peoples to the inhabitants of such splendid and sophisticated cities as Napata, Meroë, and Jenne-Jeno. Other entries cover geography, religion, economy, and many other topics that were part of ancient African life. The reader may find it useful to begin with one of the general articles—such as the ones on archaeology, dance, oral traditions, or women in ancient Africa—or to start with the entry on Africa or Kush and follow the cross-references to further and more detailed information.

When it comes to the study of ancient African history, however, it is important to note several points. First, as already mentioned, traditional historical and archaeological methods have always been difficult to pursue in sub-Saharan Africa. Beyond this, there is the whole question of oral versus written traditions. Cultures like those of Egypt, Kush, and Nubia had records and documents, and we can use these to piece together some semblance of their histories. Other cultures—in fact, the vast majority of sub-Saharan ones—relied almost exclusively upon oral history for the maintenance of their links with both the past and their own traditions. The oral historians of these peoples (or *griots* as they have been called) were responsible for passing down significant historical events and cultural practices from one generation to the next.

These oral traditions, however, often involved the inclusion of information—legends, myths, folklore, and such—that is incompatible with conventional historical methodology. As a result, such oral histories have been met with skepticism on the part of many historians. It always must be remembered, though, that, quite frequently, these oral histories are all we have to go on in our efforts to understand the pasts of many of Africa's peoples. Similarly, it is also important to remember that these histories, even when they seem to encompass magical or otherwise improbable events, often manage to give us an impressive portrait of the minds and spirits of the people who listened to them and passed them on from generation to generation. Because of this, when discussing the origins of a particular culture or the beginnings of a particular society, we often have included not just the bare facts that are known but also the legends and myths that are told about these events.

Another point to remember is that, quite often, when it comes to the history of peoples and cultures, modern scholars are forced to operate by a kind of logic of extension. We may, for example, not have much hard data about the entire ancient history of a particular people. However, we might have fairly reliable accounts of their lives and ways dating back a thousand or more years. If the study of their languages, genealogy, or culture supports the assumption that these people have lived in that same area relatively unchanged we can project what their lives may have been like 500 or even 1,000 years earlier. Such logic cannot be pushed to extremes, however, and for this reason certain groups and peoples have either not been included in this volume or else treated less extensively than it might have been wished; we simply do not have enough information.

A final point to bear in mind returns us to the opening theme of this introduction—the vastness of Africa itself. It is, quite simply, impossible to encompass everything about even ancient Africa in a manageable volume. As a result, choices had to be made about what to or not to include. On the whole, this has been done following several simple criteria. Among the most important of these are, first, What are the most established facts? second, What will be most useful and interesting for the reader? and third, What is most helpful in bringing Africa's ancient past to life for the reader?

A Final Note

Africa is not, of course, simply vast and mysterious. It also is a subject that is, for specialists and general readers alike, endlessly fascinating. It is the hope of everyone associated with this project—the writer, the editors, and others—that some of this great fascination has been communicated. It also is our hope that this work might stimulate those who read and use it to further pursue their curiosity about that land known to many Africans as "the mother of humankind."

How to Use This Book

Throughout, the attempt has been made to make this encyclopedia as accessible and easy to use as possible. Entries are arranged alphabetically, usually according to the most commonly found spelling or representation of that spelling.

The question of spelling, of course, is always a major question when dealing with languages that, for thousands of years, have been oral rather than written. In general, we have tried to give as many common variants as possible, but only within the entries themselves. For easy access to variant and alternate spellings, readers should consult the index, which lists and cross-references all of the alternate spellings that appear in the text.

In general, the entries are written to provide the reader with the basic information needed. To help those who wish to go further, we have linked the contents of each entry with other entries via cross-references. (Cross-references always are shown in SMALL CAPITALS.) Many of these cross-references are embedded within the text of the entries. But many entries also conclude with **See also** references that direct readers to other entries in one of the volumes of the encyclopedia. When using these cross-references, readers should be aware that cross-references embedded in the text have been used only for word forms that agree with the entry word itself. Other word forms are cross-referenced in the see-also references.

Many entries also include suggestions for further reading that guide readers as they search for more in-depth knowledge of a particular area. On the whole, we have included among these works those that are most likely to be easily obtained in libraries, which means that, for the most part, they have been published fairly recently and by publishers whose products are readily available to the general reader.

The volume also contains several appendices of timelines, maps, and a glossary. At the end of each volume there is a cumulative index and a bibliographic section of further readings. These are handy tools for readers with all kinds of interests.

Time Line

Prehistoric Africa

5,000,000 BCE	Period of early hominids
4,400,000 BCE	*Australopithecus ramidus* in Ethiopia
4,200,000 BCE	*Australopithecus anamensis* in Kenya
3,000,000 BCE	*Australopithecus afarensis* ("Lucy") in Ethiopia
	Australopithecines ("Taung Child") in South Africa
2,500,000 BCE	Early Stone Age; Oldowan Toolkit
2,000,000 BCE	Middle Stone Age
	Homo habilis
	Australopithecus robustus in South Africa
1,750,000 BCE	*Australopithecus boisei* in Tanzania
	Homo erectus ("Turkana Boy")
1,500,000 –40,000 BCE	Acheulean Age
200,000 BCE	*Homo sapiens* in tropical Africa
60,000 BCE	*Homo sapiens* in Ethiopia
40,000 BCE	Evidence of mining in present-day Swaziland
40,000 – 7000 BCE	Late Stone Age
20,000 BCE	San people living in southern Africa
15,000 BCE	Qada culture flourishes in Nubia
20,000 – 10,000 BCE	End of Pleistocene epoch and last ice age
9000 - 6500 BCE	Evidence of first calendar in Congo area
8000 BCE	Early domestication of cattle
	Copper discovered and used by Neolithic peoples
	Sahara begins to dry and become a desert
7000 – 4800 BCE	Neolithic Age
6000 – 5000 BCE	Sorghum domesticated in Sudan

Ancient Africa

5000 BCE	Irrigation begins to be used in Egypt
4800 BCE	Badarian culture begins in Egypt; Predynastic Period begins in Egypt
4200 BCE	Naqadah I culture in Egypt
4000 BCE	Egyptians grow food along Nile
	Badarian culture flourishes in Upper Egypt
3700 BCE	Naqadah II culture found in Egypt
3500 BCE	Bronze used for weapons and tools
	Construction of Hierakonpolis, first city in Africa
3400 BCE	Nubian A-Group flourishes
3200 BCE	Nagadah III culture found in Egypt
3050 BCE	Beginning of Archaic Period (Dynasties 1–2) in Egypt
3000 BCE	Upper and Lower Egypt are unified under Menes
	Berbers arrive in North Africa
2780 BCE	Nubian B-Group flourishes

2700 BCE	Egypt's King Sahure reaches Punt by boat
2705 BCE	Egyptian Old Kingdom (Dynasties 3–8) begins
2575 BCE	King Khufu of Egypt builds Great Pyramid
2400 BCE	Kingdom of Kerma begins in Nubia
2300 BCE	Nubian C-Group flourishes
2213 BCE	Egyptian Old Kingdom ends and First Intermediate Period begins (Dynasties 9–11)
1991 BCE	Egyptian Middle Kingdom (Dynasties 12–13) begins
1668 BCE	Egyptian Middle Kingdom ends and Second Intermediate Period (Dynasties 14–17) begins
1570 BCE	Egyptian New Kingdom (Dynasties 18–20) begins
1550–1070 BCE	Horses introduced into Egypt
1525–1417 BCE	Thuthmose I–IV in Egypt
1400 BCE	Amarna period begins in Egypt
	Iron/steel smelted in Tanzania
1375 BCE	Ramesses the Great
1200 BCE	Sea Peoples attack Egypt
1070 BCE	Egyptian New Kingdom ends and Late Period (Dynasties 21–25) begins
1000 BCE	Bantu migrations begin
	Immigrants from Saba, in Yemen, arrive in Ethiopia
	Pre-Aksumite period begins in Ethiopia
900 BCE	Napata Kingdom flourishes in Nubia
900–600 BCE	Nok culture flourishes
800 BCE	Phoenicians found Carthage
750 BCE	Kushite dynasty controls Egypt
663 BCE	Assyrian invasion ends Kushite rule of Egypt
600 BCE	Camels introduced to Egypt and Sahara
590 BCE	Meroitic period in Kush
500 BCE	Aksum emerges as a power
	Carthage dominates North Africa
	Hanno explores Africa's Atlantic coast

The Greco-Roman Period and Beyond

332 BCE	Alexander the Great conquers Egypt; Ptolemaic Dynasty begins
264–146 BCE	Punic Wars; Carthage is destroyed
200 BCE	Meroë civilization begins
30 BCE	Roman conquest of Egypt
24 CE	Roman conquest of Nubia
100 CE	Iron technology spreads throughout Africa
200 CE	Christian monasticism in northeastern Africa
	Akan migrate into what is now Ghana
250 CE	Nubian X-Group (Ballana culture) rises
400 CE	Beginning of the end of Bantu migration
350 CE	Decline and fall of Meroë
335 CE	King Ezana rules in Aksum
395 CE	End of Roman rule in Egypt
400 CE	Ancient Ghana Empire begins
	Town of Jenne-Jeno established
429 CE	Vandals arrive in North Africa
451 CE	Coptic Christians split from Roman Church
541 CE	Christian Nubia begins

A

Abu Hamed Area located at the fourth cataract of the NILE RIVER, within present-day Sudan. In ancient times, Abu Hamed was fought over by EGYPT and NUBIA.

Abu Hamed, which is dominated by an S-shaped bend of the Nile, is found in what was once Upper Nubia. This stretch of the river runs in a southwestward direction for about 150 miles (about 241 km) before returning to a northerly direction at the end of the bend. Here the river is rocky and fast, and it was often dangerous to ancient navigators.

More than 2,500 years ago, the highly sophisticated Nubian culture flourished in this area. As part of the long struggle between Egypt and Nubia for control of the area, the armies of the Egyptian king THUTMOSE I (r. c. 1493–1482 BCE) advanced through Sudan before stopping just south of Abu Hamed. The region was invaded once again, around 671 BCE, when ASSYRIANS defeated the armies of the Egyptian KUSH empire that stretched from Abu Hamed to the NILE DELTA.

Between the sixth and eighth centuries, the people of Nubia converted to Coptic Christianity and resisted invasions from Egypt, which had been under Muslim rule since the seventh century. Between the thirteenth and fifteenth centuries, however, Abu Hamed finally became Muslim-controlled. The area of the fourth cataract between Abu Hamed and GEBEL BARKAL has proved fruitful to modern archaeologists, who have discovered there many signs of ancient human life, including rock inscriptions, cemeteries, and churches.

Abusir, pyramids of Mortuary complex of Fifth Dynasty kings in ancient EGYPT; once a site of pyramids, sun temples, and funerary temples. The ancient burial grounds of the OLD KINGDOM at Abusir (also called Abu Sir) were located in northern Egypt about 10 miles (16 km) from the Giza plateau. Located between the cities of GIZA and SAQQARA, the site held fourteen pyramids, several sun temples, and tombs of royalty and officials. Only four of the pyramids remain.

Perhaps the most notable distinction at Abusir is the construction and decoration of the sun temples. In addition to the more common pyramids, mortuary temples, and tombs, several of the Fifth Dynasty kings, including NUESERRE and USERAF, built temples with great stone pillar obelisks in honor of the sun god RA.

The mortuary temples built with the pyramids at Abusir were unusually decorated; walls and columns were intricately sculpted in relief, with palm, lotus, and papyrus plants standing out from the surface. Columns with lotuses at the head, or the capital, are the oldest known examples of this type of relief sculpture.

Although they were built after the great pyramids of Giza, the Abusir pyramids are much smaller, with the tallest rising to 223 feet (68 m). The pyramids at Abusir have the typical north entrance to the chambers.

Still standing today are the unfinished pyramid of Neferefre, the unfinished pyramid of Neferikare, the pyramid of Niuserre, and the pyramid of Sahure. Some parts of the Abusir complex have not yet been excavated.

Abydos Considered the home of the ancient Egyptian god OSIRIS and an important royal site during Egypt's early Dynastic Period. Archaeological excavations of the tombs at Abydos began in 1895. These suggest that each ruler built large rectangular brick enclosures intended as funerary palaces. However, no human remains have yet been found in these structures.

Of all the royal monuments found at Abydos, the temple of the Nineteenth Dynasty pharaoh SETI (Sethos) I (r. c. 1318–1304 BCE) is the largest and most notable. Among its features are impressive representations of the god Osiris, as well as of Seti and his successor, RAMESSES II (r. c. 1304–1236 BCE). Seti's temple includes a Royal List, also called King's List, that gives the names of many of Egypt's rulers. Located in a gallery known as the Hall of Ancestors, this list is part of a wall relief that depicts Seti and Ramesses paying homage to the rulers who came before them.

Several ancient Egyptian Royal, or King's, Lists have been discovered, including the papyrus Turin Canon, the Abydos and Karnak Lists, which were found in temples, and the Sakkara List, which was found in a tomb. Although these lists tend to arrange the names of Egyptian rulers in chronological order, none of them is complete by any means. Instead, they seem to include those names that their authors determined to be important or valuable for one reason or another.

Abydos enjoyed royal favor throughout its history. However, its actual role in royal burials is unclear. With the exception of Queen Merneith, there is little indication that other rulers were buried at Abydos.

Abyssinia Ancient name for the country currently called ETHIOPIA. Scholars differ over the origin of the word. According to some, the name appeared during the rise of AKSUM in the first century. Others speculate that the word originally referred to an ethnic group that lived in old Ethiopia. Still others suggest that the word derives from the Arabic word for "mixed" in reference to the fact that the area is comprised of many ethnic groups.

See also: TIGRAY (Vol. I).

acacia gum Also known as gum arabic, this is one of the oldest and most widely used of the natural gums harvested from species of the acacia tree.

Dating back 5,000 years, to the time of the ancient Egyptians, gum arabic has been used as a binder in inks and cosmetics and as an agent in the process of mummification. Ancient Egyptian inscriptions refer to *kami*, a type of gum arabic used in painting as a pigment binder and adhesive.

Today, acacia gum is widely cultivated in tropical Africa from Mozambique to Somalia, Sudan, Ethiopia, Kenya, and Tanzania. In Sudan, there are special "gum gardens" in which the trees are propagated from seeds. Elsewhere, the gum is collected from wild trees. Oddly, the best yield of gum arabic comes from trees that are in an unhealthy condition. Hot weather, poor soil, and lack of moisture are all factors that improve gum production.

Commercial gum arabic is still widely used today in pharmaceutical preparations, in inks and other art supplies, and in practically all categories of processed foods.

Acheulean Age One of two major phases of the early Stone Age in Africa.

The Acheulean Age began approximately 1.5 million years ago and lasted for more than 1 million years. Its hallmark was the evolution of sophisticated toolmaking, specifically the development of hand axes, cleavers, and picks. (The name *Acheulean* is derived from the place in southern France where the hand ax was first discovered.) The era is often associated with the corresponding biological development of *Homo erectus*, a large-brained, bipedal toolmaker whose remains have been found in many parts of Africa.

Acheulean technology also included the development of the use of fire, which further contributed to the modification and refinement of existing tools. Tools specifically designed for hunting were another important achievement of this age.

Acheulean toolkit Prehistoric set of axes and scrapers; named for the valley in France in which early discoveries of the tools took place. Although tools of this type

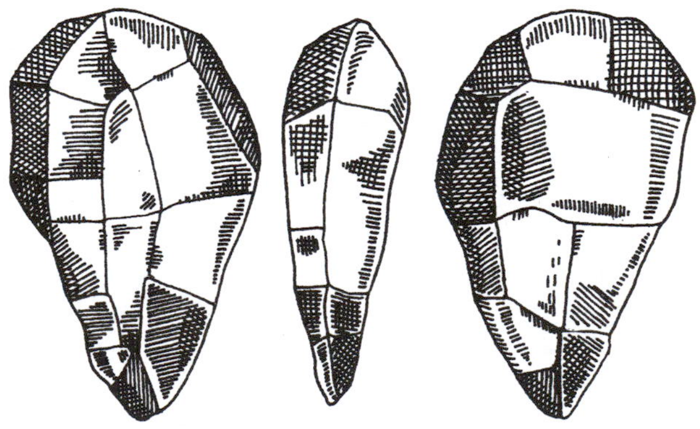

The left, top, and right-side views of an Acheulean hand ax found in Kamoa, Congo (formerly Zaïre), show the heavier, flaked construction characteristic of this Stone Age hand tool.

were first unearthed in southern France, the vast majority have been found in Africa. In general, they are sharper and heavier than the older OLDOWAN TOOLS, with chipped flakes and sharpened points. Most were used, in one way or another, in the preparation of food.

See also: STONE AGE (Vol. I).

Addis Ababa Capital and largest city of modern Ethiopia. The capital city and major kingdom of ancient Ethiopia was AKSUM (500 BCE–1000 CE).

Adefa Ancient capital city also known as Adafa, formerly located in the central highlands region of ETHIOPIA. Following the overthrow of the kings associated with the kingdom of AKSUM (c. 100–600 CE), Zagwe kings seized power and ruled Ethiopia from Adefa (c. 1150–1270 CE). From this vantage point they extended their power through trade and established Christian settlements.

See also: ADEFA (Vol. II).

Further reading: Samuel Kasule, *The History Atlas of Africa*, (New York: Macmillan, 1998); Harold G. Marcus, *A History of Ethiopia* (Berkeley: University of California Press, 1994).

Adulis Port on the Red Sea that flourished during the height of power of the kingdom of AKSUM (c. 100–600 CE). Beginning as a fair-sized village, within a few centuries Adulis expanded into a center of world trade. Merchants arrived there from ARABIA, GREECE, INDIA, and CEYLON and then traveled for several days by caravan to the Aksumite kingdom, climbing nearly 7,000 feet above sea level in the process. Adulis also served as a link to the ports that stretched to the central coast of East Africa. This enabled Aksum to continually diversify and replenish its stock of trade goods.

See also: ADULIS (Vol. II).

Further reading: David Buxton, *The Abysinnians* (New York: Praeger Publishers, 1970); Basil Davidson, *African Civilization Revisited* (Trenton, N.J.: Africa World Press, Inc., 1998); Jean Doresse, *Ethiopia* (New York: Frederick Ungar Publishing Co., 1959).

Afar People who have long lived on the arid coast of ETHIOPIA's eastern DANKIL province; also, the language spoken by the Afar people. Sedentary PASTORALISTS, the Afar apparently migrated to the Dankil area from the Ethiopian Highlands, perhaps as long ago as the prehistoric era. Living in the extremely arid conditions of the DANAKIL DESERT, even in ancient times the Afar settled as close as possible to whatever sources of water they could find. Over time, as their numbers increased and they became divided into chiefdoms, diminishing water supplies led to frequent clashes with SOMALI peoples.

See also: AFAR (Vols. II, III).

Afar Depression Low-lying area along the northeastern coast of ETHIOPIA. The Afar Depression is part of the great RIFT VALLEY, which runs from Southwest Asia to southeastern Africa. At approximately 300 feet (91 m) below sea level, the Afar Depression is Ethiopia's lowest point. The depression is occupied by the AFAR people, who also live on the nearby DANAKIL DESERT and in parts of DJIBOUTI.

Africa Name of the second largest continent of the world, covering an estimated 11,687,187 sq. miles (30,269,814 sq. km), and situated south of Europe between the Atlantic and Indian Oceans.

Over the centuries, Africa has been identified by many names: Among Greek and other ancient travelers, for example, it was known as Aetheiopia ("Land of Burnt Faces"), Corphye, Ortegia, and Libya. The Moors, Nubians, and Numidians, on the other hand, frequently called the continent Alkebulan, meaning "mother of humankind."

The name *Africa*, however, is likely to be a corruption of a Carthaginian place name originally used by the Berbers. The Carthaginians, who traced their origins to Phoenician seafarers, had come to the northern coast of Africa as early as 1000 BCE.

By 800 BCE, the Phoenician trading stations had become full-fledged colonies. Their capital was at Carthage, the site of modern-day Tunisia. There, Phoenicians and indigenous Berber agriculturalists co-existed, creating a distinct Carthaginian culture that lasted until its conquest by Rome in 146 BCE. At that time, Rome assumed control of the trading colonies, identifying the northernmost region of the continent as Africa.

Afro-Asiatic (or Hamito-Semitic) Family of languages once spoken primarily in North Africa, including the Semitic, Berber, Kushitic, Chadic, and Egyptian branches. The Semitic branch of languages from both Africa and Asia, includes ARABIC, the major spoken, religious, and commercial language of North Africa today, and the language that was spoken by the Harari. The languages in the Berber branch of the Afro-Asiatic family were spoken throughout North Africa by various nomadic peoples, including the TUAREG, in the regions of MOROCCO, TUNISIA, and ALGERIA. The KUSHITIC languages were spoken in parts of ETHIOPIA, SOMALIA and regions of East Africa. The languages of the Kushitic branch were BEJA, Agew, Burgi-Sidamo, Galla, and Omotic. The Chadic languages of Nigeria and CAMEROON included the Tubu and Zaghawa languages. The most important Chadic language was HAUSA, which was spoken in the kingdoms of the Hausaland. The Egyptian branch of languages includes the languages spoken throughout ancient Egypt.

Other languages that fell into the Afro-Asiatic family were AMHARIC, once spoken in ETHIOPIA and the language of the Solomonic Dynasty; GE'EZ, the literary language of the Ethiopian church from the fourth century CE until today; and Tigrinya, spoken in northern ETHIOPIA, ERITREA, and TIGRAY.

afterlife Concept or belief that life continues after death.

Many African societies express their belief in the afterlife through specific rituals and shared social experiences. One of the strongest beliefs is that the afterlife is an ordered world in which individuals reside after death. This world may exist in caves, in forests, or, as the Abaluyia and others believe, in a place beyond earth.

Although beliefs about the afterlife differ among societies, one common theme is that those who have passed on still have at least some role in the living community, which is why specific acts, or rituals, are performed for the dead. These rituals range from simple burial rites to elaborate ceremonies that might require creating a shrine or making offerings of food, drink, or money.

The choice of which ritual to perform generally is determined by economic circumstances, living arrangements, or long-standing traditions. Groups like the Lodagaa of Burkina Faso, for example, believe the land of the dead lies to the west, separated from this world by the River of Death. At funerals, friends and relatives provide the symbolic fee of twenty cowries, which is needed by the deceased in order to cross the river. In contrast, groups like the MBUTI place personal belongings in the grave, while other groups bury household items for the deceased's use in the afterlife.

In most societies, the funeral plays a critical role following the death of a loved one, allowing people to share their grief and reinforce the ideals they hold about life after death. The Hadza, who are hunter-gatherers, provide an interesting example. They bury their dead in a relatively simple ceremony. However, they return sometime later, always at night, to perform the Epeme dance. This dance is done to ensure the wellbeing of the living by honoring the dead. Another group, the Yombe, who live in northern Zambia, inform the community of a death by playing a special rhythm on a drum. After wrapping the deceased in a shroud, the Yombe create a grave, called a "house," that has several rooms. The Yombe then turn the deceased to face the place of their birth so they can find their way home. Some societies, such as the AKAN, hold a second burial ceremony to mark the end of a mourning period. For them, this second ceremony is a final recognition that the dead have successfully achieved their place in the spiritual realm.

Agaw (Agau, Agew) Ethnic group situated in the central and northern highlands of Ethiopia.

Through the study of regional speech patterns, linguists have traced the continuous presence of the Agaw as far back as 7000 BCE.

Mainly cultivators of the land, the Agaw were overshadowed by the neighboring kingdom of AKSUM during its rise to political statehood. Like the BEJA and NUBA, Agaw speakers were subject to Aksum's demands for tribute, as well as its repeated attempts at religious conversion. In the eighth century, Islamic expansion limited Aksum's sea trade and weakened the power of the Aksumite state. As a result, the Aksumite kingdom was relocated deeper within Agaw territory. There, Aksumite military colonies created a feudal society, while Aksumite priests continued to spread Christian religious teachings. Frequent intermarriages between Agaw women and Aksumite soldiers led to the beginnings of an intermingling of the two groups.

Between 900 and 1000, the Agaw rebelled, and continued warfare began to erode the hold of the Aksumite military. As a countermeasure, Agaw males were recruited into Aksum's military, where they adopted Aksumite culture. Over time, a number of these Agaw recruits became wealthy and joined the Aksumite ruling elite. In 1137, they established their own kingdom in the Lasta Mountains and ruled most of northern and central Ethiopia. Also known as Zagwes, these Agaw kings reestablished Aksumite culture and political ties in the region.

See also: ZAGWE DYNASTY (Vol. II).

Agbor Ancient IBO settlement located in western Iboland. Little is known about the history of Agbor, although Ibo people probably occupied the region in ancient times. Evidence from surrounding areas indicates that the earliest Ibo settlers in Agbor may have been the Ado na Idu, Nri, or Isuama. These inhabitants probably lived in a manner similar to their Ibo neighbors, subsisting primarily through agriculture. Loose village structures were centered on a council of elders who provided leadership and authority. ANCESTOR WORSHIP was the traditional Agbor religion, although they believed in a supreme god who ruled the universe.

age grades Ancient system designed to instill cultural identity through the social interaction of men from different generations.

In Africa, age grades typically involve the youngest and oldest male members of a society. Grouping these individuals by age allows a useful exchange of human interaction; youthful ideals and enthusiasm are tempered by the wisdom and experience of elders. In most groups, age grades operate on an independent basis, free from family influence, and, unlike AGE SETS, they are organized within a local residential area.

In Africa, various types of age grades have developed over the centuries, perhaps in response to changing societal needs. The earliest groups may have functioned as decision-making bodies for their communities. Over time, age grades became known for both defending their communities in times of war and participating in public work projects. In Mande society, for instance, seven age grades, each with a specific group name, are maintained at all times, while new ones are created every seven years.

See also: SECRET SOCIETIES; INITIATION RITES (Vol. I).

Age of Metals Period during which several ancient African cultures developed the technology for smelting brass and iron for use as tools and ornamentation.

The exact time period, chronology, extent, and role of the Age of Metals in ancient Africa has been a subject of controversy among historians, archaeologists, and other scholars. Much is known about the BRONZE and IRON AGES in ancient Egypt. Elsewhere, however, far less is known. Indeed, for many years the vast majority of authorities maintained that most of Africa witnessed no Bronze Age at all, progressing, instead, directly from the late STONE AGE to the Iron Age. More recently, however, evidence has been found of Bronze Age items in NUBIA and southern Sudan, as well as in present-day Mauritania. Whether these items and the technology behind them were local in origin or whether the objects or their technology were imported from a place such as CARTHAGE is not known.

According to those who have witnessed re-creations of the process, Haya steelmaking was carried out in a small furnace. The bowl of the furnace was approximately 18 inches (45.7 cm) deep and lined with mud obtained from a termite mound. (Composed of grains of silica and alumina, the termite mud does not absorb much water.) The top of the furnace was shaped like an inverted cone. Made of iron slag, it stood about 5 feet (1.52 cm) high. At its base, eight blowpipes were inserted at various depths.

A fire was lit with swamp grass and fed with charcoal produced outside the furnace. Goatskin bellows were then used to force air through these pipes and into the furnace in order to produce a fire with an extremely high temperature. After the smelting process, according to the witnesses, the Haya dismantled the furnace and recovered lumps of steel from the bed of swamp grass charcoal.

More, however, is known about the development of iron-making technology. In particular, investigations dating back to the 1970s suggest that advanced and highly complex iron making was known among the Haya people of present-day Tanzania at least 2,000 years ago. Handed down through generations of oral history, this iron-making technology apparently was sophisticated enough to create good-quality steel.

Further reading: Adu Boahen, *Topics in West African History* (London: Longman, 1964); Daniel Chu and Elliott Skinner, *A Glorious Age in Africa: The Story of Three Great Kingdoms* (Garden City, N.Y.: Zenith Books, 1965); Peter R. Schmidt, ed., *The Culture and Technology of African Iron Production* (Gainesville: University of Florida Press, 1996; Ivan Sertima, ed., *Blacks in Science: Ancient and Modern* (New Brunswick, N.J.: Transaction Books, 1989).

age sets Widespread system that assigns specific tasks to adult males from various clans and communities.

Over the centuries, age sets have played an important role in reinforcing traditions and creating stability in African societies. Age sets, for example, have been widely used in Africa for military defense. They also have been used to initiate young men into secret practices or in the knowledge of underlying systems of belief. In this way, young men learn to respect and value the knowledge of those elders who have guarded and maintained those practices throughout their lives.

Elder members of the age sets have certain rights as well, and these rights form the basis for strict social controls. For example, at a certain age young men are taught to assume responsibilities in marital and community affairs. Often, however, some elders within the system continue to exert their influence. They might do this by determining the age at which younger men are allowed to acquire adult status. Other areas in which elders often continue to have influence are testing young men's suitability for marriage and helping to choose suitable brides for marriageable young men.

Age sets play an interesting role among the MAASAI, whose young boys compete to enter age sets known as "moran." Once they enter the age set, the boys often spend an extended period preparing to become adults. This preparation sometimes goes on until the men are well into their twenties. After young men obtain moranhood, their loyalties become focused on their families and herds.

See also: INITIATION RITES (Vol. I).

agricultural revolution Process by which humans began to cultivate their food; sometimes called the Neolithic revolution.

In northern Africa, the agricultural revolution took place about 7,000 years ago and significantly changed the way food was produced. No longer simply hunting and gathering their food, the inhabitants of the region now began to cultivate their crops with the aid of tools designed specifically for that purpose. Most scientists believe that this change in food production methods was introduced into Africa from the Near East. However, there is some evidence to suggest that African agriculture may have developed on its own, in the once-fertile area of what is now the SAHARA Desert.

The major crops produced in Africa during this period included yams and rice, as well as various types of millet, sorghum, and palm oil. Other plants, such as wheat and barley, most probably were imported from western Asia at a later date.

About 4000 BCE, the NILE RIVER valley began to play an important part in the agricultural revolution. The banks of the Nile produced a variety of crops, and the Nile Valley became one of the earliest centers of food production in the region. With the increase in agriculture, grain exports and other commerce began to develop. These activities helped establish a solid and prosperous economy, and the society that emerged laid the foundations for pharonic Egypt.

See also: AGRICULTURE (Vols. I, III); CROPS (Vol. II).

agriculture The skills needed to raise animals and crops for food.

The Origins of Agriculture Of all the innovations of early humans, crop cultivation and animal husbandry are widely considered to be the two most important. Neither of these activities, however, could have occurred until the glaciers retreated and previously waterlogged landmasses dried out. Only then could people establish year-round, farm-like settlements in those areas. These settlements, in turn, led to large, dense populations and, ultimately, to stratified urban societies. These politically organized societies eventually evolved into fully developed civilizations.

Cattle may have been domesticated in Africa even earlier than 9000 BCE. A team of researchers, led by University of Massachusetts anthropologist Dr. Charles M. Nelson, recently reported on findings made at three sites in the Kenya highlands, approximately 25 miles (40 m) from Nairobi, Kenya. There the researchers found the remains of cattle. After testing their findings using radiocarbon dating techniques, the group reported that the remains apparently were 15,000 years old. The researchers' further investigations suggested that these cattle were domestic, rather than wild, animals.

The two key elements of agriculture—planting crops and domesticating animals—appear to have developed independently in at least two areas of the world, Southern Asia and South America. In Asia, this process seems to have begun in the hills north and east of the Tigris and Euphrates Rivers. Animals and farm-like establishments dating back to 9000 BCE have been uncovered in Iran, Iraq, Israel, Syria, and Turkey. From there agriculture spread to Mesopotamia by 6000 BCE. It reached China by about 2700 BCE.

The Development of Agriculture in Africa The first signs of African agriculture are evident in the fifth millennium BCE in Egypt, where crops thrived in the fertile Nile floodplain. Population growth spurned the need for increased food production through agricultural technology. With the arrival of Arab immigrants at the end of the first millennium BCE, agricultural technology passed to greater parts of West Africa. However, the use of hoes and digging sticks in much of Africa indicates that Africans did not merely borrow Arabian technology but developed their techniques over time.

Researchers representing Southern Methodist University, the Geological Survey of Egypt, and the Polish Academy of Science recently reported on discoveries they had made in the area of Wadi Kubbaniya, a now-desolate region in Egypt's Western Desert. Their report indicates that between 17,000 and 18,500 years ago—when much of Europe was still covered with ice—Africans in that area were growing barley, capers, chickpeas, dates, lentils, and wheat.

West Africa was the most important area of agricultural development with its savanna-based cultivation sustaining cereals, rice, yams, sesame, shea trees, and oil palms. East Africa savanna regions tended to produce subsidiary crops like corn, yams, cassava, and peanuts. In the humid equatorial region, root crops like yams, cassava, and taro were grown along with corn and bananas. Hearty legumes like cowpeas, kidney beans, and lima beans were cultivated throughout Africa.

African agriculture is based on either vegetation or cultivation. Vegetative agriculture is garden-style growing in which tubers or shoots are placed in the ground to yield a plant. Yams were probably the first crops used for garden-style growing. Cultivation-based agriculture depends on the use of seeds for larger crop yields and is more labor-intensive. Since crop rotation is a relatively new technology in Africa, land was traditionally overcultivated and abandoned when exhausted.

The tools found most readily in traditional agrarian African societies are the digging stick, hoe, and spade. Because plows were not traditionally used, the soil could only be cultivated for a short period of time and production was relatively low. Once the plot of land was chosen, existing plants were burned to produce a vitamin-rich ash fertilizer. After the seeds were planted and sewn, the fields had to be pruned periodically of weeds during crop growth. Wild animals and insects were always a threat to the harvest, as was drought. After the crops were harvested, the land was replanted and the process began again. Without a plow, the land could only be used for two to three years, or until the nutrients had been completely leached from the soil. It was then abandoned for up to twenty years so that native plants would have time to refortify the soil. The farmer then migrated to a new plot of land to start the process over. As populations grew, finding enough land to maintain this shifting cultivation method was difficult. Nonetheless, it continued for centuries in much of Africa, particularly the central and eastern regions. In equatorial Africa, little soil preparation was done other than stripping the land, which often resulted in extremely poor crop yields. In the semi-arid regions, the planting season was shortened to only a few months due to the long dry season.

The social implications of agrarian societies varied in different parts of Africa. Among many peoples, the men typically prepared the fields by burning and clearing them. The women usually did all the labor intensive planting, sowing, and harvesting. Other than this common male-female labor division, agricultural customs among peoples differed greatly. Division of land might have been based on age, gender, democratic allocations, or other traditional systems.

To many African people, working the soil was as much a ritualistic process as it was a way to grow food. In places like Dahomey, for example, the people appealed to a higher god whom they believed created the world by furrowing the earth. Most peoples performed elaborate ceremonies to bless the planting, sowing, and harvesting of the crops. Seeds were often passed among family members as sacred objects. Priests were called upon to ask the gods for a successful harvest. This close association between traditional cultivation techniques and religion has resulted in conservative agricultural advances throughout much of Africa.

Yams have long been a staple in many parts of Africa. Native to Africa, these wild tubers have been domesticated into the modern variety over the centuries. They were relatively easy to grow because they required simple garden-style cultivation. Although they have low nutritional value, these dense carbohydrates store well in both dry and humid climates. Combined with a variety of fruits and vegetables, they have provided a good base to the African diet for centuries.

An equally important native plant is the oil palm. It was originally found only in the forest, but with domestication, it has become one of the most important sources of oil in Africa. Plantains, a member of the banana family, were also important to much of the African population, particularly in the rainforests. Native to Asia, the plantain was probably introduced to eastern coastal Africa by Arab traders who arrived as early as the first century BCE. Over a period of several hundred years, a variety of other crops were introduced to Africa through foreign contact. Some, like the cassava, became important staples in parts of western, central, and eastern Africa.

Seed plants are more labor intensive than tubers or plantains to cultivate. In Africa, the most common traditional seed plants were the millet variety of cereals. Found in temperate savanna regions, seed plants required properly prepared fields. The field was first cleared, usually with a hoe. After the seeds were sown, the fields required constant care to keep weeds at bay and to prevent animals from pillaging the ripening plants. Once harvested, the millet was fermented or ground into flour.

One of the most important domesticated plants grown in Africa was sorghum. Native to Africa, sorghum has been grown in North Africa for nearly seven thousand years. Beginning in the first millennium, sorghum cultivation began to rapidly spread as iron tools were introduced to different parts of Africa. Other important millets included digitaria, bulrush (pearl) millet, and finger millet. Today, many of the traditional millet crops have been replaced by corn.

One of the few crops in Africa that requires wet cultivation is rice. Native Guinea rice has been cultivated around the Guinea coast and Niger basin for more than two thousand years. Indian Ocean traders brought a common variety from Southeast Asia between the ninth and tenth centuries. Because rice was easy to store and did not need to be ground before eating, it became popular among the upper classes along the coast during the following centuries.

Further reading: Adu Boahen, *Topics in West African History* (London: Longman, 1964); Bayard Webster, "African Cattle Bones Stir Scientific Debate," in Ivan Van Sertima, ed., *Blacks in Science: Ancient and Modern* (New Brunswick, N.J.: Transaction Books, 1989).

Ahmose I (Amosis) (c. 1570–1546 BCE) *First king of the Egyptian Eighteenth Dynasty and founder of the period historians call the New Kingdom.*

Ahmose was the son of King Seqenenre Ta'o II and his formidable and powerful queen, Ahhotep (Aahotep). Ahmose became pharaoh at a very young age, succeeding both his father and his older brother, Ahmose, the last king of the Seventeenth Dynasty. Because of his youth, Ahmose's mother, Queen Ahhotep, probably served as co-regent during the early years of his reign.

As pharaoh, Ahmose continued Egypt's war with its Asian enemy, the HYKSOS. Ahmose triumphed, driving the Hyksos out of Egypt. Next, he reconquered NUBIA, returning it to Egyptian control. With his borders secure, Ahmose then set about consolidating his power at home.

The last years of Ahmose's reign were devoted to reorganizing Egypt's system of government. Ahmose also built many religious and funerary monuments, although few have survived to modern times. He was particularly devoted to AMUN, the god who was to assume even greater importance during the reigns of his successors.

Ahmose ruled for about twenty-five years, and examination of his well-preserved mummy suggests that he was close to thirty-five years old when he died. He and his queen, Ahmose Nefertari, produced one son, AMENHOTEP I, who succeeded his father as pharaoh.

The face of Egyptian pharaoh Ahmose I (c. 1570–1546 BCE) is painted on this Eighteenth Dynasty mummy case. Egyptian Museum, Cairo, Egypt © *Gianni Dagli Orti/CORBIS*

Ahmosid/Thutmosid lines

Ahmosid/Thutmosid lines Group of thirteen kings and one queen who ruled ancient Egypt as the Eighteenth Dynasty (c. 1570–1320 BCE). The Eighteenth Dynasty begins what historians call the New Kingdom.

The Eighteenth Dynasty

King	Ruled (BCE)
AHMOSE I	c. 1570–c. 1546
AMENHOTEP I	c. 1546–c. 1525
THUTMOSE I	c. 1525–c. 1512
THUTMOSE II	c. 1512–c. 1504
THUTMOSE III	c. 1504–c. 1450
HATSHEPSUT (with THUTMOSE III)	c. 1501–c. 1482
AMENHOTEP II	c. 1450–c. 1425
THUTMOSE IV	c. 1425–c. 1417
AMENHOTEP III	c. 1417–c. 1379
AMENHOTEP IV (AKHENATEN)	c. 1379–c. 1364
SMENKHARE	c. 1364–c. 1361
TUTANKHAMUN	c. 1361–c. 1352
AY	c. 1352–c. 1348
HOREMHEB	c. 1348–c. 1320

Akan

Akan People, who have long lived in the forest region of modern coastal Ghana, Togo, and the Ivory Coast.

There is continuing debate about the origin of the Akan people, who eventually inhabited an area that reached from the Volta River to the basin formed by the Pra and its tributary rivers. One theory is that the Akan came from the open country in the northwestern corner of modern Ghana. Other theories suggest that they migrated to the region from areas such as LIBYA, EGYPT, ABYSSINIA, Chad, and, in particular, ancient GHANA. The association with ancient Ghana is also supported by anecdotal evidence and the fact that certain names are shared by the Akan and the Mandinka, who have strong links to ancient Ghana. The matrilineal tradition of ancient Ghana was also found in some of the Akan states, including the Ashanti.

Regardless of the precise origin of the Akan, it is widely believed that these people began migrating into the forest region 2,000 years ago. In time, distinct kingdoms began to form and occupy areas in the region. The Fante, for example, settled in the southwest, the Akwamu and the Akyem in the northeast, and the Ashanti in the northwest. The Ashanti warriors were fierce fighters, and they forged alliances with neighboring states to conquer their adversaries and become one of the most powerful nations in West Africa.

See also: AKAN (Vols. II, III); AKYEM (Vols. II, III); ASHANTE (Vol. II); ASHANTE EMPIRE (Vol. III); FANTE.(Vols. II, III); GOLDEN STOOL.(Vol. III).

Further reading: A. A. Anti, *The Ancient Asante King* (Accra, Ghana: Volta Bridge Publishing, 1974).

Akan gold weights

Akan gold weights Small, brass objects, some in the shape of plants, animals, and figures. Others are engraved with markings and designs. These weights are generally believed to be relics of the ancient Akan people of the Ivory Coast.

The Portuguese called those objects gold weights because they saw them being used for the purpose of weighing gold. Historians believe, however, that only a few of the objects, which also have been called Ashanti gold weights, were actually used as gold weights. Opinions differ about what the true purpose of these objects might have been.

Some historians maintain that the Akan gold weights were a means of artistic expression. Others believe that the objects represent a classification system used by the ancient Akan people. For these scholars, the weights represent a kind of ancient encyclopedia cataloging such entities as creatures of the land, air, and sea, as well as various other material and non-material things. Still another view is that the weights were intended to aid the memories of those citing proverbs. (A particular symbol, for example, may be nothing more than a design in itself, but when considered with its metal base, it might represent the message of a proverb. In this way a particular weight could, with its many, complex symbols, represent a very detailed text.)

Regardless of what their exact purpose, the gold weights are thought by some scholars to be examples of ancient African writing. The symbols on the objects have been shown to match symbols used in ancient Libyan writing, suggesting that the Akan people may have contributed to the development of writing in northeastern Africa. The symbols are arranged together on single metal pieces, which may mean that they stand for particular words or phrases.

Akhenaten (Amenhote, Amenophis IV) (c. 1379–1364 BCE) *Ninth king of the Eighteenth Dynasty.*

Known as the heretic pharaoh because of changes he instituted in Egyptian religion, Akhenaten, the son of AMENHOTEP III and Queen Tiye, began his reign as Amenhotep IV. He married NEFERTITI, and the couple produced six daughters. The early years of his reign reflected his traditional upbringing, in particular, the longstanding dedication to the god AMUN.

In the fifth year of his reign, Amenhotep began to promote a form of monotheism that sought to radically alter Egyptian religious and political structures. He replaced worship of Amun with devotion to a new god, ATEN, and changed his royal name to Akhenaten to indicate his allegiance to the new deity. He then moved the religious capital from its traditional site at Thebes to a newly constructed capital at AKHETATEN (also known as el-Amarna).

Akenhaten sought to impose the new religion on his subjects by suppressing the cults of other Egyptian deities. He destroyed the deities' temples, building new ones devoted exclusively to Aten. Religious services at the new capital were frequently led by the king and queen themselves, with Akhenaten serving as the one and only high priest of the new cult. This brought him into direct conflict with Egypt's established priesthood, which was devoted to the cult of Amun.

Akhenaten's new cult was never really accepted or even understood by his subjects, and most people continued to practice the old religion. Later generations came to regard the religious changes he made as heretical. After his death, Akhenaten's successor, TUTANKHAMUN, moved to restore Egypt's traditional religion, making Thebes once again the country's religious capital.

Although Akhenaten's monotheistic cult ultimately proved unsuccessful, during its brief existence, it produced significant changes in Egyptian art. These are evident not only in the temple decorations at el-Amarna but also in the literature of the period.

Akhetaten (el-Amarna) Religious capital of Egypt during the reign of the pharaoh AKHENATEN (AMENHOTEP IV) and consecrated for the worship of the god ATEN.

Also known by its modern Arabic name, el-Amarna, the city of Akhetaten was founded by the heretic pharaoh Akhenhaten (c. 1379–1364 BCE). Situated midway between Egypt's old religious capital at Memphis and the royal city of Thebes, the city was dedicated exclusively to the worship of Aten. There, Akhenaten led services devoted to the new, monotheistic deity with whom he hoped to supplant Egypt's traditional gods. The most important buildings in the city were the temples and palaces devoted to Aten, but there also were administrative offices as well as houses for nobles and artists. In addition, outside the city, there were tombs intended for the nobility and the royal family.

Akhetaten served as Egypt's capital only during the reign of Akhenaten. After his death, the city was abandoned and its monuments dismantled or destroyed.

Aksum Capital city and major kingdom of ancient ETHIOPIA that flourished 500 BCE–1000 CE; noted for its trade networks, architecture, and traditions of Christian faith.

According to many anthropologists, it is quite likely that humankind first emerged in the Great RIFT VALLEY that cuts across Ethiopia from the Red Sea to Lake Turkana. In the valley, archaeologists have found fossil skeletons dating back 3.5 million years. By the time of the late STONE AGE, several prehistoric populations inhabited present-day Ethiopia, most notably the Omotic and Kushitic language speakers. Initially HUNTER-GATHERERS, these peoples eventually learned to cultivate various grains and other crops and to domesticate sheep, cattle, donkeys, and goats. They established patterns of life that have continued, among their descendants, down to the present time.

During those thousands of years, the indigenous peoples also interacted with the numerous immigrants who came to the region, especially from across the Red Sea. One of the first groups of immigrants, the Semitic-speaking traders from Saba, or Yemen, in southwestern Arabia, began arriving about 1000 BCE, or even earlier. Actively involved in the Red Sea trade along the Arabian Peninsula, they sought to expand their trading ties along the Ethiopian coastline. Settling in the mountainous regions of TIGRAY, AMHARA, and the Shoa country to the south, these Sabean settlers produced the culture generally known as pre-Aksumite. ADULIS, near modern-day Mitsiwa, was the most important pre-Aksumite trading center, maintaining important links both along and across the Red Sea. At the same time, the immigrants added their knowledge of irrigation and hillside terracing to the plow and hoe cultivation of the indigenous Kushites. The result was an important network of farms that developed in the region's valleys and foothills.

Sabaean settlement continued for almost a thousand years, with frequent contacts and intermarriages between the Kushites and Sabaean settlers. The result of all these interchanges was a distinctive culture from which the BETA ISRAEL, or Falasha, trace their origins and Judaic faith.

By about 500 BCE, a number of descendant colonies united to form a powerful city-state whose capital, Aksum, was situated on a northeastern plateau overlooking the Red Sea. This geographical vantage point strengthened the kingdom's trading networks with EGYPT, Arabia, and other trading ports along the East African coast. Spreading out from its primary port at Adulis to secondary ports on the Gulf of Aden, Aksum's trading networks eventually extended as far as the eastern Mediterranean and the Middle East, India, and even present-day Sri Lanka.

As time passed, Aksum became a strong trading competitor with the kingdom of MEROË (also known as KUSH). *The Periplus of the Erythraean Sea,* a shipping guide recorded in the first century BCE, describes Aksum as the primary market for ivory in the northeast. The kingdom also supplied elephants for military conquests waged by the Ptolemaic dynasty in Egypt, as well as rhinoceros horn, animal hides, gold dust, spices, tortoise shell, frankincense, and myrrh.

By the fourth century, Aksum's trading ties had grown to encompass the eastern Roman Empire, which ensured the kingdom even greater prosperity and interna-

Stone monuments, or stelae, at Aksum in Ethiopia, dating from the fifth century BCE are thought to mark royal burial sites. *© Davis Bartruff/CORBIS*

tional recognition. Indeed, at the height of Aksum's power, its rulers dominated an area extending from present-day Sudan to Somalia and from the coast of the Red Sea to the Nile Valley. At times, Aksumite power even stretched across the Red Sea to the Arabian peninsula.

During this period, Aksum grew in wealth, as well as in political and military influence. Archaeological excavations have recovered everything from gold and silver (which initially may have been imported from outside the kingdom) to silk and muslin. Glassware from royal burial tombs has also been discovered, as have metal tools from Egypt and spices originating from locations as distant as the Far East. There also is evidence that Aksumite manufacturing was sufficiently developed for the kingdom to make—and even export—glassware and crystal, as well as brass and copper items.

Aksum has a number of monuments, known as stelae, that are significant for their size and purpose. Aksum's tallest stele measures 108 feet (33 meters) high and weighed between 550 to 700 tons, making it the world's largest monument of this type. These structures are believed to have served as markers for the subterranean tombs of Aksum's kings. Carved to look like multistory buildings, the stelae have doors, windows, and base-plates for offerings.

How does a building remain standing for thousands of years? Among those who apparently knew the answer were the ancient Sabean settlers of Aksum, who were one of many ancient populations who knew the secret of building with dry stone. This form of architecture uses no mortar to bind the stones together, and archaeologists have traced surviving remnants as far back as 300 CE. These remains include castles that stood several stories high and were built with stepped walls, battlements, and corner towers. Other notable examples of Aksum's dry stone architecture include St. Mary of Zion, one of the earliest churches built in the kingdom.

Aksum was one of the first African kingdoms to mint its own coins, and archaeologists have recovered Aksumite coins in sites as far away as Yemen. Although from the third to the seventh centuries, gold, bronze, and silver were all used to make the kingdom's coins, its gold coins were carefully matched, in their weights and inscriptions, to the coins of Rome. Over the years, archaeologists have been able to use these coins to undertake detailed studies of the kings and rulers of Aksum.

Aksum's most noted—and most successful—ruler was King Ezana (r. c. 320–350 CE), whose authority extended from southern Arabia to the western edge of the Ethiopian Highlands. Known by the traditional title of *negusa negast,* Ezana held dominion over numerous chiefs and princes, all of whom owed him both allegiance and monetary tribute.

The conversion of this remarkable king to the Christian faith marked a significant chapter in Aksum's history and had a profound impact on the region. Christianity had apparently come to Aksum many years before, brought to the kingdom by merchants from Byzantium. However, the religion had made few inroads in the kingdom until Ezana embraced the faith near the end of his reign.

The precise reasons for Ezana's conversion are unknown, although there is speculation that it might have been due to either influence of the Roman emperor Constantine or Aksum's close trading ties with GREECE. Another influence may have been Frumentius, a Syrian missionary who served as Ezana's tutor. Whatever the ultimate reason for Ezana's decision, its significance to Ezana and his kingdom is made clear by the way in which Aksumite coins began to bear images of the Cross of Christ rather than either symbols from Aksum's traditional, polytheistic religions or images of Ezana himself. A more lasting effect of this conversion, however, was the way in which it allied Aksum with now-Christian Rome and isolated Aksum from the people within the region who continued to follow traditional polytheistic religions.

Inscriptions left behind by King Ezana provide details about a number of wars. Some of these stemmed from religious conflicts; many others were caused by Ezana's monetary demands on the region's independent chiefdoms. (When the Tsarane, for example, refused to pay tribute, Ezana led a military expedition against them.) Other conflicts may have been resolved by enslaving and selling captives to Rome, as in the case of the BEJA nomads from the Red Sea hills, whose forced resettlement was the punishment meted out for their raids against merchant caravans.

About 350 CE, at the height of Aksum's power, King Ezana ordered an invasion of the island of MEROË. Towns and villages were razed and crops were destroyed. Prisoners and livestock were seized and many Kushites fled, settling, perhaps, in Kanem-Bornu (in what is now central Sudan). An inscription left by King Ezana states: "Twice or thrice they had broken their solemn oaths and had killed their neighbors without mercy, and they had stripped our deputies and messengers whom I sent to inquire into their raids. . . . And as I had warned them, and they would not listen but refused to cease from their evil deeds. I made war on them, they fled without making a stand, and I pursued them for twenty-three days, killing some and capturing others."

Renewed Christian fervor came to Aksum in the wake of the Councils of Nicea (c. 325 CE) and Chalcedon (c. 451 CE). The decisions made by these councils effectively made heretics of the MONOPHYSITES—Christians who had previously maintained the purely divine nature of Christ. When the councils rejected this interpretation, the Monophysites became subject to persecution and, eventually, to violence. In the wake of this, many Monophysites took refuge in Aksum. There they found asylum and ignited a period of religious enthusiasm that became known as "the second conversion." Among the more notable figures during this period were the Syrian monks known as the Nine Saints. Establishing a strong monastic tradition in the region, they ultimately helped found what became known as the Aksumite Christian or Ethiopian Orthodox Church.

After the Muslim conquests in the seventh century, the trade routes that had made Aksum so rich were blocked or even changed. As a result, the Aksumite kingdom lost its economic preeminence. Forced to resume an agricultural focus, the kingdom faced dwindling natural resources caused by soil erosion and overexploitation of trees. The Aksumites became enmeshed in serious religious conflicts when they decided to resettle in the interior central highlands. There they faced serious revolts from groups such as the Beja and the AGAW, avowed Semites who rebelled against the Christian conversion being preached by the Aksumites. The final blow to Aksum came in the tenth century, when the Banu al-Hamwiyya, an Agaw group led by a woman known as Gudit (Judith) or Isato, sacked the Aksumite kingdom.

See also: AKSUM (Vol. II) BYZANTINE AFRICA (Vols. I, II); ETHIOPIA (Vols. I, II, III).

Further reading: Basil Davidson, *The Lost Cities of Africa* (New York: Little, Brown; 1972); Elizabeth A. Isichei, *A History of Christianity in Africa* (Grand Rapids, Mich.: William N. Eerdmans Publishing, 1995); Richard Pankhurst, *The Ethiopian Borderlands* (Lawrenceville, N.J.: Red Sea Press, 1997).

Alexander the Great

Alexander the Great (356–323 BCE) *King of Macedonia, conqueror of Persia, and ruler of an empire extending from southern Europe to modern-day Pakistan and India.*

Alexander was the son of Philip, king of MACEDONIA, and Olympias, a princess of Epirus (Albania). As a child, he studied literature, science, and medicine under the Greek philosopher Aristotle. By his late teens he was taking an active part in the affairs of state, ruling as regent in his father's absence, serving as an ambassador in Athens, and commanding part of his father's army at the battle of Chaeronea.

Crowned king at twenty, Alexander quickly established his authority by executing Macedonian conspirators and enemies. He then set out to restore Macedonian rule over the Greek cities of Thessaly, Athens, and Thebes, razing the latter city and crushing all opposition to his rule. He then turned his eyes eastward in search of new lands to conquer.

In 334 BCE, Alexander attacked Persia and, with a force of only 42,000 soldiers, defeated the larger army of the Persian king Darius. Forging southward, Alexander's army arrived in EGYPT in 331 BCE. The Egyptians, who loathed the Persians, welcomed Alexander and named him pharaoh. While in Egypt, Alexander established the city of Alexandria, which became a seat of learning and economic power for 900 years.

Alexander then led his armies back to Persia, defeating King Darius once again, and marching eastward to the Indus and Ganges Rivers. Everywhere his armies went, Alexander spread Greek ideas, reformed unjust laws, and established himself as the supreme ruler. Just thirty-three years old when he died, Alexander had created an empire that stretched from southern Europe to India, encompassing virtually all of the world then known to Europeans.

Algeria

Algeria Country in North Africa that borders the MEDITERRANEAN SEA in the north, NIGER, CONGO and Mali in the south, Mauritania, Western Sahara, TUNISIA and LIBYA in the east, and Morocco in the west. Over the course of its long history, Algeria has belonged to many great empires, from the PHOENICIANS to the Romans. Algiers is its largest city and capital.

Algeria's first inhabitants were the BERBER people. According to cave paintings dating from 8000 to 2000 BCE, the Berbers were cattle herders and hunters. Around the ninth century BCE, the Phoenician civilization in present-day Tunisia established trading posts, including Algiers and Annaba, along the Algerian coast. Between the third and second centuries BCE, coastal Algeria was known as NUMIDIA and was ruled by Berber kings. From around the first century BCE to the fifth century CE, Algeria was controlled by the Roman Empire.

alphabet

alphabet Symbolic system allowing written communication. Alphabets were largely unknown among the vast majority of ancient African languages, which remained, until fairly recently, primarily spoken languages. Despite this, however, Africa did see the development of three major alphabetic writing systems: COPTIC, GE'EZ, and Vai.

Coptic The Egyptians, of course, were one of the first peoples to develop an organized system of writing, and their HIEROGLYPHICS date back to the fourth millennium BCE. Coptic script emerged more than 3,000 years later and represented the last stage of Egyptian writing. It also represented what would turn out to be the only native African writing system based on what could properly be called an alphabet, with characters clearly representing phonetic sounds.

Based largely on the Greek alphabet, Coptic script contained an additional seven letters, borrowed from the Egyptian demotic script, to denote sounds not used in the Greek language. Coptic, however, did not immediately gain acceptance in Egypt. In fact, although it was developed as early as the second century BCE, Coptic did not gain widespread use in Egypt until the third century CE. It was at this time that Christian missionaries, wanting to make their religious scriptures accessible to Egyptians, used Greek characters to translate these writings into Egyptian.

Coptic script replaced both the demotic script, which used more than 400 symbols, and the even older system of hieroglyphics—which included an unwieldy 130 characters used to convey sound and an additional 4,000 hieroglyphs used to represent ideas of enhanced meaning. The Coptic system gradually dropped some of its borrowed demotic characters and became highly standardized.

In 451, when the Coptic Church broke away from the Orthodox Church, it adopted Coptic as its liturgical language. It remained the script of the church until at least the fourteenth century.

Ge'ez An Ethiopian script, Ge'ez was used in writing the AMHARIC language and dates to c. 300 CE. In the Ge'ez script, each character stands for a syllable rather than a phonetic sound. Ge'ez became the primary written language of Ethiopia, used not only to record the lives of the saints and to compose religious poetry, but also to write stone inscriptions, philosophical tracts, and chronicles of royalty. The Bible was translated into Ge'ez between 400 and 600 CE. Ge'ez remained in use as the literary language of Ethiopia until the modern era, and it is still the liturgical language of the Ethiopian Orthodox Church today. Unlike other Semitic languages, Gee'ez is writen and read from left to right.

Other Languages and Alphabets Much later, in the nineteenth century, the Vai, a West African people who speak a language of the MANDE branch of the NIGER-CONGO family of languages, also developed a written script. Like Ge'ez, Vai (also called Vei and Gallinas) is a syllabic, rather than a phonetic, writing system. It is still used in Liberia and Sierra Leone.

Several other native African languages, including HAUSA and Swahili, adopted writing systems that borrowed Arabic script, which Arab conquerors had brought to North Africa in the seventh century CE. Arabic, however, lacks the "e" and "o" vowel sounds, as well as consonants that represent the sounds "ch," "g," "p," and "v," all of which are used in many African languages. For this reason, the Roman alphabet—which arrived with Christian missionaries and European colonists—replaced Arabic script in written African languages in the nineteenth century.

See also: WRITING (Vol. I).

Further reading: Bruce M. Fagan, *World Prehistory: A Brief Introduction*, 3rd edition (New York: Harper Collins, 1996); Ali Mazuri, *The Africans: A Triple Heritage* (London: BBC Productions, 1986).

Amanitare

(c. 12 BCE–12 CE) *Queen of ancient Kush.*

Queen Amanitare and her husband, King Netekamani, were the corulers of Musawarat es SafrA, located just 20 miles (32 km) from MEROË. Established about 1 CE, Musawarat became a trading center linking southern and western Africa, Asia, and the Mediterranean. Among Amanitare's achievements was the construction of several important temples at NAGA, some 20 miles (32 km) from Musawarat. Archaeological excavations at Naga have unearthed a Lion Temple that is distinguished by an engraved image of a four-armed, three-headed lion god. Also of interest is a nearby smaller temple whose mix of architectural influences reflects Musawarat's complex trading ties. The walls of this smaller temple contain a remarkable relief of Amanitare's son, the celebrated military hero Sherkarer.

See also: KUSH (Vol. I).

Amarna period

Era of religious and political turmoil during the reign of AKHENATEN (AMENHOTEP IV), c. 1379–1364 BCE.

After Akhenaten changed his name to reflect his devotion to the god ATEN, the young pharaoh set out to establish a new capital dedicated solely to the worship of that deity. He named this new city AKHETATEN, meaning "the Horizon of Aten." Decorations created for the religious monuments in the new city resulted in a new and unique art form. Instead of the rigid depictions of royalty that were traditional in Egyptian art, Akhenaten and his family were shown in a more human manner, engaged in everyday activities. The literature of the period, particularly its poetry, also underwent radical changes, which found expression in hymns and devotional pieces created in praise of Aten.

The Amarna period, which sometimes is called the Amarna Revolution, lasted barely three decades, coming to an abrupt end with the death of Akhenaten. Despite its relatively short duration, however, it proved to be an important phase in Egyptian religious and political history.

Amenhotep I (Amenophis)

(r. c. 1546–1525 BCE) *Second king of Egypt's Eighteenth Dynasty; son of Ahmose I and Queen Ahmose Nefertari.*

Amenhotep I was very young when he came to the throne, and, as was often the case during the NEW KINGDOM, his mother was co-regent during the early years of his reign.

Amenhotep enjoyed a relatively peaceful reign and apparently was well-liked by his contemporaries. He focused his attention on securing and consolidating the empire created by his father's successful military campaigns against the HYKSOS and NUBIA. Under Amenhotep's rule, Egypt enjoyed both economic prosperity and great artistic expression, which were manifested in the many monuments he built and restored.

Amenhotep was the first pharaoh to separate his mortuary temple from the tomb in which he was actually to be buried, a practice that continued by his successors. He died without a direct heir.

Amenhotep II (Amenophis) (c. 1450–1425 BCE) *Sixth king of the Eighteenth Dynasty; son of Thutmosis III and his second wife, Hatshepsut-Merytre.*

Amenhotep II is best remembered as a man of considerable physical strength, an avid sportsman, and a great military leader.

As a ruler, it fell upon Amenhotep II to preserve and protect the immense empire he had inherited from his father, the legendary Thutmosis III. His efforts began immediately upon assuming the throne, when the city-states of Asia revolted against Egyptian rule. Amenhotep II quickly proved his strength as a military leader. Displaying incredible fierceness in battle, he rapidly conquered his enemies. Later in his reign he conducted equally fierce wars in Syria and NUBIA. During these campaigns he was reputed to have publicly displayed the bodies of captives both on the prow of his ship and on the walls of the royal capital at Thebes.

Upon his death, Amenhotep II was succeeded by Thutmosis IV, his son by his marriage to his sister, Tio. Buried in the VALLEY OF THE KINGS, Amenhotep's tomb was unearthed in 1898. At that time it was found to contain not only his mummy, but also those of several other pharaohs.

Amenhotep III (Amenophis) (c. 1417–1349 BCE) *Eighth king of Egypt's Eighteenth Dynasty, whose reign marked a period of great artistic achievement.*

The son of THUTMOSIS IV and Queen Mutemwiya, Amenhotep III enjoyed a long and peaceful reign, during which Egypt enjoyed a period of economic prosperity. He was particularly noted for the luxury and splendor of his royal court. He also was a patron of the arts, building and restoring monuments throughout his kingdom.

Like many pharaohs, Amenhotep III maintained a large harem. However, his chief wife, Tiye, was a strong, capable woman who played an important role in the governing of Egypt. The royal couple had four daughters and two sons. When he died at the age of fifty, Amenhotep III ultimately was succeeded by his younger son, who would later change his name from Amenhotep IV to AKHENATEN.

See also: AHMOSID/THUTMOSID LINES (Vol. I).

Amenhotep IV See AKHENATEN.

Amenirdis I (r. 760–747 BCE) *Priestess and sister of King Piankhy, founder of Egypt's Twenty-fifth Dynasty (c. 747BCE).*

Amenirdis is notable as the first woman of ancient KUSH to hold the title of "Divine Wife of AMUN." Initially controlled by the powerful male priesthood of Amun, young women of ruling families were first appointed as priestesses during the eighth century BCE. Their appointment allowed kings to assert greater control over the city of Thebes as well as land and wealth consecrated to the god Amun. After he established the Twenty-fifth Dynasty of EGYPT, PIANKHY continued this tradition. Some historians have argued his decision gave greater legitimacy to the Kushite conquest.

For a brief period, Kushite priestesses formed their own dynasty, adopting the daughters of reigning kings upon whom they conferred title and responsibility. Amenirdis I passed the title on to Shepenupet II, Piankhy's daughter. Surviving records indicate this practice continued under the reign of Taharqa (690–664 BCE), whose daughter Amenirdis II inherited the title but died before her formal installation.

In keeping with the sacred traditions of the gods, priestesses of Amun lived a celibate life, attended by servants and administrators. However, the recognition granted to them was in many ways equal only to that of the reigning Kushite kings. Priestesses were given a formal coronation, royal temples, and extravagant burials that immortalized their deeds. Although they were restricted to the city of Thebes, it appears that they held a high degree of political power and amassed great wealth. The restoration and construction of public buildings, monuments, and statues reflect the good works of these ancient women. Temples built to honor Amenirdis still stand at MEDINET HABU. Their numerous wall reliefs show the priestesses making ritual offerings to Amun on behalf of the king.

See also: KANDAKE (Vol. I).

Further reading: Barbara Watterson, *The Egyptians* (Oxford, Eng.: Blackwell Publishers, 1998); *General History of Africa II Ancient Civilizations of Africa*, Abridged Edition. G. Mokhtar, ed. (Paris: UNESCO, 1990); *Black Women In Antiquity*, Ivan Van Sertima, ed. (New Brunswick, N.J.: Transaction Publishers, 1997).

Amhara An ethnic group in the central and western regions of Ethiopia.

Throughout their history, the Amhara maintained a political and cultural dominance over other ethnic groups in the region. The primary language of ETHIOPIA, for example, has long been AMHARIC, the Semitic language of the Amhara. Likewise, the Ethiopian Orthodox Church, which largely shapes religious life in Ethiopia, is closely allied with the Amhara. One of the main reasons for the success of this people is the closeness of family relationships among the Amhara themselves, for whom kinship and land ownership are closely linked.

There are at least two major accounts of the origins of the Amhara. One declares the Amhara to be descendants of Sabean settlers, or Himyarites, who crossed the Red Sea from present-day Yemen. According to archaeologists, these Sabean immigrants, who may have arrived in Ethiopia as long ago as 500 BCE, developed both the hybrid language known as GE'EZ and an original form of Ethiopic script. These settlers also brought with them their advanced knowledge of irrigation and terracing systems, which greatly aided in establishing durable methods of farming in the arid lands of Ethiopia. Throughout their history, the Amhara have earned their livelihood from the soil, raising teff (a type of cereal), as well as corn, wheat, legumes, and vegetables.

Another account of the Amhara's origins, taken from the Kebra Nagast, Ethiopia's national epic, asserts that the Amhara are descendants of King Solomon and Queen Makeda, the legendary queen of Sheba. On the basis of this, the Solomonic dynasty of Ethiopian rulers, who were primarily of Amharic descent, carried the title "Lions of Judah."

See also: AGAW (Vol. I); AKSUM (Vol. I); AMHARA (Vol. III); SOLOMONIC DYNASTY (Vol. II).

Amharic Member of the Semitic branch of the Afro-Asiatic (or Hamito-Semitic) family of languages. Amharic has served as the primary language of ETHIOPIA for many centuries and, for almost a millennium, has been both the official language of Ethiopia, used in court and government documents, and the language spoken by the dominant population group of Ethiopia.

Like other Ethiopic languages, Amharic is descended from GE'EZ, the ancient ecclesiastic and literary language of Ethiopia. The grammatical forms used in Amharic, however, clearly place it in the Semitic branch of Afro-Asiatic languages, which were introduced into Ethiopia by Arab traders during the first millennium BCE. Although it strongly resembles other Semitic languages in its use of grammatical forms, Amharic employs a syntax much more similar to that of non-Semitic Ethiopian languages.

Amharic is one of the few African languages that produced an ancient written literature. Amharic derived its written script from the alphabet of ancient south Arabia. Though originally written from right to left (as Arabic is), Amharic script—probably as a result of Greek influence—later changed direction from left to right. Amharic did retain the practice, common in many Semitic written languages, of separating words by placing two dots between them.

See also: LANGUAGES (Vol. I).

Amratian culture Early culture in predynastic Egypt.

See also: NAQADAH I AND II (Vol. I).

The ankh, right, and other ancient Egyptian amulets were thought to possess ritual power. Museo Egizio di Torino, Turin, Italy © *Gianni Dagli Orti/CORBIS*

amulets Objects, ornaments, or symbols imbued with ritual power that are worn, carried, or placed in graves; also known as charms.

Based on a number of archaeological excavations, amulets appear to have been in use in Africa from an early period. In ancient times, they were made from materials of the natural environment, including animal bone, shells, and rock. One of the earliest known charms was recovered in the Sudan and dates back to the Neolithic period (c. 5000–3000 BCE). There is speculation among ethnologists that this particular relic resembles a type of fertility charm comparable with ones still used by the FULANI.

In southern EGYPT the population of el-Badari (c. 4300–3800 BCE) was associated with recovered amulets that resembled hippopotamuses and gazelles. These items may have functioned within BADARIAN CULTURE as magic charms used for protection during the hunt. They also might have been used to prevent the spirits of dead animals from causing harm. Hunting charms were important to many African societies and, in later periods, were sewn onto hats or shirts. This practice continued in regions of South Africa and Nigeria until well into the modern era.

During the period in Egyptian history known as the MIDDLE KINGDOM (c. 2106–1633 BCE), amulets were used in a wider context. Egyptian mothers tied charms on a string and placed them around the necks of their children for their protection. This also was done as a cure for illness. High child mortality rates were not unusual in Egypt, and many such charms contained spells and prayers written on papyrus.

Charms used to protect Egyptian pharaohs in death were made of gold, lapis lazuli, and obsidian. These objects were placed between the bandages of the pharaoh's mummified remains, while large scarab amulets, containing spells and prayers, were placed on the heart to protect it. A considerable number of COWRIE SHELLS were also used in Egyptian burials as a powerful symbol of rebirth and regeneration.

The use of charms and amulets continued in many parts of Africa in ancient times, playing an important role in major RITES OF PASSAGE. Among the Pende (Bapende) of ANGOLA and Congo (formerly Zaïre), for example, elders continue a custom even today in which they carve small ivory masks known as *minyaki*. Initiates wear these masks as amulets as they undergo rituals that prepare them for adulthood.

See also: BEADS (Vol. I); CLOTHING (Vol. I); JEWELRY (Vol. I).

Further reading: Martha G. Anderson and Christine Mullen Kreamer, *Wild Spirits Strong Medicine* (New York: Center for African Art, 1989); John R. Hinnells, ed. *Dictionary of Religions* (London: Penguin Books, 1997); Gay Robins, *Women in Ancient Egypt* (Cambridge, Mass.: Harvard University Press, 1993); Barbara Watterson, *The Egyptians* (Oxford, Eng.: Blackwell Publishers, 1998).

Amun (Amun-Ra) The ancient Egyptian sun god, whose name means "concealed one."

Egyptian worship of Amun dates back to the earliest times, but Amun did not become the preeminent, all-powerful deity until the pharaohs of the Eighteenth Dynasty attributed their military successes to him. At that time, Amun was merged with the northern sun god Ra, becoming Amun-Ra, "King of the Gods." Worship of Amun became widespread, and the priests who served the deity were rich and powerful. As a result, those priests exercised great influence over the pharaohs.

Amun usually was depicted in the form of a strong young man, often with the head and curled horns of a ram. According to Egyptian mythology, Amun was married to the goddess Mut. Their son was the god Khonsu.

The cult of Amun-Ra flourished at the Egyptian capital of Thebes until the reign of the pharaoh AKHENATEN (Amenhotep IV). At that time, worship of Amun-Ra and the other gods of the Egyptian pantheon was abandoned and replaced by devotion to a single new deity, ATEN. Ahkenaten's attempt at a monotheistic revolution, however, did not last long. After his death, Akhenaten's successors restored Amun to the supreme place in the ranks of the gods.

Amyrtaeus (r. 404–399 BCE) *Egyptian pharaoh, believed to be from Libya, who was the only king of Egypt's Twenty-Eighth Dynasty.*

Amyrtaeus is believed to be a relative of another Amyrtaeus, who years earlier had tried to oust the Persians from the NILE DELTA region. After succeeding Darius II to the throne in 404 BCE, Amyrtaeus fought a successful military campaign against the Persians, who occupied Lower Egypt.

By 400 BCE, Amyrtaeus had gained control of Upper Egypt. Beyond this, little is known about Amyrtaeus's reign other than that, according to Egyptian tradition, he broke an Egyptian law that led to his son being forbidden to succeed him.

Anansi Spider god of the Ashanti people of present-day Ghana. According to Ashanti myth, Anansi, a trickster god, is the son and intermediary of the sky god Nyame, on whose behalf Anansi brings rain and floods. Traditionally, Anansi is a cunning figure, living by his wits. He is credited with creating the first human; in some legends he is also responsible for creating the separation between day and night. Anansi was also seen as having taught people how to sow grain and to use a shovel in the fields. Although in Ashanti legends Anansi is rarely bested by any human, in at least one myth he is beaten after an encounter with a girl made out of wax. When the girl refuses to speak to him, Anansi hits her with his legs. Anansi is then stuck to her, allowing people to approach and attack him.

ancestor worship Widespread tradition of worshiping deceased relatives, prevalent among West African peoples such as the Bantu, Shona, and Edo.

Ancestor worship centers on the belief that the deceased can intercede in the lives of their living relatives. Although supported by no universal set of beliefs, the practice of ancestor worship is similar in most African societies. Believers purport that ancestors who are properly honored will bring good fortune to their relatives on earth. Some ancestors may become evil spirits who haunt the living, cursing them with disease or natural disaster. The family must provide the appropriate sacrifices to appease the evil spirit. If the spirit continues to plague the living, his or her bones may be dug up and burned.

Ancestors are usually worshiped individually rather than collectively. A family or clan typically worships their relative in group ceremonies, calling upon that individual to bless them with a good harvest or protect them from a village plague. The living usually communicates with the deceased through prayer or sacrifice. While the deceased are believed to have the power to influence the living, they do not have unlimited powers and can only influence those who worship them.

In order to properly enter the ancestral realm, the deceased must be buried according to tribal custom.

When the head of a family dies, his eldest son often takes over his position of family authority. In most cases this first heir to the deceased must perform the burial ceremony for his father. With some peoples, a man who dies without a direct heir cannot be worshiped. Instead, his soul is left to wander aimlessly as a ghost. Funeral rites may continue for years until the deceased has properly passed into the ancestral realm. Ceremonies, prayers, and ritual sacrifices may aid in the process. Not until funeral rites for the deceased are complete can the son officially lead the worship services for his father.

Many peoples who practice ancestor worship believe that the ancestral realm is organized hierarchically, parallel to the living world. Thus, the deceased's rank increases only as the rank of his counterpart on earth increases. For instance, if the living son is the heir to family authority, his father's rank in the ancestral world will increase as his son's rank rises in the family and among the people.

See also: ORISHA (Vol. I); RELIGION, TRADITIONAL (Vol I); SECRET SOCIETIES (Vol. I); SPIRIT POSSESSION (Vol. I).

ancestry Founding members of families, groups, or nations identified through myths, shrines, and specific sites. In Africa, one of the most important roles that ancestry plays is in defining life purpose and traditional values. For thousands of years, oral history has helped to accomplish this through myths. In some societies, myths detail heroic deeds or hardship that give meaningful personal or national histories to future generations. It should be kept in mind, however, that not all African societies share this view. Among the Pokot of western Kenya, for example, ancestral spirits traditionally are viewed as evil and are held responsible for great misfortune. In fact, it is believed that even speaking of the dead opens the way for bad luck.

Special symbols or shrines commemorated family ancestry in many ancient African societies. In the Kingdom of Benin, in what is now the Republic of Benin (formerly Dahomey), some royal families used a special altar under which founding male ancestors were buried. Carved wooden roosters were placed on the altars of female ancestors. Commemorative figures that honor the ancestors were also used by the Baoule of Ivory Coast.

One of the most ancient symbols of ancestry in Africa, the ARK OF THE COVENANT was used to commemorate Ethiopia's national ancestry, beginning with King Solomon and Makeda, the queen of Sheba. Similarly, among the Ashanti of GHANA, a unified national ancestry was achieved through the centuries-old tradition that maintained symbolic royal stools and a royal umbrella that "covers the nation."

Ancestry may also be linked to particular sites. For Nuer groups in the Sudan, a special tamarind tree in their homeland west of Bahr el-Jebel traditionally represented the place from which many claim to have originated. Similarly, the KIKUYU treated Mount Kenya as the House of Mumbi, the spiritual dwelling place from which they originated and to which they would return as ancestors.

Traditional religion continues to make a place for ancestor reverence and worship. For example, in the annual Egungun festival of the Yoruba people, the roots of which lie thousands of years in the past, it is believed that the spirits of deceased and sometimes divinized ancestors are summoned to bring comfort and relief to the living.

See also: AFTERLIFE (Vol. I); EGUNGUN (Vol. I)

Further reading: William R. Bascomb and Melville J. Herskovits, *Continuity and Change in African Cultures* (Chicago: The University of Chicago Press, 1975); Miguel F. Brooks, trans. and ed., *Kebra Nagast* [The Glory of Kings] (Lawrenceville, N.J.: Red Sea Press, 1998). Douglas H. Johnson, *Nuer Prophets* (New York: Oxford University Press, 1994).

Angola Country on the southwestern coast of Africa; bordered on the north by the Republic of Congo, on the west by Zambia, and on the south by Namibia.

Angola has been inhabited since prehistoric times, as evidenced by early human remains found at archaeological sites in Luanda. However, many thousands of years passed before more developed societies arrived in the area. The first settlers were Khoisan-speaking hunter-gatherers. At the beginning of the sixth century a more technologically advanced people began one of the greatest migrations in history. These Bantu-speaking people, who had mastered metalworking technology, probably originated to the north, near modern Nigeria or present-day Cameroons. When they reached Angola, these BANTU speakers encountered less technologically advanced Khoisan speakers whom the Bantus thoroughly dominated with their superior knowledge of agriculture, metalworking, and ceramics. After several centuries, Bantu languages had been established throughout the region. The result was the genesis of a number of different ethnic groups who took on different characteristics and spoke languages with Bantu roots.

animism Belief that inanimate objects have a soul or life-spirit. Although the term *animism* did not emerge until the nineteenth century with the publication of Edward Tylor's *Primitive Culture* in 1871, animism has been prevalent in Africa since ancient times. The term describes a wide range of beliefs that blur the difference between the spirit world and the world of living people. In practice, elaborate funeral rites and rituals are important aspects of animism because followers of animism treat every living being and every physical object as if it is imbued with life.

See also: RELIGION, TRADITIONAL (Vol. I).

Ankaratra range Volcanic mountain range in central Madagascar. Covering nearly 2,000 square miles (5,200 sq km), the mountains lie to the southwest of what is now Antananarivo, the capital city of this island. Mount Tsiafajavona, the island's second highest peak, lies within the Ankaratra range.

Anlamani (c. 623–593 BCE) *Kushite king of Egypt.*

Anlamani and his brother Aspelta (c. 593–568 BCE) were royal descendants of the prominent Kushite rulers that included Taharqa (c. 690–664 BCE) and PIANKHY (c. 751–716 BCE). Like his predecessors, Anlamani apparently erected one of the stone pillars, known as stelae, that have provided historians and archaeologists with important insights into the inner workings of the Kushite kingdom. Among other things, Anlamani's stelae record his progress among the various Nomes, or provinces, of EGYPT. Although, as these and other records show, Anlamani kept a watchful eye over the vast territory that was controlled by Kush, he was unable to prevent warfare with the nomadic Blemmyes who inhabited the western desert.

Anlamani's reign was also noteworthy for the role played by the female members of his family. On his stelae, he describes how his mother, the KANDAKE, or queen mother, Nasalsa, attended his royal coronation at Kawa and played a prominent role in royal proceedings. He also describes the importance of his sisters, consecrated priestesses of AMUN. According to Anlamani's records, one of the chief responsibilities of these women was to play the sistrum in the holy temples that his predecessors erected at GEBEL BARKAL in honor of the god Amun.

Further reading: G. Mokhtar, ed., *General History of Africa* (Paris: UNESCO, 1990); Ivan Van Sertima, *They Came Before Columbus* (New York: Random House, 1976).

ants Insects that live together in organized groups, or colonies. There are more than 8,000 species of ants, which vary in length from .08 to 1 inch (.2 cm to 2.5 cm).

Some African ant species, like the driver ants found in the Tropics, do not live in permanent colonies. They are nomadic and carnivorous and move in long columns, devouring animals unfortunate enough to cross their path. Large armies of driver ants can even consume large mammals. Also found in the African Tropics are tailor, or weaver, ants. These ants build nests out of leaf fragments that are held together by a kind of silk secreted by their larvae.

In ancient Africa there were many interesting beliefs about and uses for ants. In Egypt, for example, ant eggs were crushed and used as cosmetic eyeliners. Elsewhere in Africa, the industriousness of ants associated them with fertility. The Pangwa of Tanzania believed that the world was created from ant excrement. According to the Dogon people of Mali and Sudan, the anthill was a symbol of female fertility.

Apedemak God worshiped by ancient kings of Kush.

Elevated to the status of a national deity, Apedemak was a highly symbolic figure. He usually was depicted as having a man's body with four arms and a lion's head. The head, according to some reports, represented Egypt's Twenty-fifth Dynasty king Taharqa.

Worship of Apedemak may have been temporarily suspended in the eighth century BCE when Kushite kings conquered EGYPT and established that country's Twenty-fifth Dynasty. Initially, the Kushites' adaptation of Egyptian religious rites included the worship of the god AMUN. By 200, however, Kushite kings returned to many of their own ancient religious practices, including the worship of Apedemak.

See also: AMANITARE (Vol I); RELIGION, TRADITIONAL (Vol. I).

Aqaba, Gulf of Northeastern arm of the RED SEA; which separates the Arabian and Sinai Peninsulas. The Gulf of Aqaba borders modern-day Israel, EGYPT, Jordan, and Saudia Arabia and has had a long history as a commercial port and strategic area. In ancient times, Aqaba was on the spice caravan route to Egypt, Greece, and other parts of Europe. Religious scholars have linked the area with the biblical port city of Ezion-Gerber, where King Solomon was said to have built a fleet of ships.

Arab coastal trade Trade between ARABS and coastal Africa.

Commerce between Arabia and coastal Africans is evident as early as the first century BCE. Early immigrants from Arabia and Yemen left their politically unstable homelands in search of new territory along the eastern coast and Horn of Africa. They crossed the Red Sea and established trading ports along the coasts of present-day Ethiopia, Somalia, and the Sudan. These trading centers connected Africa to the riches of Arabia, Asia, Persia, GREECE, and ROME for the first time. Early Arabian traders exchanged weapons for African gold, ivory, honey, tortoise shells, and slaves. As the Arab immigrants intermarried with local people, new cultures emerged. In ETHIOPIA, c. 100, the powerful trading kingdom of AKSUM was founded by people of mixed Arab and black ancestry. Although Arab coastal trade flourished over the next 200 years, it sharply declined from the third to seventh centuries with the Fall of Rome, warfare with Ethiopia, and internal conflict among African peoples.

Around the same time, as the first Arabs reached the HORN OF AFRICA and eastern coast in the first century BCE, other Arabs crossed the Red Sea further south at the Strait of Bab el-Mandeb. They too established trading kingdoms. A rich culture developed as the local people integrated the Arabian Semitic language and Sabaean religion (from Sheba) into their culture. The Arabs introduced basic writing technology and stone-building techniques, allowing for rapid advances in these early African kingdoms.

Sub-Saharan Africa, known as *bilad al-sudan*, or "land of the blacks," to the Arabs, also had early contact with Arabian traders. Southern coastal Africa along the present-day Swahili coast was connected to the African interior via extensive trade routes.

See also: TRANS-SAHARAN TRADE ROUTES (Vol. II).

Arabic Language originating in the Arabian Peninsula. The influx of Arabs into Africa, especially during the seventh century, had considerable impact, so much, in fact, that Arabic became the primary language not only of the Middle East, where it originated, but of North Africa as well.

Arabic constructs most words on the basis of three consonant sounds, with vowel sounds inserted either before, between, or after consonants. Depending upon where they come in relation to these consonants, the vowel sounds indicate associated meanings as well as number (i.e., singular or plural). The use of prefixes and suffixes attached to the root words provide further shades of meaning or indicate grammatical case (e.g., subject or object). The three consonant sounds "s," "l," and "m," for example, provide the basis for such related words as *Islam*, *Muslim*, *salaam* (peace), and *salama* (safety). Arabic sentences normally follow the pattern of verb-subject-object.

The Arabic language remained largely confined to the Arabian Peninsula until the seventh century CE, when Islamic Arabs initiated a campaign to conquer and colonize various regions of Africa (and Asia) and convert its peoples to Islam. The military—and missionary—success of these efforts had a powerful impact on many African tongues and cultures. Later settlement by Arab traders, beginning in East Africa in the fourteenth century, also served to heighten the influence of Arabic on African languages.

Even in areas in which Arabic did not replace—or at least diminish the importance of—indigenous languages, Arab conquest and trade often had a significant impact on local cultures and tongues. Arabic influence can clearly be seen in the large Muslim population of central and eastern Africa, for example.

The Arabic influence on African language and culture can be seen most readily among the Swahili and HAUSA tongues, where Arabic vocabulary has influenced the formation of words in both languages. Although most Swahili vocabulary is drawn from BANTU languages, a great number of Swahili words have been derived from the Arabic vocabulary, including the word *Swahili* itself, which means "the coast" in Arabic. In addition, both Hausa and Swahili (unlike almost all other African languages) developed a written alphabet, something which is most likely a direct result of the influence of Muslim Arabs, upon whose alphabet these indigenous Africans based their own.

The AMHARIC language of Ethiopia, affected by the migration of Arab traders in the first millennium BCE, also demonstrates a strong Arabic influence.

Indigenous African languages and dialects have influenced spoken Arabic in these regions as much as Arabic has had an impact on them. Although many North Africans now use the Arabic language almost exclusively (unlike most regions of Africa, where multilingualism is the norm), this spoken Arabic varies widely from country to country. Written Arabic, however, remains largely consistent throughout North Africa. It has become the dominant language in Mauritania, Mali, MOROCCO, ALGERIA, TUNISIA LIBYA, EGYPT, and the Sudan, as well as a language commonly spoken in SOMALIA, Chad, ETHIOPIA, and Djibouti.

See also: LANGUAGES (Vol. I).

archaeology The systematic recovery and study of material culture representing past human life and activities.

Archaeology, from the Greek words *archaios*, meaning "ancient things," and *logos*, meaning "study of," is a relatively young science, but it has already unlocked many mysteries associated with the study of AFRICA, which scientists consider the cradle of humanity. In just the last few decades, many ancient, fossilized remains have been recovered as a result of archaeological excavations, including the TAUNG CHILD in South Africa; *ZINJANTHROPUS* and *HOMO HABILIS* in OLDUVAI GORGE in Tanzania; *Homo sapiens* in Kabwe, Zambia; Nario-kotome boy in Lake Turkana, Kenya, and one of the oldest fossilized recoveries to date, Dinkenesh (or "Lucy"), recovered in Hadar, a region of the Awash River valley in ETHIOPIA.

For these finds to provide useful information, archaeologists must interpret, classify, and analyze the data that results from them and explain their significance within the correct environmental, cultural, and historical contexts. Archaeologists are often aided in their investigations by written records, ORAL TRADITIONS, and artifacts from the time period. They may also draw on the work of such specialists as geologists, botanists, linguists, and chemists, among others.

Many archaeological discoveries, in the form of human and animal remains, provide a glimpse into the day-to-day activities of prehistoric human beings—those peoples who lived before the invention of writing approximately 5,500 years ago. The time period in which these prehistoric peoples lived is generally divided into the Early, Middle, and Late Stone Ages. Excavations of STONE AGE sites have yielded a great deal of information concerning hominids, the biological term derived from the Latin word *homo*, "human being," which describes the

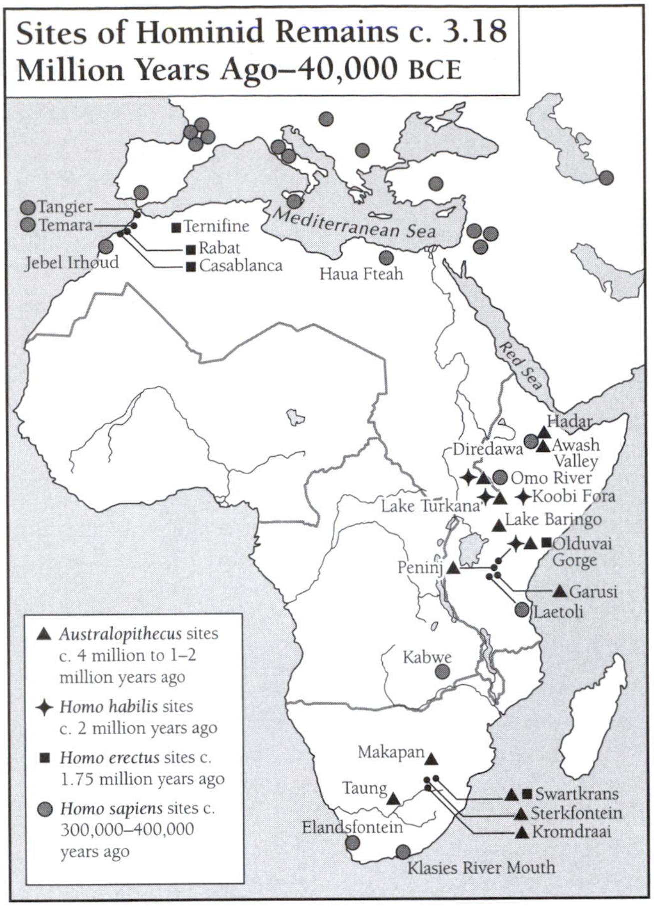

various branches of the homininidae family from which modern humans descend. Hominids were primates, who had the ability to think, stand, and walk on two feet as early as 2.5 million years ago.

Archaeologists have also been trained to identify and retrieve artifacts, or objects that are made or changed by human hands. These artifacts might include pottery, ROCK ART, cloth, or stone tools such as the ACHEULEAN AGE hand ax found in Tanzania and Kenya and dating from between 700,000 years and 1.5 million years ago. Such primitive tools, for example, are easily distinguished from the more refined cutting tools produced during the Late Stone Age by more evolved humans, known as *homo sapiens*, or modern human beings, who began to appear 100,000 years ago.

Recovered graves represent another source of artifacts and have provided archaeologists with some idea of prehistoric religion in Africa, particularly in regions where burial patterns consistently reveal some form of belief system. Such graves have been identified in Zambezi, Zambia, Zimbabwe and Malawi. In both northern and southern Africa, a number of graves have also been recovered that held the remains of *Homo sapiens* along with stone tools.

Some archaeologists specialize in certain periods and regions, such as ancient EGYPT and NUBIA, that offer an abundant degree of material culture. For example, in the Eastern Desert of Egypt, archaeologists found an ancient building that they believe was once occupied by a pharaoh. They were able to confirm that the building was a multiroom dwelling that dated back to the MIDDLE KINGDOM. These rooms contained basin rims and the remnants of pottery. In addition, a dried-up well connected with the building had many hieroglyphic inscriptions.

Archaeologists can use data from more extensive excavations to reconstruct an entire ancient civilization. For example, the ruins of Great Zimbabwe and its surrounding smaller villages, which lie in Masvingo in modern Zimbabwe, have offered archaeologists important information concerning the development of early city-states in Africa. Archaeologists who have conducted excavations at the ruins have been able to reconstruct the events that influenced Great Zimbabwe's rise and contributed to its downfall by using special tools such as trowels and small brushes to scrape away dirt and sand. This allows them to study the strata, or levels, of rock to determine the age of artifacts while causing the least amount of damage.

One of the cardinal rules in archaeology is maintaining the contextual integrity of the site. This means that items found in one soil strata cannot be lumped with others from another strata. To prevent this from occurring, all information discovered in the field is recorded on special forms known as *provenance sheets* for later analysis in laboratories. Special computer software is also used to recreate the original stratigraphic layers of ancient sites.

To gain some idea of the age of various findings, archaeologists have increasingly relied on sophisticated dating methods such as radiocarbon dating and potassium-argon dating. These methods evolved from atomic physics and involve measuring the breakdown of chemical elements in formerly living objects. Recently, archaeologists have collaborated with scientists in testing the DNA found in human and animal tissue to provide an even more complete picture of the past.

See also: HUMAN ORIGINS (Vol. I); GREAT ZIMBABWE (Vol. II); RELIGION, PREHISTORIC (Vol. I)

Further reading: Thomas R. Hester, Harry J. Shafer and Kenneth L. Feder, *Field Methods in Archaeology*, 7th ed. (Mountain View, Calif., 1997); J. Ki-Zerbo, ed., *General History of Africa I, Abridged edition: Methodology and African Prehistory* (Paris: UNESCO, 1990); Charles E. Orser, Jr., and Brian M. Fagan, *Historical Archaeology* (New York: HarperCollins College Publishers, 1995).

architecture In ancient Africa, as in other parts of the ancient world, architecture was fashioned by the climatic conditions, natural resources, and sedentary habits of its peoples, and its buildings vary from mud houses in tropical habitats to elaborate tombs and palaces in others. From Egypt to Great Zimbabwe, however, none of these

This reconstruction at Botshabelo Village, South Africa, shows a Ndebele hut of the earliest style, made only of thatch. The wooden door is decorated in a traditional motif. © *Lindsay Hebberd/CORBIS*

buildings "just happened." In fact, each of them, from the simplest mud house to a great pyramid, had to be planned and constructed with great skill.

Houses In sub-Saharan Africa, houses are among the most common architectural constructions, and their basic configurations and designs often date back thousands of years. Traditionally, most of the houses of sub-Saharan Africa are circular, a shape that offers a number of advantages to the people of this area. To begin with, the area of a circle provides more than 25 percent more floor space than a squ are with the same perimeter and more than 43 percent more space than any rectangle with that perimeter.

Beyond this, circular houses require significantly fewer materials than square or rectangular ones. Circular houses also have greater resistance to the forces of changing winds. In addition, they generally are easier to make. This was an important factor for nomadic peoples who had to abandon their homes every few months or for agricultural peoples who moved frequently because of land rotation.

Among the most notable circular house designs is that of the traditional MBUTI home, which dates back hundreds and even thousands of years. To build their homes, these small-statured people of the northeast Congo first drive saplings into the ground. Next they bend the tops together overhead, securing them with smaller twining saplings. This forms a dome-shaped structure that is covered with large heart-shaped leaves that overlap to form a waterproof enclosure. Dead branches are placed on top to hold the leaves flat. Once the leaves settle into place, even the hardest rains generally cannot penetrate a Mbuti house.

The Chagga of Tanzania, who long inhabited the fertile slopes of Mount Kilimanjaro, traditionally construct beehive-shaped houses. Interestingly, the critical dimension used in the construction of these homes is the height of the tallest man known by the builder. The diameter of the house always is two to three times the length of that man's arm span, from the fingertips of one hand to the fingertips of the other. The circumference of the house is marked off by tying a hoe to the end of a rope and attaching the other end to a peg located at the center of the planned dwelling; as the builder walks around the peg, he draws a circle with the hoe. The height of the house's doors is determined by the span of the tall man's arms; the width of the door is equal to the circumference of his head.

A number of agricultural peoples used cylindrical walls for their homes, topping them with cone-shaped thatched roofs. The walls intersect the roof to form a circle. The major distinction between this cylinder-cone design and the dome and beehive designs of the Mbuti is the material used to construct the walls. In the dome and beehive houses, the walls are made of the same material as the roof, usually saplings covered with leaves or grasses. In contrast, the walls of the cylinder-cone dwelling are usually made with mud, clay, or some other material that is plentiful in the area.

Exactly how each group or people creates these cylindrical walls—and what they do to decorate them—varies. The Kikuyu of present-day Kenya, for example, traditionally form the walls with a network of wattling that is fastened to posts and then daubed with clay. Mud is used whenever clay is not abundant. In contrast, the Hehe people of Tanzania construct a large, oblong structure with many large rooms. The walls are 10 inches (25 cm) thick and have a flat thatched roof daubed with earth. This type of construction keeps the structures remarkably cool in even the hottest weather.

Another approach is taken by the MAASAI of northern Tanzania and Kenya who, since ancient times, construct houses resembling covered wagons.The structure traditionally is covered with a mixture of mud and cow dung. Once the sun has thoroughly dried the walls, the house is clean and sanitary. Fishermen in the Lake Kyoga area also use local materials for their homes, which they construct with a thatch made of papyrus stems. The finished homes resemble inverted baskets and can be transported from place to place by canoe.

The walls of many of these houses traditionally are whitewashed and then decorated with elaborate designs. Some houses have murals painted on the inner or outer walls. Other types of ornamentation are placed around doorways or on roofs. In southern Nigeria and along the Guinea coast, murals, decorated relief patterns, and carved wooden doors and posts are found at the homes of the privileged. The outer walls of the traditional red-earth houses of the IBO, in Nigeria, are often painted in red, black, green, and white geometric patterns. Murals and mats woven with intricate designs are found in many areas of the Zambezi region of the Congo.

Larger Structures African architecture, of course, has not been limited to houses, even in ancient times. The Egyptians were among the most famous architects and builders in human history, and their works remain marvels.

The GREAT PYRAMID at GIZA, for example, was the very first on the Seven Wonders of the World to be constructed. Built as a tomb for the great king KHUFU, the pyramid is awe-inspiring in size. The length of each of the four sides exceeds 755 feet (230 m), and the corners are almost perfect right angles, astonishingly accurate to within 0.007 of a degree. The height is 481.4 feet (146.7 m) and the base covers an area of 13.1 acres (5.3 hectares). The ratio of one-half the perimeter divided by the height yields a number equal to 3.1408392 (compared with the true value of pi, which equals 3.1415927), a remarkable fact the significance of which is not yet understood.

The Great Pyramid of Giza also is one of the largest structures ever built. In its original form, it was large enough to simultaneously hold within its walls St. Paul's Cathedral, St. Peter's in Rome, the cathedrals of Milan and Florence, and Westminster Abbey. And, if they were broken into 1-foot (30.48-cm) cubes and laid end to end, its stones would stretch two-thirds of the way around the equator.

Among other monumental architectural achievements are the famous ruins at Great Zimbabwe, which give a vivid impression of the splendor of Monomotapa, one of the wealthiest kingdoms of south-central Africa. Built more than a thousand years ago, it, too, represents a major triumph of African architecture and construction.

See also: ARCHITECTURE (Vols. II, III); GREAT ENCLOSURE, GREAT ZIMBABWE (Vol. II).

Ark of the Covenant (Ark of the Law, Ark of the Testimony) Highly revered chest or cupboard, reputed to contain the scrolls or tablets of Jewish law. It is of special importance to Ethiopian Christians.

Considered the "holiest of all holies" for the Jewish people, the Ark of the Covenant has been described as a rectangular box made of hardwood and covered with gold plate. It is said to be 4 feet long, 2 feet, 6 inches wide, and 2 feet, 6 inches deep. According to various traditions, the cover of the Ark is decorated with cherubim, or angelic figures. Biblical references indicate that Moses made a case shaped like the "belly of a ship," into which he placed two stone tablets of the law.

The legends of the ark have an important role for many Ethiopians, who trace their Judeo-Christian heritage through the reported union of Solomon and the queen of Sheba, Makeda. According to the Kebra Nagast, Ethiopia's holy book of ancient secrets and traditions, the Ark of the Covenant was handed down for safekeeping from one generation to the next, from Moses to Israel's great king Solomon. In the tenth century BCE, Solomon met Queen Makeda of Ethiopia, known in the Bible as the queen of Sheba. Queen Makeda, who acquired the Ethiopian throne at a young age, had traveled from her country to Jerusalem in hope that Solomon would teach her how to govern.

The Kebra Nagast goes on to explain that Solomon used trickery to seduce the visiting queen, who eventually bore him a son. Solomon, however, later dreamed that this son, who was named Menelik, would someday be responsible for transferring responsibility of the holy laws from Israel to Ethiopia. At the age of thirteen, Menelik, who had been residing in Ethiopia with Queen Makeda, came to Jerusalem to visit his father. After being taught Jewish history and law, Menelik was anointed king of Ethiopia. At the same time, several nobles from Solomon's royal court were assigned to assist the youth in his development (see BETA ISRAEL). In spite of this, however, Menelik stole the Ark and returned with it to Ethiopia, thus fulfilling Solomon's dream.

The Ark, say many traditional legends, remained hidden away through centuries of wars and political upheaval. A number of these tales insist that the Ark was kept in a cave that had been sealed when an earthquake caused a landslide.

Obviously, the mysteries of the Ark are not likely to be solved any time soon. But many Ethiopians insist that the Ark ultimately was kept in the Kingdom of Aksum, thus forming the basis for their claim to be the Chosen People of God.

See also: AKSUM (Vol. I); AMHARA (Vol. 1); ETHIOPIA (Vols. I, II, III).

Arsinoe I (c. 282 BCE) *Queen of Egypt and the first wife of King Ptolemy II Philadelphus.*

Arsinoe I's father, Lysimachus, the king of Thrace, arranged the marriage to symbolize the union of Thrace and Egypt against Seleucus I Nicator of Syria. They married around 282 BCE and had three children. Although the length of their marriage is unknown, Arsinoe I did not remain Queen of Egypt for long. When Egypt and Thrace defeated Syria in 279 BCE, Ptolemy's recently widowed sister, ARSINOE II, arrived in Egypt. Arsinoe I was sent into exile sometime around the arrival of Arsinoe II. Some scholars believe that Arsinoe I was exiled immediately following Lysimachus's death, when Egypt's political tie to Thrace ended. Others speculate that Arsinoe II convinced her brother that Arsinoe I was conspiring to assassinate him. Whatever his motivation, Ptolemy sent Arsinoe I to Coptos in Upper Egypt and married Arsinoe II.

Arsinoe II (316–270 BCE) *Queen of Thrace, who later married King Ptolemy II Philadelphus of Egypt.*

Arsinoe's father, Ptolemy I Soter, was the founder of Egypt's Ptolemaic dynasty. He arranged for Arsinoe to marry King Lysimachus of Thrace in 300 BCE to secure the family's power within the Thracian kingdom. Arsinoe II accused the heir to the throne, her stepson Agathocles, of conspiring to kill his father. When the trusting Lysimachus ordered the execution of his son, Seleucus I Nicator of Syria declared war on Thrace. During the war, Thrace allied itself with Egypt through the marriage of ARSINOE I, Lysimachus's daughter by a previous marriage, to Arsinoe II's brother, Ptolemy II Philadelphus of Egypt. Lysimachus died from battle wounds in 281 BCE, and Arsinoe II was forced to flee Thrace. She temporarily settled in Cassandrea, a city in northern Greece that her husband renamed in her honor.

When Thrace defeated Syria in 279, Arsinoe II's half-brother Ptolemy Ceraunus tricked her into marrying him. His interest extended no further than the Thracian throne. When he arrived in Cassandrea to claim his new wife, he immediately killed Arsinoe II's two youngest sons. She fled to Alexandria, where her brother King Ptolemy II Philadelphus and his wife Arsinoe I ruled Egypt.

Shortly after Arsinoe II's arrival in Egypt, Arsinoe I was sent into exile to Coptos in Upper Egypt. Although Arsinoe I could have been exiled immediately following her father Lysimachus's death, most scholars speculate that she was exiled when Arsinoe II convinced her brother that Arsinoe I was conspiring to assassinate him. Arsinoe II then married her brother, a practice customary among the Egyptians but puzzling to the Greeks. From that point on, the name *Philadelphus*, which means "brother-loving," was attached to Ptolemy II and Arsinoe II's names.

Arsinoe II Philadelphus became a powerful force in the Egyptian monarchy. She appeared on Egyptian coins, and several towns were named in her honor. In keeping with custom, she was deified during her lifetime. A cult was established in her honor when she died, and a massive shrine, the Arsinoeion, was dedicated in her honor.

Arsinoe III (235–204 BCE) *Wife of King Ptolemy IV Philopator and queen of Egypt.*

Arsinoe III was the sister and husband of King Ptolemy IV Philopator of Egypt. Their father, Ptolemy III Euergetes of Egypt, married Arsinoe III in 217 BCE to her brother after Egypt defeated the Seleucid kingdom in Southwest Asia. During her reign, Arsinoe III had little political influence. The Ptolemaic dynasty fell into a state of decline as her husband succumbed to the influence of his corrupt court ministers. When Arsinoe III gave birth to the heir to the throne, her husband forbade her to appear in public. When Ptolemy IV died in 205 BCE, his court officials had Arsinoe III assassinated to ensure that they would retain power. Her son Ptolemy V Epiphanes was then crowned King of Egypt. At only six years of age, Ptolemy V became another puppet for the royal court.

art See ART (Vols. II, III); BEADS AND JEWELRY; MASKS; POTTERY; ROCK ART.

Asclepius Greek god of divination and healing; long associated with IMHOTEP (c. 2650–2610 BCE), the ancient Egyptian scribe, physician, poet, architect, and astronomer.

See also: EGYPT; ISIS (Vol. I).

Aspelta (Aspelto) (r. 593–568 BCE) *King of both* EGYPT *and* KUSH *during Egypt's Twenty-fifth Dynasty.*

During Aspelta's reign, Egyptian religious beliefs and rituals were retained, as were hieroglyphics, Egyptian architectural styles, and the practice of mummification. Aspelta's greatest accomplishment of record was shifting the capital of the Kingdom of Kush to MEROË, which became a center of political, cultural, and social power in 590 BCE.

See also: APEDEMAK (Vol.I).

Assyrian Of or relating to the ancient empire of western Asia situated in the upper valley of the Tigris River; the Assyrian Empire began its ascension c. 2000 BCE, and rapidly declined after c. 612 BCE. Ancient texts credit the Assyrian king Esarhaddon with the invasion of EGYPT and the capture of the capital city of MEMPHIS about 660 BCE. His son Ashurbanipal (669–627 BCE) continued the conquest of Egypt, sending armies as far as Thebes. Weapons made of tempered iron reportedly gave the Assyrians a decisive advantage over the Egyptians, whose weaponry was made of bronze and stone. The process of smelting iron to make tools and weapons is believed to have been mastered by the Assyrians as early as 1300 BCE.

astronomy Science that treats the heavenly bodies, including their motions, magnitudes, distances, and physical conditions.

The practice of astronomy has been widespread in Africa since ancient times, and instances of ancient astronomical practices have been discovered in virtually every part of the continent. In EGYPT, for example, astronomical studies led to perhaps the world's first solar CALENDAR. In Kenya stand huge, megalithic monuments that modern scientists have determined to be carefully aligned with stars and other heavenly bodies. Ancient Africans also learned that numerous earthly cycles—seasonal, planting, animal migration, animal mating, and so on—are closely related to the cycles of the Moon and Sun. From their long-term observations, they created calendars with which they scheduled planting and harvest times as well as important festivals and rituals.

Accuracy and precision were important to these ancient Africans. In part, this was a matter of survival, since the success or failure of everything from crops and hunts to annual migrations often depended upon accurate predictions of weather and seasonal events. Accurate predictions were also important, however, because the astronomer-priests with the most accurate predictions enjoyed the most power and prestige.

Another example of ancient African astronomy has been found in northwestern Kenya, where anthropologists have studied the recently discovered Namoratunga I and Namoratunga II sites date from the fourth century BCE. The first of these is a large rock-art cemetery in which the graves are surrounded by megalithic stones. These huge standing stones are marked with symbols resembling cattle brands.

In contrast, Namoratunga II, which some believe may have been used to create a calendar system as early as 300 BCE, contains only a single grave, which is surrounded by several huge standing stones. Namoratunga II also contains nineteen large stone columns arranged in rows that seem to have no relationship to the graves. The columns of Namoratunga II do, however, follow obvious patterns and seem to be related to astronomical events that are part of a complex calendar system developed long ago by eastern Kushites. This calendar links the rising of seven stars or constellations—Triangulum, the Pleiades, Aldebaran, Bellatrix, Central Orion, Saiph, and Sirius—with a 12-month, 364-day year.

See also: SCIENCE (Vols. II, III).

Further reading: Jean De Heinzelin, "Ishango," *Scientific American* 206:6 (June 1962), pp. 105–114; Alexander Marschack, *The Roots of Civilization* (New York: McGraw-Hill, 1972); Ivan Van Sertima, *Blacks in Science: Ancient and Modern* (New Brunswick, N.J.: Transaction Books, 1983).

Aswan City and state in southern EGYPT; also known as Assuan, Assouan, and Syene.

Located on the east bank of the NILE RIVER, Aswan has a long history of foreign rule. The city is situated near what is now known as Lake Nasser, across from the island of ELEPHANTINE. In ancient times, Aswan was known as Swen (meaning "the mart" in Egyptian) and was the site of an important quarry that supplied granite for Egyptian monuments. (These quarries are still used today.) Under Macedonian and Greek occupation during the last few centuries BCE, the city was named Syene. It later became a garrison post for the Romans, Turks, and British.

Atbara River Tributary of the Nile River. The Atbara River, also known as the Black Nile, is approximately 500 miles (800 km) long. It flows over Nubian sandstone northwards from the Ethiopian Highlands to the Angareb and Satit Rivers in Sudan. From there it flows into the Nile at Atbarah. The banks of the Atbara River are mainly semiarid badlands. During the dry season from November to May, the Atbara virtually evaporates to the extent that only a handful of pools remain. In the rainy season, it swells to provide more than 20% of the Nile's total water volume and carries more than 11 million tons of silt down river into the valley, which is now blocked by the Aswan High Dam, and becomes Lake Nasser.

Aten Deity of the monotheistic religion promoted by the Egyptian pharaoh AKHENATEN (Amenhotep IV).

Shortly after coming to power, Amenhotep IV declared his allegiance to a new deity called Aten. Changing his name to Akhenaten as a sign of his devotion, the pharaoh then made the worship of Aten the kingdom's official religion and set out to eliminate devotion to all other gods, especially AMUN-RA.

Under Akhenaten's direction, a new city was constructed midway between Thebes and Memphis. Named Akhetaten, meaning "Horizon of Aten," it became the center of the new cult, replacing Thebes as Egypt's religious capital, and Akhenaten the pharaoh officiated as the one and only high priest of Aten.

Akhenaten's new religion represented a radical break with traditional Egyptian theology. The supreme god of Egypt's old pantheon was Amun, usually depicted as the Sun after it had set and become hidden from view. In contrast, Aten was pictured as a bright red sun disc with extended rays. The new religion also replaced dozens of deities, each with its own powers and personality, with a single god, Aten, who was worshiped as the one and only true source of created life.

Worship of Aten did not survive Akhenaten's reign. After his death, Akenaten's successors treated the new religion as heresy. Dismantling and destroying the monuments devoted to the new god, they reestablished the old beliefs and moved the religious capital back to Thebes.

Atlas Mountains Mountain chain located in Northwest Africa. Stretching more than 1,200 miles (1,931 km), the Atlas Mountains extend from the port of Agadir, in southwestern MOROCCO, through northern ALGERIA to the Tunisian capital of Tunis in the northeast. The highest point in the range is Jebel Toubkal (Mount Toubkal) in southwestern Morocco. Formed of sedimentary rock during the late Jurassic period, the Atlas Mountains are rich in minerals, especially phosphates, coal, iron, and oil.

The most rugged areas of the Atlas range are in Morocco, where the tallest peaks can be found. In Algeria, the system becomes a series of plateaus, with the Tell Atlas and the Saharan Atlas regions surrounding the Plateau of the Chotts.

The Atlas Mountains function as a weather barrier between the MEDITERRANEAN SEA and the SAHARA Desert. The slopes facing north get enough rain to support forests and farms. Streams that flow down this side of the range are diverted to irrigate fields of crops essential to the people of North Africa.The south-facing slopes are much drier than those facing north. This southern section, called the Saharan Atlas, is covered with shrub and grasses and dotted with salt lakes and salt flats. Although too dry to farm, the Saharan Atlas can support grazing sheep.

Australopithecus Any of the prior types of hominids that are considered ancestors of the modern human species, *HOMO SAPIENS*. All evidence of the earliest known hominids, which belong to the genus *Australopithecus*, has been found on the African continent.

The genus *Australopithecus* included at least six species: *ramidus*, *anamensis*, *afarensis*, *africanus*, *boisei*, and *robustus*. All of these species originated during the Pliocene epoch (1.6 to 5.3 million years ago) and had become extinct by the end of the early Pleistocene epoch (900,000 to 1.6 million years ago).

The oldest of these species is the apelike *ramidus*, discovered in the AFAR Triangle of ETHIOPIA and dating back 4.4 million years. The 4.2-million-year-old fossil of *Australopithecus anamensis*, the second oldest hominid specimen, was found in Kenya. The third hominid species, *afarensis*, most likely was an ancestor of the Australopithecines that followed it. Like *ramidus*, it was discovered in the Afar Triangle of Ethiopia. The most famous *afarensis* specimen, Lucy, dates back 3.2 million years.

Evidence of both *Australopithecus africanus*, who lived 2 to 3 million years ago, and *Australopithecus robustus*, who lived 1 to 2 million years ago, has been found in South Africa. Fossils of the *boisei*, originally called *Zinjanthropus*, were found in Tanzania and date back 2.3 to 2.5 million years.

Fossils belonging to the genus *Homo*, which refers to more "human" species, have also been discovered in Ethiopia, Kenya, and Zambia. Although *Homo* specimens also have been found in the Middle East, Asia, and Europe, most paleontologists believe that the first hominids in Eurasia were derived from an African source anywhere from 1 to 1.8 million years ago.

The biological term *HOMINID*, from the Latin word *Homo*, or person, is used to describe the various branches of the Hominidae family. These Hominidae were closely related primates with the ability to think, stand, and walk on two feet in ways similar to modern human beings. As early as 2.5 million years ago, these hominids began to make the first tools.

Archaeologists have determined that the Australopithecines, one of the broad categories of hominids, had a brain capacity of 26 to 33 cubic inches (440 to 550 cc). Perhaps the most notable example of this species ever discovered is the TAUNG CHILD, which was found in South Africa in 1925. The Taung Child lived between 2 and 3 million years ago and lived to an age of three to six years. The child's brain capacity was 25 cubic inches (410 cc), a figure that probably would have expanded to 26 cubic inches (440 cc) had the child lived to maturity.

During the 1960s, archaeologists recovered another branch of the Hominidae family at OLDUVAI GORGE and LAKE TURKANA. Classified as *HOMO HABILIS* (meaning "handy"), *HOMO ERECTUS*, and *HOMO SAPIENS* (meaning "wise"), these species are the closest to modern humans, with brain capacities measuring up to 78 cubic inches (1,280 cc). Reconstruction of recovered remains in Africa indicates some human features and a range of size from slender to robust.

See also: HUMAN ORIGINS (Vol. I)

aware Traditional game played in many regions of Africa; also known as *awele* and *oware*.

Aware is considered one of the oldest games in the world, having its origins in ancient EGYPT, where it was reportedly used as an early bookkeeping method.

Aware may have been symbolic of early agriculture and cattle raising, since terms such as "seeds and land" and "cattle and fields" became synonymous with a player's side of the board and the small objects used to navigate it. The widespread variations of the game within Africa attest to its longevity and popularity. It is called *ayo* among the YORUBA, *giuthi* by the Kikuyu of KENYA, and *adi* in southern GHANA. In Uganda it is known as *omweso*, while the IBO call it *azig*. Among Arabs, it was known as *mancala*, which reportedly meant "to move" or "to transfer." Stone boards have been identified at ancient temples at Thebes, KARNAK, and LUXOR. Ancient forms of the game board have also been found embedded in stone ruins in ZIMBABWE, as well as in the megaliths of ETHIOPIA.

The game's popularity within the royal courts was captured in many works of sculptured art, and elegant game boards were carved from ivory and gold. Yet much has been written about the game's simplicity and spontaneity, since *aware* could be played on the ground or any other flat service on which two parallel rows of six holes or cups could be arranged. Three-row versions were played in Ethiopia, and four-row versions have been noted in the Swahili regions of East Africa. The number of holes varied as well, ranging from six to fifty. Forty-eight seeds would be divided between two players in a two-row game. A four-row game would require the use of sixty-four seeds divided between two players.

Moving counterclockwise around the entire board, each player tried to capture the majority of his or her opponent's seeds. On the surface, *aware*'s rules appear simple, but for new generations of players its many variations and complexities have been compared to chess.

Further reading: Claudia Zaslavsky, *Africa Counts Number and Pattern in African Cultures* (Chicago: Lawrence Hill Books, 1999).

Ay (c. 1352–1348 BCE) *Twelfth king of Egypt's Eighteenth Dynasty who became pharaoh after the death of Tutankhamun.*

A prominent court official at AKHENATEN's new royal city of AKHETATEN, Ay came to the throne at an advanced age and for only four years. His brief reign was devoted to restoring the traditional Egyptian religion that Akhenaten had attempted to overthrow.

Some scholars suggest that Ay married Tutankhamun's widow, Ankhesenamun, in order to become pharaoh. Ankhesenamun, however, seems to have disappeared from sight soon after the death of Tutankhamun, and it is a queen named Tiy who is depicted at Ay's side in all the decorations of the period. To further deepen the mystery, a wall painting in Tutankhamun's tomb shows Ay presiding at the dead pharaoh's funeral rites, a duty he would perform only if he already were an heir to the throne.

B

ba In ancient Egyptian religion, the part of the spirit of the deceased that could leave the tomb and travel around the earth during the day.

Not simply a composite of a person's body and soul, the ba represented all the attributes of a deceased individual. According to traditional Egyptian religion, the ba came into being at the moment of death and needed a mummy or a tomb statue in order to exist. The latter, which generally was made of wood, was believed to become magically alive in the tomb of the deceased.

The ba was most often represented as either a falcon or a bird with a human head. The closest translation of the word *ba* is "animated manifestation," the part of the deceased's spirit that had the power to leave the body, change its shape, and journey back to earth. At night, however, the ba had to return to the body of the deceased.

Many Eqyptians considered animals to be the bau (plural of ba) of deities. There also were bau that were thought to represent the various powers of kings and queens. Bau often were painted on coffins or sarcophagi. They also were seen in reliefs and architectural features.

See also: KA (Vol. I).

baboon Large, noisy monkey with a large head and a long, dog-like nose. Baboons live mostly on the plains and rocky savannas south of the SAHARA. Male baboons, which can weigh up to 90 pounds (40.9 kg) and stand up to 4 feet (1.2 m) tall, are usually much larger than females, which often weigh as little as 30 pounds (13.6 kg). Both males and females, however, have coats of harsh fur of varying colors and long, curving tails. Adult males often have capes of long hair over their shoulders.

Baboons are considered highly intelligent and sociable animals. Living in structured societies known as troops and led by a dominant male, they communicate by dog-like barks and by changing their posture and the shape of their tails. They generally live between thirty and forty years on a diet consisting of plants, insects, bird eggs, and small mammals.

In ancient EGYPT, one type of baboon, the Hamadryas, was trained to perform many household tasks. Considered sacred, the mummified remains of Hamadryas baboons have been found in tombs, and their images frequently adorned both temples and tombs. The Hamadryas were thought to be representatives of THOTH, the god of writing, who, according to the ancient Egyptians, recorded the verdicts of the dead at the last judgment.

Badarian culture Predynastic Egyptian culture that flourished around 4000 BCE. The earliest prehistoric culture of UPPER EGYPT, Badarian culture represents the height of achievement of the African Chalcolithic (or primitive predynastic) period. It was named for al-Badari, the site at which, in 1925, British archaeologists first excavated evidence of this ancient culture.

Apparently a sparsely populated agrarian community, the Badarians grew wheat and barley and herded CATTLE, sheep, and goats. The Badarians distinguished themselves through their finely made black-topped POTTERY, which included both pots and vases. These featured thin walls and ripples, both of which are signs of a level of artistic skill rarely found in so-called primitive cultures. Painted and decorated, Badarian pottery employed a variety of polished finishes.

Unlike other primitive cultures, the Badarians, while still focusing on the functionality of objects, apparently developed an aesthetic of beauty. Jewelry has been found—shells, stone and copper beads, and bracelets—that dates back to this period both in Badarian regions and in Egypt. In addition, the Badarians manufactured and utilized cosmetics, fashioning them by grinding down metal and mineral ores.

The Badarians used flint tools such as stone axes, sickle blades, saw-edged knives, and arrowheads. They wore clothing of linen as well as leather. Statuettes indicate that they probably worshiped a fertility goddess or earth mother as their main deity.

The Badarians buried their dead, along with food and goods for the AFTERLIFE in shallow oval pits. Bodies were usually laid on the left side, as if sleeping, with the head to the south and the face pointed toward the west. Women had the largest graves.

Bahriya Oasis One of approximately five oases situated at the edge of Egypt's Western Desert near LIBYA.

Ancient trade caravans relied heavily on the numerous tree-lined oases in Africa's northern desert regions. Sometimes known as *foggara*, the wells of these oases tapped into underground rivers, which may have originated as far away as the ATLAS MOUNTAINS. Some of these oases, including Bayhriya, Farafra, Dakhla, and el-Kharga, may also have supported small permanent settlements. A fifth such oasis, Dunqul, was located near ELEPHANTINE in Upper EGYPT.

See also: DAKHLA OASIS (Vol. I); KHARGA OASIS (Vol. I).

Ballana culture Beliefs, art, religious institutions, and behavior of the people who coexisted in ancient Ballana, a northern province of Nubia.

Although Byzantine texts referred to the inhabitants of Ballana as Nobatians, modern archaeologists generally use the term *X-GROUP* to describe them. This term suggests just how little firm information—either archaeological or historical—exists about the people who shared Ballana culture from approximately 250 to 550 CE.

The ancestors of the people of Ballana apparently were nomads and pastoralists who migrated to Lower NUBIA from lands west of the NILE RIVER. Although this migration may have taken place as early as the third century, Ballana's royal tombs suggest that the Ballana Kingdom was established sometime after the fall of MEROË in the fourth century.

The way of life of these people remains almost as mysterious as their origins. In part this is due to the inconclusiveness of archaeological findings at the site of Ballana itself. It is also because of the absence of historical records for the period following the destruction of nearby Meroë. Excavations of Ballana, however, do show that the culture combined elements of Byzantine, Meroitic, and Sabean cultures.

According to some sources, after 250 Ballana burials were one of the most obvious signs of this mixed culture. The kings of the region had long been associated with a tradition of burial in pyramids, much like Egyptian monarchs. During the Ballana period, however, ruling kings were buried in tumulus mounds. These consisted of great mounds of earth, large enough to include the king and his various wives, servants, horses, camels, and household effects—all of which were deemed necessary for the king's journey to the beyond.

The inhabitants of Ballana gradually adopted Christianity between the sixth and thirteenth centuries. Religious institutions unearthed in the region, however, confirm that the people infused their Christian faith with images and practices of their Nubian past.

See also: AKSUM (Vols. I, II); GOATS (Vol. I); JEWELRY (Vol. I); NUBIA, CHRISTIAN (Vol. II).

Bamana MANDE-speaking group that inhabited the mixed woodland and grassland environment near the upper Niger River. Also known, in more recent times, as the Bambara, the Bamana were identified primarily as Mande until the early seventeenth century

The origin of the people who came to be known as the Bamana is uncertain, but it is widely believed that their ancestors migrated into the area from the SAHARA, bringing with them the agricultural skills and tools that they had used there when that region could still sustain crops. Rice, as well as several varieties of millet, seem to have been their main crops. Although both iron and copper are believed to have been known in nearby regions by c. 500 to 1000 BCE, the extent of the metalworking knowledge of the ancestors of the Bamana is not known.

See also: BAMBARA (Vol. II).

bands and segmentary societies Two contrasting types of groups that can trace family lines to a common ancestor. Anthropologists usually refer to bands as stateless societies without rulers because bands often consisted of small groups of people who lived in camps. Traditionally, these groups had few institutions and based their economy on an equal exchange of goods. Typical of these among the ancient peoples of Africa were the !KUNG of South Africa, whose members were dependent on each other to hunt and forage for food.

Sometimes groups formed larger family clans when they united in times of war, epidemics, or starvation. Among the Ngombe peoples, who occupied the forest regions of northwest Kongo, any size group that claimed descent from the same ancestor was known as a *libota*. Through polygamous marriages involving several wives and numerous children, some *libotas* may have had as many as 5,000 descendants, all of whom traced their family line to Gonji, the oldest man of the oldest generation.

When family members decided to break away from the larger group, a segmentary process occurred as they migrated to other regions of the same territory. The Tiv of Nigeria were typical of this process and were organized into many small segmentary groups. Under the segment system, such groups received protection from larger groups that established institutions to settle disputes and administer justice. Some groups imposed fines, imprisoned individuals, or banished them in order to restore order, but disputes among the Tiv were settled by a singing duel!

In present-day Africa, the system of segmented societies has been greatly affected by modernization, but members of the same band often live near each other and follow ancient customs, even in urban areas.

Further reading: William R. Bascomb & Melville J. Herskovits, *Continuity and Change in African Cultures* (Chicago: The University of Chicago Press, 1975); Daniel G. Bates, *Cultural Anthropology* (New York: Simon & Schuster, 1996).

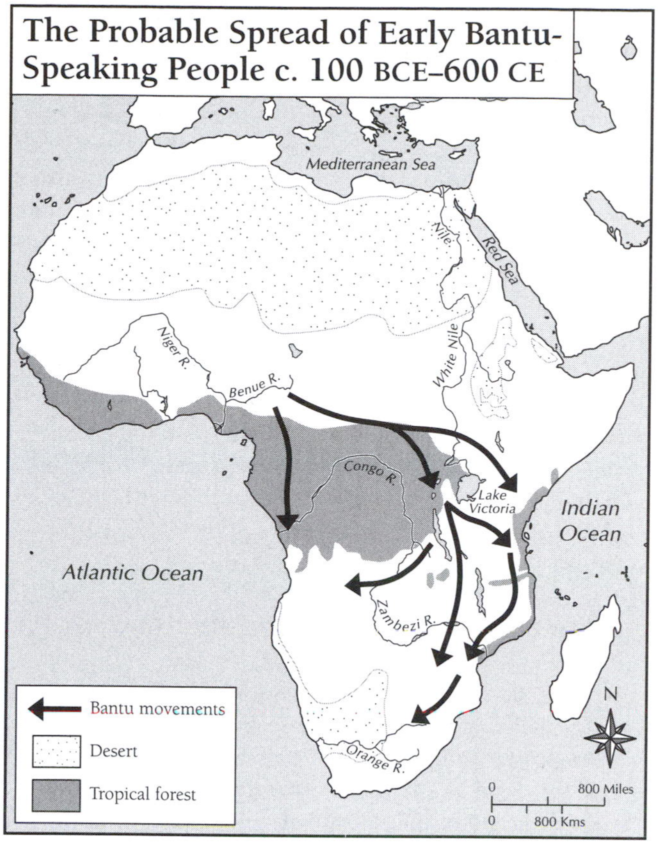

Bantu Term used to refer to more than 60 million people who speak Bantu as their native language.

Strictly speaking, Bantu is a term of linguistic classification, derived from the fact that most of the inhabitants of southern Africa use some form of the root *ntu* to mean "human being." Populating a large geographical area that straddles the equator, Bantu regions continue southward into South Africa. It is believed that the Bantu began migrating to their present areas as early as 1000 BCE. This migration, considered to be the largest in human history, continued until the third or fourth century CE.

Until approximately 200 BCE, sub-Saharan Africans lived largely in nomadic hunter-gatherer groups that were scattered over vast regions. This gave the individual groups both an abundance of resources and a protective isolation from one another and allowed them to subsist well into the first millennium by hunting wild game and gathering the fruits of the forest.

About 1000 CE, however, the Bantu-speaking people began to depend more on agriculture and stock-raising for subsistence, although some of them continued to hunt wild game and gather fruit. The transition from hunting and gathering to agri-pastoral economies coincided with the advancement from the STONE AGE to the IRON AGE.

The Iron Age came very early to some parts of Africa. Around the sixth century BCE, iron technology had already developed in ETHIOPIA, the Great Lakes region, Nigeria, and Tanzania. However, that technology spread very slowly. Indeed, it was quite possible that it was as late as 1000 CE before the smelting of iron began to diffuse throughout Africa. Steel smelting began among East Africans around 1400 BCE, when metal workers started producing steel in carbon furnaces.

Steel production was not introduced in the Western Hemisphere until the eighteenth century CE.

Bantu Migration A number of historians have suggested that the origins of the Bantu lie in CAMEROON. It is likely, however, that at least some of the Bantu might have migrated from perhaps as far north as Nigeria. One reason for believing this is that, as they migrated, the Bantu spread iron-smelting techniques across southern Africa. In fact, it was very likely that their iron tools and weapons made the Bantu militarily superior to the people they encountered along the way. The Bantu also were responsible for spreading agriculture throughout the region, particularly the cultivation of such high-yield crops as bananas, plantains, and YAMS. The result of this was an explosive growth of village life throughout Africa.

The Bantu migrated south into the rain forest regions around the CONGO RIVER and then eastward to the East African highlands. Wherever they settled, the Bantu imposed their culture and their language, by either mixing with or replacing the indigenous languages.

Anthropologists who have studied the Bantu migration have suggested several causes for this dramatic population movement. The most likely cause was an increased population and a subsequent need for more food. Ethnic warfare, which had long been a fact of life in sub-Saharan Africa, probably played a significant role, as did droughts and famines.

Bantu settlement in southern Africa, of course, was not unopposed. One of the major obstacles to Bantu settlement in the region proved to be the presence of large numbers of indigenous peoples. The largest area into which the Bantu advanced was inhabited by speakers of KHOISAN languages. Descendants of these people—the Khokhoi and the SAN—survive in small numbers today. The majority, however, were either exterminated by or assimilated into the Bantu-speaking culture.

Today, the remaining Khoikhoi are a pastoral people, skilled in basketry, metalworking, weaving, and the production of pottery. They live on the fringes of the extreme southwestern region of Africa, near Kalahari and Namib. Remnants of the San bushmen culture also remain. Still hunter-gatherers, they continue to use the Stone Age tools and weapons of their ancestors.

Further migrations displaced the earlier Bantu immigrants, pushing them farther east and south. This expansion of the Bantu migration probably began as a gradual shifting of relatively small clusters of people through the forests of the CONGO BASIN. It seems to have been most successful in East Africa, where the pastoral and food-producing peoples of eastern Africa provided stimuli for settlement and growth. The western frontier was not nearly as suitable to agricultural development, and, to the south, the Namib and Kalahari Deserts proved to be imposing barriers to settlement.

Another important event in Bantu history was a geographical split that created two major language families, the Eastern Bantu and the Western Bantu. Eastern-Bantu speakers migrated southward into Mozambique, Zimbabwe, and, ultimately, South Africa. These immigrants eventually founded the civilization of "Great Zimbabwe." Speakers of Western Bantu migrated into Angola, parts of BOTSWANA, and Namibia.

Bantu Languages A branch of the Niger-Congo family of languages, Bantu currently constitutes the largest linguistic family of all African languages. Swahili is the most widely spoken Bantu language today and it is considered the lingua franca of almost 50 million people living along the eastern coast of Africa. Beyond this, Bantu languages are spoken throughout eastern, central, and southern Africa, including regions of present-day Kenya, Tanzania, Uganda, Rwanda, Barundi, the eastern and northern Congo, northern Malawi, northern Mozambique, northern Zambia, and the Somali Republic, as well as parts of Angola, South Africa, and Zimbabwe.

The Bantu languages belong to the Benue-Congo branch of the NIGER-CONGO language family. Closely related in both lexicon and grammar, these languages are most likely descended from a single parent language that was concentrated in a much smaller area than that occupied by Bantu-speaking peoples today. The best known of the modern Bantu languages is Swahili, which is still widely spoken in Kenya and other regions of East Africa. Other Bantu languages include Rwanda, spoken in both Rwanda and Congo (formerly Zaïre); Rundi, spoken in Burundi and Congo; the South African tongues of Sotho, Xhosa, and Zulu; Makua, Thonga, and Shona, all spoken in Mozambique; Ganda, a language of Uganda; Kikuyu, a Kenyan tongue; Bemba, spoken in Zambia; Mbundu, an Angolan language; and Kongo, Luba, and Lingala, languages spoken widely in Congo and central Africa.

With the possible exception of Swahili, Bantu, like many African languages, employs different tones to indicate different meanings. In addition, such southern Bantu languages as Zulu, Sotho, and Xhosa have adopted some of the unique click noises that characterize the Khoisan languages spoken in South Africa.

Just as most Indo-European tongues classify nouns according to gender, Bantu languages place every noun in a particular class. (The method of distinguishing among Bantu noun classes, however, is difficult to discern—though they are clearly not gender-based.) Bantu languages use special prefixes to identify different classes of nouns, as well as number (i.e., singular or plural). The word *Bantu*, for example, means "people," with the prefix *ba* indicating plural, while the stem *-ntu* means "person."

In constructing sentences, the Bantu peoples then attach the same prefix to every other word—whether verb, adjective, or other part of speech—connected grammatically with a noun. In Swahili, for example, *m-thu m-zuri* means "handsome man," while *wu-thu wu-zuri* means "handsome men."

Bantu verbs start with a verb stem, which indicates meaning. As with Bantu nouns, prefixes and suffixes are then added to this stem to indicate tense, voice, mood, negation, person, and number.

See also: IRON (Vol. II); SWAHILI COAST (Vols. II, III).

Further reading: Basil Davidson, *A Guide to Africa* (New York: Zenith Books, 1965); John Iliffe, *Africans: The History of a Continent* (Cambridge, Eng.: Cambridge University Press, 1996); Roland Oliver, *The Middle Age of African History* (New York: Oxford University Press, 1967).

baobab tree One of the world's oldest and largest trees, indigenous to Africa, India, and Australia; also known as the *kuka.* Although there are different types of baobabs, those found in the dry savanna regions of Africa are scientifically classified as *Adansonia digitata.* Because its leaves only bloom for a brief period during the year, some view the baobab as an enormous upside-down bottle whose branches resemble twisted roots.

Ethnic groups in regions where the trees grow, such as Sudan, Kenya, Tanzania, Nigeria, Senegal, the Limpopo Valley, and Zimbabwe, have known for centuries that the baobab is a major sustainer of life. Some groups, in fact, refer to the baobab as "mother" because its pulp is used for healing a wide range of ailments. It has been used for treating scurvy, malaria, and rickets, as well as infections of the eye, skin, gums, and urinary tract. Beyond this, the baobab's bark has been used to make rope, fabric, and even fishing nets. The leaves, when in bloom, have been used to flavor drinks and stews and to produce a fruit, about a foot in length, called "monkey bread."

Baobabs measuring more than twenty feet wide are estimated to be about 1,000 years old. Generally, the older the tree, the more water its hollow trunk and interior roots can reserve. This is particularly critical in the more arid regions where humans and animals such as elephants seek water during long droughts and have inadvertently destroyed the trees as a result.

In ancient times, these large trunks served as burial tombs for high-ranking kings, chieftains, or founding members of family clans. This tradition was strongest among the Wolof and Serer of Senegal and the Batonga peoples of Zimbabwe, who laid their dead to rest with jewelry and surrounded by other valuable items. These groups referred to the living tree as an "ancestor," paying homage through special rites and ceremonies.

See also: SERER (Vol. II); WOLOF (Vols. II, III).

Further reading: James L. Newman, *The Peopling of Africa: A Geographic Interpretation* (New Haven, Conn.: Yale University Press, 1995).

Barawa One of several major city-states situated along the eastern coast of Africa. Centuries before the common era, this region was populated by BANTU-speaking peoples whose economy and subsistence were supported by agriculture and fishing. These people were particularly noted for their dugout canoes and the skillful use of fish traps made of wicker baskets in which they were able to catch large quantities of fish.

Baobab trees line a road near present-day Morindava, Madagascar. © *Chris Heller/CORBIS*

As the economy of the region grew, local chiefs assumed control of the market towns along the coast. By the seventh century, the region attracted the attention of traders and merchants from Arabia and India whose development of the area for large-scale commercial trading led to the founding of the Swahili kingdoms.

See also: SWAHILI COAST (Vols. II, III).

Barbary Coast North African coastal region bordered by the SAHARA Desert to the south, EGYPT to the east, the Atlantic Ocean on the west, and the Mediterranean to the north.

The name *Barbary* comes from the Latin word *barbari*, "barbarians," the term given to the people who lived on the periphery of the Roman Empire. Those people, who came to be known as the BERBERS, were the region's original inhabitants.

barter system System in which goods are exchanged for goods of equal value; TRADE by exchange of commodities.

Barter probably has been practiced since humans first began interacting with one another, and long before the invention of currency, people were exchanging items they had in abundance for items that were scarce. In many African cultures, livestock was most likely the first medium of exchange; in other cultures, grain and other agricultural products were bartered. It was not long, however, before many African cultures were using things of beauty—especially COWRIE and other seashells—as currency. In fact, copper and bronze impressions of cowrie shells were used as coins as long ago as the Late STONE AGE.

One of the prime trading centers of ancient Africa was CARTHAGE, which was located on the North African coast. Over the centuries, its extensive trading network helped transform this one-time Phoenician trading post into one of the wealthiest city-states of the ancient world. From the sixth to the third centuries BCE, Carthage imported GOLD, iron, silver, and tin in exchange for its manufactured goods. Carthage ruthlessly maintained its monopoly of the barter trade, minting gold to pay its vast mercenary army and even sinking the ships of interlopers.

Although Carthage's commerce with Phoenicia was its best known and, most likely, its most profitable, Carthaginian trade links were not limited to these. About 430 BCE, for example, the Greek historian HERODOTUS wrote of the trading voyage of HANNO, a Carthaginian writer and travaler who was reported to have journeyed as far as the Atlantic coast of MOROCCO. Hanno's voyage probably led to Carthaginian trading opportunities as far away as Río de Oro and the Cape Verde islands. According to Herodotus, Hanno employed the well-known system of dumb barter, in which merchandise was exchanged between merchants without the two parties ever meeting face to face.

Elsewhere in Africa, the extent of the gold and salt trade across the SAHARA from ancient GHANA has been well documented. SALT and gold were by far the major items involved in this trade, although CATTLE, ivory, HORSES, slaves, leather, and other items also were exchanged. The same system of dumb barter used by the Carthaginians was employed near the fabled Wangara gold fields. In this trade, however, dumb barter was used not so much to protect the traders but to guard the secrecy of the location of the gold fields.

Similarly, the region of what is now northern Somalia also saw the development of extensive trade. There, ivory, aromatic gums, slaves, and tortoise shells were bartered for cloaks, tunics, COPPER, and tin from the Arabian peninsula as well as for cotton cloth, grain, oil, and sugar from India and China. Trade with India and China also was carried out in East Africa. Although it did not develop to any great degree until much later, in the ninth century, trade there included the exchange of ivory for both glass beads and porcelain.

See also: CAPE VERDE ISLANDS (Vol. II); GOLD (Vol. II); IRON (Vol. II); IVORY (Vol. II); PHOENICIANS (Vol. I); SALT TRADE (Vol. II); WANGARA GOLD FIELDS (Vol. II).

basket making Ancient craft in which grasses or other natural fibers are woven, braided, coiled, or sewn into practical and decorative objects.

Baskets have played an important role for much of Africa's history and are generally associated with food production. Evidence of the earliest forms of basketry date back to the Neolithic Period (c. 5200 BCE) when inhabitants of the Faiyum of EGYPT, an area between the NILE VALLEY and the Gebel el-Qatrani escarpment, produced reed baskets to store cultivated grains. When made as an open type netting or box-like trap, baskets were also used by these people to catch fish. Archaeologists have also recovered a number of basket granaries lined with straw matting. Attached to homes or hung from trees, these basket granaries indicate how these people stored their food in the semi-arid environment that existed at that time. This basket-making tradition remained prevalent among later populations, including the Tuareg and HAUSA, who lived along the ancient trade routes of the SAHARA.

Along with environmental factors, societal traditions often determined the need for particular types of baskets. Traditionally held to be the work of women and their daughters, in slack periods men and boys also participated in basketry. As a result, the functions of basketry range from art forms to household items, such as bowls, grain and flour sifters, and seating mats. In some societies baskets even serve as a form of fencing, while in Uganda Tutsi women have long produced baskets woven so tightly that they can hold milk. Basketry has also been used to make masks, masquerade costumes, and musical instruments.

The uses and variations involved in basket making were largely based on the availability of natural fibers in a particular region. Unique patterns were created by alternating complementary colors. These were achieved by means of dyes or by using contrasting natural fibers, such as long grasses, straw, willow reeds, rush, rattan, raffia bamboo, or palm leaves. These natural fibers were sometimes dried or soaked for pliability. Animal hides, COWRIE SHELLS, and other decorative items were also at times sewn to finished baskets.

See also: HAUSA (Vol. II); SAHARA (Vol. II); TUAREGS (Vols. I, II).

Further reading: Barbara Watterson, *The Egyptians* (Oxford, Eng.: Blackwell Publishers, 1998); *General History of Africa, Volume I: Methodology and African Prehistory* (Paris: UNESCO, 1990).

Batn el-Hajjar Barren rocky area between the second and third cataracts of the NILE RIVER; also known as the "Belly of Stones."

The Batn el-Hajjar consists of narrow gorges flanked by rocky terrain. During ancient Egypt's MIDDLE KINGDOM, the country's southernmost border, which divided EGYPT from NUBIA, was located just south of the Batn el-Hajjar. By the start of the NEW KINGDOM, Egypt's border extended as far as the fourth cataract of the Nile.

beads Relatively small objects made from natural materials, worn for social status, ritual purpose, or personal adornment.

Beads traditionally have held an integral place in African culture and economy. Archaeological evidence has confirmed the presence of beads dating back to the prehistoric period. Some examples include Maadi, a site near el-Omari in southern EGYPT, where carnelian beads, perhaps dating from 4000 BCE, were recovered from storage pits originally thought to hold grain. Elsewhere in ancient Africa, 2,000- to 3,500-year-old rock drawings of the SAN people, in what is now BOTSWANA and the Kalahari, routinely depicted people wearing beaded jewelry that archaeologists believe was made of ostrich eggshells. Eggshell beads worn as flattened disks have also been documented among the Turkana of northern Kenya. In other societies plant seeds, straw, reed fibers, seashells, fossilized bone, and animal horns were used as well.

To make such beads, a sharpened tool probably would have been positioned over the bead and either hammered or worked until each side was pierced. Some powdery substance, possibly chalk, was most likely added to make the bead easier to string. Fibers used for the strings probably included palm leaves, sisal, and vines. The rough grainy surface of other rocks was used for polishing the finished bead, which ultimately might be round, flat, square, hexagonal, or even barrel shaped.

The analysis of some beads recovered from ancient Egypt's Predynastic Period, c. 4000 BCE, indicates that they were made of *steatite*, or soapstone, which was considered a precious stone. A glaze was used to give beads a glasslike appearance. By the Fifth Dynasty (c. 2494–2345 BCE), early forms of glass beads were being made. Blue faience, green feldspar, lapis lazuli, carnelian, turquoise, hematite, and amethyst also came into popular use in Egypt, undoubtedly carried by merchants associated with the Mediterranean and Red Sea trade.

In later eras, these beads spread from Egypt to regions south of the Sahara, most likely carried by Arab merchants along camel routes to the IVORY COAST, GHANA, and Nigeria. Various populations along the East African coast wore carnelian beads, which possibly reflects early trade in that region. In fact, beads represented an important form of currency in early regional economies. The monetary value assigned to a specific number of beads on a string might have an equivalent value to locally made items or food and in many cases served as an important form of BRIDEWEALTH.

The origins of certain types of beads have yet to be identified. In West Africa, two types of Akori beads rank among the oldest recovered in the region. Type A is the oldest, dating back to 439 CE. Other beads in the region include the Aggri, whose origins are unknown. Made of glass or porcelain material, Aggri beads have generally been found embedded in the earth and may have been associated with important ritual activity.

From the earliest times, beaded masks, crowns, and other royal objects have been associated with reigning kings in Ghana, Mali, CAMEROON, Kwazulu-Natal, and Nigeria. In Akan society, kings and priests traditionally have worn special bead bracelets to convey their royal status. However, beads may have held a particular appeal for women since they offered a creative outlet and an important source of income. Among the Ndebele of South Africa, for example, beads were used to announce an impending engagement. Elsewhere, the Pokomo and Akamba women have long performed certain important ceremonies wearing beaded "dance necklaces" or collars. The best known of this form of beadwork has traditionally been worn by MAASAI women.

Along with traditional uses, beads transmit the history and culture of a particular region, creating an outward expression of unity between generations. In South Africa, the Xhosa use ornate beadwork to designate various AGE SETS. Unique designs serve as symbolic code words relating to history, proverbs, and sometimes poetry. Similarly, countless generations of Zulu women have used beads as a form of education, transmitting social ideals to young girls in vibrant patterns that accent clothing, bags, and accessories.

As Africa's economy continued to evolve, beads and the way they were worn became more ornate, eventually coming to include a greater variety of glass, coral, bronze, ivory, amber and silver.

See also: JEWELRY (Vol. I); RED SEA TRADE (Vol. II).

Further reading: Claudia Zaslavsky, *Africa Counts: Number and Pattern in African Cultures* (Chicago: Lawrence Hill Books, 1999); J. Ki-Zerbo, ed., *General History of Africa, Abridged Edition, I Methodology and African Prehistory* (Paris: UNESCO, 1990); Barbara Watterson, *The Egyptians* (Oxford, Eng.: Blackwell Publishers, 1998).

bees Bees have been domesticated for thousands of years. The first mention of beekeeping in ancient Egypt occurs as early as 2400 BCE. The ancient Egyptians made good use of bee products: They used honey as a food sweetener and as a cosmetic for softening the skin and treating open wounds. Bee venom was sometimes used as medicine. Beeswax was used to prepare mummies and build ships, and was combined with pulverized stone to make a type of glue. Egyptians traded honey with other countries and wore jewelry decorated in the shape of bees.

Ancient Egyptian marriage contracts required husbands to provide wives with honey throughout the marriage.

Behdet Ancient city of UPPER EGYPT, also known as Edfu, whose patron god was HORUS. With the increasing instability of government rule during the First Intermediate Period (c. 2213–1991 BCE), Upper Egypt and LOWER EGYPT divided into warring kingdoms. The inhabitants of Lower Egypt reportedly worshiped SETH of Ombos, while those of Upper Egypt recognized the reigning god as Horus of Behdet. After Egypt's reunification c. 2000 BCE, Horus became the national god of the Egyptian state. From that time forward, reigning kings were known as "the living Horus." Behdet was also the site of a metal foundry, where blacksmiths, known as *mesnitu*, created religious icons, using a forge located within the city's great temple.

Further reading: E. A. Wallis Budge, *The Gods of the Egyptians: Studies in Egyptian Mythology* (New York: Dover Publications, 1969); George Steindorff and Keith C. Seele, *When Egypt Ruled the East*, rev. ed. (Chicago: University of Chicago Press, 1957); Barbara Watterson, *The Egyptians* (Oxford, Eng.: Blackwell Publishers, 1998).

Beja Ethiopian KUSHITES, also known as Hedareb nomads, who share an ethnic and linguistic affiliation with a number of groups that inhabit the Red Sea hills along the border of Sudan and ETHIOPIA. Speakers of one of the oldest dialects in Ethiopia, also called Beja, the Beja people tend to be scattered, undoubtedly the result of their traditional way of life as nomadic pastoralists. A patrilineal society composed of a number of small, related clans, the Beja were loosely organized under a chieftan's rule. The Beja contributed to MEROË's decline by raiding caravans and crippling trade. The Aksumite king Ezana, in fact, described them as constantly engaging in warfare with their regional neighbors.

See also: AKSUM (Vol. I); BEJA (Vol. II); CLAN (Vol. I); PASTORALISM (Vol. I).

Further reading: I. Hrbek, ed., *General History of Africa, Abridged Edition III: Africa from the Seventh Century to the Eleventh Century* (Paris: UNESCO, 1992); Harold G. Marcus, *The History of Ethiopia* (Berkeley: University of California, 1995); Richard Pankhurst, *The Ethiopian Borderlands* (Lawrenceville, N.J.: The Red Sea Press; 1997).

Benue-Congo Branch of the Niger-Congo language family. Benue-Congo languges are spoken from the Cape of Good Hope northward to Nigeria.

See also: BANTU (Vols. I, II); LANGUAGES (Vol. I).

Benue River West African river that is the longest tributary of the NILE RIVER. Flowing for approximately 673 miles (1,083 km), the Benue is an important water highway for the transportation of COTTON, peanuts, and other trade goods. Originating in northern CAMEROON, it flows through falls and rapids across central Nigeria. Along its course, the Benue River marks the border of Cameroon and the Nigerian state of Benue. It varies in width from 1,600 to 3,200 feet (488 to 976 m) and is joined by the Mayo-Kebbi tributary and the Gongola River before converging with the Nile, about 30 miles (48 km) from the Nigerian coast.

Berbers Pre-Arab peoples of North Africa, also known as Tuaregs, who for thousands of years have inhabited the areas from the Moroccan coast to the Siwa Oasis in EGYPT and from the Mediterranean to the SAHARA Desert.

Based on archaeological findings, the Berbers are known to have occupied parts of MOROCCO as early as 1600 BCE. Their history goes well beyond this, however, and although the exact origin of the Berbers is unknown, historical evidence dates them to at least 3000 BCE. Indeed, most scholars consider them to be the original population of North Africa. Over the centuries, however, the Berbers have mixed with so many ethnic groups that they have lost much of their independent racial identity.

Throughout time, two primary groups of Berbers inhabited the lands of North Africa. One group has historically consisted of farmers and cattle raisers living in the northern plains and mountain regions. The second group consisted of semi-pastoral nomadic peoples living in the deserts and pasturelands.

The livestock and agricultural products of the Berbers have played an integral role in their cultural and ethnic composition. In the twelfth century BCE, the PHOENICIANS established a large trading empire on the North African coast. Phoenicians relied on the Berbers to supply them with crucial foodstuffs for their settlements and for export. Not only were the Berbers exposed to the manufactured goods of the Mediterranean world, but they also fell under the influence of the Semitic culture of the Phoenicians. This helped pave way to the Berbers' later acceptance of the three major monotheistic religions: JUDAISM, CHRISTIANITY, and Islam.

Ancient Berber society was essentially feudal in structure, with distinct classes that included nobles (primarily nomads and pastoralists), the clergy (called *inislemen*), vassals, artisans (*inadan*), and laborers (called *iklan*). Berber society also tended to maintain a social and class distinction between agriculture and trade, with farming falling to the lower classes and trade to the upper.

ROME overtook the Carthaginian Empire in the second century BCE because Roman leaders wanted to control the wealth of Egypt and access the trade of Asia and the Indian Ocean. During this time, however, a wealthy and powerful Berber state existed in Numidia. The Numidian Berbers possessed an inordinate number of camels, an animal perfectly suited to the desert conditions. This provided them with great military strength and the ability to control trans-Saharan trade routes. The Romans viewed this Berber state as a threat and eventually conquered the Berbers, making Numidia a part of the Roman Empire. Rome continued to rule this area for more than 600 years, giving rise to a Romano-Berber population that still exists to this day.

See also: BERBERS (Vols. II, III); PASTORALISM (Vol. I); TUAREGS (Vol. II).

Further reading: Thurston Clarke, *The Last Caravan* (New York: Putnam, 1978); Jeremy Keenan, *The Tuareg: People of Ahaggar* (New York: St. Martin's Press, 1977).

Beta Israel (Falasha) Agriculturists who dominate the highlands north of LAKE TANA and the outskirts of GONDAR in ETHIOPIA. Also known as Falasha, they have maintained their faith in the Jewish religion over several millennia and, in small numbers, still live in Ethiopia to this day.

There are many conflicting legends and myths concerning the origins of the Beta Israel (or "House of Israel"). One of the most widespread stories involves their descent from the noblemen who accompanied King MENELIK from Jerusalem when he reportedly brought the ARK OF THE COVENANT to Ethiopia. Menelik, the first king of the Solomonic Dynasty, is traditionally identified as the son of King Solomon and MAKEDA, the queen of Sheba. Another legend, however, identifies the Beta Israel as one of the lost tribes of Israel who established their kingdom in Ethiopia following the Hebrew exodus from EGYPT.

Whatever their origin, the roots of the Beta Israel stretch back well before the arrival of Semitic farmers from southern Arabia c. 600 BCE. Many of their religious texts are ancient, attesting to the longevity of their faith. Beta Israel are strict observers of the Jewish Sabbath, and their Bible, translated into GE'EZ, is the cornerstone of their religion. Traditional priests, or *kohanim*, elected by the Beta Israel serve as spiritual leaders of the community. Outsiders have commented that their ceremonies reflect a fusion of traditional African practices, along with rites of the Christian faith; yet observance of the Jewish calendar's holy days and festivals, rites of purity, consumption of ritually slaughtered animals, and male circumcision are also strictly observed.

JUDAISM apparently was widespread in the region of Ethiopia before the adoption of CHRISTIANITY during the fourth century. At that time, those who refused to convert were persecuted and forced to live in the mountainous highlands. Subsequently, as outsiders within a predominantly Christian society, the Beta Israel lived as a segregated caste, surviving by weaving, making pottery, and working as BLACKSMITHS or goldsmiths. Although the region's ruling elite held these crafts in low regard, this expertise allowed the Beta Israel to maintain a sense of independence and identity. They were able to form their own social guidelines, elect leaders, and retain their religion and culture.

See also: BETA ISRAEL (Vols. II, III); SOLOMONIC DYNASTY (Vol. II).

Further reading: Miguel F. Brooks, *Kebra Nagast (The Glory of Kings): The True Ark of the Covenant* (Lawrenceville, N.J.: Red Sea Press, 1998); Donald N. Levine, *Wax and Gold: Tradition and Innovation in Ethiopian Culture* (Chicago: University of Chicago, 1965).

Betsileo A Malagasy people who make up the second largest ethnic group in Madagascar. The Betsileo are a mix of BANTU and Malayo-Indonesian peoples who settled on the island during the first millennium. They practice a form of ancestor worship influenced by traditional CHRISTIAN beliefs.

See also: MADAGASCAR (Vols. II, III).

Bilad al-Sudan Region of West Africa in which the ancient kingdoms of GHANA, MALI, and Songhai were located. This area was bounded to the north by the Sahara, to the south by the forest belt, in the east by the bend in the NIGER RIVER, and in the west by the middle reaches of the SENEGAL RIVER. The name *Bilad-al Sudan* is derived from an Arabic expression meaning "Land of the Blacks."

See also: SONGHAI (Vol. II).

blacksmiths Workers and skilled artisans, especially those working in iron and other metals. Since ancient times, the blacksmith has held a revered position in African society. Indeed, it is widely believed that there were two types of kings found in ancient Africa: One a warrior who ruled over a closed, stratified society and the other an artisan who reigned over a hard-working, open society.

In the SAHEL, early societies were nearly evenly divided between pro- and anti-blacksmith stratification. Although EGYPT itself was a caste-based society, the people of Ta-Seti, who according to legend invaded Egypt and established the dynastic period, were known as Mesniu ("blacksmiths") and supposedly did metal work with copper.

Egyptian legend has it that these people, who were identified with UPPER EGYPT, were followers of the god HORUS, while those in southern Egypt were followers of the god SETH. According to Egyptian mythology, after Horus killed Seth, the blacksmiths settled on land given to them by Horus. This land was located on both sides of the NILE RIVER, in what is called Middle Egypt. However, in one of several battles between the North and South at Anu, the South gained the victory.

The status of the blacksmith in African society has always been steeped in mystery, spirituality, admiration, and awe. The blacksmith is glorified and shunned, feared and despised. In many areas he is believed to have magical powers and, as a result, is afforded special privileges and bounded by special social mores. Some are humble and tactful; others are bold and arrogant.

In most African societies, because the blacksmith is considered a craftsperson, and therefore a person of respect, the products of blacksmiths are believed to have particular value; they are even said to have important powers. For this reason, works created by blacksmiths—which may be made of terra-cotta, stone, or wood as well as metal—are used to adorn and declare social status. These objects also may help establish the presence of a spirit, since a well-crafted object is believed by many peoples to be able to call forth both divine and human spirits. For this reason, these crafted objects are important in nearly every aspect of African culture, from war to births, marriages, harvest celebrations, and funerals.

Among many groups, rites of passage are a significant focus of art objects. Beyond the rituals associated with such familiar passages as birth, puberty, marriage, and death, many groups hold special induction ceremonies for healers, diviners, blacksmiths, and other skilled craftspeople; in some societies, the blacksmith performs some or all of these functions.

Blue Nile River located in northwest ETHIOPIA, approximately 850 miles (1,360 km) long. In ancient times, the Blue Nile sustained agricultural crops such as cotton, wheat, sorghum, dates, sugar cane, and legumes. Its waters provided fish for inhabitants of the region and transported merchants to and from EGYPT.

From its source at Lake T'ana in the Ethiopian Highlands, the Blue Nile descends thousands of feet through a deep gorge. It then journeys south and west through Sudan. At Sudan's capital city of Khartoum, the Blue and WHITE NILE meet above the Shabluka Gorge, forming the main stream of the NILE RIVER, Africa's longest river. Two-thirds of the Nile's waters come from the Blue Nile.

boats See GALLEY (VOL. I); SHIPBUILDING (Vol. I).

body adornment Personal adornment in Africa has always conveyed multiple meanings. Societal values, for example, associated with status, marriage, or initiation were often communicated through specific items of adornment. Early evidence for this has been found in cave paintings of the Tassili Plateau in the SAHARA, which date from c. 8000 to 6000 BCE. In one of several scenes, the woman archaeologists refer to as the *Horned Goddess* is seen performing a ritual dance. She bears the ancient markings of SCARIFICATION along with an elaborate headdress. Her image may have been meant to convey her place in society or to impart the importance of fertility; it may also have held other meanings. Other prehistoric images of this nature have been found in South Africa, where women in vulture headdress performed similar ritualized dances.

In Africa, hair, too, has always served as an important statement about the individual. The Tassilli cave provides one of the earliest images of the traditional hairstyle popularly known today as cornrows. In many parts of Africa, hair braiding evolved into what became an elaborate form of cultural identity that included family affiliations, lineage, and marital status. Married women in EGYPT, for example, reportedly wore shoulder-length hairstyles that appear to have been a series of twisted strands. By the time of the Eighteenth Dynasty in the NEW KINGDOM (c. 1550–1295 BCE), wigs made of animal wool and plant fibers were far more popular, particularly among the upper classes.

Recovery and analysis of ancient makeup palettes indicate that body adornment was also associated with the need to protect and enhance the skin. Groups like the SAN used animal fats colored by plant dyes. The Kuba used a mixture of camwood and palm oil that was applied to the face and body. Palettes containing cosmetics also indicated that both men and women in the Sudan wore makeup or facial paint. These palettes, sometimes containing alabaster or slate, have been linked to the Tasian, BADARIAN, and NAQADA I cultures that existed as long ago as 4000 BCE.

Another form of makeup began when Egyptians started to protect their eyes against the glare of the sun with powders made of pulverized lead, copper, antimony, or malachite. These powders were applied to the eye with wooden, stone, or metal sticks. Over time this form of application became highly stylized among women. Questions also have been raised about whether or not Egyptian women painted their lips. In answer, there are Egyptologists who point to the Egyptian word *seshet* as a word to describe a cosmetician, since it reportedly means "painter of her mouth."

Body adornment extended to the natural plant dyes and minerals used to create intricate patterns on the hands and feet. The application of henna leaf extract, widely used for this purpose was practiced by women in Egypt, NUBIA, and ETHIOPIA. Like other forms of adornment, this practice may have spread through interaction associated with regional trade or migration. It has also been associated with the IBO, whose patterns and methods were known as *uli*.

In Africa, men have always held strong ideals concerning adornment as well. The widely touted prenuptial contest associated with the Geerewol festival in Niger, Nigeria, and CAMEROON is a case in point. For many centuries, it has been the tradition of men of the nomadic FULANI people who are eligible for marriage to enter a contest in which women judge them on the basis of their artful use of makeup.

Eligibility for marriage has also generated other forms of body adornment in Africa. In various regions, the traditional fatting houses or fattening ceremony was usually reserved for young women between the ages of fifteen and eighteen years old. The goal of this ceremony was to add sufficient body weight to achieve a desired image of a large-sized, robust woman. Seen as adding to a woman's poise, elegance, and attractiveness, this practice was associated with wealth. The process was known to take months or as much as a year to complete. Along with an amplified diet, during this time, young women were taught social etiquette and given instructions about the proper role of a wife.

See also: BEADS (Vol. I); CLOTHING (Vol. I); JEWELRY (Vol. I).

Further reading: J. Ki-Zerbo, ed., *General History of Africa, Abridged Edition I, Methodology and African Prehistory* (Paris: UNESCO, 1990); John Middleton, ed., *Encyclopedia of Africa South of the Sahara,* Vol. 1 (New York: Simon & Schuster, 1997); Ali A. Mazrui, *The Africans: A Triple Heritage* (London: BBC Publications, 1986); Gay Robins, *Women in Ancient Egypt* (Cambridge, Mass.: Harvard University Press, 1996); Ivan Van Sertima, ed., *Black Women in Antiquity* (New Brunswick, N.J.: Transaction Publishers, 1997).

Book of the Dead In ancient EGYPT, a series of funerary texts containing magical spells and prayers. The Book of the Dead was written on PAPYRUS scrolls and often illustrated with colorful images.

The texts that make up The Book of the Dead were intended as instruction manuals for the souls of the deceased, a way to help them overcome the obstacles they would encounter while passing through the underworld. The most important of these texts are The Book of Going Forth by Day, The Book of What Is in the Underworld, and The Book of Gates.

The images in the texts originated as decorations on the walls of tombs of Egyptian royalty and nobles in the OLD KINGDOM (c. 2705–2213 BCE). Later, in the MIDDLE KINGDOM (c. 1991–1668 BCE), they were used to decorate the insides of the coffins of commoners, nobles, and royals alike. The texts themselves were not written down on papyrus scrolls until the NEW KINGDOM (c. 1570–1070 BCE). Although these scrolls were costly to produce, they became popular among those who could afford them and continued to be widely used until the end of pharaonic rule in Egypt.

The Book of Going Forth by Day was the text most frequently used by the ancient Egyptians. It is a loose collection of about 200 sections, or chapters, containing the magic spells and passwords to be recited by the deceased in the AFTERLIFE. According to Egyptian belief, these words would help ensure that the deceased would pass safely through the underworld to enjoy the blessings of paradise.

Another text, The Book of What Is in the Underworld, also was known as *Amduat*, was first found on the walls of the tomb of the pharaoh THUTMOSE I; this collection of royal funerary texts was intended as a guidebook to the underworld. According to common Egyptian belief, the book would help the deceased travel safely around the underworld and successfully reach the appropriate destination in the afterlife.

The Book of Gates stands apart from the other funerary writings because of the emphasis it places on the importance of the sun god RA. In The Book of Gates, Ra is portrayed as the creator and preserver of life, as well as the one who resurrects the dead. The work contains spells to make the Sun rise and to show the paths the deceased must travel in his or her voyage in the boat of Ra.

See also: DEIR EL-BAHRI (Vol. I); KARNAK, TEMPLE OF (Vol. I).

Further reading: Carol Andrews, ed., *The Ancient Egyptian Book of the Dead* (Austin: University of Texas Press, 1990).

Boran Oromo Also called the Borana or Borena, a subgroup of the OROMO nation. Described as pastoralists, the Boran have occupied northwest Borena and the southern region of ETHIOPIA for thousands of years. Considered the guardians of culture and tradition, their most important institution was the *gada* system, which has exerted a strong influence on its members and, like AGE GRADES, traditionally has been exclusively for men. This age system emphasized cultural identity, exerted societal control, and organized social, political, and religious activities.

Boran government consisted of the eldest men of the *gada* system. These men, known as *jarsa biyya,* presided over moral and customary law, ceremonies, and religious life. From forty-seven to fifty-five years of age, men were chosen to act as priests or *quallu.* As such, they were authorized to represent Waqa, considered the creator of life. Through different activities Boran men gained critical insights into how their society functioned. This knowledge was reflected in their outward appearance, and especially in their wooden walking staffs.

From a very young age, Boran boys and men traditionally learned to carve staffs, or forked sticks, that signify work activities, entry into adolescence, and even marriage. Married Boran women carried a *siqqe,* a staff with a point that has three layers.

Creating a wooden staff required a critical set of circumstances. For example, only specially designated trees could be cut, and only on certain days of the week. The wood of the *Haroreessa hiddo* tree was the first choice among carvers since its moist wood was considered a symbol of life. After being carved, the sticks were dyed and then oiled with butterfat to maintain the life force of the tree. Considered a living object, the wooden staff of a Boran man was broken and left on his grave when he died.

Border Cave Multilevel cave situated in the region between Kwa-Zulu Natal in South Africa and Swaziland. Excavations at Border Cave have unearthed many significant findings from the STONE AGE period.

Using radiocarbon and other dating methods, archaeologists have been able to trace recovered skeletal remains to a period ranging from several thousand to millions of years. The recovered skull and mandible fragments found in Border Cave 1 and 2, for example, are between 100,000 and 150,000 years old, a period that corresponds to what is generally considered to be the Middle Stone Age in Africa. This, in turn, has helped archaeologists identify the remains as belonging to the species known as *HOMO SAPIENS*, which is generally considered the ancestor of modern human beings.

Additional excavations at Border Cave 3 have unearthed the skeletal remains of an infant as well as remnants of a shell that may have come from ostrich or emu eggs. The cave was also a source of hematite, which, according to some evidence, ancient populations mined more than 28,000 years ago. (Hematite is a mineral that ranges in color from black to red and represents the chemical component of iron ore.) It is possible that this hematite was used as either a paint for BODY ADORNMENT or to create cave art. However, the presence of this material may also indicate iron-making activities that may have occurred in the region at a later date.

See also: PASTORALISM (Vol. I); ROCK ART (Vol. I).

Further reading: Thomas R. Hester, Harry J. Shafer, Kenneth L. Feder, *Field Methods In Archaeology* (Mountain View, Calif.: Mayfield Publishing Co., 1997); Samuel Kasule, *The History Atlas of Africa* (New York: Macmillan, 1998); James L. Newman, *The Peopling of Africa: A Geographic Interpretation* (New Haven, Conn.: Yale University Press, 1995).

Botswana Landlocked country of southern Africa bordered by present-day South Africa, Angola, Namibia, Zambia, and Zimbabwe; once known as Bechuanaland. Nearly equal in size to the state of Texas in the United States, present-day Botswana is noted for its arid, subtropical temperatures and vast, sandy plains. One of its major rivers is the Okavango that feeds into a number of inland northern deltas. The Makgadikgadi Salt Pans support diverse wildlife species, including wildebeest, antelope, and zebra. In contrast to the Kalahari Desert, or "thirstlands," in the southwest, Botswana's eastern region consists of rocky hills and shallow sand.

Botswana may be one of the oldest regions of the world, with underlying bedrock estimated at 2.5 billion years old. Based on a number of archaeological studies, the region also appears to have been populated from an early period. Historians generally agree that Botswana was first occupied by SAN hunter-gatherers between 20,000 and 30,000 years ago, if not longer. They appear to have occupied the Kalahari as well as the northern deltas. Some sources indicate that the Khoikhoi (meaning "men of men"), PASTORALISTS who occupied various regions in South Africa, arrived slightly later, and coexisted with the San in Botswana.

At the eastern site known as Depression Shelter in Tsodilo Hills, archaeologists have found evidence of continuous land use from 17,000 BCE to 1550 CE. It is believed that the highly fertile soil in this area supported large settlements of clay and thatch homes. These are believed to have been arranged in a circle around a central court or gathering place. However, it is not yet clear which of the groups occupied these settlements since the activities of San HUNTER-GATHERERS and Khoikhoi pastoralists were sometimes interchangeable, based on the availability or scarcity of food resources.

It is generally believed that BANTU-speaking farmers migrated into Botswana approximately 1,500 to 2,000 years ago. Their methods of crop cultivation relied on a method known as swidden agriculture, which involves the cutting

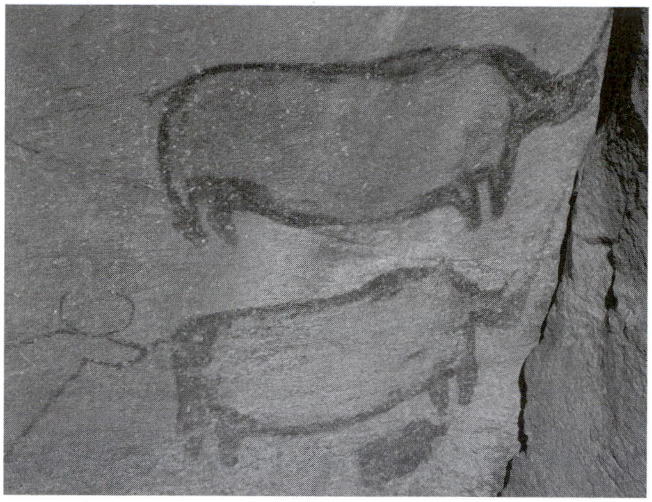

Rock paintings, some possibly 20,000 years old, created by the San peoples have been discovered in the Tsodilo Hills, Botswana. *© Galen Rowell/CORBIS*

and burning of forestland to promote fertility. This method stood in contrast to the smaller environmental impact made by the San and Khoikhoi. The Bantu were also associated with iron-making in Botswana. Remnants of an iron-smelting furnace dating to at least 190 CE have been recovered at a site in TSWAPONG HILLS near Palapye. Its use undoubtedly placed further demands on natural resources for fuel.

The Tswapong Hills have been a particularly rich source of archaeological discoveries. Located in the eastern part of the country, near the city of Serowe, the hills contain numerous caves and gorges that have yielded some of the most extensive information about early Bantu-speaking peoples yet found in southern Africa. These peoples, called the TSWANA, migrated into the region beginning about the first century CE and overcame the indigenous !KUNG SAN, who had inhabited the region for up to 300,000 years prior to this.

The extraordinary number of rock-paintings preserved in Botswana's arid environment has greatly expanded present-day knowledge of social exchange among these groups. Most of the paintings have been attributed to the San since they depict traditional healing rites, rainmaking ceremonies, animal sacrifice, and a range of other activities associated with hunting and gathering culture. A number of archaeologists, however, admit that it is possible that others were responsible for making these paintings, since some images depict relationships between the San and the Khoikhoi. Other paintings show battles between the San and Bantu and are suggestive of group conflicts. One such painting, found in the area of Gaborone, modern Botswana's capital city, is an engraving that primarily shows animal tracks and human feet. It is traditionally attributed to Matsieng, a creation myth figure who generally is considered to be an early Tswana ancestor.

According to some historians, the central issue responsible for such conflict involved farms that had been established by Bantu-speakers in the San or Khoikhoi settlements of Tsodilo Hills. Eventually the San and Khoikhoi were marginalized to outlying areas of Botswana, and the Bantu, known today as Tswana (Batswana), emerged as the region's dominant ethnic group.

Further reading: Philip D. Curtin, *African History* (Reading, Mass.: Addison-Wesley, 1995); J. Ki-Zerbo, *Methodology and African Prehistory* Vol. 1, *General History of Africa,* abridged edition (Paris: UNESCO, 1990); James L. Newman, *The Peopling of Africa* (New Haven, Conn.: Yale University Press, 1995).

boxing Traditional contact sport; in ancient times it involved the use of fists or wrestling poses. The earliest evidence for a boxing-like contact sport in Africa comes from hieroglyphic inscriptions from EGYPT that date to approximately 4000 BCE. They describe a sport whose origins can be traced to ancient ETHIOPIA, where the sport was known as TIGIL.

Boxing held a significant place in ancient Ethiopian society because it provided an outlet for the aggression of young males. It also served as a source of entertainment at public celebrations, holiday events, and harvest festivals. Generally, young men were matched with opponents of the same age, height, and level of skill or strength. Winners were subsequently paired off to fight against competitors from other villages.

The sport seems to have spread to the NILE VALLEY as a result of centuries of contact and intercultural exchange between Egypt and Ethiopia. From Egypt, it made its way to the Mediterranean world and, sometime later, became an essential part of Greek and Roman sport.

Further reading: David Buxton, *The Abyssinians* (New York: Praeger, 1970); Ali A. Mazrui, *The Africans: A Triple Heritage* (London: BBC Productions, 1986).

bridewealth A symbolic gift in the form of money, goods, services, or livestock made by prospective grooms to the family of the bride.

Bridewealth is an ancient, widespread tradition practiced in city-states as well as in outlying rural societies of Africa. One of the earliest references to bridewealth appears in Egyptian texts dating back to the seventh century BCE. Marriage contracts, known as *shep en sehemet*, detailed property and monetary items that listed the bridewealth the groom presented to the father of the bride. Although restricted primarily to the upper class, such a list provides some idea of the potential value women held as future queens, priestesses, or landowners.

More than likely, these contracts also represented a political alliance, a theme repeated in many other African societies in which marriages were arranged through a council of elders or reigning chiefs. Luxury items such as cloth, COPPER bracelets, BEADS, hoes, CATTLE, and various forms of livestock solidified the marriage, with the expense for these items borne by the entire family of the groom. This expense sometimes was so great that it was paid over several years.

In rural African societies, bridewealth was shaped by different traditions and needs. In ancient times, communities such as the IBO of southern Nigeria and the NUBA of the Sudan, required a groom spend months or even years cultivating land that belonged to the bride's family. In these regions, the agricultural labor of a woman and her future children was associated with potential land ownership. As a result, these societies required that a woman's birth family be compensated for the loss of this labor. By the time of the IRON AGE, in regions that included present-day Central African Republic, Congo, and Cameroon, where YAM, cassava, and peanut crops were cultivated, groups such as the Banda presented iron farming implements as bridewealth. In contrast, the Serer of western Senegal placed a high value on livestock and used goats, cattle, and sheep as a bride price. Cattle were used by Khoikhoi and TSWANA in the eastern region of BOTSWANA and in various regions of South Africa.

Overall, the concept of bridewealth allowed a man to obtain full conjugal benefits and full rights to any offspring produced within his marriage, along with an awareness of a woman's value to her family. It also served as a way to effectively control the number of wives a man might attain. Inversely, the custom served to discourage the likelihood of divorce, since custom demanded that, in the event of a divorce, the woman's family return the gifts that had come to them as bridewealth.

See also: FAMILY STRUCTURE (Vol. I); POLYGAMY (Vol. I); SERER (Vol. II).

Further reading: Gay Robins, *Women in Ancient Egypt* (Cambridge, Mass.: Harvard University Press, 1993); John S. Mbiti, *African Religions and Philosophy*, 2nd ed. (Oxford, Eng.: Heinemann Educational Publishers, 1999); Catherine Coquery-Vidrovitch, *African Women: A Modern History* (Boulder, Colo.: Westview Press, 1997).

Bronze Age Prehistoric period following the STONE AGE and preceding the IRON AGE, during which weapons and other implements were made of bronze, an alloy of COPPER and tin.

Copper was the first metal that people used to their advantage in large quantities. Though scarcer than iron ore, copper ore can be found in places relatively easy to access. Furthermore, because it is soft and has a low melting temperature, copper is easy to work. As a result, to this day metal workers generally need only wooden mallets and other rudimentary implements in order to shape copper into jewelry and ornaments. However, this softness also limits copper's usefulness, making it relatively weak when used for weapons and tools.

Tin, however, also is abundant and, when added to copper, has a hardening effect. This led to the production of bronze, which was used in many of the great civilizations of the ancient world. While much is known about the use of bronze in EGYPT, the Middle East, and the Mediterranean, little is known about the extent of its use in sub-Saharan Africa. Evidence shows that bronze objects were used in NUBIA and in southern Sudan. In addition, tools, arrowheads, and other weapons—all made of bronze and dating to the fifth century BCE—have been found near Akjoujt, in Mauritania. The origin of the technology needed to make this metal is unknown, but archaeologists and historians have posed the theory that knowledge of the process came to other parts of Africa from Carthage.

Iron has often been called the "king of metals," and it has traditionally brought increased military power and advanced agriculture, as well as domination of trade and control of rich natural resources, to societies with the technology to use it. If iron smelting developed as early as the Haya people appear to have accomplished it, then the need for a Bronze Age technology might have been bypassed. In fact, it is readily conceivable that, in most of western and southern Africa, many cultures went straight from the Stone Age to the Iron Age. This is further borne out by the fact that iron smelting was practiced as early as the first millennium BCE in most areas of the middle Senegal valley and the inner NIGER DELTA. As a result, the need for bronze may primarily have been for the making of symbolic and ornamental objects. If this indeed was the case, then those people who already had iron technology had the riches to import any bronze items they wanted.

Bunyoro Kingdom located in the western area of what is now Uganda; also a people of the same name. Little is known of the origins of the Bunyoro and their kingdom, but they apparently were part of an ancient kingdom called Kitara, in which agricultural Bantu-speakers were ruled by pastoralist kings and nobles called the Chwezi.

See also: BUNYORO-KITARA (Vols. II, III).

Burundi Landlocked country in East-central Africa, bordered by RWANDA, Tanzania, and the Republic of Congo. Burundi's first inhabitants are thought by some scholars to have been the hunter-gatherers known as the TWA, a physically small ethnic group that apparently was present when the first BANTU-speaking people arrived. By the fifth century, the HUTU, who were agriculturalists, began migrating into the area. This migration lasted until the eleventh century, by which time the Hutu had come to dominate the Twa and other groups in the area.

See also: BURUNDI (Vol. III).

Bushmen Term sometimes used, especially in the past, to refer to the SAN people of the Kalahari region. The term is believed to be derived from the word *bosea*, or "small," which was used by the early Dutch settlers in South Africa. Though the word *Bushmen* has been widely used, many anthropologists and historians now find the term derogatory, preferring SAN or, in the dialect of BOTSWANA, Basarwa.

Buto Chief goddess and protector of ancient LOWER EGYPT; also called Uto, Edjo, and Per Wadjit. Buto was often depicted as either a deadly COBRA wrapped around a papyrus stem or a woman wearing the RED CROWN of Lower Egypt. When portrayed as a rearing cobra with a spread hood, ready to spit poison on the pharaoh's enemies or incinerate them with her fiery glare, the image of Buto is called the *uraeus*.

Buto, the personification of the Sun's burning heat, was the queen of all the gods. She was regarded also as a goddess of the night and was honored with one of the six great festivals of the ancient Egyptians. According to Egyptian mythology, Buto, whose name literally means "she who is green," was nurse to the infant god HORUS. In this role, she protected the child from his treacherous uncle, SETH, by hiding him in the Delta marshes.

Along with NEKHBET, the vulture goddess of UPPER EGYPT, Buto was believed to defend and protect the royalty of united EGYPT. Depicted together on the royal diadem and other works of art, the two goddesses symbolized the sovereign's reign over Egypt. In addition to her role as the protector of the pharaohs, Buto was believed to bite and kill Egypt's rulers at their appointed times of death.

The goddess's name was given to the city of Buto, which was the capital of the sixth NOME, or province, of LOWER EGYPT and a major center for the cult that worshiped the goddess.

Byzantine Africa Area of Africa, including North Africa, EGYPT, and part of LIBYA, that belonged to the Byzantine Empire from the third century CE until the coming of Islam in the seventh century.

The eastern portion of the Roman Empire continued to be an important political, social, economic, and religious force after the breakup of the Western Roman Empire at the end of the fifth century CE. Historians call the Eastern Roman Empire the Byzantine Empire, after Byzantium, the ancient name of its capital city, Constantinople (now Istanbul, Turkey), but to its people and rulers it was simply the Roman Empire. Its official language was Greek, although its inhabitants spoke a variety of languages and dialects that ranged from Latin to Coptic and Armenian. It was made up of lands in northeastern Africa, southeastern Europe, and southwestern Asia. Although parts of the empire were lost to Islam and other threats, the Byzantine Empire remained significant until 1453, when the Turks captured Constantinople and founded the Ottoman Empire.

The history of Byzantine Africa begins when Octavian, by then the emperor Augustus, made Egypt a province of Rome in 30 BCE, a year after the death of CLEOPATRA. Roman colonization, coupled with Augustus's successful quieting of hostile peoples in the area, created conditions that led to four centuries of prosperity.

The Founding of Constantinople By the third century CE, the Roman Empire began to decline as a result of internal strife, famine, and war. In 306, DIOCLETIAN named Constantine (c. 288–337), later known as Constantine the Great, his successor in the West. By 312, Constantine had defeated his rivals for the throne and became emperor of the West, ruling as co-emperors with Licinius in the East until 324, when he defeated Licinius in battle, converted to Christianity, and moved his capital to the site of the ancient city of Byzantium, located on the Bosporus, the strait of water that separates European Turkey from Asian Turkey on today's map. Constantine dedicated his new capital as a "new Rome" in 330, renaming it Constantinople after himself. The move placed the new administrative capital of the empire in a place of strategic and commercial advantage between Europe and Asia. Constantine died in 337. His sons and nephews fought for control of the Empire and even wanted to restore traditional Roman religion. The Empire permanently split into its eastern and western parts after Emperor Theodosius I died in 395. The fall of the Western Roman Empire is often dated to 476, when Germanic invaders forced the last emperor, Romulus Augustulus, from the throne.

North Africa in the Byzantine Period North Africa thrived under Roman rule. The numerous and spectacular ruins at various sites in TUNISIA and Libya attest to the prosperity of the region.

Between the first and third centuries, private estates of considerable size became common, many public buildings were erected, and an export industry flourished. Many North Africans received Roman citizenship; in 193, a North African, Septimus Severus, even became emperor.

Following Constantine the Great's declaration of religious freedom for all in the empire in 313, CHRISTIANITY in North Africa grew strong. The fourth and fifth century church fathers Tertullian, Cyprian, and Saint Augustine, the bishop of Hippo, were important leaders whose writings had an effect throughout the early Christian world.

By the end of the fourth century, however, Roman civilization in North Africa was entering a period of decline. The Germanic Vandals invaded Africa and soon made Carthage their capital.

See also: BYZANTINE AFRICA (Vol. II)

C

Cacheu River River that runs approximately 125 miles (201.1 km) through central West Africa in the territory of present-day Guinea-Bissau. The river flows to the west, where it ultimately reaches the Atlantic Ocean near the town of Cacheu (formerly spelled Cacheo). The surrounding coastal lowlands produce crops of sorghum, cassava, corn, and millet and are also used for grazing cattle, sheep, and goats.

See also: CACHEU (Vol. III).

Caesar, Gaius Julius (c. 100–44 BCE) *Roman general, statesman, and dictator.*

A brilliant military strategist, Caesar joined with Pompey the Great and Marcus Licinius Crassus in a three-way alliance called the First Triumverate, which ruled Rome from 53 to 50 BCE. At that time, Rome dominated the Mediterranean region, ruling lands on both the African and European seacoasts. Operating from a Roman post in Syria, Crassus prompted a war with the Parthians. Crassus's defeat and death at the hands of the Parthians at Carrhae, in 53 BCE, destroyed the fragile alliance that had ruled Rome. Pompey attempted to seize all power for himself, but Caesar amassed his armies and drove Pompey from Rome. Pompey fled southward, ultimately to EGYPT, where PTOLEMY XII had him killed in 48 BCE.

At that time, Ptolemy and his sister, CLEOPATRA VII, were engaged in a civil war for the Egyptian throne, which had been left vacant by their father's death in 51 BCE. To settle the matter, Caesar, who had followed Pompey to Alexandria, ordered both Ptolemy and Cleopatra to submit to his judgment. Beguiled by Cleopatra's charms, Caesar had her installed as queen of Egypt. Refusing to accept the ruling, Ptolemy escalated the Egyptian civil war, and Caesar himself almost died in the battles that raged through the streets of Alexandria. But by March of 47 BCE, Caesar had overcome Ptolemy and secured Cleopatra's seat on the throne. Caesar remained in Egypt with Cleopatra for several months. The queen later gave birth to a son, Ptolemy Caesarion, whom Caesar acknowledged as his own.

After leading Roman armies in Asia Minor and quieting a rebellion in Rome, Caesar returned to Africa in 46 BCE. This time, however, he went to NUMIDIA, where King JUBA had allied himself with three mutinous Roman military leaders. Caesar swiftly and soundly defeated this alliance and declared Numidia a province of Rome.

A victorious Caesar returned home, where he declared himself dictator of all Rome. Cleopatra reunited with him in Rome later that year. Secure in his rule, Caesar drew up plans to rebuild the once-great African coastal city of CARTHAGE. Before he could see his plans come to fruition, however, he was assassinated by a group of Roman senators on March 15, 44 BCE. It was left to Caesar's grandnephew, Octavius (Augustus), who succeeded him as Rome's ruler, to carry out this plan to resurrect Carthage.

See also: ROMAN EMPIRE (Vol. I).

Caesar, Octavian (Augustus) (63 BCE–14 CE) *First emperor of Rome, who gained power by defeating the combined armies of Roman statesman Mark Antony and Cleopatra VII, queen of* EGYPT.

Born Gaius Octavius, Octavian was the grandnephew and favorite of Julius CAESAR, who adopted him as his intended successor as ruler of Rome. Upon his great-uncle's assassination in 44 BCE, Octavian took the name

Gaius Julius Caesar. By making peace with his rivals, Mark Antony and Marcus Aemilius Lepidus, Octavian ended the civil war that had followed Caesar's death.

Beginning in 43 BCE, the three ruled the empire as a triumvirate, with Lepidus ruling over Rome's extensive dominions in North Africa, which included both NUMIDIA and Mauritania. Within several years, however, Octavian had forced Lepidus from power and wrested control of Africa for himself.

In 37 BCE, Antony abandoned his wife Octavia (Octavian's sister) and married CLEOPATRA VII. Octavian felt his position as Caesar's only recognized heir to be even further threatened when Antony accepted Caesarion, Cleopatra's son by Julius Caesar, as her coruler. Five years later, claiming that Cleopatra exercised undue power over Antony, Octavian declared war on the queen of Egypt. By 31 BCE, Octavian's forces had overwhelmingly defeated those of Antony and Cleopatra. Within a few months, Octavian had captured and annexed Egypt, Antony and Cleopatra had killed themselves, and Caesarion was executed. Ultimately, Octavian also seized Cleopatra's treasure, using it to pay off the pensions of his military veterans.

Now the sole ruler of the Roman Empire, Octavian gave himself the title of augustus. He ruled the Roman Empire for more than forty years (27 BCE–14 CE), restoring the empire to peace and prosperity.

Cairo Capital of EGYPT and largest city in Africa.

Located on the east bank of Egypt's NILE RIVER, Cairo was officially founded in 969 CE. Prior to this, the city had been known by a variety of names, including MEMPHIS, Heliopolis, and Babylon. During its ancient history, it was governed by a long list of rulers, from the ancient Egyptians, Greeks, and Romans to the Arabs and Turks.

About 5,000 years ago, MENES, the legendary pharaoh who united UPPER EGYPT and LOWER EGYPT, founded the city of Memphis approximately 15 miles (24 km) south of modern-day Cairo. In 525 BCE, invading Persians established a fort, called Babylon, north of Memphis, from which they controlled Egypt until the arrival of ALEXANDER THE GREAT in 332 BCE. The region later fell under the rule of the Romans.

See also: CAIRO (Vols. II, III).

calabash Hard-shelled fruit gourds produced from a tropical vine or tree; common varieties include the white-flowered, or calabash, gourd (*Lagenariasic eraria*) and the bottle gourd (*Cuucurbitaceae*), both of which come from vines. Bottle gourds bear fruit that is edible when young but, when grown from seed, they require a great deal of time to produce. This is, perhaps, the basis for Dahomean folk tales that relate that the calabash symbolizes the earth—its two halves representing the land and the sky.

Used since ancient times as a decorative and practical item in the tropical regions of Africa, the hard-shelled gourd has also been prized most as a handy storage container. Traditionally, because of the great variation in gourd shape, the finished vessel often resembled a club, dipper, kettle, or trough, measuring anywhere from a few inches to several feet in height. In order to make containers, the gourd and its ripened fruit were soaked in water. The fruit disintegrated and was discarded and the hard outer peel became more pliable. After being dried in the sun, it was easier to carve into various shapes or to add incised decorations and symbols. Colors of calabash gourds ranged from ochre to golden brown and were often accented by the dark oil of shea nuts. Among the most elaborately decorated calabashes, which featured beads, leather or reed coverings, were those produced by the FULANI of Adamawa, in CAMEROON.

Finished calabash containers were most often used to store grains, water, milk, medicine, and tobacco. They were utilized even when broken as digging tools or as spoons for serving or eating. For centuries calabash played an important part in making MASKS. Calabash has also been used in the creation of musical instruments.

One traditional calabash instrument of ancient origin had seeds or pebbles woven into a net or macramé covering. When shaken, the beads produced a rhythmic amplified sound against the hollow gourd. Smaller hand versions had beads sealed within the calabash. In northern GHANA, the Frafras made a *duuliga*, or violin, from the calabash gourds. Generally it was covered with snakeskin and leather. The instrument's playing strings were made from horsetails with inverted twigs used as a bridge. Other instruments made from the calabash gourd include the African thumb piano, noted for its resonating sound created by a hollow cavity and metal or bamboo "keys." The *balafon*, similar in design and sound to a xylophone, was also made from the calabash.

The hard shell is capable of withstanding various manufacturing and decorative techniques. Most common were resist dye techniques, which entailed creating designs from candle wax or the paste of cassavas. Stamps made from calabash shells have also been used to decorate fabric with ornate designs, symbols, and proverbs.

Because of their durability, versatility, and beauty, calabash containers have always been highly regarded. Quite frequently the technique of making calabash art, as well as the vessels themselves, was passed down from one generation to the next, making them an important source of material culture.

See also: SHEA BUTTER (Vol. I); THUMB PIANO (Vol II).

Further reading: Laure Meyer, *Art and Craft in Africa* (Paris: Terrail, 1995); Thelma R. Newman, *Contemporary African Arts and Crafts* (New York: Crown Publishers, 1974).

calendar Arrangement of time into periods, for example, years, months, weeks, days, and so on. As many recent archaeological discoveries demonstrate, calendars have been important to the peoples of Africa since ancient and even prehistoric times.

Calendars may have been used in Africa for far longer than scientists previously believed. One of the most interesting recent archaeological discoveries is a piece of bone found in the present-day Republic of Congo. Dating back to between 9000 and 6500 BCE, the bone has thirty-nine notches carved on its surface. At first, the artifact was believed to be linked to some kind of numerical notation. Further study, however, led scholars to suggest that the notches are part of a system noting the phases of the Moon. If so, this notched bone might be one of the earliest calendars yet discovered.

Ancient societies probably first began to note time in relation to natural events or work routines that were repeated in regular ways. As a result, these people most likely divided the year into periods of planting or harvest or into times of rain or drought. At a later date, they began to notice and incorporate into their thinking patterns involving the progressions of the Sun, Moon, or stars.

The lunar calendar was one of the earliest attempts to organize these observations. Lunar calendars are based on the phases of the Moon, with generally a month assigned to each lunar cycle. Since each of these cycles is only about twenty-nine days long, lunar calendars inevitably were "short" almost eleven days when compared with the 365¼ day solar year. As a result, over the years, lunar calendars inevitably became out of step with the seasons. To rectify this, some societies developed calendars based on a different number of months; others periodically instituted various kinds of corrections to their calendars.

The Ancient Egyptian Calendar The ancient Egyptians are generally recognized as the first people to develop a calendar based on the movements of the Sun. Although it too had several inaccuracies, the Egyptian calendar represented a major step forward in the measurement and recording of time. It is uncertain exactly when the ancient Egyptians created the first versions of this calendar, but some scholars believe that its use dates back as much as 6,000 years.

The Egyptians based their calendar on their observations of the Sun, stars, and NILE RIVER. Noting that Sirius, which is one of the brightest stars in the heavens, was invisible for a period of several months, they discovered that it reappeared in the eastern sky just prior to the beginning of the Nile's annual flood. This fact became the cornerstone of their calendar, which divided the year into a system of twelve thirty-day months. They then brought the total number of days in a year to 365 by adding five festival days, each in tribute to a different major deity.

The Egyptian calendar also was divided the year into three seasons, each of which was four months long. These seasons reflected shifts in the climate as well as other changes in the natural environment. The season of *akhet*, for example, roughly corresponded to the modern season of autumn and marked the time of the Nile's flood, which lasted from mid-July to mid-November. *Peret*, the next season, lasted from mid-November to mid-March and represented the Egyptian winter. *Shomu*, the Egyptian equivalent of summer, began in the middle of March and lasted until mid-July.

The solar year's extra one-quarter day was not taken into account by the ancient Egyptians. But Egyptian civilization lasted so long that this seemingly minor error eventually became a major problem. In fact, it got to the point that the Egyptian calendar and the progression of seasons were so mismatched that the Egyptians were having winter during a time that, according to the calendar, was actually summer! The Egyptians eventually rectified the situation by creating a new calendar.

Calendars in Other Parts of Africa Elsewhere in ancient Africa, other types of calendars were used. For thousands of years, for example, astronomer-priests in West Africa based their calendars on the rising and setting of certain stars. This allowed them to link the planting and harvesting of certain crops, as well as the celebration of key religious festivals, with the predictable arrival of nature's seasons.

In other parts of Africa, variations of a lunar calendar were used. Some peoples reconciled the discrepancies between the lunar cycle and solar year by allowing for special "days of waiting," often a period in which people "waited" for the annual rainy season to begin. The individual months of the year were often named for activities typical of that time; months also were simply assigned numbers.

Other peoples dealt with the discrepancy between the lunar and solar cycles by creating twelve different months that were, in turn, divided into four unequal weeks. Thus, a month would begin with the disappearance of the Moon and then progress through weeks lasting for ten days, ten days, four days, and five days. Each of these days often had a particular spiritual significance and was believed to bring either good or bad fortune to humans, domestic animals, and wild creatures alike.

Some peoples developed particularly accurate systems for predicting the seasons. The Kamba of present-day Kenya, for example, traditionally calculated the arrival of rainy and dry seasons with the aid of the Sun. By drawing lines through certain points in their fields, they were able to measure the position of the sun and make surprisingly accurate predictions about the arrival of the seasons.

See also: ASTRONOMY (Vol. I).

Cambyses (r. 529–521 BCE) *King of the Persian Achmeunid dynasty, who ruled ancient* Egypt *in the sixth century* BCE.

Cambyses is believed to have solidified his power by killing his brother Smerdes in 529 BCE. In 525, Cambyses completed the conquest begun by his father, Cyrus the Great, who had invaded Babylon in 539. After the conquest, Cambyses became the first ruler of the Egypt's Twenty-seventh Dynasty. According to the ancient historian HERODOTUS, Cambyses was a harsh king who treated his Egyptian subjects poorly. Herodotus also claimed that Cambyses lost his sanity and committed suicide, but there is little evidence to support these claims.

camel Camels stand about 7 feet (2.1 m) and weigh approximately 1,500 pounds (680 kg). They have long necks, small ears, thick eyelashes, and powerful, sharp teeth for fighting. Their coats vary in color from dusty white to golden brown. Camels with one hump are known as dromedaries and are bred for riding.

Flat, thick-soled cloven hoofs that do not sink into the sand, double rows of protective eyelashes, and nostrils lined with hairs to protect against flying sand are all physical traits that make camels suitable to the desert environment. Camels are able to survive on coarse vegetation and can drink as much as 25 gallons (95 l) of water in a matter of minutes. Their famous humps serve as storage areas for fat and allow them to go for days without water. Capable of carrying loads of 500 to 600 pounds (227 to 272 kg), camels can travel at speeds up to 8 to 10 miles (12.9 to 16.1 km) per hour for as long as 18 hours at a time.

For centuries, camels have been used by the people of North Africa and the SAHARA as means of carrying loads across the desert. It is believed that camels originated in North America 40 million years ago and then spread to South America and Asia.

Camels had a relatively late start in Africa, having been introduced to the ancient Egyptians by the PHOENICIANS some time in the fifth century BCE. Soon after their arrival in Africa, however, camels became prized for their ability to carry trade goods across the Sahara. They were also valued for wool, meat, and milk.

See also: CARAVANS (Vol. II).

Cameroon Country in West-central Africa. Cameroon is an ethnically diverse land, featuring over 200 distinct ethnic groups, including both the FULANI and various MBUTI groups.

Cameroon borders the Gulf of Guinea to the southwest, Nigeria to the northwest, Chad to the northeast, the CENTRAL AFRICAN REPUBLIC to the east, and the Congo, GABON, and Equatorial Guinea to the south. Geographically, the country is divided into four regions. The coastal region of the southwest, which is dominated by dense rain forests and swamps, has one of the wettest climates in the world, receiving, on average, more than 150 inches (381 cm) of rain a year. Just past the coast there are a number of volcanic mountains whose slopes hold much of the country's most fertile soil. Of these mountains, Mount Cameroon is the tallest, with an elevation of 13,350 feet (4,069 m). Beyond these mountains is a dense forest in an area that is about 1,000 feet (305 m) above sea level. In Cameroon's interior is the Adamawa Massif. Rising to a height of 4,500 feet (1,372 m), it is dominated by savanna. Further north, the savanna becomes the marshy land surrounding Lake Chad. Here, the climate is drier than in the rest of the country.

In the south, the Sanaga, Wouri, Nyong, and Ntem Rivers run west into the Atlantic Ocean. The CHARI and Logone Rivers move north from the Adamawa Massif and drain into Lake Chad. A river system in the Chad Basin, which includes the BENUE RIVER, flows into the NIGER RIVER basin of Nigeria. The Ngoko River and Sangha River join together and flow into the CONGO BASIN.

Archaeological evidence suggests that Cameroon has been occupied for about 50,000 years. The first people to live in the area were MBUTI groups, known in Cameroon as the Baguielli and Babinga. For thousands of years these people have inhabited Cameroon's southern forests, hunting antelope, wild pigs, and other animals, and gathering foods like wild fruit, nuts, tubers, and caterpillars. Living in clans of ten to one hundred members, they are NOMADS, moving as needed to places where food is more readily available. As a result, they live in huts that can be fully constructed in a matter of hours.

About 2,000 years ago, different ethnic groups began migrating to the Cameroon region. The most important of these were the Sudanic-speaking Sao people, who settled around Lake Chad sometime in the first century.

See also: CAMEROON (Vols. II, III).

Cameroon grassfields Region bordered by present-day Nigeria to the west; noted for its extensive iron industries.

The early widespread use of iron in the grassfields appears to have been linked to the wealth gained from early food production and trade. Among the region's earliest population groups were HUNTER-GATHERERS known as the Baka, said to have occupied the region approximately 50,000 years ago. Early forms of food production reportedly occurred c. 4000 BCE and included the cultivation of YAMS and bananas.

Migrating BANTU-speakers from equatorial Africa later settled in the southern forests of Cameroon and the western grassfields. These groups appear to have been related by common languages and cultural practices and formed a number of diverse patrilineal societies, including the Chamba, We, and Isu. They were also among the many groups credited by some historians with bringing traditions of iron making to the region.

Radiocarbon dating has confirmed that smelting techniques were used in the region thousands of years ago. Nearly one hundred sites at which smelting occurred have been identified; they are believed to have been used to produce a wide range of items associated with agriculture, hunting, and household use. Iron may also have been used to create symbols and various other items related to royalty. At least one group, the Mbum people, made iron tokens of uniform shape. These tokens, made in varying denominations, could only be used in very specific ways, including the purchase of trade or prestige items, or as a form of BRIDEWEALTH.

It is known that later kingdoms developed as a result of successful trade. One of the most powerful and long-lived dynasties in Cameroon was associated with the Tikar. Other significant kingdoms were organized by the Bamileke, Bamenda, and Bamum.

In examining many of these ancient smelting sites, and speaking with the modern-day descendants of the ancient inhabitants, archaeologists have been able to reconstruct early METALLURGY processes. On a physical level, the process consisted of placing iron ore and charcoal into a heated foundry. The recovery of glazed material indicates that high temperatures were used for long periods at a time, which suggests that foundry workers may have processed the iron over several days.

Other aspects of iron making included such rituals as specific prayers, songs, or dances. As a result, the physical act of creating iron and the traditions that surrounded it were compared to the act of procreation. Potent herbs were traditionally buried beneath the furnace to strengthen the "birth" of a malleable form of iron.

Throughout the grasslands, there apparently were many taboos associated with iron production as well. Arguments or any acts of bloodshed—accidental or deliberate—were not allowed at iron-making sites. Menstruating women were barred as well. Married men were therefore the main keepers of the grassfield furnaces and were instructed to refrain from sexual relations prior to and during the process of smelting.

The formation of such ritual activity appears to have been based on the belief that iron could absorb the positive or negative practices associated with adult life. This was particularly true for weaponry such as spears, daggers, knives, or machetes, all of which were considered significant targets of negative influences. Masters of the forge were those men who best understood the various facets of iron production. They were among the earliest kings and were considered some of the most powerful members of early grassland societies, often credited with the power to heal or destroy.

See also: IRON WORKING (Vol. I); *NUMUW* (Vol. II).

Further reading: "Magical Iron Technology in the Cameroon Grassfields," in *African Material Culture* (Bloomington: Indiana University Press, 1996).

Canary Islanders Inhabitants of the Canary Islands, a group of mountainous islands in the Atlantic Ocean that lie about 50 miles (80 km) off the coast of northwest Africa. They include Gran Canaria (Grand Canary), Tenerife, Lanzarote, La Palma, Fuerteventura, Hierro, and Gomera, among others.

The origins of the people of the Canary Islands are uncertain. Juba II, who ruled Mauritania from 29 BCE to about 20 CE, sent an expedition to the islands, and they were found to be unpopulated. However, the expedition did find the remains of some ancient buildings on Gran Canaria.

It is believed that Roman ships visited the Canaries in the third century, as Roman amphoras (narrow-necked jars) of that era have been found off the shores of the islands.

cape buffalo Large mammal belonging to the same family as the WATER BUFFALO and CATTLE. Unlike the water buffalo, which originally came from Asia, the cape buffalo is native to the African continent and has not been domesticated. The cape buffalo is black or dark brown, and adult males can grow to nearly 6 feet (1.8 m) tall at the shoulder and can weigh up to 2,000 pounds (908 kg); females are smaller.

Cape buffalo are highly social animals that live in large grazing herds of up to 2,000 members. In ancient Africa, cape buffalo could be found throughout the sub-Saharan continent on open savannas and grassland, as well as in swamps and lowland rain forests.

Capsian culture Ancient African civilization that settled in the southern region of what is now Tunisia as long ago as c. 6000 BCE. They are generally believed to be the direct ancestors of modern-day Libyans. *Capsian peoples* and *Capsian culture* are phrases that are used to describe the large number of prehistoric tools produced during what some archaeologists call the Late Paleolithic period and that others refer to as the Late STONE AGE. The name was borrowed from the inland regions that include the great salt lakes of el-Meka located near Qafsah (Capsa). Capsian peoples were largely sedentary, and the fact that plant food products have been established as a formative part of their diet may account for an expanding population. And, although they domesticated plants, evidence suggests that the Capsians also hunted.

There have been various reports that the tools and products of this culture were in place approximately 10,000 to 6,000 years ago. Recovered tools include a type of drill created to bore holes in ostrich shell fragments, which were then strung and worn as necklaces. Many stone microliths or blades have been recovered along with pottery. Overall these finds provide a picture of a sedentary society.

The influence of the early peoples of this region is believed to have spread to the northern and eastern regions between 9000 and 5000 BCE. Evidence from the later NEOLITHIC AGE after the sixth millennium indicates that cattle became an essential source of trade at this time, perhaps through the influences of EGYPT or various groups from the Sudan.

The evolution of the Capsian people in the Neolithic period is reflected in the name *Neolithic of Capsian tradition*, which archaeologists have used to identify a significant shift in certain traditions or tool-making capabilities. Until the first millennium BCE, for instance, archaeologists speculate that because the climate and environment were well suited for hunting, the techniques for making appropriate tools developed. Therefore, this was a period characterized by the use of iron tools and weapons. Archaeologists also say that the Capsian peoples had mastered many uses of fire and probably introduced it to parts of West Africa.

Analysis of several rock carvings found in the Atlas, Ahaggar, and Tibesti Mountain ranges have linked them to Capsian culture. These carvings are of great significance since they depict animals, some long extinct, that once roamed the region. Identifiable figures include the giant buffalo, ELEPHANT, RHINOCEROS, and HIPPOPOTAMUS. Findings of large middens, or refuse heaps, indicate that the region was inhabited by land mollusks as well. The areas of their former habitation are now largely desert terrain.

One of the most unique aspects of the region involves thousands of large, stone tombs or megalithic stone structures. Estimated to have been built around the first millennium BCE, the megaliths of Mzora, or Columnata, in ALGERIA stand nearly 200 feet high and have been credited to Capsian peoples.

Further reading: Elizabeth Ischei, *A History of African Societies to 1870* (Cambridge, Eng.: Cambridge University Press, 1997); J. KiZerbo, ed., *General History of Africa I: Methodology and African Prehistory* (Paris: UNESCO, 1990); James L. Newman, *The Peopling of Africa: A Geographic Interpretation* (New Haven: Yale University Press, 1995).

caravan routes Network of trade routes that extended from the sub-Saharan kingdoms of West Africa, including GHANA and Mali, across the Sahara Desert to Europe. For almost a thousand years, trade moved over these routes from the NIGER RIVER to the city of Sijilmasa in North Africa. Beginning about the fourth century CE, this trade was controlled by the Soninke Empire of Ghana. At the height of Ghana's power, which lasted for more than 700 years, these caravan routes were the lifeblood of the empire, carrying salt, slaves, ivory, civet, gum arabic, foodstuffs, cotton cloth, metal ornaments, leather goods, and, above all, gold.

See also: CARAVANS (Vol. II); TRANS-SAHARAN TRADE ROUTES (Vol. II).

Carthage Ancient city located on North Africa's coast near modern-day TUNISIA. Carthage was the principal city of the PHOENICIAN civilization. Later, it battled with ROME in the PUNIC WARS, during which it was burnt and destroyed. Carthage was rebuilt before being destroyed for good in the seventh century CE.

Phoenician Carthage Carthage was founded by the Phoenicians of Tyre in the ninth century BCE. The Phoenicians called Carthage *Kart-hadasht*, meaning "new town." According to tradition, the city was founded by the Tyrean queen Dido, who was fleeing her brother King Pygmalion. Built on a peninsula projecting into the Gulf of Tunis, Carthage had two harbors connected by a canal. Beyond the harbors was the Byrsa, a walled fortress built on a hill.

Carthage's Phoenician settlers were sailors and merchants. Little art was produced in the city, but it became a commercial center, with wharves, markets, and factories built by slave labor. The Phoenicians grew wealthy trading pottery, textiles, ivory, lumber, slaves, fruits, and metal. (The latter included deposits of silver, which, beginning as early as 800 BCE, were brought from mines in Spain and North Africa.)

The Phoenicians made great profits taking cheap manufactured goods, like pottery or jewelry, and trading them for valuable metals. In Roman times, Punic goods, such as beds, cushions, and mattresses, were both prized and imitated. Still, because Carthage produced so little art and literature, there is scant information about the government, language, and daily life of the city. Carthaginian religious rituals involved human sacrifice to Baal, a fertility god, and Tanit, the Carthaginian version of the Phoenician goddess Astarte. The Greek gods Demeter and Persephone and the Roman goddess Juno were also absorbed into Carthaginian religion.

Carthage's Empire By the sixth century BCE, Carthage dominated the entire North African coast, from the Atlantic Ocean to the western border of EGYPT. Carthage's empire expanded to include nearby Libyan peoples and older Phoenician colonies. It also controlled Sardinia, Malta, the Balearic Islands, and part of Sicily. One Carthaginian admiral, HANNO, traveled along the coast of North Africa about 430 BCE. Another expedition, led by Himlico, traveled up the Atlantic coast of Europe as far as Britain.

Between the fifth and third centuries BCE, Carthage engaged in a series of wars with GREECE and ROME. Carthage battled with the Greeks for control of Sicily, which was only 100 miles (160 km) from Carthage and was a perfect stepping-stone between North Africa and Italy. Carthage was defeated in Sicily in 480 BCE, when the forces of Carthaginian general Hamilcar were repelled by the ruler of Syracuse, Gelon. In spite of this defeat, Carthage still held territory in the western part of Sicily. Throughout the fourth century BCE, Syracuse's rulers made repeated attempts to rid Sicily of its Carthaginian presence. In 310 BCE, the forces of Syracuse's ruler Agathocles attacked and inflicted great damage on parts of eastern Tunisia. Agathocles' forces, however, ultimately were defeated.

Roman Carthage Carthage's three wars with the Romans are known as the Punic Wars. In the First Punic War, fought from 264 to 241 BCE, the Carthaginians were defeated and lost their hold on Sicily. The Second Punic War lasted from 218 to 201 BCE and featured the famous Carthaginian general HANNIBAL. Hannibal and his war elephants marched through Spain and France and crossed the Alps into Italy. Though he was victorious at Cannae, Hannibal ultimately lost to the Romans. As a result, the Carthaginians ceded to Rome control of Spain and a number of islands. During the Third Punic War, which lasted from 149 to 146 BCE, the Romans destroyed Carthage, spreading salt over the ruins as a symbolic gesture of contempt.

In 122 BCE, after a period of twenty-five years during which Carthage lay in ruins, a new city was built, called Colonia Junonia. This city survived only thirty years. Later, in 29 BCE, the Roman emperor Augustus rebuilt the city, fulfilling a wish made by his predecessor, Gaius Julius CAESAR. This new city was known as Colonia Julia Carthago.

Ruins of the ancient city of Carthage have been preserved in present-day Tunisia. *© Nick Wheeler /CORBIS*

Roman Carthage thrived, ranking behind only Rome in wealth and importance, and the city was a favorite of Roman emperors, although none lived there. Under the Romans, Carthage was also a center of Christianity. Important Christian Carthaginians included St. Cyprian, who was Carthage's bishop in 248 CE, and Tertullian, a Christian ecclesiastical writer who lived there in the third century CE. The famous philosopher St. Augustine was bishop of nearby Hippo in the fifth century.

Carthage declined after the third century CE. In 439, the Vandal king Gaiseric captured the city, which then became the Vandal capital for almost a century. In 533, the Byzantine general Belisarius captured the city and renamed it Colonia Justiniana Carthago in honor of the Byzantine emperor Justinian I.

Between 697 and 705 CE, the city was conquered by the Arabs. Among Carthage's ruins are the remains of fortresses, temples, and an aqueduct that date from the Roman era.

Carthaginian Religion The religious beliefs and traditions practiced by Phoenician settlers of Carthage founded in North Africa c. 813 BCE. Similar to other ancient societies of Africa, Carthaginians created a framework for religious worship that centered around a supreme god known in Africa as Baal Hammon. The word *Hammon* was associated with the Sun, an attribute that the Phoenicians apparently found strong and protective. A number of lesser deities coexisted with the high god, many of whom reflected the influence of EGYPT. For instance, in Carthage the deity Eshmoun was equivalent to ASCLEPIUS, considered a sacred healer in Egypt. Even from a personal perspective, Carthaginians generally had first names that reflected religious faith.

Over the centuries, historians and archaeologists who have studied this era and region have commented on the Carthaginian traditions involving human sacrifice. Based on the recovery of skeletal remains, archaeologists have determined that the practice of human sacrifice to *Baal* flourished well into the third century BCE. Generally, the victims were small children, killed in a religious ceremony that occurred once each year. Their burned bones make it uncertain as to whether this was the sole cause of death. There have been some reports that the children were the first-born males of wealthy families. Thousands of urns containing their ashes have been found in Hadrumetum, Motya, and Cirta, which became the capital city of the ruler known as MASINISSA. The urns at earlier sites were buried under large stone markers called stelae, but it is generally believed that this practice declined in the fourth century BCE. The urns were associated with the shrine of Tanit, a goddess who was widely worshiped after the fifth century and who may also have received sacrificial victims.

Since the burials of adults have generally been described as modest, with few burial goods, questions still persist among historians and archaeologists as to why such practices were so prevalent.

See also: CAESAR, OCTAVIAN (Vol. I); TRANS-SAHARAN TRADE ROUTES (Vol. II).

Further reading: Elizabeth Ischei, *A History of African Societies* (Cambridge, Eng.: Cambridge University Press, 1997); G. Mokhtar, ed., *General History of Africa II: Ancient Civilizations of Africa* (Paris: UNESCO, 1990).

caste systems Social classes separated from one another by royal status, specialized skills, or wealth.

In many West African kingdoms, the society's castes were made up of free people with special crafts, such as weaving, making pottery, or doing leather work. There also were castes of musicians and praise singers. In exchange for their services, caste groups like these often enjoyed the special protection of a kingdom's ruling class. This relationship generally lasted until the ruling class lost power, at which time caste members were forced to sell their wares or services to anyone who would buy them.

One of the most complex and significant castes in Africa was composed of BLACKSMITHS. These artisans, who made weapons as well as essential agricultural and household items, were consistently associated with both divine kingship and spirituality. Indeed, not only did many ancient kings use the blacksmith's anvil as a symbol of royalty, but the ORISHA, or deity, of war and iron was Ogún, a legendary figure who dwelled in the blacksmith's forge.

As in other parts of the world, the castes of ancient Africa faced limitations as well as enjoyed privileges. In areas such as RWANDA, for example, only members of the Hutu ethnic group were allowed to be blacksmiths. Elsewhere, in ETHIOPIA and western Sudan, there were religious taboos as well as negative assumptions about various craftworkers. These beliefs prevented generations of craftworkers from marrying outside the cast. They also limited caste members in their choice of marriage partners, often restricting them to members of certain castes.

See also: DEITIES (Vol. I); DIVINE RULE (Vol. I); *NUMUW* (Vol. II).

caterpillar The larvae (the first stage of an insect's development after it hatches from an egg) of a butterfly or moth.

The caterpillar has long fascinated the MBUTI of the Ituri rain forest of central Africa. These people use caterpillars to make poison for their arrowheads and, before their hunts, they will pray to N'go, the caterpillar deity, to make their poison strong. In Mbuti mythology, the caterpillar is believed to have divine qualities. Along with another insect, the PRAYING MANTIS, the caterpillar is associated with Kaang, the creator god.

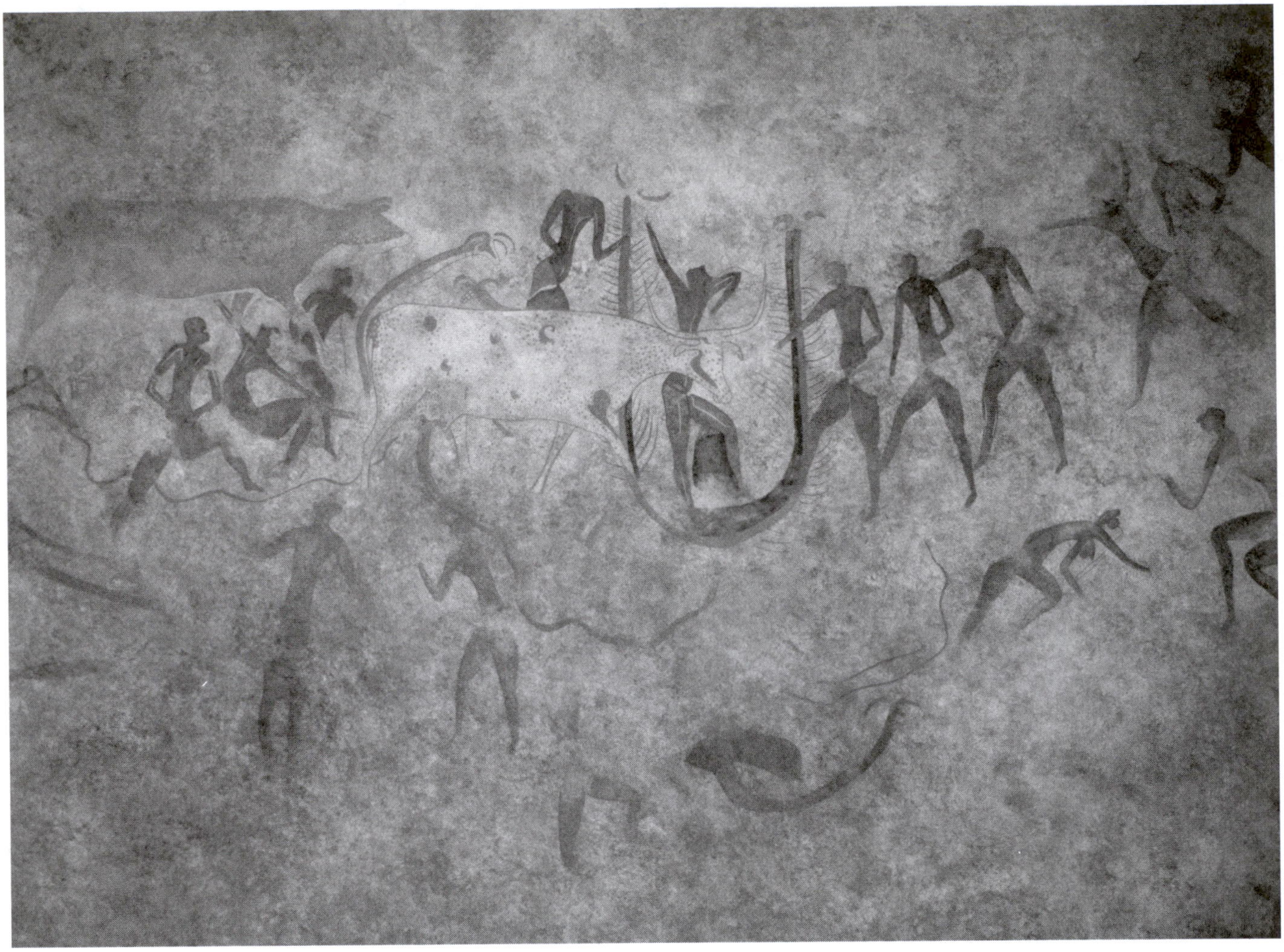

The cattle depicted in this rock painting from Algeria, created 4000–1500 BCE, are being washed in a river in the lotori festival, a Fulani initiatian rite. *© Pierre Colombel/CORBIS*

cattle Large grazing mammals raised for their milk, meat, and other products. In Africa, the domestication of cattle began between 5,000 and 10,000 years ago, following the domestication of sheep, goats, pigs, and dogs. Long-horned, humpless cattle were well-established in EGYPT'S Nile Valley by 4000 BCE. These cattle, known as the Egyptian, or Hamitic, longhorn, appear in pictographs on the walls of Egyptian pyramids. Over the next 2,000 years these animals migrated from the NILE to ETHIOPIA and into the southern reaches of the continent. Eventually, horses replaced cattle as sources of labor, leaving the primary value of cattle to be meat, milk, and leather.

Africa, like other continents, has known many breeds of cattle. Most are indigenous, having existed on the continent for thousands of years. Other breeds have evolved more recently through cross-breeding with either African or imported cattle. Regardless of their origins, however, cattle have been of profound importance to several peoples of Africa.

The MAASAI are one such example. For hundreds and even possibly thousands of years, Maasai life has revolved around cattle. Besides providing the Maasai with their basic food staple—milk—ownership of cattle determines virtually every social role as well as the social status of each individual person.

The breeds of cattle kept by the Maasai vary considerably, mostly because of the Maasai's age-old practice of clandestinely acquiring cattle from their neighbors. The Maasai traditionally have justified this tradition with a legend stating that their deity, Ngai, gave them the sole right to keep cattle. As a result, the Maasai maintain, their cattle tend to be larger and healthier than other peoples'. The truth is, however, that the Maasai have so many cattle that the offspring of both the Maasai and their cattle have more than enough milk to drink, and, as a result, are indeed healthy and sizable.

The FULANI are another people for whom cattle have been of prime importance for hundreds and hundreds of years. Mainly herders and traders, the Fulani established trade routes that fostered economic and political ties with otherwise isolated ethnic groups. As they traveled these routes, the Fulani traded with the sedentary farmers they passed, exchanging dairy products for agricultural products and luxury items. The Fulani then exchanged the latter for other goods as they continued on along their nomadic routes.

The Watusi, or Tutsi, developed a breed of cattle, known as the Ankole-Watusi, that became a favorite of breeders around the world. Medium-sized cattle with large-diameter horns, their ancestry can be traced back more than 6,000 years. Later, between the thirteenth and fifteenth centuries, these cattle were brought into northern Uganda by Hamitic peoples, leading to the eventual spread of Ankole-Watusi cattle from Lake Mobutu to Lake Tanganyika.

Among other important African breeds are the Bonswara and the Mashona, which also is known as the Makalanga or Makaranga. Another breed, the Nguni, is a subtype of the Sanga, which is associated with the pastoralist tradition of the BANTU-speaking peoples. Other important breeds include the Tswana and the Tuli.

See also: PASTORALISM (Vol. I).

Central African Republic Landlocked region bordered by present-day Chad, Sudan, Burundi, Congo, and Gabon. The Central African Republic is one of the smallest and oldest regions of the African continent, and origins of human life in the area date back a million years or more. Some historians even maintain that civilized societies were in place in this region well before the more well-known civilizations associated with ancient EGYPT.

The region was initially populated by HUNTER-GATHERER groups such as the Aka, whose lifeways were altered when the northern region was impacted by climatic changes known as pluvials, or prolonged periods of rain, that took place approximately 10,000 years ago. Many of these nomadic communities became sedentary; the people settled around the rivers, where they cultivated grain and fished. A number of these settlements bordered the CONGO RIVER in the southwest and undoubtedly contributed to the river's later importance as a prominent trade route. Unfortunately, the Congo River has also played host to many deadly diseases that decimated populations whose necessity for access to water stemmed from later annual dry seasons that sometimes lasted as long as seven months.

About 1000 BCE, migrating BANTU speakers began to dominate the region, forming a different type of social structure composed primarily of clans. Modern excavations in the region have unearthed many significant finds, which have provided telling information about the existence of these early groups and the events that shaped the region's history.

The earliest recovered stone tools were crude and worn. They have been described as "pebble tools" because of their small flakes or edges. In contrast, at a site known as Batalimo, the recovery of an advanced type of Acheulean hand-ax from the Ngoere River in Upper Sangha demonstrates how the tools used in this region evolved over time. Other finds include microlithic, or sharpened, tools made of hard flint and quartz; these date back approximately 8,000 years. Pottery associated with the Neolithic period (between 3000 and 1000 BCE), with distinctive designs and a flat bottom, distinguishes the regional inhabitants as early food producers. Overall, these findings are characteristic of a sedentary, well-developed society.

Stone megaliths erected in the Bouar region have been somewhat less easy to interpret. Megaliths like these, which generally are free-standing stones with distinctive shapes and which often weigh several tons, are usually erected by organized societies and are used as a type of burial site. (They also are known as *tumuli* or *cairns*.) Unfortunately, the absence of skeletal remains—a factor that archaeologists have attributed to high soil acidity—makes it difficult to confirm that the societies that built these stone pillars were indeed organized ones; only items made of iron have been recovered from the megalith sites during excavations.

Radiocarbon dating indicates that the megaliths of the Central African Republic range in age. The oldest megalith pillars were placed there about 5500 BCE; the most recent pillars date back from 450 BCE.

ROCK ART in the region also confirms the antiquity of early populations. Although paintings and engravings have been found in the northern and eastern regions of the Central African Republic, the northern cave sites are where archaeologists have discovered highly stylized yet identifiable human forms. They also have found numerous symbols drawn with red ochre.

The Central African Republic has been associated with early methods of food production, such as systematic planting, cultivation, and harvesting, that called for the use of specialized tools. Simple digging sticks were replaced with early forms of hoes, knives, and picks that were used to cultivate cereal grains and wild seeds such as MILLET and SORGHUM. The region has also been noted for its oil palm (*Elaeis guineensis*), a highly nutritional food product used for cooking and for making palm wine. The production of oil and wine became the basis of a significant industry in Africa. Food imports into the region included imported species of YAM. Bananas were another important food import; they were cooked in numerous ways and brewed as beer.

Other notable aspects of the region are its handicrafts, including BASKET MAKING, carved stools and masks, and a unique musical instrument known as the balafon. Made of animal horns, wood, and calabash gourds, the balafon was the forerunner of the modern day xylophone. Equally notable are the diamonds found throughout the region, which have attracted prospectors from around the world.

See also: CENTRAL AFRICAN REPUBLIC (Vol. III); COCOYAM (Vol. I); CROPS (Vol. II).

Further reading: John Middleton, ed., *Encyclopedia of Africa South of the Sahara*, Vol. 1 (New York: Simon & Schuster; Macmillan, 1997); G. Mokhtar, ed., *General History of Africa* (Paris: UNESCO, 1990).

Chari River River located in the Chad region of North-central Africa. The Chari, or Shari, is 600 miles (966 km) long and drains a 250,000 square mile (647,497 sq km) region before it flows into Lake Chad. It is the largest river system in the Lake Chad Basin.

The Chari River serves as the divider between the two contrasting regions of Chad: the SAHEL and mountain regions to the north and the Lake Chad floodplains to the south and west. The Chari River has historically offered an abundant supply of fish for the local population, and the sediments of the river create fertile soil for food crops as well as for cotton.

cheetah Swift, slender cat with long legs found on the plains and grasslands of Africa. With its powerful legs, the cheetah is well known as the fastest animal in the world, capable of reaching speeds of up to 60 miles (97 km) per hour. About 55 inches (140 cm) long, with 25-inch (64-cm) tails, cheetahs stand about 30 inches (76 cm) tall and weigh up to 130 pounds (60 kg). The coarse fur of an adult cheetah is colored a sandy yellow and is marked by small black spots. Two black streaks run down its face from the corners of its eyes.

Cheetahs usually live about twelve years. While male cheetahs live in groups of three or four, female cheetahs, except when they are raising cubs, usually live alone. Cheetahs hunt both alone and in small groups, generally during the afternoon and preying on GAZELLES, impala, and waterbuck. Cheetahs, in turn, are preyed upon by lions and leopards. Unlike most cats, their claws only partially retract, which allows the animals greater traction when they run.

In ancient times, Sumerian and Egyptian nobles trained cheetahs to aid them in their hunting expeditions. In ancient EGYPT, where cats were revered, the goddess Mafdet was often depicted as a cheetah, and, according to legend, she killed a serpent with her claws. Images of cheetahs also adorn the tomb of King TUTANKHAMUN.

child rearing Special rites and community participation associated with raising children. In Africa, the raising of children involves not only a child's immediate family but also the community at large and the child's ancestors. Child rearing also involves a reinforcement of the cultural values and traditions most cherished by each particular society.

In most African societies, community rites surrounding child rearing start at birth. The most ancient traditions of the Kikuyu, for example, call for them to bury the placenta of a recently born child in an uncultivated field. This is done because, to these pastoral people, open pastures symbolize all that is new, fertile, and strong. The Yansi, on the other hand, traditionally throw the physical remnants of birth into the river as a way of showing that the child belongs to the community. Both practices were meant to ensure that healthy children were born in the future.

Other rites were specifically designed to strengthen the bonds between fathers and newborns. Since the earliest times, Akan fathers, for example, traditionally were called upon to pour the child's first libation, or tribute, to the ancestors. Akan fathers also were required to provide the child's first pillow, which was a clean old cloth believed to carry the father's spirit.

African mothers also have been required, since ancient times, to perform special rites of purification. These rites usually begin during the earliest stages of pregnancy and might include carrying special charms and observing special taboos against the consumption of certain foods. Among the MBUTI, who have inhabited sub-Saharan Africa since the STONE AGE, women were long required to perform ritual offerings in the forest to ensure the safe delivery of their children.

One of the most significant rites associated with child rearing is the assignment of a name. Traditionally, important ceremonies accompanied the various naming practices. Among the Wolof, for example, a social event was organized in the mother's home. Taking place a week after childbirth, the child was seated on the lap of an elder. Its name (and the meaning of that name) was then whispered into the child's ear, along with a prayer, making the child the first to hear its own name. Only after this was the child's name formally announced to the jubilant attendees.

Among many African peoples, names were traditionally a sign of a strong belief in reincarnation, and children received the names of those ancestors they most resembled in physical features or behavior. A child might also have received the names of grandparents or significant community leaders. Descriptive names that might have been related to a special incident associated with the birth or the period of pregnancy might also have been given. In this way, the child might possibly acquire several names during his or her lifetime, each of which described, in some way, who he or she was.

Breast-feeding, for many peoples, represented the most critical time for young children, and it generally lasted anywhere from twelve to twenty-four months. Although this long period of nursing offered a built-in immunity for most children, once they were weaned such dangers as malnutrition and disease claimed many lives. Those children who did survive beyond this period, however, eventually came to flourish under the watchful eyes of older siblings, members of the household, and the community at large. In this way, children absorbed the social and cultural values of the society, as well as the community's codes of acceptable social behavior. Part of this process also involved identity or marks. For some societies, this sometimes meant physical markings, sometimes known as SCARIFICATION, on the face or body. In other societies, the piercing of ears or the wearing of particular kinds of jewelry or charms indicated that children had become full members of society.

Work tasks traditionally offered other learning experiences for young children. In some societies, especially in ancient times, children between two and four years old were expected to help with hunting and gathering, household tasks, herding sheep and goats, and feeding domestic animals. Rock paintings dating back to the prehistoric era tend to bear this out, showing women and children collecting fruits and nuts, as well as leaves and roots. As the children reached their middle years, more responsibilities were placed upon them, including obtaining water for the household, herding livestock, cultivating food, cooking, and running errands. By assisting adults, children expanded the food reserves of the family, providing for greater economic opportunities through trade or sale.

Puberty in ancient African societies traditionally meant greater involvement in the community. Initiation into adulthood was linked to sacred rites and secret societies. Already familiar with domestic and agricultural work patterns, the teenage girls of many societies were considered ready for marriage as soon as they were formally initiated into adult membership in the community. In some societies, particularly when BRIDEWEALTH was required, boys married anytime between eighteen and thirty years of age.

After a marriage took place, a young couple often lived within a parental household or compound (which parent, mother or father, depended upon whether the couple was part of a matrilineal or patrilineal society). In this way, a young couple was able to assist aging members of the extended family, who in turn passed on their wisdom to the couple's offspring.

See also: AGE GRADES (Vol. I); FAMILY STRUCTURE (Vol. I); RELIGION, PREHISTORIC (Vol. I); RELIGION, TRADITIONAL (Vol. I); WOMEN (Vol. I).

Further reading: Iris Berger and E. Francis White, *Women in Sub-Saharan Africa* (Bloomington: Indiana University Press, 1999); Anthony Ephirim-Donkor, *African Spirituality* (Trenton, N.J.: Africa World Press, Inc. 1998); John Mbiti, *African Religions and Philosophy,* 2nd ed. (Oxford, Eng.: Heinemann Educational Publishers, 1990).

Chiwara Mythical hero of the BAMANA people of central Mali.

According to tradition, Chiwara taught the Bamana how to farm. In his honor the Bamana hold a festival in which dancers wear masks representing antelopes, the animal associated with Chiwara.

In the Bamana language, *chiwara* literally means "farming animal." According to legend, the mythical Chiwara was the offspring of the first woman, Mousso Koroni, and a snake. Chiwara was a hard-working animal who tilled the soil using his claws and a magical hoe that had been given to him by his mother. In this way, Chiwara taught the Bamana people both the skill of farming and the value of hard work. The forgetful Bamana, however, became lazy when crops grew plentiful. Chiwara was disheartened and buried himself in the ground, never to be seen again.

In their festival in honor of Chiwara, Bamana males represent the sun, while the females are associated with the earth. Together, they symbolize the perfect balance of sun and earth that is necessary for a successful harvest. Wearing antelope masks, the dancers imitate the movements of the graceful animals by standing hunched over and carrying two short sticks as forelegs. They move to the beat of drums and songs of praise for the farmers sung by women. The word *chiwara* is also understood to mean "excellent farmer," the highest praise one can receive in Bambara culture.

See also: BAMBARA (Vol. II); MANDE (Vol. I).

Chokwe (Tchokwe, Ciokwe, Bajokwe, Badjok) BANTU-speaking people of southern Congo, northeastern Angola, and northwestern Zambia. A mixture of many indigenous groups and conquering peoples, the Chokwe can be traced back to the MBUTI, hunters and gatherers who were conquered by Bantu-speaking peoples about the sixth or seventh century.

See also: CHOKWE (Vols. II, III).

Christianity Along with Islam and JUDAISM, one of the world's three great monotheistic religions. Each believes in a single, all-powerful God, and each believes that its sacred scriptures represent the divine word of God as revealed to humanity. Christianity professes its belief in Jesus Christ as the son of God and the savior-redeemer of the world.

The Early Church in Africa According to Christian tradition, the religion was first brought to Africa when Jesus, Joseph, and Mary traveled to Egypt

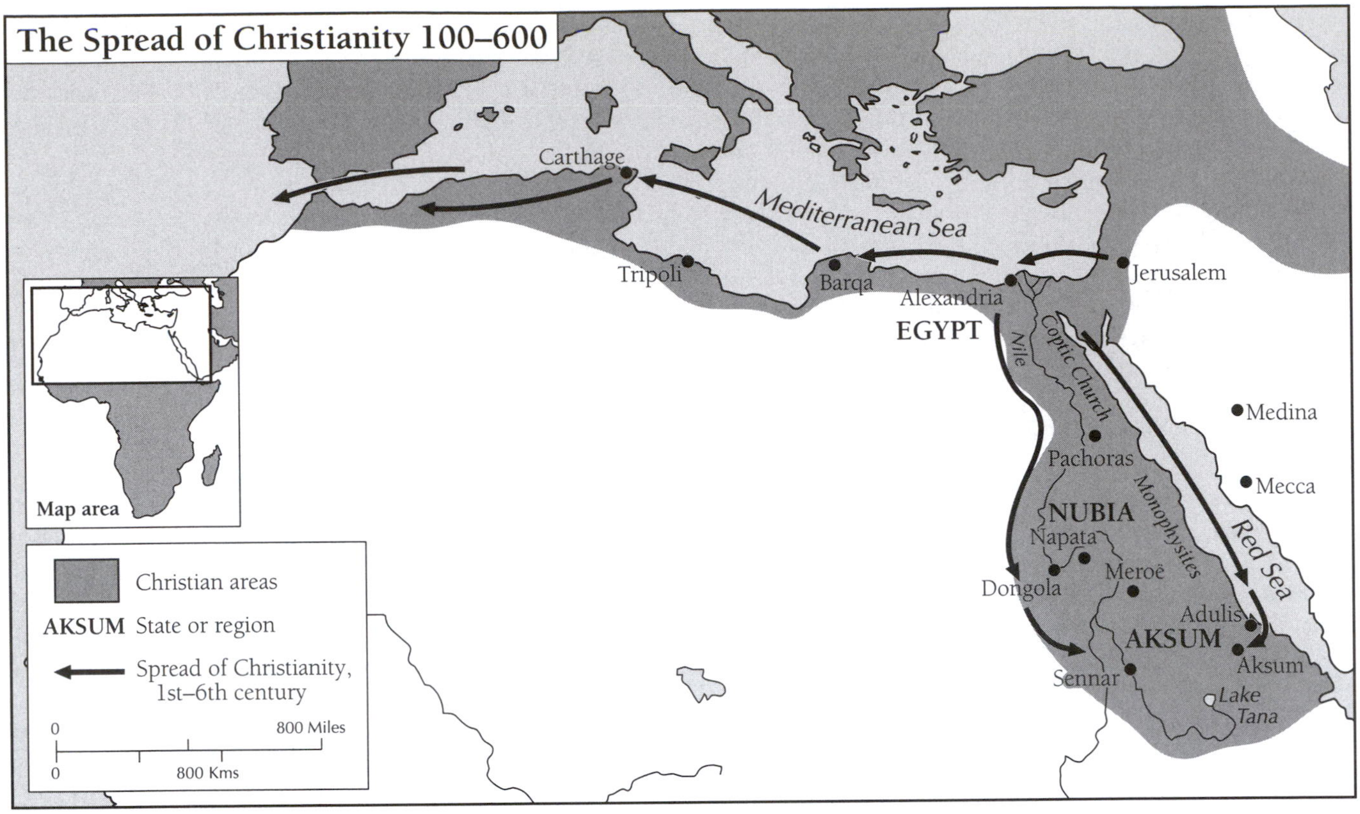

after Jesus' birth. The religion later flourished in parts of North Africa under Roman rule. The early African church had a strong presence in communities like CARTHAGE and Tangiers between the first and third centuries.

According to tradition, one of the first people to spread Christianity after Jesus' death was St. Mark, who preached in Egypt around the years 40 to 60 and founded a church in Alexandria. In Christianity's first two centuries, the religion spread quickly, with each region led by a bishop. By the year 220, Christianity had grown to the point that the province of NUMIDIA had thirteen bishops.

For many years, however, the Roman Empire continued to persecute early Christians. As late as 258, in fact, St. Cyprian, a theologian and the bishop of Carthage, was martyred for refusing to offer sacrifice to the Roman gods. By 313, however, the Edict of Milan was passed throughout the Roman Empire, allowing Christians to worship freely.

In its early days, the African church also underwent a number of controversies that resulted in breaks from the official church based in Rome. In the early fourth century, for example, the Donatist movement arose after a group of Numidian bishops objected to the appointment of the new bishop of Carthage. Instead of accepting the new bishop, they appointed their own, declaring themselves to be the true church. As a result, the Donatists, who at one time included one-half of the Christians in Africa, were persecuted and their churches confiscated.

In the fifth century, an argument involving the Monophysites also caused a schism, or split, in the church. It was at that time that the COPTS of EGYPT and Syria, who believed only in the divine—rather than the dual—nature of Jesus, broke with Rome.

Early African Christians were among the first important contributors to Latin Christian literature. One of the most influential thinkers in the early history of the Christian Church, St. Augustine, was born in Numidia. He became the bishop of Hippo, near Carthage, in 396; his writings include the *Confessions* and *City of God*. Other notable thinkers from Christian Africa include Tertullian and Cyprian.

The Catholic and Christian presence in Africa was diminished with the introduction of Islam between the seventh and tenth centuries. Still, the Christian Church in ETHIOPIA today stands as a descendent of the long tradition of Christianity in Africa.

Christianity and Traditional African Religions

Ever since Christianity spread to Africa, especially Roman North Africa, in the first five centuries, Africans have observed both Christian and traditional rituals and beliefs. At times they have even taken elements from both forms of worship.

Although there certainly is not one single traditional African religion, general similarities and differences can be sketched out between Christianity and the traditional beliefs of Africans.

Like Christians, many African peoples believe in the existence of one supreme being or creator god. However, early European visitors to the continent did not think this to be the case, partially because there seemed to be few shrines devoted to a supreme being. Since the creator was a remote being that stayed out of human affairs, few Africans offered worship to one god. Mulungu, for example, is the supreme, omnipresent god of many East African peoples. But this deity is prayed to only as a last resort, not as a matter of course or daily ritual.

Traditional African religions and Christianity also share a belief in an AFTERLIFE. Many African peoples, from the ancient Egyptians to the MBUTI of southern Africa, have buried the dead with their possessions so that they can use their belongings in the next world. Unlike Christians, however, many African peoples worship their ancestors, whom they believe have magical powers. The BANTU-speaking Fang people, for example, have long believed that the bones of ancestors can affect the fortunes of the people.

A major difference between the two belief systems is the acceptance of other deities. Unlike most African religions, Christianity does not allow its believers to worship any deity besides God. In contrast, followers of traditional African religions pray to various secondary deities as well as to their ancestors. These secondary gods serve as intermediaries between humans and the remote creator. The YORUBA people of Nigeria, for example, believe in a creator, Olorun, who watches over a group of divinities called ORISHA, to whom worshipers appeal to for guidance and support.

Another important difference is seen in the attitude toward nature and fertility. Christianity does not include rituals that celebrate nature or fertility. Traditional African religions, however, have long seen these principles as worthy of worship. The people of CARTHAGE worshiped a fertility god named Baal, who was represented as a calf and was offered human sacrifices. The Bambara people of central Africa hold an annual festival in honor of CHIWARA, the deity that was thought to have taught people to farm.

Today, missionaries have made Christianity popular in many areas of Africa. Nevertheless, African traditional religions continue to survive. In part, this is because, unlike Christianity, African religions do not observe a strict doctrine and constantly evolve to include beliefs of other religions. As a result, some African people observe a religion that combines traditional practices with Christian beliefs.

See also: CHRISTIANITY (Vol. II); CHRISTIANITY, INFLUENCE OF (Vols. II, III); MONOPHYSITE (Vol. I).

circumcision Surgical modification of male or female genitalia, or sexual organs. Although the controversy surrounding the practice of circumcision in Africa is recent, there is sizable evidence indicating that it is a cultural form dating back to antiquity.

Archaeologists have documented the earliest instances of circumcision in EGYPT in mummies, dating from at least 4000 BCE, that show evidence of the procedure. Additional evidence is provided by early travelers and writers about the region, including Herodotus (480–425 BCE), who noted that "the Egyptians and Ethiopians have practiced circumcision since time immemorial." From the NILE Valley the practice appears to have spread through resettlement and migration patterns, reaching many parts of Africa, including ETHIOPIA, the SAHARA, and the SAHEL, as well as areas populated by the FULANI, IBO, and HAUSA. Although less documentation has been found for its existence in the central and southern regions of Africa, the practice of circumcision has occurred there as well.

For those in Western society, understanding the prevalence and longevity of circumcision has meant looking beyond the dangers of blood loss, trauma, and potential death experienced by women, young boys, and girls. Its proponents have argued that one must take into account the social, cultural, and economic factors of practicing societies; it is these that reportedly account for the longevity of the practice among traditional societies, Muslims, Christians, and Jews in Africa.

Circumcision's many variations reflect conformity to specific social beliefs and values, but it appears to be most predominant in patrilineal societies in which potential bridegrooms and members of their families exercised a strong influence. For example, in those parts of Egypt, SOMALIA, and neighboring regions in the HORN OF AFRICA where female circumcision is rigidly enforced, the prevailing belief is that it keeps women chaste and pure for marriage. Although there is little fanfare for women who undergo the procedure, it carries significant economic considerations because, unless a young woman is circumcised, she is not "marketable" as a wife. The ramifications for uncircumcised women and their families generally include social isolation and condemnation. Proponents have also cited the presentation of traditional family values as a critical factor in preserving the custom.

Moreover, within traditional societies in which young males and females simultaneously experienced circumcision as a rite of passage, the practice has been viewed by many as a powerful expression of social identity and acceptance. In Kenya, accompanied by communal celebration, Akamba children are initiated between the ages of four to seven years. The greater their endurance, the greater the recognition they are accorded, since circumcision is traditionally seen among them as a commitment to the adult world of work and social responsibilities. Similarly, MAASAI males and females had to undergo circumcision before they were even considered adults deemed suitable for marriage or assignment to roles in society. After circumcision these males and females remained symbolically bound together for life within established AGE GROUPS. Those who were uncircumcised remained outside of society, considered neither male or female.

The simplest and most widely practiced form of male circumcision entails the cutting of the foreskin. Among the most extreme variations are two forms of castration. Populations such as the BEJA of NUBIA and ETHIOPIA, the Sidamo of Ethiopia, and the SAN and Khoikhoi of South Africa have traditionally practiced unilateral castration. Bilateral castration, practiced by Muslim enslavers, produced a caste of men known as eunuchs who were deemed suitable attendants for female harems.

Female circumcision in its most simple form involves clitoridectomy, or the surgical removal of the clitoris. In some societies, the labia minora and labia majora may also be removed. The most extreme form of female circumcision, practiced in regions such as Somalia, is known as the pharonic tradition. In Western society it is known as infibulation and entails the removal of the clitoris and both labia. The remaining sides of the vulva are sutured together and remain intact until the young woman's wedding night.

See also: BRIDEWEALTH (Vol. I); RITES OF PASSAGE (Vol. I); SCARIFICATION (Vol. I).

Further reading: John R. Hinnells, ed., *Dictionary of Religions* (New York: Penguin Books, 1995); John S. Mbiti, *African Religions and Philosophy* (Oxford, Eng.: Heinemann Educational Publishers, 1999); G. Mokhtar, ed., *General History of Africa II Ancient Civilizations of Africa, Abridged Edition* (Paris: UNESCO, 1990); Barbara G. Walker, *The Woman's Encyclopedia of Myths and Secrets* (San Francisco: HarperCollins, 1983).

civet Short-limbed, long-bodied mammal that, in appearance, resembles a cat and belongs to a related family of animals that also includes the mongoose. Although often referred to as a civet cat, it is not really a feline. Civets are about 30 inches (76.2 cm) long, not including a 20-inch (50.8-cm) tail. They weigh up to 25 pounds (11.3 kg) and have coats of gray or black fur, which may be marked in different patterns of stripes and spots. Their faces resemble those of weasels.

Civets are solitary animals, usually living alone in trees and rocky hillsides and going out at night for food. Some civets, such as the African civet and the Congo water civet, are semiaquatic. Although most civets live on the ground, palm civets are found in trees and eat fruit. Civets usually give birth to litters of two or three.

Civets are noted for glands, located near their genitals, that give off a musky odor. Although, in nature, these glands are used for marking territory, humans have long used them to manufacture perfume, removing the musk from captive civets every two or three weeks. As a result, civets were among the many trade items that caravans, controlled by the empires of GHANA, carried from the NIGER RIVER valley to North Africa.

clan Group of related family members who trace their family line to a common ancestor. A clan may be limited to a small geographical area or dispersed across a wide territory, but, invariably, the members of a clan share a strong bond of identity and common origin. Often, that identity is represented by a special emblem or sacred object.

A clan's sense of identity is further determined by observing the rule of exogamy, wherein men and women of the same clan are not allowed to marry. Identity also is reinforced by sharing a common name. Clans may be broken down into LINEAGE groups or into subclans, which refer to segments of a clan that have been dispersed throughout a region. The mutual support and unity created by a clan is one of its most important functions. Clans can expand through marriage and thereby strengthen their alliances with other clans.

Clans are formed when family groups become large and members spread to different areas of the same territory. Although larger in size than bands and segmentary societies, family clans may still need to unite for economic or other reasons. Among the Pokot (or Suk, as they sometimes are called) of western Kenya, for example, the clan traditionally regulated marriage and maintained other forms of social control. Clan members who trace their family line to a female ancestor are considered a matriclan. Patriclans are represented by a single male ancestor.

Over centuries, the loyalties of family clans eventually broadened and were replaced by AGE GRADES or SECRET SOCIETIES.

See also: TOTEMISM (Vol. I).

Further reading: William R. Bascomb and Melville J. Herskovits, *Continuity and Change in African Cultures* (Chicago: The University of Chicago Press, 1975); Daniel G. Bates, *Cultural Anthropology* (New York: Simon & Schuster, 1996)

Cleopatra (r. 51–30 BCE) *Queen of Egypt and last ruler of the Ptolemaic dynasty.*

Celebrated in literature and legend for her extraordinary beauty, she was equally celebrated in history for her intelligence, commanding presence, and political skills.

Like the other rulers of this dynasty, Cleopatra was descended from PTOLEMY I, one of ALEXANDER THE GREAT'S generals and the founder of the dynasty. Born about 69 BCE, Cleopatra was the daughter of Ptolemy XII Auletes; the identity and ethnic background of her mother are uncertain. Although some historians have suggested that, because of the fairly common mixing of Greek-Macedonian, Middle Eastern, and African bloodlines, Cleopatra probably had a dark-skinned complexion, she, like other Ptolemaic rulers, undoubtedly would have considered herself to be Greek. In spite of this, Cleopatra took an active interest in Egyptian culture and customs, and she was, in fact, the only member of her royal line to actually be fluent in the Egyptian language.

Cleopatra came to the throne at the age of seventeen or eighteen, reigning jointly with her father. Upon his death, she first ruled in conjunction with her brother, Ptolemy XIII. Then, after his death, she ruled with her brother, Ptolemy XIV, whom she had married, according to the Egyptian royal custom of sibling marriages.

During this time, EGYPT became embroiled in the political turmoil and civil strife of ROME. Misjudging the situation, Cleopatra, along with factions of the Egyptian court, at first sided with the Roman consul Pompey rather than Pompey's adversary, Gaius Julius CAESAR. This misstep led her brother, Ptolemy XIV, to exile her for a period. By the time Caesar visited Egypt, however, Cleopatra had regained her position and was allowed to meet the victorious Roman leader. The resulting affair between the two rulers led to the birth of Cleopatra's son, who eventually bore the name Ptolemy XV Caesarion. In time, Cleopatra ruled over Egypt as co-regent with Caesarion, enjoying the security of Caesar's protection until his assassination in 44 BCE.

Determined to keep Egypt from falling under complete foreign domination, upon Caesar's death Cleopatra quickly turned for protection to one of Caesar's protégés, the Roman consul Marc Antony. Their romantic and political liaison at first proved highly beneficial to both of them. On the one hand, it gave Antony access to Egypt's wealth and resources, which were valuable to him while he was consolidating his power and pursuing his ambitions in Rome. On the other hand, it gave Cleopatra support in her campaign to extend Egypt's borders and to maintain its independence.

Marc Antony, following Roman custom, killed himself by falling on his sword. The cause of Cleopatra's death, however, is less certain. According to popular legend, she died of a snake bite, having clasped to her breast a highly poisonous snake known as an asp. Some historians argue, though, that the actual cause of her death may have simply been some form of poison. Regardless of exactly how the two met their ends, the victorious Octavian had the lovers buried together in a single mausoleum in the city of Alexandria.

The grand designs of both Antony and Cleopatra, however, came to an end at the battle of Actium, where, in 31 BCE, Antony was decisively defeated by the forces of Octavian, later known as Augustus Caesar. Eventually, both Antony and Cleopatra committed suicide rather than face the humiliation of defeat.

See also: CAESAR, GAIUS JULIUS (Vol. I); CAESAR, OCTAVIAN (Vol. I).

Further reading: Michel Chauveau, *Egypt in the Age of Cleopatra* (Ithaca: Cornell University Press, 2000).

climate Africa's various climactic regions reflect its location in the tropical zone. Still, within Africa's relatively uniform climate are deserts, grasslands, and rich tropical forests. These changes in terrain and climate have long affected the lives of Africans. In ancient times, climate determined where Africans chose to live, their way of life, their language, and even their religious beliefs.

Climatic Zones Generally, a symmetric pattern of climatic zones extends both north and south from the equator. The equatorial tropical rain forests in central Africa are bordered to the north and south by savanna grassland regions, which are then bounded by the desert. In the extreme northwest and southwest of Africa is a region of mild, Mediterranean-type climate. There are also a few mountainous regions.

The rain forest climate can be found in the central part of the continent and the eastern coast of Madagascar. The average temperature in this area is about 80° F (26.7° C), and the average annual rainfall is about 70 inches (1,780 mm). The climate of the Guinea coast is similar to the climate of the central, except that rainfall is concentrated in one season.

North and south of the rain forest are belts of tropical savanna climate. Here, the temperatures remain high year-round. Rain falls during the summer season. These areas consist of open grasslands dotted occasionally with trees like acacias and BAOBABS.

Past the savanna lands are arid, desert climates. Less than 10 inches (250 mm) of rain fall annually in the SAHARA in the north, the Horn in the east; and the Kalahari and Namib Deserts in the southwest. In the Sahara, temperatures vary depending on the time of day and season. The highest temperatures are in July, when the average temperature is over 90° F (32.2° C). During the Saharan winter, the temperature can fall below freezing at night.

In the far northwest—Morocco, Algeria, and Tunisia—and far southwest of Africa, the climate is typically mild and wet during the winter and warm and dry during the summer.

A mountain climatic region is found in parts of ETHIOPIA, East Africa, and the Atlas Mountain region in Morocco. The weather is warm and temperate. On the highest peaks, like Mount Kilimanjaro, snow can be found.

Impact on People Climate had a tremendous influence on the migration of ancient peoples. Areas of present-day Tunisia were populated by hunter-gatherers known as the CAPSIAN people around 10,000 BCE. The dry, open country of North Africa was ideal for hunting, and it led them to migrate north to influence the Ibero-Maurusian group of present-day Algeria and east to the gulf of Sidra.

The close proximity of desert, the Mediteranean, and mountain climates in North Africa has led to a concentration of different people leading various ways of life. While Roman North Africans led sedentary, agricultural lives, the BERBERS in the Atlas Mountains lived as nomads, tending sheep and cattle. In the deserts, Arabs soon began trading along caravan routes. Their proximity to one another allowed for trade and the exchange of ideas and cultures.

By contrast, in western Africa, the densely forested regions of the Guinea coast helped to prevent large-scale migration and trade in ancient times. The boundaries of the forest promoted many distinct cultures and languages. The forests were not occupied until a relatively late time in history due to technology and crops. Ironworking needed to be introduced before tools could be made to clear the forests for farming. Furthermore, not until crops that could grow in the shade, like the plantain and taro, were brought from Asia in the ninth century could farming replace hunting and gathering as a means of survival.

The climate has also affected the religious beliefs of Africans. For example, once the necessary tools were available to farm the tropical forests of West Africa, these areas became quite heavily populated and supported fairly urban civilizations. Consequently, the religious beliefs found there were based on their states and their rulers. Kings of city-states were associated with gods, good luck, and fertility. In East Africa, however, the temperate grasslands supported cattle herding and a more rural way of life. As a result, East African religious beliefs centered around the worship of sky divinities who were associated with their ancestors.

See also: GEOGRAPHY (Vol. I).

clothing As elsewhere, humans in Africa developed clothing in response to the environment and the availability of natural resources. For HUNTER-GATHERER societies, such as the forest-dwelling MBUTI of central Africa, tree bark offered an ample supply of materials for clothing. Similarly, the Raffia palm tree, which is indigenous to central and West Africa, supplied an early source of clothing for people living in those areas, and men were the primary weavers. Other early forms of natural fibers used for clothing were jute, wild silk plants, and flax. Silk cultivators and users included the HAUSA, ASHANTI, YORUBA, and Nupe.

PASTORALIST societies tended to wear animal skins supplied by their herds. These skins were scraped and cut into forms after being dried and treated. One of the earliest known prehistoric cave paintings, found in Bechar in ALGERIA, for example, depicts men wearing animal skins and coats made of feathers. The BORAN OROMO of ETHIOPIA, and the MAASAI of Kenya also utilized their herds to make leather garments.

In the colder, mountain climates of North Africa, pastoralist groups such as the BERBERS coupled the use of animal skins with fur to create clothing that provided warmth. The fur was woven into a variety of woolen-like items ranging from clothing to tents, blankets, and rugs. It has long been the custom of women in this region to wear shawls known as *mouchitya* as a sign of their marital status. Similarly, in the Ethiopian Highlands, men and women have long worn *awollos*, or shawls, made of woven grass to protect them from the cold.

The earliest known cultivation of plant fibers used to weave cloth in Africa has been traced to EGYPT between 4000 and 3000 BCE. Along with animal skins, sedentary societies such as the Tasian culture, BADARIAN CULTURE, and NAQADA I cultivated flax. Although it is not certain what type of device was used to weave or spin the material, archaeologists have recovered bone needles that clearly were used for sewing. Looms were certainly present by Egypt's dynastic period, from which there are wall reliefs depicting looms in use. Needles, in use as early as 2686 to 2181 BCE during the Old Kingdom, were made of copper. These and other findings, such as the linen burial cloths found in ancient tombs, indicate that production of cloth was firmly entrenched during this period. However, stylized dress was reserved for the upper classes.

There is some debate as to whether the tight-fitting sheaths depicted in Egyptian art were worn by all women or only by goddesses and religious figures. More generally it is believed that by 1550 BCE, during the NEW KINGDOM, clothing for both males and females had evolved to fuller garments known as a *kalasiris*. Women wore this garment supported by shoulder straps or bodices with sleeves, while men wore this form of clothing from the waist down. Men also were known to wear kilts, dating from an earlier period, that fell to the knee and sometimes to the calf. In contrast, Egyptian laborers apparently wore a form of apron, while children and servants appear to have worn little if any clothing.

In the neighboring kingdom of MEROË, where forms of dress were comparable to that of the Egyptians, cotton cultivation and hand-spun cloth production were well under way during the fifth century BCE. The arduous tasks of drying the plant fibers, as well as cleaning and carding them, had to be performed before the fibers could be spun into threads for weaving. In both Egypt and NUBIA the task of spinning and weaving clothing was primarily carried out by women. Beyond the family's needs, this cloth production also served as a source of income. Elsewhere, the tasks involved in cloth production varied. These were sometimes divided between men and women, with the assignment of various jobs reinforced by strict taboos. Among the Kono of Sierra Leone, for example, women were the spinners and men were the designated weavers of cloth. This distinction between the work of men and women was maintained even in societies in which both men and women were weavers of cloth, with specific looms often being designed for each gender.

Once trade became a permanent and regular fixture, various regions used cloth as an important form of currency. Over many centuries, cloth became more stylized since its value was linked to its unique appearance. As a result, from the early methods of coloring that employed vegetable and mineral dyes, African cloth became widely known for specialized forms of tie-dye and resist-dye. Some forms of dye-work even became associated with specific deities. For example, the female deity known as *Iyo Mao* was known as the patron of Yorba dye-workers. Variations of such beliefs have been noted among the Wolof, Soninke, and Mandinka as well.

Stylized cloth was associated with the rise of early kingdoms that also pushed new forms of expression. Embroidery, appliqué, and other forms of embellishment with BEADS, COWRIE SHELLS, and gold threads made specialized forms of cloth a coveted luxury reserved for ruling kings. Specialized cloth was also used to make specific statements about regional culture and family lineage by using proverbs and designs of animals and plants. Raffia cloth made by the Kuba represents a prime example of this, for it was made with geometric designs that had specific names and meanings known only within the society. As such, cloth of this type became an essential component in royal ceremonies, festivals, masquerades, and ritual work.

Many ancient forms of cloth production served significant functions in modern African society, although with limited use. Bark cloth made by the Mbuti, for example, traditionally was only worn at such sacred events as funerals, ceremonial dances, and initiation rites. Beyond this, TUAREG men have long worn indigo veils and robes to announce their status as adults.

See also: MANDINKA (Vol. II); SONINKE (Vol. II); WOLOF (Vol. II).

Further reading: Mary Jo Arnoldi, Christraud M. Geary and Kris L. Hardin, eds., *African Material Culture*, (Bloomington: Indiana University Press, 1996); John Middleton, ed., *Encyclopedia of Africa South of the Sahara* (New Haven, Conn.: Yale University Press, 1997); Claudia Zas-lavsky, *Africa Counts: Number and Pattern in African Culture* (Chicago: Lawrence Hill Books, 1999).

cobra Type of venomous snake whose neck can inflate to form a hood. The short, hollow fangs at the front of a cobra's mouth contain fatal neurotoxins that act against the nervous system of various creatures, including humans. Cobras live in dry, semiarid regions. They usually hunt at night and prey on small mammals, birds, and reptiles. Female cobras usually lay eggs, although some species give live birth. African cobras include ringhals, which inhabit the southern part of the continent, and tree cobras, which are found along the equator.

The Egyptian cobra is native to Egypt. Identifiable by its small, flat face and rounded snout, the Egyptian cobra can grow up to 8 feet (2.4 m) long. In ancient Egypt, cobras were associated with the snake goddess Buto, who was often depicted as a snake coiled around a PAPYRUS roll. According to Egyptian legend, Buto helped nurse the god HORUS when he was born and protect him from his treacherous uncle SETH, who killed Horus's father OSIRIS. Buto was also believed to be the protector of Egyptian royalty. As a result, Egyptian kings wore a depiction of the cobra on their crowns.

cocoyam (taro) Tuberous root plants generally grown in the forest regions of Africa.

Known as the Asian yam or taro, cocoyams were first imported from Asia sometime during the first century. They entered Africa by way of southeastern trade routes, transported by Malaysian and/or Polynesian sailors from the South Pacific. These seafarers subsequently settled on the island of Madagascar by the second century, and some historians believe the crop spread from this point. Others hold that the cocoyam was present in Africa at an earlier period, pointing to many myths that relate to its existence.

Among the many African myths dealing with yams and cocoyams is one that has long been told among the IBO. In it, the Ibo's founding king sacrifices his children, a boy and a girl, whose burial results in the first yam and cocoyam.

The assignment of female qualities to cocoyams, which are a prominent food staple, carried over to the role of gender in their cultivation. For centuries, the cocoyam has provided a notable source of income for women farmers in Africa. Successful harvests not only provided subsistence for the woman's family but also promoted cooperative marketing strategies.

See also: CROPS (Vol. 1)

Further reading: Ralph Austen, *African Economic History* (London: James Currey, 1996); Elizabeth Isichei, *A History of African Societies to 1870* (Cambridge, Eng.: Cambridge University Press, 1997).

coelacanth Ancient lobe-finned fish known to inhabit the southern coast of Africa.

Based on fossilized remains, scientists have determined that the coelacanth was the likely ancestor of some early forms of land vertebrates hundreds of millions of years ago. This assumption is based on the coelacanth's unique physical characteristics, noted in recovered fossils. Its body, which may range in color from blue to brown, is notable for its lobes. (Lobes are the rounded, fleshy projections attached to fins and tail, which give this species the appearance of "walking" on limbs or feet.) Coelacanths have been measured at a mere 6 inches (150 mm) and up to 5 feet (150 cm) in length. They may weigh as much as 150 pounds (67.5 kg) or more.

For many years, fossilized remains served as the only record of the existence of the coelacanth in the swamps, seas, and oceans of the world. Scientists, therefore, assumed that the coelacanth had become extinct approximately 60 million years ago. These beliefs were revised in 1938 after the discovery that the species still flourished in the southeast region of the Indian Ocean near South Africa, Madagascar, and the Comoro Islands. In fact, for centuries it has been part of the regional diet. (It is generally dried and salted before consumption.)

Comoro Islands Archipelago situated in the western Indian Ocean between the island of Madagascar and the coast of East Africa. Its four major islands are Ngazidja, Mulali, Mzwani, and Mayotte, which is also known as Maore. The islands are noted for unusual wildlife, including Livingstone's flying fox, a giant fruit bat found nowhere else in the world, and the COELACANTH, a fish once thought to have been extinct for millions of years.

See also: COMORO ISLANDS (Vol. III).

Congo basin Area in tropical West-central Africa that is drained by the Congo River. The basin covers 1,600,000 square miles (4,100,000 sq km) and occupies most of the modern-day countries of Congo (formerly known as Zaïre) and the Congo Republic, as well as parts of northern Angola, western Zambia, Tanzania, and southern CENTRAL AFRICAN REPUBLIC. The basin consists of an intricate system of tributaries and channels surrounded by dense tropical rain forest. In ancient times, the area was inhabited by small-statured people and, later, Bantu-speaking peoples.

The Congo basin extends over 1,200 miles (1,900 km) from north to south from Congo–Lake Chad to Angola. It also runs about 1,200 miles (1,900 km) from the Atlantic in the west to the Nile-Congo in the east. This basin consists of a system of tributaries flowing downward along concentric slopes that range in elevation from 900 to 1,500 feet (300 to 500 m). These slopes surround a sunken area or depression known as a cuvette (which means "saucer," or "shallow bowl"). The cuvette is a sunken area containing alluvial deposits lying on sands and sandstones.

Due to its location on both sides of the equator, the climate of the Congo basin is hot and humid, with an average temperature of about 76° F. (24° C) in northern parts of the basin. In this region, it rains throughout the year, with an average of about 67 inches (175 cm) of rainfall annually. The savanna territory of the southern region is dryer. This area has distinct dry and wet seasons and averages 49 inches (125 cm) of rainfall a year.

The earliest known reference to the Congo basin occurs in ancient Egyptian records. Around 2000 BCE, the Egyptian commander Herkuf visited this region, known to Egyptians as the Land of Trees, and wrote of a "mysterious place with forests so dense they were as dark as night in the middle of the day." Herkuf also claimed to have discovered a race of small-statured men who sang and danced to their god. These tiny men, who apparently were the region's first inhabitants, became known to outsiders as the PYGMIES. Growing to an average height of about 4.5 feet (1.5 m), they survived by hunting, fishing, and gathering wild fruits and edible plants. They lived in shelters made of brush deep in the jungle.

Between 500 and 150 BCE, iron was introduced to this area. A trade route was established from Koro Toro in the north to the Likouala region, located between the Sangha and Oubangui Rivers in the basin. Around the same time, the region began to be inhabited by various Bantu-speaking peoples, who fished and farmed near the river. In medieval times, the Congo region was dominated by various empires that often traded such goods as copper and ivory.

See also: CONGO (Vol. III); CONGO BASIN (Vol. II).

Congo River Africa's second longest river, after the NILE, and one of the longest in the world; located in West-central Africa, primarily between the present-day countries of Congo and the Democratic Republic of the Congo (formerly Zaïre). The Congo extends about 2,900 miles (4,640 km), ranging in width from 0.5 to 10 miles (.8 to 16 km). It rises in the highlands of northeastern Zambia between Lake Tanganyika and Lake Nyasa (Malawi), where it is known as the Chambeshi River, at an elevation of 5,760 feet (9,216 m) above sea level and at a distance of about 430 miles (688 km) from the Indian Ocean. Formed by the junction of the Lualaba and Luvua Rivers in the southern part of the Democratic Republic of the Congo, the Congo River flows generally north to a point just south of the equator, where the Lualaba becomes the Congo River proper. From this point the course of the river resembles a huge irregular arc, looping northeast, northwest, and southwest to an outlet between Banana in Congo and Sharks in Angola, on the coast of the South Atlantic Ocean.

Like South America's Amazon, the Congo flows out of an equatorial zone in which heavy rainfall occurs almost all year. Upstream from Malebo Pool, the Congo basin receives an average of about 60 inches (15.25 m) of rain a year, of which more than one-fourth is discharged into the Atlantic. The drainage basin of the Congo is, however, only about half the size of that of the Amazon, and its rate of flow is considerably less than that of the Amazon.

More than 4,000 islands, including about fifty that are more than 10 miles (16 km) in length, are situated in the Congo River. With its numerous tributaries, which also include the Aruwimi, Kasai, and Lomami Rivers, the Congo provides the main artery of transportation in central Africa and drains the central African equatorial basin, an area of more than 1.6 million square miles (4.16 million square km). This drainage basin includes most of Congo and the Democratic Republic of Congo, as well as northern Angola, western Zambia and Tanzania, and southern Central African Republic. It is the most clearly distinguished of the various geographic depressions situated between the Sahara, the Atlantic Ocean, and the lakes of East Africa.

The Three Sections of the River From its sources to its mouth, the Congo River system has three contrasting sections. The first, the upper Congo, is characterized by confluences of lakes and rapids. At first, several streams unite to form the river, then, in about 60 miles (96 km), the upper Lualaba, Luvua, and Lukuga merge. Each stream undergoes some type of expansion, even when it does not form a lake. Rapids occur not only along the head streams but also several times along the course of the main stream. Navigation is possible along some sections of the upper Congo but only for vessels of low tonnage.

The second section, the middle Congo, flows steadily for more than 1,000 miles (1,600 km) to within 22 miles (35 km) of Kinshasa. Its course is narrow at first but soon grows wider, after which islands occur in midstream. This change in the character of the river corresponds to its entry into its alluvial plain. From that point onward, with the exception of a few rare narrow sections, the Congo divides into several arms, separated by strings of islands. It increases from a width of 3.5 miles (6 km) downstream from Isangi to widths of 5 to 7 miles (8 to 11 km) and even 8 miles (13 km). Beyond the natural silt levees occurring on either bank, some areas are subjected to extensive flooding that increases the river's bounds still further. The middle course of the Congo ends in a narrow section called the Chenal.

The Congo's third section begins upon leaving the Chenal. There the Congo divides into two branches, forming Malebo Pool, a vast area about 15 miles (24 km) by 17 miles (27 km). Immediately downstream are the first waterfalls of the of the river's final section. Cataracts and rapids are grouped into two series, separated by a fairly calm central reach, in which the altitude drops from a little less than 900 feet (270 m) to a few yards above sea level. The Congo's estuary begins at Matadi, downstream from the rapids that close off the interior Congo. Eighty-three miles (133 km) in length, it forms the border between present-day Angola and Congo (Kinshasa). At first the estuary is narrow, with a central channel 65 to 80 feet (104 to 128 m) deep, widening again downstream of Boma. There, the river, obstructed by islands, divides into several arms, and in some places the depth does not exceed 20 to 25 feet (30 to 40 m), which makes dredging necessary to allow oceangoing vessels to reach Matadi. Beyond the estuary's mouth, the course of the Congo continues offshore as a deep underwater canyon that extends for a distance of about 125 miles (200 km.).

Navigability on the Congo is limited by a series of 32 cataracts over the river's lower course, including the famous Inga Falls. These cataracts make it impossible to navigate the Congo between the seaport of Matadi, at the head of the Congo estuary, and Malebo Pool, a distance of about 250 miles (400 km). Below Matadi, however, where the Congo estuary begins, the river is navigable to the sea, a distance of approximately 83 miles (133 km). The only obstacle to navigation on the upper Congo are the cataracts near Kisangani. Between Kisangani and Kinshasa, at the northern terminus of the cataracts, the river is navigable to all river craft. Many operate on regular schedules on this route, which stretches about 1,000 miles (1,600 km), as well as on most Congo tributaries. This helps the Congo form the continent's largest network of 9,000 miles (14,400 km) of navigable waterways.

Climate and Animal Life The equatorial climate that prevails over a significant part of the Congo basin is coextensive with a dense evergreen forest that spreads out over the central depression. The forest region is bordered on either side by savanna, and the forest and savanna often meet.

Animal life in the Congo basin is close to that of the equatorial forest, which is sharply distinct from the wildlife of the savannas. Numerous species of fish live in the waters of the Congo, with more than two hundred thirty identified in the waters of Malebo Pool and its tributaries alone. The swamps often dry up at low water and are inhabited by lungfish, which survive the dry periods buried and encysted in cocoons of mucus. The waters of the Congo itself also contain various kinds of reptiles, with crocodiles being the most striking species. Semi-aquatic tortoises are to be found as well, as are several species of water snakes.

More than 265 species of birds typical of the equatorial forest have been recorded in the Congo region. Occasionally or seasonally, however, atypical birds may be seen, including such seabirds as the sea swallow, which fly upstream from the ocean. Migratory birds from Europe, including the blongios heron and the *Ixobrychus minutus* (little bittern), pass through the region, too. Species with a wide distribution within Africa, such as the Egyptian duck, also have been noted.

Aquatic mammals—HIPPOPOTAMUSES, otters, and manatees—are present but are rare. The manatee has been officially identified only on the Sangha tributary, but it appears to have given rise to legends of a sirenlike creature called *Mami Wata*.

See also: CONGO (Vol. III); CONGO BASIN (Vol. II).

copper Reddish, extremely ductile metal; an unusually good conductor of electricity. Copper is found in a free metallic state, and, in Africa, this is how it was discovered and first used by NEOLITHIC peoples around 8000 BCE.

The source of much of this copper was—and still is—the rich veins of ore found in present-day Zambia. This belt extends about 280 miles (448 km) northwest from present-day Luanshya, in Zambia, into what is now the Katanga region of Congo. Up to 160 miles (256 km) wide, this area contains more than one-tenth of the world's copper deposits.

Using copper as a substitute for stone, ancient peoples fashioned copper into crude hammers, knives, and other utensils. The malleability of the material made it relatively simple to shape by beating. Pounding hardened the copper so that more durable edges resulted. Copper's bright reddish color and its durability made it highly prized.

The search for copper during this early period led to the discovery and working of native copper deposits. Sometime after 6000 BCE people discovered that copper could be melted in a campfire and cast into a desired shape. After this came the discovery of copper-bearing rock and the process of using fire to reduce the ore to metal. This was the dawn of the age of METALS and the birth of METALLURGY.

In EGYPT, where graves have been found containing copper weapons and other implements, this metallic age began sometime between 5000 and 4000 BCE. At Gerza, just south of the modern site of CAIRO, the inhabitants learned basic copper metallurgy from immigrants from Mesopotamia. By about 3500 BCE the Gerzeans had developed an entire civilization based on copper metallurgy. During this same period NUBIANS also were fabricating instruments made of copper.

Around 3500 BCE, copper was intentionally alloyed with tin to produce BRONZE, which was both harder and tougher than either copper or tin. For this reason it was widely employed for both weapons and objects of art. From Egypt, the use of bronze rapidly spread across the Mediterranean to Europe, and the period of the metal's extensive and characteristic use has been designated the BRONZE AGE.

As copper became more important to them, the ancient Egyptians sought copper, as well as gold and antimony, in the land of PUNT. Although the exact location of Punt is unknown, it probably was along the mouth of the Zambesi River, where the gold obtained, even today, has a distinctive greenish tint, probably due to impurities of copper and antimony.

Unlike northern Africa, central Africa had no specific Bronze Age. Instead, in the last millennium BCE, central African peoples discovered the value of copper during what was, for them, the IRON AGE. These peoples prized copper for its luster and color, using it extensively for personal JEWELRY—bangles, chains, necklaces, hair ornaments, and rings. These objects were given to loved ones as well as to important personages, and were made with great craftsmanship. Copper also was used to beautify personal belongings, and copper inlaid decorations appeared on knife handles. Fine copper wire was used to bind spearheads to shafts, and burnished copper nails were used as embellishments on shields. Copper was also used in works of art used to furnish the graves of important people.

The demand for fresh copper grew with each succeeding generation, particularly as the development of new political authorities led to the need for court regalia for kings and chiefs. Copper was also used for the musical instruments that accompanied kings and their nobles on their sojourns around their domains. Not surprisingly, during this period copper frequently became more valuable than gold.

See also: COPPER (Vol. II); COPPER MINES (Vol. II).

Coptic The last form of the language of the ancient Egyptians, which evolved when Egypt was converted to Christianity. After the conquest of Egypt by ALEXANDER THE GREAT in 332 BCE, Greek replaced ancient Egyptian as the official language of the country. While the Egyptian population continued to write and speak the ancient dialects, the advent of Christianity created the necessity of translating the Hebrew Scriptures and Christian Gospels into a language the common people could easily understand. This was resolved by creating a script for ancient Egyptian utilizing a combination of the Greek alphabet and a few letters from DEMOTIC script. As a result, Coptic played an important role in the development of Christianity in Egypt, remaining the liturgical language of Egyptian Christians for centuries.

Copts Name by which the Christians of EGYPT are known. The word *Copt* is derived from an Arabic distortion of the Greek word *Aigyptos*, which itself is a corruption of the ancient Egyptian name for the city of MEMPHIS, *Ha-Ka-Ptah*.

According to Coptic tradition, Christianity was brought to Egypt in 61 by St. Mark the Evangelist, a disciple of Jesus. During the next two centuries, the new religion rapidly gained acceptance throughout the country. The center of Coptic Christianity was Alexandria, the city

The shrine celebrating the divine birth of Thirtieth Dynasty pharaoh Nectanebo I (r. 380362 BCE) or Nectabebo II (r. 360–343 BCE) at Dendara, north of Luxor, was reconsecrated as an Egyptian Coptic church by the fifth century CE. © *Vanni Archive/CORBIS*

founded by ALEXANDER THE GREAT after his conquest of Egypt in 332 BCE.

The Coptic Church still exists today in modern Egypt. Though a minority within a Moslem country, the Copts continue to practice their Christian faith, viewing themselves as direct descendants of the ancient Egyptians. Dr. Boutros Boutros Ghali, Secretary-General of the United Nations from 1992 to 1997, is but one of many Copts to figure prominently in the modern world.

The Coptic Church contributed considerably to early Christian thought, producing such well-known theologians as St. Athanasius (c. 293–373) and St. Cyril the Great, who was head, or patriarch, of the Egyptian Church from 412 to 444 CE. St. Anthony (c. 251–356), the founder of Christian monasticism in the East, was another major figure of the church in Egypt during that time. Later, during the fourth century, it was Coptic missionaries who were responsible for making Ethiopia a Christian nation.

In 451, the Coptic Church separated from the rest of Christendom following a theological dispute concerning the divinity of Christ. Known as the MONOPHYSITE Controversy, or Monophysite Heresy, this resulted in an independent national church. Although it was isolated from most of the Christian world, the Coptic Church continued to flourish on its own until Egypt was conquered by the Arabs in the seventh century.

See also: COPTIC CHRISTIANITY (Vol. II); COPTS (Vol. III).

cotton A soft, white, fibrous substance taken from the tropical plants of the *Gossypium* genus. Cotton was one of the first textile fibers manufactured by humans. Production seems to have been developed by the ancient Indus civilization between 5000 and 3000 BCE. By around

2500 BCE, the craft had developed enough that ancient Egyptians were wearing cotton clothing.

Although cotton originated outside of Africa, it ultimately bore a strong connection to the continent. Woven cloth cotton appeared by about 3000 BCE at Mohenjo-Daro, in the ancient Indus civilization. However, scholars have determined that the plant used to make the cotton of Mohenjo-Daro originated in the Kalahari Desert of southern Africa, where it still grows today. Botanists are unsure how this plant appeared thousands of miles away in another civilization, but they suspect that the cotton plant was cultivated in Africa before its arrival in the Indus Valley.

Traditionally, cotton has been woven by African craftspeople using elaborate looms, including the vertical cotton loom and the horizontal fixed-heddle loom, a device that is still used in Madagascar today.

See also: CLOTH (Vol. II); COTTON (Vols. II, III); CROPS (Vol. II); TEXTILE PRODUCTION (Vol. I).

cowrie shells Brightly colored shells that served as one of the earliest forms of money in ancient Africa. Cowrie shells are the oldest and most widely used currency in human history, having been used before the introduction of coins c. 600 BCE. Before cowrie shells, the barter system and cattle were used in business transactions.

Cowrie shells, one of the earliest forms of money in ancient Africa, were valued because they were beautiful and difficult to obtain. © *Chris Hellier/CORBIS*

Cowrie shells were valued for their beauty and the difficulty in obtaining them. The Kuba people of central Africa built vast trade networks that allowed them to obtain cowrie shells from distant places. The ancient empire of GHANA, which controlled many of the trade routes in Africa during ancient and medieval times, also traded cowrie shells. Cowrie shells were not just used for trade and currency, however; they also were used as ornaments. The Nupe, for example, used them to decorate cloth masks, and some of the peoples of Ethiopia used cowrie shells to decorate their baskets.

Cowrie shells belong to the marine snails of the Cypraeidae family that flourish in the tropical waters of the Pacific and Indian Oceans. Thick and humped, the shells are often glossy and speckled. The variety of shell most commonly used as currency was a small yellow and white type known as the money cowrie.

Crete Island in the Mediterranean Sea, located southeast of mainland GREECE. The island is long and narrow, with an area of 3,190 square miles (8,262 sq km). Crete developed one of the earliest civilizations in human history.

By 3000 BCE, Crete was part of the early Minoan civilization that produced exquisite pottery, sculpture, painting, and metalwork. During this time, Crete established trading links with northern Africa. Ancient records show that traders from EGYPT imported both Cretan cedar and oil (products that were used in the preparation of mummies), while Cretan baskets, pottery, and jewelry were traded for goods from areas in northwestern Africa.

By the IRON AGE, c. 1200 BCE, Crete was controlled by the mainland Greeks known as the Mycenaeans. In 67 BCE, the Roman Empire conquered Crete. Under Roman rule, the island was linked with the Greek civilization of Cyrenacia in North Africa. It later became part of the Byzantine and Ottoman Empires.

crocodile One of the largest living reptiles, generally recognized by its long triangular snout. Widely found in AFRICA, from EGYPT to South Africa and from Mauritania to ETHIOPIA, the Nile crocodile (*Crocodylus niloticus*) is divided into several subspecies: the East African crocodile (*C.n. africanus*), the West African crocodile (*C.n. chamses*), the South African crocodile (*C.n. corviei*), the Ethiopian Nile crocodile (*C.n. niloctus*), the Kenyan Nile crocodile (*C.n. pauciscutatus*), and the Central African crocodile (*C.n. suchus*).

Human beings eat crocodile eggs and prize their skins. In certain regions of Africa, humans also eat

Sobek, the Egyptian crocodile god, is sometimes depicted as a crocodile and sometimes as a human with the head of a crocodile, as here in a bas-relief from the Temple of Sobek and Horus (c. 205-180 BCE) in Kom Ombo, Egypt. *© Gian Berto Vanni/CORBIS*

crocodile meat. In ancient Egypt the crocodile was revered by certain sects and was represented by Sobek, the crocodile god of fertility. Worship of this crocodile deity was particularly prevalent in the province of Fayoum. Mummies of crocodiles have been found in excavations of Egyptian tombs.

crow Black bird belonging to the same family of animals as the raven and the magpie. The pied crow, which is found in tropical Africa, is distinguished by its white nape and breast. According to the folklore of the SAN, the bird's white patch comes from a lump of fat. It seems that when San did not return promptly from a long day of hunting, their wives would tie a piece of fat onto the birds and then send them out in search of the men. Although the fat is mentioned in many versions of the tale, its exact purpose is unclear. Some versions state that the fat was intended for the bird to eat during its search; others declare that it was meant to feed the hungry hunters.

cuneiform System of picture writing widely used in ancient Mesopotamia.

Cuneiform was originated in Asia by the Sumerians, who used long sharpened reeds, called *calams,* to impress characters onto soft, wet clay tablets. When the clay hardened, the writing became a permanent record. The characters, or pictograms, were ideographic, representing entire words or concepts. Most of these pictograms show such easily recognizable images as household objects, animals, and people. Making these elaborate marks on wet clay proved difficult, however, and eventually the system was simplified. What resulted was a system of abstract signs that resembled flat nails and wedges. It is from these that the name *cuneiform* originated (from the Latin *cumeus*, meaning "nail").

Similar to hieroglyphics but more abstract, cuneiform texts of Egyptian origin have been found in and around Egypt. In time, as they came to dominate Mesopotamia, the Assyrians and Babylonians transformed cuneiform into a syllabic alphabet, and the great Assyrian king, Hammurabi, used it to compose one of the first legal codes in history. Cuneiform remained in use until the first century CE.

customary law Established traditions, customs, or practices that govern daily life and interaction.

Strict adherence to verbal greetings, ritualized prayers, and public ceremonies all reflected the significance of customary laws within various societies. Largely unwritten, these laws were part of a larger oral tradition that was handed down from generation to generation within each society.

See also: LAW AND JUSTICE (Vol. II); ORAL TRADITIONS (Vol. I); RELIGION (Vol.I).

Cyrene A Greek city in North Africa. Cyrene was the capital of the ancient kingdom of Cyrenaica (c. seventh to fourth century BCE), located in a fertile region rich in natural resources. The city was established in an eroded river valley at 2,000 feet (610 m) above sea level and named after a nearby spring, Kyre.

Located in present-day Libya, Cyrene was founded in 631 BCE by a group of settlers from the island of Thera in the Aegean Sea. The settlers were led by Battus, whose descendents ruled Cyrenaica for eight generations. During the reign of the Battiads, Cyrene thrived economically, as it often traded with other Greek cities. The Battiad dynasty expanded their kingdom to include the port city of Apolliana and the towns of Barje and Euhesperides.

Around 440 BCE, the city became a democracy. Then, in the fourth century BCE, Cyrene surrendered to ALEXANDER THE GREAT and became part of Egypt's PTOLEMAIC DYNASTY. Under Ptolemaic rule, Cyrene became a center of learning, featuring great scholars and its own medical school. In 96 BCE, Cyrene became part of the Roman Empire. The city continued to flourish as the capital of a Roman province that also included Crete. Cyrene declined in the first half of the first millennium before ceasing to exist after its conquest by Islamic forces around 642.

D

Danakil Depression Basin area in the DANAKIL DESERT, between northern ETHIOPIA and southeastern ERITREA; like the Danakil Desert, it has long been populated by the nomadic AFAR people, who migrated there from the Ethiopian Highlands. The Danakil Depression is one of the lowest places on earth not covered by water, lying about 400 feet (116 m) below sea level at some points. It is part of the Great RIFT VALLEY, a geological fault system extending from the Jordan valley in Southwest Asia to Mozambique in Southeast Africa.

Like the rest of the DANAKIL DESERT, the Danakil Depression was formed after the evaporation of an inland sea. The depression is a triangular basin consisting of salt pans and active volcanoes, which separate the Danakil Desert from the Red Sea. The climate of the Danakil De-pression is hot and arid: Temperatures reach 120° F. (49° C) and less than 7 inches (18 cm) of rain fall annually. The landscape is rocky, with little vegetation or wildlife.

Danakil Desert Desert lowland area lying between northern ETHIOPIA and southeastern ERITREA, bordering DJIBOUTI. Also known as the Afar Plain or Danakil Plain, the Danakil Desert is part of the Great RIFT VALLEY, a geological fault system extending from the Jordan valley in Southwest Asia to MOZAMBIQUE in Southeast Africa.

A rocky desert area, the Danakil has little vegetation or wildlife. It reaches temperatures of 120° F. (49° C) and receives less than 7 inches (18 cm) of rain. The desert runs 350 miles (570 km) from north to south, while changing in width from 50 to 250 miles (80 to 400 km). Active volcanoes, often known as the Danakil Alps, separate the desert from the Red Sea to the north and to the east. The Ethiopian Highlands border the desert to the west. Much of the desert lies below sea level.

The Danakil Desert was once a sea that has now evaporated. As a result, 450 square miles (1,200 sq km) of the desert are covered by more than 1 million tons (1.12 metric tons) of salt. In the northern part of the desert, the Danakil depression is 400 feet (116 m) below sea level.

The area is populated by the AFAR, a nomadic people who migrated there long ago from Ethiopia's highlands.

dance Over many centuries, a wealth of dance forms have emerged in Africa that incorporate the history, religion, and traditional values of countless societies. Equally important, dance has served as an important aspect in RITES OF PASSAGE ceremonies and is a longstanding form of social recreation. An extensive and complex activity, dance in Africa has been described as earth centered, the lifeblood and expression of community solidarity. It is almost always performed in league with MUSIC such as drumming, song, and sustained audience interaction.

While no one society can be said to represent a standard dance style, the dance forms of many African peoples share several common elements and purposes. Mass dance movements are prevalent in many public ceremonies. The music might begin with an underlying rhythm created by drum, shells, rattles, or hand clapping. All areas of the body are used to punctuate the music, with quick movements of the torso and the arms or with uniform steps ranging from the very simple to the complex series of leaps and movements made by such groups as the MAASAI. The Ewe people of Togo re-create their origin stories in dance forms that imitate the movement of birds. These steps have a larger meaning that is symbolic of migration patterns.

Another form of dance common to many African societies is the ring dance, in which dancers face the middle and move in a counterclockwise circle. It is interesting to note that after the European slave trade began, this form of dance survived in the American South as the ring-shout. The ring, a vital symbol of community solidarity, also symbolizes regeneration. Processional or line dancing is often an essential part of FUNERAL CUSTOMS, and other forms include "free flow" dance formations or formations that complement a solo dancer.

In the ancient world, dance evolved in many different ways and forms. Cave paintings attributed to the SAN of BOTSWANA depict dancers in religious trances, which some sources believe may have been invoked through repetitious dance steps in ways similar to other societies that invoke SPIRIT POSSESSION. Likewise, the SHONA women of Zimbabwe believed themselves to be possessed by *mhondoro* spirits who imparted counsel after being invoked through dance. These same healing rites have also been experienced by HAUSA women in West AfricA, Kalabari women of the NIGER DELTA, and the Jukun people of Nigeria.

Early forms of dance also evolved from the daily routines of work life. Various peoples might typically display the elements involved in food production, such as using a hoe or pounding grain. The *ziglibit* dance of the IVORY COAST imitates the pounding of corn. These familiar and communal settings are also emphasized in yearly harvest dance festivals. In Nigeria, the Irigwe people imitate the growth of crops in their leaping dance steps. Nupe fishermen of NIGERIA portray their skilled throwing of fishing nets in dance. Pastoral groups in the Sudan and Kenya incorporate the movements of cattle in their dances, while groups such as hunters or blacksmiths have secret dances only known within their CASTES.

Scenes depicted in various wall reliefs lead to the conclusion that dance was commonplace in ancient EGYPT. Some scenes show dancers (primarily women prior to the MIDDLE KINGDOM) singing, dancing, and clapping. Women dancers often performed as part of religious rites and were associated with specific temples. They were also linked to the royal kingdom and were reportedly always accompanied by a female leader. The practice of having a leader of the dance line, a master of the drums, and an initiator of song are also common features in many African societies.

The indictment of "savagery" leveled against African dance by such European writers as Joseph Conrad often failed to take into account the dance's larger context. Many dances are in fact erotic, created as a central part of fertility rites, or as a part of INITIATION RITES. Dance is thus used to reinforce certain ideas concerning communal identity and the social role of young adults. In north-central Iboland, a special mask known as Agbogho Mmuo was held in the air and "danced" by young male initiates to acknowledge the beauty of young women. In GHANA, it was common for girls in Ga society to display their beauty. It should also be noted that in many other societies, dancers are traditionally segregated by gender or age. The YORUBA of Nigeria held dances in which the entire community participated, including the ruling king, and danced according to status and age.

The strength, skill, self-discipline, and endurance of dancers were also tested by traditional war dances in societies that raised armies for battle. In both the Zulu and Ndebele societies, men performed dances that honor the history of warrior kings. The need to exhibit great skill while dancing also extended to reigning kings. The Ashanti kings of GHANA were judged by their dance skills performed at their enstoolment, or coronation ceremony.

While the role of dance in African societies remains constant, styles changed and spread over the centuries as a result of migration, trade, and the development of city-states. With the advent of new religions and ideas, many traditional dances were abolished.

See also: MASKS (Vol. I): MUSIC (Vol. I); RELIGION, TRADITIONAL (Vol. I).

Further reading: *Africana: The Encyclopedia of African and African American Experience* (New York: A Basic Civitas Book, 1999); Robert B. Fisher, *West African Religious Traditions* (Maryknoll, N.Y.: Orbis Books, 1998); Samuel A. Floyd, Jr. *The Power of Black Music* (New York: Oxford University Press, 1995); Gay Robins, *Women in Ancient Egypt* (Cambridge, Mass.: Harvard University Press, 1993).

Darius I (ruled 521–486 BCE) *King of the Persian Achmeunid dynasty of the sixth and fifth centuries* BCE.

Darius succeeded CAMBYSES to the throne in 521 BCE and spent the first years of his reign crushing revolts in Persia, Media, Babylonia, and the East. A powerful leader, he expanded his kingdom to include parts of India. According to tradition, he was a good king to the Egyptians. His projects included a canal that ran from the Nile to the Red Sea, as well as a large temple to AMUN at el-Kharga. Upon his death in 486 BCE, Darius was succeeded by his son Xerxes II.

death and dying Attitudes and practices concerning death vary greatly among African societies. Geography, economy, and local customs play an important role in determining each people's view of death. Typically, groups that are sedentary tend to give more importance to death and the surrounding ceremonies than nomadic people. A plausible explanation is that nomads must quickly bury the dead and abandon the body in order to move on to new territories in search of food. For precisely this reason, the Mbeere of Kenya left their deceased in the bush to decompose naturally. More sedentary peoples, like the Lugbara of Uganda, created permanent burial grounds that could be worshiped for years. Groups like these developed elaborate funeral rites that sometimes spanned decades. They believed that a proper burial was essential to send the deceased's spirit into the realm of the ancestors, where it would be worshiped by surviving relatives.

Variations on ANCESTOR WORSHIP, a common practice among many traditional African societies, is evident in the customs of the Dogon of present-day Mali. The Dogon believe a person has at least eight souls that are separated from the body at death. Once separated, the soul journeys back to the Creator of all mankind. This journey can take several years, and it requires many expensive sacrificial ceremonies on the part of the deceased's family.

Funeral practices among groups and peoples are just as varied as views about death. In general, however, most peoples consider sudden death from disease or accident bad luck, so the body is not treated with the same respect as when an elder dies. Those peoples who bury their dead often prepare the body by simply washing it; sometimes they also clean out the stomach or intestines. Some peoples remove the fetus from women who die in childbirth because they believe the buried fetus prevents the rest of the people from becoming infertile. After a body is prepared for burial, a ceremony or mourning period usually follows. Funeral rites may last as long as the burial, or they may continue for years.

Deir el-Bahri, Temple of Modern Arabic name for the site of an ancient Egyptian mortuary complex built by the Eleventh Dynasty king MENTUHOTEP II (c. 2010–1998 BCE). Located in the cliffs to the north of Thebes, Mentuhotep's structure consisted of three levels topped by a pyramid. This design was unique for its time, differing significantly from the burial monuments of earlier rulers by combining the king's mortuary temple and tomb in one building.

Queen Hatshepsut (c. 1501–1482 BCE), who ruled Egypt during the Eighteenth Dynasty, also erected a temple at el-Bahri. Modeled after Mentuhotep's nearby temple, it has long been famous for its elegant and graceful design. The decorated reliefs on its exterior reflect the glories of Hatshepsut's rule, as well as her great devotion to the god AMUN. Of particular interest are the temple's depictions of a trading expedition to the land of PUNT, which took place during her reign. Although Mentuhotep's temple complex has not survived, Hatshepsut's monument today remains much as it was when first constructed.

deities Gods or goddesses who form the basis of religious worship and traditional practices. Deities in ancient African societies were part of complex belief systems and took many different names and forms. Many societies were monotheistic, having a belief in a central, all-powerful deity who could be contacted through prayer or offerings. Other societies combined this belief with a faith in the existence of lesser deities who served as intermediaries between the all-powerful god and the living. The rationale was that the central deity, as the powerful creator of all things, was removed from the daily affairs of humans. Therefore, the responsibilities for daily concerns were assigned to deities who had the ability to produce fertile crops, to ensure economic growth, or to generate prosperous trading. Among the Anang of Nigeria, for example, Abassi was considered a powerful, invisible giant who ruled over the universe from his compound in the sky. Lesser deities in Anang society were known as Nnem, and they served as helpers or messengers to God. Among the Mossi of Yatenga in Upper Volta, Wennam was the principal deity who assigned earth custodians, Tenga Wende and Tido Wende, to provide earthly abundance through farm crops. Prayers and offerings were given to the earth custodians through specially built shrines. The YORUBA of Nigeria recognized OLORUN as their supreme deity but depended upon the ORISHA for resolving dilemmas or meeting day-to-day needs.

Many such deities were portrayed in artwork or appeared as carved figures throughout the ages. In some societies these figures represented the power of the deity or served as a means of transferring spiritual power. Some figures were placed on shrines within the living compound or family homes. Other figures were carried by dancers during rituals honoring specific deities.

See also: ANCESTOR WORSHIP (Vol. I); MONOTHEISM (Vol. I); POLYTHEISM (Vol. I); RELIGION, TRADITIONAL (Vol. I); SPIRIT POSSESSION (Vol. I).

Further reading: William R. Bascomb and Melville J. Herskovits, *Continuity and Change in African Cultures* (Chicago: University of Chicago Press, 1975); E. Bolaji Idowu, *African Traditional Religions: A Definition* (New York: Orbis Books, 1973).

demotic Flowing, cursive script that served as the final stage of hierolyphic writing in ancient Egypt.

Although probably developed expressly for use in government documents, demotic script became the most common everyday script in Egypt from around 660 BCE until the early fifth century CE. (Its name is derived from the Greek word *demotikos*, which means "for the people.") In addition to being utilized for government documents, demotic script became common in correspondence, business, literary texts, wood carvings, and stone inscriptions. Only priests, who continued to use the older HIERATIC script (more closely linked to ancient HIEROGLYPHICS) in writing religious texts, avoided using the more prevalent demotic script.

Like modern cursive handwriting, demotic script joined the letters of words, employing quick strokes of a reed brush or pen to create a flowing handwriting. Although harder to read than hieratic script, the demotic script allowed more standardization—that is, everyone wrote its characters in essentially the same way. The last dated example of demotic text is a stone inscription from 425.

The ROSETTA STONE (discovered in 1799 and translated in 1822) is inscribed in demotic script, hieroglyphs, and a Greek translation. The presence of both written languages provided the key to deciphering ancient Egyptian hieroglyphics.

Dendara Village in EGYPT; site of a well-preserved ancient Egyptian temple. Dendara, on the west bank of the Nile in central Egypt, was the principal site of the cult of HATHOR. The ancient Egyptian goddess of the sky, fertility, women, and childbirth, Hathor was represented either as a cow or as a woman whose crown consisted of a sun disk held between the horns of a cow.

The Hathor temple at Dendara is one of the best preserved buildings of ancient Egypt. Built primarily during the Ptolemaic Period (c. 323–30 BCE), it was completed by the Roman emperor Tiberius early in the first century. The influence of classical Roman styles, as well as earlier Greek styles, can be seen in the relief carving. This is especially true of the human figures, which feature the heroic, voluptuous, larger-than-life proportions characteristic of the Greek style.

deshret Reddish yellow desert land of the Sahara that covers approximately 95 percent of Egypt; from the Egyptian word meaning "red earth" or "desert."

Ancient Egyptians distinguished the dry, sandy, infertile deshret from the land they called *KEMET* ("black earth"), the extremely fertile soil of the NILE RIVER valley. This silt-layered, fertile soil washed over the fields of ancient Egypt every year when the Nile flooded over its banks. Its richness allowed the Egyptians to carve out from the desert a band of green fields bordering each side of the river.

The distinction between *deshret* and *kemet* is characteristic of the Egyptian adherence to dualism, the notion that any totality consists of two elements joined in harmonious opposition. Capitalized, the terms refer to UPPER and LOWER EGYPT; *Deshret* was also the name of the RED CROWN, the symbol that represented the Delta region of Lower Egypt.

Dida Galgalla Lava desert, found in Kenya, consisting of gray sand and brown and gray boulders. The Dida Galgalla lies north of Marsabit and west of LAKE TURKANA. It is part of the Great RIFT VALLEY, a geological fault system that runs about 3,000 miles (4,827 km) from the Jordan valley in southwestern Asia to Mozambique in southeastern Africa. Although Dida Galgalla is a harsh environment, it is home to many rare birds.

diet Ancient Africans obtained food in several ways: they hunted, fished, gathered, scavenged, herded, and farmed.

The earliest peoples were HUNTER-GATHERERS. Their diet included large game, rabbits, birds, fish, mice, grasshoppers, crabs, snails, mollusks, fruit, nuts, wild cereals, vegetables, fungi, and other plants. Some hunter-gatherers were also pastoralists, and, as a result, they had meat and milk, which they obtained from domestic animals. (While some pastoralists consumed the milk produced by their livestock, others did not. This difference is thought to stem from cultural mores or perhaps from the belief that some peoples were lactose–intolerant.)

Even in ancient times, hunting and gathering only used a portion of people's time, allowing opportunity for other activities, including social interaction and artistic expression. Some historians, therefore, believe that were it not for population growth, ancient peoples would not have taken up farming, since it represented a much more time-consuming activity. (In fact, it has been said that hunger has been the motivating force behind the development of agriculture, migrations, revolutions, wars, and the establishment of dynasties.)

When the ancient African population grew larger than the food sources could support, people began to engage in agriculture. While the hunters and gatherers did consume some wild cereal, the advent of farming meant that a steady supply of grain was available and that a surplus could be amassed to provide food in lean times or as currency in trading necessities and other items.

Geography was a determining factor in the diet of the hunters and gatherers. Different regions supported different wild plants and animals. In parts of West Africa, for example, people harvested forest snails, while groups living on the shores of Lake Victoria used water flies as an ingredient in soup.

In the case of agriculture, the type of terrain and amount of rainfall determined the kinds of crops that grew best. The ancient Egyptians grew barley, beans, cucumbers, dates, figs, grapes, leeks, melons, and wheat. The people of ETHIOPIA domesticated *noog*, an oil plant, and *teff*, a tiny grain, which was not found elsewhere in Africa. Many varieties of wheat and barley were cultivated in Ethiopia, where the altitude was conducive to their growth. The peoples of West Africa's "yam belt" cultivated a variety of plants used in soups, including fluted pumpkins. The IBO used yams as a carbohydrate staple, rolling pounded yams into a ball and dipping them into a sauce before eating them. The peoples of marginal areas experimented with a fluctuating blend of farming, hunting and gathering, and fishing. Climate change also affected diet. For example, gradual desiccation in western Sudan affected the development of cereals.

Yet another factor influencing the diet of ancient Africans was social mores. The MAASAI were pastoralists and loathed hunting and farming. Consequently, only in times of famine would they take up cultivation and hunting, although some Maasai groups did adopt agriculture.

Foods from Asia were also part of the diet of ancient Africans. It is thought that the settlers of Madagascar brought bananas, rice, and COCOYAM from Asia. It was previously thought that these foods spread to the mainland and then across the continent. However, it is now believed more likely that they spread very gradually around the shores of the Indian Ocean.

The importance of food staples was reflected in the languages of ancient Africans. Among the Ibo, a successful yam farmer was referred to as a "yam king," and the Ibo language has numerous words for yams. The Chagga have twenty different words for *banana*. To the Nuer and Dinka peoples, fish and grain were more important than meat. Thus Dinka priests were referred to as "Masters of the fishing spear." In the Sudan, the word for *life* refers to SORGHUM. In the SAHEL, the same word refers to MILLET.

The preparation and consumption of food was often associated with rites and rituals. For example, the peoples of the MAGHREB ate communal meals built around couscous, which was made from pulverized grain. The women prayed aloud during the grinding process, and the communal consumption of the couscous was an expression of solidarity. Among the Ibo, the eating of yams was forbidden before the New Yam festival. This was most likely done to allow the tubers to grow to maturity.

The amount of food available sometimes determined who would live and who would die. Some hunters and gatherers would be forced to abandon their infants and elders in times of famine. The diets of the ancient Africans also affected their life span and health. A diet lacking in certain nutrients could be responsible for illness, and many people suffered a lifetime of pain due to such health problems as arthritis and tooth decay.

See also: AGRICULTURE (Vols. I and II); CROPS (Vol. II).

Diocletian (245–316 CE) *Emperor of Rome who, during his more than twenty-year rule, strengthened the empire's position in northern Africa.*

Gaius Aurelius Valerius Diocletianus, an officer in the Roman army, was proclaimed emperor by his troops upon the death of Emperor Marcus Aurelius Numerianus (Numerian) in 284. Carinus, Numerian's brother and co-emperor, challenged Diocletian's claim to the title of emperor, but was assassinated by his own troops during the battle for the throne.

Diocletian recognized the difficulty of one man ruling the vast Roman Empire. So in 286, he chose to share the throne—and the title of augustus—with Marcus Aurelius Valerius Maximianus (Maximian). Seven years later, Diocletian named two younger men, Gaius Galerius Valerius Maximianus (Galerius) and Constantius I Chlorus (Constantius I), as subordinate rulers with the title caesar. Each of the four rulers had administrative control over a portion of the Roman Empire, with jurisdiction over Africa being divided between Diocletian, who ruled over Egypt, and Maximian, who ruled over the rest of Roman Africa.

Through a combination of warfare and administrative reorganization, Diocletian restored the strength of the Roman Empire, which had deteriorated under several prior rulers, and extended its boundaries in Persia and Africa. In 296, Diocletian's armies recaptured Egypt, which had declared its independence from the Roman Empire. As part of his reorganization of the empire, Diocletian divided Cyrenaica, a region of North Africa, into two provinces: Libya Superior (Pentapolis) and Libya Inferior (Sicca). He then assigned a permanent military force to the region—the first such contingent placed in Africa by an emperor.

In 305, Diocletian abdicated and forced Maximian to do the same, leaving rule to his handpicked successors, Galerius and Constantius I.

See also: CYRENE (Vol. I); ROME (Vol. I).

Further reading: Peter Brown, *The World of Late Antiquity.: From Marcus Aurelius to Muhammed* (New York: W. W. Norton, 1989); Jackob Burkhardt, *The Age of Constantine the Great* (Berkeley: University of California, 1983).

disease in ancient Africa Disease has plagued the African continent for thousands of years. The African people have long coped with disease-causing organisms by adapting to their environment. Threatening diseases were kept at bay with simple changes in diet, water sources, or migration patterns. Subtle genetic mutations over the centuries have allowed Africans to effectively deal with many diseases.

However, new diseases emerged in response to the changing African environment. Parasites and microbes that cause diseases are directly affected by geography. Some thrive in the savanna grasslands or semiarid deserts, while others prefer the tropical rain forests of the western coastal regions. Parasitic diseases like malaria depend upon mosquitoes for transmittal; thus, the disease survives only in areas with pools of water. Temperature and altitude also play an important role in determining where microbes are able to live. Extreme climate changes can affect the susceptibility of the population to otherwise nonthreatening diseases.

The Role of the Seasons The seasons affect diseases both directly and indirectly. The wet season allows mosquitoes and other parasitic hosts to breed, while the dry season can contribute to heat exhaustion, which may negatively affect human immune systems. Dry seasons have always been a time of travel for the African people; they abandon their crop fields to visit neighboring villages for trade. However, diseases travel along with their human hosts, often with devastating effects.

Particularly before the time of Euopean involvement, the seasons determined the state of health of Africa's agriculturalists. Barring periodic catastrophes like drought, the wet season supplied a bounty of food for local African inhabitants. The nourishment this food provided enabled the people to increase their body weight, thus strengthening their immune systems against disease. The dry season brought drought and hunger, which increased the susceptibility of the immune system. On the other hand, the dry season prevented parasitic larvae from hatching and, accordingly, reduced disease in any given year. For much of their history, African peoples lived in equilibrium with microbes and parasites.

Parasites Parasites are some of the most common diseases in Africa. Like all parasites, those found in Africa rely on a secondary organism to transport them to the host. Common parasites include filarial worms like the *Loa loa* and the *Calicoides*, which are both transmitted by flies. Intestinal worms are passed to humans from monkeys, although they are not life threatening.

Echinococcus granulosus is a tapeworm common in sheep, cattle, camels, dogs, and many other mammals in Africa. Ingesting their larvae causes hydatid, or echinococcal, disease, which causes severe cysts throughout the body, particularly in the liver. In the Turkana region of Kenya, where dogs are important to society, hyatid disease is spread predominately through the feces of dogs. Children are particularly susceptible to the disease because mothers use dogs to guard their children while they work.

Another native African parasite is *Leishmania*. It is transmitted by tropical sand flies that bite humans and animals. Some strains of *Leishmania* cause minor disfigurement by producing open sores on the body and face, while others have more serious side affects. One form of *Leishmania* has long been evident in the regions surrounding present-day Ethiopia, where inhabitants often sought shelter in nearby caves. The parasite was contracted from sand flies that feed on cave-dwelling rodents.

Schistosomes are parasites that are passed through the feces of snails. The origins of this parasite can be traced to the lakes of central and eastern Africa, where many species still exist that infect both humans and baboons. Humans are infected by coming into contact with infected water. The disease can cause serious liver, bladder, and kidney problems.

Viruses Viral diseases are abundant in Africa. Many have never left the continent, but some have caused substantial problems abroad. Most are harbored in animals and then passed to humans via tick or insect bites, although the bites rarely result in disease. More often the virus is destroyed by the immune system or protects its host from a more dangerous virus.

Malaria Malaria has long been a serious health threat in Africa. Mosquitoes transmit all four strains of the disease. One of the more lethal strains has been largely controlled after thousands of years of genetic selection. The sickle cell blood trait common to Africans developed as a direct response to the malaria parasite. Sickle cells limit the parasite's ability to grow once inside red blood cells, thus largely protecting the host. In tropical regions outside of Africa where sickle cells are not common, this same malaria strain is a serious life-threatening disease.

Disease in Ancient Egypt Evidence gathered from ancient Egyptian papyri and the medical examination of mummified remains suggest that the people of ancient Egypt suffered from many of the same diseases that afflict people of the modern world; these included malaria, poliomyelitis, smallpox, trichinosis, bubonic plague, tuberculosis of the bone, arthritis, gout, tooth decay, bladder stones, and gall stones.

Among the most common diseases in ancient Egypt were parasitic infections. Malaria, characterized by recurrent chills and fever, as well as anemia and enlargement of the spleen, may have been the disease that claimed the life of ALEXANDER THE GREAT in 323 BCE. Another parasitic infection, schistosomiasis, also was common in ancient Egypt.

See also: DISEASE IN MEDIEVAL AFRICA (Vol. II); DISEASE IN PRECOLONIAL AFRICA (Vol. III).

Further reading: Aidan Cockburn, Eve Cockburn, and Theodore Reyman, *Mummies, Disease and Ancient Cultures* (Cambridge: Cambridge University Press, 1998); Joyce Filer, *Disease* (Egyptian Bookshelf) (Austin: University of Texas Press, 1996).

divination Ritual expertise in foretelling events or determining the hidden roots of illness. Widely prevalent throughout Africa, divination has long served as a central component in African religion. It has also played a prominent role in political and cultural areas, as well as in the succession of kings, and, as such, offered practitioners the ability to gain the confidence of rulers. For example, divination was prominent in the enthronement or installation ceremonies of ancient kings in EGYPT. It also serves as an important means of reinforcement of family and community identity.

Over the centuries, a vast number of divination systems have developed in Africa. The ritual skill required to master these systems included a thorough grounding in names, signs, and figures, along with their interpretative counterparts, such as proverbs, parables, or symbolic riddles. For centuries, these systems have appeared deceptively simple to outsiders. For instance, the Dogon traditionally read the tracks left by animals from an ancient period, while the Bamum, or Mum, of West Africa interpreted the movements of spiders. More frequently, divining involved the casting down and "reading" of various objects, such as COWRIE SHELLS, divination stones, or gourds. Other diviners interpreted vital information from numbers, from reading palms, or from images in water. Many divination experts were linked to spiritual deities either through an ORACLE or some other form of mediumship.

Other types of divination reflect a very complex science, such as the system of IFA. Traditionally administered by a BABALAWO, or "father of mysteries," divination has been a dominant tool and feature of the religions shared by the YORUBA and Fon peoples of Nigeria, Dahomey, Togo, and GHANA. It has long been associated with the deity Orunmila, who was considered the god of divination, and involved the use of sixteen palm nuts cast on a divining tray. Each throw of the palm nuts offered a numerical formula whose meaning was revealed through the appropriate verses; the procedure was repeated every five days.

A common thread among various forms of divination is that ritual specialists often created them to explain the unexplainable, including droughts, storms, depleted soil, or ruined crops. On a personal level, divination can almost be compared to a form of "preventive medicine," foretelling impending illnesses and diagnosing their underlying causes. Whenever misfortune stemmed from neglect of family or ancestral spirits, diviners were able to offer the appropriate actions to repair the results of this neglect. Overall, divination served as an important means of keeping society in harmonious balance.

There has been considerable debate as to whether the practitioners or specialists who were able to perform divination were customarily men or women. This may have depended on the particular society. The skills involved probably were passed down as an inherited body of information from family members. Diviners also served as apprentices to master teachers for a fixed number of years. It is also possible that the ability to divine may have occurred more quickly as a result of SPIRIT POSSESSION. The diviner's function has been described as multidimensional and may have included healing skills as well. Among the Zulu of Kwazulu-Natal, for instance, Izangoma was the title used for females who traditionally served as a diviner/healer for one of several goddesses, such as Nomkhubulwane. Similarly, the Nganga was a variation of the same title used by the BaKongo peoples of West Africa. The primary tools of the Nganga diviner generally included herbs and special medicines whose contents remained a secret. For societies of the CONGO, Nkisi figures were also employed by Ngangas. The chief responsibility of identifying WITCHCRAFT, and the application of appropriate remedies for the harm caused were often accomplished through divination.

See also: ANCESTOR WORSHIP (Vol. I); RELIGION, TRADITIONAL (Vol. I); SPIRIT POSSESSION (Vol. I).

Further reading: John R. Hinnells, ed., *The Penguin Dictionary of Religions* (London: The Penguin Group, 1995); John S. Mbiti, *African Religions and Philosophy* (London: The Heinnemann Group, Ltd., 1999); T.N.O. Quarcoopome, *West African Traditional Religion* (Ibadan: African Universities Press, 1987).

divine rule Belief among some ancient African societies that kings obtained the right to rule from the society's deity or deities. Exempt from ordinary laws and customs, many ancient kings served dual functions as rulers and intermediaries for the deity.

In Africa, the concept of divine rule can be traced back to ancient EGYPT, where from even the earliest dynasties pharaohs claimed to be descended from various deities. Elsewhere in Africa, royal claims to divine rule entitled kings to wear special royal garments and crowns. They might also carry sceptors or other objects to signify their power and status. Among some peoples, kings even lived in special areas removed from the general popoulation.

Some societies simply replaced kings who became ill, wounded, or disabled. Others believed that, even if a king's power was divinely based, kings could be overthrown or replaced if their actions became cruel or unjust. In Senegal, for example, a king who had been wounded in battle would be replaced by a paternal brother. Other societies legitimized regicide, the actual or symbolic killing of the king, in situations that called for the king's removal. This practice, too, dates back to the ancient Egyptians, among whom aged pharoahs faced death. In Egypt, this practice was eventually transformed into a symbolic ritual known as the SED FESTIVAL, which represented the periodic rejuvenation of the pharaoh.

See also: ANCESTOR WORSHIP (Vol. I); DEITIES (Vol. I); GOVERNMENT, SYSTEMS OF (Vol. II); LAW AND JUSTICE (Vol. II).

Further reading: William R. Bascomb and Melville J. Herskovits, *Continuity and Change in African Cultures* (Chicago: The University of Chicago Press, 1975); Basil Davidson, *The Lost Cities of Africa* (New York: Little, Brown, 1987); E. Bolaji Idowu, *African Traditional Religions: A Definition* (New York: Orbis Books, 1973); Robert Farris Thompson *Flash of the Spirit* (New York: First Vintage Books; Random House, 1984).

Dja River Also called the Ngoko River, the Dja forms part of the border between Cameroon and Congo. The river stretches nearly 450 miles (724 km) before it feeds into the Sangha River, a tributary of the Congo. Much of the river is navigable by small craft.

Djeme Site of the mortuary temple of RAMESSES III (1184–1153 BCE); later known by the Arabic name Medinet Habu. During a reign of more than thirty years, Ramesses III was revered as a military hero who not only defeated invading LIBYAN forces but also successfully expanded Egypt's territorial boundaries. Ramesses' victories ushered in a period of great prosperity for EGYPT, which in turn generated the construction of many buildings and temples. One of the outstanding works of the period known as the NEW KINGDOM, Ramesses's memorial temple housed a library and contained numerous inscriptions and wall reliefs related to his battles with the Libyans.

Djerid Largest salt lake in Africa, also known as Chott Djerid and Shatt Al-Jarid. Located in southwestern TUNISIA near the Sahara Desert. Djerid occupies an enormous salt-flat basin of about 1,900 square miles (4,900 sq km). Except after heavy rains, only the lowest parts of the lake are covered with water.

Djibouti Present-day country occupying an area on the northeastern coast of the Horn of Africa. Inhabited since STONE AGE times, it was the ancient homeland of the AFAR and other Somali PASTORALISTS.

dog Domesticated mammal belonging to the canine family, which also includes the coyote, wolf, and FOX; highly valued in ancient EGYPT. Although they come in a variety of shapes, sizes, and colors, all dogs share such common traits as a long muzzle, sharp canine teeth, and a tail. The largest dog, the Irish wolfhound, can stand as tall 39 inches (99 cm) and the smallest, the Chihuahua, only 6 inches (15 cm). They are bred and trained by humans as hunting animals, guides, and pets. Dogs are intelligent and social animals with highly developed senses of hearing and smell. They live about fifteen years and give birth to their young in litters of up to ten.

Dogs held a special place in ancient Egyptian society. Only people of royal blood were allowed to own purebred dogs, which were treated lavishly during their lives. When their masters died, these dogs would be placed in tombs with them to provide protection in the AFTERLIFE. One of the earliest known breeds of domestic dogs in Egypt is the Basenji, a short-haired, medium-sized dog that whimpers rather than barks. Basenjis were raised in the courts of Egypt's pharaohs.

Africa is also home to a wild dog known as the African hunting dog, a long-limbed animal with large, pointy ears. African hunting dogs prey on antelopes south and east of the Sahara.

Dongola Bend Ancient region encompassing the lands situated between the third and fourth cataracts of the Nile River; also known as Dongola Reach and The Land of Yam.

Originally populated by farming and fishing communities, Dongola is a fertile river valley described as the garden of the Upper Nile. It spans more than 200 miles (320 km) of unbroken terrain and produces abundant crops of millet and cotton, as well as cattle and other domestic stock.

At the beginning of ancient Egypt's Twelfth Dynasty (c. 2000–1780 BCE), a trading post was established in Dongola, which was by then considered a province of the Egyptian Empire. The ruling dynasty's plans to push further south into NUBIA were interrupted by the Hyksos occupation of EGYPT, c. 1700–1670 BCE. After the Hyksos invaders were expelled, the rulers of the newly founded Eighteenth Dynasty resumed the expeditions to the area.

In 1525 BCE, THUTMOSE I, the third pharaoh of the Eighteenth Dynasty, led an army to Dongola, venturing beyond the fourth cataract to Kurgus. There, in the region that later became the capital city of MEROË, Thutmose left an inscribed marker noting his conquest. Although a number of revolts by Kushites occurred in Dongola after Thutmose I's death, they were suppressed by a succession of Egyptian overlords.

donkey Domestic ass used throughout Africa for transportation and as a beast of burden.

The introduction of the domestic donkey to the African continent was an important factor in the improvement of transportation and labor productivity for many peoples. Wild asses have inhabited the continent of Africa for thousands of years. Two varieties still thrive in northeastern Africa, the Nubian and the Somali asses. Rock paintings indicate that ancient Egyptians hunted Nubian asses, so their range must have extended from the Nile to the Red Sea. Today, small numbers of wild Nubian asses inhabit parts of Sudan. Their Somali relatives are much larger and live in the desert region between the Red Sea and the plateaus of present-day Somalia.

The ass was one of the first animals domesticated in Africa. Bred by the Egyptians from its wild counterpart, which was native to North Africa and Arabia, the donkey became one of the most important domestic animals in Africa. Donkeys were used in early Egypt as the principal means of transportation and as labor animals. As populations spread from North Africa to the Sahara and eastern coast, indigenous peoples began using the donkey for labor and transport. It was particularly important to early Semitic and Hamitic peoples.

drums Oldest known musical instrument in the world; drums date back to 4000 BCE in ancient EGYPT. The music produced by the drum—and the drum itself—varied from group to group in ancient Africa.

A drum is a percussive instrument that is constructed by stretching a skin over a vessel or frame; the sound comes from the vibration of the stretched skin as it is struck. The earliest drums were probably made from hollowed-out tree trunks with a reptile or fish skin stretched across it. These drums were struck with the hands. When animal skins took the place of fish or reptile skin as the stretched membrane, sticks were then used to beat the drum. Eventually, a double-headed drum was produced by attaching tension cords through holes in the skins in order to hold the two ends together. Perhaps the best-known double-headed African drum is the Ethiopian *kebero*, which was used to accompany the music of important religious ceremonies.

Drums were also important throughout sub-Saharan Africa. In religious festivals and rituals, dancers often performed intricate movements to the syncopated rhythms of drums, which were played primarily by males. Drums were played by one person, in pairs, or in a larger group known as an ensemble.

Dyula People of western Africa who speak a MANDE language of the Nilo-Congo family. Also known as the Dioula, Diula, and Jula, they are chiefly Muslims and have long been noted as commercial traders. Most of the Dyula inhabit the trade routes of the IVORY COAST, but Dyula clans have also settled in lands that became Burkina Faso, Mali, Ghana, and Guinea-Bissau. The word *dyula* means "itinerant trader," and the Dyula are respected for their abilities in commercial dealings. The Dyula were active gold traders as long ago as the third century CE, flourishing during the periods of ancient Ghana and the empire of Mali. During this period they provided a link between the gold-producing forests in the south and the trading net-

E

eagle Predatory bird belonging to the HAWK family.

Because of their powerful build and majestic bearing, eagles have long been associated with power and warfare. According to the traditions of the ancient Egyptians, for example, the king was granted the authority to rule over the earth by Holse, the god of the eagle. In Egypt, eagles also were associated with the phoenix, a bird that was part of Egyptian mythology from early times.

ebony Valuable timber tree (*D. dendo*), native to various parts of Africa as well as to parts of Asia, the Americas, and the Pacific; also known as black ebony, billetwood, and Gabon, Lagos, Calabar, and Niger ebony. The best ebony is from the heartwood of the tree. Heavy and almost black in color, this hard, dense wood can be polished to a beautiful sheen, which makes it one of the world's most exquisite, as well as most durable, woods.

Ebony was highly prized in ancient times. The Greek historian HERODOTUS, for example, wrote that the Ethiopians sent a tribute of 200 logs of ebony to Persia every three years. Ebony from NUBIA was used to make some of the famed treasures of the Egyptian kings and contributed significantly to Egypt's material wealth.

See also: EBONY (Vol. III).

economics Modes of production and distribution of wealth. As with most ancient peoples, economic issues were major considerations in many African cultures. Not surprisingly, dynamics such as climate, terrain, subsistence, shelter, natural resources, technology, trade, and even art were all related in one way or another to economics.

Subsistence Once people moved from the hunter-gatherer stage of subsistence and began to develop tools and settle into village life, most economic decisions resulted from a combination of experience and the availability of resources. In hunting as well as fishing societies, for example, an individual's status often was determined by that person's continued success in the hunt or catch or by the size and number of fishing vessels owned by the individual. Elsewhere, the availability of water sources and grazing land determined whether an ethnic group pursued a pastoral or a nomadic form of subsistence. Among many of these peoples, CATTLE raising became the dominant means of meeting their subsistence needs. In addition to providing meat and dairy products for human consumption, cattle were used as currency, as BRIDEWEALTH, and as a means of settling debts. In this way cattle became a determining factor in social stratification within these cattle-raising societies.

Shelter In many parts of Africa, housing was not as problematic as it was in colder, harsher environments. Thatched-roof homes were erected in wet, heavily forested areas, while mud and clay structures were built in more arid climates. However, wealth and status often were linked to the number and size of the dwellings owned by a person. Thus, economic considerations were linked to the availability of the materials needed to erect dwelling places.

Natural Resources and Technology Settlement in close proximity to fertile fields and mineral deposits could be the means of the acquisition of immense power. Ancient GHANA offers a perfect example of the exploitation of both types of resources. Because of its proximity to the Wangara gold fields and its taxation of commercial traffic on the trade routes, Ghana received immense revenues without any substantial capital outlay. This wealth facilitated the production of iron tools, which in turn provided the kingdom with a distinct advantage in agricultural production. These high agricultural yields provided Ghana with an additional source of revenue apart from the Saharan trade.

Trade Trading or bartering game and fish for other goods was an intricate part of the early hunter-gatherer economies. Likewise, the open market, at which people laid out their produce and other goods, was a part of the African scene for hundreds of years.

The gold and salt trade, which developed in later years between Sahara merchants and Ghana, Mali, and Songhai, was interesting for three reasons. First, it was the source of tremendous wealth for the rulers of these ancient empires. Second, because salt was scarce and gold was so abundant, salt became more precious than gold. Third, due to the secrecy associated with the location of the Wangara gold fields, trade was conducted by dumb barter, a process in which the merchants did not actually meet face to face, but instead left appropriate amounts of goods in a prescribed place in exchange for the gold.

Art Artists and blacksmiths have long been revered in Africa, in part because in the minds of many African peoples, art is "functional." For these people, birth, death, and countless other events that occurred during a person's life were believed to depend on appeasing various ancestors and deities. This required creating icons and fetishes to be used in certain observances and ceremonies. Those who fashioned these objects were thought to possess magical powers. Since the well-being of entire communities often depended on adequate yields from the hunt or harvest, the perceived importance of these objects—and of the people who made them—was very closely associated with the economics of the community.

See also: ARAB COASTAL TRADE (Vol. II); COPPER (Vol. II); GOLD (Vols. I, II); INDIAN OCEAN TRADE (Vol. II);. *NUMUW* (Vol. II); TRANS-SAHARAN TRADE ROUTES (Vol. II).

Edfu

Town in central Egypt; location of the Temple of HORUS.

Located on the west bank of the Nile River, about 65 miles (105 km) from Aswan, Edfu, or Idfu as it has also been called, houses the best-preserved cult temple in Egypt, the Temple of Horus. The town itself has been known by many names, having been called Tbot by the early Egyptians, Apollinopolis Magna by the Greeks, and Atbo during Coptic times. Around 3400 BCE, it was the capital of a predynastic Upper Egyptian kingdom that worshiped the god Horus.

The large sandstone temple is second in size only to the great Temple of KARNAK, and it bears an abundance of inscriptions and HIEROGLYPHICS. These tell of religious ceremonies and recount tales of the pharoahs' wisdom and might. The temple, which was discovered in 1860, was well preserved by its long submersion under desert sands. Excavations on the site have yielded a magnificent black marble statue of Horus and a Roman necropolis, as well as Coptic and Byzantine remains.

Edo

Kwa-speaking group that has long inhabited the southern forest region west of the NIGER RIVER. These peoples have inhabited this area, in what is now the Benin province of present-day Nigeria, for upwards of 3,000 years. Originally, single-family settlements dominated the region. However, about the fifth century, village communities began to be formed in order to provide families with better defenses. These communities also facilitated more efficient use of natural resources.

See also: BENIN (Vol. II).

Egungun

In Yoruba society, a masking cult representing the return of the dead from the spirit world. According to traditional Yoruban belief, an Egungun, the supernatural being after whom the cult is named, is the embodiment of the spirit of a male ancestor who returns from the spirit world to visit his family. Not every ancestor is invoked as an Egungun, only those who have lived a good life on earth and who, because they are in favor with OLORUN (Olodumare), the creator, are permitted to enter heaven and return to the world of the living. Such ancestors are seen as worthy of true worship, not just veneration, and may be used by the living to appeal to the creator. The Egungun can either intercede with angry divinities to protect the living from harm or simply bless the living and receive their offerings.

The living person who puts on the family's Egungun attire also puts on the ancestor's spiritual power. He wears a special outfit made from cloths of different colors that cover him from head to foot. His feet are obscured, and he wears a veil that allows speech but conceals the wearer's identity. Many Egungun also wear special masks and charms. The person wearing the Egungun attire is accorded the respect due an honored visitor from heaven; women and the uninitiated may not touch the Egungun on penalty of death.

Egungun are sometimes summoned by an individual to bring spiritual benefits and comfort to his descendants. They are also summoned by entire villages to go from dwelling to dwelling and bless the living at the start of the yam season or the planting season and at other festivals. Egungun are also called on at times of calamity to carry a propitiatory offering to an offended divinity.

See also: ORISHA (Vol. I); RELIGION, TRADITIONAL (Vol. I); SPIRIT POSSESSION (Vol. I).

Further Reading: Omosade Awolalu, *Yoruba Beliefs and Sacrificial Rites* (White Plains, N.Y.: Longman Group, 1979).

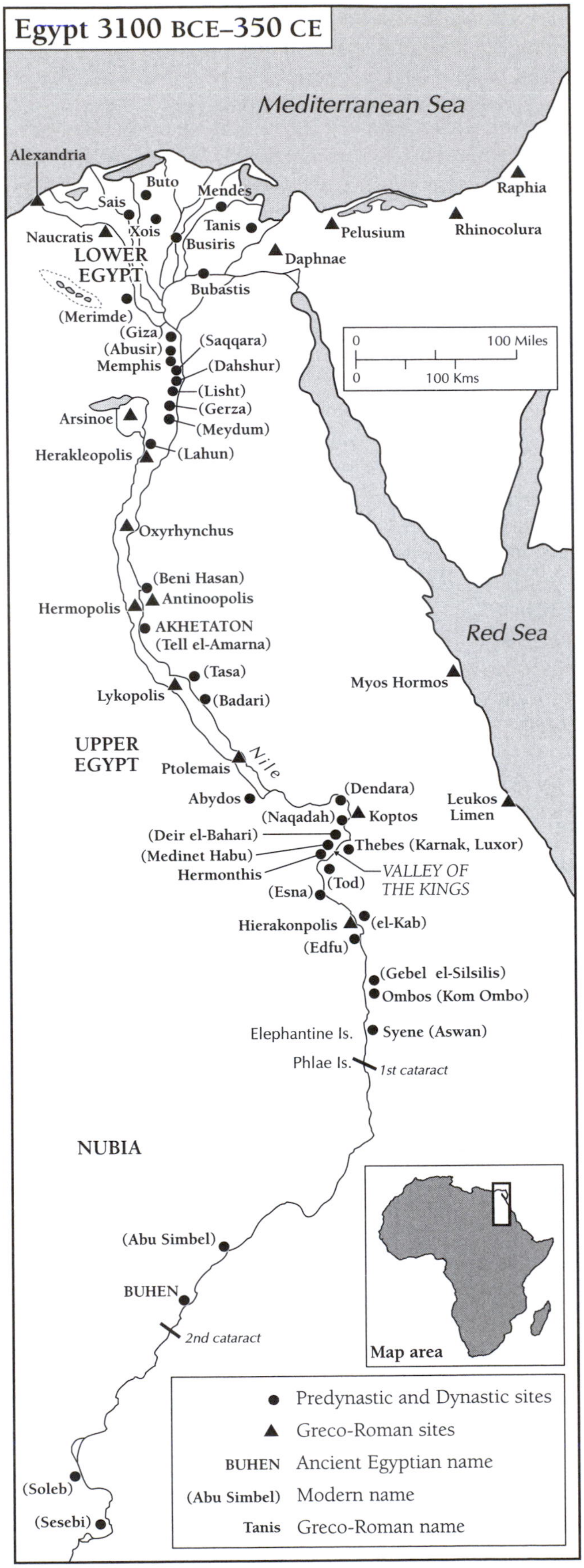

Egypt Country situated on the northeastern part of the African continent. Egypt is mostly desert, with the Nile River running, south to north, for 600 to 700 miles (960–1120 km) through the center. On either side of the river lies a narrow strip of land known as the Nile Valley. The northern part of Egypt, known as the Nile Delta, is where that river empties into the Mediterranean Sea.

The name *Egypt* is derived from the Greek word *Aigyptos*, but the ancient Egyptians called their country KEMET, or "black land," for the dark, richly fertile soil that results each year as the Nile overflows its banks and floods the river valley. In sharp contrast to this is the "red land," or desert (*deshret*), which makes up much of the rest of the country. Until the country was unified c. 3050 BCE, the ancient Egyptians divided their land into two kingdoms, UPPER EGYPT and LOWER EGYPT. Lower Egypt was the northern part of the country, and Upper Egypt was the part to the south.

Although a majority of Egyptologists interpret the ancient Egyptian word *kemet* to mean "black land," some Egyptologists and other scholars dispute this interpretation. *Kemet*, according to them, means "Land of the Blacks," a reference to the black-skinned Africans they believe were the actual inhabitants of the ancient kingdom.

Egyptologists divide the long history of ancient Egypt into kingdoms and intermediate periods. These are in turn subdivided into thirty dynasties of rulers.

Predynastic Period	
Badarian Culture	c. 4800–4200 BCE
Naqadah I, II, III	c. 4200–3050 BCE
Early, or Archaic, Period	
Dynasties 1–2	c. 3050–2705 BCE
Old Kingdom	
Dynasties 3–8	c. 2705–2213 BCE
First Intermediate Period	
Dynasties 9–11	c. 2213–1991 BCE
Middle Kingdom	
Dynasties 12–13	c.1991–1668 BCE
Second Intermediate Period	
Dynasties 18–20	c. 1668–1570 BCE
New Kingdom	
Dynasties 18–20	c. 1570–1070 BCE
Late Period	
Dynasties 21–25	c. 1070–650 BCE
Kushite Domination	c. 742–650 BCE
Saite Period	
Dynasty 26	c. 663–525 BCE

Persian Period	
Dynasties 27–31	c. 525–332 BCE
Greco–Roman Rule	c. 332 BCE–395 CE

After the end of Roman rule, Christianity flourished in Egypt for several centuries, only to be replaced by Islam when the country was conquered by Arabs in the seventh century.

The Egyptian contribution to the history of civilization is immense. Foremost among these contributions are the introduction of writing, the advancement of medical science, the development of sophisticated agricultural programs, and the creation of lasting architectural monuments.

Since the latter half of the twentieth century, the racial makeup of the ancient Egyptians has been a subject of considerable controversy. The traditional view of Western scholars is that, from the beginning, the ancient Egyptians were a light-skinned but suntanned people. According to these scholars, darker or black-skinned people only began to be seen in Egypt from the time of the Eighteenth Dynasty and afterwards. A very different view, however, is held by other scholars, who believe that, from predynastic times onward, the ancient Egyptians were in fact black Africans. The most prominent of these scholars is the Senegalese historian Cheikh Anta Diop. Diop points to the writings of the fifth-century BCE Greek historian HERODOTUS, who described the Egyptians of his time as black and as having a culture that was African in orientation.

See also: EGYPT (Vols. II, III).

elephant The African elephant is the largest living animal on land, weighing 8 tons (7 metric tons) and standing 10 to 13 feet (3 to 4 m) at the shoulder. Elephants are usually gray or brown in color and have little body hair. They breathe through their powerful trunks, which are also used to suck up water and to pick up food. On either side of an elephant's trunk are tusks. Ivory is made from elephant tusks.

Elephants are found in sub-Saharan Africa and live in both jungles and savanna, moving in small groups led by older cows (female elephants). Adult members of the groups can each eat more than 500 pounds (225 kg) of grasses and other vegetation a day, and can live up to sixty years.

Elephants have played an important part in Africa's history and culture. In the mythology of many African peoples, elephants symbolize strength, leadership, and greatness. The Baule people of Ghana and the IBO people of Niger, for example, traditionally have carved masks in the form of elephants. The Samburu people of present-day Kenya have, for hundreds of years, worn ivory charms made from the tusks of elephants who had died in the wild. These charms were put on babies to protect them from harm. Another Samburu custom has been to burn elephant dung on the floor of the house of a newly married couple to bless them with a long, happy marriage.

Elephantine Former name of the site known today as Aswan, situated along the Egypt's NILE RIVER. Ancient accounts of Elephantine emphasize its importance as a route to the lands south of Egypt. Some of the most important of these accounts were those of Harkhuf, an Egyptian governor who took part in four expeditions to the area during the Sixth Dynasty (c. 2420–2260 BCE).

Harkhuf's journeys took him as far as KERMA, in the Kingdom of KUSH, near the third cataract of the Nile, where he sought to discover trade routes and establish economic relations with the rulers he met. Harkhuf's travels along what he called the "forty-day road" ultimately brought him praise from his royal masters. As he wrote in approximately 2300 BCE: "The majesty of Mernere, my lord, sent me, together with my father, the sole companion, and ritual priest Iri to Yam in order to explore a road to this country (south). I did it in only seven months and I brought all gifts from it.... I was very greatly praised for it."

Elgon, Mount Extinct volcano found within the Great RIFT VALLEY along the border of modern-day Kenya and Uganda. Mount Elgon consists of a crater up to 5 miles (8 km) wide with several peaks rising from it. The highest of these peaks is Wagagi, which has an elevation of 14,178 feet (4,321 m).

On its eastern and southeastern slopes, Mount Elgon blends gently with the Uasin Gishu Plateau, which stands at 6,200 feet (1,890 m). But on its western and northwestern slopes, high cliffs separate Mount Elgon from the plains of eastern Uganda. Within the volcano's crater are forests and swamps, which are drained by the Suam and Turkwel Rivers. The area has long been occupied by the Gishu, a BANTU-speaking people.

Eritrea Former province of Ethiopia, approximately 36,000 square miles (93,600 sq km) in area, including regions in the Horn of Africa and the mountainous plateaus bordered by the RED SEA. Much of Eritrea's ancient history has been overshadowed by the kingdom of AKSUM, which was founded within its borders about 350 CE.

However, numerous cave paintings recovered in the region attest to a regional history dating back to at least 6000 BCE. During these ancient times the area was primarily populated with indigenous AGAW, Nilotic-speakers from the forests of southern Sudan, and Kushite pastoralists who originated in the desert in the north. During the pre-Aksumite era (c. 800–300 BCE) these peoples were joined by Semitic speakers originating in southern Arabia (Yemen). As the recovered temple at Ilmuquah reveals, the region's religious traditions have also been diverse, reflecting elements of Judaism, Christianity, and Islam.

See also: ERITREA (Vols. II, III); ETHIOPIA (Vols. I, II, III).

Eshu (Esu, Eshu-Elegba) One of the principal divinities in traditional YORUBA religion.

In Yoruba belief, Eshu is the divinity who must be propitiated first, before any other divinities or ancestors. Eshu delivers sacrifices and offerings from humans to the gods and from one divinity to other divinities, thus maintaining the relationship between the human and the supernatural worlds. Eshu must be taken seriously because he is the god who tempts and tests, rewarding and punishing humans, regardless of rank and influence, to determine their true character. He prompts human beings to offend the gods, whose anger they must then mollify with sacrifices. It is said that without Eshu, the gods would go hungry.

Eshu is neither the Christian Satan or the Muslim Shaitan; traditional Yoruba belief does not look upon the world as a contest between absolute good and absolute evil. Eshu can create hatred between brother and brother, and he can reconcile them after years of dispute. He can kill a firstborn child and provide offspring to the childless. He punishes those who do not offer the required sacrifices and rewards those who do. In Yoruban religion, Eshu personifies the coexistence of good and evil in the world.

See also: RELIGION, TRADITIONAL (Vol. I); SPIRIT POSSESSION (Vol. I).

Further Reading: Omosade Awolalu, *Yoruba Beliefs and Sacrificial Rites* (White Plains, N.Y.: Longman Group, 1979).

Esna Site of the important cult of Khnum, the ancient Egyptian god of fertility, water, and procreation; located south of the city of Thebes. According to Egyptian myth,

The temple of Khnum at Esna, Egypt, built during the reigns of Ptolemy VI (180–145 BCE) to Decius (249-251 CE), lay buried under Nile mud until the nineteenth century, when this hall was excavated. The town of Esna still covers the rest of the temple. *© Richard T. Nowitz/CORBIS*

Khnum used a potter's wheel to create humankind from clay. The temple at Esna shows Roman influence in its reliefs and columns.

Ethiopia Vast country in East African bordered by modern-day Eritrea, Djibouti, Kenya, Somalia, and Sudan. Based on the unearthing of skeletal remains of humans who lived millions of years ago in HADAR, the Omo Valley region, and in Aramis in the Awash Valley, Ethiopia is considered one of the cradles of humanity. A region in which the cultivation of grain and domestic herding dates back to the STONE AGE, its diverse population includes eastern Kushitic speakers consisting of the OROMO, SOMALI, AFAR and Saho, who were primarily nomadic herders. Other groups, such as the Amhara and TIGRE, reflect a mix of Arabic influence, carried by immigrants from the Arabian Peninsula in the centuries before Christ.

Royalty in Ethiopia includes the Solomonic dynasty, initiated, according to Ethiopian tradition, by the queen of Sheba. Ethiopia's tradition of literacy dates back more than 2,000 years and includes a popular form of script known as *lessana ge'ez*, or simply GE'EZ, meaning "the language of the free." However, Ethiopia's embrace of Christianity, initiated during the rule of AKSUM, generated the most unique forms of religious devotion and architecture in the world.

See also: ABYSSINIA (Vol. I); AGAW (Vol. I, II); ARK OF THE COVENANT (Vol. I), BLUE NILE (Vol. I); ETHIOPIA (Vols. II, III); GE'EZ (Vol. II); SOLOMONIC DYNASTY (VOL. II); TIGRAY (Vols. I, II).

Further reading: Anthony Appiah and Henry Louis Gates, eds., *Africana: The Encyclopedia of the African and African American Experience* (New York: A Basic Civitas Book, 1999); Samuel Kasule, *The History Atlas of Africa* (New York: Macmillan, 1998); James L. Newman, *The Peopling of Africa* (New Haven: Yale University Press, 1995); Roland Oliver and Brian M. Fagan, *Africa in the Iron Age: c. 500 BC to AD 1400* (New York: Cambridge University Press, 1994); Richard Pankhurst, *The Ethiopian Borderlands* (Lawrenceville, N.J.: The Red Sea Press, Inc, 1997).

Ethiopian Highlands Plateau region in eastern Africa. The Ethiopian Highlands, which cover almost two-thirds of ETHIOPIA and much of central ERITREA, were produced by the lava flow of long-extinct volcanoes. The average elevation of the region is about 5,500 feet (1,676 m). Many rivers and deep valleys cut through the landscape, often dropping 2,000 feet (610 m) below the plateau. The highlands are split into two sections by the Great RIFT VALLEY, a geological fault system that stretches 3,000 miles (4,827 km) from Southwest Asia to Southeast Africa.

The rift cuts through the highlands diagonally, from northeast to southwest. The western highlands is the larger section, running from central Eritrea and northern Ethiopia to the basin of Lake TURKANA in the south. The rugged western highlands are divided by the valley of the Abay, also known as the BLUE NILE. The western highlands are also the location of Mount RAS DASHEN, which, at 15,157 feet (4620 m), is the highest peak in Ethiopia. Inhabitants of the western highlands include the TIGRE, the descendents of a Semitic people who established the Christian AKSUM kingdom, and the AMHARA, also descendants of Semitic peoples and political rivals of the Tigre. Found in the much smaller eastern highlands is Mount Batu, which stands at an elevation of 14,127 feet (4306 m).

The Ethiopan Highlands are the most farmed and most densely populated regions of both Eritrea and Ethiopia. They are also home to many forms of wildlife, including the rare Simien fox.

Ewaso Nyiro River River in Kenya that, along with the Tana River, drains Mount Kenya. The Ewaso Nyiro is a brown, muddy river that winds through the northern Frontier Desert. The rich jungle banks of the river contrast with the surrounding desert and support animal life such as the CROCODILE, the ELEPHANT, the WATER BUFFALO, the LION, the GIRAFFE, the ZEBRA, and the MONKEY.

The Ewaso Nyiro River is part of the Great RIFT VALLEY, a geological fault system extending 3,000 miles (4,827 km) from the Jordan valley in Southwest Asia to Mozambique in Southeast Africa.

F

Falasha See BETA ISRAEL

family structure In African societies, an extended family unit consisting of grandparents, parents, children, brothers, sisters, and cousins.

In ancient times, family units were based within large households or compounds, and the larger the family, the more secure its members felt. Responsibility, obligation, and authority were the cornerstones of family life, but decision making was often left to the wisdom of family elders.

From an economic standpoint, family structure generated food production and therefore contributed to the local economy. Archaeological reconstructions of the lives of ancient hunter-gatherers show that, while there frequently was a division of labor among the sexes, there also was a certain level of gender equality. Among the !Kung, whose population extended over Botswana, Angola, and Namibia, women looked after the children, supplied the family with water and firewood, and prepared the family dwelling. Women also contributed a large portion of the community's food in the form of wild plants. On the other hand, men were responsible for providing the community with a sufficient supply of meat. As hunters—often of large predators—men performed tasks that were considered more dangerous and more complex. In spite of this, however, men may also have assisted within the household and frequently were joined by women in the decision-making process.

Because marriage often represented the unification of families, kingdoms, and countries, political power was also tied to family structure. The ancient rulers of EGYPT and NUBIA, for example, often made marriage arrangements between siblings and first cousins precisely in order to exercise political control over a particular region or kingdom. This type of family structure also allowed people, especially wealthy or royal households, to transfer or maintain material resources. Although children were coveted in all societies, the offspring of royal marriages were particularly valued—and rewarded. It was they who were the recipients of the crown or, at the very least, of such inherited forms of wealth as land, cattle, or money.

See also: WOMEN IN ANCIENT AFRICA (Vol.I); WOMEN IN MEDIEVAL AFRICA (Vol. II); WOMEN IN PRECOLONIAL AFRICA (Vol. III); POLYGAMY (Vol. I).

farming techniques The various methods of clearing and cultivating land and planting and harvesting food crops; used by the farmers of ancient Africa.

Prior to about 10,000 BCE, ancient peoples got their food by hunting, gathering, and fishing. Groups of people moved seasonally in order to be near food sources. When the transition to farming came, most historians believe that it was made independently in several different regions of the world.

While it was previously believed that the first farming was carried out in Mesopotamia about 8000 BCE, there now is evidence to suggest that the ancient peoples of EGYPT and NUBIA may have grown barley as early as 16,000 BCE. Likewise, it appears that wild SORGHUM was harvested in the area of KHARTOUM as early as 6000 BCE. This and other evidence, while not yet universally accepted, has done much to change long-held views of human technological development.

Most likely, the first food production method used by ancient Africans was gathering and storing grain, or cereal, produced by wild grasses. Gatherers then began actively to encourage the growth of the grasses, possibly by weeding to remove competing plants. Stone hoes were invented to accomplish this task. The next step was to collect and sow seed from the strongest plants.

The transition to food production was made during the STONE AGE in different ways in different areas of Africa. The people of the NILE RIVER valley took advantage of the fact that while the WHITE NILE flowed continuously, the BLUE NILE flooded annually, leaving behind deposits of dark, fertile soil along its banks. When the water receded, the people pushed seeds into this muddy deposit, and a crop would grow as the soil dried out.

Between 8000 and 4000 BCE, the climate of the SAHARA was much wetter than it is today, and a series of rivers and lakes there provided good fishing. As the Sahara gradually became drier, however, from about 3000 to 1000 BCE, the desert spread, and lakes and rivers became smaller and smaller. The emphasis on fishing gradually shifted to farming the savanna grasslands that bordered the desert. Stone Age farmers of the area used sickle blades for cutting grasses and grinding stones to make flour.

The crops chosen for domestication depended on the conditions of the area. For example, along the edges of the spreading desert, pearl millet was domesticated, probably because it was fairly drought-resistant. In contrast, in the wetlands of the upper NIGER RIVER, wild rice was grown. The peoples of the tropical forest planted root crops, rather than cereals, and in the highlands of ETHIOPIA, farmers grew oil plants and cultivated banana-like plants for their starchy stalks.

The development of farming in forested areas required tools to clear the land. New techniques of grinding and polishing stone resulted in improved axes and adzes. To make them, a stone was ground against a harder stone to create a sloping, sharp-edged surface. This was an improvement over the earlier method of sharpening a stone by striking it against another stone to chip away flakes. Other techniques for clearing forests included killing trees by ringing them and setting fires to burn the undergrowth. Forest farmers also took advantage of natural clearings to grow yams and palm nuts. The advent of the IRON AGE brought further improvements in farming tools.

As the transition to farming spurred Africans to invent new tools and cultivation methods, the social, political, and economic fabric of their lives also changed. People no longer had to move constantly in order to gather food. Consequently, permanent settlements sprang up, and more enduring housing was built. The population increased, too, as women bore more children who could be kept safe within the settlement. More children meant more hands to work the farms, so surplus food could be produced and traded to other peoples for raw materials and other necessary items. Not surprisingly, the changes brought about by the rise of agriculture led to the formation of rich and poor classes, with those who controlled the land and food production becoming the wealthy class.

See also: AGRICULTURAL REVOLUTION (Vol. I); AGRICULTURE (Vols. I, III); CROPS (Vol. II).

festivals Celebrations that often combine religious, historic, and cultural themes. Widespread in Africa, festivals frequently occurred on an annual or seasonal basis. In many societies festivals were a means of restoring spiritual balance and maintaining a strong sense of community. Ancient rulers also used community festivals as a way to reinforce their regal power. One of the earliest—and most noteworthy—examples of this was the ancient Egyptian SED FESTIVAL, which was a celebration of divine kingship. In western Africa, festival dates are often determined by divination and are often unknown until the last minute.

Harvest Festivals One of the most important festivals in agricultural communities is the annual harvest festival. The Ibo people of Nigeria celebrate Ikeji, meaning "new yam eating," by serving only dishes made of yams to symbolize the abundance of the crop. The New Yam Festival, marking the end of one planting season and the start of the next, is a time to thank the yam spirits through the ancestors for a bountiful harvest. The king or the oldest man in the community traditionally eats the first yam, his position bestowing on him the role of intermediary between the people and the spirit world. The first day of this four-day festival is the holiest and most important. Sacrifices are offered to the ancestors, who it is believed walk among the living on that day. All male children are expected to attend and offer reverence. The remaining days of Ikeji provide masquerades for the entertainment of guests. Marriages are often contracted at this time.

The peoples of the Niger Delta celebrate the Ikwerre, Kalabari, and Okrira festivals in honor of the water spirits. Masqueraders wear MASKS that resemble fish or water birds. Rituals include divinations and sacrifices, followed by songs and dances depicting these spirits, who, it is believed, are present within the masqueraders who wear masks representing them.

Festivals Honoring Ancestors Reverence for ancestors and belief in SPIRIT POSSESSION are important aspects of traditional Yoruban religion. The EGUNGUN festival, which honors the ancestors and requests their blessings, lasts twenty-four days. On each day of the festival, a masked dancer called an Egungun, believed to be possessed by a different ancestor, dances through the town or village. The body of the dancer is totally concealed so that he becomes the disembodied spirit of the ancestor his dance honors. On the final day of the festival, a priest sacrifices animals at the shrine of the ancestors and pours their blood on the shrine. The sacrificed animals are consumed at the feast that follows.

Festivals in Honor of Divinities The YORUBA celebrate many festivals to honor the many divinities, or ORISHA, in the pantheon of their traditional belief system. One commonly celebrated festival honors Shango, the god of thunder and lightning and the orisha of drum and dance, who is feared and respected among the people. Shango's followers come to him for protection from their enemies, for legal problems, and for solutions to assorted difficulties. Shango's festival lasts twenty days, during which his hereditary priest makes sacrifices at Shango's shrine. On the final day, the priest becomes possessed by Shango and gains magical powers, including the ability to eat fire and, much later, swallow gunpowder. A procession ending in a feast concludes the festival.

Festivals of Secret Societies Many peoples throughout Africa have formed SECRET SOCIETIES, bound by oath, in response to a special local or cultural need. The secret societies also conduct festivals, an example of which is the Yoruban Gelede festival, held annually from March until May, before the rainy season. This festival, intended to appease the destructive powers of the ancient mothers, is the remedy for the distress caused by the threat of drought or infertility. Males wearing female masks dance in pairs, their faces uncovered, the masks perched on top of their heads. The faces on the masks show the serenity and composure considered desirable in Yoruban women. Because the dancers' identities are not secret, they are not thought to be possessed by a god and may walk freely among the people in costume before and after the masquerade.

Other Festivals Celebrations also generally accompanied the RITES OF PASSAGE into adulthood, following circumcision or clitoridectomy and their associated rituals. In these and in other ceremonies, the importance of blood must be noted. Spilling blood when making a sacrifice means that life, whether human or animal, is being given back to God, who is the ultimate source of life. Among the Mbuti who live in what is now the Republic of the Congo, blood shed during circumcision is thought to bind the person to the land and to his ancestors in a solemn covenant or agreement. Once the individual's blood is shed, he joins the stream of his people. There is, however a widespread belief in African societies that menstrual blood is ritually dangerous and taboo, forcing women, even priestesses, to absent themselves from shrines and banning them from handling any ritual objects. Even though women frequently functioned as mediums with the spirit world, the task often belonged to a girl before she reached puberty or to an older woman past childbearing age.

See also: DIVINATION (Vol. I); EGUNGUN (Vol. I); MASKS (Vol. I); ORISHA (Vol. I); RELIGION, TRADITIONAL (Vol.I); SPIRIT POSSESSION (Vol. I).

Further reading: Anthony Ephirim-Donker, *African Spirituality: On Becoming Ancestors* (Trenton N.J.: Africa World Press, Inc., 1998); Mary H. Secrecy Noote, *African Art that Conceals and Reveals* (New York: Museum for African Art, 1993); Benjamin C. Ray, *African Religions: Symbol, Ritual, and Community* (Englewood Cliffs, N.J.: Prentice-Hall, 1999).

Fezzan (Fezan)

Fezzan (Fezan) Saharan region of the present-day North African country of LIBYA. The Fezzan was the site of ancient settlements, and cave paintings dating back to prehistoric times can be found in and around the surrounding hillsides. Controlled by a people known to the ancient Greeks as the GARAMANTES and sometimes called the Garamantian Empire, the area later became part of the Roman Empire under the name Phazania.

See also: FEZZAN (Vols. II, III); LIBYA (Vol II).

fire

fire Fragments of burned bone found in a cave at Swartkans, South Africa, provide evidence of the intentional use of fire in Africa just 1 million years ago. In other parts of Africa, hearths were probably not commonplace as centers of human habitation until about 60,000 years ago,when there was a pronounced rise in social and cultural activity.

Anthropologist Louis Leakey has pointed out that the same primitive tool used to make fire—a hard, pointed stick twirled between the palms to make a piece of soft wood smolder—can also be used as a hand drill to make holes in shell and bone. Fire and such drilled objects, perhaps used as personal ornamentation, enter the archaeological record in Africa at the same time.

Fire also has its place in African mythology. For example, in the creation stories of the Dagara people of what is now Burkina Faso and Ghana, fire is the first element on the wheel of life. Water is the second element. According to these stories, in the beginning there was no world as humans know it, but only a burning ball of fire moving at great speed. When this ball of fire encountered a massive body of water, the shock forced fire into the underworld, leaving a hot, steamy surface that was fertile for living things. This surface, called Earth, is the third element on the Dagara wheel of life. The minerals and stones and other hard components of the earth hold things together and thus make up the fourth element. The fifth element, vegetative nature, came into existence when the clouds of steam in the atmosphere subsided, allowing plant life to grow.

In tropical Africa, the nights are close to twelve hours long year-round, and darkness falls abruptly. The first uses of fire were to provide protection from animals and, later, to help in hunting and toolmaking. Control of fire made the night safe. Fires caused by lightning and set by humans helped thin the vast African forests and turn woodlands into grasslands, making cultivation and passage easier. The main areas of migration and settlement in African prehistory tended to be in the savanna regions.

fishing Early inhabitants of Africa were primarily nomadic foragers, but archaeological evidence indicates that several groups also established very early fishing communities. The Ishango people of Lake Albert were active fishermen around 23,000 BCE, as were the inhabitants of Wadi Kubbaniya in EGYPT 5,000 years later. Not until 7000 BCE did fishing communities start to emerge in abundance. In addition to the NILE and NIGER RIVERS, the riverbanks of the Congo and the Zambezi emerged as abundant fishing areas. Harpoons and net weights were found in some of the settlements, indicating that early nomadic people were able to live a semi-sedentary life for the first time.

With a plentiful food supply, these early fishermen were able to establish villages of up to 1,000 people living in permanent dwellings. Their social structure changed from loose ties between families (which was typical of nomadic peoples) to more structured communities. New concepts, like property and inheritance, emerged as they accumulated nets, harpoons, and other tools necessary for fishing.

Although the social progression of these early fishing communities is unclear, they were successful enough to flourish for thousands of years. As agricultural technology was introduced, fishing villages began to trade fish for the crops and commodities of neighboring villages.

See also: FISHING (Vol. II).

flamingo The African flamingo is reddish with black wing feathers. In ancient EGYPT, however, these birds were frequently found in lakes, a fact that led to a striking difference between the birds of ancient Egypt and those of the rest of the continent. Flamingos actually are white in color; their pink hue comes from eating tiny pink shrimp. Since brine shrimp are rarely found in Egyptian lakes, even today many Egyptian flamingos are only a very pale pink.

During the height of the Roman Empire, flamingo tongues were consumed as a great delicacy. In fact, flamingoes were such a popular food in ancient ROME that the birds were threatened with extinction. To protect them, the Romans established a law forbidding the hunting of flamingos.

fly Small, winged insect. An adult fly measures between .25 and .5 inches (0.6 and 1.2 cm) in width. Some flies are known to carry malaria and other serious diseases. For example, the tsetse fly, which lives throughout tropical areas south of the Sahara, is a known carrier of the parasite that causes sleeping sickness.

In ancient EGYPT, flies were considered symbols of valor and determination. Often, gold medals in the shape of flies were given to accomplished soldiers. Flies were also recognized as pests. Egyptians covered their doors and windows with mats to keep them out. According to the Bible, an infestation of flies was among the ten plagues sent to Egypt by God to persuade the Egyptians to release the Israelites from slavery.

See also: TSETSE FLY (Vol. II).

folklore Proverbs, stories, tales, beliefs, customs, codes, and literature of a culture passed on from generation to generation, usually as ORAL TRADITION.

In ancient Africa, since the stories and proverbs were typically told and not written, much of what we know about folklore from even the early part of the common era comes from the versions of folklore that exist in modern Africa. Scholars believe that this folklore is very old and has been passed down for centuries; thus, people today can get a glimpse of the past from these stories and proverbs.

In Africa, as in other parts of the world, folklore takes different forms for different purposes. Generally, though, figures in these stories can go beyond the constraints of everyday life. They may amass great wealth, visit imagined places, or perform actions that if carried out in real life would merit punishment or even death. Though folklore can contain magical elements, the rationale for telling the stories is often to help real people better understand their world.

Creation myths are among the most common types of ancient folklore, and they often explain how things came to be. Hundreds of creation myths exist. In almost every such African myth, the gods give humans everlasting life, but someone distorts the message. The YORUBA of Nigeria are among the African people who have a particularly rich tradition of folklore, and their creation myth is well known. However, among the Yoruba, the myth varies, showing that, even within a culture, folklore can differ from region to region.

The Yoruba creation myth, like most African myths, includes a god in the sky ruling over earth from above. More specifically, however, the Yoruba myth tells that before there were people on earth, there was only water and flooded marshland. Therefore, the chief god, OLORUN, decided one day to make land and sent another god to make it, giving him a snail shell of earth and a hen. Even though he had been given an important task, this god stopped to get a drink on the way, and, as a result, fell into a drunken sleep. His brother, Oduduwa, hearing and seeing what had happened, took the gifts from Olorun and went to earth to accomplish the feat. He poured the earth from the shell and set the hen on it so that the hen could peck and scratch the earth to form land. The hen continued until there was a sizeable piece of dry land. When the drunken god awoke and saw what had taken place, he fought with Oduduwa over the claim to this land, and Olorun made Oduduwa ruler over earth. The other god was given the less important task of creating figures, which became people when Olorun breathed life into them.

One variation of this myth explains that the god who came to form land on earth became bored and began to create humans out of clay but stopped in the middle to drink. Because of the god's drunkenness, some of the humans were not formed well, thus explaining how deformed people came to be. This is another example of how folklore explains a part of real life.

The African trickster tale is another common form of folklore; in fact, it is perhaps the best-known of all. In it, the trickster often outsmarts the gods or gets out of an impossible situation. In one such trickster tale of the Yoruba, the trick is played on the tortoise himself, as he tries to steal knowledge from the gods. The knowledge is contained in a shell that he carries around his neck, but, angry that he cannot traverse a tree trunk because of the shell, the tortoise breaks it. As a result, knowledge spills out and spreads throughout the earth. Scholars speculate that this type of folklore shows the quirks and flaws of humans, as well as the lessons we can learn.

ANANSI, a spider figure, is one of the well-known tricksters of western Africa. Among the BANTU, the trickster takes the form of a hare, while in Nigeria and Benin, the tortoise is the trickster.

Much African folklore centers on animals, as well as on spirits of the natural world. In this type of folklore, there are gods and spirits to represent most of the things on earth and in the sky, including animals, the Sun, Moon, stars, and lightning. A spirit may be strong or weak, depending on the power that its natural counterpart has on earth. For example, a river or a snake has great power because it can kill people, and so both are among the nature spirits that are strong. In folklore, animals often have greater powers than in real life and can talk, climb to the sky, and accomplish other amazing feats, even speaking to the gods.

The purposes of honoring or praising something in nature and of teaching about nature are often served in folklore. For example, in one Tanzanian myth, a GIRAFFE asks a god for wisdom, and the god consents. The god tells the giraffe that it will be allowed to see and listen but not talk. This, the deity explains, is because those who talk much are foolish, while those who remain silent show wisdom. This, according to myth, explains why a giraffe never utters a sound.

Folklore also explains what may at first seem inexplicable. One story of how fire was brought to earth is an example. In this myth, the insects and birds came together to find a way to bring fire to earth from the sky so that they could stay warm at night and cook. The Mason Wasp agreed to fly high into the sky, past the clouds, where it was thought the gods kept fire. The vulture, eagle, and crow decided to go with him, but after many days of flying, the vulture died. Many days later, the eagle died, followed by the crow. Only the wasp remained, flying higher and higher until, after thirty days, the gods did indeed give fire to the wasp to bring to earth, and then decreed that only the wasp, who would rule the birds and insects, would be able to build a nest near fire.

Traditionally, in Africa, those who knew folklore and, in particular, proverbs, were thought to be wise. They were respected and were generally thought of as people who understood the culture and how it functions. One of the reasons why ancestors were revered in many African cultures may have been because of their knowledge of the folklore that was orally passed from generation to generation. Stories, tales, proverbs, customs, explanations, and codes of behavior have all been passed down for centuries in Africa in the great tradition of oral literature. Some of these stories were so elaborate that they took days to tell. This folkloric tradition served to honor or praise, explain, teach, preserve history, pass down morals and virtues, and elevate people in their everyday existence.

Further reading: Leo Frobenius and Douglas C. Fox, *African Genesis: Folk Tales and Myths of Africa* (New York: Dover Publications, 1999).

fox Carnivorous mammal belonging to the canine family of animals; other canines include the DOG, the JACKAL and the wolf. Foxes have long, pointed muzzles, thick coats, and long tails. They generally are solitary animals, living alone most of the year and sleeping in grasses or thickets. During the breeding season, pairs of foxes establish dens, homes burrowed in the ground, to raise their families.

Foxes eat a variety of foods, including insects, small birds, rodents, lizards, eggs, and fruit. They are, in turn, hunted by larger animals like wolves, as well as by humans. The most common fox, the red fox, is found in northern Africa and can be as long as 23 inches (58 cm) and weigh 5 to 10 pounds (2 to 4 kg). The fennec, or desert fox, which is found in the Sahara, has large ears and fluffy cream-colored fur. The desert fox is between 9.5 and 16 inches (24 to 40 cm) long and weighs between 1.5 and 3.5 pounds (3 to 8 kg). It is the smallest type of fox.

Foxes appear in the mythology of various African cultures, often as a mischievous trickster character. In ancient Egypt, many people carried *was*-scepters, fetishes with carvings of dog or fox heads that were thought to hold life-giving powers.

Fula Term that refers both to a language in the West Atlantic branch of the NIGER-CONGO family of LANGUAGES and also to the nomadic people who speak that language. Though most prevalent in present-day Guinea and northern Nigeria, the Fula (also called FULANI) are a wandering, pastoral people with roots going back to ancient times. Fula, which consists of four distinctive dialects, is closely related to Wolof, another Niger-Congo language spoken on the western coast of Africa.

Fulani Muslim people of West Africa who inhabit the area from Lake Chad to the Atlantic coast. The Fulani, also called the Fulbe, are of mixed BERBER and sub-Saharan African heritage and are found in present-day Nigeria, Mali, Guinea, CAMEROON, Senegal, and Niger. The Fulani language, known as Fulfulde or Fula, belongs to the West Atlantic branch of the Niger-Congo family.

The Fulanis' origins are somewhat obscure, and a great deal of conjecture has been raised by historians and archaeologists regarding their past. Some scholars speculate that they are related to the PHOENICIANS, but others believe that the Fulani came from somewhere in the Senegambia region. Ancient travelers in West Africa who noted their appearance made claims that they were a mixture of black African and Berber peoples. Many Fulani groups do not have the features associated with darker-skinned Africans. But, despite their straight hair and aquiline features, recent genetic studies have shown that the Fulani have always been linked to black Africa.

Originally, the Fulani practiced pastoralism, although their culture evolved as they conquered and absorbed neighboring peoples. Their expertise in the area of animal husbandry made it their dominant way of life, and their cattle were rarely killed for meat. The Fulani moved in nomadic groups, living in camps comprised of portable huts, and every season they traveled with their cattle along the north and south corridors of Senegambia in search of grazing land and water. Certain pastures were more appropriate for summer months, while winter may have restricted some groups and led to temporary settlement.

The Fulani survived mostly on dairy products, although they often exchanged their produce with farmers for grains and luxury items. Because marriage was a common feature of trade relations, there is speculation that the wide variation of skin color and hair texture of the Fulani may be linked to their trading practices.

Historians generally view the unique social structure of the Fulani as egalitarian, with men and women playing equal and interchangeable roles to support their households. Intermarriage between cousins and polygymous relationships among Fulani men were also a prevalent feature in the ancient period. At the height of their power, in the eighteenth and nineteenth centuries, the Fulani established a Muslim kingdom that included much of the western Sudan.

See also: FULANI (Vols. II, III).

funeral customs Burial rites and associated beliefs practiced by various societies.

The staggering number of different funerary customs practiced among the populations of Africa provides some idea of their significance. Funeral rites have held an integral place in society from ancient times and often appear to have developed to express a belief in reincarnation or regeneration. These themes influence every aspect of life in Africa and have served as the underlying source of many of its cultural forms. It is a theme most apparent in each new generation, which is believed to embody returning ancestors.

Funerals have long been considered a crossroads where the worlds of the living and the dead briefly coexist. In the unsettling period following death, funerary rites have also offered grieving people a way to reinforce the continuity of kinship while reinforcing the all-important sense of community. The appearance of food, libation, gifts, and personal possessions in and on graves can be traced back to many ancient populations. The custom may have initially begun as an appeasement to the gods or as a way to avert calamities, such as drought or failed crops. In ancient EGYPT, for example, it was customary to bury people with their possessions, and status was a determining factor in how the deceased was to be sustained, protected, and compensated in the next world. Archaeologists have excavated the mummified remains of pharaohs in beautiful sarcophagi with a wide array of grave goods, including precious jewels, weapons, household items, and such means of transportation as chariots and small boats or replicas.

In comparison, some 10,000 to 25,000 years ago, the HUNTERS-GATHERER ancestors of the modern day SAN in BOTSWANA and the Khalahari Desert in southern Africa buried their dead with simple possessions, such as stone tools. Some sources indicate that they placed the bodies in a fetal position, knees bound by rope close to the chest, with the body lying on its left side facing east. Archaeologists' excavations have failed to offer a complete picture of what formal funeral ceremonies, if any, the San conducted. Instead, it appears that following the family's farewell, the San dismantled their camps and abandoned the area except for periodic visits. If true, the absence of elaborate rites may reflect the San's nomadic existence.

Many funeral customs were shaped by the environment. Ritual imagery of rivers, lakes, and other bodies of water confirm a widely held view of death as a journey. The Mende of Sierra Leone believe that the last gasps of a dying person are efforts to climb the hill of death. A few days later, a "crossing the river ceremony" acknowledges the person's arrival in the land reserved for the dead. The Lodagaa, farmers in northern GHANA, maintain that the land of the ancestors is found in the west, across a river of death. The fee to cross the river is twenty cowries, and those who attend the funeral pay for the journey. The impact of environment on belief was further demonstrated by the Chagga of what is now Tanzania, who hold that it takes nine days to travel the rugged desert terrain between the physical and spiritual worlds. As a result, for protection from the sun, their deceased loved ones are "fed" with milk and wrapped in animal hides.

Some of the traditions practiced by the Abaluyia people of Kenya are considered representative of many African societies. For example, although men and women demonstrate strong displays of grief, widows often have a well-prescribed path to follow. As soon as death is apparent, wives and their cohorts begin to wail and their children take up these laments as well. Wailing is considered by many societies to be an essential rite, and the inability to cry is offensive. Among the BaManianga of the Congo, women whose "strong eyes" shed no tears are considered a disgrace to their family and community. The underlying impulse involved is reciprocity—"Today we cry for you, tomorrow you will cry for me."

As in many African societies, the Abaluyia keep their deceased unburied for a brief period to allow relatives and friends to gather. They hold night vigils and festive ceremonies, which are also common in many societies. Vigils are often organized to ward off the possibility of WITCHCRAFT, generally associated with inexplicable deaths. Festive ceremonies, on the other hand, are traditionally held to please the deceased while offering communal solace to the grieving family. It should be noted, however, that one funerary custom that remains within the cultural sphere of the pastoral Abaluyia society is the recognition given to women who have been faithful to their husbands. At the burial ceremony, such a widow is encouraged to dance holding her husband's spears; if past childbearing age, she may wear his garments.

The timing and logistics of burial are influenced by societal beliefs. For instance, the Lodagaa bury their dead in the morning or evening because in the afternoon the soul of the dead person might be apart from the body, basking in the sun. The Abaluyia, on the other hand, bury everyone except for chieftains in the afternoon; chieftains are traditionally buried at sunset.

While the practice of a "double funeral" is largely misunderstood by outsiders, there is both a practical purpose and a societal purpose behind it. The dead are first buried quickly to prevent a polluting presence. In the interval before the more formal funeral, many traditional rituals intended to elevate the deceased to ancestral status are celebrated. The SHONA of Zimbabwe, for example, held a *kugadzira*, a communal meal, a year after death. This meal not only allowed the family to reaffirm kinship ties, it also called for the distribution of former possessions belonging to the deceased, including former wives, lands, and titles. Later, in Zulu society, the *ukubuyisa idlozi* ("bringing home of the spirit") ceremony is held by the bereaved family within two years of death. When the ceremony is performed for men of high position, an ox is sacrificed to the ancestors; the name of the deceased is added to the praise list; and the ceremony culminates with the eldest son dragging a tree branch, symbolic of the spirit, from the gravesite to the homestead.

Many societies that perform double funerals present sacrificial offerings at shrines during the interim period or participate in sacred DANCE. The Dogon or the FULANI, for example, perform a dance to reunite spirit and community. Not only do these ceremonies "invite back" the departed, in many regions they served as an official notice that the period of mourning, pollution, and disorder that are thought to accompany death is at an end. The formal funeral, a community event, climaxes this period of grief.

Following the funeral, the work of maintaining the memory of the deceased continues. The AKAN of GHANA still invoke their ancient traditions of remembering the ancestors and their continuing deeds for the community through the *adae wukudae* or *kweisidaie* ceremonies performed on Wednesdays and Sundays. Announced by drumming on the morning of the event, the ceremonies begin after ancestor stools are ceremonially blackened and water poured by a female elder. This symbolic gesture allowed the ancestors to wash their hands before eating. Beginning with the oldest stool, rulers or priests traditionally gave an offering of plantains, meats, and wine, and they invited the ancestors to participate:

My spirit grandfather,
Today is Wednesday Adae
Come and receive this mashed plantain and eat
Let this town prosper . . .

Rites such as these continue to be used by many African societies in order to maintain ties to the deceased. Funerary customs have a timeless quality that blends past, present, and future in a celebration of life over death.

See also: AFTERLIFE (Vol. I); ANCESTOR WORSHIP (Vol. I); RELIGION, TRADITIONAL (Vol. I).

Further reading: Simon Bockie, *Death and the Invisible Powers: The World of Kongo Belief* (Bloomington: Indiana University Press, 1993); S. Cederroth, C. Corlin, and J. Lindstrom, eds., *On the Meaning of Death: Essays on Mortuary Rituals and Eschatological Beliefs* (Uppsala: Almqvist & Wiksell International, 1988); Pierre de Maret, "Archaeological & Other Prehistoric Evidence of Traditional African Religious Expression," in Thomas D. Blakely, Walter E. A. van Beek, Dennis L. Tomson, eds., *Religion in Africa: Experience & Expression* (Portsmouth, N.H.: Heinemann, 1994); John S. Mbiti, *African Religions and Philosophy* (Portsmouth, N.H.: Heinemann Educational Publishers, 1999); Dominique Zahan, *The Religion, Spirituality and Thought of Traditional Africa.* Translated by Kate Ezra Martin and Lawrence M. Martin (Chicago: The University of Chicago Press, 1970).

G

Gabon Country along the cost of West Africa. Spearheads dating back to c. 7000 BCE have been discovered in the area, but little is known about the region's early inhabitants who used them. BANTU ethnic groups have been migrating into the area since the twelfth century CE.

See also: GABON (Vols. II, III).

galley Type of seagoing ship powered by oar and sail that was used by Egyptians, PHOENICIANS, and other ancient peoples for commerce and war; the galley was used, with variations in design, for thousands of years.

Though galleys had a single mast and sail, the primary source of power for the ships was human. The first galleys had one series of rowers on each side of the long, narrow, shallow boat. Shields, which were sometimes made of animal hide or heavy cloth, hung from a rail to protect the rowers. The galleys were used for transporting goods for trade, but also for war. From about 850 BCE on, galleys often were fashioned with a large ram at the bow.

Around 700 BCE, the Phoenicians introduced a new kind of galley, a bireme, which had two rows of oars. These were arranged with an upper and lower bank of rowers on each side of the ship. The Greeks are credited with the first three-banked galley ship, c. 500 BCE. These three-banked galleys, or triremes, were also used by ROME and other kingdoms in the Mediterranean, primarily because they achieved greater speed and had more power with which to ram enemy ships. Some of the three-banked ships held two or three masts and sails. Galleys with four and five banks of oars followed.

Galleys were used to carry trade goods in the Mediterranean and Red Seas. Over time, the galleys used in commerce were built differently than those used in war. The merchant ships became deeper and wider, with a greater storage capacity. They also came to rely more on sail and wind power than on the strength of human rowers. In contrast, the long, narrow fighting galleys were primarily powered by rowers and were built for speed and ease of maneuverability.

See also: SHIPBUILDING (Vols. I, II).

Garamantes Inhabitants of northern Africa, in the vicinity of the Fezzan region in present-day LIBYA; they were eventually absorbed into Roman Africa. Although their exact origins are unclear, the roots of the Garamantes go back to ancient, and probably even prehistoric, times. According to some historians, they may be related to the SEA PEOPLE who, at various times, challenged Egyptian power in eastern Africa. Other scholars, however, see the Garamantes as related to the various indigenous STONE AGE peoples of North Africa whose rock drawings and other remains have only recently begun to be studied.

As early as the fifth century BCE, the Greek historian HERODOTUS described the Garamantes as successful warriors who were noteworthy for their mastery of four-horse chariots. These war chariots allowed the Garamantes to establish military dominance in the region. For the most part, it seems that these lightweight, maneuverable chariots were used primarily to raid and plunder neighboring areas. The speed and power of the Garamantes' chariots allowed these raids to go on over an area that, according to Herodotus and the Roman geographer Strabo, stretched from ETHIOPIA in the east to the Atlantic coast in the west.

The Garamantes' military power gave them effective control over much, if not virtually all, of the trade passing through their territory. Evidence also suggests that the Garamantes themselves might have used their chariots as part of their own trading efforts: Many of the numerous rock paintings found in the Fezzan depict the Garamantes' vehicles in action, and some seem to show ox-drawn carts that might have been quite suitable for transporting trade goods. In addition, some of the ancient pathways across the region seem capable of handling traffic from vehicles larger and heavier than the Garamantes' war chariots. Unfortunately, there is little other hard evidence—in the form of discoveries from other regions, for example—to support the notion that the Garamantes maintained trans-Saharan or, indeed, any other significant trade routes.

Beyond controlling the trade, the Garamantes also conducted extensive raids against neighboring peoples, including the far more powerful Carthaginians. Even when CARTHAGE was a major force in North Africa, in the sixth century BCE, the Garamantes remained a significant problem for the city-state's outlying regions, and conflicts between the Garamantes and Carthaginians were frequent. The pattern continued after Carthage's defeat in the PUNIC WARS, with the Garamantes raiding and plundering areas that had fallen under Roman dominion. This continued until ROME, determined to solve the problem of the Garamantes once and for all, launched a major military expedition against them. By the year 19, this Roman force had effectively stamped out the Garamantes' opposition and brought them under the rule of Roman Africa. Later, in the sixth century, the Garamantes fell under the control of the Eastern Roman Empire.

See also: LIBYA (Vol. II).

gazelle

Type of antelope found in North Africa and eastern and central Africa. Gazelles are slender, graceful animals standing from 2 to 3 feet (60 to 90 cm) at the shoulder. They live on open plains and in desert areas. Their fur coats are usually brown, though their bellies and rears are white. Light stripes run down from the sides of their faces from above the eyes to the muzzles. Their horns are short and have slightly upturned rings at their ends. Female gazelles have horns that are usually smaller and more slender than those of males.

There are about twelve species and fifty forms of gazelles. Of these, the Dama gazelle, found in North Africa, is the largest. The most common gazelle found in East Africa is Thomson's gazelle. It has black stripes along its sides and white stripes on its face. No matter what type, gazelles move in herds that usually include five to ten members, though they can contain several hundred.

Gazelles were a familiar part of ancient Egyptian daily life. Egyptians used bows and arrows to hunt gazelles, which had an important place in their diet. Later, some Egyptians even raised gazelles on farms. The animal's appearance in Egyptian mythology underscored its importance. Anunket, a goddess worshiped at ELEPHANTINE, was often associated with the gazelle. Another Elephantine goddess, Sati, is represented with a human head, the crown of UPPER EGYPT, and the horns of a gazelle.

Gebel Barkal

Sacred mountain in the ancient Kushite (Nubian) city of Napata. Situated between the third and fourth cataracts of the Nile, Gebel Barkal (also known as Djebel Barkal) was a spiritual center for several generations of Kushite kings. A 303-foot (100 m) high tabletop mountain made of sandstone, the *gebel*, or mountain, was believed by worshipers of the Egyptian god AMUN to have a deity's spirit residing deep within its interior.

Rulers of KUSH established Napata as their capital in the eighth century BCE, after which they constructed numerous temples, statues, pyramids, and stelae at Gebel Barkal. They installed the priesthood of Amun there as well. One of the Gebel Barkal temples, erected by King PIANKHY (r. 751–716 BCE), housed a famous example called the Stele of Victory. Comparatively lengthy, the text on this stele contained 159 lines in Meroitic script detailing both Piankhy's military conquests and his responsibilities as king. Other stelae at the site discussed the nature of the Kushite kingdom and proclaimed the supremacy of the god Amun. Similar monuments were constructed by King Shabaka (r. c. 716–701 BCE), who succeeded his brother Piankhy as king and continued the policy of monument building. One of Shabaka's more noteworthy creations was a pyramid, also located at Gebel Barkal, that later served as his burial site.

Other successors, including Piankhy's sons, Shabataka (r. 698–690 BCE) and Taharqa (r. 690–664 BCE), also built temples at Gebel Barkal. Considered one of the greatest builders of the era, Taharqa demonstrated his devotion to the god Amun by building and restoring temples and sanctuaries at Gebel Barkal as well as at Thebes, KARNAK, MEMPHIS, Kawa, and the Isle of Argo. He also made offerings of precious jewels and gold plate, along with equipment and endowments for the sanctuaries and priesthood. His projects at Gebel Barkal included the reconstruction of the Temple of Amun, to which he added an inner chamber to house his altar. Taharqa's work also included the construction of a series of colossi that stood in the forecourt, a rock temple dedicated to Amun, and a separate temple honoring the goddess Mut, the wife of Amun.

Still later, King ASPELTA (r. c. 593–568 BCE) left several stelae at Gebel Barkal that provide some idea of what it meant to become a king. One of these contains what has become known as *The Enthronement or Coronation Text*. It depicts the Kushite army standing near Gebel Barkal, their leaders consulting the god Amun about Aspelta's kingship. Another of his stelae, the Stele of Excommunication, offers important insights into the authority of the priests of Amun, who reportedly held the power of life or death over Kushite kings. Based on the writings of the ancient historian Diodorus of Sicily, the power of the priesthood at Gebel Barkal ultimately was destroyed by the Kushite king Arkamani.

Further reading: Basil Davidson, *Africa in History*, rev. ed. (New York: Touchstone, 1991); Basil Davidson, *African Civilization Revisited*, (Trenton, N.J.: Africa World Press, 1991); Barbara Watterson, *The Egyptians* (Oxford, Eng.: Blackwell Publishers, 1990).

Gebel Silsila Narrow gorge on the NILE RIVER in southern EGYPT, forming a natural barrier that, in Egypt's Predynastic Period, marked the boundary between Nubian and Egyptian cultures.

As the Nile flows north past the fertile plain of Kom Ombo, it is hemmed in by nearly barren sandstone hills where the water courses through a tight bottleneck at Gebel Silsila. Beyond the gorge, the river reemerges in limestone cliffs that form the reaches of the lower Nile River valley to the Delta. In ancient times, the area extending south from Gebel Silsila to the second cataract and beyond was the territory of lower Nubian farmers and herders. Described by archaeologists as the NUBIAN A-GROUP, these people established themselves in the area some 5,800 years ago, developing a culture that lasted from approximately 3800 to 3000 BCE.

Deluged annually by rising waters, the gorge at Silsila was a site for the A-Group's sacred fertility ritual, which was performed at the time of flooding. These rites were dedicated to the goddess Taweret (also known as Thoueris and Taurt). The protector of childbirth and fertility, she was portrayed as part hippopotamus, part crocodile, and part lion. The narrows were also the location of shrines and offerings to the deity Hapi. Shown as a fat man with pendulous breasts, Hapi represented fertility and personified the annual inundation of the Nile River.

Further reading: William Adams, *Nubia: Corridor to Africa* (Princeton: Princeton University Press, 1977); David O'Connor, *Ancient Nubia: Egypt's Rival in Africa* (Philadelphia: University of Pennsylvania Press, 1994).

Ge'ez Ancient language of ETHIOPIA; part of the Hamito-Semitic language family. Ge'ez apparently developed from the language of the Sabean settlers who crossed to Ethiopia from southern Arabia as early as the first millennium BCE. By the third and fourth century, it was being used for written inscriptions. It continued to be used, both as a spoken and a written language, for hundreds of years, including in the scriptures and services of the Ethiopian Orthodox Church, where it is still used today. The Ge-ez alphabet, which is called *fidel* (meaning "the alphabet" or "the writing system") by its users, dates back to approximately 100 BCE, making it one of the oldest African alphabets and certainly the oldest one still used in modern times. Like English, the Ge'ez alphabet consists of twenty-six letters, but all of those letters represent consonants.

See also: ALPHABET (Vol.1); GE'EZ (Vol. II).

geography The second largest continent in the world, surrounded by two oceans and two seas and home to rich and varied resources and physical features, the African land mass was first recognized as the continent called AFRICA by the ancient Romans. (The word *Africa* may come from Latin or Greek words that mean "sunny" and "without cold.") Before that, the Greeks referred to the continent as LIBYA.

Africa is bounded by water, with the Atlantic Ocean on its west coast, the Indian Ocean and RED SEA on its east coast, the MEDITERRANEAN SEA to the north, and the Indian and Atlantic Oceans to the south. The African continent comprises more than 11.5 million square miles (4,439,000 sq km), or one-fifth of the land on earth, and is almost as wide from east to west (4,600 miles or 2,882 km) as it is long from north to south (5,000 miles or 3,100 km). Most of the continent has a tropical climate.

Africa is divided by the equator (0° latitude), which runs through the central part of the continent, crossing GABON, the Congo Republic, the Congo Democratic Republic, Uganda, and Kenya. The tropic of Capricorn runs through the southern part of the continent and through southern Madagascar. In addition, the prime meridian, or 0° longitude, traverses Africa from north to south.

The lowest point in elevation on the African continent is Lake Assal, which is located in Djibouti, near the coast of the Gulf of Aden. It is 515 feet (157 m) below sea level.

Among the massive continent's unique physical features is one of the largest islands in the world—Madagascar. Africa also contains one of the world's largest bodies of fresh water—Lake Victoria—and some of the largest deposits of natural resources, including gold, diamonds, and fossil fuels. Africa has the longest river in the world, the NILE, and the most species of freshwater fish and hooved mammals of any continent.

The climate and vegetation of Africa are thought to have remained basically the same for many years, with most of the changes taking place during the past 1 million—and especially the past 2,000—years. These latter changes have been caused, in large part, by the impact of humans on the land as they became more advanced in farming, toolmaking, and building, and as populations increased and cities grew.

Mount Kilimanjaro, a dormant volcano on the Kenya–Tanzania border, is one of a series of volcanoes formed at the same time as the Great Rift Valley. *© Shama Balfour; Gallo Images/CORBIS*

In turn, Africa's geography has contributed in significant ways to the history of the continent. The vast amount of desert in the northern part of the continent, in particular, has had a great influence on human settlement. Indeed, for long periods in African history, some areas were entirely unoccupied. Even today, the world's second largest continent contains only 10 percent of the world's population. The continent's mountains and deserts imposed barriers to settlement and communications between settlements, but they also became home to peoples who were able to take advantage of what these areas had to offer.

High Plains In general, Africa is thought of as a massive plateau with three divisions: the northern plateau, in which the SAHARA Desert and the Atlas Mountains lie; the central and southern plateaus, which encompass southern and West-central Africa; and the eastern highlands. Some of the highest plateau land is in ETHIOPIA, in the eastern highlands, where the altitude reaches heights of up to 15,000 feet (4,572 m).

Other plateau areas that reach significant altitude are the CAMEROON highlands, the Guinea highlands (which reach into Sierra Leone and Liberia as well as Guinea), the Fouta Djallon, which is also in Guinea, the Jos Plateau in Nigeria, and the Adamwa area that lies in CAMEROON and Nigeria.

Mountains Although Africa has many groups of mountains and several well-known mountain peaks, mountains comprise a smaller percentage of land in Africa than they do on any other continent. In the Great RIFT VALLEY, which spans almost 4,000 miles (6,400 km), volcanic and seismic events created the highest peaks in East Africa. Kilimanjaro in Tanzania (central Africa), the tallest mountain peak in Africa, rising to 19,340 feet (5,895 m), is actually a dormant volcano. Other tall, volcanic peaks that are now extinct include Mount Kenya (17,058 feet or 5,199 m), in Kenya; Mount Meru (14,978 feet or 4,565 m), in Tanzania, about 40 miles (64.4 km) west of Kilimanjaro; and Mount Elgon (14,178 feet or 4,321 m), which is on the border of Kenya and Uganda. Mount Cameroon, an active volcano in western Africa, peaks at 13,435 feet (4,094 m).

The Atlas Mountains lie in the northwest. They cross through what is now MOROCCO and the northern tip of ALGERIA near the Mediterranean and Atlantic coasts. The Virunga Mountains are still actively volcanic, and every ten years or so an eruption produces a lava flow. A flow that took place in the distant past was responsible for the creation of Lake Kivu.

Unlike so many of Africa's great mountains, the Ruwenzori range was not formed as a result of volcanic activity. Also called the Mountains of the Moon, these peaks are located in the central African countries of Uganda and

Physical Map of Africa in 2001 CE

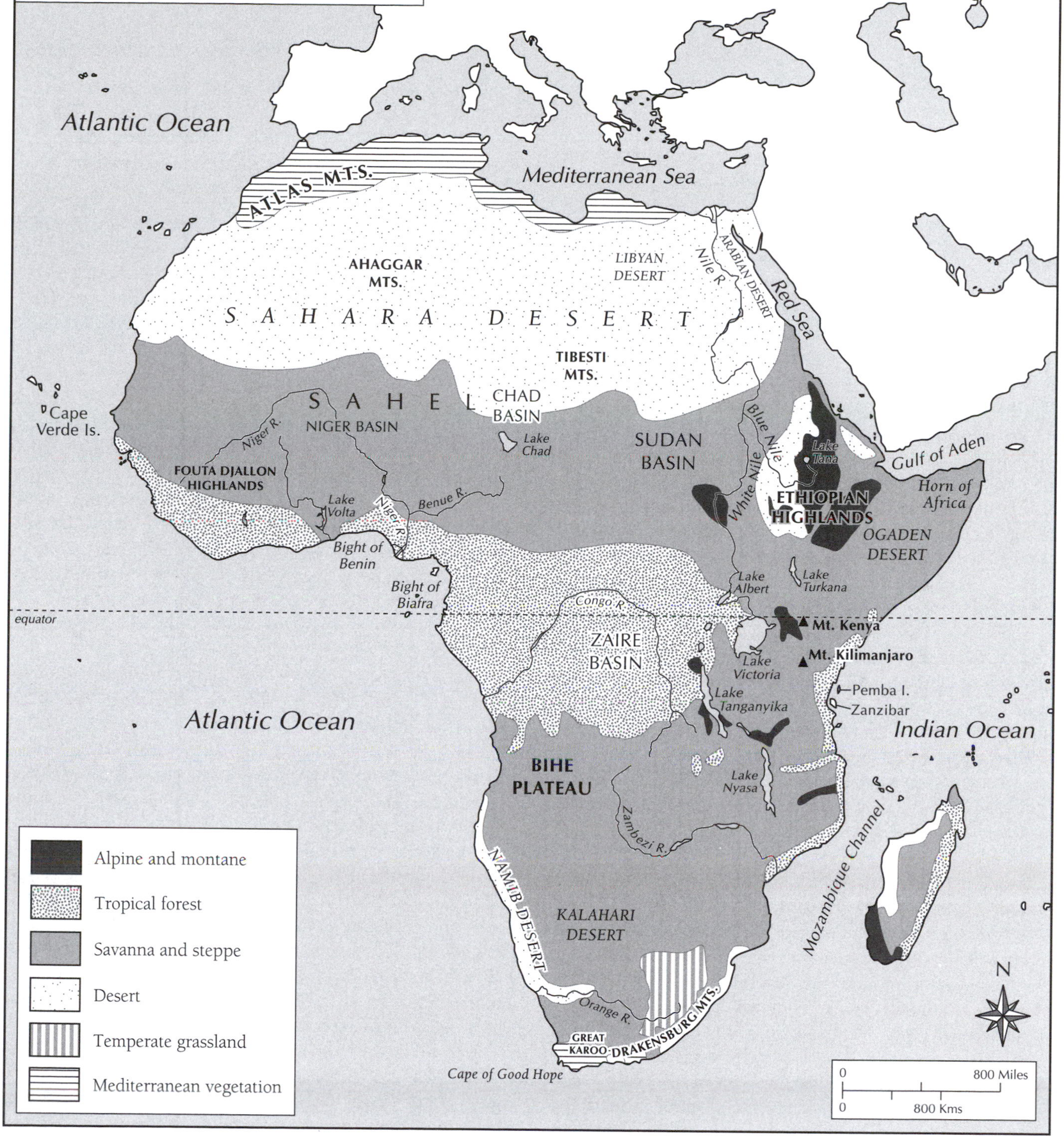

the Democratic Republic of Congo (formerly Zaïre). The highest mountain in this range is Margherita Peak, at 16,795 feet (5119 m). In southern Africa, the Drakensberg Mountains rise to a height of 11,425 feet (3,299 m) at Ntlenyana (also called Ntshonyana) and to 10,823 feet (3280 m) at Mont-aux-Sources.

Lakes The western Rift Valley is the location of Lake Tanganyika, among others, while lakes found in the eastern Rift include Nyasa, Natron, and Manyara. These equatorial lakes were part of a system that also formed one of the largest freshwater lakes in the world, Lake Victoria. Lake Chad, another large freshwater lake, is located in the central Sudan.

Rivers and Tributaries Africa is home to many great and famous rivers, including the CONGO, the NIGER, the Zambezi, the ORANGE, the Vaal, and the NILE. Water supply and control of water have historically been of concern throughout Africa. As a result, rivers and tributaries have played an important role in agriculture, irrigation, and drainage, as well as in travel, trade, and political history.

The Nile River, at 4,150 miles (6,677 km), is the longest river in the world. The Nile flows out of Lake Victoria (the Victoria Nile) north into Lake Albert (the Albert Nile), where it continues north as the al-Jabal River, the WHITE NILE, and the Nile. Finally, after winding through Uganda, Sudan, and EGYPT, the Nile spills into the Mediterranean Sea.

Several tributaries flow from the Nile as it makes its journey north, but the major tributaries on the right bank are the Sobat, Atbara, and BLUE NILE. The al-Ghazal is the major tributary on the left bank. Together the Nile and the tributaries flow north and west before entering the Mediterranean Sea. There, the Nile basin covers a vast area of Egypt north of CAIRO.

Another of Africa's great rivers, the CONGO, travels 2,900 miles (4,666 km) from its source in Zambia to the Indian Ocean. It is responsible for the drainage of most of central Africa. Like the Nile, it descends rapidly through a series of steep gorges, rapids, and waterfalls, including the Boyoma Falls, which extends for 60 miles (96.5 km).

The Niger River begins in Guinea. Then, with its largest tributary, the BENUE, it winds through Nigeria before entering the Atlantic Ocean. About 2,600 miles (4183 km) in length, the Niger has the largest river basin in western Africa. As with the Nile, swamps make parts of the river difficult to navigate.

The Zambezi River travels 2,200 miles (3,540 km) and forms the magnificent Victoria Falls. One of the largest waterfalls in the world, it is located on the border of Zambia and Zimbabwe. The Zambezi's two main tributaries are the Kafue and the Luangwa, which join the Zambezi past Lake Kariba and then empty into the Indian Ocean at the river's 37-mile-wide (59.5 km) mouth. Swamps of reeds and other water plants clog the river in places, impeding travel and fishing.

The Orange River, flowing from the Drakensberg Mountains to the Atlantic, is, along with its tributary, the Vaal, about 1,300 miles (2,092 km) long. It is one of the six important drainage systems in Africa and drains southern Africa.

Grasslands Two wide areas of vast grasslands (one north of the equator and one south), which used to be known as savannas, lie between the deserts of the north and south and the rain forests near the equator. These are large, open, grassy areas, in which only a few trees might be found, among them the BAOBAB, which has been domesticated for farming, and the acacia. On average, these grasslands receive moderate rainfall of 20 to 45 inches (50.8 to 114.3 cm) per year.

The Highveld grassland area of South Africa is a true grassland, with trees or woody plants comprising ten percent or less of its land. This is likely due to the natural occurrences of lightning, which often cause fires.

Grass was long thought of as being "sweet" or "sour." Sweet grass was good for grazing; sour grass was not. One of the best-known sweet grasses in Africa is the *Themeda* variety. *Andropogon* is one of the better-known sour grasses.

Africa has had the longest history of human life on earth. During the period of human habitation, grasslands generally have increased and treed areas have decreased. In part, this has been caused by the burning of woodlands, which has occurred for centuries and has caused tall grasses to take over large areas of plateau. Among these grasses is *Hyparrhenia*, a grass that, although it is quite common, is not good for grazing; tall and coarse, it can be home to disease-spreading insects.

These human-induced grasslands are no longer home to many, if any, original trees. On the other hand, farmers have been domesticating trees for thousands of years, planting them to create park-like areas within their farms. The exact effects of this prolonged human use of Africa's grasslands have been—and most likely will continue to be—a topic of debate.

Africa's grasslands and woodlands are home to many species of animals, among which are the LION, the African ELEPHANT, RHINOCEROS, antelope, GIRAFFE, deer, ZEBRA, WATER BUFFALO, BABOON, CHEETAH, LEOPARD, JACKAL, hyena, and various types of MONKEY. In the equatorial rain forests, the magnificent gorilla (the largest ape in the world) lives, as do monkey, bats, and lemurs.

Deserts The deserts of Africa cover about one-third of the continent. Today, these deserts are among the hottest and driest in the world, but millions of years ago, rain fell there in abundance for long periods of time. The last great rainfall that fell on the deserts of northern Africa occurred about the sixth millennium BCE. Today, the African deserts receive less than 16 inches (40.6 cm) of rain per year, with some areas receiving only 5 inches (12.7 cm) per year.

More than 25 percent of Africa is made up of the vast SAHARA Desert, which has an area of 3.5 million square miles (9,065,000 sq km). This massive desert reaches from the Atlantic coast in the west to the RED SEA in the east, and it has long been a natural barrier between the northern coastal areas and the rest of Africa. Within the great Sahara are the Nubian and Libyan Deserts, as well as the western Sahara. Fewer different types of vegetation grow in the Sahara than in any other arid region in the world. Several animals are found in the Sahara today, including hares, desert FOX, GAZELLE, and a type of small rodent called a jerboa, which is famous for its ability to jump great distances. However, evidence of a prehistoric hunting culture that probably existed on the edge of the Sahara shows that many animals—including the elephant, rhinoceros, HIPPOPOTAMUS, and giant buffalo—once roamed what are now desert areas.

The spread of the desert southward, c. 8000 BCE, caused a change in the way of life of the HUNTER-GATHERERS who lived near these areas. The gatherers, for example, learned ways to plant seeds and grow crops. In north central Africa, in particular, hunters and gatherers began an AGRICULTURAL REVOLUTION, learning to produce more and more food by planting seeds and improving their methods of fishing.

Among the driest deserts in the world is the Namib Desert, which is located on Africa's southern Atlantic coast. Being near the ocean coast, some succulents are able to survive on the moisture from the constant fog. The other great desert in Africa is the Kalahari Desert, located in southern Africa.

Over the centuries, the course of African history also has been affected by the continent's vast supplies of natural resources. These resources have included GOLD, nickel, fossil fuels, diamonds, COPPER, manganese, platinum, iron, zinc, lead, tin, beryllium, limestone, graphite, and gypsum. They also have included a wealth of animal and marine life and a rich array of vegetation.

See also: GEOLOGY (Vol. I).

Further reading: A.T. Grove, *The Changing Geography of Africa* (New York: Oxford University Press, 1993).

geology One of the oldest continents on earth, Africa is particularly rich in such mineral resources as GOLD, silver, COPPER, iron ore, gypsum, limestone, and granite, which were all used extensively by ancient Africans.

Geological history The continent of Africa was not always in the form that it is in today. According to the theory of plate tectonics, the mysterious geological occurrence known as the Pan-African event brought together the West African plate and the central African plate about 200 to 300 million years ago. After this, Africa became part of a supercontinent called Gondwanaland in which were joined Africa, South America, Antarctica, Australia, and the subcontinent of India. Eventually, a series of geologic events and eruptions, about 175 million years ago, caused Gondwanaland to separate into the present continents. Over time, the Atlantic Ocean widened, separating the continents even further.

Rock formations Several types of rock are found throughout Africa. These contain a wide variety of minerals and natural resources. In western Africa, crystalline rock is found under or outcropping over half of the area and this is known as the West African Shield. The oldest activity that formed shield rock is thought to have occurred over 2.5 billion years ago. The shield rock here and in other parts of Africa contains a rich supply of resources, including gold, manganese, diamonds, copper, lead, iron ore, zinc, low-grade uranium, and several other minerals.

In general, sedimentary rock comprises less of the rock found in Africa than igneous or metamorphic rock. Sedimentary and partially metamorphosed sedimentary rock, however, cover parts of the shield rock throughout Africa. This type of rock tends to form on or near the surface and is the only type of rock in which certain valuable resources like natural gas are deposited. Limestone, shale, and sandstone are among the sedimentary rocks commonly found in Africa, and they have been often used for building, especially by the ancient Egyptians.

Sedimentary basins formed in the west in Congo and Gabon, near the coasts of Senegal, Sierra Leone, Ivory Coast, and southern Nigeria, and then later in large basins inland in Chad and other areas. Within these basins, rich natural resources were formed of petroleum, natural gas, coal, potash, gypsum, zinc, and uranium.

Igneous activity produced many geologic features in Africa, including the cliffs and plateaus in Sierra Leone, Ivory Coast, Guinea, and Liberia. When magma intruded and created dikes and plugs and then later eroded, many diamond deposits formed in these areas. Volcanic activity also created cliffs, plateaus, and outcropping that eroded, allowing for the deposits of diamond, tin, and other minerals to form. Granite is a common type of igneous rock found in Africa and was used extensively in building and sculpture by the ancient Egyptians.

Geological features The geologic features of Africa have had an enormous impact on human settlement and history. For example, the Mediterranean coast along northern Africa has for many millennia been considered uninviting because of its rocky coastline and lack of harbors. Since TUNISIA offers some of the best access to Africa, cultural advances often entered Africa from there and moved westward. As a result, from the time the PHOENICIANS entered Africa and founded CARTHAGE, c. 800 BCE, the east coast of Tunisia became an important and prosperous area that changed the course of African history.

Geologic resources have been exploited in Africa since prehistory. Archaeological evidence shows the first known mine was dug more than 40,000 years ago in Swaziland. This mine was probably dug to locate ochre, which is a variety of the mineral hematite. It was used for ornamentation and funeral customs.

Gold was one of the first metals to be used extensively by human beings. As early as about 4000 BCE, gold was found in Egypt, which was the main producer of gold until the first century CE. In ancient times, gold was found in the bottoms of streams and mined from the sand and gravel. Bronze (a copper-tin alloy), copper, silver, and iron were among other metals found and used extensively in ancient Africa.

In addition to using the natural mineral resources, ancient people discovered the use of rock for building and sculpting. Egypt, in particular, had a wealth of limestone, sandstone, and granite, all available from the exposed surface of the earth. The development of natural stone resources in ancient Egyptian building marks an era of incredible human and technological achievement, a period when human beings mined, quarried, and constructed on a large scale without the benefit of the wheel, the pulley, or smelted iron tools.

The exploitation of mineral and stone resources in Africa contributed greatly to economic wealth in ancient times. The continent contains some of the largest deposits of mineral resources in the world, and at least some or most of the minerals known to exist in the world can be found in Africa. Major deposits of fossil fuels include natural gas, coal, and petroleum, as well as some of the greatest deposits of gold, diamonds, cooper, manganese, nickel, platinum, and phosphates. Iron ore, tin, zinc, and lead are among the other important minerals found in Africa.

Gerzean culture Early culture of predynastic Egypt.

See also: NAQADAH I AND II (Vol. I).

Ghana, ancient Kingdom founded in the SAHEL between the fifth and eighth centuries; also known as Akwar and Ouagadou. The roots of what was to become one of Africa's richest and most powerful kingdoms lay in migrating nomads from the North African coast who began settling in the region before the fifth century. The exact ethnic makeup of early Ghana's inhabitants is unclear; however, they are likely to have been a combination of BERBERS, black Africans, and other ethnic groups. The ancient kingdom and empire of Ghana should not be confused with modern coastal Ghana, located 500 miles (805 km) to the southeast.

See also: GHANA EMPIRE (Vol. II); KINGDOMS AND EMPIRES OF THE WEST AFRICAN SAVANNA (Vol. II).

Further reading: Daniel Chu and Elliott Skinner, *A Glorious Age in Africa: The Story of Three Great Kingdoms* (Garden City, N.Y.: Zenith Books, 1965).

Gibraltar Southernmost area of the Iberian Peninsula. A rocky promontory called the Rock of Gibraltar forms the southernmost point. Gibraltar has an area of 2.3 square miles (5.8 sq. km). At its highest point, the rock is 1,396 feet (425 m) above sea level. While the ancient history of the area is obscure, many prehistoric relics, including a Neandertal-type skull, have been found in its caves. No town existed at Gibraltar before 1160 CE.

The narrow waterway that flows between the Rock of Gibraltar and the northernmost point of northwest Africa is called the Strait of Gibraltar. "Pillars of Hercules" is the name given by the ancient Greeks (c. 1100 BCE) to the two peaked rocks that flank the entrance to the straight. Ancient Calpe was the name for the northern rock (Rock of Gibraltar); ancient Abila was the southern rock (Jebel Musa). To the ancient Greeks, the Straight of Gibraltar signified the ne plus ultra, the end of the world as it was known at that time, although it was believed that somewhere beyond that point lay Atlantis, the mythical continent supposedly engulfed by the Atlantic Ocean.

From the fourth through the seventh centuries, there was a thriving Christian civilization in existence. However, the transition from the previous Greco-Roman era to Christianity was not without problems. Northern Africa was sharply divided between two cultures. To the west of the Gulf of Syrtis (Sidra) were speakers of Latin, while in Egypt and Cyrenaica were Greek-speaking people. The conflicts within and between the eastern and western arms of the church, and the failure of either sector to bring the marauding ethnic nomads in the south into the fold, greatly weakened the region. The invasion of the Roman Empire by the VANDALS, who settled in Africa in 429, set the stage for the arrival of Islam and Muslim rule, which began with the coming of Tarik-ibn-Zeyad in 711.

giraffe Long-necked, hoofed mammal that belongs to the same animal family as the OKAPI. Giraffes stand about 18 feet (5 m) and are the tallest mammals on the earth. Giraffes live on the savannas and open grasslands south of the Sahara.

Giraffes have highly developed senses of sight, hearing, and smell. Although they move in a trot that might look slow, they are able to achieve speeds up to 30 miles (48 km) per hour. They mainly eat acacia leaves and are preyed upon by lions and sometimes leopards. Though it is commonly thought that giraffes make no sounds, they actually are able to emit a low moan. They live between fifteen and twenty years.

Because of their unique appearance, giraffes have been noted throughout Africa's history. In ancient Egypt, giraffes were considered exotic animals and their tails were among the trade items brought from faraway lands. An inscription from ELEPHANTINE shows a giraffe brought by King Wenis of the Fifth Dynasty from a trade expedition. In Zimbabwe, rock paintings have been found of giraffes, which were considered to have the same essential quality, *nlow*, as humans.

goat Hoofed, horned mammal belonging to the same animal family as the sheep.

Wild goats often live in rocky areas. Female goats (does) and their offspring (kids) travel in herds of thirty or forty. Male goats (rams) live alone and only return to the herd during mating season. Wild goats include the ibex, which is found in Sudan.

After the dog, goats were probably the first animals domesticated by humans, and they have provided meat, milk, and wool to humans for thousands of years. During the BANTU migration, goats were an important part of the people's diet since goats could survive on almost any vegetation and required less maintenance than cattle.

Goats appear frequently in African mythology. One CAMEROON myth tells the story of a girl who fed flour to a hungry goat. To thank her, the goat told her about a great flood. Because of this warning, she and her brother were the only survivors.

Goba Ancient site noted for its rock-hewn church, located within the southeastern state of Bali, or Bale, in ETHIOPIA. Ethiopian sources maintain that Goba's church was built in an ancient tradition that predates the rock-hewn churches credited to King Lalibella of the Zagwe dynasty (r. c. 1185–1225 CE). Similar rock churches have been found in such regions as AKSUM, TIGRAY, and ERITREA. The sources maintain that these edifices were built by Christian communities whose faith moved them to build churches able to withstand the ravages of time.

See also: LALIBELA, CHURCHES OF (Vol. II); ZAGWE DYNASTY (Vol. II).

Further reading: Richard Pankhurst, *The Ethiopian Borderlands: Essays in Regional History from Ancient Times to the End of the 18th Century* (Lawrenceville, N.J.: The Red Sea Press, 1997).

gold A yellow, soft, lustrous precious metal that does not tarnish or corrode; gold was mined and panned in several locations throughout Africa from ancient days to the present.

Gold has been important in Africa since the time of ancient Egypt. The pharaohs of Egypt exploited the alluvial gold found in or along streams in NUBIA and KUSH. Egyptian gold, categorized as white gold, included a high percentage of silver, whereas yellow gold was called *noub*. In addition to using gold as currency, the Egyptians used gold to make jewelry, to adorn burial furnishings, and to decorate buildings.

Archaeological evidence at sites between the Nile River and the Red Sea reveals the mines of Kush in Nubia as one of the greatest gold-producing operations of the ancient world. Because it remained an essential trading commodity within Nubia well after its conversion to Christianity in the middle of the sixth century, some estimates have placed overall gold production of Kush at more than 3.5 million pounds (1.6 million kg).

Trade within Africa between northern merchants and indigenous populations was the first link in the trading chain. More than 2,000 years ago, HERODOTUS (c. 490–425 BCE) wrote about the gold trade between the Carthaginians and the chiefdoms in Mauritania. The Carthaginians had devised a means of communicating their arrival and desire to trade by creating a large fire on the shore near their ships, with smoke serving as a signal. Then the Carthaginians stacked items such as COPPER, cloth, cowries, and salt from the Sudan in heaps at a designated site. The Carthaginians then moved away and the local traders came forward to stack gold next to the Carthaginian trade goods. The tenth-century Arabic traveler al-Mas'udi noted this same method of trade being carried out in various parts of West Africa and commented that the process continued until both sides were satisfied that an equal exchange had been made.

The gold trade first became significant in Tunisia in North Africa during the fourth century BCE, but the sources of that gold are unknown. Evidence of early mining activities in the Sirba River valley in what is now Niger, has led to speculation that the gold of Carthage came from there because the Sirba Valley is closer to Carthage than Bambuk, Bure, or the other gold fields that later became the major African producers of the gold. Archaeologists working in West Africa believe that gold crossed the Sahara as early as the fourth century CE because standard Roman weights used to measure gold have been found that date from the time of Constantine the Great (r. 307–337). The fact remains, however, that no gold artifacts have been found in sub-Saharan Africa that date from this period. The earliest gold object from West Africa is an earring dating to c. 800 found in the city of ancient Jenne in the upper inland Niger Delta of the middle Niger.

See also: GOLD (Vol. II); GOLD TRADE (Vol. III); TRADE (Vol. II); TRANS-SAHARAN TRADE ROUTES (Vol. II); WANGARA GOLD FIELDS (Vol. II).

Great Pyramid Pyramid built during the Fourth Dynasty, by ancient Egypt's King KHUFU.

The Great Pyramid of Giza (also called the Great Pyramid of Khufu) is one of three great pyramids built near the city of Giza, Egypt. Originally a necropolis of ancient MEMPHIS, it is today part of Greater Cairo. Built by King Khufu to serve as his tomb, the Great Pyramid of Giza is the only surviving wonder of the Seven Ancient Wonders of the World.

The pyramid is believed to have been built over a twenty-year period. However, it is not known how the great blocks of stone from which it was constructed were put in place. One theory is that long levers were used. Another theory suggests that a ramp was assembled and raised as the building advanced. The ramp, which may have been either straight or spiraled, may have been coat-

Four hundred eighty-two feet (147 m) high, the Great Pyramid was built as the tomb of the pharaoh Khufu in 2530 BCE. *© Charles and Josette Lenars/CORBIS*

ed with mud and water in order to ease the movement of the blocks as they were put into place.

When first built, the Great Pyramid of Giza was 481 feet (159 m) high. Over the centuries, approximately 30 feet (10 m) has been lost from its top. For more than 43 centuries, the pyramid ranked as the tallest structure on earth. Each side measures 750 feet (248 m) long, is angled at 51 degrees and 51 minutes, and is carefully oriented with one of the cardinal points of the compass. The entire structure consists of around 2 million blocks of stone, each weighing more than 2 tons (1.8 metric tons). A smooth limestone casing once covered the pyramid, but much of this was plundered to provide materials to build Cairo. The vastness of the Great Pyramid of Giza can perhaps best be fathomed by considering that the cathedrals of Florence and Milan, St. Peter's Basilica in Rome, as well as Westminster Abby and St. Paul's Cathedral in London, could all fit inside.

The Great Pyramid of Giza represents the prototype of a private necropolis built on a huge scale according to preconceived, organized plans. This pattern for construction, which was established by King Khufu, was followed by most of his successors during the Fourth Dynasty. On both sides of the Great Pyramid of Giza there are streets of nearly seventy aligned *mastabas*, or platform tombs, built for Khufu's officials. There also are four subsidiary pyramids. The first three were built for Khufu's mother, Hetepheres; Queen Mereyites; and Queen Henutsen. The fourth pyramid is smaller, and its purpose is debated. Clearly not a tomb, it may have been constructed as a residence for the king's KA, or spirit.

The entrance to the Great Pyramid is on its north face. Inside are a number of corridors, galleries, and escape shafts, some of which lead to the king's burial chamber. At the heart of the pyramid is the king's sarcophagus, which is made of red granite. The interior walls fit so closely together that not even a card can fit between them, another indication of the sophisticated level of construction. Inside are inscriptions bearing the cartouche, or symbol, of King Khufu, along with the names of the work gangs involved in the project.

Khufu did not rely solely, or, perhaps not even, on slave labor for his pyramid-building project. Instead, he utilized those portions of the population that were left idle, unable to farm, during the Nile River's annual flood. This provided more than tens of thousands of Egyptians with food and clothing during what often was a difficult time. More than this, the project also served to unite the population behind a single, national goal.

Excavations of the site of the Great Pyramids began in 1869 under the leadership of Auguste Mariette, the founder of the Cairo Museum. These excavations continue to this day.

The pyramid currently is maintained as part of a much-visited tourist area that also includes the pyramids of Kings Khafre and Menkaure. A museum in the area houses the sun boat, a funerary boat discovered on the site in 1954. This boat is believed to have carried the body of Khufu to his burial place inside his Great Pyramid.

See also: ARCHITECTURE (Vol. I).

Great Sphinx Mammoth stone sculpture representing a mythological being that possessed a lion's body and a king's head; created in ancient EGYPT at Giza as the royal portrait of King Khafre (c. 2575–2465 BCE).

Perhaps the most well-known of all Egyptian sphinxes, the Great Sphinx at Giza, was massive, at 187 feet (570 m) long and 66 feet (201 m) high. The entire structure was constructed from limestone. The head of the creature was a sculpted portrait of King Khafre, the fourth king of the Fourth Dynasty. The use of the sphinx as a portrait for royalty continued throughout Egyptian history, and the influence of the mythological sphinx spread from Egypt to Asia and on to Greece, where it first appeared c. 1600 BCE. Scholars theorize that the Great Sphinx at Giza was most likely built to serve as the guardian of the royal mortuary complex.

Greco-Roman Period In northeastern Africa, the epoch (c. 332 BCE–642 CE) comprising the Ptolemaic (332 BCE–30 BCE), Roman (30 BCE–c. 330 CE), and Byzantine dynasties (c. 330 CE–642 CE).

For nearly a thousand years, a succession of three foreign dynasties ruled Egypt, first from GREECE, then from ROME, and finally from Byzantium. These rulers held sway over a vast empire that covered much of the Mediterranean world. The city of Alexandria was its administrative center, while its borders at times extended across LIBYA and as far as Syria and the Aegean Sea.

The Ptolemaic era saw the rise of Alexandria as a world center of Greek learning, knowledge, and culture, as well as a crossroads of international trade. Greece sent troops to Africa in support of local rebellions against the Persian rulers of Egypt as early as the mid-fifth century BCE. By 450 BCE, the Greek historian HERODOTUS had journeyed to Egypt. The spread of Greek language and culture, called Hellenization, did not begin in earnest, though, until ALEXANDER THE GREAT of Macedonia overthrew the last Persian ruler of Egypt in 332 BCE. Alexander stayed there only a few months. But during that time he established the port city of Alexandria (naming it after himself) and moving the royal capital there from Memphis. These actions served to reorient Egyptian trade and society outward toward the Mediterranean.

Upon Alexander's death, his empire was divided, and the Greek general Ptolemy became the ruler of Egypt. Taking the title of pharaoh, he founded the PTOLEMAIC DYNASTY that ruled Egypt for more than 250 years. The succession of Ptolemies maintained their power, in part, by adopting Egyptian religious iconography, actively promoting Egyptian religion and culture, and claiming the same divine status that the Egyptians had attributed to preceding rulers. At the same time, they guarded and developed free science, literature, art, and culture, and classical Greek literature and drama became popular, especially in the nation's urban centers.

Great mathematicians and physicists such as Euclid and Archimedes were among the many Greek scholars who worked in Egypt. The desire to encompass all this Greek learning prompted Ptolemy III to found the famous Library of Alexandria. Unfortunately, the thousands of papyrus scrolls that made up the great library have not survived.

As the economic and political power of Alexandria grew, an undercurrent of conflict among Egyptians, Greeks, and the immigrant populations who occupied the crowded streets developed within the city. Faced with popular revolt, depleted finances, and poor international relations, the later Ptolemies found themselves gradually reined in by Roman power. The able queen CLEOPATRA, who was linked to both the Roman general Julius CAESAR and later to Marc Antony, led a war against Rome. Egypt's armies, however, were routed at the battle of Actium, in 30 BCE, and with Cleopatra's suicide the next year, direct rule from Rome began.

Transformed into an imperial province, Egypt served as both a granary and a military stronghold for Rome. For three and one-half centuries the Roman Empire exploited the land and resources of Egypt, extracting grain and taxes in ways that ultimately proved socially and economically ruinous to the local population.

Egyptians were granted Roman citizenship in 212. Under the emperor Diocletian (284–305), however, the once mighty Roman Empire was divided into East and West, and Egypt was divided into three provinces. By the latter stage of Roman domination, Christianity became Egypt's official religion, and, within a few decades, the country's predominant faith. When Constantine I (c. 280–337) defeated Licinius in 324 and became sole empror of the Eastern and Western Roman Empire, he moved the capital of the empire to the city of Byzantium in Asia Minor, beginning the Byzantine period of the Greco-Roman era. A fifth-century religious split led to the MONOPHYSITE movement in Egypt, in support of a doctrine stating that Christ had only one, divine nature. The persecution of the Monophysite Coptic Church, as it was known, stiffened Egyptian resistance to Byzantine rule. Heavy taxation further disaffected the Egyptian population from the empire, and in 642 the people stood by as the unpopular Byzantine rulers of Alexandria fell to invading Islamic armies.

See also: BYZANTINE AFRICA (Vol. II); COPTIC CHRISTIANITY (Vol. II); COPTS (Vol. I); ISLAM (Vol. II).

Greece Hellenic city-states of the ancient Mediterranean that influenced African history, science, technology, and cultures through settlement and dynastic rule; Hellenic influence was particularly noteworthy in EGYPT in the years 332 to 30 BCE.

One of the first discussions of Hellenic influence in Africa dates to *The Histories* of HERODOTUS, c. 430 BCE, which describes the founding of the Grecian colony of CYRENE almost 200 years earlier. The settlers, according to Herodotus, had come from the drought-stricken island of Thera and had sailed to northern Africa, where they settled at a place called Aziris. After six years, they were led by the North African inhabitants to a spring known as Apollo's Fountain, which became the site of the Cyrenean colony. The moist soil of this city, which allowed crop cultivation and horse breeding, enabled the settlement to thrive and expand through the region.

This, of course, was not the only mention of Africa by the ancient Greek historian. Elsewhere, Herodotus maintained that shields and helmets had first entered Greece from Egypt and that the Greek word *aegis* (a goatskin harness) was derived from the goatskin robes worn by North African women. He also claimed that these were the people who had taught the Greeks how to harness a chariot with four horses.

Other descriptions of Greek colonization in Africa are more deeply rooted in myth and legend. In the tale of Jason and the Argonauts, for example, the hero is said to be sailing to the oracle at Delphi when a sudden gale blows his ship off course. Landing in northern Africa, Jason gives a tripod to the god Triton in exchange for safe passage from Lake Tritonis. The deity then predicts that when a descendant of the *Argo's* crew removed the tripod, 100 Greek cities would be built there. Upon hearing this, the Africans reportedly hid the tripod.

In the end, however, it was ALEXANDER THE GREAT who ultimately brought extensive Hellenic influence to the African continent. Indeed, Alexander's military victory over Egypt's Persian rulers in 332 BCE inaugurated three centuries of Greek domination. (The name *Egypt* itself comes from the Greek; the Egyptians actually referred to their own country as KEMET.)

Under the Ptolemaic Dynasty (320–30 BCE), which was founded by Alexander's successors, the new capital city of Alexandria quickly rose as a place of both commerce and learning, becoming the center of Mediterranean life for centuries. During this time, the museum (or temple of the muses) at Alexandria, along with the city's famous library, represented an attempt to encompass all of Greek learning in a center very much like a modern university.

During the era of the Ptolemies, Greek poetry, drama, and literature were spread chiefly by Greek immigrants, whose culture remained isolated from the local African communities. Greek science, however, had a more wide-ranging influence. Among Alexandria's scholars, writers, and artists were Apollonius Rhodius, the composer of the epic *The Voyage of the Argo*; Aristophanes of Byzantium, who was credited with the invention of punctuation marks; Aristarchus of Samothrace, the first grammarian; and Theocritus of Syracuse, the first bucolic poet. The mathematician Euclid, the most important figure in the history of geometry, taught in Alexandria during the reign of Ptolemy I Soter (306–283 BCE). The mathematician Archimedes, also a resident of Alexandria, discovered the ratio 3:2 between cylinder and sphere; he also invented the Archimedean screw for raising water, a development that permanently revolutionized irrigation and agriculture in the NILE RIVER valley. Other leading scientists of Alexandria included the geographer Eratosthenes of Cyrene, whose map of the world was the first to use lines of latitude and longitude, and Herophilus of Chalcedon, the physician who discovered the nervous system.

The Ptolemaic rulers solidified their power by adopting and adapting Egyptian religion and symbols. Following the example of their predecessors, they claimed divine status as pharaohs. They built temples and fostered the cult of Sarapis, a Hellenized version of the Egyptian cult of OSIRIS. Brother-sister marriage was evidently common practice within the dynasty, as well as in the population at large.

The change from HIEROGLYPHICS to the DEMOTIC form of language signaled the new order, as the Hellenized language became the official language of both the state and the bureaucratic elite. Demotic remained predominant until the introduction of COPTIC, much later in time.

For the Ptolemies, Egypt was a business proposition to a great extent, and Alexandria served as the center of commerce and trade. Unfortunately, this only served to increase social tensions among immigrant Greeks, Egyptians, and other Africans. With the fall of Egypt to Rome, the social disintegration of Alexandria became inevitable. The Greek culture, science, and art that influenced Alexandria's life for that period, however, have endured.

See also: GRECO-ROMAN PERIOD (Vol. I).

Guinea Name formerly used to describe the entire western coast of Africa. Guinea's history stretches back 30,000 years, with archaeological evidence from the area indicating early agricultural cultivation.

Three independent modern nations in the this region of modern Africa use the name Guinea—the Republic of Guinea, Guinea-Bissau, and Equatorial Guinea.

The region closest to the Atlantic coast is called Lower Guinea. Its earliest inhabitants were the Baga and the Nalu, who were later displaced by the Susu and Mandinka. The Lower Guinea Forest region, nearest to the borders of modern Sierra Leone and Liberia, was occupied by the Kpelle (Guerz), the Loma (Toma), and Kissi ethnic groups, who lived in small villages. The NIGER RIVER originates in this dense forest, where the region's heaviest rainfall occurs. Archaeologists studying the southeast areas of the forest have strong evidence that cultivation of yams, oil palms, and other agricultural crops was well under way by 100 BCE. Later, rice and KOLA NUTS were grown. The Lower Guinea highlands, which peak in the Nimba Range, are approximately 5,780 feet (1,762 m) above sea level.

The northeastern plains of the region are called Upper Guinea. The area's characteristic grasslands, or savanna, supported a number of useful trees, including the BAOBAB and the shea, which was used to produce SHEA BUTTER. The central area of Upper Guinea contains strong evidence of MILLET cultivation from as early as 1000 BCE. Archaeologists have uncovered many stone figures carved in human and animal likeness. These figures, known as *nomoli*, were made of steatite or granite and were probably made for fertility rites that attempted to ensure successful harvests.

Archaeologists have also been able to create a link between early forms of metallurgy and the growth of Guinea's early city-states. It appears that iron smelting was done from at least 200 BCE, as a number of tools and pieces that are likely ritual objects have been found throughout the area.

See also: GUINEA (Vols II, III); GUINEA-BISSAU (Vol. II).

H

Hadar Site of the discovery of the skeletal remains of an example of an early primate species.

Located in the Afar region of ETHIOPIA, 217 miles (347 km) northeast of ADDIS ADABA, Hadar became the focus of media attention in 1974 when archaeologists recovered the remains of an early primate species later identified to be *Australopithecus afarensis (A. afarensis)*. Archaeologists who made the discovery gave these nearly complete skeletal remains of a young woman the name Lucy. Ethiopians, however, refer to her as Dinkenesh ("she is wonderful") and regard her as the mother of human civilization.

Estimated to be between 3 million and 3.18 million years old, Lucy's bones are among the oldest fossilized remains of the human family ever found.

With a slender but powerful body, Dinkenesh stood just under four feet tall when she died at about the age of twenty. Her robust arms were longer than those of a modern human, although her hands and brain were no larger than those of a chimpanzee. An agile climber, Dinkenesh also was fully bipedal, meaning that she could stand upright and walk on two feet. Her upright stance helped her get food from the trees as well as from the ground and allowed her to survive by scavenging meat, hunting smaller animals, and feeding on fruits, vegetables, roots, and tubers. Such remarkable food-gathering abilities helped Dinkenesh's species survive and evolve for more than 2 million years.

See also: *HOMO ERECTUS* (Vol. I); *HOMO HABILIS* (Vol. I); *HOMO SAPIENS* (Vol. I).

Hannibal (c. 247–183 BCE) *Carthaginian military commander renowned for his leadership, daring, and brilliance as a tactician.*

As commander of the forces for the North African city-state of CARTHAGE, Hannibal led a daring march over the Alps from Spain to Italy. Taking place during the Second PUNIC WAR (218–201 BCE), this feat is considered one of the greatest in military history.

Born in Carthage, near present-day Tunis, Hannibal was the son of the great Carthaginian general Hamilcar Barca. Following Carthage's defeat by Rome in the First Punic War (264–24 BCE) Hamilcar Barca led Carthaginian forces to Spain, where he conquered much of the country. He brought his son to Spain at about nine years of age, making the boy swear undying hostility to Rome.

Hannibal remained in Spain following his father's death in 229 or 228 BCE. There he led troops under the command of his brother-in-law, Hasdrubal, who succeeded in consolidating Carthaginian dominion over the Iberian Peninsula. When Hasdrubal was assassinated in 221 BCE, Hannibal was proclaimed commander in chief by the Carthaginian troops. This field promotion was later ratified by the Carthaginian government.

As commander, Hannibal's first priority was to solidify Carthage's position in Spain. To accomplish this, he married Imilce, a Spanish princess, and conducted a series of battles against various Spanish tribes. In 219, he attacked Saguntum, a city in Spain that, although within Carthaginian territory, was considered a friend by Rome. Although Saguntum fell to Hannibal's troops after an eight-month-long siege, Rome demanded the surrender of the Carthaginian general. Hannibal refused, despite the fact that he had been severely wounded in the siege. Rome responded by declaring war against Carthage, thus initiating the Second Punic War.

In 218 BCE, Hannibal initiated an ambitious attack that targeted Rome itself. Leaving his brother (also named Hasdrubal) to defend Carthaginian Spain and North Africa, Hannibal mobilized his forces. Marching from Cartagena, the capital of Carthaginian Spain, Hannibal's force included between 40,000 and 102,000 troops, HORSES, and thirty-eight ELEPHANTS, which were to be used in battle as well as to carry baggage.

In the autumn of 218 BCE, Hannibal's troops marched north along the eastern coast of Spain and over the Pyrenees mountains, where his soldiers battled several local peoples. The Carthaginian army then crossed the Rhône River, where Hannibal commandeered small boats for his troops and built rafts for the elephants. The most treacherous part of Hannibal's march, however, was the alpine crossing, which took Hannibal fifteen days. Many troops died, some of exposure, some in landslides or falls from mountainsides, and some from the attacks launched by local mountain peoples.

By the time the Carthaginian army finally arrived in northern Italy, more than half of Hannibal's troops had died, leaving just 20,000 infantry, 6,000 cavalry, and only a few elephants. In spite of this, however, the Carthaginian army—behind Hannibal's skill as a general—won impressive victories. Defeating the Taurini people, Hannibal's troops conquered their chief town, the modern-day city of Turin. The Carthaginians also destroyed the Roman forces in battles at the Trebia River and Lake Trasimene. With each victory, Hannibal added reinforcements, recruiting Ligurian, Gallic, and Celtic soldiers to add to his forces.

After resting throughout most of the summer of 217 BCE, Hannibal's troops resumed their movement south through Italy. In 216 BCE, the Carthaginian and Roman armies finally battled in full force at Cannae in southeastern Italy, where the Romans maintained a large supply depot. During the battle, Hannibal ordered the center line of his troops to yield, retreating but not breaking their line. By pushing both flanks forward and breaking through the Roman lines, the Carthaginians were able to circle behind the Roman center and surround the Roman army. The Romans were overwhelmed, with an estimated 60,000 Romans dying in the battle. Fewer than 6,000 Carthaginian troops were lost.

Hannibal's army occupied Italy for the next thirteen years. Though Hannibal had hoped to use this occupation to rally the Italian population into a rebellion against Rome, neither his own countrymen nor the subjugated Italians supported him in this effort. Rome's dominant strength at sea, moreover, not only made Hannibal's troops dependent on local provisions, but also cut them off from reinforcements. As a result, Rome slowly regained the territories subjugated by the Carthaginians.

In addition to eating away at Hannibal's victories in Italy, the Romans also began waging successful military campaigns in Carthaginian Spain. In 207 BCE, Hannibal's brother Hasdrubal, who had been bringing Carthaginian reinforcements from Spain to northern Italy, was intercepted, defeated, and killed by the Romans.

When Rome invaded Carthage itself in 203 BCE, Hannibal finally abandoned Italy and returned home. The Carthaginians had just accepted harsh Roman terms of surrender and negotiated an armistice when Hannibal attacked Roman troops at Hadrumetum (present-day Sousse, in TUNISIA). In a battle at Zama later that year, Hannibal's army suffered a crushing defeated at the hands of an alliance of Roman troops led by Scipio Africanus and Numidian troops led by Scipio's ally MASINISSA. In the battle, which brought an end to the Second Punic War, the Carthaginian army lost 20,000 men. Hannibal, however, survived.

Defeated by Rome, Hannibal then served as a civil magistrate in Carthage. While paying the harsh tribute demanded by Rome, Hannibal reformed the government of Carthage. He overthrew the oligarchic power structure, introduced constitutional and administrative changes that reduced corruption, and initiated a renewed period of financial prosperity.

Fearful that the still-powerful Hannibal might initiate another war, the Romans demanded that he surrender. Instead, he fled to Ephesus, in Asia Minor. There, King Antiochus III of Syria, preparing an attack on Rome, put Hannibal in command of a fleet in Phoenicia. Hannibal was inexperienced as a naval commander, and he suffered a quick defeat at the hands of the Roman fleet.

Once again fleeing the Romans, Hannibal arrived in Bithynia, on the southern coast of the Black Sea, in 190 BCE. There, he served King Prusias II in his war against Pergamum, another ally of Rome. Once again, however, Hannibal was defeated, and, once again, the victorious Romans demanded Hannibal's surrender. This time, though, he was unable to escape, and, in the Bithynian village of Libyssa, he killed himself by taking poison.

Further reading: Serge Lancel, *Hannibal* (Malden, Mass.: Blackwell, 2000); J. F. Lazenby, *Hannibal's War* (Norman: University of Oklahoma Press, 1998).

Hanno (c. 530-470 BCE) *Carthaginian explorer who led an important voyage of colonization along Africa's Atlantic coast.*

Hanno's voyage was recorded in an eighteen-line Carthaginian inscription hung on plaques in the Temple of Chronos, the Greek god of time.

Translated into Greek as the *Periplus of Hanno*, it was one of the earliest written geographical narratives in the ancient world. Around 430 BCE, HERODOTUS wrote of Hanno's voyages in relation to the founding of Carthaginian trade on the Atlantic coast of Africa. According to the *Periplus*, Hanno set out with sixty ships bearing 30,000 colonists, although these figures have long been disputed and may have been greatly exaggerated. (Five thousand settlers would have been more in line with colonizing missions during this period.)

Also in dispute is the extent of Hanno's voyages. The Roman Pliny the Elder, in his *Natural History*, stated that Hanno had circumnavigated Africa and reached Arabia, a feat that was not impossible. As the places described in the narrative suggest, however, it is more likely that he sailed beyond the western SAHARA and Mauritania to Senegal, and possibly as far as CAMEROON or GABON. Some of the places mentioned can be associated with known sites, while others remain in dispute. No other subsequent written reports about these regions are known to exist until those of the Portuguese, some 2,000 years later.

Carrying out orders to found colonies along the African coast, Hanno deposited groups of settlers, known as Libyphoenicians, at seemingly suitable places along the way. Afterward, he founded a trading post on an island near Mauritania. The survival of Carthaginian barter methods on the coast was described by the Arab authors Sharif al-Idrisi and Yacout in the twelfth and thirteenth centuries CE, a remarkable persistence that has led some scholars to speculate that trade may in fact have been the primary mission of Hanno's colonizing voyage.

Noted for its literary style, the *Periplus of Hanno* is an early example of popular travel writing. The account, which may not have been written by Hanno himself, contains a report of an active volcano and the earliest extant written description of gorillas. It tells of sometimes hostile encounters with natives and animals, as well as of music, raging fires, and aromatic trees, which were valued as potential trade goods. The use of the word "gorilla" may have been a corruption of *kikongo ngo diida*, meaning an animal that violently beats itself (i.e., thumps its chest). The description in the *Periplus* of the gorillas as a race of hairy men and women may cast doubt upon this aspect of the account, but our modern concept of human and nonhuman primate species may cloud our judgment as to exactly what kind of creatures Hanno's men saw (and skinned).

An annotated summary of Hanno's chronicle, based on the Greek translation, follows.

Hanno was sent by the Carthaginians beyond the Pillars of Hercules [GIBRALTAR], in order to found cities of the Libyphoenicians. He sailed with 60 ships, 30,000 colonists, and provisions.

The ships sailed for two days beyond Gibraltar and founded the city of Thymiaterium ("Altar of Incense") in the middle of a great plain.

The party then sailed westward to Solois in Libya, a heavily forested area [possibly the Lake District of Morocco].

The voyagers consecrated a temple to the Phoenician lord of the sea and then sailed eastward into thick marshes that were a feeding ground for elephants and other wild animals. Sailing one day's journey to the sea, they founded cities called Caricus Murus, Gytta, Acra, Melitta, and Arambys.

They sailed to the River Lixos (or Lixus), flowing out of Libya, where they had friendly relations with a nomadic herding people, the Lixites [BERBERS].

Living above the Lixites were hostile people with burnt faces [presumed to be Ethiopians], wild animals, and mountains inhabited, according to the Lixites, by cave-dwellers who could outrun horses.

Taking Lixite interpreters aboard, Hanno sailed southward for twelve days, then turned east for a day's journey. Settlers were left on a small island in a bay, where they founded a city they called Chernah ("last habitation"). Based on distance, they judged this place to be situated on the shore directly opposite Carthage.

Sailing past a great river called Chretes, the voyagers came to a lake with three islands [probably the Tidra archipelago, near the coast of Mauritania]. A day's journey beyond these islands they came to a mountain range inhabited by people wearing animal skins. These people threw stones at the ships and drove off Hanno's expedition before it could make a landing.

Next, Hanno came to a broad river [probably the SENEGAL RIVER], which the expedition found teeming with CROCODILES and HIPPOPOTAMUSES. Turning back, the party retreated to Chernah.

Sailing southward for twelve days along the coast [probably as far as modern-day Guinea, Sierra Leone, or even Liberia], the party encountered "Ethiopians" [possibly Kru speakers] who fled from them and whose speech was unintelligible to the Lixite interpreters.

Dropping anchor by a tall mountain range, the party noted forests of aromatic wood. Two days beyond the forests was open sea with a plain on the landward side, where many nighttime campfires were observed.

Replenishing the party's freshwater supplies, the crew sailed along the coast for another five days [probably reaching present-day Ivory Coast]. They then came upon a great bay that the Lixites called the Bay of the Horn of the West [probably Cape Three Points in Ghana, the entrance to the Bight of Benin].

Disembarking on an island, they saw only forests during the daytime. At night, however, the bay was ringed with fires, and they heard the sound of flutes, cymbals, drums, and many voices. The sailors were afraid, and their soothsayers advised them to leave the island.

Sailing away quickly, the party passed a burning country of aromatic forests, with huge torrents of fire flowing down into the sea that made landing impossible.

Hurrying on in fear, they sailed another four days past the burning coastline. In the middle was a taller flame that seemed to rise up to the stars. In daylight, they saw that it was a high mountain called Chariot of the Gods [most likely the active Mount Cameroon].

After three days of sailing alongside the fires, Hanno's party reached a bay called Horn of the South [possibly in Gabon].

In the bay they came to an island with a lake, within which was another island "full of savages." Most of these creatures were "women" with hairy bodies; the interpreters called them "gorillas." Hanno's party gave chase, but the males escaped by climbing trees and throwing stones. Three females were taken, biting and clawing their captors, who killed them, skinned them, and brought the skins back to Carthage. [Here the *Periplus of Hanno* ends.]

Haoulti Archaeological site of the pre-Aksumite culture of present-day ETHIOPIA, dating to the fourth or fifth century BCE. Haoulti and its archaeological remains demonstrate the influence of South Arabia upon northern Ethiopia in its ARCHITECTURE, art, and culture.

The objects discovered at Haoulti provide insight into the complex cultural influences on the region before the rise of the ancient Christian kingdom of AKSUM, around the second century CE. The richest example of the influence of South Arabia upon Haoulti in the fourth and fifth centuries BCE are a *naos*, or throne, and various statues that were discovered there. The *naos* was carved from a single block of local limestone and stands 56 inches (142 cm) tall. It has four feet shaped like bulls' hooves that support a base decorated with two bars with a small niche covered with ornamentation. The niche is topped by a dais in the shape of a depressed arch. Along the edge of the niche, two rows of reclining ibexes converge to form a stylized tree, which stands at the top of the throne. Each side of the throne is decorated with a bas-relief of a small figure, holding a staff, who precedes a larger bearded man holding a fan. The figures have aquiline features, which suggest a Semitic appearance, with their eyes depicted as small lozenges. The smaller figure wears a plain robe down to his ankles, while the larger figure wears a baggy loincloth.

The same bulls' hooves on the throne are seen in a marble statuette from Marib, and the reclining ibexes occur in decorations from the Sabaean region, including Marib and Haz. The facial features and clothing are parallel to figures represented in bronze sculpture also from Marib. These similarities suggest the South Arabian influence.

The statues also recall artifacts accidentally discovered at Addi Galamo on the western edge of the Tigre plateau. The Haoulti statue represents a seated woman with her hands on her knees dressed in a long, pleated robe. Over the robe she wears a wide necklace made of three thick, ringed strands, from which hangs a shield that lies across her chest. The shield is counterbalanced by an ornament in the shape of a trapezoid that rests between her shoulder blades. The woman's posture, the position of the hands, and the necklace with its counterweight all bear a strong resemblance to the statues of Addi Galamo. Statues with the same pose of a seated woman wearing a long fluted robe, with a necklace with hanging beads, a shield, and a counterweight are in the National Museum in Rome as well. However, the posture and decoration of the statue is most similar to statues of women from the region under Syro-Hittite control, which seems to be the real point of connection between Ethiopia and Asia Minor in the seventh and eighth centuries BCE.

Other objects, such as two earthenware amulets and a carnelian amulet, were found at Haoulti and are Meroitic in origin. These objects show the relationship between Ethiopia and the NILE VALLEY before the common era. The influence of MEROË on Ethiopia was primarily in metal-working techniques that are seen in bronze, iron, and gold objects discovered at the site.

Harkhuf (governed c. 2290–2270 BCE) *Egyptian trade expeditionist and royal governor.*

Harkhuf led notable journeys into NUBIA and to inner Africa during the Sixth Dynasty. Much of what is known about Harkhuf derives from the biography found in his *mastaba*, the inscribed stone tomb of common Egyptians. Originally from ELEPHANTINE, Harkhuf was appointed as governor of a southern section of UPPER EGYPT during the rule of King Merenre. He was mainly responsible for trade—both the discovery of new trade routes and the safe maintenance of existing ones. In this capacity, he led four documented expeditions into NUBIA and Yam (Sudan). The Nubian route was a particularly important link to central Africa and the goods to be found there, which included incense, MONKEYS, DOGS, GIRAFFES, EBONY, skins (likely LEOPARD and panther), ivory, and other unusual goods.

During early expeditions through the territories of Irtjet and Zatju, Harkhuf traveled along the NILE RIVER. But when these territories later became hostile to EGYPT's efforts to exploit and colonize Nubia, Harkhuf was forced to take alternate routes or to travel under the protection of the ruler of Yam. He sometimes traveled with his own military or armed escort in order to keep the trade routes open.

One of Harkhuf's most famous journeys was his fourth documented expedition, during which he traveled south to Yam. On this trip, Harkhuf arranged to bring an MBUTI back to the court of King Pepi II, who, as a collector of the unusual, was very pleased with the gift.

Hathor Ancient Egyptian goddess, known as the protector of pregnant women and patron of music and dance.

In the mythology of ancient Egypt, Hathor was the daughter of Nut and RA. In early myths, Hathor was the mother of the sky god Horus, but in time this capacity was attributed to ISIS. Hathor became the protector of Horus, and her name translates to "house of Horus." She was depicted either as a cow or as a woman crowned by a sun disk held between a cow's horns.

In the story of Ra, Hathor was created by her father Ra as "Sekhmet" the destroyer of men who wronged him. Later, however, Ra changed his mind and disguised beer as blood, which Sekhmet then drank. Intoxicated, she could no longer kill and became Hathor, goddess of love.

Hathor was particularly worshiped as a goddess of fertility. It was believed that, when a child was born, seven Hathors came to announce the infant's fate. The seven Hathors were regarded as having the power to exchange a prince born to ill-fortune with a luckier child, thereby protecting the dynasty and the nation.

In later times, Hathor was also regarded as a goddess of the dead, giving food and water to the deceased as they arrived in the underworld.

Hausa Language of the Afro-Asiatic family. Hausa has been spoken throughout North-central Africa, from the Sudan west to the regions south of the SAHARA. Compared to other African languages, the Hausa language demonstrates remarkable uniformity of pronunciation, vocabulary, and grammatical structure wherever it has been spoken. This most likely indicates that Hausa originated relatively recently and spread rapidly through the lands south of the Sahara, since older languages tend to have more differences in their dialects, which are variations that evolve based on geographical distance.

See also: HAUSA (Vol. II); HAUSA STATES (Vols. II, III).

Hawara, Pyramid of Along with LAHUN and LISHT, part of the mortuary complex for kings of the Twelfth Dynasty of EGYPT. The pyramid was built c. 1938 to 1770 BCE.

The pyramid at Hawara, built by King Amenemhet III c. eighteenth century BCE, was one of the most elaborate pyramids of the time, and was described by ancient Greek geographer Strabo as being as great as the GREAT PYRAMID of GIZA. Strabo named it "the Labyrinth," and it is still one of the most visited of all of Egypt's ancient sites. Ancient scholars believed that the Labyrinth was designed as a meeting place, but it was probably built as a mortuary complex.

The Greek historian HERODOTUS described the Labyrinth as having twelve courts and 3,000 rooms, of which half were above ground and half below. The roof of every room was made of stone, and the walls were filled with sculptures. Each court was built of white marble. Herodotus speculated that the money and labor to build the Labyrinth must have outweighed all the public works of the Greeks put together.

hawk Bird of prey; biologically related to the EAGLE, the kite, and the vulture. In ancient EGYPT, hawks, like falcons, were admired for their grace and power. In Egyptian mythology, the hawk was associated with Menthu, the god of war. Menthu was often depicted as a man with a hawk's head. Because Ra, the sun god, was also portrayed as a man with a hawk's head, the two gods were often confused with one another.

Heracleopolis Greek name for the ancient Egyptian city of Henen-nesut, EGYPT'S capital during the FIRST INTERMEDIATE PERIOD (c. 2213–1991 BCE).

Heracleopolis, the Greek name of the town called Henen-nesut in ancient times, was located in present-day Bani Suwayf. The Ninth and Tenth Dynasties, often referred to as the Heracleopolitans, were founded by King Khety and controlled Middle and LOWER EGYPT from Heracleopolis.

About the same time, the Eleventh Dynasty, which claimed UPPER EGYPT, was flourishing in Thebes. The presence of two dynasties, which lasted nearly seventy-five years, was the source of great conflict. Each dynasty sought dominion over the other, and boundaries continually changed. This period was finally brought to an end about 1968 BCE by King MENTUHOTEP II (sometimes called Mentuhotep I), who defeated the Heracleopolitans, reunified Egypt, and launched the MIDDLE KINGDOM.

Scholars believe that the group of literary works describing the strife of this time was most likely written after the reunification of Egypt, during the Middle Kingdom.

herder See PASTORALISM.

Herihor (r. c. 1080 BCE) *Ancient Egyptian official and usurper of the throne.*

A high official during the reign of RAMESSES XI. (Ramesses ruled from 1100 to 1070 BCE and was the last king of the Twentieth Dynasty.) Although it is known that Herihor was a military officer and high priest during Ramesses' reign, details about his exact origins are obscure. It is thought, however, that he came to Egypt to help stop a rebellion led by a former high priest of AMUN. The ineffectual Ramesses was unable to stop Herihor from making himself first a high priest, and later vizier of both Upper and Lower Egypt. Herihor's fight to control the throne is depicted in reliefs found in the temple of Khons in Thebes.

Herodotus (484–425 BCE) *First Greek historian, often referred to as the Father of history.*

Born in Halicarnassus, a Greek colony in Asia Minor, Herodotus devoted himself to literary pursuits during much of his life. His great work, *The Histories*, is the story of the war between the Persian Empire and the much smaller Greek city-states.

Known as the first historian to make investigation the key to history, Herodotus researched his book by traveling extensively throughout the ancient Mediterranean world. His African travels took him to places throughout Egypt, including ELEPHANTINE, in the southern part of Egypt, as well as the Arabian frontier in the east.

Herodotus was an inquiring reporter, talking to many people, including actual witnesses to the events he later wrote about. Interwoven throughout his book are descriptions of the people and countries he visited. In the course of telling his story, Herodotus reports on the customs of the Egyptians, the Hittites, and others he met during his travels. Much of what we know today about many of the ancient peoples comes to us from Herodotus.

Despite the fact that he has been criticized for including inaccurate and often highly implausible anecdotes in his work, Herodotus greatly influenced later historians by clearly establishing the principle that history must begin with research.

Native to Africa, the goliath heron is the largest member of the heron family. Ancient Egyptians associated the heron with the phoenix, a symbol of rebirth. *© Brian Vikander/CORBIS*

heron Family of large, long-legged wading birds that also includes the bittern and the egret. Herons have broad wings, long and straight pointed bills, and soft plumage. They are usually found in tropical areas, where they wade in streams and marshes and feed on frogs, fish, and other water animals. Herons stand with their long necks bent in an S-shape, but fly with their heads folded back onto their shoulders.

Africa is home to the European night heron and the shoe-billed heron, which is found along the WHITE NILE. Also found in Africa is the goliath heron, which has a reddish head and neck, and is the largest heron of all at up to 59 inches (150 cm) in length.

In ancient Egypt, herons were associated with Bennu, the ancient Egyptian phoenix. According to legend, there was only one phoenix and it was a servant of the sun god. Every 500 years, this phoenix would build a nest that would serve as a funeral pyre. Once the phoenix was consumed by the pyre's flames, a new one would arise from its ashes in a process that represented the rising and setting of the sun, as well as resurrection and eternal life.

Hierakonpolis City in UPPER EGYPT, c. 3500–3400 BCE, believed to be the earliest known African city; also known as Nekhen. Archaeological studies conducted over the past twenty years have uncovered a wealth of information about the life and culture of this city built along the western bank of the Nile. The remains of palaces as well as artifacts and artwork all indicate that Hierakonpolis was the residence of both early kings and royal officials. Mud-brick and stone temples found there have been proved to be burial sites, which, according to some archaeologists, provided models for the great pyramids built by later Egyptians. Religious beliefs among the residents of Hierakonpolis included devotion to the god HORUS as the patron deity of the city. In addition, the many temples, as well as the ritual masks and grave goods (also known as *nekhen*) that were buried with the dead, suggest a belief in an AFTERLIFE. This would seem to be reinforced by the fact that Hierakonpolis's cemeteries contain some of the earliest forms of mummification found in EGYPT. There, the dead have been found padded and wrapped with linen and covered with pitch in order to seal out decay-causing moisture.

Hierakonpolis also is considered the birthplace of Egypt's long tradition of pharaonic dynasties, which developed after long periods of warfare with the rival kingdoms of Nekeb, in the north, and NUBIA, to the south. Eventually, between 3200 and 3000 BCE,

Hierakonpolis emerged as the dominant kingdom in the region. One of the prime pieces of evidence is a stone table called the NARMER PALETTE. The palette's depiction of the famous warrior-king Narmer (more frequently known as MENES), who is seen wearing both the RED CROWN of Lower Egypt and the WHITE CROWN of Upper Egypt, is generally interpreted as a symbol of Egypt's unification into a single nation. Besides King Menes's name, the tablet contains details of the many military victories he won while consolidating his power.

With unification came the earliest form of centralized government in Africa. King Menes founded the First Dynasty and relocated the capital to MEMPHIS. Egypt then entered a period of rapid development that included the regulation of trade links and the construction of palaces, large funerary tombs, and religious temples. In addition, greater emphasis was placed on creating methods of irrigation to produce the abundant crops needed to sustain Egypt's growing population.

hieratic Form of ancient Egyptian writing used from the First Dynasty (c. 2925–2775 BCE) to about 200 BCE. Hieratic script was a cursive form, which meant that its characters were written in a flowing style in which letters of words were joined together. Hieratic script was usually written in black ink with a reed pen on PAPYRUS. It was used in literary and religious texts, as well as such everyday documents as letters, catalogs, and official writs.

Hieratic script was introduced around the time that HIEROGLYPHICS were first being used in carved or painted inscriptions. It represented a simplified form of hieroglyphic writing that was quicker to write, especially on papyrus. Although the symbols used in hieratic script were similar to hieroglyphic writing, hieratic symbols were less detailed. Also, the spelling of words was occasionally different.

Hieratic script was written from right to left. It was first written in vertical lines, starting from the top, then, in 2000 BCE, horizontally. Around 660 BCE, another form of writing, DEMOTIC script, began to replace hieratic script in daily use.

hieroglyphics Egyptian writing system consisting of pictures or symbols that was used in ancient Egypt for more than 3,000 years. (The name *hieroglyphics* comes from the Greek *hieros*, meaning "sacred," and *glypho*, meaning "inscription.")

Priests and scribes carved hieroglyphics on temples and tombs, public monuments, furniture, and wrote on PAPYRUS. This writing form was popular from the end of prehistory until about 396 CE. The most recent hieroglyphic text appears on the walls of the temple of Isis on Philae Island.

Hieroglyphics most likely were developed to record crop yields, determine tax rates, or set down the histories of kings. The writing form soon took on a religious significance, however. The Egyptians themselves called hieroglyphics *medou netjer*, or "words of the gods." The average Egyptian of the time would not have been able to read hieroglyphics, which can be read right to left, left to right, or in vertical columns. There was no hieroglyphic dictionary; thus, scribes often made up symbols or created new symbols for what they wished to express.

Several hundred picture signs make up the hieroglyphic writing system. There are three basic elements of hieroglyphic writing: phonograms, ideograms, and determinatives. Words could be created by using only phonograms, only ideograms, or by using a combination of the two.

A *phonogram* is a sound in picture form. Egyptians did not usually include vowels in their writing, so hieroglyphic phonograms depict consonant sounds of the spoken language.

An *ideogram,* or logogram, is a symbol or picture representing a specific object. Typical hieroglyphic ideograms are birds, cats, Egyptian gods, and items connected with daily life, like crops, fish, and boats.

A *determinative* is a type of logogram. There were several hundred hieroglyphic determinatives, which were used to further explain the meanings of words. Because vowels were not shown in the written language, two words with similar consonants would appear alike unless distinguishd by determinatives. Both *pot* and *pet,* for example, would be written *pt* according to the Egyptian system. Similarly, with the addition of one particular determinative, the phonogram *mr* would mean "canal"; with a different determinative, it would mean "love." Determinatives also were used to show plurals.

HIERATIC and DEMOTIC were both derived from hieroglyphics. *Hieratic*, a word that comes from the Greek *hieratikos* meaning "priestly," is best described as cursive hieroglyphics. This writing form is as old as hieroglyphics and was written mostly with a brush on papyrus. In it, smaller signs are joined together to form word groups. Like hieroglypics, hieratic was used mainly by priests and scribes. Demotic, also called enchorial, came into use during the Twenty-fifth or Twenty-sixth Dynasty, about 712–525 BCE. Demotic evolved from hieratic and was a style of penmanship. Demotic pen strokes were quicker and less defined than hieratic. With demotic, new signs were created, and the connection between hieroglyphics and hand-written text faded. This less formal language was used mostly in official, business, and personal writing.

For centuries, the signs and symbols of hieroglyphics were locked in mystery. While many were fascinated by the carvings, they mistakenly believed hieroglyphics were just decorative symbols. The discovery of the ROSETTA STONE in 1799 by Napoleon's soldiers became the key to interpreting the ancient Egyptian writing. The Rosetta Stone features the same text carved in three different languages: hieroglyphics, demotic, and Greek. By comparing the texts, scholars were able to decode the hieroglypghic incription. The Rosetta Stone has been on display at the British Museum in London since 1802.

When inscribing tombs or memorials to pharaohs, ancient Egyptians often disguised the true meaning of the hieroglyphics by creating new signs or by giving new forms to old signs. Later kings, trying to erase the history of earlier pharaohs, often destroyed monuments to past leaders. With this in mind, coded hieroglyphs were carved inches deep into the stone or statues. For example, one statue to RAMESSES II contained a sun god (RA), the king as a child (*mes*), and a sedge plant (*su*), which was seen as equalling Ra-mes-ses. In this way, the hieroglyphs of the pharaoh's name could be preserved for eternity.

high-water canalization Creation of man-made waterways; used in ancient times for irrigation, drinking water storage, drainage, and travel that allowed for greater trade opportunities between eastern Africa and the Persian Gulf.

Early canals in the Middle East were most likely built to satisfy the need for drinking water and irrigation. However, during periods of high water, travel on the canals was possible. The most notable canal of ancient Africa linked the NILE RIVER to the Red Sea by way of the Isthmus of Suez. Built more than 3,000 years ago as an irrigation canal, it was used during periods of high water by sailors seeking to extend trade between the East African coast from Sofala, on the coast of what is now Mozambique, up to the Persian Gulf. This ancient canal is the ancestor of the modern Suez Canal.

Although some researchers believe that excavation may have begun under either SETI I or RAMESSES II, during the thirteenth century BCE, the ancient canal was possibly built during the period of the Twelfth Dynasty (c. 1938 BCE to 1756 BCE). Still other researchers say that DARIUS I, king of Persia built the canal c. 500 BCE. The canal was maintained and modified until sometime in the eighth century CE.

See also: AGRICULTURE (Vol. I).

hillside terracing Process by which crops are grown on hillsides or mountains. Crops grown using this technique are planted on graduated terraces built into the slope. This labor-intensive method of AGRICULTURE has been practiced in sub-Saharan Africa since the IRON AGE, starting around 3000 BCE. Hillside terracing reduces soil erosion and water loss and maximizes the amount of land available for agricultural production.

Each terrace is built on a low, flat ridge of earth that runs across a slope. The terraces are built with a slight gradation, so that water may run off. In areas where there is not an excessive amount of rainfall, the terraces may be built on the same level. This type of agriculture has been used in Africa for cultivating cassava, YAMS, rice, MILLET, and SORGHUM, among other crops.

hippopotamus Large, amphibious mammal found in the lakes and rivers of sub-Saharan Africa. Hippopotamuses live in groups of seven to fifteen, preferring to rest during the day in the water and feed on grasses at night. They are fast swimmers and can stay under water for up to ten minutes before coming up for air. Hippopotamuses are aggressive animals, and during mating season, males often have battles that result in death.

Tomb inscriptions in ancient EGYPT portrayed serpent-like creatures threatening people and crops. In these inscriptions, hippopotamuses were often pictured being harpooned. According to Egyptian legend, the dead whose hearts failed to be lighter than the feather of Truth (MA'AT) were destroyed by a monster named Ammut, who was part hippopotamus, part lioness, and part crocodile.

In spite of these views, hippopotamuses were also revered by Egyptians as a symbol of fertility. The hippopotamus was, for example, associated with female pregnancy. During the MIDDLE KINGDOM of ancient Egypt, earthenware sculptures of hippopotamuses became popular.

Hittites Indo-Europeans who established an empire in Asia Minor during the fourteenth and thirteenth centuries BCE.

Originally known primarily through a brief mention in the Bible, the importance of the Hittite Empire has been reaffirmed within the last hundred years by archaeological discoveries in Turkey and Syria. (The name *Hittite* was derived from the Hatti people of Asia Minor.) Around 1400 BCE, during the reign of the great pharaoh AMENHOTEP IV, the Hittite king Suppiluliumas I conquered the Mitanni, a powerful Syrian empire. This established the Hittites as an empire in Asia Minor and a rival to Egyptian power. This rivalry came to a head in 1285 BCE when the Hittite leader Mutwatallis fought an indecisive battle against the Egyptian pharaoh RAMESSES II at Kadesh. Although Ramesses was forced to flee the scene of the conflict, the battle stopped the Hittite advance toward Egypt. Peace between the two powers was sealed by a marriage between a member of Ramesses' family and a Hittite princess.

At the peak of its power, the Hittite Empire extended from upper Mesopotamia and Syria to what is now southern Lebanon. During this time, the Hittites began smelting iron, signifying the beginning of the IRON AGE. Hittite religion included the worship of thousands of deities, and their literature displays a level of emotion not usually found in ancient Near Eastern texts. In addition, the Hittite code of law appears to express more humane treatment than other legal systems of that time and place. The empire flourished until around 1200 BCE, when it was overthrown by the Aegean SEA PEOPLES.

Homo erectus Scientific term used to describe members of the Homindae family; humanlike species living in the prehistoric era.

In 1975, scientists working on the western shore of ETHIOPIA's Lake Turkana recovered the fossilized remains of a twelve-year-old boy. Named *Homo erectus* (*H. erectus*) because he stood "upright" and traveled extensively over wide areas, scientists believe that the boy probably traveled from the Ethiopian coast to Harar. From there, the boy, who lived about 1.5 million years ago, traveled to the Awash Valley and then southwest into the Omo Valley and to Lake Turkana. Based on his ability to travel, scientists have theorized that *H. erectus* was the first member of the human family to migrate from Africa to parts of Europe and Asia. This belief is supported by the discovery of other human remains in this region.

The features of *H. erectus* seem more human than those of earlier members of the human family. His brain capacity, for example, was 70 cubic inches (1150 cubic cm), and he appears to have had vocal chords, giving him the ability to speak. *H. erectus* lived a relatively long life as well. He also may have learned varied techniques for survival. Among the most important of these was the use of fire, which helped *H. erectus* with cooking, self-protection, and warmth. *H. erectus* also developed advanced tools like knives, choppers, scrapers, and cleavers, all of which helped him hunt large animals and prepare them to be consumed as food.

See also: *HOMO HABILIS* (Vol. I); *HOMO SAPIENS* (Vol. I); HADAR (Vol. I).

Homo habilis Scientific term used to describe certain humans of the prehistoric era who, over centuries, evolved into *HOMO ERECTUS*; members of the now-extinct Homindae family that includes the modern human beings known as *HOMO SAPIENS*. During the 1960s, the remains of six species of *Homo habilis* (*H. habilis*) were recovered at Olduvai Gorge in Kenya and at Lake Turkana in ETHIOPIA. Scientific analysis indicates that *H. habilis* lived between 1.5 and 2.5 million years ago, providing further evidence that human life began on the continent of Africa.

Scientists distinguish between humans and primates by the size and development of the brain and jaw and by their posture. The first hominids are called *Australopithecus*. The earliest known hominid, nicknamed "Lucy," is also known by the Ethiopian name Dinkenesh. A nearly complete *A. afaransis* skeleton roughly 3.18 million years old, Lucy is the ancestor of *A. africanus*, an upright-walking, intelligent hominid, the first skull shown on this chart. At that point development branched in two directions. *A. robustus* ("strong"), which became an evolutionary dead end, had large molars and powerful jaws but a brain capacity about the same as its predecessor, *A. africanus*. The other branch became the antecedent of modern humans: *Homo habilis* ("skillful") developed about 2 million years ago; *H. erectus* ("upright in posture") appeared about 1.75 million years ago; and *H. sapiens* ("wise") evolved between 300,000 and 400,000 years ago.

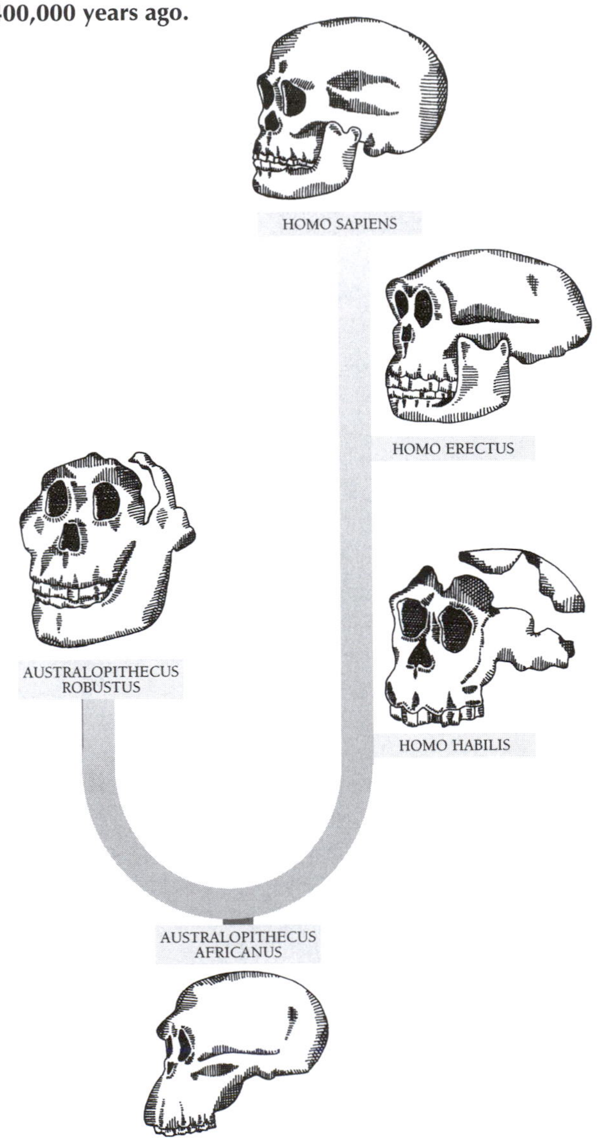

Given the name *habilis*, meaning "clever," "handy," or "skillful," *H. habilis* belonged to a group of hunters and gatherers who used simple stone tools. These tools, which often have been found with or near the skeletal remains of *H. habilis*, were stones that had been flaked, or broken off, to form cutting points. They were used as knives, hand axes, or choppers and may have provided some form of defense against large predators. Despite this tool-making ability, *H. habilis* apparently had a small brain capacity, ranging from 40 to 61 cubic inches (650 to 1,000 cubic cm), according to most estimates.

See also: *HOMO ERECTUS* (Vol. I); *HOMO SAPIENS* (Vol. I).

Homo sapiens

Term used by scientists to describe the most evolved members of the Homindae family, which closely resemble modern human beings. *Homo sapiens* (*H. sapiens*) had the largest brain capacity of all recovered hominids, measuring 79 to 85 cubic inches (1,300 to 1,400 cm). This is a close comparison to modern-day humans, whose brain capacity measures roughly 88 cubic inches (1,450 cubic cm).

H. sapiens, which means "wise," lived in tropical Africa some 100,000 to 200,000 years ago. The earliest known example of *Homo sapiens*, dating back approximately 60,000 years, was found in the Dire Dawa region of ETHIOPIA. *H. sapiens* were believed to have traveled over a wide terrain, leading some scientists to theorize that members of *H. sapiens* eventually colonized other parts of the world. Generations of adaptation, according to some theories, would have caused differences in skin color and appearance between these migrating *H. sapiens* and their African ancestors.

See also: *HOMO ERECTUS* (Vol. I); *HOMO SAPIENS* (Vol. I).

Horemheb

(c. 1348–1320 BCE) *Thirteenth and last king of ancient Egypt's Eighteenth Dynasty.*

Horemheb became pharaoh after the death of AY, who died without an heir. A general, Horemheb had risen through the ranks of the Egyptian army, having served under the pharaohs AMENHOTEP III, AKHENATEN, and TUTANKHAMUN. Horemheb's wife, Mutnodjme (Mudnodjme), may have been the sister of Akhenaten's queen, NEFERTITI. If so, this marriage firmly established his link to the royal family.

The main thrust of Horemheb's rule was the restoration of traditional Egyptian religion, law, and order. Seeing himself as the rightful successor to Amenhotep III, the last pharaoh before the ARMANA PERIOD, Horemheb sought to erase the memory of the four pharaohs who preceded him, all of whom he believed to be connected to the cult of ATEN. Abolishing the changes and reforms instituted under Akhenaten, Horemheb firmly reestablished devotion to Egypt's old gods, restoring old temples and building many new monuments in the process. Horemheb's death marked the end of the Eighteenth Dynasty.

Horn of Africa

Term used to describe the odd-shaped "horn" jutting out along Africa's northeastern coast on the RED SEA.

According to some historians, the Horn was the fabled Land of PUNT that figured prominently in the history of ancient Egypt and which was visited by Egypt's Queen Hatshepsut. Other sources indicate that trade in a variety of goods, including frankincense and myrrh, flourished at the port of Zelia, on the Horn, as early as the sixth century CE.

Much of the land of the Horn is characterized as dry or even arid, forming a semi-desert covering almost 23,000 square miles (59,570 sq km). Its mountainous terrain includes Africa's third-highest mountain, Ras Dashan, which measures 14,000 feet (4,270 m). Nearby Dijoubuti represents Africa's lowest point, at 455 feet (140 m) above sea level. With one of Africa's longest coastlines, the Horn has the continent's largest area of geological rifting. (Rifting occurs when shifts of the earth, over time, form deep valleys.)

horse

Many historians believe horses were first introduced to Africa from Asia as long ago as the time of the HYSKOS, who invaded and conquered EGYPT c.1650 BCE. Although it is unclear precisely when horses were first used in battle, images and skeletal remains of horses have been linked to Egypt's NEW KINGDOM (c. 1550–1070/69 BCE). This suggests that horses played a role in Egypt's war of liberation against the Hyskos. Exactly what that role was, however, is not certain. The iron bits, bridles, saddles, and stirrups unearthed in recent excavations, for example, would have allowed riders to control a horse while simultaneously using weapons. However, it also is possible that, since horses were considered a powerful symbol of prestige, they initially may have been used only for hunting or for pulling chariots. Regardless of their precise military role, though, it is clear that horses were used in the Saharan trade caravans before being replaced by camels.

By the first millennium BCE, horses had become a valuable trade item and were widely used in both the MAGHREB and the kingdom of KUSH (Nubia). The geographer Strabo (c. 22 CE) detailed battles in which mounted warriors fought on horseback with javelins, describing the horses as small but spirited and tractable. According to Strabo, the horses wore cotton or hair collars, from which hung a lead rein. Some of these horses, Strabo continued, were so well-trained that they followed the warriors like pet dogs, without even being led.

See also: CAVALRY (Vol. II); DOMESTIC ANIMALS (Vol. II).

Horus Ancient Egyptian sky god, important for the pharaohs' claim to be his earthly embodiment.

In Egyptian mythology, Horus was generally known as the son of OSIRIS and ISIS and was represented by a falcon or a falcon-headed man. The Sun and the Moon were thought to be his eyes. In predynastic times, the followers of Horus invaded EGYPT, and he was venerated as a triumphant warlord. Horus also was an important part of the state religion. As a result, many pharaohs took on his name.

Horus is believed to be a synthesis of two earlier deities, Horus the Child and Horus the Elder. As Horus the Child, Horus was often depicted as a child suckling at the breast of his mother, Isis, which may have inspired the more modern image of the Madonna and Christ Child. As Horus the Elder, he avenged the death of his father, Osiris, against the evil SETH. Horus lost his left eye in the eighty-year battle, but he eventually rallied to defeat Seth and victoriously unite UPPER and LOWER EGYPT. The image of the eye of Horus, a human eye combined with falcon markings, became a powerful Egyptian amulet.

human origins The commencement of the existence of humans; generally believed to have taken place on the continent of Africa.

In 1974, archaeologists working in the region of Hadar, ETHIOPIA, discovered the 3.18-million-year-old remains of a woman. "Lucy," as the woman was called, provides strong evidence of a common human ancestry originating in Africa. Skeletal remains, rocks, and fossils also have been uncovered in Africa's Great RIFT VALLEY—some dating back 5 million years—that help support this theory.

Olduvai One of the most important sites in paleoarchaeology, OLDUVAI GORGE is located near Lake Eyasi in the north-central part of what is now Tanzania. Located in the area of the Great Rift Valley, the gorge is 9 miles (14.5 km) long and 330 feet (100.6 m) deep and exposes a virtual timeline of prehistory in nearly 2 million years of sedimentary rock. Excavation of the rock layers has revealed the fossilized remains of many ancient hominids, including *AUSTRALOPITHECUS*, *HOMO HABILIS*, and *HOMO ERECTUS*. The discoveries made there, most anthropologists agree, established the African origins of all humankind.

A family of English archaeologists, the LEAKEYS, is largely responsible for Olduvai's fame. Between the 1930s and the 1960s, Louis Leakey unearthed a number of stone tools of the OLDOWAN tradition. His wife, Mary Leakey, was the first to find a hominid fossil in the gorge, a 1.75-million-year-old *Australopithecus boisei* that was unearthed in 1959. Since then, Olduvai Gorge has yielded many fossilized skeletal remains, including some dating back 700,000 to 1.8 million years.

Kenya Evidence of early human presence, including fossils of *Homo erectus* and *Homo habilis*, has also been discovered in modern-day Kenya. Western Kenya, in particular, where sedimentary deposits have been dated back 12, 14, and even 20 million years, has been a major source of information about the course of human evolution.

In 1972, for example, a hominid skull was unearthed at Koobi Fora, a sand spit east of Lake Turkana in the northern part of the country. Discovered by Bernard Ngeneo—a member of a team of researchers led by the famous paleoarchaeologist Richard Leakey—the skull was identified as belonging to *Homo habilis* and was dated as being from 1.8 to 1.9 million years old. Designated "1470" for its museum accession number, it has proven a controversial find because its discovery suggests that many types of hominids apparently coexisted in East Africa for many millennia, a fact that makes it hard to delineate any clear path of human evolution.

An even more famous Kenyan hominid specimen was found in 1984 by Kimoya Kimeu, the foreman of another Leakey-led team, this one working at Nariokotome on the western shore of Lake Turkana. The TURKANA BOY, as the discovery was called, represents one of the most complete fossil hominid skeletons ever found. Living approximately 1.6 million years ago, the Turkana Boy was a *Homo erectus* of about twelve years of age. Analysis of the bones has led archaeologists to conclude that a mature *Homo erectus* would have been about six feet tall and would have boasted a large brain.

Botswana A lime quarry at Taung, in modern Botswana, revealed one of the earliest glimpses of the extended human family tree in the form of a small skull, its braincase intact. Found in 1924, it was identified as belonging to a young hominid, an *AUSTRALOPITHECUS AFRICANUS*—a new species of upright-walking, intelligent hominid. The TAUNG CHILD, as the discovery was called, was not accepted by the scientific community until additional Australopithecus finds were made in the 1960s.

It is believed that the area's three modern rivers—the Zambezi, Okavango, and Chobe—once formed a single mighty river, which is thought to have flowed across an arid, desertlike northern Botswana. When this river divided, it apparently formed the Okavango Delta, which is the world's largest inland river delta. There, archaeologists have found parts of heavy-duty stone picks and axes, which constitute evidence that tool-making hominid inhabitants were present in the delta somewhere between 200,000 and 600,000 years ago.

Further reading: Brian M. Fagan, ed., *The Oxford Companion to Archeology* (New York: Oxford University Press, 1966); Richard Milner, *The Encyclopedia of Evolution* (New York: Facts On File, 1991).

hunter-gatherers Term used to characterize societies whose main form of sustenance is derived from a combination of hunting, fishing, and the collection of wild plant foods grown in nature

Hunter-gatherer societies were widespread on the African continent for thousands of years. Until about 3,000 years ago, southern Africans depended exclusively on hunting and gathering. Many groups lived nomadic lifestyles, tracking game animals and fresh sources of food. They gradually lost most of their land and livelihood to pastoralists, gardeners, and farmers. The remaining bands were, by and large, eventually assimilated into neighboring populations. Today, relatively few African peoples survive primarily as hunter-gatherers, and much of what is known about hunter-gatherer societies of the past is based on observations made during historic times. The largest and best-known such population today are the KHOISAN of the arid Kalahari region in southern Africa.

Hunter-Gatherers in Prehistory Pre-human populations subsisted in Africa by means of hunting and gathering millions of years ago. Fossil finds uncovered in Bouri, ETHIOPIA, during the 1990s indicate that by 2.5 million years ago hominids were already using stone tools to carve meat and scrape bone marrow. The increase in protein and fat provided by a carnivorous diet may have been a factor in the evolution of bigger brains and longer legs in protohuman populations. Paleolithic evidence remains scarce for the evolutionary period during which the genus *Homo* and the human species emerged in Africa.

Southern African hunter-gatherers have dwelled continuously in the Kalahari region since at least 9000 BCE. Although the area is now desertlike, there have been relatively wet periods over the past 11,000 years. Even today, although surface moisture is rare, water trapped below the surface of the absorbent sand sustains hardy species of plant life, including grasses, thornbushes, and fruit-bearing trees. The vegetation is thus highly resistant to drought and provides fodder for many animals, including large antelopes. The combination of edible plant life and game animals has enabled nomadic hunter-gatherers to survive in the arid climate for many generations.

Tools and Weapons Archaeological research reveals that around 8000 BCE, hunter-gatherers in Africa had developed sophisticated means of acquiring food. At Gwisho springs in Zambia's central Kafue Valley, the moist soil has preserved many tools and artifacts, some of which date from circa 2000 BCE and demonstrate the successful adaptation of hunter-gatherers in the region. Microlithic blade technology was in use across vast areas of savanna and forest throughout sub-Saharan Africa. In the drier climates, rock paintings and carvings on cave walls have been preserved from ancient times. Many of these artworks, created using paints mixed from animal fat, vegetable dyes, and ochres, depict beasts of prey and scenes of hunting and fishing. However, in the northern part of southern Africa, there are few paintings, and no Kalahari SAN people are known to have made rock art in historic times.

In heavily forested regions, a variety of weapons—from axes and spears to dug-out pits and trap lines—were employed from the Middle STONE AGE and into the Late STONE AGE. In the savanna grasslands during the Late Stone Age, prolific hunters killed animals of all sizes with the bow and arrow, as well as multipronged spears fashioned from carefully hewn microliths attached to shafts of wood. Arrowheads of stone or bone were tipped with slow-acting poisons. With this technology, small, highly mobile hunting parties could track and bring down large, fast-moving, far-ranging ungulates such as antelope and buffalo. Small game could be caught in traps, nets, and snares, or tracked with DOGS and clubbed. Reptiles and bird eggs also provided a source of food. In the swampy Okavango of the northern Kalahari, fishing, rather than game hunting, was a mainstay of subsistence.

In addition to meat, one of the main by-products of hunting was bones, which were made into tools, weapons, and ornaments. Skins were another by-product, and hides were scraped with stones, treated to become soft, and made into such useful items as clothes, house-coverings, and carrying bags.

The Gatherers Gathered plant and animal foods were an important part of the human diet. Far less ancient vegetal material has survived as evidence than the more durable stone and bone, but, as an example, hunter-gatherers living today depend upon gathered foods for more than half of their nutritional needs. The !KUNG obtained as much as 80% of their food supply from plants, which despite being seasonal, are more abundant and reliable sources of food. While men were most likely the primary hunters, ranging far afield in pursuit of game, gathering was principally the job of women, who also had to care for the young. The gatherers' principal tools were sharpened digging sticks and carrying bags. They picked fruits, berries, and melons and dug tubers and edible roots. Women also caught insects such as caterpillars, locusts, and termites, providing a highly concentrated source of nourishment.

Social and Political Organization The typical political organization of early hunter-gatherer bands was probably loosely stratified, with a relatively undefined social hierarchy compared to later settled populations. The predominant forms of social organization among hunter-gatherer bands have sometimes been characterized as communal, reflecting the loose hierarchy and mobility which would allow small, kin-based groups to remain flexible and highly adaptive to the challenge of environmental conditions. Even today, for example, MBUTI and others living in the rain forests of central Africa maintain few material possessions and do not greatly value private individual ownership. Their hunting territories are strictly defined, however.

Researchers have inferred much about ancient African hunter-gatherer populations from the practices of surviving groups in the Kalahari. Much of this information is drawn from field studies carried out during the 1950s and 1960s. In the past, these peoples were often thought to have descended from refugees fleeing other regions. However, the combined evidence of archaeology, historical linguistics, and the highly developed degree of adaptation of these peoples show that they have occupied the Kalahari for millennia. Likewise, the societies, cultures, and ways of life of these peoples were thought to have undergone little change over the centuries. More recent archaeological and historical studies, though, indicate that contact with herders and farmers has been influential for the past 2,000 years.

Names and Languages Outsiders referred to these hunter-gatherer groups by a variety of generalized names, none of which reflected historical ethnic origins or the self-descriptions of local and kin groups. BANTU-speaking agriculturalists referred to the hunter-gatherer peoples as Sarwa (or Twa); Khoekhoen herders living to the north knew them as the SAN (or Sonqua); later European settlers called them Bushmen. The latter name, originally meaning simply "those without cattle or other domesticated livestock," became a derogatory term in the context of the racialized social politics of modern southern Africa. Today the preferred term for the hunter-gatherer peoples of the Kalahari is *San*, a word taken from the Nama language and whose original meaning is obscure. Anthropologists have created a general term, *Khoisan*, to describe the peoples of the Kalahari, who are descended from the historical intermingling of Khoekhoen (Khoi-khoi, or Hottentot) herders and San hunter-gatherers.

Southern African hunter-gatherers spoke a great many different languages. For the most part, these fall into three major language families, nearly all distinguished by the use of "clicks." Cultural differences among modern populations, such as those found between the !Kung in the northwest of southern Africa and their neighbors, suggest that hunter-gatherer societies as a whole were heterogeneous and diverse. Following the introduction of herding, strict divisions between hunter-gatherer societies and pastoralists may not have always existed.

The unusual symbols and letter patterns in the names of the !Kung, /Gui, //Gana, Kxoe, //Ng-!Ke, and /'Auni languages and dialects stand for clicks. The Khoisan family of languages employs three kinds of clicks, almost always as the beginning consonant of a word. These are an ingressive click, for which air rushes into the mouth; an egressive click, for which air rushes out of the mouth; and a labial click, made with the closing of the lips, which sounds like a kiss.

Staple Foods and Diet Studies of Kalahari hunter-gatherers in historic times paint a somewhat different picture than the familiar image of a society of big-game hunters. Although large antelopes were hunted, most meat came from such smaller game as hares, ostriches, guinea fowl, porcupines, and small antelope breeds. In fact, meat provided a relatively small part of the food supply. Gathered foods were the true staples of these peoples' diets. Throughout the Kalahari edible plant foods included the fruit of the BAOBAB tree, sour plum, and a variety of other species. In addition, the !Kung lived in an area where the nutritious mongongo nut grew in abundance.

The chief significance of hunting in Kalahari societies was as a source of status and prestige. Hunters marked their arrows for easy identification, and the kill belonged to the hunter whose arrow first struck the felled beast. He was the one responsible for dividing up the spoils, following strict rules in distributing the meat to the network of kin who made up the band. Everyone received a share and no one ate alone, although the parents of the victorious hunter's wife were favored.

Large animals were butchered by men in the field for easier transport, and women did the cooking. Unlike meat, plant foods were relatively abundant and did not have to be shared beyond the immediate family.

In the dry southern regions of the Kalahari, melons and roots were an important source of water. CALABASHES and ostrich eggshells were hung in trees to collect water during the rainy season. Later in the year, groundwater was extracted through sucking tubes. Winter droughts often forced people to move near the few underground springs, even though such sources were still in a relatively dry state.

Nomadic and Settled Lifestyles The scarcity of water and edible plants enforced a regime of movement throughout extensive and well-defined territories of the Kalahari. The !Xo of the dry southern desert remained on the move throughout the year, pausing in their annual rounds only for the boys' puberty ceremonies in the fall. In the central savanna, //Gana and /Gui peoples came together and collected water during the brief rainy season before dispersing. In the western central Kalahari, the Nharo people enjoyed a more abundant water supply and consequently lived in larger and more stable settlements. In the Upper Karoo region, hunter-gatherers known as /Xam camped on hilltops and followed game animals. Prior to colonial contact and Dutch settlement, hunter-gatherers whom the Khoekhoen called the Soaqua inhabited the coastline of the western Cape. They ate shellfish and fish, game animals, ostrich eggs, and tortoises as well as plants. The Soaqua often used caves, generally located at a high elevation, for shelter from the elements; these caves also gave them a panoramic view of the land. The Soaqua may also have gone on seasonal migrations for hunting purposes.

Bands and individuals, as well as family units, interacted frequently, visiting their neighbors for extended periods. Individuals also could move between bands, which, therefore, were often in flux as corporate entities. Ties of marriage and fictive kinship were built up, facilitating a high degree of social mobility among bands and providing networks for the common sharing of water and other resources in times of scarcity. Families lived in semicircular thatched shelters of branches and twigs. Campfires were central gathering places, with families moving from one hearth to another in ritualized visitation rounds. Marriages were usually arranged between members of different bands. Although POLYGAMY occurred, it was rarely practiced, since there was a shortage of marriageable females and few men could afford to support more than one wife.

The highly mobile, nomadic lifestyle of most southern hunter-gatherers meant that few material goods or possessions were kept, and manufacturing was kept to a minimum. Houses were temporary shelters that were abandoned when people broke camp. Personal items were limited. In addition to clothing, tools, weapons, fire drills, and implements for food gathering and processing, southern African hunter-gatherers made musical instruments, pipes, boxes, and other items of wood, bone, shell, and stone. Later, metal obtained in trade was used for knives and blades.

Clothing and Dress Typical animal-skin clothing in the Kalahari consisted of loincloths for men and aprons for women. Women also wore cloaks that doubled as slings for carrying babies and for collecting foodstuffs or firewood. Some groups made skin hats and leather sandals. Children's clothing, although varied, was typically patterned after adult garments.

Ornaments were worn by men, women, and children. Small disks made of ostrich eggshell were strung into necklaces and waistbands or sewn onto headpieces and clothing. Other decorative wear was made of roots, seeds, reeds, and animal horn. Young women powdered their hair. They also painted their faces with either red ochre or a mixture of crushed wood and animal fat. Women in particular bore ornamental tattoos—made by rubbing ash into cuts in the skin—on the face, buttocks, and thighs. Men received scarification marks at the time of their initiation into adult status; facial tattoos were earned through successful hunting.

The Khoisan People Today Today, most Khoisan people in the Kalahari are adapted to herding and agriculture, with only about 5 percent subsisting primarily by hunting and gathering. Most of the previous hunter-gatherer populations have been decimated by disease, assimilation, poverty, economic dependency, and the encroachment of others on their former lands. In Botswana and Namibia, small reserves of land have been set aside for Khoisan people living a traditional lifestyle, but these modern hunter-gatherers live under the constant threat of losing their remaining territory.

Hutu (Bahutu, Wahutu)

BANTU-speaking people who have long inhabited a region of present-day BURUNDI and Rwanda. Believed to have entered the area around the first century, the Hutu encountered and overcame the small-statured hunters of the TWA ethnic group. The Hutu brought with them a way of life dedicated to small-scale farming and cattle herding. Their social structure involved into a CLAN system, with *bahinzas* (petty kings) ruling small regions.

See also: HUTU (Vols. II, III).

Hyksos

Foreign invaders who occupied EGYPT in the seventeenth century BCE.

Little is known about either the origins of the group of Asians known as the Hyksos or about the way they conquered large parts of Egypt. The most common assumption is that the Hyksos dominated Egypt by military force, although political control is another possibility.

Under Hyksos rule, Egypt seemed to have enjoyed peace and prosperity. The Hyksos respected the native religions, mainained ancient Egyptian as the official language, and allowed many Egyptians to serve at high levels of government. Although later Egyptians depicted the period of Hyksos rule as one of chaos and misery, there were indisputable technological advances during the era, including the use of both copper and bronze. The Hyksos were also the most likely source of many new tools and weapons, including both horses and war chariots.

Hyksos rule in Egypt enabled KUSH to gain its independence. After a century of Hyksos rule, the southern Egyptian city of Thebes asserted its independence. The war that resulted led to the expulsion of the Hyksos in 1567 BCE.

Hyrax Hill

Archaeological site located near Lake Nakuru in west-central Kenya. The hill, which lies in Kenya's portion of the Great RIFT VALLEY, is about 3 miles (4.8 km) from Lake Nakuru and stands about 300 feet (91 m) above the lake level. In 1926, famed paleontologist Louis LEAKEY first observed evidence of prehistoric life in Hyrax Hill. Leakey's wife and fellow paleontologist, Mary Leakey, began excavating the site in 1937. Her excavations revealed a STONE AGE site that included a walled enclosure and a burial mound. In total, there are three separate sites, the oldest dating back 3,000 years and the most recent from two or three centuries ago.

I

Ibo (Igbo) People living chiefly in southeastern Nigeria who speak Igbo, a language of the Kwa branch of the Niger-Congo family.

There is little agreement among historians about the origins of the Ibo people. One school of thought sees Ibo culture as a development of the Nok, Ife, and Benin cultures. Another widely accepted view is that the Ibo originally migrated southward from EGYPT. Dates for the Ibo's arrival in the area of Nigeria vary widely, from the early common era to the eighth or fifteenth centuries CE.

See also: BENIN (Vol. II); IBO (Vols. II, III); IFE (Vol. II); NIGER-CONGO (Vol. II); NOK CULTURE (Vol. I).

idolatry Worship of drawn, carved, sculpted, or painted images representing religious figures, legends, and myths.

The religions of ancient Africa often relied on images to teach and maintain cultural traditions. This frequently was accomplished by the appearance of religious images on such everyday objects as coins, jewelry, weapons, tools, and buildings. Egyptians and Nubians, in particular, were noted for such art, which included representations of the Egyptian moon god Khonsu, the sky goddess Nut (who sometimes was portrayed as a cow), and APEDEMAK, the Nubian lion god.

See also: ART (Vol. I); EGYPT (Vol. I); NUBIA (Vol. I); RELIGION, TRADITIONAL (Vol. I).

Ifa YORUBA divination system made up of a series of verses that are chanted to drive away evil.

Ifa was an ancient divination system practiced by the Yoruba people of southwestern Nigeria. The Ifa system was a series of verses that were chanted to alleviate a client's suffering. In it, a learned Yoruba priest appealed to the gods by reciting the verses that fit the sufferer's needs. The verses applied to all aspects of life, from physical ailments to natural disasters, and they served to encourage the ideal tribal life by supporting the accumulation of wealth, wives, and children. These materialistic goals helped instill an entrepreneurial spirit within the community. Through the Ifa chantings (a single chanting could last several hours), an individual was believed to directly connect with the gods.

The Yoruba people originally supported a pantheistic society. The Yoruba believed that mankind originated in Ife (ILE-IFE), a sacred city that supposedly arose when one of the gods turned water into land. As the first Yoruba city, Ife was the center of Ifa divination. At the height of its influence from the eleventh to fifteenth centuries, Ife was the focal point for surrounding kingdoms. Neighboring kingdoms even sent their deceased rulers to be buried in the sacred town.

Ifa, the divination god, was the backbone of the Yoruba divination system. During a ceremony, a Yoruba priest called on Ifa with an ivory tapper (*iroke-Ifa*). Sixteen sacred palm nuts were tossed onto a dusted divination board (*opon Ifa*). The Yoruba priest then studied the pattern left in the dust to determine which verses to recite. The process was repeated until the priest had a complete message to chant.

According to Yoruba belief, Eshu-Elegba, the messenger god, delivered the divine messages chanted by Yoruba priests to the gods. Eshu's image was used extensively in Ifa art, particularly on divination boards and bowls. His hair was always depicted half-shaved to symbolize his friendship with Ifa.

Yoruba priests shaved their heads to honor Eshu and to symbolize the beginning of an initiation ceremony. Other Yoruba shaved their heads for ceremonies, believing that spirits entered a person through the head.

During an Ifa ceremony, a Yoruba priest carried a special iron staff that symbolized his power over death. A cock was often sacrificed and tied to the staff because the Yoruba believed that the screams of the birds tricked the gods into believing that a person has been sacrificed, thus avoiding human death. This Ifa staff was believed to protect the priest and the sufferer during the ceremony.

See also: IFA (Vol. III); IFE (Vol. II); YORUBA (Vol. II).

Further reading: E. Bolaji Idowu, *African Traditional Relgion: A Definition* (Maryknoll, N.Y.: Orbis Books, 1973); Benjamin C. Ray, *African Religions: Symbol, Ritual, and Community* (Upper Saddle River N.J.: Prentice-Hall, 2000).

Ile-Ife

Ile-Ife Yoruba city in the southwestern part of modern-day Nigeria; also known as Ife and Ife-Lodun. Probably the oldest center occupied by the Yoruba people, Ile-Ife dates back 1,000 years or more. Excavations at the site have revealed Ile-Ife to have been, even in its early days, a remarkably urbanized community. This has led some historians to theorize that Ile-Ife's first settlers, who supposedly immigrated there from the north, had experience with living in towns or even larger communities.

See also: ILE-IFE (Vol. II); YORUBA (Vol. II).

Imhotep

Imhotep (fl. c. 2650 BCE) *Vizier of the pharaoh Djoser; recognized as a deity during the Third Dynasty of ancient Egypt's Old Kingdom.*

One of the few Egyptian gods other than the pharaohs who was a real person, Imhotep was a priest, scribe, poet, doctor, and a founder of the Egyptian studies of astronomy and architecture. As the vizier of King Djoser (r. 2630-2611 BCE), Imhotep also was skilled in a wide variety of royal enterprises and administration.

As an architect, Imhotep is best known for designing the STEP PYRAMID OF DJOSER at SAQQARA. Located near MEMPHIS, the step pyramid is known as the first human-made structure to be fashioned entirely of stone. The pyramid was intended to be a tomb for Djoser, but it ultimately inspired a style of architecture that embodied the spiritual ideas of the Egyptian people. Containing temples, pavilions, corridors, chapels, halls, and storerooms, the pyramid also was distinguished by fluted columns attached to its limestone walls, a clear link with ancient styles of Egyptian architecture.

Imhotep was first honored as a god during the OLD KINGDOM because of his wisdom and his work as a scribe. Later, during the NEW KINGDOM, scribes venerated Imhotep as the patron of scribes, pouring out a few drops of water as an offering to him before beginning to write.

During the Late Dynastic Period, Imhotep was fully recognized as a god. He was associated with the god THOTH and seen as a patron of medicine. Anyone—god or man—who suffered with pain was thought to be tended to by Imhotep, and feats of miraculous healing were attributed to him. This led the Greeks eventually to identify Imhotep with Asclepius, their god of medicine.

A small temple of Imhotep was built on the Island of Philae during the Ptolemaic Period (c. 332–44 BCE). The Roman emperors Claudius and Tiberius commissioned praises to Imhotep that were inscribed on the walls of their Egyptian temples. In art, Imhotep was represented as a seated priest with a shaved head holding a papyrus roll. At times he was shown without divine insignias, clothed in the garb of an archaic priest.

initiation rites

initiation rites Culturally based practices designed to introduce adolescents to the values, history, and social guidelines of their societies. Many of these practices date back to ancient times, and a number of them survived, in one form or another, well into the modern era.

In Africa, the initiation of the young has always represented an important vehicle for passing on knowledge about community affairs, economics, religion, and such social responsibilities as courtship, sexuality, marriage, and childbirth. Male and female elders were usually assigned the task of directing or participating in specific initiation activities. These activities were drawn from elements of nature, song and dance, morality tales, ORAL TRADITIONS, and ritual objects to create a learning experience. The length of the actual ceremonies varied, with some lasting a day and other, more complex rites lasting months or even years. Researchers have noted three common themes in many initiations: The first was separation from the community and familiar surroundings; the second was a period of seclusion; and the third, or final, step involved integration or rebirth within the initiate's community.

For many adolescent girls, initiation often began with the onset of menstruation. The Akan of GHANA, for example, held a sacred feast for young women. It included libations and prayers designed to invoke protective guidance and future fertility. The young initiates remained with older female adults for a specified period in order to learn about taboos, sexuality, marriage, diet, and other social responsibilities. In contrast, young women of the Nandi society in Kenya traditionally underwent rigorous training, including the symbolic cutting of firewood, spirited dancing, and, ultimately, female CIRCUMCISION.

Many societies regard the initiation of young men as a test of strength. The Nbemdu of ANGOLA traditionally called their initiation *mukanda.* A rite that sometimes lasted several months, it included feasting, song and dance, and sexual freedom. The young men were taken to a special site known as "the place of dying," a symbolic metaphor for the loss of their youth. After they were circumcised and forced to endure physical ordeals and verbal abuse, they were formally educated in the ways of adult males. They then returned to their villages wearing white clay masks to symbolize the process of rebirth. There they performed the dance of war for public recognition of their adult status.

See also: AGE GRADES (Vol. I); EGYPT (Vol. I); OLD KINGDOM (Vol. I); SECRET SOCIETIES (Vol. I); RITES OF PASSAGE (Vol. I); WOMEN IN ANCIENT AFRICA (Vol. I).

Further reading: John S. Mbiti, *African Religion and Philosophy,* 2nd ed. (Oxford, Eng.: Heinemann Educational Publishers, 1989); Paul Spencer, "Age, Aging and Age Organization," in John Middleton, ed., *Encyclopedia of Africa South of the Sahara*, Vol. 1, (New York: Charles Scribner's Sons, 1997).

ink Fluid or paste first used for writing and drawing in ancient Africa c. 2500 BCE. The Egyptians were among the earliest people to use ink, reed pens, and brushes for writing. One of the oldest sources for ink was the cuttlefish, which was fairly common in the MEDITERRANEAN SEA. Sometime later, the Egyptians began to use colored dyes such as indigo, white lead, charcoal, and soot. They, and later the Ethiopians, used specially designated colors to honor the gods mentioned in sacred texts. Other sources for making ink included extracts from juices, plants, and minerals. After it was molded and dried into sticks or small cakes, lampblack mixed with glue or gum was also used.

Ink and PAPYRUS were used to create the early form of books known as *papyrus rolls.* Papyrus comes from a reed-like plant found in the marshes of the NILE VALLEY and NILE DELTA regions. The ancient Egyptians sliced these stalks into thin sections. Then they laid them side-by-side and pressed them into sheets approximately 5 to 6 inches (12 cm to 15 cm) wide. When the sheets were dried in the sun, they achieved a paperlike consistency. Although seemingly fragile, many papyrus documents were preserved beneath Egypt's hot desert sands for more than 4,000 years.

See also: EGYPT (Vol. I); ETHIOPIA (Vol. I).

Inscription of Mes Inscription on the walls of a tomb at SAQQARA that details the court records of a land dispute fought over several generations during the thirteenth century BCE. The inscription was carved to prove the legal right, by inheritance, to the land in question. It also provides evidence of the substantial legal rights of ancient Egyptian women, showing that they had the right to administer property, to serve as witnesses before a court of law, to file lawsuits, and to appeal court rulings.

The subject of the inscription, Mes, was a descendant of Neshi, an Egyptian admiral whom King AHMOSE I had rewarded with a large tract of land south of MEMPHIS. Before he died, Neshi insisted that the land never be divided, decreeing that his heirs (and their heirs) would hold joint ownership and share in the income generated by the land, but that it would be under the management of a single heir who would act as trustee.

Mes's descendants, however, eventually separated into two branches, with one branch of the family eventually being, in effect, disinherited from both trusteeship and joint ownership. During the reign of King HOREMHEB, however, Werenra, a woman from the disenfranchised branch of Neshi's family, filed suit in the high court of the vizier, one of the king's highest civil officials. As a result, she won back both trusteeship and joint ownership.

Werenra's sister, Takharu, later sued to demand division of the estate among six heirs. After the vizier decided in Takharu's favor, Werenra and her son Hui appealed this verdict, which, after many years, finally was overturned. Eventually, the position of trustee was inherited by Hui's wife, Nubnefret.

Nubnefret's right to the position, though, was challenged by Khay, a member of the rival branch of the family. Falsely claiming that his trusteeship had been taken from him by Hui and Nubnefret, Khay bribed a court official to forge tax records supporting his claim. With the help of this evidence, Khay won the case. Nubnefret's son, Mes, however, reappealed to the vizier. Producing the authentic tax records as well as witnesses who testified to his family's long trusteeship, Mes won a reversal, settling the case once and for all.

Iron Age Period in ancient times during which iron was the primary metal used for weapons, tools, and other implements. For many years, it has been widely believed that the earliest human use of iron was by the HITTITES of ancient Turkey, who passed their knowledge of ironworking to the Assyrians who, in turn, used iron weapons to help create an empire stretching from EGYPT to India. Ironworking was also practiced by the PHOENICIANS, whose North African colony of CARTHAGE lay in what is now TUNISIA. It was, according to this view, extensive trade with Libyans, Algerians, and Moroccons that was most likely responsible for carrying Phoenician iron technology to western Sudan and sub-Saharan Africa.

Elsewhere in Africa, ironworking flourished in AKSUM, NUBIA, and, in particular, KUSH. Of all these ancient peoples, the Kushites were the most notable ironworkers, and their capital city of MEROË was a center of ancient iron technology. Even today, tall mounds of iron slag—the dirt removed from iron during the smelting process—can be found among the ruins of Meroë, testimony to the major role ironworking played in Meroitic culture. Meroitic ironwork was especially important in the creation of weaponry, with which the Kushite armies were able to conquer Egypt c. 750 BCE. Kush's domination of Egypt lasted until the Assyrian invasion of 660 BCE.

Recent discoveries have shown that, contrary to some long-held theories, sub-Saharan Africans developed metalworking technology at a very early stage in history. By about 1400 BCE, for example, East Africans were already producing steel in carbon furnaces, even though steel was not invented in western Europe until the eighteenth century CE. Iron technology, however, spread slowly across Africa, and it was not until the first century CE that the smelting of iron began to rapidly diffuse throughout the continent.

One of the main instruments for spreading iron technology was the BANTU migration, which carried Bantu iron-smelting techniques across southern Africa. Proficiency with the production of iron weapons made it possible for the Bantu migrants to subjugate most of the indigenous peoples with whom they came in contact in southern Africa. As a result, the natives of the newly found areas were assimilated into Bantu culture or exterminated. Once assimilated, these peoples became proficient in making iron tools and weapons for themselves, enabling many to develop agricultural communities.

In time, the use of iron became widespread in sub-Saharan Africa. During the first millennium, for example, the people of what eventually became the kingdom of GHANA used iron weapons to gain prominence in West Africa. The use of iron farming tools gave them agricultural superiority over their neighbors as well. No evidence of widespread ironworking within Ghana itself has been found, however; a fact that leads most archeologists and historians to believe that Ghana used its well-known gold supplies to purchase iron weapons and tools from Saharan traders to the north and east.

Elsewhere, the people of the Nok culture, located in the northern area of what is now Nigeria, were smelting iron by 500 CE. Ironwork has been known among the Haya people of western Tanzania for even longer, possibly, it is believed, for at least two thousand years.

irrigation System of applying water to land in order to aid AGRICULTURE; invented by the ancient Egyptians, c. 5000 BCE.

Before the invention of irrigation, people typically gathered food as it grew in the wild. By about 5000 BCE, however, irrigation techniques were being used along the NILE RIVER. The Nile was particularly well-suited to this since the course of the river runs from south to north at an angle of 5 inches per mile (12.7 cm/m). In addition, its riverbanks slope downward at a greater angle, allowing for the flooding of the desert on both sides of the river.

As the only source of water in EGYPT, the ancients came to associate the Nile with feast or famine, as the likelihood of one or the other directly depended on a good or poor season of flooding. Irrigation became a necessity, and irrigation systems constructed to help control the water of the Nile led ancient Egyptians to develop such other sciences as surveying, soil classification, and river engineering.

The Nile River would flood each year as a result of the seasonal rains running into the Nile's tributaries—the BLUE NILE, the WHITE NILE, and the ATBARA. From highlands in ETHIOPIA and Lake Victoria in Uganda, the waters would flow into Egypt and flood the Nile River valley. By July, the floodwaters would reach ancient MEMPHIS in Egypt. The high-water peak of the season would be reached in September. In November and December, the water would recede rapidly, reaching its lowest water level sometime between March and May. This seasonal cycle repeated itself for thousands of years until the Aswan Dam was completed in 1970. Its completion finally allowed the flooding of the Nile to be controlled, assuring sufficient water for irrigation and other purposes for both Egypt and the Sudan.

Beginning about 7,000 years ago, Egyptians planted seeds in the mud and dirt left behind when the floodwaters receded. Over time, the Egyptians experimented further with irrigation techniques, and their early techniques led to more sophisticated techniques that were used in Africa until the conquests by the Roman Empire, begining about 30 BCE.

King MENES, the legendary Egyptian ruler who unified UPPER and LOWER EGYPT c. 3000 BCE, was also credited with another irrigation technique, which involved the construction of irrigation canals. According to tradition, he redirected the course of the river and then built the ancient capitol of MEMPHIS on the land where the Nile River had run. By 2000 BCE, after more than a thousand years of developing basin irrigation, both sides of the Nile River formed an intricate pattern of basins, dikes, levees, canals, and sluices.

Under this system, the fields on the Nile floodplain were divided into great basins by earth embankments. The largest basin may have covered as much as 50,000 acres (20,235 ha). A series of high-water canals carried the water from the Nile at flooding time to the basins through a series of dikes, levees, and feeder canals.

The feeder canals connected the river to the basins, typically filling by mid-August, a few weeks before the river crested. After around forty days of filling, the entrance was unblocked, allowing the water to fill the basin. The water soaked the ground and the rich layer of silt and soil from the river settled onto the land. In October, as the Nile floodwaters receded, water was drained out of the basins into discharge canals, which fed the water back to the river.

Planting took place from mid-October to November. Seeds were typically sown directly in the soil, though sometimes, after a poor flooding, fields were ploughed first. The new soil left by the Nile floodwaters usually was wet enough to grow a crop without any other watering. Harvesting took place in March or April. A single crop was generally planted; however, in lower areas of the valley and in basins, where the land remained wet, a second crop could sometimes be planted and harvested.

Ancient Egyptians grew crops of many kinds and had an abundance of food not seen anywhere else in Africa at the time. Among the crops cultivated were grains such as wheat and barley; vegetables such as onions, lettuce and radishes; legumes such as chickpeas, fava beans, and lentils; as well as clover, olives, dates, and figs.

In addition to flooding fields for planting, irrigation was also used to store water in a type of reservoir that could be used to water crops at a later time. In these basins, clay was applied to the top of the soil to prevent the water from being lost into the ground. The *shadoof* was an ancient Egyptian bucket, which was put on a pole with a counterweight; this device allowed for the raising of water from a stream or low area to a higher field. The Archimedes' screw was a type of pump also used for moving water from one place to another.

Drainage was an important part of ancient irrigation, and the Egyptians were known to have built underground drainpipes of COPPER by about 2500 BCE. Some of these pipes were used in pyramids as a type of bathroom for the dead, as Egyptians believed that the deceased had the same needs as the living in their journey from one state of life to the next. The refinement of drainage pipes led Egyptians to produce clay pipes that were used to drain the lower areas of the NILE VALLEY.

Egyptians were not the only Africans using irrigation in ancient times. A civilization of Proto-Saharans, or what is now called the Fertile African Crescent civilization, lived in the highlands of middle Africa c. 4000 BCE across the then-fertile SAHARA. These Proto-Saharans practiced agriculture vigorously, fertilizing the land and using such tools as the hoe. Water storage and irrigation were among the other agricultural methods employed by the Proto-Saharans.

An increase in agriculture, or in the production of food, generally meant an increase in population in the ancient world—as it still does today. A surplus of food often fostered the growth of towns and settlements. The areas of Africa that used irrigation, such as the Nile River valley and the Proto-Saharan settlements, had ample food supplies. As a result, they experienced a growth in population, which led to the development of urban areas and civilization in general. The population of ancient Egypt grew more than anywhere else in Africa, largely due to the abundance of crops harvested along the Nile, where irrigation was used heavily. Those areas of Africa that had not yet discovered irrigation, and where the climate or land didn't lend itself well to farming, experienced little population growth as people continued to hunt and gather for subsistence.

See also: HIGH-WATER CANALIZATION (Vol. I).

Ishango Bone Oldest known mathematical tool, which was found in an ancient mountainside settlement near the Lake Edward region in present-day Uganda and Congo (Kinshasa).

The Ishango Bone is named after the Ishango people, who inhabited the area sometime between the seventh and tenth centuries BCE. Little is known of the Ishango people except that they hunted, fished, and farmed in the area before volcanic eruption destroyed their village.

Although the dates of the Ishango civilization are uncertain, scientists believe the Ishango Bone was made around 8500 BCE. It was originally considered a simple tally record, but recent microscopic analysis has revealed additional notch marks indicating that it may have been used as a lunar calendar. The bone itself has a quartz writing tool at one end, while the body is made of bone etched with three rows of notched marks with each row having its own mathematical significance. The first row is a series of calculations based on the number ten, the second row contains prime numbers between ten and twenty, and the third is a multiplication table.

The Ishango Bone is an important indicator of the scientific progress in Paleolithic Africa. With the advancement of trade among societies, knowledge of mathematics and units of measure became increasingly

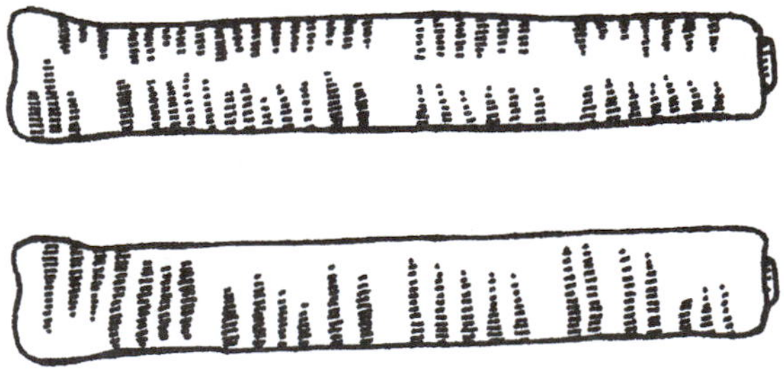

Found in 1960 and dating back to 8500 BCE, the Ishango Bone is the world's oldest mathematical tool. It is kept in the Royal Institute for Natural Sciences in Brussels, Belgium, and can be seen only by special arrangement.

important. Basic mathematical calculations were also used to predict the effects of drought or floods on crop yields. With the discovery of the Ishango Bone, the long-held assumption that African societies were slow to develop mathematical technology has been disproved.

Isis An ancient goddess considered the source of life and divine motherhood. In Egyptian mythology, Isis was considered to be the daughter of the earth god Neb and the sky goddess Nut. The best-known myths about her involve the resurrection of her husband OSIRIS and the virgin birth of her son HORUS. In these, she was best known for finding—and then putting back together—the pieces of her husband's body when he was dismembered by his brother SETH. Over time, the recurring themes of resurrection, virgin birth, and the trinity of Isis, Osiris, and Horus came to influence Christian thought and philosophy.

The earliest religious rituals honoring Isis apparently took place in prehistoric NUBIA among the Anu, an ancient people who inhabited the region that eventually became the Kingdom of MEROË. Even after the establishment of Meroë, the ruling queens of the realm—the KANDAKES—traditionally served as priestesses of Isis.

In EGYPT, worship of Isis dates back to 2500 BCE, and Egypt became a primary site for rites and ceremonies honoring the goddess. It was commonly held by Egyptian pharaohs, for example, that their prosperity stemmed from the NILE RIVER, which they believed to have been formed by the tears Isis shed for her husband. Egyptian worship of Isis reached its peak during the period spanning the Twenty-seventh and Thirtieth Dynasties (525–332 BCE), when worshippers built the great temple at Philae, an island situated in the Nile River.

After Egypt was conquered by the Greeks in 332 BCE, temples devoted to Isis were established in the new city of Alexandria. In time the religion spread beyond North Africa to Greece, where it was known as the Eleusianian Mysteries, and even to Italy, where the remains of an Isis temple have been recovered at the site of the city of Pompeii. By 86 BCE, the worship of Queen Isis had become a cornerstone of Roman religion and remained so until being supplanted by Christianity.

The worship of Isis occurred in many regions of the world, generating hundreds of images of the goddess that reflect distinct cultures. Isis has been shown holding the sistrum, an instrument believed to have originated in NUBIA, as well as both a healing wand and the Egyptian *ankh*, another symbol of life and immortality. In the form of the Black Madonna, images of Isis and the infant Horus have been found in regions as far-flung as Afghanistan, Portugal, northern England, France, and Mexico.

This statue of the goddess Isis, daughter of the earth god Neb and the sky goddess Nut, from the Twenty-sixth Dynasty (1680–1560 BCE) is 35.5 inches (90 cm) high. Cairo Museum, Cairo, Egypt *© Roger Woods/CORBIS*

Further reading: Ean Begg, *The Cult of the Black Virgin.* (London: Arkana Press, 1985); R. E. Witt, *Isis in the Ancient World* (Baltimore, Md.: Johns Hopkins University Press, 1997).

Itjawy Capital of ancient EGYPT at the beginning of the MIDDLE KINGDOM, c. 1991 BCE to 1962 BCE.

Following a brief civil war, Amenemhet, also called Amonemhet, seized power from the reigning king, Mentuhotep III, c. 1991 BCE. He then reunified Egypt under a central government.

Previously a vizier to Mentuhotep III, Amenemhet was an experienced administrator; so when he became king he recognized the advantage of having a more centrally located capital. Thus, he moved the capitol from Thebes to Itjawy (also Itj-towy or Itj-Tawy). Located near the Fayyum Oasis, south of MEMPHIS, and on the border of UPPER EGYPT and LOWER EGYPT, the name of the new capital meant "seizer of" or "one who takes control of two lands." The relocation of the capital ushered in a prosperous and powerful period for Egypt, one that saw a rebirth of art, architecture, and literature.

Ituri forest Dense tropical rain forest in central Africa that is home to two ancient peoples, a BANTU-speaking group of village agriculturalists and the MBUTI, a nomadic HUNTER-GATHERER group once known as PYGMIES. The forest is named for the Ituri River, which flows through it, running east to west.

Though inhabited by the Mbuti for thousands of years, the Ituri forest, which is home to giant hardwood trees that rise to a height of 170 feet (51.8 m), was thought by many people to be completely impenetrable. Walking through the forest is not easy, as the floor contains a thick mass of plants, trees and tree roots, and fallen fruits and nuts. In some areas, the thick tree canopy prevents almost all sunlight from reaching the forest floor. Humid, with a high annual rainfall, the Ituri forest has a wide variety of plants and animals, including the greatest variety of primates of any region in the world. Throughout history, the seeming inhospitable nature of the forest has afforded its inhabitants protection from enemies. Even today, there is no easy access to the forest in the way of improved roads or navigable waterways.

As far back as the Sixth Dynasty, the ancient Egyptians knew of the Mbuti. Pottery of ancient EGYPT shows representations of small-statured people, and Pepi II (c. 2325–2150 BCE) was known to have some of these people living at his court. Four groups of these peoples, collectively known as the Bambuti, still live in Africa today. Though there is not much archaeological evidence of the ancient Mbuti, scholars believe that they have inhabited the Ituri forest since about 2500 BCE, hunting and gathering for subsistence.

Besides the Mbuti, a group of agriculturalists has inhabited the Ituri for at least 2,000 years. Most of these people speak one of the Bantu languages, and traditionally they have lived in small villages, cultivating crops and raising livestock. In parts of the forest, the Mbuti and these agriculturalists trade food and goods with each other and even share languages and customs.

Ivory Coast West African country whose name comes from the region's thriving trade in ivory elephant tusks; also known by its French name: Côte d'Ivoire. Because bones are difficult, if not impossible, to preserve in the region's extremely moist climate, archaeologists have not yet been able to determine exactly when humans first settled the area. However, scraps of tools and weapons that have been found suggest that people were present in great numbers by the upper Paleolithic Age. Traditional accounts note that the first masters of the land were short and bearded —much like the MBUTI of East Africa—who supposedly lived in trees and hunted with spears and arrows. It is theorized that these people are likely to have arrived in the area by the fifth millennium BCE, having been forced from their previous homelands as the Saharan forests began to disappear.

See also: IVORY COAST (Vols. II, III); STONE AGE (Vol. I).

Further reading: H. Sugar, *Côte d'Ivoire* (Santa Barbara: ABC Clio, Inc., 1996).

J

jackal Carnivorous mammal belonging to the same canine family as the DOG, FOX, and wolf. Jackals live in deserts, grasslands, and open brushland, alone, in pairs, or in packs. Jackals are nocturnal animals that sleep during the day in holes or hidden in the brush. Like hyenas, jackals usually feed on the dead carcasses of already hunted animals, although they also prey on rodents and young gazelles. Like coyotes, they howl and yap before their evening hunt. The golden jackal, found in Northeast Africa, usually hunts in small packs. The black-backed jackal and side-striped jackals are found on southern and eastern Africa. The black-backed jackal is red with a black back. The side-striped jackal is gray with with a stripe on its sides.

Perhaps because they scavenge dead animals, jackals have had a somewhat dark reputation in African folklore. In ancient EGYPT, Anubis, the god of the dead, was depicted either as a jackal or a man with a jackal's head. Anubis embalmed mummies in the afterlife. Another jackal-headed god, Wepwawet, was worshiped in Syut, a commercial center south of CAIRO. In Hellenistic times, Syut became known as Lycopolis, which means "City of the Wolf."

Jenne-Jeno Ancient city on the Bani River, a tributary of the NIGER RIVER, in what is now Mali. Jenne-Jenno is the most thoroughly excavated site of the early first millennium in West Africa, and much of what is known about that region is the result of these investigations.

For centuries, the area surrounding the site of Jenne-Jeno was subject to the regular flooding that typified the inland NIGER DELTA at that time. Between the effects of the flooding itself and the diseases that resulted from it, the land remained virtually uninhabitable for centuries.

About 1000 BCE, however, this began to change, when, like virtually all of northern Africa, this area began to become increasingly dry. As a result, by the third century BCE, pastoralists and agriculturalists, driven from the once-fertile southern SAHARA, began to migrate into the region. Archaeological discoveries indicate that a settlement was founded at Jenne-Jeno sometime during this period. Evidence of crowded cemeteries indicates that a substantial town existed on the site by at least 400 CE.

The simplicity of Jenne-Jenno's buildings, which were constructed from sun-dried mud, may have contributed to the town's successful early urbanization, as well as to the development of the region as a whole. Nearby towns using similar building techniques dotted the middle Niger valley, especially at Timbuktu, about 300 miles (483 km) away.

Old Jenne was surrounded by smaller settlements. Although nothing is known of their early agricultural practices, it is very likely that the people there were growing their own food. Unlike the arid conditions in that region today, rainfall was plentiful from about 300 to 1100. There was more than enough rainwater to keep the fertile floodplains around Jenne-Jenno well irrigated for crops.

IRON use existed in this part of Africa even before the beginning of the common era, and the inhabitants of Jenne-Jeno apparently were gifted metal workers. Their products consisted not only of tools but also of jewelry. POTTERY was another local product, and artifacts have been located that indicate an ability to manufacture sophisticated, thin-walled pottery.

Jenne-Jeno was part of a well-developed West African trading system, and TRADE was an important part of its economy. Exactly how extensive this system was is open to some debate. But to some scholars, the absence of any local sources of iron ore for Jenne-Jeno's ironworking industry indicates a trade network that must have reached well beyond local boundaries. The presence of Roman and Hellenistic beads also is indicative of at least some trading contact with peoples having links beyond simply West Africa.

Much later, Jenne-Jeno became an important trading and cultural center for the Muslim world.

See also: JENNE (Vol. II); JENNE-JENO (Vol. II); JEWELRY (Vol. I); PASTORALISM (Vol. 1).

Further reading: Susan Keech McIntosh, *Excavations at Jenne-Jeno, Hambarkatolo, and Kaniana: The 1981 Season* (Berkeley: University of California Press, 1995).

jewelry With the advent of the IRON AGE in Africa, metal forms of jewelry gained an equal and sometimes higher place than the rocks, shells, or animal bones used by previous generations. Bronze, COPPER, GOLD and silver reflected societal growth and served as an important medium for communicating social rank, marital status, and age. An expression of cultural affiliation, metal jewelry served as an important form of BRIDEWEALTH.

Creating metal jewelry fell within the domain of the BLACKSMITHS, who were often associated with magic. Blacksmiths often learned such techniques as the lost wax process from local or regional craftsmen. This process was used for thousands of years by such groups as the Baule and Dan of the IVORY COAST—who reportedly learned of this technique from the Akan—who forged in gold at an early date. Other groups associated with the process from an early period were the Fang, the Bamum, the Tuareg, and the HAUSA. Each of these regional groups refined their techniques of jewelry making over time.

In general, the lost wax process relied on beeswax obtained from honeycombs. The wax was crushed, boiled, and filtered through cold water until hardened. This wax, which served as a mold, was briefly placed in the sun in order to become pliable. Once it was given a form or design, *sprues*, or tubes, were attached to it. While heated metal was being poured into one side, gas and liquids escaped from the other. (Instead of wax, the Tuareg and Hausa used crucibles to obtain the same effect.) Other groups poured heated metal into preset molds and then hammered intricate designs into the finished product. Regardless of how it was created, once the metal jewelry cooled, it was usually given a final coating of wax or oil.

The most intricate and often the heaviest jewelry was cast as a sign of prestige for ruling chiefs or kings. These heavier pieces, which might weigh several pounds, were also believed to be imbued with ritual power that protected the wearer. Heavy metal collars and necklaces, ankle and arm bracelets, such as those made by the Fang, often required the assistance of the blacksmith since these items were made for permanent wear. Over the centuries metal crafting evolved to make these forms of jewelry hollow so they would provide more flexibility for the wearer.

Cultural motifs were engraved in most metal work and consisted of ancestral figures, images of fish, animals, or birds that signified ritual meaning for both the wearers and their peers. The Bamum used the image of a spider, for example, to symbolize attainment of inner wisdom. Senufo initiates of the Ivory Coast wore traditional "rings of silence," which were cast in the form of a buffalo head, upon entering adult society.

In Africa, the type of metal chosen for jewelry was especially significant. The belief, for instance, that silver was "pure and blessed" made it the primary choice among the Tuareg and other Islamic groups of the SAHEL. Brass was preferred by the Baule, who patterned their jewelry by laying decorated strips of wax on the charcoal core and then pouring heated metal on top.

Trade imports and the presence of gold in NUBIA accounted for the staggering array of jewelry and ritual objects recovered from the ancient kingdoms of EGYPT and KUSH. The Kushites, like their Egyptian neighbors, became experts at the forge, particularly after moving their kingdom to MEROË c. 590 BCE. This may account for the high levels of craftsmanship and ornately designed jewelry found throughout the NILE VALLEY region. One of the oldest items that has been recovered is a diadem, a type of crown or headband, made during Egypt's Fourth Dynasty (c. 2575–2465 BCE). Decorated with an array of symbols, including papyrus flowers and ibis, it may have belonged to a reigning queen or other high-ranking person.

In contrast, much of the jewelry of ETHIOPIA denoted Christian themes, including many variations of interlaced design. Like other regions, Ethiopians used the lost wax process to create amulets as well as hand, neck, and processional crosses of brass, iron, silver, and copper. Some crosses were also covered in beads or precious stones.

See also: BEADS (Vol. I); BERBERS (Vols. I, II, III); BODY ADORNMENT (Vol. I).

Further reading: Mary N. Hooter, *Secrecy: African Art that Conceals and Reveals* (New York: The Museum for African Art, 1993); Laure Meyer, *Art and Craft in Africa* (Paris: Terrail, 1994).

Jos Plateau Centrally located Nigerian highland known for its association with the ancient NOK CULTURE.

Measuring almost 3,000 sqare miles (7,800 sq km), the Jos Plateau has a tropical climate and is the origin of several rivers that feed the larger NIGER, Gongola, and BENUE Rivers. Parts of the plateau were once a vast forest but have since been turned into grasslands through human intervention.

Although other peoples such as the Biram, Numan, YORUBA, and IBO have occupied the area, the Jos Plateau is historically known as being the dwelling site of the Nok people. From c. 900 BCE to c. 200 CE, the Nok inhabited the region and produced bronze castings, intricate terra-cotta pottery sculptures, and tools made out of iron and stone.

Juba I (FL. c. 45 BCE) *Ancient king of northern African kingdom of Numidia.*

The independent BERBER kingdom of NUMIDIA, with its roots in the fourth century BCE, eventually extended from the eastern region of present-day Algeria to Mauritania. Populated by a mix of nomadic mountain pastoralists and coastal farmers, it became a frequent battleground as the Roman Empire attempted to secure its hold on North Africa.

Juba I was a descendent of a family dynasty that traced its roots to MASSINISSA (died 148 BCE), who first took power in the neighboring region of CARTHAGE about 206 BCE. According to several legends, Juba, as a child, was publicly humiliated by Julius CAESAR, an event that served as a catalyst for his lifelong opposition to Caesar.

During Rome's First Triumvirate, during which power was shared by Pompey, Crassus, and Caesar, Numidia was placed under the jurisdiction of Pompey, and Numidia's king, Juba I, became his ally. When Caesar defeated Pompey in 60 BCE, Juba seized the opportunity to resist the domination of Caesar. By 46 BCE, however, Juba was defeated by Caesar, and Juba's son, Juba II, was taken to ROME. Caesar then extended direct Roman rule over much of what had been the semi-independent kingdom of Numidia. Numerous forts and frontier zones, known as *limes*, were used by the Romans to systematically control both the former kingdom and the surrounding area. As a province of the Roman Empire, Numidia supplied grains and olive oil through enslaved labor.

See also: MAGHRIB (Vol.I); NUMIDIA (Vol.I).

Further reading: Samuel Kasule, *The History Atlas of Africa* (New York: Macmillan, 1999); James L. Newman, *The Peopling of Africa: A Geographic Interpretation* (New Haven, Conn.: Yale University Press, 1995).

Judaism Religion and culture that encompasses the laws, customs, and practices of the Jewish people.

The history of the introduction of Judaism to ancient Africa is not altogether clear. The oldest of the world's three major monotheistic religions (Chrstianity and Islam are the others), Judaism arose in the Middle East, in the land of the modern-day state of Israel. In the view of the ancient Israelites, God (Yahweh in Hebrew) rewarded his people with bountiful harvests. But, it was believed, Yahweh also punished wrongdoers with misfortune. According to the Jewish scriptures, the Israelites were descended from a single ancestor, Jacob, whose twelve sons became the progenitors of twelve separate but related Jewish tribes.

A handful of the tribes, led by the prophet Moses, migrated to EGYPT around 1600 BCE where they were eventually forced into slavery. Following their conquest of the land of Canaan in Palestine, the early Israelites began to assert an influence over Egyptian culture. Under the leadership of King Saul in 1020 BCE, and later under King David, the Israelites were able to capture Jerusalem and establish a powerful kingdom. In 586 BCE, however, the Jewish people were conquered and exiled to Babylonia, where early Judaism started to take on some of the characteristics of modern Judaism. Over the next 500 years, Judaism was influenced by Greek, and later Roman, culture as these western empires conquered parts of the Middle East.

The basic doctrine of early Judaism centered on the belief that God created the universe and is its sole ruler. God's word and commandments were revealed to his people in the writings known as the Torah, the teachings of which had been revealed to the prophet Moses on Mt. Sinai when the early Semites migrated back from Egypt. The Jewish people believed that a covenant, or *berith*, existed between them and God that stemmed from a promise God made to their ancestors at Sinai. According to that covenant, if the Jewish people acknowledged God as their sole leader and obeyed his laws, he would make them his chosen people and watch over them. God also promised to send his Messiah to offer redemption and restore Jews to the Holy Land. Eventually, the concept of Messianic redemption led to the belief that individuals could hasten the Messiah's arrival by strictly adhering to God's commandments.

The first evidence of Judaism's spread towards Africa occurred in the fourth century BCE when it was established as a valid religion at Alexandria, the new Ptolemaic capital of Greek Egypt. An important Mediterranean trade center, Alexandria was influenced by all aspects of Greek society, and contact with other Greek trading centers in Egypt facilitated the spread of Judaism to the African coast.

Prior to this, the PHOENICIANS established port towns along the African coastline as they joined the Greeks in developing Mediterranean trade. Historical evidence indicates the Phoenicians originally may have come from Palestine, the land occupied by the Israelites, thus linking their ancestors to the Jews. Some of the larger Phoenician settlements were established in present-day TUNISIA, a fertile agricultural area inhabited by the BERBER people. The

Berbers provided food for the Phoenicians in exchange for Mediterranean products, and, in the process of establishing this trade relationship, many of the Berbers integrated aspects of the Phoenician's Semitic culture into their own.

By 65 BCE, the Hebrew kingdom of Judea had come under control of the Roman Empire. Around the same time, the Horn of Africa and South Arabia emerged as important sources of frankincense and myrrh, aromatic resins that were important for Roman funeral pyres and perfumes. As Roman trade increased, Judaism spread through these coastal communities. In 70 CE, the Romans destroyed Judea, forcing Jews to migrate to new lands. Many settled in Egypt and North Africa, allowing Judaism to penetrate as far inland as the Sahara Oasis. It was during this period that Judaism fully developed into its modern rabbinic form, with emphasis on the role of study, prayer, and religious observance in personal salvation.

See also: BETA ISRAEL (Vols. I, II); CARTHAGE (Vol. I); CHRISTIANITY (Vols. I, II); CHRISTIANITY, INFLUENCE OF (Vols. II, III); ISLAM (Vols. II, III); MONOTHEISM (Vol. I); PTOLEMIES (Vol. I).

Jugurtha (160–104 BCE) *Militant king of Numidia; grandson of Masinissa (c. 238–148 BCE).*

King Jugurtha struggled not only to gain the throne but also to free NUMIDIA from the Roman domination under which MASINISSA had placed it. After the death of Masinissa's successor, King Micipsa, in 118 BCE, Numidia was divided among his heirs, who included Micipsa's two sons and Jugurtha. Eager to gain even more power, Jugurtha soon managed to have one of his rivals, Hiempsal, killed. The other, Adherbal, was forced to take refuge in ROME. Swayed by a personal appearance by Jugurtha, the Romans divided Numidia between the remaining two heirs.

Mistakenly believing that he had Rome's full support, in 112 BCE Jugurtha attacked Adherbal, and, in the process of achieving victory, massacred a number of Roman citizens. Incensed, the Roman Senate declared war on Jugurtha. Jugurtha, however, proved himself an able military leader, using Numidia's desert terrain to avoid major pitched battles and, in general, humiliating the Roman forces. A peace settlement in 111 BCE that greatly favored Jugurtha failed to satisfy the Numidian leader, and war was resumed quickly. Once again, however, Jugurtha managed to defeat the Romans, effectively ending their control of Numidia by 110 BCE.

Ultimately, Rome could no longer bear Jugurtha's rebellion, and, under Gaius Marius, a new Roman offensive was begun in 107 BCE. Initially, Jugurtha was able to repeat his early successes against the Romans, but Marius eventually won the support of King Bocchus I of Mauritania, Jugurtha's father-in-law, whose betrayal led to Jugurtha's capture in 105 BCE. Taken to Rome, the Numidian king was subjected to a series of public humiliations and died there in 104 BCE.

K

ka In ancient Egyptian religion, the spiritual double of every person and the source of his or her life powers.

Ancient Egyptian religious beliefs held that the spirit, or soul, of a person consisted of three parts: the ka, the BA, and the ankh. Egyptians believed that at each person's birth, the god Khnum created that person's ka. Upon death, a person was said to have "gone to his or her ka." The ka needed a body in order to survive, however. As a result, if the deceased was not mummified or if the deceased's mummy decomposed, the spiritual double was thought to die and the deceased lost the chance for eternal life.

Egyptians saw the ka as the origin and giver of all that is desirable, especially eternal life. The ka also was believed to act as a protecting spirit, guarding the deceased against dangers found in the AFTERLIFE.

According to tradition, most mortals had a single ka. Kings, however, were thought to have multiple kas. The great pharaoh RAMESSES II, for example, was reputed to believe that he had more than twenty kas. Gods also had kas, and Egyptians worshiped the deities' kas in order to receive favors. OSIRIS, for example, was known as the ka of the pyramids. In HIEROGLYPHICS, ka was represented as two raised arms bent upward at the elbow.

Kadesh Ancient Syrian city on the Orontes River and, for many years, a major crossroads of the trade routes in western Syria.

During the early fourteenth century BCE, Kadesh was the scene of conflict between EGYPT and one of its main Asian rivals, the HITTITES. During the reign of the Egyptian pharaoh SETI I, Kadesh was captured and brought under Egyptian rule. The Hittites, however, soon advanced on Kadesh and gained control of the city, which they considered to be sacred. For the remainder of Seti's reign, Kadesh remained in the hands of these invaders from modern-day Turkey.

Around 1300 BCE, just four years after succeeding to his father's throne, the young pharaoh RAMSESSES II set out to reconquer Kadesh. Unfortunately, false information from captured spies led the pharaoh into a trap. Ramsesses and a force of 20,000 Egyptian soldiers soon found themselves surrounded by a Hittite army that outnumbered them two to one. This predicament lasted until the rest of the Egyptian army arrived and drove off the Hittites. Ramsesses II claimed victory, even putting a victory inscription on the Temple of KARNAK. Historians, however, believe the battle ended in a truce.

Kalahari Desert Arid desert region that stretches over the central plains of southern Africa, covering parts of modern Botswana, Namibia, and SOUTH AFRICA. The Kalahari region is mostly sandy and lacks surface water, but it is heavily vegetated with brush and low grasslands. The occasional rainfall creates viable grazing areas and collects in basins that support an abundance of wildlife, including wildebeest, elephants, giraffes, gnus, zebras, and springbok. For hundreds of years prior to the great BANTU migration, the inhospitable Kalahari was inhabited by the !KUNG San, a group of HUNTER-GATHERERS who called themselves the Zhun/twasi, or "the real people."

During the great BANTU migrations (c. 1000 BCE–500 CE), the harsh environment of the Kalahari prevented easy passage through the region, and the !Kung therefore remained the sole inhabitants of its interior. They were masters of the desert environment, developing a thorough knowledge of the local flora and fauna. Though they occasionally killed large mammals for their meat and hides, more often they survived on edible roots and berries, BAOBAB fruits, and *mongongo* nuts. Their diet was supplemented with meat from birds, including flamingoes and geese, and reptiles, including lizards and crocodiles.

The Kalahari, which covers nearly 360,000 square miles (232, 400 sq km), contains the Okavango Delta to the north, and the Makgadikgadi salt pans to the northwest.

See also: GEOGRAPHY (Vol. I); KALAHARI DESERT (Vol. II).

kandake Title of supreme royalty held by the ruling queens of ancient KUSH.

During its Meroitic period, Kush had a number of queens who held the sovereign title of *kandake*, meaning "queen mother." Reigning by themselves or in conjunction with their husbands or sons, the kandakes ruled from royal courts at Napata or MEROË or from the temples established at Musawarat es-Safra. Shankiakhete (ruled 170–160 BCE) was one of the earliest known kandakes. Those who followed her included Amanishakhete (ruled 45 BCE) and Amanirenas (ruled 24 BCE). In addition to being rulers and warriors, kandakes often served as priestesses for the Egyptian god AMUN, as well as for the goddesses ISIS and Nut. In addition, the kandakes were highly influential in both local and national matters, and their duties even included presiding over coronation ceremonies.

Reliefs and sculptures give dramatic portrayals of the kandakes' role as warriors and military leaders. During Greco-Roman times, one of the most celebrated kandakes was Amanirenas. About 24 BCE, she led her soldiers against Kush's Roman overlords, engaging the enemy at ASWAN, 70 miles (112 km) north of Kush's border with EGYPT. There she defeated three units of the Roman army. In a symbolic gesture, she decapitated a statue of Augustus Caesar and buried the head of the statue in the doorway of a public building. After this act of defiance, Amanirenas supposedly led her troops further into the interior of Kush before finally being captured at Primis (Qasr/Brim).

Karnak, Temple of Modern Arabic name for the site of an elaborate series of temples, the largest and most spectacular of which was dedicated to the god AMUN. Karnak is located on the east bank of the NILE RIVER, near the ancient city of Thebes. Covering more than 200 acres (80 ha), the religious complex includes not only temples and chapels, but also obelisks, columns, and statues. Construction of the site was undertaken by a succession of pharaohs and went on for thousands of years. One of the many impressive features of the site's architecture is a series of monumental gateways called pylons.

Built during the MIDDLE KINGDOM (c. 1991–1668 BCE), Karnak was originally the site of a modest shrine to Amun. But the rulers of the NEW KINGDOM (c. 1570–1085 BCE) expanded the scope of the temple complex by enlarging it into three sections. The pharaohs who contributed to its basic development during the Eighteenth Dynasty were THUTHMOSE I, Queen Hatshepsut, and THUTHMOSE III. Their work was continued on an even grander scale by the Nineteenth Dynasty pharaohs SETI I and RAMSESSES II.

The Temple at Karnak was at the heart of Egyptian religion, and the ancient Egyptians regarded it as a national shrine, calling it *ipet-isut*, of "the most revered of places." They were dazzled by its magnificent architectural monuments and by the great wealth and power of the priests dedicated to the service of the supreme god Amun. The faithful made Karnak the focus of their devotion to the god. The Opet festival, a yearly celebration held in honor of Amun, was one of the most important religious events to take place there. During the festival, the image of Amun was carried in solemn procession from his great temple to the banks of the Nile. Amid much public rejoicing, the image was then transported on a barge to the temple at LUXOR, where it remained for several weeks before being returned to Karnak with similiar solemnity.

Kash (Kasu) Names used for the ancient KINGDOM OF KUSH and its inhabitants.

Kash was the Egyptian name for Kush during the MIDDLE KINGDOM (c. 2000–1780 BCE), when Kush was considered a province of the Egyptian Empire. *Kasu* was the term generally used by King Ezana of AKSUM, who sent armies to destroy the region about 350 CE. It is widely assumed that the major battle of Ezana's invasion took place at the capital city of MEROË at the junction of the Atabara and NILE Rivers.

See also: EGYPT (Vol. I).

Kashta (r. c. 806–750 BCE) *Early king of Napata in the kingdom of Kush; noted for leading the first phases of Kush's invasion of Egypt.*

For hundreds of years, KUSH had been dominated by EGYPT, but by the Twenty-first Dynasty (c. 1085–945 BCE), Egyptian power had begun to decline. As time passed, Kush's trading links propelled it to economic prominence, and the area began to assert its autonomy. Ultimately, an independent kingdom was established at Napata, and under King Kashta's guidance, plans were made to invade Egypt.

Just how successful Kashta's invasion was is unclear, but it was not long before Kashta's sons, PIANHKY (r. c. 750–716 BCE) and Shabako (r. c. 716–701 BCE) completed Kush's conquest of Egypt. After this, a succession of Napatan kings ruled in Egypt as the Twenty-fifth Dynasty, holding power over the country as a whole for fifty years and over UPPER EGYPT for more than a hundred years. This period represented the height of power for Kushite kings, who ruled a kingdom that extended from modern-day Khartoum to the MEDITERRANEAN SEA. Beginning around 663 BCE, Assyrian invasions forced a Kushite retreat, but it is clear that the Kush's occupation of the area left an indelible mark on customs, religion, and architecture in both lands.

Kei River River emptying into the Indian Ocean on the Eastern Cape of South Africa; also known as the Great Kei River.

Although not a particularly large river, the Kei was important geographically to the region's IRON AGE residents. Since the weather north of the Kei River was far more suitable for agriculture than the climate to the south, the river formed a kind of southern border, separating one region from another. As a result, the area north of the Kei, which was marked by summer rainfall, ultimately became the home of many SAN- and BANTU-speaking farmers and cattle-herders.

Kemet Ancient Egyptian word for "Egypt."

Ancient Egyptians called their land Kemet, or Kmt, which meant "black land," after the fertile, silt-layered soil left behind each year during the annual flooding of the NILE RIVER. Black land *(kemet)* was distinguished from the surrounding red land *(deshret*, or desert), so-called because of the reddish yellow ochre color of the sands. By the time of the ancient Greeks, however, this meaning had been transformed, since, according to some authorities, the Greeks referred to Kemet as the "Land of the Blacks."

Kemet in 2000 BCE covered nearly 400,000 square miles (1,000,000 sq km). Districts were divided into "nomes," and the entire region was divided into two halves: UPPER EGYPT and LOWER EGYPT. Upper Egypt was also known as the NILE VALLEY, and it consisted of a narrow valley on either side of the NILE RIVER. Lower Egypt, also known as the NILE DELTA, was the place where the Nile River split before reaching the MEDITERRANEAN SEA.

A VULTURE symbol was traditionally used to represent Upper Egypt; a COBRA symbol signified Lower Egypt. The two areas were quite different; they were separate kingdoms before they united during the reign of MENES (r. 3100 BCE).

Kerma Chiefdom or kingdom that flourished in Upper Nubia from c. 2400–1500 BCE; ultimately it became the kingdom of KUSH. Kerma, which traced its origins to people possibly related to the NUBIAN C-GROUP, was marked from the first by a highly organized chiefdom or monarchy. Its early history, extending from about 2400 to 2000 BCE, saw the rise of the town of Kerma as a religious and governmental center. Protected by a sophisticated network of walls and ditches, it held not only a large mud-brick royal hut but also a massive religious structure that grew steadily over time.

From 2000 to 1650 BCE, Kerma was in virtually constant conflict with its Egyptian neighbors. This conflict, however, seems not to have lessened Kerma's considerable trade with EGYPT. An Egyptian trading post, built at Kerma during the early 1900s BCE, for example, showed signs of both Egyptian and Kushite artisans producing glazed POTTERY, beads and other jewelry, metalwork, and even cabinetry. For the most part, these goods showed a basic functional Kushite style with an overlay of Egyptian influences.

As time passed, however, Kerma's aristocracy seems to have begun to adopt Egyptian styles, language, and customs. Eventually, Kerma's traditional art and religion also began to succumb to this Egyptianization. This process continued even during the disintegration of Egypt's MIDDLE KINGDOM in the eighteenth century BCE. During this period, Kerma (or Kush, as it had begun to be known), assumed control of the territories left behind by the retreating Egyptians. (Often, however, they left Egyptians in charge of the territories, allowing the Egyptians to rule on their behalf.) As it gained in power, however, Kerma became increasingly Egyptianized, with its royals and nobles adopting Egyptian-based religion, language, and customs on an even more widespread scale than before.

By the sixteenth century BCE, Egypt began to emerge from the weakness of its post–Middle Kingdom (or Second Intermediate) Period. At this time, c. 1660 to 1550 BCE, Egypt became strong enough to launch a number of successful military offensives against its Kushite neighbors, and it was not long before Kerma itself fell to Egyptian invaders.

Further reading: David O'Connor, *Ancient Nubia: Egypt's Rival in Africa* (Philadelphia: University of Pennsylvania Press, 1994).

Khafre's Pyramid Second-largest pyramid complex at Giza. Khafre, also known as Rakhaef or Chephren, was the son of the pharaoh KHUFU. Khafre ruled Egypt from c. 2520 to 2494 BCE and is most famous for building his pyramid complex, which includes the GREAT SPHINX, a mortuary temple, and a valley temple. Khafre's pyramid is smaller than his father's, but since it is built on higher ground and at a steeper angle, it appears taller. Khafre's pyramid stands 450 feet (137 m) high with a base of 704 feet (215 m). Its overall volume is estimated at 58.1 million cubic feet (1.6 million cubic m). The pyramid is also distinctive in that its topmost layer of smooth stones is the only remaining casing of stones on a Giza pyramid.

More than just a pyramid-builder, Khafre also was renowned for the statues he ordered created. These works, which included the Great Sphinx, earned him the reputation as the greatest statue-maker of the Pyramid Age. Fifty-eight statues have been found in Khafre's pyramid temples, including four gigantic sphinxes, each measuring more than 26 feet (8 m) long; twenty-three life-size statues in his valley temple; nineteen large statues of himself in and around his mortuary temple; and another ten colossal statues of himself in the sphinx temple.

Kharga Oasis Largest oasis parallel to the NILE RIVER in Egypt. Approximately 138 miles (222 km) long and 16 miles (25.7 km) wide, Kharga is the largest and most advanced of the five oases near CAIRO. The Bagawat Tombs, consisting of 300 painted Christian tombs dating back to the fifth and sixth centuries, are located in the Kharga oasis. The tombs are found in the Temple of Ibis, a sandstone temple supposedly built by the Persian emperor DARIUS in honor of the god AMUN. The al-Nadura Temple, which dates to Roman times, also is located in the oasis. At one time, Kharga was the only stop on the Forty-Day Road, the slave-trade route between North Africa and the tropical south.

Khartoum Capital of modern-day Sudan and site of ancient NUBIAN communities. Archaeological excavations conducted near Khartoum offer strong evidence that the cultivation of crops and the domestication of animals occurred at an early date. In fact, goats, sheep, and cattle most likely have been present in the area since at least the fifth millennium BCE.

Several different types of pottery have been recovered from the region around Khartoum. One of these, probably dating back 6,000 years or more, is distinguished by a basket-weave design made by catfish spines. Another design contains dotted wavy lines virtually identical to pottery found in the Tibetsi region of the Sahara. The link between these two potteries has led some archaeologists to suggest that, as the once-fertile Sahara began to dry up, people may have begun migrating to the north and east. Eventually, according to the archaeologists, these people may have colonized Egypt and, ultimately, the area around Khartoum.

The discovery near Khartoum of pottery dating back even earlier than the fifth millenium BCE is another indication of the level of sophistication reached by the hunting–fishing communities that inhabited the region.

Khasekhem (Khasekhemwy, Khasekemui) (r. c. 2800–2790 BCE) *Last pharaoh of ancient Egypt's Second Dynasty.*

Little is known about ancient Egypt's Early Dynastic Period (also called the Archaic Period), which lasted from 3100 to 2686 BCE. It appears, however, that despite the refinement of Egyptian culture that took place during the First Dynasty, the close of the era was marked by civil strife. The main cause of this apparently was conflict between two religious groups, the cult of HORUS, which dominated the south, and the cult of SETH, which was the main religion of the northern NILE DELTA region.

Struggles between adherents of Horus and Seth continued into the Second Dynasty, leading to a decline in the pharaohs' authority. This seems to have led to rival claims to the throne, each claimant allied with one of the deities. Various rulers made attempts to resolve the conflict, most notably Hotepshekhemwy (also known as Raneb). His name, which means "peaceful in respect of the two powers," is probably a reference to his mediation of the strife.

Hotepshekhemwy, however, was unable to resolve the conflict permanently. The situation worsened, possibly even leading to a civil war between UPPER and LOWER EGYPT. Although few details are known, peace seems to have been restored, at least temporarily, by Khasekhem, who reigned from approximately 2800 to 2790 BCE. His royal name translates as "the two lords are at peace in him," suggesting both a meeting of the gods, Horus and Seth and a temporary resolution of the conflicts disrupting the kingdom. Khasekhem's tomb, the largest in ABYDOS, was discovered in the late nineteenth century.

Khoisan Least widespread of the four major families of African LANGUAGES. The Khoisan languages—including Nama and !KUNG—have nearly become extinct today and are kept alive primarily by the Khoikhoi and SAN peoples of South Africa, whose origins apparently lie in prehistoric times.

Like many other African tongues, Khoisan languages use differences in tonality to distinguish meanings. Vocal inflection is employed, especially in the Khoikhoi and San languages, to indicate case, number, and gender. The unique feature of Khoisan languages, however, is the use of special consonants known as *clicks*. (Khoisan is also called the Click family of languages.) English speakers use similar click sounds in a very limited way: *tsk-tsk*, for example, or the *chk-chk* noises used to signal horses. In Khoisan languages, however, these click sounds function not as words themselves, but only as parts of words.

Khoisan languages employ a wide variety of click sounds, all produced through a sucking action of the tongue. By altering the positioning of the tongue and the way one releases air into the mouth, a Khoisan speaker can create a great number of different click sounds. Khoisan speakers produce various clicks by placing the tongue against the teeth, the palate, the alveolus (the inner surface of the gums of the upper front teeth), the inside of the cheek, or the lips. Curling the tip of the tongue up and back so that the underside of the tongue touches the palate produces yet another kind of click.

San languages feature six different types of clicks—though no single San language employs all of them. The Khoikhoi employ four kinds: dental (with the tongue against the teeth), palatal (against the palate), lateral (against the inside of the cheek), and retroflex (with the underside of the tongue against the palate). Over time, the use of some Khoisan click sounds eventually spread to nearby BANTU languages, including Zulu, Sotho, and Xhosa.

See aslo: KHOIKHOI (Vols. II and III).

Khormusan Early Stone Age people of prehistoric NUBIA. Fishers and HUNTER-GATHERERS, the Khormusan are believed to have settled in Lower Nubia's NILE RIVER valley about 50,000 years ago, coming originally from the then-fertile area of the SAHARA. Excavations at Khor Musa, near Wadi Halfa, and other sites have revealed examples of Khormusan stone tools as well as remnants of the substantial settlements in which the Khormusan lived.

Khufu (Cheops) (r. c. 2550–2526 BCE) *Pharaoh of ancient* Egypt *who was the builder of the Great Pyramid of Giza.*

Assuming the throne about 2550 BCE, Khufu, also known as Cheops, was the second king of the Egyptian Fourth Dynasty, ruling ancient EGYPT for approximately twenty-four years. His most famous accomplishment was the construction of the GREAT PYRAMID of Giza, one of the Seven Wonders of the Ancient World.

The construction of the Great Pyramid provides important insights into Khufu's rule, for he transformed the project into a great socializing force for the nation. By using workers who would otherwise have been idle during the annual flooding of the NILE RIVER, Khufu provided his subjects with both employment and a unifying national goal. Beyond this, the pyramid's construction required major achievements in science, astronomy, mathematics, and art, all of which were direct results of Khufu's ability to inspire, mobilize, and organize his people.

Khufu's ability to lead, however, was not the result of any liberality or generosity on his part. Indeed, in contrast to his father, the beneficent King Sneferu, Khufu was reputed to be a cruel despot. In spite of this, however, Khufu was renowned throughout Egyptian history, and even as late as the Twenty-sixth Dynasty he was worshiped as a god.

A tiny statuette depicting Khufu, discovered in the temple of OSIRIS at ABYDOS, has become famous. In 1954, a funeral ship belonging to Khufu was also uncovered in a pit near the Great Pyramid. It is currently displayed in the Boat Museum on the site of the original pit.

Kikuyu Language and people of East Africa living in present-day Kenya. Although no exact dating of their arrival in the area is possible, the Kikuyu have long been a diverse mix of tribal peoples who trace their ancestry to the Thagicu, Igembe, Tigania, Gumba, Athi, and MAASAI people.

According to the Kikuyu's oral history, the Kikuyu god (Ngai) commanded Gikuyu, the forefather of the Kikuyu, to build his home near Mount Kenya. Gikuyu settled in the center of the land. It was full of fig trees, so he named it the Tree of the Building Site (Mukurue wa Gathanga). Ngai sent Gikuyu a wife, Mumbi. Gikuyu and Mumbi had nine daughters. Along with one other child, their daughters became the progenitors of the ten ancestral clans of the Kikuyu.

The merging of multiple cultures produced an eclectic mix of Kikuyu rituals over the centuries. From the Thagicu people they adopted ceremonial dances and initiation rites, and initiation ceremonies became a pillar in Kikuyu life. Young men and women were fully integrated into village life after circumcision and clitoridectomy ceremonies. Males became warriors at this time, and female social responsibilities increased beyond the village proper.

kola nuts Seeds rich in caffeine, chewed as a stimulant and used in various ceremonies in traditional African cultures.

The kola, or cola, tree, native to West Africa, is related to the cacao tree, from which chocolate is made. Its seeds, called *guru* or *goora* nuts in West Africa, are about 1.5 inches (3.8 cm) long and are traditionally chewed as a stimulant. Kola nuts contain large amounts of caffeine as well as smaller amounts of other stimulants and may be mildly addictive. Like gum, they are chewed to quell thirst and refresh the breath. The nutritional value of the kola nut is negligible. Beverages made from kola nuts are prized by Muslims, whom the Koran does not permit to drink alcohol.

In western Africa, the kola nut is less important as a crop with value in the economy than as a tool of communication and ritual. As a stimulant, it serves the culturally important function of a social lubricant. Kola nuts have long been a core element in religious and magical ceremonies, used as offerings to deities, to make love potions, and to foretell the future. The nuts also are used as symbolic currencies to pay off debts of a ritual nature.

From September to June, the nuts are harvested by climbers. The seeds are extracted from their star-shaped pods and processed by sun-drying or piled into heaps for "sweating."

!Kung Ancient people inhabiting isolated areas of southern Africa for thousands of years; known among themselves as the *Zhun/twas*, or "the real people."

HUNTER-GATHERERS, the !Kung are believed to have lived in southern Africa for thousands of years before the BANTU migrations began about 2,000 years ago. Over the centuries, exposure to the easier lifestyle of their Bantu-speaking neighbors has led many !Kung to modify or even abandon their traditional way of life, although a few !Kung continue their ancient lifestyle, despite its difficulties.

For thousands of years the environment inhabited by the !Kung has been made up of harsh, semiarid areas in what is now BOTSWANA, ANGOLA, and Namibia. Composed of small hills and flat plains, even today the region's landscape is dominated by brush and grass. Trees and water have always been scarce. The area experiences extreme temperatures ranging from below freezing in the winter to well over 100° F (38° C) in the summer.

For millennia, the !Kung have lived in villages with populations ranging from ten to thirty people, and the ways of those currently following the !Kung's traditional lifestyle provide a good indication of how these people have lived since prehistoric times. The women spend two to three days each week foraging for food in the desert. Given the nature of the land, this can be an arduous task, although it ultimately yields an apparently adequate supply of fruits, berries, nuts, and roots of various kinds. !Kung men are responsible for hunting. Game is scarce, however, and the hunters often have to travel long distances before they can find and kill the wildebeest and other animals that are their prey. The hunt remains a communal activity, with the !Kung fairly sharing whatever meat is obtained. Weapons include poison-tipped spears and arrows, which are made and maintained by the hunters themselves.

Traditional !Kung villages consist of an array of small grass huts arranged in a circle. The !Kung consider the middle of the circle to be common space, and it is in this central area that virtually all !Kung life—except sleeping—goes on. The !Kung play and cook here, as well as make the decisions upon which the village's survival depends. Unlike many other groups, the !Kung function without a chief or formal leader, governing, instead, by consensus. Agreement is reached by long discussions in which everyone is given a chance to voice his or her opinion.

The !Kung believe that the spirit world is active in daily events ranging from sickness and death to the presence of water or food. Ills and misfortunes, they believe, are caused by invisible arrows shot at the unfortunate ones by spirits. The !Kung believe, however, that they can prevent, or even reverse, the action of these arrows through various activities. The most notable of these is the healing, or trance, DANCE. In it, dancers circle a fire until they reach a trance. There, it is believed, they come into contact with *n/um*, a powerful spiritual force that allows everyone gathered around the fire to be healed.

See also: ANIMISM (Vol. I); RELIGION, TRADITIONAL (Vol. I).

Further reading: Richard B. Lee, Irven DeVore, et al., eds. *Kalahari Hunter-Gatherers: Studies of the !Kung San and Their Neighbors* (Cambridge, Mass.: Harvard University Press, 1976); Marjorie Shostak, *Nisa: The Life and Words of a !Kung Woman* (Cambridge, Mass.: Harvard University Press, 2000).

Kurru Part of the area known as Napata, capital of ancient KUSH, in what is now northern Sudan; renowned for the ancient burial grounds of the royalty of Kush, c. 900 to 700 BCE.

Kurru, also known as al-Kurru, was once the burial site of some of the great Kushite (also called Cushite) kings of the Twenty-fifth Dynasty. The Egyptian tradition of burying royalty beneath a pyramid was passed to the Kushites when they conquered Egypt, and the first Kushite leaders to build pyramids did so at Kurru. The existence of the burial sites at Kurru is thought to be the first evidence of a Kushite state, though scholars have not confirmed that it is the only burial ground of the Kushites of the time.

Shabaka (also called Shabako or Sabacon), the founder of the Twenty-fifth Dynasty after EGYPT was conquered by the Kushites, and Shebitku (Sebichos), his successor, were both buried in pyramids at Kurru. A later pharaoh, Tunuatamun (also known as Tanutamon), who was defeated by the ASSYRIANS at MEMPHIS and Thebes, was also buried at Kurru.

Kurundi People who have long occupied the area now known as BURUNDI; also the name of the BANTU language they speak.

The Kurundi people, also called Rundi or Kirundi, consist of three ethnic groups of Kurundi-speaking people (a Bantu language), the TWA, the HUTU, and the Tutsi. The Twa were likely the first Bantu-speaking people to come to the area. The Hutu made their living from agriculture, while the Tutsi were mainly pastoralists. The precise reasons for why and how these Bantu-speaking peoples began supplanting the native SAN people are not known. As a result, the influx—and dominance—of Bantu-speaking peoples, which dates to the beginnings of the common era, has been attributed to everything from the Bantu speakers' skill at ironworking to their possible control of trade routes. It has even been associated with the Bantu speakers' successful cultivation of the newly imported banana. The Kurundi language is in the Benue-Congo branch of the NIGER-CONGO subfamily that is commonly known as the Bantu languages.

Kush Ancient capital and kingdom of Nubia, based between the first and second cataracts of the NILE RIVER. The term *Kush* was apparently first used by Egyptians during their Twelfth Dynasty to refer to the first Kushite kingdom established at KERMA. (The Egyptians also used the names *Kush, Kash,* and *Khenet-hennferwere*. By the eighteenth century BCE the name *Ta-Seti*, or "Land of the Bow," was also used in recognition of the kingdom's famed archers.)

Kush was actually a series of kingdoms that rose to prominence when left in isolation or declined when dominated by EGYPT. Kerma (c. 2400–1570 BCE), which was situated between the Nile's third and fourth cataracts, was the earliest Kushite kingdom, and it went through several phases of development, beginning as an agricultural society that cultivated cereal grains (most likely SORGHUM and MILLET).

As in much of the ancient world, these activities fostered Kerma's development and helped to establish a class structure of ruling elites, priests, craft workers, and laborers. Evidence also suggests that cultural practices in Kerma included sacrificial offerings and the use of burial tumuli, or grave mounds.

As time passed, trade relations elevated Kush to an important position in the mercantile world of the RED SEA and the MEDITERRANEAN SEA. Kush's abundant resources included GOLD, semiprecious stones, livestock, EBONY woods, IVORY, COPPER, and quarried stones. Trade routes were apparently expanded, creating what some historians have labeled a "Nubian Corridor" linking the NILE RIVER valley to both the Mediterranean and the southern regions of Africa. The Kushites accomplished this by laying a form of track, known as a *doilkos*, that allowed boats to be pulled on land.

Unfortunately for Kush, its resources and accessibility also provided strong incentives for Egypt to assert its trading interests in the border areas of UPPER EGYPT and Lower Nubia. Egypt repeatedly invaded and occupied Kushite territory, reducing it to the status of a province. Archaeologists and historians speculate that these periods saw a process of Egyptianization that was reflected in numerous Egyptian-made artifacts and religious icons.

During the fall of the MIDDLE KINGDOM and Egypt's subsequent evacuation of Lower Nubia, the Kushite kingdom absorbed the territory abandoned by the Egyptians. These lands included the towns of Buhen and Mirgrissa, which had once been held by the Egyptians and in which important trade relations were already in place. A second Kushite rise to prominence occurred when Egypt relinquished political control to the HYKSOS, during its Second Intermediate Period (c. 1786–1550 BCE).

Only after the influence of the Hyksos came to an end was Egypt able to resume its domination of Kush. At this time it even launched a number of military strikes, ostensibly undertaken in retaliation for trade and military alliances that the Kushite rulers had formed with the Hyskos. Kushite soldiers, known as the MEDJAY, reportedly fought on both sides of the war.

Continued assaults against the Kushite kingdom culminated in the destruction of Kerma, c.1500 BCE. With their nation annexed and transformed into an Egyptian province, the former inhabitants of the Kushite kingdom dispersed to outlying regions, including Napata, and Kush entered a lengthy period of decline. Indeed, it was not until the end of the Egyptian NEW KINGDOM (c. 1186–1070 BCE) and the beginning of the Twenty-first Dynasty at Tanis (c. 1070–69), that Nubia, along with other remnants of the Kushite kingdom, regained independence and reestablished the kingdom at Napata.

The Napatan Period (900–300 BCE) For more than 100 years, beginning around 900 BCE, the second Kushite kingdom grew in isolation. Although little is known of this transition between Kerma and the Napatan periods (c. 900–590 BCE), the latter is generally considered to be a period of reconsolidation among the Kushite rulers. This reconsolidation, which took place in the wake of Egypt's internal wars and subsequent invasion by Libyan forces during the eighth century BCE, led to the emergence of a powerful Kushite family dynasty.

Historians speculate that, during the early Napatan period, at least seven generations of kings ruled Kush. Among the earliest of these was King Alara, whose son, King KASHTA (c. 806–750 BCE), was the first of this family dynasty to be documented fully in Egyptian and Kushite records and stelae, which are stone monuments with inscribed texts.

King Kashta was considered a notable leader, and he extended Kushite political control north through Lower Nubia and UPPER EGYPT. Kashta began his campaigns during a period in which Egypt was wrestling with political disruptions brought on by conflicts with independent nomes, or provinces, and Libyan chiefdoms. As a result, he was able to achieve several important victories, which led Kush to reclaim Lower Nubia and to establish control over the outlying city of Thebes (or Waset, as it was sometimes called).

The battle for control of Kush's and Egypt's political structure was continued by Kashta's son PIANKHY (751–716 BCE), who defeated an army of Libyans sometime between 750 and 730 BCE. Although Piankhy ruled from Napata, he exercised a strong measure of control over the Egyptian cities of Hermopolis and HIERAKONPOLIS, as well as over smaller nomes in the delta region. Under Piankhy, the Kushite kingdom eventually included a vast tract of territory that extended from its southern base at Napata to the northern Nile Delta.

Under Piankhy's vigorous rule, the Kushites engaged in numerous military expeditions and were prolific builders. Piankhy has been credited with introducing many architectural innovations and traditions at this time, including the development of Egyptian-styled pyramids for use as burial chambers.

Piankhy was also the first Kushite king to install his sister (in this case, AMENIRDIS I) as a priestess of AMUN. The tradition of creating women priesthoods was probably begun as a means of ensuring political loyalty to the king. It also represented a way to keep enormous wealth and property within the ruling family. In time, Amenirdis even ruled from Thebes in place of King Piankhy. This, however, was an unusual situation for Kushite women, although they appear to have held other important positions. Royal installation ceremonies at Napata, for example, were generally conducted (or at least strongly influenced) by the KANDAKES, or queen mothers. Kushite women also participated in military campaigns and often served as corulers with their husbands or sons.

Piankhy's heirs ruled all of Egypt for approximately fifty years; the retained control of southern Egypt for another fifty years beyond that. During this time they engaged in strong military expeditions to quell rebellions. They also were known for their architectural innovations, including Piankhy's introduction of Egyptian-styled pyramids for burial chambers. Taharqa, (ruled c. 690–664 BCE) was perhaps the family's most prolific builder and religious visionary, and he is credited with building numerous religious temples at Memphis, Thebes, Karnak, as well as in Nubia. He was also considered a model pharaoh, and by some accounts assisted Egypt in regaining its independence. During his reign, however, Assyrian armies sought to oust the Kushite rulers, and despite the fact that he was considered an excellent military strategist, Taharqa was eventually defeated by the Assyrians.

Archaeological evidence supports the widely held view that Napata represented a materially wealthly capital city. Excavations of royal tombs at NURI, al-Kurru, and GEBEL BARKAL indicate that wealthy Kushites adapted many outward displays, emblems, and religious icons of Egyptian culture. These included both the WHITE CROWN and winged sun discs. Kushite nobles also began to use sacred barks for burials in place of their traditional tumuli (the circular structures used to cover burial pits and grave goods). Similarly, burials had formerly positioned the deceased in a fetal position; the deceased were now mummified and laid out in Egyptian-style coffins. Similarly, the Kushites adopted the use of canopic jars, amulets, and *ushabties*—small figures made in human likeness—that were traditionally used by Egyptians in place of the entombment of the royal family members buried with the king.

Speculation about the Kushites' outward displays of Egyptian culture has generated much discussion among historians. Some scholars believe that this Egyptianization was an represented an attempt, by these kings, to legitimize their rule over Egyptian territories. (Both King Kashta and King Piankhy, for example, used the royal title of King of Upper and Lower Egypt.) Other historians insist that, rather than being subsumed into Egyptian culture, Kushite culture coexisted with Egyptian influences.

Meroë While headed by King Tanwetamani, the nephew of Taharqa, the Twenty-fifth Dynasty finally collapsed c. 663 BCE. By 590 BCE, the Kushite kingdom relocated to Meroë in the southern region of Nubia.

This relocation brought the kingdom to an area between the fifth and sixth cataracts of the Nile and initiated what is generally known as the Meroitic Period (590–350 BCE). At this time, access to the nearby island of MEROË provided the kingdom with a primary source of forest land and iron ore, which helped make Meroë one of the earliest and largest sites of iron production in the region.

Napata, however, was not completely abandoned. In fact, it remained a holy city and place of burial. This was primarily because of Gebel Barkal and the Temple of Amun, both of which had been established by earlier Kushite kings. Napata was also the site of the royal installment ceremonies that were conducted (or at least heavily influenced) by the kandakes.

Among the traditions reclaimed by the Nubians when they reestablished the kingdom at Meroë was matrilineal succession, through which the crown passed from the king to one of his sisters' sons. Another example of the importance of women within the royal family was the fact that, from a religious perspective, the king and his mother personified HORUS and ISIS. As a result, the queen assumed much of the king's power and visibility.

Under the reign of ASPELTA (ruled c. 593 BCE), the Kushites expanded their territories further south and west, developing strong trading ties with both ROME and India. As time passed, its vast resources of gold, ebony woods, and iron-rich deposits helped make the Kushite kingdom in Meroë into a prosperous trading power. For a period of several hundred years, its wealth and power were recognized by traders in Egypt, the Red Sea, and in the regions south of the SAHARA. By the first century of the common era, it had achieved recognition as one of the wealthiest trading cities in the ancient world. This period is also noted for a return to indigenous religious practices, which included the worship of APEDEMAK, a national deity whose origins most likely predated Egyptian rule. No sooner had it reached this peak, however, then the Kushite kingdom began to decline. A number of contributing factors have been cited, including the deforestation caused by the process of smelting iron. Also noted among the causes of Kush's decline are overgrazing and the development of alternative trade routes passing through AKSUM.

The final destruction of the Meroitic kingdom came c. 350 CE, when King Ezana dispatched Aksumite troops against the city. Although Ezana left records of his accomplishment in conquering Meroë, little is known of the reasons for the invasion or of the events leading up to it. Nor is much known about the aftermath of the Aksumite conquest.

See also: BALLANA CULTURE (VOL. I); NAGA, TEMPLES AT (VOL. I); NUBIA, CHRISTIAN (VOL. II); X-GROUP (VOL. I).

Further reading: Anthony Browder, *Nile Valley Contributions to Civilization* (Washington: Institute of Karmic Guidance, 1992); Phyllis M. Martin and Patrick O'Meara, eds., *Africa* (Bloomington: Indiana University Press, 1995); Frank Snowden, Jr., *Blacks in Antiquity* (Cambridge, Mass.: Belknap, 1970).

Kyoga, Lake Body of water located north of Lake VICTORIA in the Great Lakes region of central East Africa. Lake Kyoga is about 80 miles (129 km) long and is formed by the Victoria Nile in its middle course. The lake sits at 3,390 feet (1,033 km) above sea level and is shallow, with swampy sections and PAPYRUS reeds covering much of its shores.

See also: KYOGA, LAKE (Vol. II).

L

labor In ancient Africa, people engaged in many types of labor, including hunting, gathering, fishing, herding, agriculture, and trading. Cooking and other domestic arts were also undertaken, as were various other trades, such as carpentry, copying manuscripts, healing, and even library-keeping. Forced labor, such as slavery, likely existed as well.

Hunter-Gatherers Before the advent of the purposeful cultivation of food, or agriculture, labor consisted of nomadic wandering in search of the food needed for subsistence. Success for these HUNTER-GATHERER peoples required knowing where to find food sources—and then moving on when those sources became depleted. Ancient Africans who hunted and gathered likely formed societies of families that moved around together and stayed in one place for a few days or several weeks. These societies mainly hunted game and gathered wild berries, roots, and herbs. Though hunting and gathering activities were dramatically reduced by the expansion of agriculture, some societies continued this way of life; a few such societies, including the KHOISAN of the arid Kalahari region in southern Africa, still exist today.

Historically, the domestication of animals probably occurred before the cultivation of plants. DOGS may have been the first of these domesticated animals, being tamed perhaps as early as 10,000 BCE. In the Middle East, the GAZELLE was probably one of the first grazing animals to be domesticated. Later came pigs, sheep, and CATTLE. Prior to 4000 BCE, nomadic societies of cattle-herders wandered the vast African savannas that provided pastures for their herds.

Agriculture Near the end of the Pleistocene glaciation, about 10,000 years ago, AGRICULTURE is thought to have begun and, with it, civilization. The agricultural methods developed in early MESOPOTAMIA influenced the entire ancient world, including EGYPT. Records of ancient agriculture in Egypt show that farming thrived along the NILE RIVER. These ancient Egyptians not only built IRRIGATION and drainage systems employing the use of canals, they also advanced the use of tools for farming.

Early African crops included such grains and legumes as wheat, barley, MILLET, oats, rye, chickpeas, lentils, vetch, and horsebeans. Fruits that were commonly cultivated included grapes, olives, dates, apples, and figs.

As agriculture took hold, many people began to settle into communities, leaving behind their nomadic way of life and becoming full-time farmers. Successful societies raised animals that helped support both herders and farmers and created surplus crops; these surpluses allowed for trade, which helped cities prosper.

Urbanization Trade routes were developed from West Africa south to what is now Congo (formerly Zaïre) and across the SAHARA Desert to the coastal societies. Among the goods traded and sold were animal skins and leather, GOLD, ivory, and timber. The trading centers grew into great cities where governing bodies were formed to oversee trade, charge taxes, and control the land.

As farming methods began to produce reliable results, people no longer had to worry about their food supply in the same way they once had. When people had to rely strictly on hunting, gathering, and fishing, they were well fed when food sources were plentiful, but they went hungry when food was scarce and hard to find. Most members of the hunter-gatherer societies spent their time looking for food. After successful herding and farming systems were invented, not everyone had to labor for subsistence. People had time for other things, including experimenting, thinking, and observing. By 3500 BCE, following the example set by the farmers in permanent settlements along the Nile, many people were choosing to live in urban areas, working in a variety of trades. Over time, this change in labor patterns allowed for the advancement of science, art, government, and religion, forming the basis of modern civilization.

Some scholars believe that another result of the development of agriculture was the introduction of forced labor. As agriculture advanced and permanent societies formed, the need for laborers grew and gave rise to SLAVERY. Though forced labor takes many forms and the origin of owning or bonding people is not known, the most common form in ancient times and throughout history was slavery, or the consideration of laborers as property that could be owned, sold, or traded. By the time of the Roman Empire of the second century, slavery had been legalized and was practiced in some North African cultures.

Labor in Ancient Egypt Our knowledge of ancient Egypt gives us insight into the labor trends of one early civilization. By about 1000 BCE, most Egyptians lived in houses given to them by the state, for which they worked. Instead of receiving money for their work, they received rations in the form of food, animals, clothes, and other necessary items, and people often traded their extra food or other rations for luxuries.

Though some of the male children of the upper classes attended school, most boys became farmers. Some learned a trade, such as carpentry or POTTERY making, taught to them by a skilled craftsman. Other trades included mudbrick making—such bricks were typically used to build houses for the wealthy—and medicine, which required years of training with a practicing doctor after a boy had completed a regular school career.

Though some Egyptian girls did attend school, most were trained to perform the labor of the home, such as cooking, which called for food to be baked in a clay oven in a kitchen yard. They also learned sewing and other domestic arts. In ancient Egypt, however, this did not seem to imply a lesser status. In contrast to women in other times and places, ancient Egyptian women were allowed to sell, buy, and trade goods, as well as to own property.

Lahun, pyramid of

Lahun, pyramid of With the pyramid of HAWARA and the pyramid of LISHT, part of the mortuary complex for kings of the Twelfth Dynasty of EGYPT (c. nineteenth century BCE).

Lahun is the site of the ancient Egyptian pyramid built for King Sesostris II, also called Senwosre II. As the fourth king of the Twelfth Dynasty, Sesostris II ruled Egypt from about 1844 to 1837 BCE. No one is sure why this king chose to build his pyramid 30 miles (48.3 km) from Lisht, where the first two kings of the Twelfth Dynasty built their pyramids. Unfortunately, Sesostris II's pyramid, along with many others in ancient times, was repeatedly robbed, but an outstanding collection of jewelry was later discovered in the wall in the tombs of the princesses. Technically and artistically, the jewelry is among the best pieces of the time.

Laikipia Escarpment Steep-sided cliff facing Lake Bogoria in present-day Kenya. Both the Laikipia Escarpment and Lake Bogoria are part of the Great RIFT VALLEY, the geological fault system that extends 3,000 miles (4,827 kilometers) from the Jordan valley in Southwest Asia to Mozambique in Southeast Africa. The Laikipia plateau area leading up to the escarpment has been traditionally occupied by the MAASAI.

lakes and rivers Lakes and rivers are found throughout Africa and serve as resources for food, as means of transportation between regions, as natural boundaries between various ethnic groups, and, along their banks, as sites for agriculture.

Lakes are inland bodies of water, usually freshwater, that are formed by rivers, or glaciers. The main lakes of Africa are: Lake CHAD of the central Sudan, and Lake VICTORIA, Lake TANGANYIKA, and Lake Malawi of southeastern Africa. These lakes were the focus of several different populations because of the varied resources that the lakes provided.

Rivers are natural streams of water that are larger than a creek and empty into an ocean, a lake, or another river. The longest, and arguably most important, rivers of Africa are the NILE RIVER of Egypt, the NIGER RIVER of West Africa, and the CONGO RIVER of central Africa. These rivers create arteries for TRADE, provide food, and function as a means for the dissemination of ideas and goods by connecting disparate cultures.

languages Since prehistoric times, Africa has seen wide linguistic diversity. In part, this is due to the ancient origins of many African languages. It also is the result of centuries of migration and dispersal, which have created a mosaic of languages and dialects that in no way reflect whatever national borders existed at various times in Africa's history. As a result, no general linguistic feature can be said to characterize all, or even most, African languages. In general, however, African languages have been classified into four major language families, as the chart on page 138 shows.

See also: AFRO-ASIATIC (Vol. I); AMHARIC (Vol. I); BANTU (Vol. I); COPTIC (Vol. I); GE'EZ (Vol. I); FULA, (Vol. I); HAUSA (Vol. I); KHOISAN (Vol. I); KISWAHILI (Vols. II, III); NIGER-CONGO (Vol. I); NILO-SAHARAN (Vol. I).

Further reading: Derek Nurse and Bernd Heine, *African Languages: An Introduction* (New York: Cambridge University Press, 2000).

Four Major Language Families of Africa

Nilo-Saharen
Main Languages Chadian, Eastern Sudanic, Songhai
Where Spoken South of the Sahara, from the Nile to the middle of the Niger
Comments May have common ancestry with Niger-Congo Languages

Afro-Asiatic
Main Languages Afro-Asian, Amharic, Arabic, Berber Kushite
Where Spoken North Africa and eastward toward Horn of Africa
Comments Many African languages reflect hundreds, even thousands of years of trade and migration between Africa and the Middle East

Niger-Congo
Main Languages Bantu-Congo, Eastern Adamawa, Kwa, Mande, Voltic
Where Spoken Across much of Africa,from present-day Senegal to the Cape of Good Hope
Comments Bantu languages, in all their many forms, are the most commonly spoken on the continent

Khoisan
Main Languages Khoi, San
Where Spoken Southwestern Africa
Comments Distinguished by the use of "click" sounds

The Languages of Africa to 2500 BCE

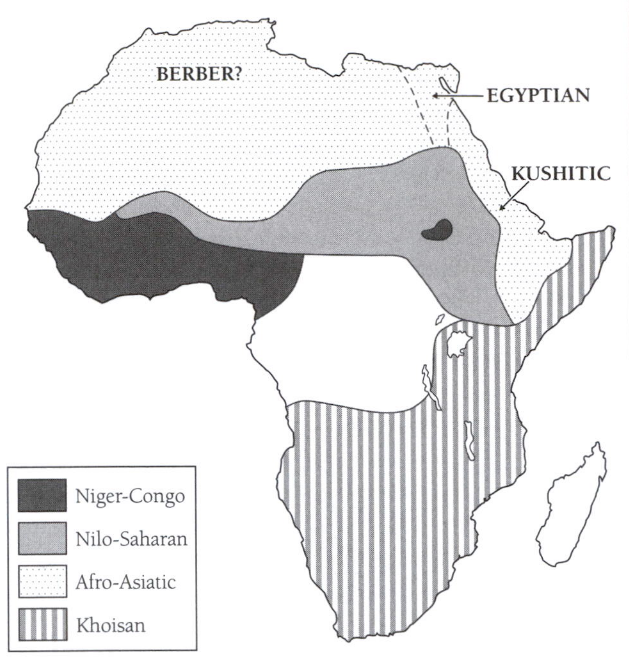

The map, based on the research of University of California–Berkeley anthropologist Joseph Greenberg, shows the languages of Africa before the Bantu migrations of 100 BCE to 600 CE. The Bantu languages, a branch of the Niger-Congo family, eventually reduced the range of the Khoisan languages to just the southern portion of the continent.

Leakeys, the Family of anthropologists, archaeologists, and paleoanthropologists noted for their discoveries of early human remains in Africa.

The son of missionary parents, Louis Leakey (1903–1972) was raised in Kenya and despite a formal education in England, remained close to the local KIKUYU and other peoples of the area throughout his lifetime. At an early age, Leakey began focusing on the study of early humans, and by the 1920s he had gained wide recognition for his discoveries of artifacts relating to HUMAN ORIGINS. Believing that the human race had its origins in Africa rather than in Europe or Asia, Leakey carried out extensive investigations in Kenya. In 1949, his discovery of a *Proconsul* skull helped establish a clear evolutionary link between monkeys and apes. Later discoveries, especially those at OLDUVAI GORGE, contributed to a clearer understanding of the development of early hominids.

Although Louis Leakey garnered the majority of the accolades and fame during his lifetime, his wife Mary (1913–1996) was generally considered to be not only a better scientist but also a more significant contributor to the knowledge of early human beings. After marrying Leakey in 1936, she carried out major excavations, both with her husband and on her own. Indeed, many of the greatest discoveries made at the Olduvai Gorge site, upon which so much contemporary knowledge of early humans depends, were the work of Mary Leakey. Her discovery of *Zinjanthropus* (*Australopithecus boisei*), or "Lucy," as the fossilized remains of this prehistoric female became known, not only brought her and her family fame but also helped revolutionize the way in which early hominids were seen.

It was Louis and Mary Leakey's son Richard (b. 1944), however, who seemed destined from the very first to carry their pioneering work to new heights. Learning well from his brilliant and famous parents, Richard became a serious field anthropologist. In the late 1960s, he was working at sites in present-day ETHIOPIA when he began a series of discoveries that rocked the scientific world and did much to fill in the gaps in our knowledge of early hominids: In 1972 he found a fossilized *Homo habilis* skull; in 1975 he discovered the skull of a *Homo erectus*; and in 1984, his team unearthed both a nearly complete *Homo erectus* skeleton (popularly known as TURKANA BOY) and the first skull ever found of the species *Australopithecus aethiopicus*.

Richard Leakey's wife, Meave Gillian Leakey (b. 1942), a trained zoologist, has also made several important discoveries, including an apparently new hominid species, *Australopithecus anamensis*.

In recent years, Richard Leakey has focused his energies on both politics and animal conservation, but the Leakey scientific legacy has been ably carried on by both Meave and their daughter Louise.

Further reading: Virginia Morell, *Ancestral Passions: The Leakey Family and the Quest for Humankind's Beginnings* (New York: Touchstone Books, 1996).

The excavations of anthropologist-archaeologist Louis Leakey, shown here in 1972, and those of his wife Mary and son Richard established that the first humans lived in East Africa rather than in Asia, as was previously thought. © *Hulton-Deutch Collection/ CORBIS*

Legba shrine Household altar in YORUBA and Yoruba-derived religions; said to protect practitioners' households.

Over the years the deity Legba has been known by several names, including Eshu, Elegbara, and Elegba. Legba shrines generally are erected in front of the home or in an entry way. Usually made of carved wood, lacitrite, or stone, they vary in form and appearance. In some regions, a small head and shoulders are set within a dish or bowl. Elsewhere, other types of altars include a slender wooden statue sitting atop a mound (known as a *kpe*). The elements of the shrine that are said to hold its protective powers are often hidden in mounds of earth that contain a pottery jar. Inside that jar are leaves, remnants of fabrics, grain, beads, or other natural materials.

See also: RELIGION, TRADITIONAL (Vol. 1)

Further reading: William Bascomb, *African Art in Cultural Perspective* (New York: W. W. Norton, 1973); Mary H. Foote, *Secrecy: African Art That Conceals and Reveals* (New York: Museum for African Art, 1993); Robert Farris Thompson, *Flash of the Spirit* (New York: Random House, 1984).

leopard Large carnivore belonging to the same feline family of animals as the LION and tiger. Leopards weigh between 110 and 200 pounds (41 and 74.6 kg), stand between 25 and 30 inches (63.5 and 76.2 cm) at the shoulder, and measure around 7 feet (2.1 m) in length, not including its 3-foot (1-m) tail. Leopards' coats are usually yellow above and white on the belly and are patterned with dark spots or rings. Leopards are solitary, nocturnal animals that live in Africa's bush and forested areas south of the SAHARA.

Leopards appear often in Africa's folklore and history. In ancient EGYPT, leopards were hunted and their skins were extensively traded. Leopards were also associated with OSIRIS, the god of the dead, and Seshat, the goddess who invented math and writing. Among the IBO people, the leopard was associated with fertility.

In one Nigerian folktale, a leopard entered villages disguised as a seductive man. One woman followed this leopard man away into the forest, where he turned back into a leopard. The leopard then chased the woman, but could not catch her.

lesser wives In many African societies, a term describing women who enter an existing marriage arrangement and share husband and household with other wives.

In this type of arrangement, known as POLYGAMY, the oldest or senior wife usually acts as the dominant authority figure. Newly married or lesser wives are expected to defer to her age and experience. The origin of this practice, widespread in much of ancient Africa, is not known. According to some theories, it may have been handed down by rulers who retained hundreds of wives for political power. Other sources indicate that the practice may have evolved from religious beliefs.

See also: FAMILY STRUCTURE (Vol. I); WOMEN IN ANCIENT AFRICA (Vol. I).

Further reading: Iris Berger and E. Frances White, eds., *Women in Sub-Saharan Africa* (Bloomington: Indiana University Press, 1999); Catherine Coquery-Vidrovitch, *African Woman: A Modern History* (Boulder, Colo.: Westview Press, 1997).

Libya North African country on the coast of the MEDITERRANEAN SEA that has a rich history dating back to the eighth millennium BCE; part of the SAHARA Desert is located in Libya. Ancient farmers of the NEOLITHIC AGE likely occupied the plains of the northern coast from as early as 8000 BCE. This society was advanced in AGRICULTURE, growing crops and raising CATTLE.

More than 5,000 years ago, the area that is modern-day Libya was a great savanna, or grassy plain. But, except for a narrow strip of land along the Mediterranean coast, most of this area is now part of the Sahara Desert. Nomadic people, called savanna people, hunted wild game and wandered the great plain with their herds. Some time after 2000 BCE, the nomadic society began to fall apart as the desert advanced and other, horse-riding peoples began invading the area. Some of the savanna people moved south into the Sudan, while others became part of the invading BERBER culture.

The Berber migration into LIBYA was recorded in inscriptions in EGYPT, c. 2700 to 2200 BCE. These inscriptions also comprise the first recorded history of Libya. Though the origin of the Berbers is not known, the remains of their culture and language support the idea that they may have come from southwestern Asia. They probably moved into North Africa sometime in the third millennium BCE, and over the next centuries they migrated from Egypt all the way to the basin of the NIGER RIVER. Egyptians referred to the Berbers as the Levu, or Libyans. The Twenty-second and Twenty-third Dynasties of Egypt, often called the Libyan dynasties, are thought to have been Berbers.

The GARAMANTES, who are the probable ancestors of today's Tuareg people, colonized the FEZZAN area c. 1000 BCE. From their capital at Germa, the Garamantes controlled several oases in the Wadi Ajal area. They also controlled much of the trade in the area, having been hired

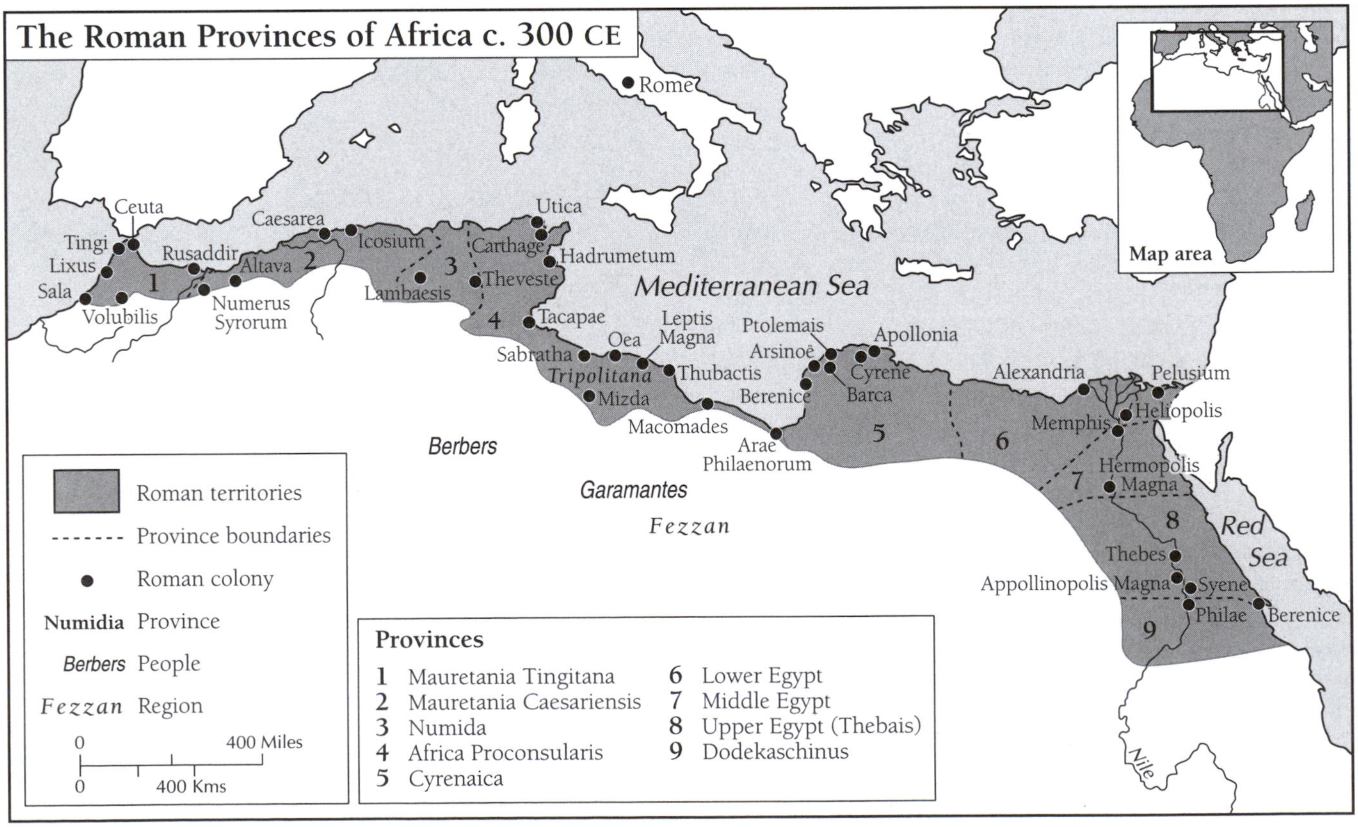

by the Carthaginians to carry GOLD and ivory on the trade route between western Sudan and the Mediterranean coast. It was at this time, too, that Libyans began to deal with Africans living south of the Sahara Desert.

Known for their skill in breeding horses, the Garamantes also kept herds of longhorn cattle. They were able to cultivate part of their hot, dry land by developing an irrigation system that used *foggares*, a series of connecting underground tunnels that carried water.

Significant remnants of the Garamantes' culture and civilization have been discovered and examined, including more than 50,000 pyramid-like tombs and several cities built of stone, including Germa, the capital, Zinchera, and Saniat Gebril. Researchers also have found Geramente inscriptions in the ancient Berber writing called *tifinagh*, which is still used by the Tuareg today. The power of the Garamantes was threatened by ROME, which launched several attacks against them. The Garamantes eventually allied with Rome sometime in the first century CE.

Some time in the seventh century BCE, Greeks moved into Cyrenaica on the Mediterranean coast of northeastern Libya and established CYRENE, which became known as a city of great art and science. It was to Rome, however, that Libya was most important, since it was situated just across the MEDITERRANEAN SEA from Italy. Rome's first conquest was the northwestern region of Libya on the Mediterranean coast. Later called Tripolitania, this region became known for exporting olive oil as well as for the gold trade and the slave trade. Then in 74 BCE, Cyrenaica came under the control of the Romans. This region was known for its wine and horses. Although the Romans ventured into the Fezzan and brought it under their control, they were mainly interested in the regions of Africa from which they had something to gain economically. They also sought regions in which local people could be used to defend the area from hostile forces.

Near the end of the first century CE, Romans finally secured the route between Tripolitania and Cyrenaica, and for more than 200 years protected the trade routes between them. With trade and communication guaranteed by Rome, Tripolitania and Cyrenaica generally thrived until c. 400. During this time, they used the same language and legal system as the Romans.

Evidence of Roman influence in Libya, as in virtually every part of the Roman Empire, included baths, forums, markets, and other familiar institutions of Roman urban life. Roman ruins discovered in Libya also show how much the area prospered under Roman rule. Scholars believe that the rich tradition of art and music that exists today in Libya is due in part to the influence of the Romans, who decorated temples and homes with such ornamentation as beautifully crafted mosaics.

Around 70 CE, after the Romans put down the Jewish revolt in Palestine and conquered the area, significant numbers of Jews made their way to Cyrenaica, where many Jews already resided. Then, in 115, Jews in Cyrenaica led another revolt against the Romans that was stopped within three years. Scholars now believe that perhaps more than 200,000 people were killed during that time.

The term *Libya* was first used as a name for the province by Emperor DIOCLETIAN about 300 CE when he separated the area of Cyrenaica into Upper Libya and Lower Libya. When the Roman Empire was divided in 395, Libya was governed by the Eastern Empire, which ruled from Constantinople, while the Western Empire was ruled from Tripolitania.

The VANDALS, a Germanic warrior people, entered North Africa from Spain and seized power in the regions of Tripolitania and Cyrenaica in about 429 and attacked the city of Rome in about 455. However, by the end of 100 years of rule in Africa, they became less interested in making war and were conquered by Byzantines, c. 533, on behalf of the Roman Empire, which was trying to reclaim northern Africa for its own.

See also: BYZANTINE AFRICA (Vols. 1, II); CARTHAGE (Vol. I); LIBYA (Vols. 1, II); SLAVERY (Vols. I, II, III); TUAREGS (Vols. II, III).

lineage Basic distinction used in social grouping of most African societies.

Lineage is a descent group determined through either patrilineal or matrilineal ancestry. The founder of a particular lineage is usually the child or grandchild of the founder of that lineage's CLAN. Though lineages serve as bridges between various segments of a clan, lineages, unlike clans, are smaller in the number of living members and of generations. A lineage represents a single body of members, but the members do not necessarily all share a common name. A lineage may hold property jointly, but a single leader often exercises authority over the members and serves as its representative. Lineages can be traced back for many generations, and, since lineages generally are considered permanent groups, the inclusion of different generations creates a more stable social structure. African lineages also function as basic political units if centralized authority—in the figure of a king or chief—does not exist.

According to a typical social model, various lineages live together as autonomous groups that make up a society. This type of lineage system, sometimes referred to as a segmentary social order, is common throughout Africa. It is particularly prevalent among pastoral peoples, who often lack a form of centralized political authority or government. The balance of power among these segmented social groups is usually determined by force through WARFARE, with the decision to engage in armed conflict usually made by a member of the group who is believed to possess ritual, or even mystical, authority.

lion Large carnivore belonging to the cat family. Adult lions are about 7 feet (2.1 m) long, stand 3 feet (1 m) at the shoulder, and weigh up to 400 pounds (182 kg). They have short-haired coats of tawny fur, and 3-foot-long tails that end with a tuft of dark hair. Male lions have manes of darker hair on and around their heads. They are found in open grasslands, savannas, and semi-desert areas.

The power and grandeur of the lion has long been admired on the African continent. One of its earliest appearances in mythology occurs with the sphinx. According to Egyptian legend, sphinxes had the bodies of lions and the heads of humans. Lions were also associated with Sakmet, the Egyptian goddess of war and vengeance, and Mahes, the Egyptian personification of the summer heat.

In Ghana, a popular folktale involved a lion and a clever rabbit. The rabbit overheard the lion saying he would eat him. But instead of running away, the clever rabbit went to the lion's cave and told him of another, more powerful lion. The rabbit led the lion to the lake and pointed to the water, and when the lion attacked his own reflection, he drowned, leaving the rabbit in peace.

Lions are social animals that live in prides with up to thirty members. They usually hunt zebras, wildebeest, and antelopes. Lions claim their territory by scent-marking and roaring.

Lisht, pyramid of Along with the pyramid of LAHUN and the pyramind of HAWARA, part of the mortuary complex for kings of the Twelfth Dynasty of EGYPT; Lisht, also called al-Lisht, is the site of two notable pyramids that were built by AMENEMHET I, also called Amonhemet I, the founder of the Twelfth Dynasty, who ruled c. 1938 to 1908 BCE.

During his reign, Amenemhet I moved the capital of Egypt from Thebes to Lisht, where he built his pyramid from mud brick that was then covered with stone. Unfortunately, the pyramid did not survive the ages well and is in ruins. Though Amenemhet I was the first ruler of the MIDDLE KINGDOM period, the style of his pyramid resembled older pyramids.

Sesostris II (also called Senwosre II), the son of Amenemhet I, was the second king of the Twelfth Dynasty and ruled for ten years with his father. Sesotstris I built his pyramid next to his father's. The first layer of his pyramid was made of sand compartments covered with limestone. Meri, the governor in charge of the construction of the pyramid, is remembered due to a stele, a slab of stone inscribed with a record of his accomplishments, which can be seen today in the Louvre Museum in Paris.

locust Short-horned migratory grasshopper. Like other grasshoppers, locusts have long, powerful rear legs for jumping and can produce chirping sounds with these hind legs and their wings.

Traveling in large swarms known as plagues, they tend to migrate for a number of reasons, including population density and heat. These plagues can be so large and dense that they darken the sky for several square miles. Plagues can migrate hundreds of miles, and, once they settle in an area, they can devour large amounts of vegetation.

Locusts have been considered threats to agricultural crops since ancient times. The desert locust, which is found in EGYPT and other arid parts of Africa, probably formed the plagues that were described in ancient Egyptian records. In the book of Exodus, the Bible also mentions a swarm of locusts as the eighth plague that God inflicted on Egypt.

Logone River Main tributary of the Chari (Shar) River, which empties into Lake Chad. The river is 240 miles (386 km) long and is fed by the Mbere River and its tributary, the Vina, of present-day Cameroon, and by the Pende of present-day Central African Republic. During the rainy season the river becomes linked to the BENUE River system through the swamps of Lake Fiango and Tikem, and the Mayo Kébi River in Cameroon. The regular loss of water to the Benue system is detrimental to the dry region of the Lake Chad basin. Extensive PAPYRUS swamps line much of the river's course.

Lower Egypt Delta land of the NILE RIVER; along with UPPER EGYPT, one of the two kingdoms of ancient EGYPT. The annual flooding of the Nile, which overflows its banks and deposits mineral-rich silt over 15,000 square miles (38,850 sq km) of land, turned this one-time swamp into the fertile soil that the Egyptians called KEMET, or the "black land."

The NILE RIVER flows northward, and the distinction between the "upper" and "lower" Nile follows that flow. Thus, Lower Egypt refers to northern Egypt, where the river empties into the MEDITERRANEAN SEA. In ancient times, Lower Egypt stretched from just south of present-day CAIRO northward to the city of ALEXANDRIA, located at the Nile Delta.

Lower Egypt was symbolized by a RED CROWN and had a bee as its emblem. The chief god of Lower Egypt was HORUS, the son of OSIRIS and ISIS. In Egyptian mythology, Horus eventually avenged the murder of his father at the hands of his uncle, SETH, who was the god of UPPER EGYPT.

Prior to unification with Upper Egypt, c. 3000 BCE, Lower Egypt consisted of a great number of independent and autonomous Delta towns. Each one functioned as a trade center, a political center, and a center of cult worship. These towns eventually unified into the kingdom of Lower Egypt.

According to Egyptian legend, MENES (also known as Narmer) was the founder of the First Dynasty of Egyptian kings and the first king of a unified Upper and Lower Egypt. This unification resulted from Upper Egypt's victory in war c. 3000 BCE. The unification of the two kingdoms not only centralized authority but also facilitated massive administrative, building, and IRRIGATION projects. Widespread food distribution and the regulation of trade also were undertaken, leading to a rapid multiplication of Egypt's wealth.

See also: BADARIAN CULTURE (Vol. I), NAQADAH I AND II (Vol. I); NARMER PALLETTE (Vol. I).

Lucy (Dinkenesh) Nickname for the earliest Australopithecine skeleton found in Africa.

See also: HADAR (Vol. 1).

luntiu-setiu Highly skilled archers of ancient KUSH (Nubia), who played a prominent role in the military success of the kingdom. In ancient times, the Kingdom of Kush was widely known as Ta-Seti, or "Land of the Bow" in tribute to these highly trained soldiers who were even more famous for their mastery of the art of the bow and arrow than for their use of swords and javelins. The well-earned reputation of these soldiers was recognized by the ancient Greeks and Romans, as well as by the Arabs, whom they defeated in battle at Dongola, c. 652.

Luxor Famous temple located in the southern part of the ruins of the ancient city of Thebes.

The temple of Luxor was commissioned by the late Eighteenth Dynasty king AMENHOTEP III, who reigned from 1390 to 1353 BCE. Built close to the NILE RIVER, the temple runs parallel to the riverbank. Its entrance features a long colonnade of fourteen pillars, each 50 feet (15.2 m) tall, which lead to a large court and a complex of halls and chambers. The temple was eventually completed by TUTANKHAMUN and HOREMHEB. RAMESSES II also made additions.

The peristyle court is one of the oldest parts of the Luxor temple in Thebes, which was built for Amenhotep III about 1380 BCE. In the foreground is a relief carved for Tutankhamun. *© Roger Wood/CORBIS*

The temple was dedicated to AMUN, the king of the gods, his consort Mut, and their son Khons. The Luxor Temple is linked by an avenue of sphinxes to the Great Temple of Amun at KARNAK, the northern part of the ruins of the city of Thebes.

M

Maasai African pastoralists named for the Maa language; they are known to have lived a nomadic life in the Nile Valley of Sudan as far back as 500 BCE.

Historically, the Maasai people are a part of a larger group of ancient peoples known as the NILOTES (sometimes referred to as Nilo-Hamitic). All Maasai speak the same Nilotic language called Maa or Ol Maa or Masai.

Because the ancient Maasai did not leave written records, not much about their life is documented. According to ORAL TRADITION, the Maasai originated in the area near Lake Turkana. Archaeological evidence suggests that the Maasai may have left the NILE VALLEY of Sudan for Kenya around 500 BCE, probably moving first into the Great RIFT VALLEY, and then on to modern-day Tanzania, sometime in the first millennium CE. The Maasai inhabit areas of Kenya and Tanzania to this day, living a pastoral life rich in tradition, custom, and ceremony.

Much of what is known about the ancient Maasai and their way of life comes from nineteenth- and twentieth-century observations. This is due, in large part, to the firm traditionalism of the Maasai themselves, who are a people with a deep respect for the past. Indeed, 75% of today's Maasai (who number between 250,000 and 350,000) continue to follow their traditional social and religious customs.

The Maasai have a long and rich tradition of religious beliefs and practices that includes many rituals and celebrations. An important part of this tradition is the *laibon* who serves as a diviner or ritual leader. The *laibon* is expected to be a healer of body and spirit, a rainmaker, and a source of good pasture land.

Maasai mythology plays an important part in explaining the traditional Maasai way of life. One documented myth explains the division of the Maasai people into two main groups. According to one version, a great ladder was built for the Maasai to climb up the long, steep slope leading to the Gishu basin. When the Maasai climbed the ladder, however, it broke, leaving one group on top of the plateau and the other at the bottom.

Several myths emphasize the importance of CATTLE to the Maasai people. One such myth names the god Engai (also called Enkai) as the creator and explains that his three children were given gifts. The third son, who was given a stick with which to herd animals, became the father of the Maasai. Another Maasai myth explains that when the earth and heavens split apart, the god of rain, Ngai, gave all cattle to the care of the Maasai. In yet another, Engai uses roots of the holy wild fig tree to help cattle make their way from the sky to the earth. To avoid harming the sacred root, the Maasai traditionally do not break the ground. In fact, it was not until quite recently that they began to cultivate the earth.

The Maasai have long honored cattle, having lived off them for thousands of years, as they wandered seasonally with their herds to more fertile grazing lands. Not surprisingly, a typical Maasai expression is "I hope your cattle are well." Among the Maasai, a large number of cattle signals wealth, and cattle are traded, sacrificed, used to pay fines, and given as dowry.

The Maasai are well-known for their beautiful ornamentation of beadwork, bangles, coils, and elaborate hair styles. The patterns of beads identify AGE-GRADES as do styles of hair, which is sometimes worn long and plastered with ochre and sometimes shaved. Another noteworthy Maasai art is dance, which is famous for the dancers' endurance and their high jumps.

Known for being great warriors, Maasai boys pass through an age-grade system in which they go from junior warrior to senior warrior (at which time they are allowed to marry). From there they pass to junior elder and then to senior elder. Morans are men between fourteen and thirty who traditionally live in the bush alone, learning traditional customs and the ways of the warrior. According to Maasai traditions, a warrior is expected to kill a lion using only his spear.

Young Maasai women typically are married to older men, and they are allowed to have sex prior to marriage (but not outside sex after marriage). In Maasai society, both boys and girls are thought to pass into adulthood around puberty by rites of passage that include circumcision and clitoridectomy.

The traditional home of the Maasai is the *enkang* or *kraal*, a complex of ten to twenty small mud-dung homes enclosed by a fence made from thornbushes. Each structure is built by women and may contain only two rooms with no window other than a small hole in the roof. Traditionally, an enkang is used temporarily, and a new one built as the band moves on. In typical Maasai culture, women tend the home and milk the cows, while the men herd the cattle and protect the home and herd.

Though it is not known for sure how many of the present-day customs and ways of the Maasai date back to ancient times, the Maasai have been resistant to change and modernization. Most prefer to live a traditional nomadic life of herding cattle, as their ancestors have done for thousands of years.

See also: MAASAI (Vols. II, III); PASTORALISM (Vol. I).

ma'at The ancient Egyptian concept of truth, justice, and cosmic order. Sometimes ma'at was personified as the daughter of the sun god RA and associated with THOTH, the god of wisdom. She was usually represented as a figure with a feather in her hair.

According to the ancient Egyptian religion, all people were judged upon their deaths. During the Judgment of the Dead, the deceased person's heart would be placed on a scale balanced by ma'at, represented only by an ostrich feather.

As a concept, ma'at also played an important part in Egyptian understanding of kingship. The king, according to traditional Egyptian notions, was a representative of the gods. His duty was to follow divine will and establish ma'at. This concept was a central part of Egyptian religion and daily life.

See also: EGYPT (Vol. I).

Macedonia Ancient kingdom in the northeastern corner of the Greek penuinsula. During the reign of ALEXANDER THE GREAT (c. 330–323 BCE), Macedonia extended its borders to EGYPT by liberating the North Africans from the Persians.

Macedonia was founded during the seventh century BCE. After 338 BCE, Philip II unified the Greeks and strengthened Macedonia, transforming it into an important kingdom. Macedonia was eventually expanded by Philip's son, Alexander the Great, into the Middle East, Egypt, and western India.

The people of Egypt welcomed Alexander, and he was able to take control of the country without a war. According to legend, Alexander traveled to the Oracle of AMUN, where he was told that he was the son of the god. This strengthened Alexander's claim to the Egyptian throne, since, for thousands of years, Egypt's rulers had believed themselves to be the descendants of the country's chief god, Amun. It also furthered Alexander's belief in his own divinity. Upon adding Egypt to the Macedonian kingdom, Alexander founded the city of Alexandria on the NILE RIVER.

Upon Alexander's death in 323 BCE, his empire was divided, and PTOLEMY ruled Egypt as a civilian official. Ptolemy's rule continued even though a Macedonian general, Perdiccas, made an unsuccessful attempt to take Egypt from him a few years after Alexander's death.

Mafia Island 170 square mile (440 sq km) island in the Indian Ocean 10 miles off the coast of Tanzania in eastern Africa. Mafia Island has been a stop on the African coastal trade route for possibly two thousand years.

Mafia is the largest island of an archipelago, or group of islands, in the Indian Ocean. Situated south of Zanzibar, the island lies close to the Rufiji River delta. The closest city on the mainland, the modern Dar es Salaam in Tanzania, is eighty miles away. The surrounding ocean area presents a variety of coral reefs and gardens that are home to a wide variety of fish. The many species of birds on the island differ from the mainland. The island's geography includes beaches, bays, and forests.

Scholars theorize that BANTU-speakers were the first inhabitants of the island. An ironworking, agricultural Bantu culture may have crossed from the mainland and settled the island from about 200 CE to 400 CE. Other inhabitants of the island included the Triangular Ironware culture, a later indigenous people thought to have been present on the island when Arab settlers from what is now Yemen took control of the island in c. 975.

Some scholars believe that the island called Menouthias, as described in *The Periplus of the Erythraean Sea,* written by PTOLEMY in 50 CE, is Mafia Island, while other scholars think the ancient writing describes Zanzibar or Pemba.

See also: INDIAN OCEAN TRADE (Vol. II); MAFIA ISLAND (Vol. II).

Maghrib Arabic word for the region in northwestern Africa that includes the areas of present-day TUNISIA, MOROCCO, and ALGERIA. The Maghrib (also called Maghreb or Magrib), not unified until Arab rule began in about the year 700 CE, was home to many prehistoric and ancient peoples.

Archaeological evidence shows that ancestors of modern-day humans inhabited the central Maghrib as early as 200,000 BCE, and tools from Neandertal people indicate that prehistoric humans were in the area by about 43,000 BCE. Some scholars believe that, by about 30,000 BCE, the population of this area had tools, tool-making methods, and craftsmanship that were highly developed for this era.

At Tassili-n-Ajjer, north of Tamanrasset in the central Maghrib, cave paintings give evidence of a group of prehistoric peoples who inhabited the area between c. 8000 and 4000 BCE. These cave paintings depict vivid scenes of prehistoric life in Africa. Research indicates that a NEOLITHIC AGE people, the Capsians, who lived on the plains in the Maghrib region, conquering the original inhabitants.

In ancient times, the people in this region came to be known as BERBERS, and they have continued to inhabit the area since that time; in fact, about one-sixth of the people who live in the Maghrib today still speak a Berber language.

Makeda, queen of Sheba (d. 955 BCE) *Powerful ruler who played a prominent role in the social and economic history of ancient Ethiopia.*

Some sources indicate that Queen Makeda was part of the dynasty originally founded by Za Besi Angabo in 1370 BCE, with her grandfather and father being the last male rulers of the royal line. The family's intended choice to rule ETHIOPIA was Makeda's brother, Prince Nourad, but his early death led to her succession to the throne. She apparently ruled the Ethiopian kingdom for more than 50 years.

Biblical references and ancient texts have often cited the young Queen's inexperience as the basis of her relationship with King Solomon of Israel, explaining that the young queen traveled to Israel seeking advice from the wiser, more experienced Solomon. The historical facts, however, indicate that Queen Makeda had become a well-respected administrator, empire builder, and international trader before her meeting with Israel's famous king. Exactly when she made that visit is uncertain, but it is clear that, while there, Queen Makeda adopted the Jewish faith and conceived a child with King Solomon. This child, named David, eventually was crowned king of Ethiopia as MENELIK I.

The empire that Queen Makeda controlled was extensive and encompassed all of Ethiopia as well as parts of Upper Egypt, Syria, Armenia, India, and southern Arabia (where she was known as Belkis). Direct access to the Mediterranean and the Red Sea, as well as the many land-based caravans that passed through Ethiopian territory, also gave Queen Makeda a vast and wealthy trade empire. For the most part, however, this was administered by specially appointed merchants rather than by the queen herself.

See also: ARK OF THE COVENANT (Vol. I); SOLOMONIC DYNASTY (Vol. II).

Malawi Present-day country in central Africa, bordering Mozambique and Tanzania, that is the site of important discoveries regarding early humans and HUMAN ORIGINS. Areas within Malawi apparently were inhabited by early hominids as early as 2 million years ago. Recent studies have unearthed evidence of settlements inhabited by ancestors of the SAN people dating back almost 100,000 years. Much later, beginning in the first millennium BCE, the area came under the influence of the massive BANTU migration, during which the indigenous peoples were, like others throughout this part of Africa, dominated by the Bantu speakers, whose ironworking and advanced agricultural techniques gave them decided technological advantages over the previous inhabitants. This pattern continued during the early centuries of the common era as other Bantu-speaking peoples came into the region from the Congo and the present-day countries of Tanzania and Congo (formerly Zaïre).

mamba Venomous snake belonging to the COBRA family. Mambas have narrow heads and large eyes, large scales, and long front teeth. Unlike other cobras, they do not have hoods around their necks. Mambas are found in tropical and southern Africa and are among the swiftest snakes. Their poison, if not treated, is often fatal to humans.

The SAN people of southern Africa, who have long been familiar with the mamba, have a folktale explaining why the snake has no legs. Long ago, says this legend, there was a terrible drought, and all the people and animals had to move away; only the lazy and arrogant snake was left behind. Eventually, all the grass and food disappeared. The snake decided to leave too, but began to sink in the sand as soon as it started moving. The snake called out for help, and the Moon, taking pity on the snake, shrank its legs, which allowed it to glide on the sand.

The black mamba can grow up to 14 feet (4.3 m) in length and is considered to be the most aggressive. It usually lives on the ground and typically preys on small mammals and lizards.

Despite its name, the black mamba actually has dark brown or gray skin. When it attacks, the black mamba raises the front of its body above the ground and strikes the head or trunk of its prey. Another variety, the green mamba, can grow up to 9 feet (2.7 m) and usually lives and hunts in trees.

Mande Family of languages used by a number of different peoples in West Africa.

The area in which Mande languages are spoken includes a wide variety of terrains and peoples ranging from such savanna dwellers as the BAMANA to the forest-dwelling Kono, Vai, and Susu. By the tenth and eleventh centuries CE, Mande-speaking cultures were well-established in the region. Exactly when and how they first peopled the area, however, is unclear. It has been suggested that Mande speakers inhabited the upper NIGER RIVER valley between 5000 and 2000 BCE, but this is not a widely held view.

See also: BAMBARA (Vol. II); BAMBARA KINGDOM (Vol. III); MANDE (Vol. II).

Manetho (305–285 BCE) *Egyptian author and priest; famous for his study of the history of ancient Egypt.*

Manetho lived in Sebennytos, the capital of Egypt during the Thirtieth Dynasty, and was a priest during the reigns of Ptolemy I and Ptolemy II. A thorough knowledge of both Egyptian HIEROGLYPHICS and Greek, as well as firsthand experience with Egyptian religious beliefs and customs, made him especially well-suited to the task of studying Egyptian history.

Commissioned by Ptolemy II to write *Aegyptiaca*, a collection of three books about the history of ancient EGYPT, Manetho was given access to the archives of the temple in which he served as a priest. Ranging in content from mythological texts to official records, from magical formulas to scientific treaties, the archives were rich with all the sources needed to write the history of the country. Given the diversity of these sources, it is not surprising that in Manetho's account, myths and folktales are neatly interwoven with the facts of Egyptian history.

When complete, *Aegyptiaca* chronicled the kings of Egypt from the earliest times, when gods and demigods supposedly ruled, to the historical dynasties, from MENES down to ALEXANDER THE GREAT's conquest of Egypt. Although many of the specific details—such as the names of kings and the exact dates of their reigns—are often incomplete and inaccurate, Manetho's work remains the basis for the conventional numbering of the dynasties of the Egyptian pharaohs.

Marra Mountains Mountains in the western region of the modern day Republic of the Sudan.

Located halfway between the NILE and Lake CHAD, the Marra Mountains once formed part of an ancient caravan route—winding northwest toward the Nile at DONGOLA BEND. From there travelers could continue north to EGYPT or south towards KUSH. Some historians believe this was the route known as the Forty-Day Road mentioned in the accounts of HARKHUF, an Egyptian governor who traveled from Egypt to KERMA, the Kushite kingdom.

See also: ELEPHANTINE (Vol. I).

Mashonaland Homeland of the SHONA people in northeastern Zimbabwe. The region is comprised mainly of a large plateau running north to the Zambezi River valley. Primarily grassland dotted with sparse woodland areas, for many centuries Mashonaland has supported the agricultural and cattle-herding lifestyle of the Shona.

Masinissa (240 BCE–148 CE) *Ruler of the ancient North African kingdom of Numidia.*

The son of a chief who headed the Massyli society of NUMBIDIA, Masinissa was reared in CARTHAGE. Although his father militarily supported Carthage against ROME during their battles on the Iberian Peninsula (modern-day Spain), Masinissa aligned himself with Roman forces after 206 BCE, when the Carthaginians were routed and driven out of Iberia. He is noted for assisting Rome in other territorial invasions of Carthaginian-held lands. In return, Roman officials helped him to achieve his goals of becoming the next ruler of Numidia. Syphax, his political foe, was chieftain of the Massaesyl and strongly favored Carthaginian rule. It was Masinissa who provided the cavalry of 4,000 men to the Roman army that brought about Syphax's defeat.

In 201 BCE, a treaty drawn up between Carthage and Rome had several important aspects that increased Masinissa's power. It was decreed that Carthage relinquish her fleet and territorial lands and be forbidden to engage in any warfare without notification to Rome. Notably, a written clause contained within the treaty stipulated that any lands formerly belonging to Masinissa's ancestors could be reclaimed. As a result, Masinissa was given the lands formerly held by Syphax, including Zama, which allowed him to extend his rule over both the Massyli and Massaesyl nations. He effectively organized the settlement of these nomadic societies by replacing early methods of cultivation with the more advanced agricultural methods used in Carthage.

Masinissa established his capital at Cirta, the modern-day Algerian city of Constantine, where he ruled for approximately fifty years. Even then Cirta had the urban flavor of a growing city. Carthaginian language, religious rites, and art forms were in evidence, and greater emphasis was placed on limited trading. The coins minted at Cirta and used for trade appear to have been made from bronze, lead, and COPPER.

Masinissa is noted for having developed and maintained his political alliance with Rome, thus ensuring that his political goals and aspirations were met. However, in 155 BCE, his power was checked when a Roman commission came to Numidia to settle disputes between Numidian- and Carthaginian-held territories. Over Masinissa's objections, the commission decided to destroy Carthage, and the Romans subsequently burned the city to the ground and performed ritual ceremonies to curse the land.

See also: JUBA I (Vol. I).

Further reading: Philip Curtin, Steve Feierman, Leonard Thompson, Jan Vansina, eds., *African History: From Earliest Times to Independence*, 2nd ed. (London: Longman Group Limited, 1995); G. Mokhtar, ed., *General History of Africa: Ancient Civilizations of Africa*, vol. 2 (Paris: UNESCO, 1990).

masks Decorated coverings for the face, often worn at times of religious or social significance.

Masks play important roles among many African peoples and are used in everything from agricultural festivals to funerals. They also are used in warfare and in ceremonies for curing the sick.

One of the earliest uses of masks was probably to discipline children. As an extension of a mother's habit of making nasty faces to frighten children into obedience, masks were used to instill discipline. Masks were also often worn by judges, generally either to show that they represented a spiritual or ancestral authority or else to protect themselves against reprisals by those they judged. For the same reason, they were worn by secret societies that punished malefactors.

As long ago as the time of ancient Egypt, masks were also an important part of funerals. From as early as 2000 BCE, the faces of the Egyptian dead were covered with plaster-covered cloths that were painted with representations of the deceased. The funeral masks of important people—such as people of royal blood or very wealthy citizens—often were decorated with gold and silver. Elsewhere in Africa, masks frequently were made of wood and, as a result, archaeologists have found few examples surviving from ancient times.

The YORUBA peoples are among the most famous African mask makers. Their masks often are used for ritualized reenactments of battles, especially ones featuring the deeds of legendary and heroic warriors. In the Oyo area, masks are also part of elaborate ceremonies honoring the peoples' ancestors. These brightly painted masks are covered with cloth, with a new layer of cloth being added each year.

The Nigerian Epa festival, for which this contemporary Epa Society mask was created, honors the Great Mother, from whom all women and female sorcerers are traditionally said to be descended. The mask is 36.5 inches (92.7 cm) high. *© North Carolina Museum of Art, Raleigh, N.C./CORBIS*

The Dogon of present-day Mali and Burkina Faso are also noted for their elaborately carved masks. Their masks, some of which date back to the early common era, play an important role in funeral ceremonies. When a family member dies, the survivors make figures, which are intended to house the spirits of the deceased during the official period of mourning. When that time is up, masks are used to drive away the deceased's spirits. Dogon rituals also make use of a Great Mask. This mask is never actually worn. Instead, a new one is made, every sixty years, to represent the Dogon's primordial ancestor.

See also: DOGON (Vol. II).

Matara One of three cosmopolitan centers in ancient AKSUM (300 BCE –600 CE). Situated on the high plateau region near the Ethiopian/Eritrean border, Matara overlooks the RED SEA coast. Once a leading cosmopolitan city, Matara had TRADE markets that attracted a cross section of ethnic and religious groups, including Egyptians, Kushites, Arabs, Jews, and Indians. Testifying to Matara's wealth and success are the ruins of former structures, including a small palace complex used by the nobility, and stelae, or stone monuments. The recovery of Roman and Byzantine objects further confirms Matara's role in Aksum's trade network, which linked the Nile, the Mediterranean, and the Indian Ocean.

Matsieng Figure in TSWANA creation mythology.

See also: BOTSWANA (Vols. I, II, III).

Mbuti (Bambuti) Group of peoples of the ITURI FOREST in present-day Democratic Republic of Congo. The Mbuti are among several peoples whose small stature has led them to be referred to as PYGMIES, a term that is no longer popular with anthropologists, who prefer to call them Mbuti. The Mbuti reach an average height of 4 feet 9 inches (1.4 m) and an average weight of 100 pounds (45 kg). They have long subsisted by hunting game and gathering fruit. The Mbuti are still masters of the jungle, hunting and gathering as they have for perhaps as long as 4,500 years.

The Mbuti peoples, whose groups include the Sua, Aka, Efe, and one called the Mbuti, are probably the original inhabitants of the great Ituri forest. They are nomadic and territorial, with patrilineal CLANS of up to 100 members claiming segments of the forest. Clans migrate to new camps within their territory every three to four weeks to follow their herds and maximize their access to plant resources. Their beehive-shaped huts, made of phrynium leaves, require only a few hours to build, thus facilitating their nomadic lifestyle.

Traditionally, the Mbuti have maintained a symbiotic relationship with BANTU-speaking villages and agriculturalists of the southern Sudan. In exchange for crops, CLOTH, pots, axes, and SALT, the Mbuti hunt and gather food for the villages, providing them with wild game, as well as honey, fruit, nuts, mushrooms, caterpillars, and termites from the forest. To the west, the Sua and the Mbuti have aligned with the Budu (Babudu) people; the Aka Mbuti live near the Mangbetu; the Efe Mbuti inhabit the north and eastern areas of the forest with the Mamvu and Lese (Walese); and the group that calls themselves Mbuti live near the Bila (Babila) in the heart of the forest. The Mbuti take up the languages of their village neighbors and try to stay within several hours' walking distance of them. Relationships between Mbuti individuals and their respective villages are common, and family ties between the two are passed from generation to generation.

Hunting techniques among the Mbuti vary. Some use bows and arrows or spears when they track large game, while others rely on nets to catch smaller animals like antelope. Mbuti women often assist the villagers by tending the fields while the men hunt. Starchy foods like beans, YAMS, and squash acquired from the villages provide the bulk of calories in the Mbuti diet.

The Mbuti were long thought to be only imaginary beings. Four thousand years ago, during ancient Egypt's Sixth Dynasty, an Egyptian expedition reported seeing "dancing dwarfs" in a "land of spirits," but, even when requested to do so by the pharaoh himself, the expedition was unable to bring back one of these "dancers of god." Later, tales of these small forest people appeared among the Greeks, Romans, and Arabs. But, since so many of the stories seemed too outlandish to be believed, smaller peoples generally were considered to be only a myth. It was not until the 1800s that the outside world finally had proof of the existence of the small-statured Mbuti.

A formal political system or social hierarchy does not exist in Mbuti society. Instead, all disputes are settled by general discussions between the disagreeing parties. Music, song, and dance are important to Mbuti culture, particularly during INITIATION RITES or to celebrate the gifts of the forest. They worship a forest deity but do not seem to believe in an afterlife. The dead are buried near the temporary phrynium huts and are abandoned when the Mbuti moves to a new location.

One of the more unusual Mbuti customs is the practice of "sister exchange." In order to marry, a man must find a woman of his own clan to marry with a man of his prospective wife's clan.

medicine The science and art of diagnosing, treating, and preventing disease as well as improving health; also the substance or means (spell, ceremony, etc.) by which health is improved. Medicine and the medical arts took many forms in ancient Africa, from simple herbal cures to procedures that were the result of many years of study and training on the part of the healers.

As early as the Predynastic Period, the ancient Egyptians practiced medical arts of one kind or another. Indeed, the BADARIAN CULTURE, as well as the subsequent NAQADAH I and II cultures, all seem to have been adept at treating illnesses and other disorders with herbs, drugs, and flowers. By Egypt's Third Dynasty (c. 2700 BCE) the training of physicians had become formalized, and the Egyptian population was treated by the world's first trained, practicing physicians. These healers treated diseases, performed surgery, and prescribed medicines. In large part, this was due to the effects of the legendary IMHOTEP, architect, royal adviser, and, in the eyes of many, the world's first physician. As a minister to King Djoser (c. 2725–2640 BCE), Imhotep established schools for doctors and produced twenty volumes of medical texts that helped spread the use of medicinal herbs throughout Africa.

In general, ancient Egyptians believed that illness and disease were the result of the activities of the demon goddess Sekhmet. Cures, they believed, were aided by the healing deities, RA, THOTH, and ISIS. Because of this, the sick were given a combination of spiritual and physical treatments that included everything from specialized incantations to the applications of herbs and other medicines. The incantations were employed in order to rid the patient's body of any evil demon or god that might be causing a particular ailment. Physicians also gave out prescriptions, set broken bones, and treated wounds.

Though the ancient Egyptians were advanced in the techniques of embalming and doctors were known to have various surgical tools such as forceps, drills, and hooks, they did not have extensive knowledge of anatomy. As a result, with the exception of trepanning, which involved creating a small hole in the skull of an ill patient for the purpose of allowing disease to break free of the body, they performed only a few, relatively minor surgical operations

Among the specialists in medicine in ancient Egypt were dentists, veterinarians, and gynecologists. The *Kahun Papyrus* (also called the *Kahun Gynecological Papyrus*), which is dated c. 1825 BCE, provides evidence that Egyptian physicians were capable of a wide range of procedures, such as recommending birth-control methods, performing pregnancy testing, and diagnosing reproductive problems. (Sour milk, crocodile dung, and honey were among the contraceptives prescribed.)

A record of disease, deformities, and treatments has been collected from the remains of mummies, art, and medical texts. Two of these texts, the *Edwin Smith Papyrus* and the *Ebers Papyrus*, provide remarkable insights into Egyptian medical practices.

Egypt may have been home to the invention of medicine as a healing practice, but Egyptian medical practices spread to other parts of Africa and influenced the healing arts there. In addition, other traditions and systems developed on their own. One of the most important of these has been linked with the YORUBA people, whose roots can be traced to ILE-IFE and beyond. Primarily herbal and homeopathic in orientation, Yorubic medicine is part of a long line of practice that extends from Africa through the Caribbean to the Americas.

Of equal interest is the tradition of the Djembe, a sacred drum used in healing ceremonies and other important rituals. Dating back to at least 500 BCE, the Djembe has been called "the healing drum" because of its use in traditional healing rituals.

medicine men Religious healers who try to cure disease and ailments by appealing to supernatural powers. Common figures throughout history in ancient African societies, medicine men have traditionally served as an important link between the real and supernatural worlds. Many traditional African societies believe that offending otherworldly powers causes disease and illness. Therefore, it also is maintained, the cures lie in appeasing the spirits. In the appeals they make to otherworldly spirits, the medicine men provide hope that diseases can be cured or illnesses avoided. The types of cures vary from culture to culture, or even among various healers within a single culture, and an appropriate cure might involve anything from exorcisms to religious ceremonies to herbal remedies.

Medicine men were found among some of the earliest inhabitants of Africa, including the SAN, who originated, according to most estimates, 20,000 to 30,000 years ago. The San traditionally believe in two gods. The first is the Creator; the second is the Creator's subservient messenger, Gauwa. Despite the fact that, in San society, the medicine men would often interact with Gauwa, the great Creator is the being who is seen as bringing illness and death. Ironically, it is that same Creator who is seen as instilling the medicine men with the power to facilitate cures. That power, however, has limits and could easily be disrupted. Therefore, the medicine men are always on guard to avert any bad will that the Creator might send their way through Gauwa.

Medicine men are abundant among the San, with virtually everyone playing the role of medicine man at some point in time. The San believe that curing powers can be delivered through dance, so large village dances are held several times a month, much as they have throughout the San past. At these gatherings, the San believe, the sick would be cured and future evil would be avoided. The medicine man performing at any given dance enters into a trance, placing his hand first on the sick person and then on the rest of the villagers. The healer then grunts softly, fluttering his hands as he does so. His sounds and movements become progressively louder and more animated to draw out the sickness that is affecting the infected person.

As the dance develops and the sickness becomes more difficult to extract, the medicine man's grunts turns into high-pitched shrieks. He then tramples the fire of the dancing area and sets his own hair afire in an attempt to spark his healing powers. The villagers then put out the fire in the healer's hair as the medicine man hurls flaming sticks into the darkness to chase away Gauwa and the evil spirits. He then goes into a deep trance that supposedly enables his spirit to leave his body and confront Gauwa. During the trance, the people watch over his body, chanting for his safe return from this state of half-death. When he awakens from the trance, the medicine man has done all he that he can to cure the sick.

Although each society appeals to the spirits in its own particular way, the purpose of the process is generally the same: They all attempt to alleviate illness by removing evil from the sick. Some groups use ceremonies akin to the dances of the San. Others use good-luck charms, love potions, or sacred objects to drive away evil spirits. Some even used magical remedies involving sacrifice, usually in the form of small, domesticated animals.

The concept of evil, and thus the root of a person's illness, varies among groups as well. Evil spirits might be in the form of an all-powerful god like Gauwa. Other groups, such as the Suku, believe in WITCHCRAFT. Among the Suku, witches are not gods but people who were turned into evil spirits after being fed human flesh at birth. As adults, these witches could inflict illness or death on humans. Medicine men perform rituals to protect the people from witches and heal those already cursed by illness.

See also: RELIGION, TRADITIONAL (Vol.1)

Medinet Habu Arabic name for the town known as DJEME, which occupied the original site of the mortuary temple of RAMESSES III (1184–1153 BCE). During a reign of more than thirty years, Ramesses III was revered as a military leader who not only defeated invading forces from Libya but also expanded Egypt's territorial boundaries. Ramesses' victories ushered in a period of great prosperity for Egypt, which in turn generated the construction of many buildings and temples. One of the most outstanding works of the period known as the NEW KINGDOM, Ramesses' memorial temple housed a library and contained numerous inscriptions and wall reliefs related to his battles with the Libyans. The name *Medinet Habu* is believed to have been given to the site by later inhabitants who erected Christian churches within temple walls.

See also: COPTS (Vol. I); COPTIC CHRISTIANITY (Vol. II).

Mediterranean Sea Largest inland sea in the world. The Mediterranean borders Europe, Asia, and Africa, and covers an area of 965,000 square miles (2,499,350 sq km). It connects with the Atlantic Ocean through the Straight of Gibraltar, in the west. It is also connected with the Black Sea in the northeast through the Dardanelles, the Sea of Marmara, and the Bosporus. In the southeast, it is connected to the RED SEA by the modern-day Suez Canal. Among the rivers that flow into the Mediterranean are the Po, Rhône, Ebro, and NILE.

Since ancient times, cultures have flourished around the Mediterranean. Egyptian merchants navigated it as early as 3000 BCE. The Egyptians were followed by the Aegeans and the HITTITES. Around the twelfth century BCE, the PHOENICIANS began to gain prominence in the region. They established trading posts along the North African coast, the largest of which was CARTHAGE. By the fifth century BCE, an entire trading empire known as the Punic civilization was based around that city. By the first century CE, the Mediterranean was almost entirely dominated by ROME. The Romans called it Mare Nostrum, meaning "our sea." By the fourth and fifth centuries, the Byzantine Empire controlled the area, and eventually, following the conquests of the seventh and eighth centuries, Arab peoples controlled the Mediterranean.

See also: ALGERIA (Vols. I, II, III); BYZANTINE AFRICA (Vols. I, II); MOROCCO (Vols. I, II, III); LIBYA (Vols. I, II, III).

Medjay Mercenary troops and traders of KUSH who served in the Hyksos and Egyptian armies.

The military relationship between Egyptian rulers and the Medjay appears to have begun sometime between 1700 and 1670 BCE, following the Hyksos invasion of Egypt in the Seventeenth Dynasty. Based in KERMA in Lower NUBIA, some Medjay soldiers chose to join forces with the Egyptians in opposition to Hyksos rule. Ironically, it appears that the Medjay used many of the same superior weapons that initially led to EGYPT's defeat: bronze swords, powerful bows and arrows, and HORSES and chariots. These fierce Medjay warriors helped expand and develop Egypt's military power, enabling the Egyptian ruler Kamose (c. 1576–1570 BCE) to begin the process of dislodging Hyksos control. However, it was left to his brother, AHMOSE I, to finally end Hyksos rule and reunite Egypt under the Eighteenth Dynasty (1570–1085 BCE). In retaliation against Medjay soldiers who fought against Egypt, Ahmose waged war on Kerma until about 1450 BCE, when the capital and the kingdom were destroyed. Even this did not obliterate the Medjay's history—it lived on in Egyptian vocabulary in the form of a word that meant "policeman."

Memphis Capital city of ancient EGYPT during the OLD KINGDOM (c. 2705–2213 BCE). Memphis is located south of the NILE RIVER DELTA, about 12 miles (19.2 km) from the modern city of Cairo. Memphis is also the site of a number of ancient necropolises, or cemeteries, including Giza and SAQQARA.

According to tradition, Memphis was founded in 2925 BCE by MENES, the legendary king who first united UPPER EGYPT and LOWER EGYPT. Memphis was located on the boundary of these two lands and was deemed a good site for a capital. Its primary god was PTAH, for whom a prominent temple was built. The city was originally named "the White Wall," possibly in reference to the king's palace.

Memphis reached the height of its dominance during the Third and Fourth Dynasties (c. 2650–2465 BCE). Some of ancient Egypt's most spectacular monuments were built during this time. Djoser, the second king of the Third Dynasty, constructed the impressive STEP PYRAMID OF DJOSER entirely of stone.

During the MIDDLE KINGDOM (c. 1991–1668 BCE) and the NEW KINGDOM (c. 1570–1070 BCE), Memphis's influence remained strong, even after Thebes was established as the new capital. Later, during Greek and Roman rule, Memphis was second in importance only to Alexandria. Memphis was abandoned after the Arabs conquered Egypt in 640 CE.

Menelik I (c. 10th century BCE) *Ruler of ancient Ethiopia and the son of Queen Makeda and King Solomon.*

Menelik was reared in the royal court of the Ethiopian kingdom ruled by Queen MAKEDA. His mother's adoption of the JUDAISM led Menelik to observe the traditions of his mother's faith, and he journeyed to Jerusalem at the age of thirteen. It appears that Menelik may have rejected the opportunity to remain in Jerusalem, however. Instead, after being crowned king of ETHIOPIA by his father, Menelik left Israel, traveling with a number of Israelite nobles. According to the *Kebra Nagast*, Ethiopia's national epic, it was at this time that Menelik and the nobles stole the sacred ARK OF THE COVENANT from Solomon. This traditional account states that Menelik carried out the will of God by removing the Ark of the Covenant from Jerusalem.

See also: SOLOMONIC DYNASTY (Vol. II).

Menes (Narmer) (r. c. 2925–c. 2863 BCE) *First pharaoh of ancient Egypt.*

Menes ruled c. 2925 BCE and, according to traditional Egyptian belief, was responsible for uniting UPPER and LOWER EGYPT. He is also attributed with establishing the city of MEMPHIS, which served as his capital.

According to the third-century BCE historian MANETHO, Menes ruled for sixty-two years before being killed by a hippopotamus. Manetho also wrote that Menes originally came from THINIS, a province in Upper Egypt. Menes has been identified, if inconclusively, with ancient Egyptian kings known as Scorpion and Aha.

Menkaure (c. 2575–2465 BCE) *Fifth king of Egypt's Fourth Dynasty; son and successor of Khafre who built the third and last pyramid at Giza.*

Although his pyramid is the smallest of the pyramids of Giza, it was made of costly Aswan granite. Inside the pyramid was a basalt sarcopaghus and many fine slate sculptures. These depicted Menkaure himself, his wife Khamerernebti II, and the god HATHOR. Menkaure's reign lasted about twenty years, and he was said to be a just and pious king. The epitaph on his pyramid—which his son and successor, Shepseskaf, finished after Menkaure's death—noted that he was called Man-kau-Ra, the deified one.

Mentuhotep II (Nebhapetre) (r. c. 2008–1957 BCE) *Egyptian king of the Eleventh Dynasty who reunified Egypt.*

Mentuhotep II, sometimes identified as Mentuhotep I, defeated Lower and Middle Egypt of the kingdom of HIERAKONOPOLIS and became the first king of the MIDDLE KINGDOM. At the time of his ascension, Mentuhotep II ruled only UPPER EGYPT, which had been battling the kingdom of Hierakonopolis in LOWER EGYPT for about sixty years. During the fourteenth year of his reign, Mentuhotep II began a new military campaign against Hierakonopolis, and by 1968 BCE, he had gained control of all of Egypt.

Once Egypt was unified, Mentuhotep II established Thebes as his capital and built many monuments commemorating his military victories. His most memorable building is his funerary complex in Thebes.

Meroë Kushite kingdom established between the fifth and sixth cataracts of the NILE RIVER. Meroë was founded c. 590 BCE and became one of the leading cities of the ancient world. Its growth and development were linked to international trade, iron smelting, agriculture, and the expansion of its territories. Recovered evidence suggests that between the third and second centuries BCE, MILLET served as a chief diet staple. Flax and COTTON were cultivated and spun on an early type of loom.

Archaeologists had hoped that the recovery of a written script would help to address many aspects of Kushite culture. Known as Meroitic writing, it had apparently been inscribed on various monuments and stelae. (Stelae are stone monuments, of various sizes, that usually bear

The pyramids of the kings of Kush at Meroë (300 BCE–300 CE) in ancient Sudan were built on a smaller scale than the pyramids in Egypt's Valley of the Kings. *© Jonathan Blair/CORBIS*

inscriptions regarding important people and their deeds.) However, archaeologists have not been able to decipher the texts. Instead, their attention currently is focused on various art forms recovered in the region. Meroitic pottery, considered by some to be among the most well- made in the ancient world, shows evidence of Egyptian, Greek, and Roman influences, along with distinctive Kushite motifs. Highly detailed wall reliefs confirm the presence of CATTLE and horses in Meroë, and there are also reports that ELEPHANTS were trained there for use in military battles. Archaeologists have also recovered the ruins of a temple dedicated to their national deity APEDEMAK and speculate that it signaled a return to earlier cultural beliefs.

Various ruins in Meroë have also provided a strong sense of kingdom's prosperity, including the recovery of a royal palace and bathing compound. There also was a proliferation of pyramids used for royal burials. (Although created using the same principal as Egyptian pyramids, Meroitic pyramids were built on a much smaller scale.) The homes of the wealthy appear to have been built in fired red brick, while other homes were constructed of more modest materials.

Ironically, the destruction of the kingdom may have been hastened by the use of its iron foundries. Dependency on timber for fuel most likely resulted in deforestation, which in turn had a significant impact on agriculture. Little is known about this period or the events that led to repeated clashes with Ezana, the king of AKSUM. However, in 350 CE, the Ethiopian king dispatched armies to Meroë, and the kingdom was razed. Its inhabitants may have retreated from the Ezana's army or they may have been absorbed by other ethnic groups that overran the region. Because of the uncertainty about who occupied the region in the aftermath of its destruction, archaeologists collectively refer to this population as the X-GROUP.

See also: ASPELTA (Vol. I); BALLANA CULTURE (Vol. I); ETHIOPIA (Vols. I, II, III); GEBEL BARKAL (Vol. I); MEDJAY (Vol. I); NAGA, TEMPLES AT (Vol. I); NUBIA (Vol. I); NUBIA, CHRISTIAN (Vol. II).

Further reading: Joseph E. Harris, *Africans and Their History* (New York: Penguin, 1998); Frank Snowden, Jr., *Blacks in Antiquity* (Cambridge, Mass.: Belknap, 1970)

Meroë, Island of Part of the ancient kingdom of KUSH, with its northern end situated between the fifth and sixth cataracts of the NILE RIVER.

Once MEROË was established as the capital of Kush, the neighboring Island of Meroë became an important part of the kingdom's economic life. There, the combination of climate and fertile land produced a wealth of fast-growing agricultural crops, including tropical cereals such as SORGHUM and MILLET. The land also proved to be excellent for grazing cattle and other livestock.

Rich in hardwood timber, the Island of Meroë also contained numerous deposits of iron ore, and early iron smelting flourished on the island. Axes and plows were produced for clearing and cultivating the land, while spears and arrows, used to defend the kingdom from invaders, were highly valued by traders. Resources and activities like these helped make Kush a major political and commercial competitor to both Egypt and the Kingdom of AKSUM.

Mesopotamia Site of one of the world's earliest civilizations. Although recent archaeological discoveries have shown that the earliest humanlike creatures, the *Australopithecines*, developed on the African continent as early as 4 million years ago, the Middle East was the scene of some of the first human civilizations. Many of these developments took place in Mesopotamia, the region between the Tigris and Euphrates Rivers. This area, sometimes referred to as the "Fertile Crescent," covers parts of modern-day Turkey, Syria, and Iraq.

Although little is known of Mesopotamia's early inhabitants, it is clear that they had established villages and other settlements in the area by about 7000 BCE. By 3500 BCE—at about the time that the AMRATIAN and GERZEAN CULTURES were developing in EGYPT—new peoples began migrating into the region, eventually establishing the community of Sumer. Considered to be the world's first civilization, Sumerian culture included the earliest known form of writing.

As time passed, other peoples and civilizations rose in the area, including Akkadia, Babylonia, and Assyria. By the sixth century BCE, however, Mesopotamia fell under the sway of the Persian Empire, which also eventually counted Egypt among its conquests. Later, the region was conquered by ALEXANDER THE GREAT and, eventually, by the Romans.

See also: BALLANA CULTURE (Vol. I).

metallurgy The art and science of extracting metals from ores and modifying the metals for use. Metallurgy has been practiced in Africa since ancient times. The early metalsmiths of SUMERIA, Babylon, and EGYPT were highly prized members of their society. These people were so valuable that invading armies made a special effort to capture them and carry them off.

At Gerza, on the Nile River just south of the modern site of CAIRO, a civilization developed based on the metallurgy of COPPER. The people of this GERZEAN CULTURE had learned basic copper metallurgy from immigrants from MESOPOTAMIA by about 3500 BCE.

Copper was the basic metal used in ancient Egypt, as important to the ancient Egyptians as iron has been to the modern technological world. Early metal workers quickly learned that copper became less brittle and easier to shape if it was heated before hammering. Called tempering, this process put an edge on a tool or weapon that was both hard and durable. Tools made with this process were so strong that they were used to construct the pyramids and other great buildings of Egyptian civilization. The Egyptians also learned that copper was malleable, meaning that it could easily be hammered into useful and artistic shapes.

Copper was especially valued for its color and luster. As a result it often was used to create beautiful and intricate jewelry, such as rings, bangles, chains, necklaces, and hair ornaments. Copper was also used to decorate weaponry. Knife handles were inlaid with copper designs, spear shafts were bound with fine copper wire, and shields were embellished with burnished copper nails. The ancient Egyptians also used copper for more practical purposes, such as water pipes.

Many examples of copper craftwork were preserved in ancient Egyptian tombs. Most of the surviving relics are made of cast copper. The Egyptians are commonly credited with inventing the lost-wax method of casting metal, which uses as a mold a beeswax model of the object to be cast. Molten liquid copper is then poured into the mold, and the metal is allowed to cool and harden. The mold finally is broken away to reveal the cast metal object, which is finished with a chisel and other hand tools.

IRON was being worked in Anatolia as early as 2000 BCE, and it soon became a valuable commodity, both in wrought bars and in such weapons as dagger blades and spears. Iron technology spread across Africa along with the BANTU migration, but it was not until the first century CE that the smelting of iron was common throughout the continent.

Around 1000 BCE, ancient Egyptians also developed the technology for making elementary forms of steel. Hot iron was hammered to expel impurities. Then it was broken into pieces and heated with wood chips in clay containers until the pieces of iron absorbed carbon and melted. This converted it into steel. The steel pieces could be reheated and forged into bars for later use. There is evidence that East Africans began producing steel in carbon furnaces around 1400 BCE.

metals Various opaque, malleable substances used to create durable tools, works of art, and other goods. Metals, and especially COPPER, bronze, and precious metals such as

GOLD and silver, were an essential part of Egyptian culture from the earliest dynasties onward. To a large extent, the civilization of ancient Egypt depended on these metals.

Most copper is not found in its usable form, that is, as a pure reddish brown metal. Instead, copper usually has to be extracted from ore, such as the mineral malachite. (Ore is a mineral or aggregate of minerals from which a substance, usually a metal, can be extracted.) The Egyptians mined malachite, preferring it over other copper ores like azurite and cuprite because of the ease with which usable copper could be extracted from it. The Egyptians mined for copper in the Sinai Peninsula on such a large scale that it can be considered the first real industry of the ancient world

The process of extracting copper from the ore is known as smelting, and it requires a fire that is much hotter than a normal cooking fire. In order to achieve this intense heat, early metalsmiths had to design intricate bellows systems and special ovens. Smelting was also used to make bronze, an alloy, or mixture of metals, made from copper and tin. Bronze appeared between 3000 and 2500 BCE, beginning in the Tigris-Euphrates delta. Although it is possible that independent development of bronze occurred in different regions, it is more likely that the bronze culture spread through trade and migration, beginning in the Middle East and then moving on to Egypt, Europe, and possibly China.

The Sumerian city-states were the first great metal-using civilization. The Sumerians traded up and down the Euphrates River, transporting copper from Armenia to the north. The Sumerian word for copper, *urudu*, is also used for the Euphrates, which was their "copper river."

Brass, an alloy of copper and zinc without tin, did not appear in Egypt until about 30 BCE, when it was rapidly adopted throughout the Roman world. Brass was especially valued for making coins.

Egypt exploited NUBIA for its precious metals, including gold and electrum. The gold mines of Nubia were located in the valleys and mountains on either side of the NILE RIVER. Nubia was also an important source of copper, which was used to make the stone-working tools necessary for Egypt's monumental building projects.

The ability to work iron probably first emerged in the Near East, in Egypt and Mesopotamia. Several drops, special forges used to harden metal, have been found in Egypt, and have been dated to about 3500 BCE.

See also: BRONZE AGE (Vol. I); METALLURGY (Vol. I).

Middle Kingdom Period of strength and achievement in Egyptian history, lasting from 1991 to 1668 BCE. Following the period of decline known as the First Intermediate Period (c. 2213–1991 BCE), the Twelfth Dynasty emerged as a powerful force. Founded by Amenemhet, a usurper who came to power in 1991 BCE, the dynasty included such notable figures as Sesostris I and Sesostris III. These and other pharaohs of the dynasty helped Egypt regain the wealth, power, and glory of its earlier years. A hallmark of the era was the Egyptian conquest of NUBIA. By the seventeenth century BCE, however, the kingdom was in decline. This culminated in what has come to be called the Second Intermediate Period, an era during which Egypt was dominated by the Hyksos.

See also: NEW KINGDOM (Vol. I); OLD KINGDOM (Vol. I).

millet Edible cereal grain widely cultivated in Africa; called *gero* and *acha*. Easy to cultivate and quick to grow, millet seeds are extracted from Poaceane grass and its many varieties. Similar to SORGHUM, millet seeds were domesticated in various regions of Africa dating back to the period of the Late STONE AGE, c.18,000 BCE, and even earlier.

Pearl millet (*Pennisetum*), which originated in the western Sahel, is one of the heartiest varieties of this grain, and comes from a variety of grass known to grow as tall as 10 feet (3.05 m). The early cultivation of pearl and bulrush millet has been linked to the inhabitants living on the border areas of the SAHARA Desert. Archaeologists have documented its use as far back as between the second and third millennium BCE, at a site known as Dhar Tichitt, where these crops were likely to have been planted in response to the growing impact of desiccation. Another variety of millet is known as eleusine (*Eleuisine coracana*). Described as a type of finger millet, it is indigenous to eastern Africa, particularly ETHIOPIA, where archaeologists have identified its cultivation in the former kingdom of AKSUM.

Ground into flour by women using stones or *kerns*, millet is rich in protein and has a bitter, nutty taste. It has been traditionally cooked as porridge or used as a side dish with meats and stews. It also was fermented to make beer. The enduring popularity of millet in Africa stems from the variety it provides and its ability to flourish under extreme environmental circumstances, including drought.

See also: AGRICULTURE (Vol. I).

Further reading: Elizabeth Isichei, *A History of African Societies to 1870* (New York: Cambridge University Press, 1997).

Mokele-mbembe Giant mythological animal believed to live in West Africa. According to MBUTI lore, Mokele-mbembe has the body of an ELEPHANT, a long neck, one horn, three-toed claws, and an enormous tail. Although believed to be a vegetarian, Mokele-mbembe has been said to attack hippopotamuses and small boats.

Mokele-mbembe is said to inhabit the swampy Likouala region of the present-day Republic of Congo, going on land only to travel or eat. Mokele-mbembe is a Lingala name for "one that stops the water." Although proof of its existence has not been confirmed, some believe Mokele-mbembe to be closely related to sauropod dinosaurs. In recent times, the native people of Likouala, a region that has not changed much since the dinosaur age, have identified Mokele-mbembe with pictures of sauropod dinosaurs.

Mokele-mbembe is said to be between 16 and 32 feet (4.9 and 9.8 m) in length, not including a neck between 5 and 10 feet (1.5 and 3 m) long, and a tail that is also between 5 and 10 feet (1.5 and 3 m) long. It is reputed to have reddish brown skin and a ruffled hood of skin on its neck, like the comb of a male chicken. According to the Mbuti, Mokele-mbembe feed mostly on the malombo plant. In the twentieth century, a number of scientists attempted to confirm Mokele-mbembe's existence but were unable to do so.

money Anything that is commonly used for making payments and accounting for debts and credits. Money developed independently in different parts of the world, eventually replacing barter as the principal means of TRADE.

In ancient Africa, there were several driving forces that spurred the development of common currencies. For example, rulers imposed taxes, and prospective bridegrooms were required to compensate the head of the bride's family for the loss of his daughter's services (this was called the bride price). Also, payments of tribute or sacrifices of one kind or another often were made to fulfill religious obligations. Many societies even had laws requiring people who committed crimes of violence to compensate their victims (or victims' families) in one way or another.

Types of Money To accomplish all this, ancient Africans, like people all over the world, experimented with different types of money. At first, commonly desired commodities were used. This commodity money, as it is called, had value independent of its value as money. By around 9000 BCE, African people were herding CATTLE and growing crops, and various African societies began to use both cattle and grain as commodity money.

COWRIE SHELLS and manillas were other common forms of money in ancient Africa. A type of mollusk shell found in the shallow waters of the Pacific and Indian Oceans, cowries are both rare and beautiful. As a result they acquired a value that often led to their use as decorations and ornaments. They also were used as money, and represent one of the most widely and longest-used currencies in history. Manillas, which are ornamental metallic objects worn as jewelry in West Africa, also were used as money for thousands of years.

Since the domestication of animals generally came before the cultivation of crops in ancient Africa, it is likely that cattle are the oldest form of money.

Precious METALS, which had ornamental uses before they were adopted for use as money, served as currency in many ancient societies. As early as 2500 BCE, for example, the peoples of MESOPOTAMIA were using silver as a means of payment. Similarly, Egyptian tomb paintings show gold rings being exchanged according to weight, indicating that these were being used as a type of currency. Precious metals in weighed quantities were a common form of money in ancient times; however, the transition to quantities that could be counted (such as coins) rather than weighed came gradually.

Money in Ancient Egypt The monetary history of ancient EGYPT appears to be based on AGRICULTURE. Egyptian farmers deposited their grain in local warehouses for safety and convenience. This practice eventually led to a vibrant banking industry.

When Egypt came under the rule of the PTOLEMIES (c. 323–30 BCE), the traditional system of warehouse banking reached a new level of sophistication. The Ptolemies linked the regional warehouses into a network and established a central bank in Alexandria, where all the accounts were kept. Farmers continued to deposit their grain in local warehouses, but now payments could be transferred from one account to another all over Egypt without any paper actually changing hands.

Grain banks continued to enable local transactions even after coins were introduced. However, in an effort to economize on the use of the precious metals that went into coins, the Egyptians used coins primarily for foreign purchases and activities involving the military. (This was also a tacit recognition that grain deposited in a bank in Egypt would be of little use to a third party in Asia Minor.) Eventually, however, a metal-based monetary system replaced grain as a medium of exchange.

The Use of Gold Gold eventually emerged as the preferred money, with virtually a universal appeal to peoples across the world. In addition to its aesthetic beauty, gold resists corrosion and does not change color as it ages. There are other characteristics that make gold suited to monetary transactions, including its associations with magic, divinity, and the Sun. For whatever reason, gold became something like a common denominator and was generally accepted everywhere, unlike cattle, grain, salt, or cowrie shells, which had limited value outside of the local areas in which these commodities had appeal. As gold (and silver) money grew in popularity, other types of money were used less frequently, until they eventually became obsolete.

Money was one of several criteria, along with owning livestock and the ability to mobilize militias, that enabled societies to increase in size and complexity. In western Africa, a number of kingdoms emerged, including Ghana and Mali, that depended on their control of the gold trade routes linking the land south of the SAHARA Desert to North Africa and the world.

See also: BARTER SYSTEM (Vol I); GHANA EMPIRE (Vol. II); MALI EMPIRE (Vol. II); MONEY AND CURRENCY (Vol. III).

monkey Mammal belonging to the primate family of animals, which also includes apes, lemurs, and humans. With their intelligence and resemblance to humans, monkeys have often intrigued the people of Africa. As a form of tribute, ancient Nubians would give monkeys to the Egyptians, who viewed these animals with great respect. In their mythology, African peoples often portrayed monkeys as servant guardians. To make crops grow, for example, the BAMANA carved masks representing the monkey. Among the Baule people, the *Gbekre*, a figure that was half-man and half-monkey, was a spirit that protected good people in the AFTERLIFE and punished the wicked ones. The Gbekre was often represented in the carved sculptures made by the Baule.

Monophysite Referring to a fourth- and fifth-century theological controversy based on the belief that Jesus Christ has a single nature, which is divine; also known as Eutychianist, after the Greek monk Eutyches (c. 378–c. 454 CE), one of its early proponents. Monophysite theology was declared heretical by the Council of Chalcedon but remained a central tenet of the COPTIC Church.

The word *monophysite* is from two Greek words meaning "one nature." Belief in the single nature of Jesus Christ was strong among Coptic Christians, whose church was governed by the Patriarch of Alexandria, in Egypt. However, at the Council of Chalcedon in 451 CE, church leaders from the rival partriarchates of Rome and Constantinople upheld the church's traditional belief in two separate human and divine natures within Jesus Christ and declared the Monophysite belief in a single nature heretical. The declaration of the council caused a schism, or split, within the church; some Coptic Christians submitted to the council's authority, but many broke with the council and set up an independent Coptic church, with its own bishops and clergy. Monophysite congregations continued to exist thereafter in EGYPT, Syria, and Mesopotamia.

See also: CHRISTIANITY (Vol. I); COPTIC CHRISTIANITY (Vol. I)

monotheism Belief in a single supreme being.

Along with pantheism, monotheism is one of two critical elements found in traditional African religion, thought, and philosophy. Molded to fit cultural identity, place of origin, and language, the same supreme being that was known as OLORUN among the YORUBA was called Mwari among the SHONA, or Chukwu in Iboland (Nigeria). Numerous origin myths surround the concepts of these supreme beings, providing an important way for religious beliefs to be passed from generation to generation. Rituals that were performed on a daily or seasonal basis by community-based mediums, prophets, or priests served to reinforce these beliefs and concepts. These rituals often called for the use of special shrines and altars.

See also: AFTERLIFE (Vol. I); PANTHEISM (Vol. I); RELIGION, TRADITIONAL (Vol. I).

Morocco Modern country in North Africa. The name *Morocco* derives from Marrakech, the first of four imperial capitals established by the Almoravids in the middle of the eleventh century.

The original people of present-day Morocco were the BERBERS, who inhabited the region as long ago as the second millennium BCE. Like much of North Africa, the area fell under the influence of Phoenicia, when, as early as the twelfth century BCE, PHOENICIAN traders established trading posts along Africa's Mediterranean coast. From these trading posts there eventually developed an empire, stretching from North Africa to modern-day Spain, dominated by CARTHAGE. The fall of Carthage in 146 BCE left the area under the control of ROME.

Roman domination lasted for more than 500 years, coming to an end with the VANDALS' invasion of North Africa in 429 CE. This was followed, beginning in 533, by a period during which Morocco was under the control of the Byzantine Empire. Ultimately, however, Morocco was swept up in the Islamic invasions of the seventh century, falling to Arab troops in 682.

See also: ALMORAVIDS (Vol. II); BYZANTINE AFRICA (Vols. I, II); PHOENICIANS (Vol. I).

mummy A dead body that is preserved or embalmed prior to burial. For the ancient Egyptians, the mummification process was closely linked to their religious beliefs concerning the AFTERLIFE. The body was preserved for the next life.

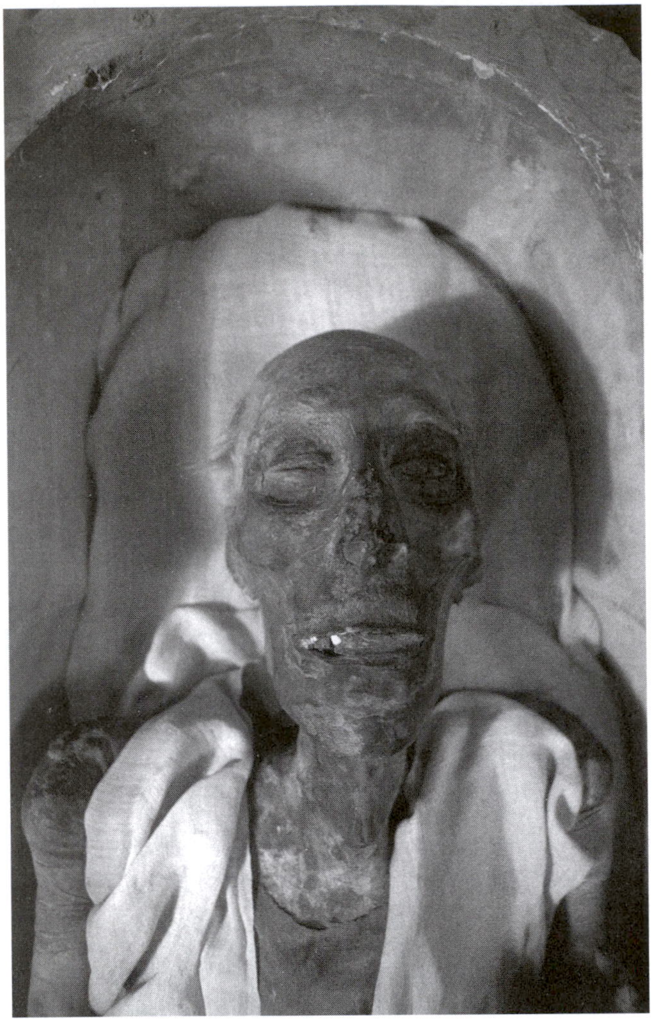

The mummified body of Ramesses II (r. 1304–1236 BCE) is located in the Mummy Room at the Egyptian Museum in Cairo. *© Richard T. Nowitz/CORBIS*

The mummification process began with the ritual cleaning of a corpse. An incision was made into the side of the corpse and the vital organs were removed, treated with preservatives, and placed in special jars. The body was then placed on an embalming table and covered with preservatives to dry. After forty days, the corpse was wrapped in linen bandages. In all, it took seventy days for a body to be properly mummified.

Although some mummies of ancient EGYPT were destroyed over the centuries by robbers, many still exist, some dating back 5,000 years. The best-preserved mummies usually belong to pharaohs, who had elaborate funerals and burials. Mummies of some of the later pharaohs are so well preserved that it is possible to determine some of the pharaohs' medical problems. For example, scholars have learned from the mummy of RAMESSES II that the king suffered from both poor circulation and arthritis. Originally, only kings were mummified, but, later, their courtiers were also preserved to serve the kings in the afterlife. Sacred animals, like cats, DOGS, and hawks, also were embalmed.

music African music has often been described as highly innovative. Its wide diversity and inherent power reportedly stem from the keen ability of early societies to translate the sounds of the natural world into a vital social framework. These efforts form the underlying structure of African music and impart a unique vitality to the music that lends itself to improvisational patterns.

African music is often discussed in three broad categories by musicologists: Movement, for example, has always been an essential part of music, and in many societies, song is inseparable from DANCE. Timing is another category that has been discussed by musicologists because it provides African music with a distinctive flavor while providing a cohesive element that allows for the layering of complex polyrhythmic patterns. Tonality is the last category, and it includes natural harmony and pitch levels akin to human speech. The YORUBA of Nigeria, for example, use a polyphonic tone that reflects their own language patterns. The resulting sound has dual or overlapping melodies and is viewed as a unique art form. In some societies, music substitutes for speech and is punctuated by movement or facial expressions that may be used to educate or to entertain.

Evidence of how long music has been present in Africa comes from one of the oldest surviving relics from ancient times, a rock painting made in Tassili-n-Ajer in ALGERIA. This painting depicts music and dance styles that some sources say are comparable to modern movements. Archaeologists note that this scene dates back to the time of Africa's Neolithic hunters, c. 6000 to 4000 BCE. An early form of a harp with six strings has been depicted on a c. 700 BCE rock painting uncovered in the SAHARA. The instrument was apparently in common use when the painting was made.

This harp and its many variations belong to the category of African instruments known collectively as *chordophones,* which included simple music bows in ancient times and, in later periods, harps, lutes, and zithers. Another category of instrument that is common in Africa but varies among regions is the *aerophone*. Included are such instruments as reeds, bullroarers, flutes, horns, and oboes. Their use is sometimes practical. In Lesotho, for example, herders use a *lesiba,* or mouth bow, to graze their cattle. *Membranophones* encompass primarily DRUMS in various forms, such as the ones depicted in terra-cotta in the ancient YORUBA city of IFE. Drums were often associated with the royal court and were used to accompany unique praise-songs. They were also used for announcements concerning the king or queen and the society over which they ruled. *Indiophones* are rhythmic instruments such as rattles or bells and include *lamellophones* like the *mbira,* or thumb piano, which was reportedly used in religious rites and SPIRIT POSSESSION dances, as well as for entertainment.

The human voice has always been considered one of the greatest of all instruments in Africa. Like instrumental music, songs have often been described as multilevel or polyrhythmic in structure. Some songs held central or controlling themes while relying on repetitive phrases. Religion undoubtedly influenced music since it has played an integral role in every RITE OF PASSAGE from birth to the grave. Music was also influenced by community, and among the most notable features of African music are the call and response associated with vocal skills or instruments. This style of music may have derived from the simple "call and response" of pastoralists, agriculturists, or other workers in the ancient world.

See also: FUNERAL CUSTOMS (Vol. I); GRIOT (Vol. II); MUSIC (Vols. II, III).

Further reading: Robert B. Fisher, *West African Religious Traditions* (Maryknoll, N.Y.: Orbis Books, 1998); Samuel A. Floyd, Jr., *The Power of Black Music* (New York: Oxford University Press, 1995).

N

Naga, temples at Great center of worship in the steppe-country south of MEROË. King Natakamani (ruled 15 BCE–15 CE) and his coruler Queen AMANITARE were among the greatest builders in the Meroitic Period, and their names have been found on many monuments, including the eight temples they constructed at Naga. Among them is the Temple of AMUN, the high god worshiped by Egyptians and Nubians alike. This temple, despite its recognizable Meroitic features, appears to have been influenced by both Roman and Egyptian architecture, the latter of which is particularly evident in its decorated entrance.

The most famous temple at Naga, however, is the Temple of the Lions, with its impressive wall reliefs paying tribute to APEDEMAK, the warrior god of Kushite origin. (Lions played an important, if little understood, role in the religious ceremonies of royal officials at Meroë.) Other Kushite gods were immortalized at Naga as well.

King Natakamani and Queen Amanitare's efforts resulted in the last of the great construction projects during the Meroitic period. Several of their temples have survived into the modern era.

See also: KUSH (Vol I.); NUBIA (Vol I.).

Further reading: Stanley Burstein, ed. *Ancient African Kingdoms: Kush and Axum* (Princeton, N.J.: Markus Wiener, 1998); Pamela F. Service, *The Ancient African Kingdom of Kush* (Pelham, N.Y.: Benchmark Books, 1998).

Naqadah I and II Two early cultures of Predynastic EGYPT dating roughly between 4000 and 3000 BCE; named for the town in UPPER EGYPT in which artifacts from these cultures were first excavated.

Also known as the AMRATIAN and GERZEAN cultures, respectively, the Naqadah I and II periods followed the earlier BADARIAN CULTURE in Upper Egypt. Excavations have revealed advanced cultures that apparently already possessed skills such as pottery making and mud-brick architecture.

The Naqadah I, or Amratian period, c. 4200 BCE, was clearly influenced by the Badarian culture, which was the earliest known Egyptian civilization to farm, hunt, and mine. Like the Badarians, the people of Naqadah I based their economy on AGRICULTURE, hunting, fishing, and CATTLE-raising. Unlike the Badarians, however, the people of the Naqadah I period lived in fairly large settlements, usually in homes made out of mud-brick.

The POTTERY of this era also was more highly developed, usually featuring black-topped red or dark red burnished ware. Whereas Badarian pottery was decorated with simple bands of paint, the Naqadah I artisans used geometric designs and pictures of animals on their ceramics, either painted on or carved into their surfaces. On one fragment is a drawing of a RED CROWN, the earliest known representation of the red pharaonic crown of UPPER EGYPT.

The Naqadah II, or Gerzean, period dates as far back as 3400 BCE and was a further development of the Naqadah I period. This culture was based around Naqadah and HIERANKOPOLIS in Upper Egypt and Sayala in NUBIA. Artifacts from this period include pottery made from buff-colored desert clay decorated in dark red paint, a tube-shaped drill used for stonecutting, and flint knives. Naqadah II culture also developed irrigation systems and traded with other countries. The presence of foreign materials like lapis lazuli indicated that trade was conducted with places as faraway as Afghanistan.

On the wall of the first-century BCE Temple of the Lions at Naga, Sudan, the lion-headed god Apedemak is depicted receiving offerings. © Paul Almasy/CORBIS

As the Naqadah II culture developed, displays of wealth increased. In particular, graves became increasingly elaborate and featured remarkable vases made of stones that came from remote areas of the Eastern Desert. The tombs also included large ceremonial knives as well as cosmetic palettes decorated with elaborate designs in the form of animals, birds, or fish.

Around this time, pictographic writing first appeared and was inscribed on pottery, slate palettes, and stone. These objects usually bore the iconography of the earliest known line of pharaohs. The pottery indicates that late in the Naqadah II period (c. 3200 BCE), a dominant political force was already beginning to form the first united kingdom of ancient Egypt. The resulting dynastic culture, which followed the Naqadah II period, was heavily influenced by its predecessor.

Narmer Palette Slate tablet from the First Dynasty (c. 2920–2770 BCE) that depicts the legendary Egyptian king

Narmer uniting EGYPT. The tablet, about 25 inches (63.5 cm) tall, was discovered in HIERANKOPOLIS, the capital of Egypt during predynastic times. Originally, the palette was probably used as a table on which cosmetics were pulverized. The engraving shows Narmer defeating his enemies and creating one state from UPPER EGYPT and LOWER EGYPT. On one side of the palette, Narmer is shown wearing the WHITE CROWN of UPPER EGYPT, and on the other, he wears the RED CROWN of LOWER EGYPT.

The palette depicts Narmer as a powerful figure. Near the top, he is associated with bulls. Further below he is portrayed in a procession, passing in front of ten decapitated corpses lying on the ground with their heads between their legs. Over the corpses, a ship is drawn that contains a harpoon and a falcon. These images are believed to symbolize a conquered region in Lower Egypt. On the back of the palette Narmer is shown ready to strike a foe, whom he is grabbing by the hair.

Some believe that Narmer was MENES, the king traditionally associated with Egypt's unification around 2900 BCE. Since the unification might have taken place over several generations, though, others speculate that the figure of Narmer represents several kings, including his probable successor, Aha.

Nefertiti (Nefer-Nefer-Aten) (c. 1379–1344 BCE)

Queen of ancient Egypt's Eighteenth Dynasty and "Great Royal Wife" of Akhenaten (Amenhotep IV).

Nefertiti played a prominent role as Akhenaten's queen. Along with her husband, she frequently presided over the rites connected with the worship of the god ATEN. The Aten rites represented radical changes in Egypt's state religion of the time and are sometimes referred to, collectively, as the AMARNA PERIOD, or the Amarna Revolution. Depictions of her participating in the cult's religious observances were part of the temples at el-Amarna, the new capital that Nerfertiti and Akhenaten established for the cult. In the service of the new religion, she was renamed Nefer-Nefru-Aten, meaning "Beautiful is the Beauty of Aten."

However important a role Nefertiti may have played in the early years of Akhenaten's reign, it appears that, by the twelth year, she had fallen into obscurity or died. At that time, one of her daughters, Merytaten, assumed the role of Akhenaten's principal wife. There is evidence that Nefertiti was buried in the royal tomb at Amarna, but her remains have never been found.

Renowned as a great beauty in her own time, Nefertiti's fame grew with the discovery of a painted limestone bust that is now in the Egyptian Museum in Berlin, Germany. Dramatically depicting Nefertiti's graceful and delicate features, the statue is one of the most familiar of the Egyptian art treasures to have survived from that period.

See also: AKHENATEN (Vol. I).

Nekhbet

Vulture goddess of ancient Egyptian mythology. In Egyptian art, Nekhbet was often portrayed as a vulture or as a woman with a vulture's head, wearing the WHITE CROWN of UPPER EGYPT.

Nekhbet was the protector of the kings of UPPER EGYPT, often portrayed with her wings spread above the pharaoh, and she was often associated with the cobra-goddess, BUTO. Together they guarded the pharaoh and symbolized a united Egypt.

Nekhbet was also a goddess of childbirth, said to be present at the births of gods and kings. In ancient times, she was worshiped in al-Kab and in HIERAKONPOLIS (also known as Nekhen), on the west bank of the NILE RIVER.

Neolithic Age

Period that witnessed the advent of a series of sophisticated and specialized stone tools.

The era most likely began shortly after the area comprising the modern-day SAHARA Desert began to dry up, beginning about 8000 BCE. Besides stone-ground and polished tools, other innovations of the Neolithic Age included the invention of baskets and pottery, which took place by about 2000 BCE. These new creations allowed people to store and transport goods. Another innovation—permanent huts for shelter—came at about the same time. Perhaps the most important advance, however, was the discovery that animals could be domesticated and seeds could be planted and cultivated. This helped transform HUNTER-GATHERERS into herdsmen and farmers.

As a result of these innovations, Africans were no longer limited to small bands that seasonally trekked through the wilderness in search of wild animals, wild plants, and water. Larger, more sophisticated and organized settlements could now be located close to bodies of water. Likewise, food could be preserved both for human consumption and for the feeding of livestock. In short, life could be sustained year-round, usually without fear of drought or flood.

These changes led to larger concentrations of people, which meant that some people could be assigned to such tasks as producing pottery or baskets. Others could take on the jobs of making weapons and tools, administering justice, running the government, or making war. Along with the Neolithic invention of writing and the discovery of methods for smelting metal ores, these developments would forever change the adventure of mankind as inhabitants of the earth, allowing civilizations to emerge in Africa and in many other regions of the world.

See also: AGRICULTURAL REVOLUTION (Vol. I); AGRICULTURE, ORIGINS OF (Vol. I); STONE AGE (Vol. I).

New Kingdom

Following the glories of the MIDDLE KINGDOM (c. 2000–1650 BCE), EGYPT entered a period of decline and foreign domination known as the Second Intermediate Period, which lasted from approximately 1650 to 1575 BCE. The emergence of the Eighteenth Dynasty, however, saw the reemergence of a revitalized Egypt, during which the Egyptians drove out the Hyksos, who had dominated them since the end of the Middle Kingdom. This coincided with a realignment of the forces within Egypt's state religion that brought to the forefront the god AMUN. As the New Kingdom went on, Egypt expanded its territories in Asia, eventually, under the pharaoh Thutmose III, reaching the banks of the Euphrates River. The period also saw Egypt's renewed influence in the lands to the south, as it reestablished control over KUSH and NUBIA.

The New Kingdom was also marked by what has become known as the AMARNA PERIOD, during which the pharaoh Amenhotep IV changed his name to AKHENATEN and attempted a wholesale transformation of Egyptian religious life. This included everything from the institution of an entirely new state religion based upon monotheistic principles to the movement of the seat of governmental power from Thebes to el-Amarna, 300 miles (480 km) to the north.

Akhenaten's actions, which took place during the mid-fourteenth century BCE, plunged the nation into unrest, which, despite the era's many artistic achievements, doomed the Amarna experiment. The turmoil was quelled only upon Akhenaten's death and the succession of the young king TUTANKHAMUN, who began the process of reinstituting the traditional Egyptian religion. This process was continued by HOREMHEB, the last of the dynasty's kings.

The New Kingdom managed to survive for several hundred more years, flourishing under such noted rulers as RAMESSSES II and the other warrior-kings and monument builders of the Nineteenth Dynasty. Ultimately, however, like the OLD KINGDOM before it, the Middle Kingdom fell victim to strife between ambitious officials and priests, and the nation fell into disarray.

Niger-Congo One of the four major families of African languages. Niger-Congo is comprised of more than 900 separate languages and is the most widely distributed of all the African LANGUAGE families, spoken in all parts of the continent. Most of the indigenous languages of central and southern Africa belong to the Niger-Congo family. Speakers of Niger-Congo languages cover an area that stretches through virtually all of West Africa south of the SAHARA—from Senegal to South Africa. In addition, migration of Niger-Congo peoples brought this language family as far as eastern and southern Africa too. The Niger-Congo family includes six related branches: West Atlantic, Mande, Gur, Kwa, Benue-Congo, and Adamawa-Eastern.

Languages in the West Atlantic branch include Wolof, spoken in Senegal; Temne, a language of Sierra Leone; and FULA, a language spread by nomads south of the SAHARA from Senegal to Chad, though primarily in Nigeria and Guinea. The best known Mande languages are Mende, a Liberian tongue, and Malinke, of Mali, as well as languages spoken along the valley of the NIGER RIVER and in Sierra Leone. The Gur, or Voltaic, branch of the Niger-Congo family includes Mossi, a Burkina Faso tongue, as well as Dagomba and Mamprusi, languages from North Ghana. The best known of the Kwa tongues are YORUBA and ASHANTI.

The BANTU languages, spoken throughout central and southern Africa are the best known of the Benue-Congo languages. Others include Tiv, Jukun, and Efik, spoken in Nigeria and CAMEROON. The Adamawa-Eastern branch includes Banda, Zande, and Sango, tongues spoken primarily in Nigeria and Cameroon.

Kordofanian, the primary group of languages of southern Kordofan (the central Sudan), is often classified as a seventh branch of the Niger-Congo family. Made up of about thirty languages, classified in five small groups (Koalib, Tegali, Talodi, Tumtum, and Katla), the Kordofanian is considered by some linguists to be a completely separate language family.

Like many African tongues, Niger-Congo languages employ different tones to indicate shades of meaning. Nouns are divided not just according to gender (masculine, feminine, or neuter), as in many Indo-European languages, but according to as many as twenty classes—for example, human beings, liquids, and animals. Each noun class employs a unique pair of affixes (i.e., suffixes or prefixes) to indicate singular or plural. Verbs consist of a verb root, which seldom changes, with attached particles or auxiliary verbs used to denote tense or mood. (The use of the infinitive, for example, indicates the future tense in many Niger-Congo languages.)

Like most African languages, the Niger-Congo group has maintained an ORAL TRADITION. With the significant exceptions of Swahili (the major Bantu tongue) and Vai—a Mande tongue that developed an indigenous script during the modern era—the Niger-Congo languages remained entirely unwritten until quite recently. Similarities between the Niger-Congo tongues and members of the NILO-SAHARAN family of languages suggest that these two families may share the same ancestor language.

Niger Delta The largest river delta in Africa. Located in NIGERIA, the delta covers about 150 miles (241 km) of coastline and extends over an area of about 14,000 square miles (22,531 sq km). The delta lies at an elevation of 500 feet (152 m) below sea level. It is made up primarily of mangrove swamps, which join with freshwater swamps to the north. It is through a series of channels in the Niger Delta that the Niger River flows into the Gulf of Guinea.

At Lokoja, the Niger merges with its main tributary, the BENUE RIVER. Together, they form a stretch of river

A boat crosses the Niger River at the present-day town of Mopti in Mali. *© Nik Wheeler/CORBIS*

measuring two miles (3 km) in width. At Aboh, the river separates into a network of channels (known as rivers) within the delta. The Nun River is considered the Niger River's most direct link. Among other important channels are the Forcados, the Brass, the Sambreiro, and the Bonny. Sandbars block almost all the mouths of these channels.

Niger River The main river in West Africa and the third-longest river on the continent after the NILE and CONGO. It flows for about 2,600 miles (4,184 km) through Mali, Niger, and Nigeria to the Gulf of Guinea. The NIGER DELTA is the largest river delta in Africa.

The Niger River flows in a northeastward direction, rising in Guinea about 150 miles (241.4 km) from the Atlantic Ocean. It receives its upper tributaries—the Mafou, the Niandan, the Milo, the Sankarani, and the Tinkisso—before entering Mali. Past Bamako, Mali's capital, the river drops about 1,000 feet (305 m) within 40 miles (65 km) into a valley. Today, the rapids of this section have been submerged in the backed-up waters of the Sotuba Dam near Sansanding.

From here, the Niger flows about 1,000 miles (1,600 km) in an east-northeastward direction. At Mopti, it is joined by a main tributary, the Bani, then flows into a region of lakes and creeks known as the Niger's "internal delta." The largest lake in this region is Lake Faguibine, which is almost 75 miles (121 km) long, 15 miles (24 km) wide, and more than 160 feet (49 m) deep in places.

The lake region ends at Kaburu, a major port in TIMBUKTU. Here, the river runs in an almost eastward direction. The river then narrows at a rocky ridge, before moving in a southeastward direction and widening to a floodplain that flows through Gao. This is the northernmost bend of the river, running through the southern edge of the SAHARA Desert.

From Jebba in Nigeria, the river flows east-southeastward through a broad, shallow valley. Soon afterward, it is joined by two important tributaries, the Kaduna River and the BENUE RIVER. Once joined with the Benue, the Niger widens to a 2-mile (3.2-km) wide stretch that is occasionally interrupted by small islands and sandbanks. At Aboh, the Niger breaks off into many branches, moving through the Niger Delta into the Gulf of Guinea.

The river passes through such diverse vegetation as grasslands, rain forests, and swamps. Among the wildlife living in and along the Niger are HIPPOPOTAMUSES, three different types of CROCODILES, herons, and storks. The average rainfall along the Niger varies from more than 160 inches (406 cm) in the delta area to less than 10 inches (25 cm) in Timbuktu. Depending on the region, the annual flood season occurs at different times of the year. In upper Niger, the river floods in June. In the middle Niger, flooding first occurs between July and October, and is known as the "white flood" because of the light sediment in the water. The "black flood" occurs in December, when the water is carrying more sediment from upstream. The high-water period of the lower Niger lasts from May to October.

For thousands of years, the Niger River has served as a key source of irrigation, fish, and transportation for humans. Between the fourth century BCE and the second century CE, the NOK CULTURE, the earliest known people of Nigeria, lived on the JOS PLATEAU, the area above where the Niger and the Benue joined.

See also: NIGER EXPEDITIONS (Vol. III); NIGER RIVER (Vol. III).

Nile Delta Marshy, alluvial plain in northern EGYPT where the NILE RIVER empties into the MEDITERRANEAN SEA. In ancient times, the Nile split into at least seven smaller channels just north of the city of CAIRO. As long ago as 4000 BCE, farmers were cultivating the borders of this marshland in order to reap the benefits of its exceptionally fertile soil.

By pharaonic times, c. 3000 BCE, farming dominated the area, and, by the time of the NEW KINGDOM (c. 1570–1070 BCE), the cultivated area of the delta exceeded the area of the entire Nile Valley. During ancient times, the arms of the Nile River were named the Pelusiac, the Tanitic, the Mendesian, the Phatnitic, the Sebennyic, the Bolbitine, and the Canopic. Today, because of heavy cultivation and a changing climate in the area, there are only two arms, the Damietta and the Rosetta.

Nile River World's longest river, located in northeastern Africa. Measuring about 4,150 (6,677 km) long, the Nile is one of only two rivers in the world that flow from south to north from twin sources: The WHITE NILE in UGANDA and the BLUE NILE in ETHIOPIA. Described by geologists as an "exotic stream," the Nile travels for 2,000 miles (3,218 km) across the desert to KHARTOUM, where the two tributaries meet above the Shabluka Gorge. The Nile continues its route through present-day Sudan, where it is joined by a third tributary, the Atbara River. Eventually the Nile empties into the MEDITERRANEAN SEA.

Over thousands of years, the powerful ebb and flow of the Nile has created, through the constant process of erosion, the narrow corridor known as the NILE VALLEY. The rise of Nile Valley civilizations such as NUBIA and EGYPT were largely documented in Egyptian sources and the writings of ancient Greek and Roman travelers. From a geographical perspective, Egypt's location between the Eastern and Western Deserts made it the beneficiary of fertile alluvium carried by the river during its journey north. As early as 6000 BCE, Nile Valley inhabitants were cultivating food crops, including SORGHUM, MILLET, and YAMS. Settled farms were in place by 5000 BCE as migrating populations learned to harness the waters of the Nile to their advantage. This allowed people to supplement their hunting-and-gathering activities with the cultivation of clover, wheat, beans, cotton, corn, and rice.

The Nile also influenced the creation of the world's earliest CALENDAR. The first season of the year was called *akhett*, named for the flood waters that began to rise and saturate the fields for four months at a time. The next season, *peret*, was named for the receding waters. The third and last season of the year was known as the harvest, or *shemou*.

The Egyptians noted each year that Sothis, or SIRIUS—the largest star in the constellation Canis Major—would rise on the horizon just before Nile's waters would swell. Therefore, the study of ASTRONOMY was directed, to a great extent, toward predicting the timing and the causes of the rising of the Nile in order to prevent the disastrous effects of flooding.

Beyond the calendar, other sciences and technologies developed that were related to the Nile. For example, the Egyptians became experts in the building of dykes, dams, and canals in order to protect their fields, and their methods eventually gave way to more sophisticated methods of IRRIGATION. Also, the practice of surveying the area around the river led to the rise of a state bureaucracy to oversee the lands.

Other notable aspects concerning the Nile include its impact on religious belief. The deity HATHOR came to represent the rising waters of the Nile as a symbol of fertility; Hapi represented the actual flood or inundation. Equally important was the Nile's role in international trade, linking Egypt and NUBIA to the Red Sea trade and the lands to the south and east of the African continent.

Nile Valley Region where the Egyptian civilization began to develop c. 3100 BCE. Because of the annual flooding of the NILE RIVER, the land on either side of the river is exceptionally fertile. Intensive cultivation of the Nile Valley has sustained the population of the Egypt for almost 5,000 years.

Nilo-Saharan One of the four major families of African LANGUAGES. Nilo-Saharan has been spoken in nearly all parts of the continent, from the SAHARA southward to Congo (formerly Zaïre) and Tanzania as well as among some pastoral peoples in eastern Africa. The wide dispersal of the speakers of Nilo-Saharan languages has made this family difficult to study and classify. Linguists have nonetheless identified six branches of the Nilo-Saharan family: Songhai, Saharan, Maban, Furian, Koman, and Chari-Nile.

Like the NIGER-CONGO family of languages, most Nilo-Saharan tongues traditionally use tones to differentiate meaning. Also like the Niger-Congo family, Nilo-Saharan remained largely unwritten oral tongues (with the important exception of the Nubian language) until modern-day attempts at transcription using the Arabic and Roman ALPHABETS.

These similarities to the Niger-Congo family of languages suggest that these two families may share a common ancestor language. Yet unlike the Niger-Congo languages, some Nilo-Saharan tongues use inflection to indicate the case of nouns, some have gender classifications for nouns, and many feature conjugation of verbs—characteristics that mark the Nilo-Saharan tongues as unique among African language families.

Nilotes A people of the Later IRON AGE who were pastoralists in southern Sudan and who migrated to various areas of eastern Africa, where they mixed with the native peoples and formed new cultural groups.

The Nilotes were established as a people by about 1000 CE in southeastern Sudan. Their languages belonged to the Nilo-Saharan group, and their society was based on kinship. They were nomads and pastoralists who moved with their flocks. It is believed that they migrated into East Africa as a result of drought, overpopulation, or, possibly, an increase in the size of their herds.

An early migration of the Nilotes took place during the period 200 BCE to 1000 CE, when the southern Nilotes, known as the Paranilotes, who were ironworkers, cereal farmers, and pastoralists, moved into the highlands east of Lake Victoria Nyanza. About the same time, other ironworkers, who were BANTU-speakers, migrated to the area from the southwest. The region was already peopled by Kushites, who used stone tools. The Kushites were absorbed by the Paranilotes; the merger gave birth to the Kalenjin people of the Kenyan highlands. After about 1000, the Kalenjin people extended their range and intermingled with other Iron Age peoples. The Elgeyo, Nandi, and Pokot peoples came into being from these mergers.

Around 1500, the western Nilotes of the southern Sudan moved in clan groups to the area northeast of Lake Victoria Nyanza. One of these Luo-speaking clans, the Bito, deposed the Chwezi, took control of the Kitara state, and began the new dynasty of Bunyoro-Kitara. The Bito established several other kingdoms, including Buganda, Koki, Kiziba, and Toro. The Bito minority adopted some of the traditions of the Chwezi and also adopted the Bantu language. Thus the Bito ruled without much opposition from their Bantu subjects, and the merger of the two cultures formed a new culture that had elements of each of the parent cultures.

In other cases, the Luo-speakers were the assimilators, imposing their political systems and language on the indigenous people. In the highlands, the Luo sent out chieflets from already established chiefships to rule over the non-Luo groups.

The impact of the Nilote migrations went beyond the assimilation and integration of other cultures, however. Some peoples responded to the invaders by withdrawing into other areas. For example, the pastoral Bahinda withdrew into Ankole, Karagwe, and Ruanda, and established new kingdoms there.

The later migrations of the eastern Nilotes, also called Paranilotes, were responsible for the formation of the Karamojong of northeast Uganda and the MAASAI of central Kenya.

See also: KUSH (Vol. I); CHWEZI DYNASTY (Vol. III); CHWEZI KINGDOM (Vol. II).

Ninetjer (Nynetjer) (r. c. 2800 BCE) *Egyptian pharaoh and third king of Egypt's Second Dynasty (c. 2890–2686 BCE).*

Ninetjer ruled for almost forty years and established MEMPHIS as his capital city. He was renowned for his festivals and temples. A military expedition during the thirteenth year of Ninetjer's reign is chronicled on the PALERMO STONE.

Little is known about the kings of the early Second Dynasty, but the name of Hotepsekhemwi, the first king of the dynasty, means "the two powers are in peace," which may suggest a reunification of EGYPT following the tumultuous First Dynasty. The Second Dynasty kings are believed to be of Lower Egyptian origin, as evidenced by the relocation of the capital to Memphis and placement of the royal burial grounds at SAQQARA in LOWER EGYPT.

Nkisi Power, or spirit, figures used by the BaKongo peoples of western Congo (formerly Zaïre), along the Congo coast, the Mayombe Forests, and in Angola; also known as Nkondi and Nkongi, their use is believed to date to ancient times. Generally carved from wood, the Nkisi, which were sometimes erroneously referred to as a "nail sculpture," are considered by many to be among the most complex ritual objects in Africa. Although the creation of the sculptures traditionally has been controlled by a ritual authority or priest, the work has often been based on specific requests by those who came for consultation. Made in the form of humans, they were considered spirits from the realm of the dead who would carry out specific assignments if the appropriate sacrifices were offered. The spirit could then be grounded or controlled when placed within a natural object, such as a special bag, gourd, or shell.

Several types of Nkisi figures have been used in this way to represent good or evil. Benevolent types have been said to embody ancestral spirits; when the nose or forehead of the figure was rubbed, it was comparable to praying or communicating with the dead. Smaller types of Nkisi have been used for healing or for overcoming personal difficulties; these contained bags of medicine and herbal remedies. Menacing figures armed with spears or knives have been used to represent opposing or malevolent forces of evil.

Opinions vary as to the function of these figures. There have been some reports that certain Nkisi figures have been meant to cause suffering or death, while others have reportedly been used to protect property. There are also those who believe that the primary function of the Nkisi was to destroy those who practiced WITCHCRAFT.

When the Nkisi were created to cause harm, mixtures known as *bilongo*, consisting of grave dirt, blood, gunpowder, and other potent magical substances, were inserted into open cavities of the wooden figure, usually in the abdomen or the back of the head. These mixtures were then covered with mirrors, COWRIE SHELLS, or clay and were activated by inserting metal blades or nails into the figure. Some believe that each such blade or nail was supposed to represent a specific request being made. It was not unusual for a figure to be almost completely covered by blades or nails, suggesting that numerous requests were being made.

See also: DIVINATION (Vol. I); masks (Vol. I); RELIGION, TRADITIONAL (Vol. I); SPIRIT POSSESSION (Vol. I).

Further reading: Mary H. Nooter, *Secrecy: African Art that Conceals and Reveals* (New York: The Museum for African Art, 1993); William Bascom, *African Art in Cultural Perspective: An Introduction* (New York: W. W. Norton, 1973); Benjamin C. Ray, *African Religions: Symbol, Ritual and Community*, 2nd ed. (Upper Saddle River, N.J.: Prentice Hall, 2000).

Nok culture Modern name given to the IRON AGE society whose sculptures, iron tools, and stone artifacts were found near the Nigerian town of Nok. The figures are the earliest known sculptures of a highly developed people from sub-Saharan Africa and date from roughly 900 BCE to 200 CE.

The Nok culture, also called the Nok Figurine culture, was both highly skilled and technologically advanced. It is best known for its terra-cotta sculptures of humans and animals, which ranged from life-size to 1 inch (2.5 cm). It also is known for its early use of iron.

Nok sculptures are remarkable for their striking craftsmanship and intricate design. Heads are often long and tubular, an exaggeration typical of Nok style. It is thought that many of the surviving heads may once have been part of life-sized sculptures. Faces were created with much care and detail, sometimes showing teeth, mustaches, curved brows, full lips, open mouths, delicate eyes with representations of eyelashes, and scars or tattoos.

Though the exact function of the sculptures created by Nok culture is not known, scholars speculate that the elaborate human figures may represent a god or a notable deceased person, while the plainer sculptures may indicate a person of lower social status. Some sculptures, in which the animal or person is supported by a round base, may have been used as decorations for the outside of homes, tombs, or shrines.

Most sculptures were formed from coarse clay, made by hand, and covered with a mixture of finer clay and water called slip. The sculpture was then polished until the surface appeared smooth, giving the finished piece the appearance of a person with shiny skin. The large heads were hollow, with several holes in them. Though scholars do not know the exact method used for firing these sculptures, today's firings in Nigeria last about two hours, and the clay pieces are first covered with grass, leaves, and sticks.

The first sculpture was found in 1928 in Nok, a town in central Nigeria near the confluence of the NIGER RIVER and the BENUE RIVER. Since the style of sculpture had never been seen before and nothing was previously known of the people who created it, the culture was named after the town. Since that time, hundreds of sculptures, tools, and other artifacts belonging to the Nok have been discovered in the area. The Nok figures are the earliest known examples of sculpture in Nigeria, but similarities to modern YORUBA art lead scholars to believe that the Nok tradition may have continued throughout Africa for thousands of years.

Because of the discovery of iron tool artifacts at Nok, scholars now know that the Iron Age was ushered into West Africa at least 800 years earlier than in the northern plains. The oldest known iron-smelting works is attributed to the Nok as early as the fourth century BCE. Scholars do not know if this Iron Age technology was brought to this area by another people or if the Nok discovered it themselves. It is believed, however, that the Nok, unlike most other cultures making the transition from the NEOLITHIC to the Iron Age, did not first use bronze or COPPER, but progressed directly from stone to iron.

nomads Name for people who wander, either periodically or in cycles, for subsistence. Ancient nomadic peoples of Africa are known to have lived a nomadic lifestyle for thousands of years.

Although many nomads still wander in areas of Africa today, the nomadic way of life was much more common in ancient and prehistoric times, when hunting and gathering was the main means of subsistence. In general, nomads wander in bands or small groups of people, usually as the seasons change or as animals move to more fertile pastures.

The life of the nomads is not without direction, however. On the contrary, nomads have great knowledge of the land, seasons, climate, and habits of animals, and they use this knowledge to direct their wanderings. When agriculture became known, some nomads cultivated crops in one area but then moved from time to time in order to find better areas to grow crops.

Perhaps some of the earliest known nomads are the prehistoric HUNTER-GATHERER societies of the SAHARA and the BERBERS, considered the original people of North Africa. Evidence of nomadic PASTORALISTS on the shores of the ancient lakes of the Sahara show that by c. 5000 BCE this area was home to various prehistoric cultures. Pastoral nomads raised livestock and moved to more fertile pastureland as the need arose, which especially was the case in areas near the mountains or where the land was poor or particularly wet.

The ancient Berbers, who are known to have lived in Africa since about 3000 BCE, occupied settlements west of EGYPT and south of the MEDITERRANEAN SEA. Berbers have had the reputation of being nomadic desert wanderers throughout their history. Aided by camels, many Berber merchants did indeed travel the Saharan trade routes to bring goods from the south to the big cities of the north. The truth, however, is that most Berbers became settled farmers.

As cities and urban areas grew, nomadic peoples came into conflict with settlers. They never posed much of a serious threat to the settlers, though, and even the great rebellion of the nomadic Tacfarinas, which took place in TUNISIA in 23 CE, was put down.

When ROME took control over most of North Africa, it opened up land, leading to the spread of urban life. During this time, it is thought that as many as 80,000 people moved into Africa from Rome and its surrounding area. Only in such locales as the ATLAS MOUNTAINS did North African culture remain outside the sphere of influence of the new settlers. The influx of Roman conquerors forced more and more North African nomads to move into the Sahara to avoid the fighting and the accompanying turmoil. As a result, competition for resources became fierce and the desert oases increasingly came under attack by nomads like the Sanhaja, a Berber group that advanced by camel.

Evidence shows that as more people moved into an area, more interdependence was created, more trade occurred, and nomads were forced to become more mobile. This, and the fact that the Sahara Desert was becoming drier, contributed to the nomads' increasing use of CAMELS. Though the use of Egyptian camels dates back to the sixth century BCE, they were not widely used in the Sahara until c. 200 CE.

Roman invasions and urban settlements, along with advances in AGRICULTURE, IRRIGATION, and tool making, led to a decline in the nomadic way of life.

See also: BERBERS (Vols. II, III); TRANS-SAHARAN TRADE ROUTES (Vol. II); TUAREGS (Vols. II, III).

nomarch Title assigned to rulers of small villages that became provinces of ancient Egypt.

In predynastic EGYPT, c. 3500 BCE, a number of small villages cropped up along the banks of the Nile River. Their rulers controlled and organized the villages' trade, which was based on pottery, alabaster vessels, and glass beads. The most successful of these villages developed into larger chiefdoms, which, after the Egyptian state became politically organized, were recognized as provinces called nomes. Their rulers were referred to as nomarchs.

Nuba (Noba) Ethnic group indigenous to southwestern Sudan.

A non-nomadic agricultural people who have lived in the area since ancient times, the Nuba apparently have long subsisted on a diet based on SORGHUM and the meat from their domesticated CATTLE and goats. More than 100 languages have been attributed to the Nuba clans, which include such subgroups as the Anag, Karla, Tagali, Tumtum, and Temein. For centuries, the Nuba's most significant religious rituals have been performed by the Kudjur, or priest, whose responsibilities include making rain and contacting departed ancestors.

Among the many unanswered questions about the Nuba is their exact origin. Various burial sites and artifacts have led some archaeologists to suggest that the Nuba were one of several ethnic groups (collectively known as X-GROUP) who migrated to MEROË some time after its decline from power. Later, they retreated inland, where the Nuba Hills formed a natural barrier that protected them from marauding nomads and Arab slave traders.

See also: AKSUM (Vol. I, II); BALLANA CULTURE (Vol. I); NUBA (Vol. III); ZANJ (Vol. II);

Further reading: Basil Davidson, *The Lost Cities of Africa* (New York: Little, Brown, 1987).

Nubia See KUSH.

Nubia, Christian Period of religious conversion that took place in the Nubian kingdoms of Nuba (Nobatia), Makurra (Makouria), and Alwa (Alodia) following the destruction of MEROË in 350 CE.

See also: NUBIA, CHRISTIAN (Vol. II).

Nubia, Lower Ancient region of northeastern Africa located between the first and second Nile cataracts of present-day EGYPT. Lower Nubia was part of the larger region of Nubia (KUSH) that extended from the NILE RIVER valley east to the RED SEA, and south to KHARTOUM in present-day Sudan.

Lower Nubia saw one of the earliest phases of state formation from 3800 BCE to 3100 BCE with the NUBIAN A-GROUP cultures, whose remains were found in large tombs in the cemetery at QUSTUL in the 1960s. These remains demonstrated the A-group's wealth and provided evidence that they were ruled by early pharaohs. The A-group cultures traded COPPER, incense, GOLD, and semi-precious stones with the north for manufactured goods and agricultural products. The rise of the First Dynasty in Egypt (c. 2950 BCE) resulted in the end of the A-group culture and Lower Nubia's independence.

There are no archaeological finds from the area for the next 500 years, until the emergence of the NUBIAN C-GROUP cultures, who lived from 2300 BCE to 1550 BCE, during the Egyptian Sixth Dynasty. Lower Nubia was known then as WAWAT. The C-group settled along the Nile from Aswan to the second cataract. Their culture was dependent upon cattle. As Egypt began to fragment politically, the C-group migrated to the north. Some members rose very high in Egyptian society, playing a pivotal role in the struggles that founded the MIDDLE KINGDOM around 2050 BCE.

In 1950 BCE Egypt conquered Lower Nubia and controlled the region until 1700 BCE. The C-group cultures remained culturally distinct under Egyptian rule, but the land of Kush to the south and the MEDJAY people of the Eastern Desert remained independent from Egyptian rule. As a result, Kush became a strong power in the south and when disunity threatened Egypt again in 1700 BCE at the end of the Middle Kingdom, Kush took over Lower Nubia, with its C-group populations and its Egyptian soldiers. These peoples now looked to the ruler of Kush as their leader, and he was represented as a pharaoh.

During the rule of the NEW KINGDOM, from about 1550 to 1100 BCE, the C-group peoples of Lower Nubia became increasingly Egyptianized, and eventually their culture disappeared; little is known of Lower Nubia between 1100 and 750 BCE.

In 750 BCE, MEROË was founded as the new capital of Kush in the southern part of Lower Nubia. This event would establish Lower Nubia's independence from Egyptian rule, although its leadership was still pharaonic. Meroë was a great city with large industrial complexes and enormous temples. After battling the Romans in the north, the Meroites reached an agreement in 23 BCE establishing Aswan as a new home for their settlers. This event launched an age of prosperity for Lower Nubia. The wealth of trade created many achievements in art and architecture. (The culture also flourished due to the decision of Roman emperor Diocletian to withdraw Roman soldiers from Lower Nubia and to establish the first cataract as the southern boundary of the Roman Empire in 272 CE.) Meroitic culture, which had become increasingly Africanized as Lower Nubia was cut off from Egypt, continued to dominate the region until around 300 CE, when it was destroyed by the Blemmyes of the Eastern or Arabian Desert.

Around 375 CE the kingdom of Nobatia, by then known as Nubia, was established, with its capital near the present-day Sudanese border. Evidence of this post-Meroitic culture was found in archaeological remains in cemeteries and villages ranging from the first cataract to just north of the third cataract. The remains of the culture did not show a dramatic break with the Meroitic traditions, but the formal differences in the pottery—especially in its size, shape, and design—show the new characteristics of the Nobatian culture. Great tombs with jewels, crowns, and weapons of the BALLANA CULTURE were found at Qustul. The iconography of these objects showed that Nobatian culture used pharaonic symbols and worshiped ancient gods like the Meroites. The Nobatian kingdom ended around 550 CE with the rise of Christianity in Egypt and Lower Nubia.

See also: X-GROUP (Vol. I)

Nubian A-Group Farmers and herders who established themselves, c. 3800 BCE, in the area south of GIBEL SILSILA in the lower NILE RIVER valley; also known as Ta-Seti ("The Land of the Bow"). Many modern researchers believe that the politically centralized Lower Nubian A-Group was ruled by kings, making it the earliest kingdom in the Nile River basin. Before unification of UPPER and LOWER EGYPT, c. 3100 BCE, the Nubian civilization, which lasted from about 3800 BCE to c. 3000 BCE, evidently was a dominant power in Upper Egypt. Nubian A-Group burials and artifacts found upriver from the modern site of Aswan resemble those of the contemporaneous Upper Egyptian Amratian culture NAQADAH I.

While the Nubian A-Group apparently preceded the kingdoms of Upper and Lower Egypt, archaeologists disagree over whether the Nubian culture developed independently or as an offshoot of the AMRATIAN CULTURE. Icons associated with the Nubian A-group's political elite, most notably the symbols of the HORUS-falcon and the WHITE CROWN, were later adopted by the rulers of the unified Egyptian state. Cave temples built at Gibel Silsila by Egypt's Eighteenth Dynasty ruler HOREMHEB depict his disputed claim of military victory over the Nubians.

Further reading: William Adams, *Nubia: Corridor to Africa* (Princeton, N.J.: Princeton University Press, 1977); David O'Connor, *Ancient Nubia: Egypt's Rival in Africa* (Philadelphia: University of Pennsylvania Press, 1994).

Nubian C-Group Cattle-raising PASTORALISTS of Lower Nubia (Kush) who established a culture that lasted from c. 2200 to 1500 BCE. The C-Group, which apparently moved eastward into the NILE VALLEY c. 2300 BCE, was, like the earlier NUBIAN A-GROUP, organized into structured chiefdoms. Throughout their 700 year history, they remained dependent primarily upon cattle-herding, a fact that was reflected in their art and POTTERY as well as in their leather clothing.

During the Egyptian First Intermediate Period (c. 2200–2000 BCE), the C-Group was under more or less constant threat from EGYPT, which used its full military and economic might against the smaller culture. Despite frequent conquests by the Egyptians, however, the C-Group successfully maintained its own traditions well into Egypt's MIDDLE KINGDOM (c. 2000–1650 BCE). As the Middle Kingdom came to an end and Egyptian power in the area waned, however, the C-Group fell victim to another invader, this time from the Nubian culture based at KERMA. In time, the C-Group was effectively absorbed into the kingdom of KUSH, and C-Group people began adopting Egyptian customs on a major scale. Eventually, C-Group culture became virtually identical to that of the Egyptians.

Further reading: David O'Connor, *Ancient Nubia: Egypt's Rival in Africa* (Philadelphia: University of Pennsylvania Press, 1994).

Nuer Seminomadic group that has lived for thousands of years in areas of present-day Sudan and ETHIOPHIA. According to their own oral tradition, the Nuer originally made their home in Koat-Liece, a village west of Bahr al-Jebel. There, a sacred tamarind tree, its branches laden with offerings of bracelets and tobacco, was a living altar to the Nuer's supreme being, Kwoth Nhial.

The Nuer traditionally have had no kings or chiefs. Instead, prophets and religious leaders were the most powerful and influential members of the Nuer communities, which usually consisted of several extended families or CLANS. These religious leaders frequently have been members of the Spear Master clans, a group that has long been deeply rooted in Nuer culture.

Considered sacred by the Nuer, CATTLE have played a number of roles in the lives and beliefs of these people. Ritual sacrifice of a cow, for example, has been an important part of Nuer RITES OF PASSAGE, including the birth of a child, the onset of puberty, marriage, and funerals. Cattle also have been considered a symbol of manhood, and, upon reaching the age of sixteen, Nuer boys have traditionally been given an "ox name" as part of their INITIATION ceremonies. Beyond this, however, cows have been important to the Nuer for their physical survival, especially for milk, which traditionally has made up a large part of the Nuer diet. Although cattle hides, bones, and internal organs have been used in the construction of beds, tools, weapons, and even musical instruments, there is some question about whether or not the Nuer consumed the meat.

See also: NUER (Vol. II); PASTORALISM (Vol. I); POLYTHEISM (Vol. I).

Further reading: Elizabeth Isichei, *African Societies to 1870* (London: Cambridge University Press, 1997); James L. Newman, *The Peopling of Africa* (New Haven, Conn: Yale University Press, 1995).

numeration systems Methods of numerical calculation used by individual peoples. Traditional systems differed from people to people, expanding and evolving as mathematical needs changed.

Although it is impossible to date the development of numeration systems, descriptions of finger counting, believed to be the earliest forms of reckoning, are found in the Egyptian BOOK OF THE DEAD. A reverence for the ability to calculate is described.

The most common numbering system is to express a greater number in terms of the sum of two smaller numbers. In the system that the Mawha language of Mozambique uses, for instance, the word for six means "five plus one," the word for seven means "five plus two," the word for twenty means "two tens," and the word for thirty means "three tens." Some languages use a base-10 system; some use base 5; other languages, such as YORUBA, use 20 as a base for counting.

The Yoruba system perhaps originated from using the combined digits of hands and feet to count off. Numbers are more precisely defined by subtraction and, to a lesser extent, addition. For example, the word for forty means "two twenties," and the word for seventy means "four twenties minus ten." Sometimes smaller numbers from one to five are employed in the enumeration.

The subtractive system is thought to have developed from counting cowrie shells, the Yoruba's earliest currency. Large bags of shells would be swiftly grouped by a counter into lots of twenty, and these groups would then be reckoned into whatever amount was needed by subtracting shells from the nearest multiple of ten. As the economy and numbers developed, the system expanded to accommodate larger sums. Then multiples of 200 formed the base. The Yoruba's concept of infinity is illustrated by the image of countless locusts swarming a large area.

Yoruba children still learn their numeration system in the traditional way, with their parents at marketplaces, and through the use of ancient mathematical games. The Yoruba language has adapted to the use of larger numbers.

The Bambara of Mali and Guinea have a ten-twenty system that exemplifies the everyday origin of many traditional counting systems. The word for twenty means "one person" because one person has twenty digits in all;

the word for forty means "mat" because, as it is explained, a husband and wife sleeping on a mat together have twenty fingers and twenty toes, forty digits in all.

Gesture systems of counting are used by some peoples. The Yao people of MALAWI and Mozambique point to the first four fingers of their left hand to count from one to four and then make a fist to indicate five; to make ten, the fingers of both hands are raised and the hands are joined. In other gesture systems, a tap on the chin means ten.

The most elementary system of written notation is the tally mark. Use of this kind of notation, as shown on the ISHANGO BONE, dates as far back as 8500 BCE.

The FULANI people of West Africa measure their wealth in terms of the number of CATTLE or other animals they own. They place sticks in patterns in front of their houses to display their wealth to neighbors. Sticks placed in the shape of a V mean "100" cattle. Sticks crossed in the shape of an X mean "fifty." Placed flat, the sticks each stand for ten; placed upright, the sticks stand for ones. Thus, the owner of a house with sticks in the pattern VVX— — III in front of the house is telling neighbors that he or she possesses 273 cattle.

Numidia An area in North Africa (present-day ALGERIA) that was part of the empire of CARTHAGE before the PUNIC WARS. During the second Punic War (218–201 BCE), the East Numidian king MASINISSA allied himself with ROME; following the Roman victory over Carthage in 210 BCE, Masinissa was rewarded with the throne of a united Numidia.

For almost 150 years, the country maintained its cultural and political independence. King Masinissa's grandson, King JUGURTHA, however, engaged in several conflicts with Rome, the last of which led to his downfall in 105 BCE. Later, during the Roman civil wars of the first century BCE, Numidia's King JUBA I sided with Pompey against Julius CAESAR, a decision that, following Caesar's victory, cost Numidia its independence. Numidia continued, however, as a subject kingdom and even, under King Juba II, enjoyed a period of revival that lasted until the invasion of the VANDALS during the fifth century CE.

Nuri Ancient Kushite city on the NILE RIVER at the fourth cataract. Nuri is the site of the royal burial grounds of the NAPATA dynasty (c. 747–200 BCE). The Napatan kings battled with EGYPT over control of the NILE DELTA. Their culture was a unique fusion of African and Egyptian influences.

More than twenty generations of kings are buried in Nuri. The Napatan tombs at Nuri feature stepped pyramids made of stone. Built against the eastern face of these pyramids were small chapels where priests could make offerings to the dead.

Napatan pyramids were much smaller than those built in Egypt. The pyramid of King Taharqa is the largest, measuring 90 feet (27 m) along the base. In contrast, the GREAT PYRAMID AT GIZA measured 750 feet (229 m). Napatan pyramids were also steeper than their Egyptian counterparts. Each pyramid usually had two or three small rooms underneath it. The king's body was placed in the room directly below the pyramid. Like Egypt's pharaohs, these kings were mummified, and their bodies were placed in wooden or stone coffins. Napatan queens also had pyramid tombs, though they were smaller and less elaborate than those of the kings.

Although they have been looted by thieves, the tombs at Nuri shed light on the culture and history of the Napatan period. Many of the goods and inscriptions found at the tombs attest to the strong influence Egypt had on the culture.

O

Ogun (Ogoun) In traditional YORUBA religion, the god of iron and of war.

Ogun is one of the earliest of Yoruba divinities. Two traditions exist regarding his origins. In one, he is a deified ancestor, a heroic individual who made important contributions to the people. In the other, stronger tradition, he is a primordial being who, when the gods first came to earth in the dawn of days, cut a path for the other gods through an impassible thicket by using his sharp iron machete. Thus, Ogun is associated with clearing away barriers, protecting against accidents, and opening a path for health and prosperity. He is the tutelary, or guardian, divinity of hunters, blacksmiths, goldsmiths, and butchers.

In still other traditions, Ogun reigned over a territory in Yorubaland. In one such telling (perhaps a myth for the origin of iron), Ogun is the first king of the town of Irè. On coming home from a battle, he discovers that empty kegs of palm wine, instead of being turned upside down as they should have been, were left standing upright. Ogun becomes enraged and slaughters many of his subjects until, realizing what he has done, he repents, dramatically drives his sword into the ground, and sits on it until both he and his sword sink slowly deep into the earth, promising to return when they are needed.

In modern times, Ogun has become the divinity of truck drivers, mechanics, and others who work in or with iron and steel. In law courts, traditional believers swear on Ogun instead of the Bible or the Koran and kiss a piece of iron that represents him. Swearing falsely breaks a covenant with Ogun and can lead to ghastly accidents.

See aslo: CHRISTIANITY (Vol. II); EGUNGUN (Vol. I); KORAN (Vol. II); *NUMUW* (Vol. II); RELIGION, TRADITIONAL (Vol. I).

Further Reading: Omosade Awolalu, *Yoruba Beliefs and Sacrificial Rites* (White Plains, N.Y.: Longman Group, 1979).

okapi Cud-chewing, hoofed mammal belonging to the same animal family as the GIRAFFE. Unknown to science until the early twentieth century, the okapi, because of its stripes, was at one time thought by Europeans to be a kind of zebra.

Because the okapi seemed to be a combination of several creatures, the ancient Egyptians associated the creature with the god SETH, the troublesome deity who killed his brother, OSIRIS. Often depicted with a dog's body, a forked tail, and a long, pointy nose, images of Seth incorporated elements of several creatures. As a result, like such other creatures as the aardvark and the long-nosed mouse, the okapi often was considered a kind of inspiration for the deity.

Old Kingdom Period in ancient Egyptian history lasting from approximately 2700 BCE to 2200 BCE. Following the initial unification of UPPER and LOWER EGYPT, the nation was ruled, for a period of almost 400 years, by two royal dynasties. During this time the Egyptians not only developed their life-sustaining irrigation system but also constructed the first of their impressive architectural wonders, the pyramids.

By the beginning of the Old Kingdom, the Egyptian government had been centralized enough to take effective control of both public life and public works. The resulting burst of pyramid and monument building forever changed the social and physical landscape of the country.

The first of these was the great STEP PYRAMID at SAQQARA. But it was not long before the great pyramids of KHUFU and KHAFRE were constructed at Giza. The organization necessary to perform these feats not only testified to the sophisticated level of Egyptian society but also helped create the social fabric that was to endure within the nation for several millennia.

The three dynasties of the Old Kingdom ruled relatively successfully for 500 years. Then, however, unrest and conflict among the ruling elite of priests and public officials led to a decline in royal power. By the end of the Sixth Dynasty, about 2181 BCE, Egypt fell into the hands of several dynasties of weak, ineffectual rulers. As a result, the kingdom suffered a decline from which it did not emerge until the dawn of the MIDDLE KINGDOM, more than 200 years later.

See also: EGYPT (Vol. I).

Oldowan tools One of the oldest known sets of stone tools used in the STONE AGE or Paleolithic period (c. 2.5 million years ago). Oldowan tools, named for their discovery at OLDUVAI GORGE, in Kenya, were used by inhabitants of the region at least 1.75 million to 2 million years ago. Sometimes described as Oldowan Technology, the tools represent an improvement over the earliest digging sticks and simple stones that gave the Stone Age its name. The series of stones with flaked, or sharpened, edges made at Olduvai were used for cutting, scraping, and chopping food. Scientists have determined that to create a flaked tool, our human ancestors had to strike one stone against another repeatedly. Gradually pieces were chipped away until a sharpened edge was formed. About 1.5 million years ago, a more advanced set of instruments, called the ACHEULEAN TOOLKIT, came into use.

Olduvai Gorge Area in the Great RIFT VALLEY that has been the source of many important discoveries in paleoarchaeology; located near Lake Eyasi in modern-day Tanzania.

See also: HUMAN ORIGINS (Vol. I).

Fossils 2 million years old have been dug from the walls of 25-mile (40-km) long Olduvai Gorge in the Great Rift Valley. © *Brian Vikander/CORBIS*

Olorun (Olodumare, Oludumare)

Creator deity in traditional YORUBA religion.

According to traditional belief, Olorun is present in all of creation as the intrinsic energy that brought about its being. In this view, the tree, the rock, and other aspects of nature are manifestations of Olorun's essence, and it is this essence that believers revere and worship, not their visible forms. Accordingly, human beings must see the Creator in all things and see themselves as part of creation, thus strengthening the Yorubas' connection between themselves and the world in which they live.

See aslo: RELIGION, TRADITIONAL (Vol. I)

Oludumare

See OLORUN.

oracle

Generally considered an oral response from a divine god accomplished through the use of human mediums. From ancient times, oracles have served various populations in Africa, providing dire predictions, meting out appropriate justice, and offering solutions and guidance. These various oracles were believed to have been the embodiment of living gods, and they spoke at specially appointed sites or times through chosen mediums. Oracular predictions also occurred in dreams and as visions, or took place when individuals were in the throes of SPIRITUAL POSSESSION. In this way oracles represented a critical aspect of RELIGION in Africa and were honored with traditional rites, customs, and the observance of taboos. In ancient EGYPT and NUBIA, the primary oracle shared by both regions was AMUN, who was believed to reside in the holy mountain of GEBEL BARKAL. Similarly, in Nigeria, the Aro-Chuku oracle represented an important divinity for the IBO.

Although the traditions and rites of each region varied, the men and women serving as oracles usually received many years of training. In a number of societies, priests or priestesses served as the primary mediums and offered responses in everything from parables and riddles to symbolic figures. Many of the men and women who spoke on behalf of the gods also acted in the capacity of divine kings.

Others, such as the priests and priestesses of GHANA, who were known as Okomfo, were community-based. Relying on the oracle for guidance, they were able to cure illnesses and to provide tangible, communal solutions to social problems. The Okomfo worked with attendants trained to interpret their words and remedies. In other communities, oracles were recognized as village elders, healers, doctors, or medicine men.

The oral traditions of the Chwezi, from the region of Lake Victoria, relate stories of oracles in place prior to the advent of early kingdoms in the fifteenth century. The long-standing practice of Chwezi spirits reputedly was to enter the body of several women at a time. Family members then consulted these spirits about specific matters. In the past these mediums traveled widely through Chwezi territory, stopping at specific regional shrines. Others worked directly with the king.

One of the most notable aspects of oracular deities was their choice of who would receive the gift of mediumship. In the society of the Lugbara, of modern-day Uganda, it was held that at a young age, the deity chose specific girls as divine representatives on earth. When an individual was so identified, the girl was left in the woods, where certain divine revelations or visions were revealed. After returning to her village, she presided over a specially built shrine.

It appears that many societies commonly retained women as oracles, although the reasons are not completely clear. These women were often responsible for the upkeep of the religious site, which often meant performing purification rites, maintaining appropriate materials, and other sacred duties.

See also: AROCHUKU ORACLE (Vols. II, III); DIVINATION (Vol. I); NKISI (Vol. I); RAINMAKER (Vol. I).

Further reading: Philip Curtin, et al, *African History: From Earliest Times to Independence,* 2nd ed. (London: Longman Group Limited, 1995); John R. Hinnells, ed., *The Penguin Dictionary of Religions* (New York: Penguin Books, 1995); John S. Mbiti, *African Religions and Philosophy*, 2nd ed. (Oxford, Eng.: Heinemann Education Publishers, 1999).

oral traditions

The social values, guidelines, and history that form the spoken record of societies. From ancient times, oral traditions have enabled African societies to remain connected with their past as part of an endless cycle of regeneration. Belief in this cycle of regeneration (and the sense of community that it fosters) has shaped oral traditions into a relative chronology rather than a timetable of absolute dates.

In some African cultures, conveying knowledge about the past in spoken form was considered a sacred responsibility. Accordingly, there was an associated belief in the divinity of the spoken word. Among the FULANI, for example, it was believed that the spoken word, or *haala,* had the power to activate all things. Similarly, the Dogon tell of how the seventh of eight ancestral spirits became the architect of world order by weaving a cloth that conveyed the power of the word, known as *soy,* to humans. These examples underscore why oral tradition should be understood as encompassing a wide body of songs, folklore, myths, and proverbial wisdom, yet transcending each specific form.

One reason why oral traditions transcend each specific form is that traditions have the ability to make the distant past a present, living reality. Africanists and historians in general have remarked that oral traditions in African societies appear to embody three distinct forms: The first form of oral tradition has been linked to the creation myth. Many societies created these early traditions by using mnemonic, or memorization-assisting, devices to retain their founding histories, religious ideals, and other vital information. Mnemonic devices often contained formulaic words that, when combined in certain ways or repeated as an incantation, were known to bring about solutions or resolve hardships. This interplay of historical events and religious beliefs has led many historians to reduce to the level of myth the oral traditions associated with the ancient period, to question their historic validity, and to criticize their limited reality and "coded messages."

The second form of oral history is said to reflect the societal development and interaction of early city-state formation. These were the oral traditions that were not shared with outsiders. Early city-states had powerful political systems with accomplishments that its rulers sought to preserve through an organized system of oral history. The griot, or court historian, often served this purpose as a "talking mouth." These oral traditions, often set to MUSIC, incorporated the genealogy of early founders, the lives and exploits of kings, and the formation of dynasties. In societies where a high value was placed on such traditions, those entrusted with the position retained their knowledge by chanting or by undergoing a long period of memorization.

Oral traditions of this type are generally considered most reliable. Described by some historians as a fixed text, they cover up to eight centuries or more of a people's history. In this way, the epic deeds of kings such as Sundiata of Mali (r. c. 1230 CE) were maintained and embellished, while keeping many historical details intact. The Kuba peoples of southeastern Congo (Kinshasa) can relate historical data that dates back more than fifteen centuries.

The third form of oral tradition is based on the memory of the oldest living members of a population. These oral traditions, described as free texts, are not the responsibility of any single individual. In many instances, a council of elders might serve the purpose of transmitting oral traditions; this is an important way of maintaining many of Africa's oldest institutions, such as AGE SETS, SECRET SOCIETIES, and INITIATIONS. Within this time reference, oral traditions also aided in settling property disputes and agricultural concerns and were significant in religious ritual, incantations, and prayers. Such traditions have also influenced the social aspects of courtship, marriage and family life.

Because free texts often embody the personality of the teller, controversy continues as to their reliability or selective memory. These views have been challenged by African scholars who argue that the purpose of all history is to select that which is most courageous, productive, or artistic about a particular society. They also maintain that written history has often been based on "firsthand accounts" supplied by the oral traditions of informants.

While there are disadvantages in dealing with oral history—such as the oversimplification of ideas, the years it takes for outsiders to understand them, and concerns about the errors of informants—oral traditions represent an important source of historical information and cultural insights from a unique African perspective. These traditions have played a crucial role in leading archaeologists to ancient sites in East Africa and have been used to explain ruins in other regions. Although many historians have begun to see how well oral traditions work with written records and archaeological projects, holders of the oral tradition and their "living memories" are quickly vanishing from the cultural landscape of Africa.

See aslo: MALI (Vol. II); SUNDIATA KEITA (Vol. II).

Further reading: J. Ki-Zerbo, ed., *General History of Africa I: Methodology and African Prehistory* (Paris: UNESCO, 1989); Phyllis M. Martin and Patrick O'Meara, eds., *Africa*, 3rd ed. (Bloomington: Indiana University Press, 1995); John S. Mbiti *African Religion and Philosophy*, 2nd ed. (Oxford, Eng.: Heinemann Educational Publishers, 1999); Claudia Zaslavsky, *Africa Counts: Number and Pattern in African Cultures*, 3rd ed. (Chicago: Lawrence Hill Books, 1999).

Orange River River in Southwest Africa near the Cape of Good Hope.

From an early date, the Orange River aided in the migration and settlement patterns of the KHOIKHOI, the SAN, the BANTU, and other peoples. The lush landscape and wildlife along its banks offered a variety of food resources for HUNTER–GATHERERS, pastoralists, and farmers alike. The river and nearby pastures also supported such livestock as goats, sheep, and CATTLE, which were present in the region by about the second or third century BCE. However, it is not completely certain how they arrived there. Sometime later, pastoralist CLANS settled into community clusters around the springs and tributaries of the river. Later, these communities were formed into the nation-states that eventually played major roles in South Africa's history.

See also: ORANGE RIVER (Vol. III).

orisha In traditional YORUBA religion, forces in nature that act on behalf of humans.

Believers in traditional Yoruba religion use DIVINATION, prayer, DANCE, ritual, and sacrifice to ask the orisha to intervene in human affairs and correct or heal a bad situation. The orisha are part of nature, too, but they exist at a higher plane, closer to OLORUN, the Creator. They represent the ability of humans, through their powers of reflection, to enter into a consciousness of the divine. Worship of the orisha, it is said, leads to balance and harmony. Each of the some four hundred orisha has its own cult and priesthood.

See also: ESHU (Vol. I); OGUN (Vol. I); RELIGION, TRADITIONAL (Vol. I); SPIRIT POSSESSION (Vol. I).

Orisha Oko YORUBA deity associated with AGRICULTURE and general fertility; his emblem is an iron rod. The Yoruba, who have most likely inhabited the savannas west of lower Niger since the fourth millennium BCE, are largely dependent upon agriculture for their survival, and, not surprisingly, Orisha Oko is one of their primary deities, honored by many temples and served by numerous priests. The most important festival in honor of Orisha Oko is celebrated at the time of the YAM harvest. Beyond a general sharing in the harvest, in which virtually everyone eats yams, there is a general sense of freedom and license. In ancient times, it is believed, this even included a degree of sexual license that allowed men unrestricted access to women from certain groups or classes.

See also: ESHU (Vol. I); OGUN (Vol. I); RELIGION, TRADITIONAL (Vol. I); SPIRIT POSSESSION (Vol. I).

Oromo (Galla) Kushitic people of ETHIOPIA, formerly called the Galla. Studies of ancient LANGUAGES show that the Oromo were one of several groups present in Ethiopia at least 7,000 years ago. Beyond that, the Oromo trace their origins to the dry savanna northeast of Lake TURKANA and to the southern highlands near the Shabele and Juba Rivers. For thousands of years, CLAN systems have been based on patrilineal descent, a system that helped maintain their ancient tradition of PASTORALISM. In Oromo society, all male children of the same generation form an indissoluble group that moves through all the AGE SETS together. The Oromo also used this system, sometimes called the *gada* system, to address political, social, and economic issues within their society. Except for such subgroups as the BORAN OROMO, their way of life continued relatively uninterrupted until the Islamic-Ethiopian wars of the fifteenth and sixteenth centuries.

See also: OROMO (Vols. II, III).

Further reading: David Buxton, *The Abyssinians* (New York: Praeger Publishers, 1970); James L. Newman, *The Peopling of Africa: A Geographic Interpretation* (New Haven, Conn.: Yale University Press, 1995).

Osanyin YORUBA deity presumed to be the younger brother of IFA, the god of DIVINATION.

Osanyin is generally seen as being in control of the principles that govern Yoruba MEDICINE. For the Yoruba, medicine invariably involves an understanding not just of the human body but also of the patient's emotional and spiritual nature. For this reason, Yoruba healing traditionally is seen not simply as a matter of medical practice but also as a matter of religion, involving the visible and invisible worlds. This results in a complex system governing everything from how certain herbs or other materials are gathered to how and when they are applied. Even the movements, gestures, and sounds of the healer are prescribed. It is this entire system that is seen as being controlled by the deity Osanyin.

See also: RELIGION, TRADITIONAL (Vol. I).

According to an ancient and well-known Yoruba myth, as soon as Ifa entered the world, he wanted to have a slave to work for him. He sent the slave to work cutting grass. As the slave started to work, he noticed he was about to cut the grass that was used to cure fever, so he adamantly refused to destroy the useful grass.

Moving on to another kind of grass, the slave started to cut. But, as before, he noticed that he was about to destroy a useful grass. This one he recognized as the grass that was used to cure headaches, and again he refused to cut it. This continued with the next kind of grass as well, which turned out to be a cure for stomachaches.

Astonished at how much the slave knew, Ifa asked the slave, who turned out to be Osanyin, to teach him everything he knew about the uses of plants, herbs, and other materials.

Osiris One of the major deities of the state religion of EGYPT, and the principal god of the dead and lord of the underworld.

The cult of Osiris first began during the OLD KINGDOM, at which time Osiris became fused with the funerary god Khentimentiu, "Foremost of the Westerners," and became associated with the rebirth of the earth after the flooding of the NILE RIVER. The myth of Osiris relates that Osiris's parents were the earth god Geb and the sky goddess Nut. His brother was the god SETH, and his sister, the goddess ISIS. Osiris married his sister, and eventually they produced a son, the god HORUS.

According to the story, Seth became so jealous of his brother that he drowned Osiris in the Nile. Isis retrieved the body of her dead husband, but the evil Seth intervened. Dismembering his brother's corpse, Seth scattered the pieces throughout Egypt. However, the resourceful widow managed to collect her husband's remains and put them back together again. Using her magical powers, Isis resurrected him and eventually became pregnant with Horus. Later, Horus went on to avenge his father's murder, defeating Seth in battle and establishing himself as an earthly ruler much like the pharaohs.

According to Egyptian belief, Osiris began to rule the underworld once he was resurrected. Together with a tribunal of forty-two other deities, he sat in absolute judgment over the souls of the departed. By the time of the MIDDLE KINGDOM, Osiris was firmly established as the most important deity associated with the cult of the dead. The cult was centered at ABYDOS, where, according to common belief, Osiris's head was buried.

Osiris's prominence was a constant throughout the history of Egyptian religion. In fact, his position as "weigher of souls" and judge of all mortal beings lasted well beyond the rule of the pharaohs and traveled beyond the boundaries of Egypt.

ostrich Large, long-legged, flightless bird. Male ostriches, which can measure 8 feet (2.4 m) in height and weigh more than 300 pounds (111.9 kg), are the largest living birds in the world. The ostrich's powerful thighs have no feathers but instead help it to run up to speeds of 40 miles (64.4 km) per hour.

In prehistoric times, ostrich eggs were used by ancient people for ornamentation. The SAN and Nubian peoples, for example, would engrave patterns and pictures of animals on these eggs. The ancient Egyptians made beads out of ostrich shells.

The SAN people of southern Africa were fascinated by the odd, flightless behavior of ostriches. According to one of their legends, the ostrich once held fire beneath its wings. Humans, however tricked the ostrich and stole the fire. Afterward, the ostrich no longer flew and kept what little fire it still had tucked underneath its wings.

P

Palermo Stone Stone fragment from the Fifth Dynasty (c. 2565–2420 BCE) of ancient EGYPT that is inscribed with hieroglyphic symbols. It is a valuable source of information about Egypt's history during the first five dynasties (c. 2925–2325 BCE).

The Palermo Stone is made of black basalt and was once part of a larger stone that probably stood in an ancient Egyptian temple. The stone is inscribed on both sides with HIEROGLYPHICS, which are arranged in horizontal rows. At the top of the stone is a list of predynastic rulers, followed by time lines for different kings that list the memorable events of that king's reign by year. It includes, for example, information about the extent of the flooding of the NILE under various rulers.

The Palermo Stone is a fragment of a larger original tablet that is thought to have measured approximately 7 feet (2.1 m) in length, 2 feet (0.61 m) in height and 2.5 inches (6.3 cm) in thickness. This larger tablet was probably a detailed chronicle of all of Egypt's kings from the First to the Fifth Dynasty. The last king mentioned on the Palermo Stone is Neferirkare, the third of nine kings of the Fifth Dynasty. Other, smaller fragments of the original monument are found in the Egyptian Museum in CAIRO and the University College of London. The Palermo Stone is named after the Italian city where it is kept.

pantheism Belief that the sacred essence of deities is represented in all aspects of the natural world; a view found in virtually every region of the African continent. The term *pantheism* has been widely used to describe the way in which many African religions were organized around the natural cycles of their environment. During ancient Egypt's OLD KINGDOM (c. 3200–2200 BCE), for example, a family of nine deities represented every element of the universe. Known as the Ennead, this family included Atum, identified with the sunset; Shu, god of the air; and his twin sister, Tefnut, goddess of the dew.

Other aspects of pantheism can be seen in the beliefs of the Akan farmers of GHANA, who expressed their reverence for the earth in a myth in which the supreme deity, Nana Nyame, created the sky, the earth, order, and destiny. According to the myth, Nana Nyame completed the task in the northern region on a Thursday (Asase Yaa) and in the southern region on Friday (Asase Efua). It therefore was decreed that on those days the earth could not be plowed, defiled by the spilling of blood, or subjected to any other misuse.

See also: DOGON (Vol. II); NUER; (Vol. I) POLYTHEISM (Vol. I).

papyrus Writing surface used by the ancient Egyptians; also, the common name for the *Cyperus papyrus* plant from which the Egyptians made their writing material.

For centuries, papyrus, which resembled parchment, was the main writing material of ancient Egypt. Its use was probably widespread by about 3000 BCE, although the earliest known example dates back only to 2500 BCE. Eventually, papyrus was also used in GREECE, the Middle East, and ROME. Books, as we know them today, are more closely related to the papyrus rolls of ancient Egypt than to any ancient writing material that preceded it.

The papyrus plant was cultivated along the banks of the NILE RIVER. According to Pliny the Elder, the paper was made by first removing strips of the pith from the stem of the plant. The strips were then laid alongside each other, and another row of strips was placed crosswise over the first row. The two rows of strips were dampened with water and pressed together. The sap of the plant acted like glue and sealed the strips together into a sheet that was hammered before drying.

The result was a sheet of white material that, if all went well, had no marks or defects. The size of the sheet varied, but a typical sheet was 5 to 6 inches (12 to 15 cm) wide. The sheets were then pasted together to form long rolls. The length of the rolls varied, but usually no more than twenty sheets were pasted together into a roll. Sheets could be added to a roll as needed.

Perhaps the best-known use of papyrus was for the mortuary texts collectively known as the BOOK OF THE DEAD. Egyptians, preoccupied with an interest in the AFTERLIFE, wrote texts that would safely see the dead to another world. Many of these papyri remained well-preserved.

Being an organic substance, papyrus was subject to gradual deterioration. Keeping the material out of the light and free of organisms helped to preserve it, as did the dry climate of Egypt.

Just as scribes working with clay tablets had previously created a decorative style of writing that incorporated HIEROGLYPHICS, papyrus inspired Egyptians to create new styles of handwriting. Two cursive styles were created, one considered priestly and called HIERATIC, and the other a more simplified style of hieratic called DEMOTIC. The actual writing was usually done by SCRIBES, well-respected government officials who worked in the temples and pyramids. Papyrus was also used to write down prose, poetry, religious and scientific texts, myths, and stories.

Although the main use of the papyrus plant was to make paper, ancient Egyptians also used it to make sails, rope, mats, sandals, garlands, wreaths, and baskets. When dried, the roots of the plant were used for fuel. Caulk was derived from the pith of the stem, and the pith also was boiled and eaten.

The papyrus plant is a perennial and comes back year after year. An aquatic plant, it thrives in flowing water and has been described as grasslike and graceful. The common form grows to approximately 15 feet (4.6 m) in height, although a dwarf variety is often used today as an ornamental plant.

pastoralism Way of life characterized by the upkeep of domestic animals, including CATTLE, goats, sheep, CAMELS, zebus, and yaks. Pastoralists and their domesticated animals have a long history of mutual dependence. According to archaeological evidence, one of the earliest African pastoralist cultures dates back to the period 3800 to 3000 BCE (and perhaps to as early as 7000 to 5000 BCE). Excavations from Kadero and Esh Shaeinab in the NILE VALLEY suggest that these early pastoralists, generally known as the NUBIAN A-GROUP, migrated through this region with their herds, eventually encountering the STONE AGE Akban culture near the second cataract of the Nile.

Herds supplied many important products for these and other ancient pastoralists. Meat, milk, and blood provided nutritional food products. Animal skins were used for making clothing and tents, while bones were made into tools and other household items. Because their herds were so vital to their survival, it was important to early pastoralists to maintain the health and numbers of their herds.

The populations of the pastoralists' herds were maintained by the techniques commonly associated today with animal husbandry to control the breeding of the animals. Food supplies for the animals were equally important, and they often were maintained by a migratory process known as transhumance. In some areas, transhumance was affected by seasonal changes. In wet seasons, for example, groups frequently remained sedentary, cultivating grains of various kinds. In dry seasons, however, entire communities often had to pack their belongings onto their animals and go in search of new pastures. The

This undated drawing from the tomb of Puimre shows papyrus plants being harvested in the time of Thutmose III (c. 1504–1450 BCE).
© Bettmann/CORBIS

FULANI of the Sahel; the MAASAI, Turkana, and NUER of East Africa; and the Chwezi and KHOIKHOI of the south all practiced forms of transhumance. Other forms of herding, usually described as nomadic, occurred in drier regions in or near the Sahara. The TUAREGS, Moors, and Bedouin of these areas maintained herds that consisted mainly of camels and goats. These herds were successful because of these animals' ability to feed on tree leaves when pastures could not be located.

Over the centuries, pastoralism determined where people lived and influenced their economic, social, and cultural outlook. Economically, ownership of animals defined wealth and power, often causing local wars over pasturelands and water rights. From a social and cultural standpoint, herding became a tradition passed down from one generation to the next via RITES OF PASSAGE. Other traditions among pastoralists included an array of celebrations, from sacrifices to dances, that acknowledged the importance of herds to the people's culture and suvival.

See also: BORAN OROMO (Vol. I); GEBEL SILSILA (Vol. I).

Persian conquest Period during which EGYPT was conquered and ruled by Cambyses II of Persia; lasted from 525 BCE to 405 BCE.

With roots in parts of modern Iran and Afghanistan, ancient Persia became the center of a vast empire under its most famous rulers Cyrus the Great (r. c. 550–530 BCE), DARIUS I (550–486 BCE), and Xerxes I (r. 486–465). Cyrus the Great first vanquished the Medes, Persia's neighbors on the Persian Plateau. He then began a series of conquests that established the Persian Empire: Lydia fell around 545 BCE, and, by 539, Cyrus had been named king of Babylon.

The Persian Empire soon included most of the known world, from North Africa and southeastern Europe in the West to India in the East. At the height of its power, Persia ruled an area almost as large as the continental United States.

Cyrus's successor, Cambyses II (r. c. 529–521 BCE), crossed the harsh Sinai Desert in 525 BCE and attacked Egypt, which was well into the 700-year-long period of decline and foreign domination that began in 1070 BCE, toward the end of the Twentieth Dynasty. Betrayed by the Greek mercenary soldiers they had hired, the Egyptians were defeated by the Persians in the battle at Pelusium.

Cambyses II was succeeded by Darius I and then by Xerxes I, who faced revolts in Babylon as well as Egypt. Egypt successfully revolted against Persian rule in 405 BCE, during the reign of the Persian emperor Artaxerxes II. Egypt remained an independent state until it was conquered again, first by the Persians in 341 BCE, and then, in 332 BCE, by ALEXANDER THE GREAT, the young Macedonian ruler who added Egypt to his growing empire.

Phoenicians Ancient Semitic sea-faring people who were noted as merchants, traders, and colonizers. They inhabited the area that is now Lebanon and part of Syria and Israel. Phoenician civilization flourished in the first millennium BCE.

Little is known of the Phoenicians' roots, but the Greek historian HERODOTUS, among others, preserves an ancient tradition that places their original homeland in the Persian Gulf. The Phoenicians migrated to the Mediterranean region about 3000 BCE and soon began to extend their influence along the southeastern coast of Asia Minor, with settlements at Joppa (or Jaffa, modern Yafo), Acre, Dor, and Ugarit along the coast; in EGYPT, where they carried on extensive trading; and the northern coast of Africa, where, sometime between 814 and 750 BCE, they founded CARTHAGE. That city became a wealthy trading center, the head of a western Phoenician empire, and one of the most important cities of Africa.

Perhaps the most significant Phoenician contribution to culture and progress was the development of a twenty-two-letter ALPHABET that became the basis of the Greek alphabet and the ancestor of the Roman alphabet, in which most European and African languages are written. The Phoenicians are also credited with using Polaris, the North Star, as an aid to navigation. Their name for themselves was the Kena'ani and they are, very likely, the Canaanites of the Bible. Their chief cities or, more properly, city-states, exclusive of their colonies, were Tyre, Sidon, Byblos (modern Jbail), and Berot (modern Beirut), each of which had its own king. Sidon was famous for its embroideries; Tyre was well-known for its fine cloth, dyed with Tyrian purple made from the snail *Murex*; and Byblos—the word *bible* is derived from its name—was a trading center for PAPYRUS. Ivory and wood carvings and metalwork became Phoenician specialties. It is thought that the Phoenicians originated the art of glassblowing, or shaping glass without the use of molds, some time during the first century BCE.

The Phoenician Homeland The Phoenicians' early history is tightly linked with Egypt's. By the sixteenth century BCE, the two countries were carrying on extensive TRADE. Egypt controlled the Phoenician states for a time, but by the fourteenth century BCE, Egypt had lost its hold over them and the Phoenician states were independent once more. Their independence was threatened again in the ninth century BCE by attacks from the ASSYRIANS. In 868 BCE, the Assyrian king Ashurnasipal II exacted tribute from the Phoenician states and started a pattern of Assyrian supremacy and occasional collection of tribute that lasted almost 200 years. In 678 Sidon rebelled against the Assyrians, who destroyed the city and rebuilt it on the mainland. Tyre resisted Assyrian sieges in 672 and 668 but succumbed toward the end of the reign of Ashurbanipal (668–627 BCE), the last great king of Assyria.

As patterns of dominance in the Middle East shifted, so did Phoenician independence. Nebucharrezzar II, the king of the new Babylonian Empire from 605 to 562 BCE, sacked Jerusalem in 597 and then besieged Tyre, which held out for thirteen years before it finally fell. The Persians were next, capturing the Phoenician states in 538 and making them—along with Syria, Palestine, and Cyprus—a province of the Persian Empire. The ships of Tyre and Sidon were considered the finest vessels in the fleet that Persian emperor Xerxes assembled in 480 BCE to invade Greece. They fought at and were defeated in the famous battle of Salamis, which helped end the Persian threat to Europe. In 345 BCE, Persia quelled an unsuccessful revolt against its empire by Tyre and Sidon.

The pattern of domination by the major empires of the age continued unabated. ALEXANDER THE GREAT captured Tyre in 332 BCE and brought Phoenicia under Macedonian rule. His successors fought among themselves for control of the Phoenician city-states and their commercial resources. At the same time, the cities prospered and became centers of learning as well as trade, and a distinctive Phoenician cultural identity began to disappear. Greek replaced Phoenician as the language of culture and learning, and Aramaic became the language of the common people. In 64 BCE, the Roman general Pompey the Great made Phoenicia part of the Roman province of Syria, although Tyre and Sidon remained self-governing. Phoenicia and the rest of Syria fell to Muslim invaders in the seventh century CE.

Phoenician Colonies The Phoenicians never developed any kind of central federation or common government. The city-states had their own kings, whose power always seemed to be limited by the wealthy merchant families. Because their primary interest was commercial, the Phoenicians were not looking for lands to settle; instead, they were in search of anchorages and staging points from which they could mount trading expeditions. They often chose offshore islands and impregnable-looking promontories that offered maximum protection and safety.

The Phoenicians had settlements on the island of Cyprus in the Mediterranean in the ninth century and on Malta by the seventh century BCE. Both islands were stepping-stones on the route to Spain, an important source of silver and tin. Tradition has it that a Phoenician colony was founded at Gades (modern Cádiz) as early as 1130 BCE, but no Phoenician artifacts dating back earlier than the eighth century BCE have been found. Gades became one of the most important outposts of Phoenician power and, around 205 BCE, the Romans seized it from the control of the Phoenician colony of CARTHAGE. Later, after the Muslim invasions of Spain, it became a Moorish stronghold.

The oldest Phoenician colony in Africa was Utica, founded in the seventh century BCE and located about midway between present-day Tunis and Bizerte, TUNISIA. Utica and its neighboring colony of Carthage, which was founded around 750 BCE on a peninsula near modern Tunis, were almost equal in power. These colonies, along with Motya (modern Mozia) in Sicily, gave Phoenicia practical control of the Strait of GIBRALTAR. Carthage itself established a number of settlements in Tunisia, Algeria, Morocco, the Balearic Islands, and southern Spain.

Carthage was unique among Phoenician colonies because it was not politically dependent on the city-states back home. Babylonian pressure on the city of Tyre in the Phoenician homeland forced Carthage to act independently and respond to pressure from the Greek colonies on the island of Sicily in the Mediterranean. The Carthaginians successfully defended their colonies of Motya and Panormus (modern Palermo) and limited the Greek presence in Sardinia. An alliance in 450 BCE with the Etruscan cities on the Italian mainland successfully kept the Greeks from contact with Spain. The worth of the alliance was short-lived, however, as Etruscan power declined after 500 BCE. In 480 the Greeks vanquished a Carthaginian army at Himera, in Sicily. Because the Phoenician fleet sailing in Persian service was all but destroyed by the Greeks at the battle of Salamis that same year, the Phoenician homeland could offer no help.

Carthage's presence in Sicily started to increase about 410 BCE; eventually, Carthage came to rule much of Sicily at various times. In the years following 265, however, an expanding ROME vied with Carthage for control of the island. Carthage lost the three PUNIC WARS, fought against Rome from 264 to 241, from 218 to 201, and from 149 to 146 BCE. During the second Punic War, a daring invasion of Italy was launched by the famed Carthaginian general HANNIBAL (247–183 BCE), who almost won the war for Carthage. Hannibal led an army of 60,000 soldiers from Spain across the Pyrenees, into France, and across the Alps to invade the Italian Peninsula. In 216 BCE, at the battle of Cannae, he dealt the Romans their worst military defeat up to that time. Nonetheless, Carthage lost the second Punic War when its army was defeated at the battle of Zama in North Africa. Totally destroyed at the end of the third Punic War but rebuilt as a Roman colony in 44 BCE, Carthage later became an important city in the Roman Empire. Punic, the last extant dialect of the ancient Phoenician language was spoken in North Africa until the fifth century CE, when it, too, died out.

The city was overrun by the Vandals around 430 CE. The final destruction of Carthage came in 698 at the hands of Arabs.

See also: KINGDOMS AND EMPIRES OF THE MAGHRIB (Vol. II); LIBYA (Vol. II).

Piankhy (Piye, Peye) (r. c. 750–716 BCE) *King of ancient Kush.*

Piankhy appears to have inherited the throne of KUSH from his father, King KASHTA (c. 800–750 BCE), who first initiated Kush's invasion of EGYPT. A number of conflicting dates are given for Piankhy's continuation of his father's efforts, but it is generally believed that the Kushite conquest of Egypt was completed by around 750 BCE. In the course of this invasion, Piankhy had to rid LOWER EGYPT of the last of the ASSYRIANS and to quell growing rebellions initiated by Tafnak, prince of Sais in the northern delta region.

On a monumental stone stele now housed at the Cairo Museum, Piankhy left engraved details of both his life as a king and his many battles. The Stele of Victory, as it is known, contains a long description of Piankhy's martial achievements. Another stele describes the Kushite empire and proclaims the glory of the Supreme Being, known as AMUN or Amon.

Despite his victories, Piankhy did not remain and rule in Egypt (something his successors would do over the next 100 years). Instead, he and Kenensat, his "Great Royal Wife," ruled Egypt from Napata.

The kings who founded Egypt's Twenty-third Dynasty (c. 850–725 BCE) started a long-standing tradition of powerful women priests. Their purpose was to diminish the growing power of the priesthood by transferring the power held by the priests to the daughters of the royal house. The women acquired large estates, as well as political authority. Given the title "Divine Wife of Amun," they became priestesses, living only in Thebes and remaining celibate for life. They were attended by servants who also were expected to be celibate.

Images of the priestesses are prevalent in Egyptian artwork, where they generally are depicted making the ruler's ritual offerings to the gods. The tradition continued for 200 years, with each female successor symbolically adopting a daughter of the ruling king. When the priestesses died, they were given royal burials, and memorial temples were established in their honor.

This tradition was already well-established when Piankhy conquered Egypt. Adapting it for his own ends, he installed his sister Amenirdis on the throne as "Divine Wife Apparent." Amenirdis was then "adopted" by the priestess Shepenupet I and, in turn, adopted her own niece—Piankhy's daughter—Shepenupet II.

polygamy

polygamy The generic term for plural marriage, or marriage to more than one spouse at the same time.

The word *polygamy* refers to plural marriage in general. The marriage of a woman to more than one man is more specifically called *polyandry*. The marriage of one man to more than one woman is called *polygyny*. Of the two forms, domestic situations involving polygyny are far more common. It is said that about 80% of of the world's societies recorded by anthropologists have practiced polygyny. Polyandry often takes the form of brothers sharing the same wife. Polygyny often takes the form of sororal polygyny, in which two or more sisters are married to the same man.

Historically, bigamy, or marriage to one additional spouse, appears to be the most common form of polygyny, although Muslim law permits a man four wives, provided that he can support them. Hindu religious law and customary marriage, as practiced in Africa and other places, puts no specific limit on the number of multiple spouses.

The marriage patterns followed in remote rural areas may shed light on probable practices of centuries ago. In West Africa, where polygyny was commonly practiced, families often consisted of a man with several wives, each of whom was the head of a household that consisted of herself and her children. The children might address each woman as "mother," but everyone knew to which subfamily the children belonged. The first, or senior, wife in such circumstances often had some measure of primacy or authority over the other wives. Such ranking, which extended to lesser wives as well, was an attempt to avoid or decrease jealousy among wives over perceived inattention from their shared husband. It also lessened rivalry between children, especially when there was something of significance, such as a royal title, to inherit. Traditionally, the oldest son of the senior wife was the heir apparent.

BRIDEWEALTH, or a bride price, was traditional among many African peoples, such as the matrilineal Makonde of what is now Tanzania, as well as many patrilineal societies in sub-Saharan Africa. The bride price involved the groom's giving items of high value to the bride's father. The practice, seen as an act of respect for the bride and her family, at the same time compensated them for the loss of her services and gave the husband the right to future children. (Wives and children were considered the property of the husband.)

The CATTLE herders of East Africa paid their bride prices in cattle. Among the MAASAI, the NUER, and the Turkana, the groom often had to borrow cattle from kinsmen to pay the bride price and, as a result, stayed in debt to older male relatives for many years.

Polygynous marriages most often occurred among kings, chiefs, very wealthy merchants, and nobles, who, depending on local practice, may also have kept concubines. Most males could afford only one wife, or, at the most, two wives.

In contemporary Africa, polygyny in traditional societies is disappearing under pressure from church, governmental, and civil rights groups that are committed to protecting the rights of women and children.

polytheism In Africa, the sacred belief in lesser deities as an extension of a supreme being.

Many African religions observe both MONOTHEISM and polytheism. As recent studies have shown, throughout history a number of significant African religions have recognized a supreme being.

Although not every group supported the idea of lesser deities, the groups who did appear to have been widespread. For example, the Dogon of Mali, one of the more ancient ethnic groups of West Africa, recognized eight mythical ancestors, known as the Dyongou Serou (the Octad). The Dogon believed that, along with a Supreme Being known as Amma, these ancestors were the creators of civilization. In a somewhat different vein, ritual possession by the Mboatsia, or "little people" of the forest, was considered a high religious calling among the Fante of coastal Ghana. However, the Fante also acknowledged that the Mboatsia derived their power from the high god Nyame. Similarly, Wennnam, the supreme deity of the MOSSI, designated power to earth custodians known as Tenga Soba Nama. Through offerings, these custodians controlled the natural environment and enabled farmers to survive.

See also: DOGON; FANTE (Vol. II); PANTHEISM (Vol. I); RELIGION, TRADITIONAL (Vol. I); TOTEMISM (Vol. I).

Further reading: William R. Bascomb and Meville J. Herskovits, eds., *Continuity and Change in African Cultures*, (Chicago: University of Chicago Press, 1959); Cheik Anta Diop, *The African Origin of Civilization: Myth or Reality?* (Chicago: Lawrence Hill Books, 1975).

pottery Vessels molded from wet clay and hardened by applied heat. Recovered pottery in Africa has been linked to the rise of early civilizations whose economies developed as a result of the mass production, storage, and trading of food. The range of pottery types and sizes provides some idea of the variety of food grown and consumed in ancient periods.

The Process of Pottery Making Some of the earliest evidence of pottery making comes from the fishing and foraging communities that inhabited the banks of the NILE RIVER near KHARTOUM, c. 7000 BCE. Since the process of making pottery almost always begins with the collection of clay, it is not surprising that archaeologists recovered pottery shards, or fragments, in this region. Using digging sticks and hoes, the clay was collected from pits, transported to a designated site, and allowed to dry. Then it was pounded with mortars, cleaned of unwanted particles, and left to soak in water for several days. Potters often used tempers to strengthen the clay, including straw, animal dung, chaff (discarded grain husks), river pebbles, and old pottery. Adding this material also helped reduce shrinkage and avoid cracking during the firing process. For example, around 5200 BCE, inhabitants of Faiyum, 45 miles (72 km) southwest of modern-day CAIRO, made pottery from coarse clay tempered with chaff. This community produced small bowls, cups, cooking bowls, and pots with knobbed feet or rectangular patterns.

Specialized techniques used to create pottery included the coil technique, which was developed by women potters along the Guinea coast. This technique involved adding and shaping a continuous roll of wet clay to the pot with one hand while it was rotated on a flat surface with the other. Other societies used a convex mold method. It involved pounding a flattened piece of clay on a rounded surface. This was done in order to form the shape of the pot, then more clay was added to lengthen it.

Adaptation to particular soils led to variations in these methods. When the clay achieved the desired shape, two final phases completed the process. During the pre-firing phase, the pots were turned down over small fires that helped dry out any remaining moisture from the clay. Direct firing, which occurred sometime later, was the final phase, usually taking place in wide-open areas. The clay pots were stacked over layers of fuel such as dried grass, millet chaff, or wood. Then, after being "fired" for a few hours, they became hardened, serviceable vessels.

As the methods of pottery improved, distinctive styles and patterns were linked to specific societies. Archaeologists have been able to determine that these styles and patterns spread to neighboring regions. For example, during the Early IRON AGE, dimple-based pottery was first used along the northeastern shore of Lake Victoria and some time later in Urewe, Kenya, southern Uganda, northwestern Tanzania, Rwanda, BURUNDI, and the Kivu province of Congo (formerly Zaïre). Named for the thumbprint found on the base of recovered bowls and pots, dimple pottery was notable for its decorative patterns.

Pottery-Making Cultures The presence of pottery shards at archaeological sites generally indicates a settled farming community. IRON AGE farmers were skilled in making baked clay pots, which they decorated with patterns of grooves and other shapes. These pots were used to carry and store water and other liquids and to cook foods.

Ancient Zambia and Zimbabwe are particularly rich in examples of pottery. Some of the oldest examples are from the NOK CULTURE, which flourished from about 500 BCE to 200 CE. The Nok left behind many terra-cotta figures, some as large as 4 feet (1.2 m) tall, that show evidence of a highly advanced mastery of technique. Animal figures are presented very naturalistically, while humans are in stylized poses. Most of the Nok figures are heads, which appear to be parts of larger figures.

Examples of small, fine, thin-walled pottery dating from before 450 CE have been found at JENNE-JENO, an ancient city on the inland delta of the NIGER RIVER in western Sudan. Most of their ceramics have been dated from 500 to 1400, though the dating is questionable, since many of the items were not originally found by archaeologists.

Bambata pottery made by peoples living near Mabveni in southern Zimbabwe date from the second century. Later pottery styles in the region are usually grouped as Gokomere-Ziwa ware and date from the third through the fifth centuries. Found near Lydenburg, South Africa, were a number of hollow ceramic heads dating from about 500 that historians think were used as religious or ceremonial masks.

See also: POTTERY (Vol. II).

praying mantis Large, slender, slow-moving insect. The praying mantis measures between 1 and 5 inches (2.5 and 12.7 cm) in length. It has two large eyes and long, spiny front legs that it uses to hold the insects on which it preys. While waiting to feed, the mantis stands with these front legs raised, in a "praying" position. These insects are usually green or brown, which allows them to blend in among dried leaves and twigs.

The word *mantis* means "diviner" or "prophet" in Greek. The Greeks, however, were not the only people who thought these insects had supernatural powers. In southern Africa, the mantis is associated with Kaang, the creator god of the SAN people. Many myths are told about Kaang, including some in which he comes back from the dead.

According to one San myth, Kaang, a praying mantis, was eaten by an ogre, who then vomited him up. In another myth, Kaang was killed by thorns and had his bones picked clean by ants. Kaang then reassembled his skeleton and rose again. The Bushmen believe that Kaang created the Moon from an old shoe.

Ptah Creator god of Egyptian religion and patron of arts and crafts.

Always depicted in human form, Ptah was especially venerated in MEMPHIS, the oldest and longest-lasting capital of ancient Egypt and the city that, according to popular belief, owed its commercial success to the patronage of Ptah. Though supported by a strong and wealthy priesthood, his cult enjoyed little popularity throughout the rest of ancient EGYPT. As a result, although there was a temple dedicated to him at KARNAK, Ptah never attained the rank of a national god in the state religion in the manner of OSIRIS or AMUN-RA.

In the myth of Ptah, the ideas of creation and creativity were closely linked. The theology developed at Memphis taught that the god had brought the universe into being from nothingness by his thought and speech. He was believed to be the driving force behind even the most ordinary human activities, but particularly those of an artistic nature.

Ptolemies Dynasty, founded by ALEXANDER THE GREAT, which ruled EGYPT from the fourth to the first century BCE. In 323 BCE, after Alexander's death, control of Egypt passed to one of his leading generals, Ptolemy. Assuming the throne, Ptolemy quickly launched a series of moves that, in the following years, effectively merged Egyptian and Greek cultures. Settlement by Greeks and Macedonians was encouraged, improvements in agriculture were made, and new industries were introduced. African trade with the Greek-oriented world increased, as did intellectual and literary ties.

Like the dynasty's founders, succeeding Ptolemaic rulers continued to balance Greek and Egyptian interests, leaning heavily, however, toward Greek culture. Nevertheless, during the Ptolemaic period, Egypt regained much of its lost splendor, if not its territorial and military power. The Alexandrian Library became a center for learning and scholarship. Leading thinkers in everything from philosophy to mathematics to SCIENCE took part in the Egyptian revival.

In the end, Ptolemaic Egypt lacked the military power to stand up to the growing influence of ROME. As a result, by the time the famous Queen CLEOPATRA came to the throne, she had to rely on political intrigue in order to maintain Egypt's independence. Eventually, around 30 BCE, a victorious Octavian claimed Egypt as a province of the Roman Empire.

See also: CAESAR, OCTAVIAN (Vol. I).

Punic Wars Series of three wars, fought between 264 and 146 BCE, in which ROME vanquished the North African city-state of CARTHAGE. The first conflict (264–241 BCE) erupted over Carthage's attempt to exert its power in Sicily, just off the Italian coast. Rome, which had limited sea power at the time, was forced to rapidly develop its naval forces in order to meet the Carthaginian threat. However, after more than twenty years of primarily naval strife in which both sides suffered significant losses, Rome's fleet vanquished the Carthaginians and forced their retreat.

Barely twenty years later, in 218 BCE, war broke out again, this time over Rome and Carthage's competing interests on the Iberian Peninsula. During the conflict, Carthaginian forces, led by HANNIBAL, succeeded in crossing the Alps and invading the northern and central Italian provinces, which they eventually occupied. Ultimately, however, Hannibal's forces were unable to subdue Rome, and their defeat in 202 led to the end of the Second Punic War, in 201 BCE.

The terms of the peace that ended the second conflict exacted a great toll on Carthage in terms of monetary payments, loss of territory, and restrictions on its further development. Straining against them, Carthage rebelled and the Third Punic War (149–146 BCE) broke out. Once again, Carthage was defeated, this time even more soundly than before, and it never again became an effective force in the region.

See also: GRECO-ROMAN PERIOD (Vol. I).

Punt Ancient trading region situated between the RED SEA and the Gulf of Aden in present-day coastal ETHIOPIA and DJIBOUTI.

For centuries, Punt was a source of vast wealth for EGYPT. Because of the abundant riches—incuding ivory, animal skins, ostrich feathers—they obtained there, Egypt's pharaohs were in the habit of referring to Punt as "God's Land" and the "Land of Spirits."

Trading expeditions between Egypt and Punt began as early as the First and Second Dynasties, c. 3100–2686 BCE. The water route led traders first to ELEPHANTINE, then to the Red Sea ports of Koseir or Leucos Limen, and south to Punt. In contrast, trading caravans made their way from Punt to Egypt via overland routes along the BLUE NILE and Atabara Rivers. By the Fifth Dynasty (c. 2494–2345 BCE), local residents along the way were making such extensive demands for tax and tribute that traders abandoned the traditional routes. They were replaced by direct sail, with most of the journeys being made during the summer months of June, July, and August.

Although others had journeyed there earlier, Egypt's King Sahure (2708–2697 BCE) made the first recorded attempt to reach Punt by boat. Inscriptions tell how, during his journey, Sahure acquired vast quantities of myrrh, electrum (a natural alloy of gold and silver), and ebony, as well as staves of wood for making storage. In return, the Egyptians supplied the Puntites with hatchets, daggers, and jewelry.

The Hyksos invasion of Egypt, about 1700 BCE, temporarily halted expeditions to Punt, but trade resumed once the NEW KINGDOM was established, in 1570 BCE. One of the most famous expeditions of this era was made in 1495 BCE by Queen Hatshepsut. Images and inscriptions detailing that journey appear on three wall reliefs in Hatshepsut's temple of Deir-el-Bahri in Thebes. There, ships "journeying in peace to the land of Punt" are shown returning with myrrh resin, myrrh trees, ebony, ivory, "the green gold of Emu," and eye cosmetics. The reliefs also depict Puntites and their children being brought on board waiting ships, along with apes, MONKEYS, DOGS, and the skins of the southern panther.

Because it was held in such high favor in Egypt, Punt remained an unconquered region, and its trade with Egypt continued until the reign of RAMSESSES II. Punt's own trading networks eventually spread beyond Egypt to AKSUM and the neighboring East African ports. In time, these links extended to the Mediterranean, Arabia, and Persia, as well as to India and the islands of the Indonesian archipelago.

Pygmies Name, considered pejorative, for four small-statured, nomadic HUNTER-GATHERER societies, collectively called MBUTI (or Bambuti). They have inhabited the ITURI FOREST in the northeastern part of present-day Congo (formerly Zaïre) for millennia. (The word *pygmy* derives from the Greek word meaning "fist," which was used as a measure of length; the Mbuti were first described by Europeans in the writings of Greek authors.)

python Constrictor snake found in warm, tropical areas. Unlike cobras, pythons are not venomous; instead, they usually kill by strangling their prey with their coiled bodies. The largest pythons have expandable jaws that allow them to swallow whole such large prey as goats or pigs. The African python, also called the rock python, often reaches a length of 21 feet (6.4 m). The 5-foot (1.5-m) ball, or royal, python lives primarily in equatorial western Africa. It curls itself into a tight ball with its head inside.

The Naayire people consider pythons to be sacred, noble animals. Long ago, according to one legend, a group of Naayire hunters decided to sleep in the jungle around a giant tree. During the middle of the night, a python fell from the tree onto one of the hunters. The hunter woke up and discovered that a group of enemies was about to attack them. Because the python alerted the hunters to the attack, the Naayire decided never to hunt pythons again.

Q

Qada culture Late STONE AGE culture that flourished in NUBIA 10,000 to 15,000 years ago. Made up of people who were hunters and gatherers, the Qada culture is the source of the earliest human remains yet found in the region of the NILE VALLEY. These remains have been found in cemetery-like areas clearly separated from other settlement areas, with corpses carefully arranged in fetal positions.

quartzite A commonly found rock made up largely of quartz; related to sandstone and granite. Quartzite comes from sandstone, which changes to quartzite when silica is deposited between the grains of quartz found in the sandstone. Quartzites are usually powdery white in color, although some forms are pink and gray. They are granular rocks that have smooth surfaces when broken. Many quartzites are ancient rocks, belonging to the Cambrian or Precambrian systems. Since they weather slowly and little soil grows on them, they are often found on the surfaces of hills or mountains.

In EGYPT, sandstone and granite—a rock that is also mainly composed of quartz—were often found in deposits above ground. Around the time of Egypt's Fourth Dynasty (c. 2575–2465 BCE), cut blocks of sandstone and granite were used to construct temples and pyramids; before then, buildings were made of mud bricks. Quartzite blocks were often used inside these sandstone monuments, and they have been found in the burial chambers of Neferhotep and Ankh-Hor in Thebes. They were also used in the LUXOR temple and in the shrine to RAMESSES II in Tanis. The gold coffin of King TUTANKHAMUN was placed in a quartzite sarcophagus, which was then enclosed in four gilt shrines. Quartzite was also used for carvings, including a large sculpture of Tutankhamun, a statue of Nedjem from the reign of Ramesses II, and a door lintel depicting Senwosret III between the minor gods Atum and Re-Horakhti.

Qustul Burial site of the rulers of the NUBIAN A-GROUP culture. Between approximately 3800 and 3100 BCE, Qustul was the center of a kingdom, known as Ta-Seti, that was situated between the first and second cataracts of the NILE. Qustul was also the royal burial site of the later Nubadian dynasty

The wealth and grandeur of the stone-lined pit graves in Qustul equal or surpass the Egyptian royal tombs found at ABYDOS, NAQADAH I AND II, and HIERAKONPOLIS. By about 2900 BCE, the A-Group's kingdom was destroyed by a newly unified Upper Egyptian state based in Hierakonpolis. Then, during the First Dynasty (c. 3050–2775 BCE), MENES conquered Lower Nubia. It was probably about this time that the royal cemetery at Qustul was looted and destroyed.

Thousands of years later, Qustul would again be a royal burial site, this time for the kings of the Nobatian dynasty. The Nobatians (also known as Blemmyes or the X-GROUP) came from east of the Nile and took over much of Lower Nubia around 350 CE. The Nobatian kings used pharaonic symbols and worshiped ancient gods.

The Nobatian graves were made up of a collection of rooms with brick walls and vaulted roofs built inside a large pit dug into the earth. Aside from the body of the ruler itself, these rooms were filled with furniture, pottery, food, and weapons, which kings believed they would need in the AFTERLIFE. Often animals were sacrificed at the tomb's entrance. The tomb would then be buried in a mound of earth.

The Nobatian dynasty ended around 550, when they were defeated by the Nobatae, a group of recently converted Christian Nubians.

R

Ra Sun god and one of the most important of all dieties in the Egyptian religion. Since Ra was worshiped in the city of Heliopolis, an ancient center of the cult of the Sun, he is often referred to as "Ra of Heliopolis." The cult of Ra began in the early dynasties of the OLD KINGDOM, at which time he assumed many of the attributes of an earlier god, Atum. His prominence as the sun god is closely associated with the architectural development of the pyramids. Ra is depicted as a man with the head of a falcon, on top of which is a COBRA.

Ra is the god most closely identified with the pharaohs of ancient Egypt. About the time of the Fifth Dynasty, c. 2494–2345 BCE, the concept that the pharaohs were the sons of the deity was firmly in place, and Sa-Ra, "Son of Ra," became part of the royal title. This divine claim continued throughout the rest of Egyptian history until the end of pharaonic rule.

Later, in the NEW KINGDOM, Ra became merged with Amun, the sun god worshiped at Thebes. He thus become Amun-Ra, the supreme god of the state.

See also: AMUN (Vol. I).

rainmaker Ritual authority believed to hold the power of producing rain. Pastoral and agricultural societies look to the life-giving qualities of rain for their survival, since their lives are dependent upon crops and animal herds. Rain is considered a sacred occurrence, particularly in the arid eastern and southern regions. These societies center their beliefs and expectations around special intermediaries or ritual authorities, who either acquire or inherit the appropriate knowledge and rites necessary to produce rain. Rainmakers perform annual public rites and festivals in order to focus community awareness. Privately they conduct formulaic prayers, invocations, and sometimes even animal sacrifices in order to keep the proper balance between rainy and dry seasons.

Similar to those chosen to perform as an ORACLE, a rainmaker often wields great power, serving alternately as a king or other ruling official. Rainmakers, for example, have always been prominent among the Tonga, BANTU speakers of southern Zambia, northern Zimbabwe, and BOTSWANA, who have deities that may be invoked to create rainfall. Similarly, the Lotuko of southern Sudan have always deferred to the rule of rainmakers. Having inherited the title and ritual knowledge, these individuals have traditionally presided over nine designated rain areas and have controlled the AGE SETS of their region.

Members of rainmaking castes often organize to regulate fees, notably among such peoples as the Mwari of South Africa and the Ibibio-speakers of southeast Nigeria. The rainmaking castes among the Fur people of Sudan inherit their abilities and collectively carry out ritual sacrifice at designated shrines, including the tombs of their ancestors.

With few exceptions, rainmakers have primarily been men. The Luvedu of South Africa, however, traditionally choose a queen to perform these rites. Their rain queen also serves as the political and divine ruler of the kingdom, with powers so closely tied to rainmaking that her death or anger could, according to Luvedu beliefs, generate drought. The knowledge she used to make or stop rain was inherited from her predecessors and decreed by divine gods.

In ETHIOPIA, the Koma rainmakers take up residence in caves. Their rainmaking ritual calls for petitioners to bring gifts along with animal skins containing water. Once the water is consumed by the Koma in a public ceremony, rain generally follows. In contrast, the Udhuk, who also are from Ethiopia, use colored rain stones, which they maintain have fallen from the sky for that purpose. Other traditional practices include the burning of special leaves whose smoke pulls the rain down.

Aside from mystical rites associated with rainmaking, many of the ritual authorities traditionally relied more on methods involving the study of nature, the stars, sky, and the habits of animals. Many were reportedly taught at a young age about the names and characteristics of leaves, roots, and tree barks in their surroundings. When coupled with ritual practices, their practical and esoteric knowledge created a formidable body of information. Occasionally when such knowledge failed to produce rain, or to stop it, or caused flooding, rainmakers were imprisoned or killed.

See also: RELIGION, TRADITIONAL (Vol. I).

Further reading: William R. Bascomb and Melville J. Herskovits, eds., *Continuity and Change in African Cultures* (Chicago: University of Chicago Press, 1959); John R. Hinnels, *Dictionary of Religions*, (New York: Penguin Books, 1995); John S. Mbiti, *African Religions and Philosophy*, 2nd ed. (Oxford, Eng.: Heinemann Education Publishers, 1999).

Ramesses I (Ramses I) (r. c. 1320–1318 BCE)

Founder and first king of ancient Egypt's Nineteenth Dynasty.

Ramesses I came to the throne at a fairly advanced age, succeeding HOREMHEB, the last king of the Eighteenth Dynasty. Like Horemheb, Ramesses I was a military officer, and he might have been the favorite of the heirless Horemheb because they had been comrades in arms.

Ramesses was not without experience when he came to power, however, having held a number of important government posts after leaving the army. Both his personal name (Ramesses, meaning "RA has fashioned him") and his royal name (Menpehtyre, meaning "Eternal is the power of Ra") emphasize his devotion to the traditional religion of Egypt, rather than the newer cult of the AMARNA PERIOD. His reign lasted barely two years, and he was succeeded by his son SETI I.

Ramesses II (Ramses II, Ramses the Great, King Useraf, Ozymandias) (r. c. 1304–1236 BCE)

The third pharaoh of ancient Egypt's Nineteenth Dynasty; called "The Great" because of his impressive accomplishments, scope, and length of his reign.

Ramesses II is considered by many to have been the greatest pharaoh ever to rule ancient Egypt, and he is surely the best known. The "Ozymandias" of the ancient Greeks, he may also have been pharaoh at the time of the biblical exodus of the Jews from Egypt. The son of SETI I and Queen Tuya, Ramesses was co-regent with his father before becoming pharaoh in his own right at the age of about twenty-five.

Ramesses II (r. 1304–1236 BCE) is depicted as the god Osiris in this 33-foot (10-m) tall statue from the Temple of Ramesses II in Abu Simbel, Egypt. © *Gian Berto Vanni/CORBIS*

Ramesses was a great warrior whose victories over the HITTITES restored Egypt's supremacy over its neighbors. Ramesses resolved his final conflict with the Hittites with a masterpiece of diplomacy that is generally considered one of history's first international peace treaties.

At home, Ramesses carried out building programs on a massive scale. The most impressive were his mortuary temple, the Ramesseum, at Thebes and Abu Simbel, a temple containing four gigantic seated figures of Ramesses. Another of his important constructions was a temple dedicated to OSIRIS, which was located at ABYDOS. A grand master in the art of self-promotion, Ramesses was not content with simple monument building. In his campaign to make his presence felt throughout his kingdom, he went so far as to put his name on the monuments built by other pharaohs.

In addition to having several concubines, Ramesses married many times throughout his very long life, fathering, it is reported, more than 100 children. His first and most important "Great Royal Wife," however, was Queen Nefertari. After her death, she was succeeded as queen by Istnofret.

Ruling for sixty-seven years—longer than any other pharaoh—Ramesses II lived well into his nineties, outliving all but his thirteenth son, Merneptah, who succeeded him c. 1236 BCE.

Ramesses III (Ramses III, King Usermare-Meryamen) (r. c. 1198–1166 BCE) *Second king of Egypt's Twentieth Dynasty.*

The last great warrior-pharaoh and temple builder of the NEW KINGDOM and the son of Sethnakhte, the founder and first king of the Twentieth Dynasty, Ramesses III came to the throne after his father's short, three-year reign.

Ramesses III was eager to follow in the footsteps of his illustrious predecessor and hero RAMESSES II. Although he fell short of this goal, Ramesses III nevertheless managed several significant accomplishments during his thirty-year reign. As a warrior, he waged two successful campaigns against the Libyans and defeated the confederation of invaders the Egyptians called the SEA PEOPLES. As a monument builder, his major achievement was the mortuary temple at the site known today as Medinet Abu.

Unlike many other pharaohs, Ramesses III lived well into old age. He not only survived a failed assassination attempt plotted by one of his minor wives, but he also outlived many of his sons and daughters. Ramesses III was buried in the Valley of the Kings and succeeded by his son and heir Ramesses IV.

Ras Dashen The highest mountain in ETHIOPIA and the fourth-tallest peak in Africa. Reaching 15,157 feet (4,620 m), Ras Dashen's nine jagged peaks and round craters tower above Ethiopia's northern landscape. Bordered by the Tacazze River on its southern and northeastern side, the mountain is often capped by snow during the winter season. Ras Dashen is part of the Simen mountain range, which was formed more than 25 million years ago as a result of volcanic activity.

See also: RIFT VALLEY (Vol. I).

red crown Crown of the ancient Egyptian pharaohs that represented northern or LOWER EGYPT, also called Deshret. Until UPPER EGYPT and Lower Egypt were unified under one rule, c. 3050 BCE, each region had its own representative crown: red for Lower Egypt and white for Upper Egypt. The tradition of wearing both the red and white crowns is credited to MENES or Narmer, founder of the FIRST DYNASTY. The NARMER PALETTE, recovered in HIERAKONPOLIS, was inscribed with his name, and images on one side show him wearing the WHITE CROWN of Upper Egypt as he battles his enemies in the delta. On the other side of the palette, he is wearing the red crown as he inspects the bodies of his slain northern opponents.

Further reading: E. A. Wallis Budge, *The Gods of the Egyptians: Studies in Egyptian Mythology* (New York: Dover Publications, 1969); Barbara Watterson, *The Egyptians* (Oxford, Eng.: Blackwell Publishers Ltd., 1998).

Red Sea Long, narrow waterway separating the Arabian Peninsula from the African continent. Measuring more than 1,400 miles (2,240 km) long and 220 miles (352 km) wide at certain points, the Red Sea reaches depths of an estimated 1,765 feet (582 m) to 9,974 feet (3,291 m). This waterway is part of the Great RIFT VALLEY System extending from eastern Africa to southwestern Asia. Geologists speculate that the Red Sea was formed millions of years ago, when Arabia and Africa broke apart as a result of great pressures within the earth's core. Its name comes from the unusual underwater algae found beneath its surface, which creates a reddish brown appearance.

For centuries, scholars have debated whether the Red Sea might actually have parted during Moses' escape from EGYPT, as described in the Torah, Bible, and Koran. There is little doubt, however, that the Red Sea was one of the most active and important waterways of the ancient world. Its southern end was important to ancient expeditions from Egypt to the Land of PUNT, and sometime later, the trading ties between AKSUM and ROME, GREECE, and Asia. The Red Sea also provided a route for Egyptians, Romans, Arabs, BERBERS, and Turks to transport enslaved Africans from Nubia and the NILE VALLEY.

Salt, one of the most important trade goods of ancient Africa, accumulates in deposits here along the shores of the Red Sea. © *Steve Kaufman/CORBIS*

religion, prehistoric The religious practices or rites associated with *HOMO SAPIENS* or *HOMO ERECTUS* prior to recorded history. Because of the various excavations in Africa, archaeologists have been able to formulate significant theories about the place that religion held in the prehistoric era. Physical and cultural remains such as fossils, bones, and artifacts suggest that many early rites and worship practices were in place in this period.

In part, the development of these religious practices may have been linked with the growth of hominid populations, as, apparently, a relatively large hominid population existed at the time. The size of this population may have generated the need for a social structure that formally recognized RITES OF PASSAGE such as birth, marriage, and death. Eventually, growing food, raising animals, and other aspects of the struggle for survival also became part of these rites. Indeed, based on evidence found among the Samo in Burkina Faso and the IBO in Nigeria, it is believed by some historians and archaeologists that early hominid settlements or villages were generally organized around a central altar.

Burial patterns have also helped archaeologists understand early belief systems. At sites located in Zambezi, Zambia, Zimbabwe, and Malawi, archaeologists have identified scenes in which various kinds of funeral rites were being performed. Elsewhere, particularly in northern and southern Africa, excavations of mid Paleolithic grave sites, have uncovered stone tools that apparently were buried along with the remains of *Homo sapiens*. Caves located at Afalou-bou-Rhummel, in ALGERIA, and Taforalt, in MOROCCO, also show evidence of use as burial sites.

Excavations made at the NAQADAH I AND II sites, which date to the Predynastic Period (c. 4000–3500 BCE) of ancient EGYPT, also have revealed artifacts bearing directly on prehistoric religion. There, archaeologists have unearthed engraved POTTERY, axes, stone pots, tools, and both arrow- and hammerheads, as well as COPPER objects, all associated with BADARIAN CULTURE. A number of the objects found in the graves at these sites contain drawn figures, and it is believed that some of these figures were used for ritual purposes. The exact meaning of these drawings—or exactly what those rituals were—is not clear. However, the rituals may be linked with the fact that a number of the graves, which generally are oval or circular in shape, contained multiple burials; beyond this, some of the corpses in these graves apparently had been deliberately dismembered.

Finally, there are many ancient megaliths in Africa, such as those found in present-day Gambia-Senegal and the Central African Republic. Many of these burial sites, which also apparently represented belief in the AFTERLIFE, date back to the Neolithic period. Although much about these sites is not clearly understood, they may have been dwelling places for those buried within.

See also: FUNERAL CUSTOMS (Vol. I); RELIGION, TRADITIONAL (Vol. I)

religion, traditional Spiritual belief in and devotion to various forms of supernatural power. Since ancient times, there have been literally thousands of religions in Africa, each shaped by the society that created it. The common thread that ties them all together is the underlying structure of social order they represent.

For centuries, the interpretations of outsiders concerning non-Christian and non-Islamic worship practices in Africa have often been clouded by prejudice and ignorance because of the lack of comparable church structures, holy texts, or other sacred forms in Africa with which they could identify. This often led to a complete misreading of ritual devotion in the form of sacrifice, prayers, song, DANCE, artwork, myth, and ORAL TRADITION. Time-honored rituals were derided as well, including animal sacrifice, libations, and highly expressive forms of prayer.

For this reason, some ancient Greek and Roman travelers remarked that Africans had no religion.This view has prevailed for many centuries, somewhat influencing even modern historians and anthropologists who attempt to establish interpretations or terms for aspects of religion they could not otherwise understand. For example, outmoded words like *paganism*, *fetish*, and *animism* were coined by anthropologists to describe highly complex and sophisticated concepts of deity, the physical tokens of this devotion, and the spiritual essence that animates the universe. These forms of expression have been passed down through generations, dating back to the prehistoric period.

Like the people of most ancient societies throughout the world, African peoples have learned how to make sense of the natural universe and its predictable and unpredictable attributes. Often, they did this by observing the cycles of night and day, plant life, the stars, and the phases of the Moon. Such attempts to understand the mysteries of the universe also meant learning to cooperate with the forces that ranged from life and death to the disastrous occurrences of floods, famine, and desertification. Cooperation and placation may have given way to forms of prayer incorporated into the routines of daily life in various forms of worship. These adaptations added a deeper meaning to life and attempted to answer essential questions about existence and purpose. Based on archaeological findings of burials, the remnants of offerings, and sacrificial remains, it appears that religion and religious rites were organized to depict the relationship between humans and the unknown.

Characteristics The term *traditional religion* generally refers to religious thought and philosophy that has its roots in African culture before and separate from contact with CHRISTIANITY or Islam. Traditional religion includes specific beliefs, ceremonies, and rituals carried out by designated ritual specialists, which include elders of the community, priests, RAINMAKERS, ORACLES, MEDICINE MEN, and prophets. The values associated with these rituals are embodied in the presence of the ritual specialists and then passed down from generation to generation, during the process of which they are, of course, modified. It this way religion incorporates the history of the society through such oral sources as myths, proverbs, personal names, and language.

Rather than formalized patterns of liturgical prayer, the traditional worship that typified much of ancient Africa found expression in outward actions that included invocation, poured libation, offerings, prayer, and forms of MUSIC. (The latter usually called for drumming accompanied by song and dance.)

Ancient African societies generally made no distinction between sacred and secular activities; a devotional act was a vital force regardless of whether it was performed at designated shrines, in daily work chores, or in community FESTIVALS. Although no two societies worshiped in exactly the same way, there apparently were many shared beliefs. Scholars have compared these beliefs to an inverted triangle with categories and examples in the following way.

Supreme Being The Supreme Being was known by many names in ancient Africa. The IBO of Nigeria traditionally refer to this being as Chukwu; the Akan of GHANA use the name Onyame, while the Ewe used Mawu. The YORUBA of Nigeria used the name OLORUN, or Olodumare, and the Mende of Sierra Leone refer to Ngewo. Considered the Creator, from time immemorial the Supreme Being has been viewed as omnipotent, omniscient, and compassionate; the highest form of life and the shaper of human destiny.

Many African societies, even in ancient times, have shared common myths that tell of the Supreme Being's omnipotence. These myths also explain that, while communication between this being and humans continued, direct contact was somehow altered by the folly of humans. This contact was also affected by the fact that the deity placed intermediaries within the human sphere to meet the daily needs of people. The Mende of Sierra Leone provide an example of this pervasive belief, for, even in ages long past, they maintained that at one time their god, known as Ngewo, was close to humans. The Mende say that this changed when, after being given permission to ask Ngewo for what they needed, the people made so many requests that, in order to escape their demands, Ngewo retired to the heavens. In spite of the prevalence of such beliefs among ancient Africans, it was widely understood and accepted that the deity continued to serve as an active part of life but that divine intermediaries were the appropriate means through which people were to communicate their needs.

The Religious Pantheon Another common feature of traditional African religion that dates back to ancient times is the pantheon of gods that represent various aspects of the natural world and serve as intermediaries to the Supreme Deity. The names of many gods and goddesses linked to the natural world have survived in traditional folklore and myths.

Annual festivals, many of which are still celebrated today, represent one of the earliest traditional forms of communal thanksgiving. These are especially common as expressions of gratitude to DEITIES for a successful or bountiful harvest of YAMS or other such agricultural product. For the Mbaye of Chad, for example, water, lighting, and sun have long been considered powerful spiritual influences that require specific ritual offerings. In much the same way, the goddess Anuket, who personified the way in which the NILE RIVER nourished the fields in the regions bordering Aswan, was honored in ancient EGYPT.

Sun and moon gods were worshiped by early Sabeans who crossed the RED SEA from Yemen, bringing their religious beliefs to the Highlands of ETHIOPIA. It has been reported by some that MAKEDA, the famous queen of Sheba, who ruled over AKSUM and the region of southern Arabia, was originally a sun worshiper. But, following her involvement with Solomon and the embrace of his religious convictions, Ethiopia's unique form of Judaism came into being.

The ORISHA, who are associated with YORUBA religion, represent the most widely known intermediaries in Africa. Like other lesser gods or deities, each orisha has its own attributes of nature, as well as its specific favorite foods and taboos. There are also prayers, songs, and dances performed on certain days of the week. Generally, Yoruba devotees become aware of and familiar with the requirements of their own orisha through DIVINATION.

Ancestors The worship of ancestors in Africa is not a religion in itself, nor is it a cult, as it has erroneously been portrayed by some historians. Instead, it represents a misundertood aspect of African religion. In traditional African religions, ancestors may personify the male and female founders of society. They also may be kings or even family members who provide a good example of morality in their daily lives. As such, they are viewed as important parts of the ongoing social structure.

Many forms of power have been attributed to ancestors, especially in ancient times, but this power generally lies within the scope of the society's needs and the ability to seek and receive help in a crisis. To offer the ancestral spirits both recognition and gratitude, certain types of shrines are erected at which prayers, animal sacrifices, masquerades, or similar ceremonies are performed.

In Chad, the *qir ka,* for example, has long been regarded as a powerful ancestral male figure and plays a prominent role among the Sara people. Since theirs is a patrilineal society, legal rights, identity, and land are part of the power that is conferred to succeeding generations through links to this ancient individual.

Death, the Afterlife, and Burial Rites In Africa, death has always been considered a final RITE OF PASSAGE. Viewed as an act of inevitable fate from prehistoric times, the grave goods buried by early *HOMO SAPIENS* underscored an early belief in an AFTERLIFE. As time passed, these beliefs evolved, and the stone tools once found in prehistoric graves gave way to jewelry and to money for use in the afterlife. Belief in the hereafter, which often was held to be a replica of life on earth, supported the practice of human sacrifice in CARTHAGE. It also spurred the construction of the burial tumuli of NUBIA, which contained royal families, their close advisers, and their servants.

A number of ancient African societies also believed that, when death occurred, the deceased had to give accountings of their lives. This belief is reflected in ancient temples, most famously in EGYPT. There, wall paintings and other artifacts show the gods of the underworld waiting to devour the dead as their hearts are weighed on the sacred scales of justice by MA'AT. Similarly, some societies, such as that of the Akan, believed in what they referred to as Asamando, the place at which the dead are judged for their past behavior. According to the Akan, this judgment was carried out by former kings, and wrongdoers were returned to earth, possibly to be born blind, lame, or deformed.

Many ancient African societies actually held two burial rites. The first was often done to remove the polluting presence and disruption caused by death. The second was to apply every possible ritual aspect to ensure that the spirit of the deceased had been satisfied. Because the second funeral often was one of extravagance, accompanied by appropriate displays of mourning, it was remembered long after by younger generations. In this way, African religion was self-perpetuating, creating an endless cycle of birth and rebirth that affirms the creative abilities of the deity.

See also: ANCESTRY (Vol. I); ARK OF THE COVENANT (Vol. I); BAOBAB TREE (Vol. I); CHRISTIANITY (Vols. I, II); CIRCUMCISION (Vol. I); DIVINATION (Vol. I); ISLAM (Vol. II); MASKS (Vol. I); MONOTHEISM (Vol. I); PANTHEISM (Vol. I); POLYTHEISM (Vol. I); RELIGION, PREHISTORIC (Vol. I); SPIRIT POSSESSION (Vol. I); WITCHCRAFT (Vol. I).

Further reading: John R. Hinnells, ed., *The Penguin Dictionary of Religions* (London: The Penguin Group, 1995); John S. Mbiti, *African Religions and Philosophy*, 2nd ed. (Oxford, Eng.: Heinemann, 1999); T. N. O. Quarcoopome, *West African Traditional Religion* (Ibadan: Africa Universities Press, 1987).

rhinoceros In mythology, the rhinoceros served as inspiration for the unicorn, a mythical horned horse. It is also associated with the ancient Egyptian mythological creature Amenti, a serpent that devoured sinful people in the AFTERLIFE. The rhinoceros was an exotic animal to ancient Egyptians. According to inscriptions, it was one of the prizes King THUTMOSE I brought back with him from an expedition in Nubia. Later, the Empire of AKSUM, in ETHIOPIA, exported rhinoceros horns to lands as far away as China.

rhythm pounder Uniquely carved wooden figure used in funeral processions.

Among the Senufo of the IVORY COAST, the rhythm pounder symbolizes respect for the elders who were once important within the community. When these elders pass away, certain rites are needed to help them achieve the status of ancestor. As a rite of passage, this wooden carving, about 3 feet (92 cm) high and swaying in accompaniment to the music of drums and horns, is carried by a procession of mourners.

See also: AFTERLIFE (Vol. I); ANCESTOR WORSHIP (Vol. I); FUNERAL CUSTOMS (Vol. I); SCULPTURE (Vol. I).

Rift Valley The geological fault system that spans 3,000 to 4,000 miles (4,828 to 6,437 km), from southwestern Asia to eastern Africa, and was home to the earliest prehistoric people on Earth.

The Rift Valley—*rift* meaning "depression," "trough," or "crack"—is also known as the Great Rift Valley, the Afro-Arabian Rift Valley, and the Eastern Rift Valley. It is one of the longest rifts on the planet. Geologists think the valley was created in a fault zone more than 50 million years ago. The Rift Valley has a wide variation in elevation from around 1,300 feet (396.2 m) below sea level in the Dead Sea to about 6,000 feet (1,828.8 m) above sea level in KENYA. The width of the valley is 30 to 40 miles (48.3 to 64.4 km) on average. It measures only a few miles wide at its narrowest point and expands to 100 miles (160.9 km) at its widest point. From space, the Rift Valley in Kenya is clearly visible.

The Rift Valley enters Africa from the Red Sea, moves into ETHIOPIA, stretches southwest into Kenya, extends south through Tanzania, MALAWI, and finally proceeds into Mozambique, going through the lower Zambezi River valley to the Indian Ocean. The Rift Valley in Africa is typically considered to be the main valley, with a western branch extending north along the eastern coast of the CONGO. Several freshwater and alkaline lakes are in the valley, the largest of which are in the western rift valley and include Lake Nyasa (also called Lake Malawi) and Lake TANGANYIKA.

Of the several Rift Valley lakes in Kenya, the largest is Lake TURKANA. It was along the shores of this lake that archaeologist Dr. Richard Leakey discovered hominid remains thought to be millions of years old. Using archaeological discoveries and oral history, scholars have gathered evidence that seems to support the theory that the human race originated in this area of Rift Valley. Evidence suggests that as early as the STONE AGE, c. 50,000 BCE, people lived near Lake Turkana and manufactured stone hand-ax tools. Then, around 10,000 BCE, the discovery of fire allowed for the invention of new ways of toolmaking. Cultures of hunting-and-gathering people developed in the area, and AGRICULTURE likely began around 1000 BCE in the Rift Valley, probably having been introduced by Kushites from Ethiopia.

Ancient IRRIGATION systems have been discovered from this time, too. The Rift Valley is the location of an important IRON AGE site at Engaruka. This area in northern Tanzania was home to a large settlement of agriculturalists who irrigated the land for more than 1,000 years.

Several other lakes fall in the Rift Valley, including Lake Naivasha, Lake Nakuru, Lake Baringo, Lake Bogoria, and Lake Baringo. Lake Naivasha is a freshwater lake and the highest of the Rift Valley lakes. Lake Nakuru is noted for the million or so pink FLAMINGOS that make their home there. Within the Kenyan part of the Rift Valley, animal life is abundant, including HIPPOPOTAMUS, ZEBRA, white and black RHINOCEROS, LEOPARD, GIRAFFE, buffalo, waterbuck, and several hundred species of birds.

See also: KUSH (Vol. I); RHINOCEROS (Vol. I).

Further reading: V. Morell, *Ancestral Passions: The Leakey Family and the Quest for Humankind's Beginnings* (New York: Simon & Schuster, 1995); Anthony Smith, *The Great Rift: Africa's Changing Valley* (London: BBC Books, 1988).

rites of passage Term used by anthropologists to describe the special ceremonies that mark a person's development.

Rites of passage occur in all societies of the world, the most common marking birth, the onset of adulthood, marriage, and death. Many of these rites have remained intact for thousands of years. Most have been carried out in culturally distinctive ways that include the use of ritual objects, feasts, song or DANCE, and special CLOTHING or JEWELRY.

Marriage in Africa offers a prime example of a series of smaller rites that culminate in a final ceremonial rite of passage. Some societies begin this process during early childhood. The Udhuk of ETHIOPIA, for example, traditionally marry at an early age, but individuals are permitted to choose their future spouses. After approaching their parents and gaining approval, the future bride wears BEADS, indicating that she is engaged. In contrast, parents in the Kiga society of Uganda make all the arrangements for marriage, and the young bride and bridegroom do not meet until the day of the wedding. Prospective husbands of the Wolof culture, in what is now Gambia, ask intermediaries to carry KOLA NUTS, clothing, and other gifts to the family of the prospective bride. The presenting of gifts, known as BRIDEWEALTH, is a crucial rite of passage that dates back to the times of Egyptian rule. The ruling elite, in particular, required that contracts, known as *shep en sehemet*, be drawn between the groom and the father of the bride. It was generally held that the gifts strengthened the relationship between families united by marriage.

The actual marriage ceremony is the culmination of these rites and ranges from a simple act to highly demonstrative displays. TORO bridegrooms in Uganda carry their new wives on their shoulders to their new home in order to demonstrate to the community the high esteem that they have for their brides.

Funerals have traditionally been the most elaborate rite of passage performed in Africa, and they provide insight into the life of the deceased, while also affirming belief in the AFTERLIFE. For example, many societies bury their deceased with personal objects, a practice that dates back at least to the early Egyptian and Nubian kings who built lavish tombs to ensure a comfortable setting in the afterlife. In contrast, many nomadic hunting-and-gathering societies conduct a more simple form of burial, although it is no less significant to the living.

Among the lesser rites associated with funerals is the act of purification. In Ghana, when a married man or woman dies, the family of the deceased performs a traditional rite that simultaneously protects the surviving partner from the polluting effects of death and dissolves the marriage. When the period of mourning is completed, the former spouse is free to marry again.

See also: BURIAL RITES (Vol. I); CHILD REARING (Vol. I); EGYPT (Vol. I); INITIATION RITES (Vol. I).

Further reading: John S. Mbiti, *African Religions and Philosophy*, 2nd ed. (Oxford, Eng.: Heineman Educational Publishers, 1989); Gay Robins, *Women In Ancient Egypt* (Cambridge: Harvard University Press, 1993).

rock art Engravings and paintings, often in color, made by ancient peoples on stone surfaces. The earliest rock paintings date from the period 5000 to 2000 BCE and contain depictions of game animals. Some 30,000 examples of ancient rock art have been sound in the SAHARA alone. Human figures, if shown, carry clubs, bows and arrows, and other weapons used for hunting. Rock art is very likely connected to the creators' religious beliefs or rituals.

Rock art in the Sahara, South Africa, and the NILE VALLEY offer strong examples of the relationship between the human and the unknown. In the Nile Valley, between Wadi Abbad and Wadi Hammama, for example, archaeologists have found evidence on rocks and POTTERY that show images and rituals that may preserve the roots of Egyptian religion.

Early rituals are more clearly depicted in southern Africa, where paintings of the eland have been attributed to the SAN. In these drawings, the animals appear to symbolize prosperity, and the scenes generally include ritual DANCE that probably recognized this. Likewise, archaeologists have found rock art in the Kongo region that dates back to the Late STONE AGE. Modern-day interpretations by people in the region indicate that one such rock bears symbols for the Moon and stars that have been in widespread use since ancient times.

A number of rock paintings with religious themes have been found in BOTSWANA, including scenes of a rainmaking ceremony in which a sacrificial animal is seen being led by what may have been priests. In caves found in Natal, South Africa, a rock painting of what is likely a religious scene shows women clapping for masked dancers. Elsewhere, in the Sahara region, including southern Oran and Tassili N'Ajjer, images have been found that show oxen with Egyptian-style discs, which many archaeologists believe predate the human form later assigned to the Egyptian deity HATHOR. Similarly, images of a ram with a sphere apparently predate the similar figure, but with a human form, later assigned to the Egyptian god AMUN.

In southern Africa, no site has been reliably dated to any time before the common era. The San, among others, continued the tradition of rock painting well into the nineteenth century, although some of these sites may contain the work of KHOIKHOI and Bantu-speaking artists.

See also: ENNEDI (Vol. II)

Rome Italian city-state, republic, and empire that, by the beginning of the common era, ruled much of the European and Mediterranean world. The area of the Palatine Hills was originally settled by a people known as the Latins, who were inhabiting the area by about 1000 BCE. For a brief period the Latins fell under the dominance of a rival Italian people, the Etruscans, but they eventually freed themselves of Etruscan rule and, in 509 BCE, established the Roman Republic. Over the next 225 years, Rome gradually conquered neighboring peoples and territories until it had control of the entire Italian Peninsula. Then, with the PUNIC WARS, which began c. 264 BCE, Rome battled with CARTHAGE, its main rival in the western Mediterranean. In the ensuing conflicts, in which Rome defeated the powerful Carthaginian Empire in three separate wars, Rome came to dominate the islands of Sicily and Sardinia and, later, parts of Iberia and the North African coast.

By the end of the Punic Wars, however, the Roman republican system was crumbling. During the period dominated by Julius CAESAR, Rome was caught up in turmoil that eventually brought on the end of its relatively democratic form of government. Eventually, the republic was replaced by an empire in 27 BCE, when Octavian, the adopted son of Julius Caesar, assumed the name Augustus and became the first Roman emperor. During these years, c. 130–30 BCE, Rome expanded into northern Europe, Asia, EGYPT, and North Africa, forging a mighty empire that controlled the region for almost 500 years.

Rome in Egypt As Rome expanded its power into Asia, it encountered the Egypt of the PTOLEMIES, the rulers who assumed control of Egypt after the death of ALEXANDER THE GREAT (356–323 BCE). Egypt finally fell securely into the Roman sphere of influence during the period of Queen CLEOPATRA (r. 51–30 BCE), who struggled to maintain her nation's independence by playing one side against the other in the dangerous game of Roman politics. She first sided with Pompey, an adversary of Julius Caesar, in their bitter and violent rivalry. Then, switching sides, she supported the victorious Caesar. Her subsequent affair with the Roman leader—and the birth of their son Caesarion—helped her achieve an uneasy peace with the Mediterranean power, which gave Egypt a semblance of autonomy.

After Caesar's assassination, however, Cleopatra and her country were once again drawn into Roman politics. Marrying Caesar's protégé, Marc Antony, she set about trying to reestablish Egypt's full independence, as well as its position of power in Africa and Asia. The combined forces of Cleopatra and Antony, however, proved no match for Octavian, who defeated them at the famous naval battle of Actium, in 31 BCE. After his victory, Octavian assumed full control of Rome. Egypt became a Roman province, which it remained until the empire split into eastern and western spheres in 355 CE.

Rome in Kush and Nubia Once it was in control of Egypt, Rome began to exact tribute from the nearby kingdom of KUSH. Despite this tribute, however, Roman forces repeatedly made advances into Kush, penetrating ever deeper towards Nubia. As a result, Kushites began to attack Roman outposts, which led to quick retaliatory attacks by the Romans. Roman forces seized several Kushite towns and then marched on Napata, which they soon conquered and destroyed.

Although this three-year conflict resulted in a clear victory for Rome, the Kushites did benefit from the results. The KANDAKES, who played a major role in the Kushite military and government, appealed to the Roman leader, Julius Caesar, who, feeling that he was putting Rome in a tenuous position by overextending his troops, pulled back the Roman forces. He then restored the Egyptian-Kushite borders to their previous state, leaving Kush and Nubia relatively independent of Rome in the years that followed.

Rome in North Africa Rome became a major power in North Africa as a result of its victories in the Punic Wars. Inheriting the power of the once-dominant Carthaginian Empire, Rome at first tried to rule northern Africa through a series of colonies—known as Africa Vetus—and client states, including NUMIDIA and Mauritania. For the most part, these client states, ruled by native kings, enjoyed a great deal of autonomy, and they were able to prosper despite both the Roman presence and the occasional raids of indigenous Berbers. However, JUGURTHA, one of the native kings of Numidia, abused his power, angering the Romans and plunging Numidia into a six-year war that ended in Jugurtha's public humiliation in Rome. Later, in the turmoil that resulted from the conflict between Julius Caesar, Pompey, and Crassus (c. 55–46 BCE), another Numidian king, JUBA I, managed to consolidate power and establish a substantial degree of independence for his kingdom. The final victory of Julius Caesar in 46 BCE, however, marked the beginning of the end of this independence, as Juba's young son was taken to Rome to be raised, in Roman fashion, in Caesar's own household. As time passed, Caesar extended Roman power and rule, eventually transforming Numidia into what became known as Africa Nova. Later, in 33 BCE, the death of King Bocchus left Mauritania under direct Roman rule as well. Increased resistance to the Romans, which followed the death of JUBA II, led to further Roman intervention. By 40 CE, Rome had firm control of the region, retaining it until the empire began crumbling in the fourth and fifth centuries.

Rosetta Stone Ancient stone bearing an inscription written in HIEROGLYPHICS, DEMOTIC, and Greek; it provided the linguistic clues that led to the first translation of Egyptian hieroglyphics.

The Rosetta Stone was discovered by one of Napoleon's soldiers in August 1799 during the French military expedition to EGYPT. It was found near the Delta town of Rashid, whose ancient name was Rosetta. The stone itself is a slab of black basalt 46 inches (115 cm) high by 28.5 inches (72 cm) wide. The text of the stone is basically an inscription written in 196 BCE by the reigning king's priests. It honors the Egyptian king Ptolemy V Epiphanes in three different languages—hieroglyphics, demotic (a simple version of hieroglyphics), and Greek. Through a comparison of the Greek and Egyptian texts, for the first time linguistic scholars were able to decipher ancient Egyptian hieroglyphics. From their study, they concluded that hieroglyphs are mainly phonetic, not the symbolic signs they previously were thought to be.

In 1802, Johan David Akerblad and the French scholar A. I. Silvestre de Sacy were the first to make headway in the translation of the markings on the stone. After identifying a few of the letters and some of the proper names in the demotic section of the text, the two scholars compared them with the same names found in the Greek section. Thomas Young, a British physicist, built on these findings by proving that proper names in hieroglyphics had phonetic value. Young also introduced the concept of *cartouches*, the writing of proper names enclosed by ovals. In 1814, Young further revealed that hieroglyphics should be read by studying the direction in which the bird and animal signs were facing.

The final breakthrough in the translation, which occurred in 1822, is credited to the French scholar Jean-François Champollion. Champollion recognized the signs used to write royal names such as Ptolemy. He then was able to draw on his knowledge of Coptic Egyptian to unlock the phonetic values of the remaining hieroglyphs. One year later, Champollion published his work in the famous *Lettre à M. Dacier*.

In 1802, under terms set forth in the Anglo-French Treaty of Alexandria, the stone was given to the British Museum in London, England, where it is still displayed.

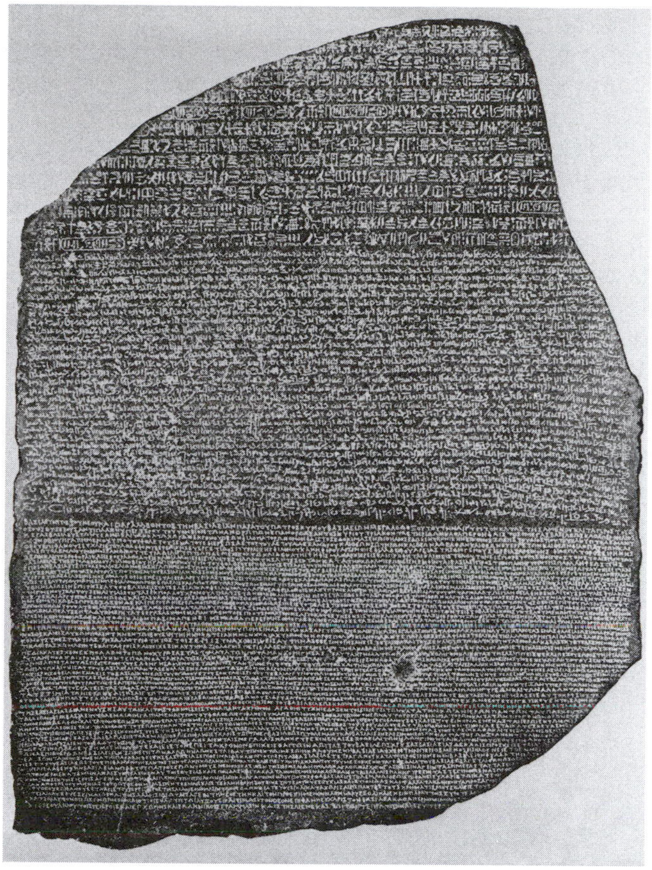

Because it provided the same text in three different languages, the Rosetta Stone enabled Champollion and Young to decipher the riddle of hieroglyphics. British Museum, London, England *© Bettmann/CORBIS*

Ruvuvu River One of the major rivers in the largely mountainous East African nation of BURUNDI. Fed by streams seeping from the plateaus east of Lake Kivu and Lake TANGANYIKA, the Ruvuvu (sometimes spelled Ruvubu) originates not far from Burundi's capital city, Bujumbura. The river, approximately 300 miles (480 km) in length, flows northeast across the country, forming a portion of the eastern border with Tanzania. After it joins with the Kagera River in Rwanda, the two rivers together form the southernmost source of the NILE and finally spill into Lake VICTORIA.

Ruzizi River River that marks part of the borders between the present-day Democratic Republic of the Congo (Congo-Kinshasa) to the west and BURUNDI and Rwanda to the east.

The Ruzizi River, also called Rusizi, traverses a 100-mile (161-km) course through the Western RIFT VALLEY from Lake Kivu, the highest lake in Africa, south to Lake TANGANYIKA. Providing drainage for Lake Kivu, the river flows along the Rwanda-Congo border before entering the Imbo valley in Burundi. Forming the Burundi-Congo border, the Ruzizi River then enters Lake Tanganyika. Volcanic activity forces Lake Kivu's drainage to flow south through the Ruzizi River.

In Burundi, the Ruzizi basin of the Imbo plains forms a freshwater system that includes twenty-two rivers and is one of the systems that contributes to the ample supply of freshwater in the area.

Rwenzori, Mount Mountain range in East-central Africa on the western branch of the RIFT VALLEY.

The Rwenzori Range, also called the Ruwenzori Range or Mountains, stretches along 80 miles (128.7 km) of the present-day Uganda-Congo border. The widest point spans 30 miles (48.3 km) and the highest point reaches over 16,700 feet (5,090 m) at Mount Margherita. Though this range lies just north of the equator, it has a permanent snow line at around 14,800 feet (4,511 m). The peaks typically lay under a blanket of mist or clouds. Several lakes, glacial lakes, and glaciers are found in the mountains. Ancient crystalline rock makes up the range, but the mountains contain substantial deposits of cobalt and copper.

In ancient times, these mountains were mistakenly thought to be the source of the NILE RIVER. Scholars think that the famous "Mountains of the Moon" described in the second century by Ptolemy are the Rwenzori Mountains.

S

Sahara The world's largest desert and the only true desert found at 0° longitude.

The Sahara, which means simply "desert" in Arabic, covers one-third of Africa, including most of North Africa, and extends approximately 3,320,000 square miles (8,598,800 sq km), an area roughly the size of the United States. The great desert measures 3,000 miles (4827 km) from east to west and between 800 to 1,200 miles (1287 to 1931 km) from north to south. It stretches from the Atlantic Ocean on the west to the RED SEA on the east. Its northern boundaries are the Atlas Mountains and the MEDITERRANEAN SEA; its southern boundary lies along latitude 16° N and extends through parts of Chad, Niger, and Sudan. The Sahara is one of the harshest environments on earth.

Geography The Sahara is crossed by the NILE and the NIGER Rivers, which sustain most of the human population. Only 2.5 percent (80,000 square miles/200,000 sq km) of the Sahara are oases, which are areas of farming and settlement. The water in an oasis (which is almost always below sea level) comes from wells or springs fed by underground basins. The Sahara has about ninety large oases and many small ones that may support only one or two families. Some large oases have thousands of date palm trees planted, and farmers grow barley, wheat, and other crops. However, even the largest settlements on the oases sustain fewer than 2,000 inhabitants.

The main geographic features of the Sahara include shallow basins called *chotts* and *dayas*; gravel-covered plains called *regs*; rock-strewn plateaus; and sheets, dunes, and seas of sand, collectively called *ergs*, which cover about one-quarter of the desert's surface. The shifting, wind-blown sands in an *erg* can form dunes as high as 600 feet (180 m). (Scientists have yet to explain the "singing" or booming of the sand dunes.)

Mountains and uplands cover the central portion of the Sahara. The plateaus of the Sahara, such as the Tademait Plateau in Algeria and the Ennedi Plateau in Chad, are covered with angular weathered rocks. The Ahaggar Mountains in Algeria rise 9,573 feet (2,918 m) high. Mount Koussi in the Tibesti Mountains of Chad reaches a height of 11,204 feet (3415 m). The lowest point in the desert is Egypt's Qattara Depression, 436 feet (133 m) below sea level.

Climate The highest temperature recorded is 136° F (58° C) at al-Aziziyah in Libya; yet in other places, frost can be seen in the wintertime. The annual rainfall measures no more than 0.08 inches (2 mm), and some areas may go for years with no rainfall at all. A narrow strip of the western coast enjoys a relatively cool, uniform temperature year-round, due to ocean currents; however, most of the Sahara experiences a cycle of extremely hot summers and mild to cool winters.

Climatologists estimate that the Sahara has been a desert since the Early Pliocene epoch, or for roughly 5 million years. It has been subject over time to a cycle of drier and more humid conditions, though for the past 2,000 years, its climate has been very stable.

Strong winds, given such names as *sirocco, khamsin,* and *shahali,* can blow unpredictably for days. They move vast amounts of sand and create an ever-changing landscape, burying everything in their path and decreasing visibility to hazardous levels.

Animal Life Most desert animals can go for long periods of time without drinking and are able to take some water from the plants in their diet. The smaller animals are

Most oases, like this one in Algeria near the Moroccan border, are large enough to support only a handful of families. *© Robert Holmes/CORBIS*

nocturnal, staying in their borrows during the heat of the day and exiting during the cooler night to find food. These animals include gerbils, snakes, lizards, and small foxes called fennecs. Among the larger animals living in the Sahara are white gazelles and a rare antelope called an addax, an extremely hardy animal that resembles its much larger relative, the oryx. Barbary sheep live in the rocky plateaus.

Archaeology and History The region of Africa that includes the Sahara had a much wetter climate during the ice ages of the Pleistocene epoch, which ended about 9500 BCE. Archaeological evidence indicates that forests and grasslands covered the region, which was inhabited by antelopes, elephants, giraffes, extinct buffaloes called bubaluses, rhinoceroses, ostriches, and warthogs.

The widespread presence of stone artifacts, fossils, and ROCK ART give evidence of human habitation throughout the region. Almost 30,000 engravings and rock paintings date from the fifth millennium BCE. Archaeologists have also found bone harpoons and accumulations of shells on the shores of long-dried-up Saharan lakes. Evidence of the presence of domestic livestock and the associated lifestyle of nomadic PASTORALISM in the region can be traced as far back as 5000 BCE. Direct evidence of formal AGRICULTURE—the cultivation in Egypt of barley and emmer wheat introduced from Asia—dates from as early as 4000 BCE. Native African plants were first domesticated by the Gangara people, ancestors of the modern Soninke, in roughly 1000 BCE.

In about 4000 BCE the climate became more arid, and the region began to turn into a desert. At the same time, TRADE began to start between neighboring settlements and, eventually, between the Sahara region and the outside world. By 2000 BCE, COPPER from Mauritania found its way to the BRONZE AGE people of the Mediterranean. The people of CARTHAGE, one of the great cities of ancient times, apparently continued these Bronze Age trade relationships as their city rose to prominence after 600 BCE.

The growing aridity of the Sahara had its effect in the transition from CATTLE and HORSES to CAMELS, which are well adapted to life in the desert. Camels were used in Egypt by 600 BCE, although in other parts of the Sahara they were unknown until some 600 or more years later when they were introduced from the Middle East. Camels all but replaced cattle as the pack animals of choice on the trade routes.

The Movement of Peoples The North African city of Carthage, destroyed at the end of the Third PUNIC WAR in 149 BCE, later became an important city in the Roman Empire. After the city was overrun by the VANDALS, a Germanic people, around 430 CE, a major shift in population occurred. Various Berber clans, camel-mounted NOMADS who once lived along the northwest coast of Africa, entered the desert to avoid the anarchy and warfare following the defeat of the Romans and gradually became established throughout the Sahara. The clans often plundered caravans and attacked oasis dwellers. Later, other groups of Berbers—prompted by the rise of Islam—and Arab peoples who desired to maintain traditional beliefs, also moved into the Sahara. Within 500 years, Islam had spread to the southern borders of the Sahara, and Arabic became the main language of the desert.

Of the major black African kingdoms known to the Arabs at the beginning of the Islamic period, most were located north of Lake Chad and the Senegal and Niger Rivers, close to the southern edge of the Sahara. Historians speculate that these kingdoms found it more beneficial to locate themselves closer to the ends of the trade routes than in lands more suited to agriculture. In exchange for GOLD, ivory, foodstuffs, and slaves, these kingdoms could import luxury goods and, most important, SALT—a precious commodity readily available only on the coastlands.

There is archaeological evidence for a mixed pastoral and agricultural economy among an intermingled group of Libyan Berbers and black agriculturalists in the Sahara by 4000 BCE, about the same time Egypt began to flourish. However, the growing desertification of the Sahara region seems to have forced its black population to migrate to the more fertile and welcoming savannas of the SAHEL region south of the Sahara.

See also: KINGDOMS AND EMPIRES OF THE WEST AFRICAN SAVANNA (Vol. II); LIBYA (Vol. II); MAGHRIB (Vols. II, III); TRANS-SAHARAN TRADE ROUTES (Vol. II).

Further Reading: David Ball, *Empires of Sand* (New York: Bantam Doubleday Dell, 1999); Babs Suzanne Harrison, Staefan Eduard Rada, et al., *The Lion in the Moon: Two Against the Sahara* (New York: Rainbow Books, 1994); Anthony G. Pazzanita and Tony Hodges, *Historical Dictionary of Western Sahara* (New York: Scarecrow Press, 1994).

Sahel Hot, dry band of grasslands that lies south of the SAHARA.

The Sahel, which means "border" in Arabic, lies south of the Sahara and extends through modern Senegal, Mauritania, Mali, Burkina Faso, Niger, Nigeria, Chad, and Sudan. The area was initially populated by the southward migration of desert-dwelling black peoples in search of more hospitable living conditions. All the major black kingdoms of ancient western and central Africa arose in the Sahel as way stations and terminus points for the TRADE routes to North Africa. The largest and the longest lasting was GHANA, which originated in the late fourth century but did not reach its peak until about 1000. Mali, the Songhai Empire, and Kanem-Bornu are important Sahelian kingdoms that came into being after the decline of Ghana.

See also: MAGHRIB (Vols. II, III); MALI EMPIRE (Vol II); SONGHAI EMPIRE (Vol. II).

salt One of Africa's major natural resources and an item in great demand in trade in the ancient world; in ancient Africa, it was often used as a form of currency.

Salt has been used as MONEY and in barter for thousands of years in Africa. In fact, the word *salary* is derived from a Latin word meaning "salt." Like all things used as currency, salt was easy to distribute, readily transported, not perishable, and valuable beyond its use as money. In hot climates like that of western Africa, salt was used to season and preserve food. Ingesting salt helped prevent a person from losing bodily fluids.

The rise of AGRICULTURE may have contributed to the increased use of salt. Nomadic people who lived off meat that was either raw or had been roasted to keep in the natural salt, had little need for salt. The proliferation of trade around the MEDITERRANEAN SEA, however, gave rise to settlements and urban trading areas, which led to an increase in agriculture. And as agriculture increased, diets changed to include more vegetables, grains, and boiled meats, all of which required salt as a supplement.

In ancient times, therefore, salt became a valuable item and one of the most commonly traded commodities. In fact, it was more precious than GOLD to some ancient peoples. North African traders in salt and gold are believed to have begun crossing the SAHARA Desert by at least the fourth century.

See also: BARTER SYSTEM (Vol. I); SALT TRADE (Vol. II).

In ancient times, because they valued salt so much, the people of West Africa frequently traded equal weights of salt for gold.

San (Bushmen) HUNTER-GATHERERS who most likely were the original inhabitants of Botswana, Namibia, and northwest South Africa. The San belong to the group of language speakers known as the Khoisan, an umbrella term that includes the Khoikhoi, !Kung, G/wi, and other speakers of "click" languages. Despite similarities in language and appearance, the San and Khoikhoi represent two distinct ethnic groups who, at various periods of history, coexisted in the same regions. The name *San* reportedly comes from their word *sa,* which means "gatherers of fruit" or "harvest." As such, it is a better description of the San way of life than BUSHMEN, a term that is now considered to be derogatory and unsuitable.

The San's longevity in southern Africa ranges between 20,000 and 30,000 years, although the San actually may date back to an even earlier period. The complex nature of their society has been avidly studied and offers critical insights into the Late STONE AGE period. For instance, a recovered collection of tools associated with the San dates back some 15,000 years, and is known as the Wilton Stone Kit. The tools were named for the cave shelter in Cape Province, South Africa, where they were discovered. The kit demonstrates an advanced level of toolmaking ability, including scrapers, borers, and microliths, which are long, blade-like pieces of stone produced by striking a larger stone or core. These tools most likely were used to butcher animals. Although the San hunted in small groups, they developed highly effective methods for bringing down animals like the eland, kudu, impala, and bushbuck using nets and animal traps, along with spears and arrows coated with a poison made from vegetables. After a successful hunt, every part of the animal was consumed, and the skin made into clothing and bags.

It remains uncertain how often meat could be made available by hunting, and women and children, who were primarily the gatherers, provided nearly 80 percent of the San diet. Food items most likely to have been consumed on a daily basis included honey, berries, mongongo nuts, insects such as grasshoppers, fruit, and smaller animals such as tortoises and mole rats. Recovered digging sticks and grinding stones suggest that women also obtained wild roots and plants from the more than 100 types available in the region. Adding further variation to their diet, San who lived closest to the coast caught fish, rock lobsters, seals, and mussels in reed baskets.

This cooperative system of hunting and gathering allowed the San to share food resources among the members of their family group or bands. These groups ranged from ten to sixty people, but often shifted in size as a result of POLYGYNY, as well as resettlement and natural loss from death or disease. San society has often been described as egalitarian because of their emphasis on shared work responsibilities and leadership chosen from a group of elders.

Between 20,000 and 15,000 BCE, San culture had developed to the point of burying the dead in accordance with specific rites. Their spiritual belief system centered around a single, all-powerful god as well as lesser deities, possibly land or animal spirits. However, notions of land ownership remain questionable since the San were a highly mobile society. Their homes, made of interlocking branches and thatch, were designed for transport over long distances.

Because they applied time limits and organized efforts to their subsistence activities, the San were able to devote a generous amount of time toward developing their cultural practices. As a result, their cave paintings and ornamental jewelry made from ostrich eggs represent one of the most widespread forms of prehistoric art in southern Africa. A variety of musical instruments have also been attributed to the San and may have been used in social or ritual practices. For example, the !KUNG San who live in Kalahari bordering BOTSWANA, have been depicted in cave paintings as participants in healing DANCES performed as a safeguard against spirit-induced illnesses or similar misfortunes.

One of the questions that still remains to be answered about the San involves the recovery of their skeletal remains at sites as far away as Tanzania, Uganda, southern Sudan (Nubia), ETHIOPIA, and SOMALIA. Archaeologists are uncertain whether these findings reflect forced resettlement following Bantu migrations into South Africa some 2,000 years ago or whether it relates to hunting-and-gathering activities.

See also: KHOIKHOI (Vols. II, III); SAN (Vol. III).

Further reading: Elizabeth Isichei, *A History of African Societies to 1870* (Cambridge, Eng.: Cambridge University Press, 1997); G. Mokhtar, ed., *General History of Africa*, Abridged Edition (Paris: UNESCO, 1990); Kevin Shillington, *History of Africa* (New York: St. Martins Press, 1995).

sand drawings, Chokwe Geometric patterns drawn in the sand by the Chokwe people of northeasern Angola.

The Chokwe people, also called Tchokwe, are thought to be the descendants of an old culture of savanna hunters that once lived in central Africa. They are well-known for their engravings, tattoo designs, and sand drawings, which are called *lusona* (plural, *sona*). The designs that the Chokwe use in their *sona* have a double function: They are both highly stylized, mathematically interesting figures and mnemonic (memory-aiding) devices. Specific drawings refer to ancient fables, proverbs, riddles, and other topics and serve as a way to transmit traditional knowledge from one generation to the other. Boys learn how to form the easier *sona* as part of their preparation for adult initiation ceremonies. The more intricate *sona* are mastered only by specialists. The designs are expected to be executed in smooth, continuous movements as the speaker retells the associated story. Any lack of fluidity is seen as an imperfection worthy of scorn.

To make a sand drawing, the storyteller first smooths the ground and then, with his fingertips, prepares a grid of equidistant points that will be used to simultaneously create the figure and tell the story. As the story progresses, the design is completed. Depending on how the storyteller used the marks, he can draw an abstract bird, snake, chicken, or any other design that he has memorized.

Sango (Shango) In traditional YORUBA religion, the divinity associated with lightning and thunder.

Yoruba divinities are sometimes primordial spirits and sometimes deified ancestors—heroic individuals who made important contributions to the life of the people. In popular legend, Sango, the god of lightning and thunder, had human origins. He may once have been the fourth *alafin*, or ruler, of the town of Oyo, which much later became a city-state of some importance in the region. Sango discovered a charm that let him call down lightning and thunder but destroyed his own palace and family when he used it. The loss so horrified him that he hanged himself.

The cult of Sango as the god of lightning and thunder may have displaced worship of Jakuta, an earlier deity, who hated immorality and would hurl stones of fire at those who acted against the will of OLORUN (Olodumare), the Creator. Today, traditional believers sometimes worship Sango and Jakuta interchangeably.

Other versions of the Sango legend paint him in darker terms. In one version, he was a tyrannical ruler who, tired of domestic disputes, left his family in disgust. He was drawn up into the sky on a chain and expresses his royal rule by lightning and thunder. In other versions, he was versed in magic and instilled fear in his subjects by breathing fire and smoke. Despite the stories, however, contemporary devotees revere Sango for his sense of justice and his hatred of sorcery.

Sango communicated with his devotees by means of SPIRIT POSSESSION. The spirit of Sango is said to "mount" a human spokesman as a person might mount a horse. The person loses consciousness, and the god speaks through his mouth. The one possessed becomes capable of performing preternatural and superhuman acts without getting hurt.

See also: RELIGION, TRADITIONAL (Vol. I).

Further reading: Omosade Awolalu, *Yoruba Beliefs and Sacrificial Rites* (White Plains, N.Y.: Longman Group, 1979).

This twentieth-century Sango staff provides a contemporary depiction of the Yoruba god of lightning and thunder. It stands 13 7/8 inches (34.4 cm) high by 7 1/4 inches (8.5 cm) wide. North Carolina Museum of Art, Raleigh, NC © *North Carolina Museum of Art /CORBIS*

Saqqara Site of an ancient burial ground, known for its elaborate private tombs from the OLD KINGDOM period.

As the primary burial site of the ancient Egyptian capital of MEMPHIS, Saqqara was used by almost every dynasty at least through the First Intermediate Period. The most elaborate mastabas, or private tombs, at Saqqara were built as "houses of eternity." These structures sometimes contained more than twenty separate chambers, with numerous burial shafts for family members. Thousands of HIEROGLYPHIC inscriptions decorate the multicolored walls.

The step pyramid of Djoser at Saqqara, dating from the Third Dynasty (2630–2611 BCE), was the first pyramid built in Egypt. *© Richard T. Nowitz/CORBIS*

Late OLD KINGDOM private tomb architecture culminated at Saqqara in the mastabas of the Fifth and Sixth Dynasty (2465–2181 BCE), in which the greatest variety of wall scenes may be found. These tombs were intended for such high-ranking administrators as Ti and Ptahhotep and were dominated inside by large-scale figures of the deceased. On one level, these figures were meant to signify the importance of the deceased. On another level, these scenes of people, objects, and activities were believed to have been endowed with reality in the afterlife. Thus, they offered provisions for the deceased's spirit. Other representations included scenes of craftsmen at work, herdsmen leading bulls, boating games, and ritual pilgrimages to holy sites.

The Old Kingdom mastabas at Saqqara have become a major source of information about life in the Old Kingdom, providing the opportunity to reconstruct a picture of daily life during the period. As a result, the site remains a primary Egyptian tourist attraction.

Satire on the Trades Name given to the ancient Egyptian text, written c. 2000 BCE, that recorded the hard life of TRADE laborers, as well as the scorn with which the upper class regarded the laborers.

Sometimes described as a poem and sometimes as a text, *Satire on the Trades* is thought to have been written by an aristocratic father who wanted to warn his son of the dangers of the trades and to persuade him instead to enter a training school for SCRIBES. According to the author of the satire, scribes remain free of an employer's control, are not subject to heavy or dirty labor, and want for nothing as members in the court of the king. As a scribe, the son is promised "life, prosperity, health."

The text describes the life of trade laborers as hard, dirty, miserable, and dangerous. The builder, for one, is portrayed as being covered with clay, physically battered, and miserable. The arrow maker is similarly miserable as he ventures into the desert looking for flint. The launderer, meanwhile, lives a dangerous life because this work is done on the riverbank where CROCODILES also reside.

This poem or text also shows the disdain that the ancient Egyptian upper class shows the working class. It poses that the people of the trades are thought to be "wretched through and through." The author of the satire speaks from his experience and seems to sum up his view of the tradesman when he writes, "I have seen how the belabored man is belabored."

See also: MERCHANTS (Vol II); TRADE (Vol. II).

scarab beetle Large, heavy-bodied oval insect.

In ancient EGYPT, scarab beetles would occasionally appear in great numbers along the muddy banks of the NILE. As a result, the scarab beetle was associated with resurrection, renewal, and immortality. Re-Khepri, the sun god, was often depicted as a scarab, a man with the face of a scarab, or as a man whose head was surmounted by a scarab. According to tradition, Re-Khepri rolled the Sun before him across the sky, carrying it safely to the other world after sunset in order to renew it for the next day.

The ancient Egyptians used exquisitely carved and inscribed stone figures of scarabs as seals to commemorate important events, and scarab figures have also been found buried with MUMMIES. Roman soldiers often wore scarab rings as military symbols.

scarification Marking the body or face for the purpose of cultural identity, status, or group affiliation; also known as *cicatrix.*

Although it has not been determined when the practice of scarification began, evidence of its antiquity has survived in an ancient terra-cotta recovered in the Fayum region of EGYPT. The sculpture, which appears to have been made during Roman occupation of Egypt, is of a Sudanese woman whose cheeks bear distinctive scarring. It serves as an important reminder that scarifications appeared on many MASKS and human-like figures sculpted from wood, metal, or clay. Created to represent ancestors or deities from the spiritual realm, these identity marks were also created in imitation of the living, whose incisions or burns of distinctive patterns on the skin raised keloid scars. (Keloids, a trait found in many dark-skinned populations of Africa, resulted from the reformation of connective tissue.)

When taken collectively, the scarifications displayed in representational art and by particular groups offer a visual statement concerning spirituality, social origins, and a sense of community, past and present. For instance, the Sonjo of Tanzania traditionally marked their left shoulders

This undated ancient Egyptian fresco of a scarab beetle is from a tomb in the Valley of the Kings, Luxor, Egypt. *© Bojan Brecelj/CORBIS*

The cheeks on this contemporary Ivory Coast gold mask of a queen mother shows a pattern of decorative scarification. Musée National des Arts Africaines et Oceaniens, Paris, France. *© Archivo Iconografico, S.A./CORBIS*

with an *Ntemi*, a symbol representing their ancient founder. Although the exact reasoning behind this practice is unclear, it is known that one of the Sonjo's primary beliefs centered on the necessity of recognizing this being when he made his eventual return to earth. In a somewhat similar vein, the Lozi of BOTSWANA marked their arms and ears, apparently in order to gain recognition in the spiritual realm after death. Elsewhere, in societies in which infant mortality rates were high, children were given special identity marks that supposedly would change their appearance and prevent their return to the spirit world.

Over the centuries, scarification evolved into one of Africa's most widespread forms of BODY ADORNMENT. However, scarification clearly had more important roles to play than simple ornamentation, especially in the RITES OF PASSAGE undergone by the young men and women of many peoples. Such rites have often required some form of modification to the head, limbs, or torso. Initiation into adult society required Okiek women to have their heads and eyebrows shaved. Among the Mende of Sierra Leone, "teeth marks" of the Poro deity are made with a razor on the backs of male initiates. Tooth modification has also been associated with transitional rites and often involved the removal, chipping, or filing of incisor teeth. Both the NUBA of the Kordofan region of central Sudan and the Luo of KENYA traditionally removed the lower front incisors as part of initiation. Other forms of body modification have included the wearing of wooden plugs designed to stretch the earlobes. This has been a common practice among the MAASAI and Turkana of Kenya, as well as the Ndebele of South Africa, who begin to wear earplugs at ten years of age.

See also: CIRCUMCISION (Vol. I).

Further reading: John Mbiti, *African Religion and Philosophy,* 2nd ed. (Oxford, Eng.: Heinemann Educational Publishers, 1999); Thelma R. Newman, *Contemporary African Arts and Crafts* (New York: Crown, 1974); Frank M. Snowden Jr., *Blacks in Antiquity* (Cambridge, Mass.: Belknap, 1970).

science The role of Africans in the history of the physical sciences has often been overlooked in modern academic studies; however, because it can be argued that the history of natural science begins with the dawn of humanity, it was likely that humans in Africa were the first to explore the laws of science and use their accumulated scientific knowledge to their advantage.

From the beginning, humans had to face the issues of subsistence—locating nourishment, building shelter, and manufacturing CLOTHING—and the first pseudoscientific observations were likely made in conjunction with the development and utilization of tools for hunting. Humans most likely came to understand the basic laws of physics and mechanics as they learned to manufacture weapons, shelters, and tools.

When agriculture developed in EGYPT, nearly 17,000 years ago, knowledge of ASTRONOMY and mathematics, as well as the development of units of measure and time, became of paramount importance. In fact, the CALENDAR the Egyptians developed more than 6,000 years ago is a prototype of the one we use today.

Egypt was a highly advanced society thousands of years before the progressive European civilization of ancient Greece, so the Greeks considered Egypt the center of scientific study. Much of what the Greeks knew of astronomy and geometry was handed down from the Egyptians, and the most brilliant Greek scholars studied in Egypt.

The Egyptians also made advances in the fields of mining, METALLURGY, AGRICULTURE, SHIPBUILDING, and MEDICINE, and the extensive engineering knowledge of Egypt's pyramid builders still perplexes scientists today.

Due to adverse climatic conditions on the continent below northern Africa, there is a dearth of early archaeological evidence from these regions. It is difficult, therefore, to ascertain the scientific and technological advances made in those areas. However, discoveries such as the ISHANGO BONE in central Africa have forced archaeologists to rethink prior theories regarding the scientific knowledge of ancient African peoples. This notched bone, which is thought to be an early calendar and counting tool, dates to c. 8500 BCE, suggesting that the peoples of central Africa were capable of rather sophisticated mathematics during the Paleolithic era. The knowledge of mathematics and units of measurement that the Ishango Bone represents are the bedrock of scientific thought.

See also: FARMING TECHNIQUES (Vol. I); IRRIGATION (Vol. I); ISLAMIC CENTERS OF LEARNING (Vol. II); SCIENCE (Vols. II, III).

scribe Practioner of the ancient profession of WRITING and transcribing records, letters, and texts of various kinds; typically, in ancient EGYPT, a highly respected priest or government official.

The profession of scribe dates back nearly to the invention of writing, c. 3200 BCE. According to Egyptian myth, the scribe of the gods, THOTH, invented writing and gave it to the people. Though PAPYRUS is fragile, it revolutionized writing, and the earliest known example dates back to about 2500 BCE. Stone carvings show scribes carrying rolls, indicating that scribes may have been writing on papyrus even earlier. Although papyrus was the most common writing material of scribes, they also wrote on pottery, pieces of limestone, and wooden boards. Scribes used a pen or brush made of reed as well as INK made of various pigments. (Red and black were the most common colors.) More complex than alphabetic systems of writing, Egyptian HIEROGLYPHICS contained approximately 700 separate signs that could be used individually or in combination with other signs. As a result, the number of literate people in Egypt was low, and well-trained scribes were greatly respected.

The profession of scribe was thought to be a noble one, and scribes were often honored by representation in art. Egyptians were generally aware that writing was a major asset of civilization, and scribes facilitated that contribution. The School of Life, a training school for scribes, was so named because scribes achieved a sort of immortality through writing; it was thought that their books and records had the potential to last forever.

Scribes were required to pass through a difficult and laborious training, which was often rough and severe. (In fact, the Egyptian word for teach was *seba*, which means "to beat.") After a long period of training and apprenticeship, scribes were certified to practice their profession. Some schools for scribes in the NEW KINGDOM were part of a government department. Having completed their training, scribes typically were employed as priests or officials of the government and worked in temples, at pyramids, or in the court of the king. They were thought of as educated people, and were allowed to advance in position, often obtaining important posts in government.

Scribes wrote or transcribed many types of records, including letters, taxes, legal reports, religious texts, hymns, poetry, stories, myths, medical and scientific texts, and official proclamations of the court. In other words, they were involved with written communications and records of every kind. Perhaps the most famous works of the scribes were the mortuary texts that are now collectively called the Book of the Dead. On tomb walls, coffins, and on papyrus, scribes wrote magical formulas and other texts intended to help guide the deceased safely to the AFTERLIFE. This funerary text writing was thought to have provided much work for the scribes at the time.

See also: DEMOTIC (Vol. I).

sculpture The avenue of human artistic expression using three-dimensional or relief forms; found in ancient Africa as early as c. 6000 BCE.

Archaeological excavations so far have not told the entire story of ancient African sculpture. Evidence, however, suggests that sculpture was created far back in prehistoric times. Rock carvings of the Tassili and Ennedi found in the SAHARA date to as early as 6000 BCE.

Other ancient African sculpture includes the small fired-clay animals found at Daima near Lake Chad. These works, which were done by a NEOLITHIC AGE people, date back to the fifth and sixth century BCE. Many scholars believe that these suggest the existence of even earlier non-fired clay sculptures.

About the same time, the amazing terra-cotta figures of the ancient Nok people, an IRON AGE culture, were being made. The NOK CULTURE produced hundreds of fired-clay figures ranging from pendant size to life size. Plain features and holes in the eyes typified these sculptures, which were masterful in technique and detail.

The ancient Sao culture of the Chari valley in CAMEROON also sculpted human figures. These most likely were depictions of ancestors or gods and were made from about the fifth century BCE and continue to be made even today. Elsewhere, in the area near Lake VICTORIA and Lake TANGANYIKA in Uganda, a sculpted head and torso are regarded as the earliest art of this part of Africa. Although much of this ancient African sculpture probably was created at about the same time, each culture produced a distinctly different style.

Unfired clay was perhaps one of the earliest and most commonly used materials for sculpture in ancient Africa. Other media for sculpting were fired clay, wood, stone, and metals such as GOLD, COPPER, and IRON. Ivory and bone also were used. Ancient sculptors most likely carved, cast, modeled, or built sculptures in ways similar to methods used by artists today, using tools such as hammers, gauges, chisels, and saws. Large stone carvings, likely created in pieces and fixed together, may have required some support.

The people of ancient EGYPT were prolific in sculpture and other arts for at least 3,000 years before the common era. Egyptians sculpted monuments and portrait statues, as well as relief sculpture honoring the gods and royalty. Another common subject of Egyptian sculpture was the SCRIBE, usually depicted with PAPYRUS and pen in hand. Much of what is left of ancient Egyptian sculpture today is mortuary sculpture, originally created for tombs and temples. Relief sculpture in tombs dates back to the Third Dynasty, c. 2705 BCE. Egyptian sculpture is also known for the colossi, or larger-than-life sculpture, of which the GREAT SPHINX, and the mammoth portrait sculptures of RAMESSES II are perhaps the best known.

Sculpture of ancient times was not created for artistic expression alone, however, and went beyond the simple decoration of a house, building, or tomb. Portrait statues of rulers often were created to make a political statement that attested to the greatness of a kingdom. Honoring the dead was another common reason for sculpting, as was paying homage to a god. In Egypt, sculpting may have been thought of as an early recording of history, religion, and culture, as kings, ancestors, and gods were sculpted in three-dimensional forms and in reliefs that often accompanied hieroglyphic texts. Sculpture was also thought to aid the deceased in making a safe journey to the AFTERLIFE, an activity of particular concern to the Egyptians.

Ancient African sculpture ranged from simple, plain figures made from one medium by one artisan to the work of many highly skilled craftsmen assembling one mammoth piece. Though the creation of the colossal sculptures of ancient Egypt were unique to that time and place, many of the techniques used by ancient sculptors are still used today, and many of the traditions of early African sculpting continued into the common era.

See also: IVORY (Vol. II); POTTERY (Vols. I, II).

Sea People Groups of forceful traders and explorers who roamed the MEDITERRANEAN SEA and Aegean Sea and warred with established peoples, such as the HITTITES and the Egyptians.

The Sea People generally wrecked havoc in the ancient world around the Mediterranean and the Aegean. Some scholars say that the Sea People were the ancestors of the PHOENICIANS, while others say they were Philistines from what is now southwestern Palestine. Still other scholars trace the origin of the Sea People by using Egyptian documents that may identify them as several different peoples, including Greeks, Sicilians, Sardinians, the Teresh (from which the Etruscans in Italy descended), as well as the Philistines. Whatever their origin, they were widely known by the name "Sea People" in the ancient world.

During the NEW KINGDOM, EGYPT gained more territory than it had ever controlled before or after, and then it actively defended its borders. Two known wars between Egypt and the Sea People took place—one was during the reign of King Merneptah and the other during the reign of RAMESSES III.

The Sea People were also known to have destroyed the great trading port of Ugarit, which Egyptian merchants and travelers often visited to TRADE. Also credited with the destruction of the Hittite Empire, the Sea People were infamous in the ancient world. Their skill at sea was advanced, and some scholars even credit the Sea People with making the first trip around the African continent, in about 600 BCE. If true, this feat was not to be duplicated for another 2,000 years.

secret societies Formal organizations united by an oath of secrecy. In Africa, members of secret societies generally have come from a vast cross section of age groups and regions. Since ancient times, these groups have used distinctive symbols, LANGUAGE, CLOTHING, and special rituals to reinforce group identity and to gain public recognition. Because of the secretive nature of these groups, little is known about their inner workings or when they first developed in Africa. Some groups may have been formed in response to adverse conditions such as war or its aftermath. They may have also developed to ensure political goals, to maintain ritual activities, or to protect isolated communities. Like other independent groups, these societies found various ways to maintain themselves through monthly dues or accepting fees in return for special services.

The MENDE people of Sierra Leone in West Africa, for example, established two of the best-known societies. These apparently were created in order to strengthen the community, its traditional beliefs, and its way of life. Male members of the Poro people served as a judicial team, handling personal disputes or disagreements over land, property, and other aspects of Mende life. The women of the Sande were responsible for the care and maintenance of ritual objects used in special ceremonies. Equally important, the women cultivated the herbs that were made into special medicines and sold to generate the group's income. Both groups played a traditional role in the INITIATION RITES of young boys and girls into Mende society.

See also: AGE GRADES (Vol. I); CIRCUMCISION (Vol. I); MASKS (Vol. I); RITES OF PASSAGE (Vol. I).

Further reading: Captain F. W. Butt-Thompson *West African Secret Societies* (London: H. F. & G. Witherby, 1929).

secretary bird Bird renowned for its ability to hunt reptiles; indigenous to SOMALIA. Except for its long, powerful legs, the secretary bird closely resembles a hawk or eagle. Standing more than 4 feet (1.2 m) high and armed with superior vision, the secretary bird is able to stalk its prey from a long distance. Its primary mode of attack is surprise, and it grips its victim with its powerful, razor-sharp talons. The bird continues to flap its wings after attacking to avoid getting bitten and to render its prey helpless.

Ancient Egyptians who visited the land of PUNT, as modern-day Somalia was known, most likely observed the secretary bird's hunting skills. There is speculation that these visitors may have woven fables or myths about the creature's power. Primary examples of this are the Egyptian myths of HORUS, who was immortalized as a falcon hawk, and SETH, the serpent that he successfully battled.

Sed festival Celebration held by ancient Egyptian kings symbolizing a renewal of their leadership of the world and a long reign in the AFTERLIFE. The Sed festival (also known as Heb-Sed) was usually held after a king's thirtieth year on the throne and repeated every three years thereafter. The festival was a joyous event that included ceremonies representing a ritual reenactment of the unification of EGYPT under MENES, Egypt's first king.

The ceremony began with the king's presentation of offerings to the gods. Then, sitting on a double throne, the king was crowned twice. His first crown would be white, symbolizing UPPER EGYPT; the second crown was red, symbolizing LOWER EGYPT. Finally, the king put on a short kilt with an animal's tail in the back and ran a ritual course four times. This race was held to prove the king's vitality. He was then carried away in a great procession to visit shrines to the gods HORUS and SETH. During the ceremony the king held an oar and a ritual object. The ceremony was also performed in front of a stature of Min, a god of masculine fertility.

Much of what is known about the Sed festival has been learned from wall-reliefs and paintings, including a large granite gateway found in Bubatis. Another source of information concerning the festival is the Heb-Sed court in the STEP PYRAMID OF DJOSER, in SAQQARA. The funerary complex was built during the Third Dynasty, in approximately 2600 BCE. Its design was credited to IMHOTEP, an adviser of King Djoser, who was later deified for his work as a doctor. The structure was a walled compound made from stone, rather than the mud bricks of earlier buildings; the roof was made of timber. A long colonnade led to a court that held two altars. It was in this court that the Sed Festival was held. Although the complex was in ruins for many centuries, it has been rebuilt in modern times.

Some scholars believe that the Sed festival was held in place of human sacrifice. Long ago, these historians believe, the king was killed during the prime of his life so that his virile power could be transferred to his successor. By dynastic times, this custom was replaced by a ceremonial sacrifice—the Sed festival. Later, when Egyptian kings were closely associated with OSIRIS, the periodic Sed festival apparently dramatized the king's death and resurrection, which echoed that of Osiris himself.

See also: FUNERAL CUSTOMS (Vol. I).

Semna forts Series of military forts established along EGYPT's southern boundary with NUBIA during Egypt's MIDDLE KINGDOM (c. 2106–1633 BCE). To protect Egypt's trading interests, King Sesostris III (r. c.1862–1843 BCE) erected eleven mud-brick forts at Semna, near the second cataract of the NILE. He also ordered a blockade of the Nile in order to restrict Nubian travel and limit trade to that designated by the king. Senwosret strictly enforced the complete subjugation of Nubia, leaving behind an inscription boasting of how he had established boundaries further south than any other ruling pharaoh.

See also: KUSH (Vol. I).

Senegal River West African waterway that flows from the Fouta Djallon highlands in Guinea for more than 1,000 miles (1,600 km) north and west through Mali, forming the border between Senegal and Mauritania before entering the Atlantic Ocean.

The Senegal River, one of the major African rivers, is the only permanent river between MOROCCO and Senegal. It empties into the Atlantic Ocean at St. Louis, on the border of Senegal and Mauritania. Its major tributary is the Falémé River, which forms the border between Mali and Senegal.

The river's seasonal cycle has had a strong impact on the agriculture of the area, with crops being produced only after the recession of floodwaters. For thousands of years, pastureland in the valley has been used by the livestock of nomadic peoples, including the FULANI.

Since ancient times the Senegal River bed was known to contain great deposits of GOLD. The famous voyage of HANNO of CARTHAGE, who led exploratory trade expeditions in western Africa, may have been motivated in part by the knowledge of gold to be found in the Senegal and NIGER Rivers. Scholars believe that Hanno probably explored the Senegal River around 500 BCE. In *The Periplus of Hanno*, Hanno writes what many scholars believe is a description of the Senegal River: "Sailing thence, we came to another river, very great and broad, which was full of crocodiles and hippopotami. . . ."

After 300 CE, the ancient empires of Ghana, Mali, and Songhai each controlled the local trade in the Senegal River valley.

See also: FOUTA DJALLON (Vol. II); KINGDOMS AND EMPIRES: WEST AFRICA (Vol. II); SENEGAL RIVER (Vol. II).

Seth

Seth Ancient Egyptian god of chaos, war, deserts, and storms.

Also known as Set or Suetekh, Seth was, according to the mythology of ancient Egypt, the son of Geb and Nut, the gods of earth and sky.. He also was supposed to be the brother of ISIS, Nephythys, and OSIRIS and the husband of both his sister Nephthys and Taurt, the protectress of childbirth and fertility. He is most often represented as a doglike figure, although he is sometimes portrayed as a pig, JACKAL, DONKEY, or HIPPOPOTAMUS.

For almost 2,000 years, Egyptians considered Seth to be a god of positive qualities, especially a protector against storms and warfare. Many pharaohs even named themselves after him as a tribute and offering to his power.

After the UPPER and LOWER KINGDOMS of Egypt were unified, around 3050 BCE, the perception of Seth changed. According to mythology, Seth's predilection for causing trouble increased, and he supposedly resisted the authority of his brother, Osiris, and ultimately murdered him. According to traditional myths, this in turn led to an eighty-year-long war that pitted Seth against HORUS. Eventually, Horus was victorious, emerging as the ruler of the unified kingdoms of Upper and Lower Egypt. By the Twenty-sixth Dynasty, Seth's reputation had soured so greatly that he was usually depicted with red eyes and hair, the embodiment of evil to the ancient Egyptians.

Seti I (Sethos)

Seti I (Sethos) (r. 1318–1304 BCE) *Second king of Egypt's Nineteenth Dynasty and a noteworthy warrior and monument builder.*

The son of RAMESSES I and Queen Sitre, Seti succeeded to the throne after the end of his father's brief reign. Like Ramesses, Seti served in the military and held several prominent government posts before becoming pharaoh.

Concerned with legitimizing his family's right to the throne, Seti sought to establish a link between himself and the pharaohs who preceded the "heretic" pharaoh, AKHENATEN (Amenhotep IV). In what is called the King's List (aslo called the Royal List) at his temple at ABYDOS, Seti celebrated the memory of monarchs, from the beginning of dynastic rule in EGYPT to himself. King's lists were subjective. Often omitted were lesser kings, usurpers, and those whom the current ruler considered illegitimate. Conspicuously absent from that list were those who had reigned during the Amarna Period (1379–1364 BCE) during which all gods but Aten were banished along with Queen Hatshepsut (1501–1482 BCE), who, for a queen, had wielded unprecedented power.

Seti's military expeditions in foreign lands demonstrated his intent to restore Egypt to the glory it had seen before Akhenaten's reign. To reach this goal, he conducted several campaigns in Syria and Palestine, the last of which pitted the Egyptians against the HITTITES near the city of KADESH. Seti also waged war against LIBYA.

An impressive number of monuments were either built or restored during Seti's reign. Among the finest examples of these was the Hypostyle Hall in the Temple of Amun at KARNAK. Other architectural achievements included the temple dedicated to the god OSIRIS at ABYDOS and Seti's own tomb in the VALLEY OF THE KINGS at Thebes.

The temple of Seti I at Abdyos, Egypt, commemorates the Nineteenth Dynasty (1320–1200 BCE) pharaoh, who was an important warrior and monument builder during his reign from 1318–1304 BCE. *© Robert Holmes/CORBIS*

This seventeenth-century BCE Egyptian sculpture of a funerary boat shows the positioning of the ship's mast at the bow of the ship. The Bowers Museum of Cultural Art, Santa Ana, California *© The Bowers Museum of Cultural Art/CORBIS*

shea butter Waxlike, fatty matter extracted from the nut of the shea tree. The shea tree (*Butyrospermum*) was present in West Africa, as part of the continent's ecological mix, as long ago as prehistoric times. However, archaeologists have not established a starting date for either its economic value or its widespread use in cooking and as a cosmetic item.

When crushed, shea nuts yield a waxy butter suitable for cooking. This material has also been used as a form of margarine and as a key ingredient in chocolate. For centuries, it has been widely used in Africa and elsewhere as a remedy for dry skin.

The ability to store shea butter over long periods undoubtedly made it a useful and long-standing export item. Women reportedly did much of the work involved in producing shea butter, and they have long regarded it as an important source of income.

Further reading: Elizabeth Isichei, *A History of African Societies to 1870* (New York: Cambridge University Press, 1997); Phyllis M. Martin and Patrick O'Meara, eds., *Africa* (Bloomington: Indiana University Press, 1995).

Sheba, queen of See MAKEDA, QUEEN OF SHEBA

shipbuilding Since ancient times, various types of boats have been used for the transport of people and goods in Africa.The design of the first boats is a matter of speculation. They may have been constructed from single trees, hollowed out to form dugout canoes, or from logs crafterd together to form rafts. The first paddles were probably human hands. Surviving Egyptian clay tablets record the use of boats for transportation as early as 4000 BCE. The earliest record of sailing ships is found on a Theban tomb painting from c. 1400 BCE that shows a grain ship being unloaded in Egypt.

Egypt, with its Nile-centered riverbank culture, is credited with many innovations in ship design. Since the NILE flows north but the prevailing winds in the region blow south, these innovations allowed the Egyptians to take full advantage of the river in both directions for transportation and communication.

The oldest Egyptian boats were made from bundles of papyrus reeds lashed together to form a spoonlike hull. Between 4000 and 3000 BCE, the Egyptians discovered sails and used them to propel the boat. The first sails were probably leafy branches that caught the wind, but by 3500 BCE Egyptian boats had stronger, more watertight hulls made from planks of wood. These boats also featured square sails, probably woven from reeds, attached to a mast.

By 2500 BCE, Egyptian ships made the transition from paddles to oars. A ship pushed by hand-held paddles requires a low waterline, limiting the size and displacement of the vessel, so that the paddles can reach the water. Oars, on the other hand, are attached to fixed points on the hull. This design allows the sides of the vessel to rise higher and lets the oars be longer, providing the additional leverage needed to move stone blocks and other heavy cargoes. Later, as vessels increased in size, multiple rowers manned each oar. A large steering oar was used at the stern of these vessels. The Greeks and Romans later improved on these designs by adding more banks of rowers, as many as twelve, in cargo ships called GALLEYS.

The third major Egyptian innovation was in the position of the mast relative to the vessel. By 1800 BCE, the mast had moved from its earlier position at the prow, or bow, of the ship to a more advantageous position amidships, where the sail could catch crosswinds, not just tailwinds, to push the boat forward. These sails still had booms, or long poles, at the bottom of the sail. By 900 BCE, the PHOENICIANS improved on these designs by using a loose-footed square sail, which was more practical for a seagoing vessel.

By the fifth century BCE, merchant ships weighing 400 tons were carrying cargoes across the MEDITERRANEAN SEA. Heavier ships were not built in the West until the nineteenth century. The largest ship of ancient times was a 2,000 ton merchant ship built by Hiero II (270–215 BCE) of Syracuse to carry grain from Egypt.

See also: AGE OF DISCOVERY (Vol. II); INDIAN OCEAN TRADE (Vol II); SHIPBUILDING (Vol. II).

Shona Ethnic group that has lived in the area of present-day Zimbabwe for more than 1,000 years. Predominantly farmers, the Shona grow maize, MILLET, SORGHUM, sweet potatoes, and pumpkins and raised chickens, CATTLE, and sheep. Around 600, Shona ancestors built Great Zimbabwe and many other walled cities in the region, but in the recent past, they have lived in small, scattered communities made up of extended families. The Shona language is related to BANTU, and the Shona most likely moved into the Zimbabwe area some time during the great BANTU migration.

See also: GREAT ZIMBABWE (Vol. II); MAPUNGUBWE (Vol. II); SHONA KINGDOM (Vol. III), ZIMBABWE (Vols. II, III).

Sirius The brightest star in the constellation Canis Major; noted by ancient Egyptians as rising just before the annual flooding of the NILE DELTA and so signaling the beginning of a new growing season and year.

Sothis, as Sirius was called by ancient Egyptians, rises each year just around the time of the rising of the NILE RIVER in midsummer. The rising of the Nile River was an important event in ancient Egypt, as it brought much-needed water and nutrients to the soil. It even brought new soil from the mountains to the plain for the start of a new growing season. As a result, Sirius became associated with fertility and a prosperous harvest. The Egyptians believed that Sirius made the river rise, and according to at least one myth, Sirius was also known as the female god Sopdet.

Sirius, which is now known to be a binary star, is roughly double the size of the Sun. It also is relatively close to the earth, and is the brightest star in the constellation Canus Major, which is located to the southeast of Orion's Belt.

Many Egyptian temples were designed so that the inner chambers received the light of Sirius—evidence of the importance of this great star to this ancient civilization.

See also: DOGON (Vol. II)

slavery Forced servitude. Slavery is rare among HUNTER-GATHERER and other primitive peoples because these societies generally lack social or class distinctions among members, a key condition that allows slavery to flourish. Slavery among more developed societies in Africa has a long history. Slaves were used in ancient EGYPT and Nubia and are known to have been killed to accompany their owners into the AFTERLIFE and tend to their needs. The Old Testament Book of Exodus chronicles the end of the Egyptian enslavement of the Jews during the reign of the pharaoh RAMESSES II (r. 1304–1236), when the prophet Moses led his people to freedom. The tasks that slaves in Egypt performed are uncertain; it is now thought, for instance, that peasant labor, rather than slave labor, was used between growing seasons to build the pyramids.

CARTHAGE in North Africa, a Roman province after its conquest in the PUNIC WARS (264–146 BCE) and a major commercial center until its decline towards the middle of the third century, very likely followed the Roman model and used slaves to row its GALLEYS and to tend its farms. It is thought that Carthage acquired at least some of its slaves through TRADE with sub-Saharan Africa, although most of the slaves were very likely Nubians or indigenous black inhabitants of North Africa.

The extent to which slavery was practiced in sub-Saharan Africa is not known. If the pattern that existed during early Islamic times can be used as an indicator of prior behavior, neighboring peoples may have sent warriors on slave raids against one another's settlements to secure women for childbearing and children as field laborers. Males were not prized because they were likely to run away, so they were often killed.

See also: SLAVERY (Vols. II, III).

Further reading: Kallen, Stuart. *The Lost Kingdoms of Africa: Black Africa Before 1600.* (Edina, Minn.: Abdo & Daughters, 1990); Suzanne Miers and Igor Kopytoff, eds. *Slavery in Africa: Historical and Anthropological Perspectives* (Madison: University of Wisconsin Press, 1977).

Smendes (r. c. 1070–1044 BCE) *Founder of ancient Egypt's Twenty-first Dynasty.*

The High Priest of AMUN who shared power with HERIHOR when the latter usurped the throne of RAMESSES XI, Smendes ruled LOWER EGYPT during the earlier half of the eleventh century BCE. He founded his capital at Tanis, a northeastern city on the NILE DELTA. A damaged inscription on a pillar found at Gebelen is the only record of Smendes' reign.

Smenkhare (Smenkhkared)(c. 1364–1333 BCE) *Tenth king of the ancient Egypt's Eighteenth Dynasty, and successor to Akhenaten.*

Smenkhare married AKHENATEN's daughter Merytaten, who had succeeded her mother, NEFERTITI, as Akhenaten's Great Royal Wife, or principal wife. Evidence suggests that Smenkhkare was co-regent during the latter part of Akhenaten's reign and that he assumed the religious name, Neferneferuaten, of his mother-in-law, Nefertiti. This new name, which some scholars believe means "Perfect One of the Aten's Perfection," seems to indicate that, during his two-year reign, he perpetuated the cult of the god ATEN at el-Amarna.

After the death of Merytaten, Smenkhkare married another of Akhenaten's six daughters, Ankhesenpaaten, who later became the wife of Smenkhare's successor, TUTANKHAMUN (C. 1361–C.1351BCE). The condition of the royal mummy suggests that Smenkhare was in his early twenties when he died.

Somalia Africa's easternmost coastline situated between the Gulf of Aden and the Indian Ocean; also known as Somaliland. Somalians are part of the major language group of Eastern KUSH speakers that include the OROMO and AFAR of ETHIOPIA, as well as the Reendille and Boni of Kenya. Known for their vibrant poetry and verse, Somalians emphasize a shared national identity borne of family CLANS. Their poetry also reflects the freedom and hardships associated with being farmers and NOMADS. However, since it was a stateless society for so long, much of what we know about Somalia's history has come from early patterns of migration and TRADE links in the ancient world.

Origins and Migratory Patterns Several theories have attempted to explain the origins of Somali peoples. Initially, historians believed that they originated on either the western coast of Africa or southern Arabia. However, recent evidence suggests that they migrated from the highlands of southern Ethiopia. Exactly when they began to migrate is not clear, but archaeologists generally believe that they established settlements along the Omo and Tana Rivers, near Lake TURKANA, centuries before the common era. The Somali, known as the Samaale or Sam, reportedly migrated away from the main group in Ethiopia during the first millennium BCE. Traveling along the plains of northern Kenya, by the first century CE the Samaale had established communities along the Tana River as far as the coast of the Indian Ocean. It is also believed that, in this same period, segmented groups of the Samaale crossed the Ogaden, or Ogaadeen, Plains along the southern shore of the RED SEA. There they occupied the region that came to be known as HORN OF AFRICA.

Social Structure and Economy The clan structure of the Somali appears to have been in place at an early period. Comprised of descendants who traced their lineage to a common ancestor, Somali clans spoke a common language and maintained similar cultural and religious beliefs.

One of the most controversial aspects of Somalia's social and economic structure has involved the widespread tradition of female CIRCUMCISION. Believed to date back thousands of years, the form of circumcision practiced in Somalia was a severe RITE OF PASSAGE for young women. A crude, surgical procedure that altered the female genitalia, the goal of circumcision was to ensure sexual abstinence before marriage. It was also considered a sound economic practice that emphasized entitlement to BRIDEWEALTH, a critical factor for prospective brides and their families.

The region's dry, grassy plains undoubtedly influenced the tradition of nomadic herding. The mobility of animals like CATTLE, oxen, and CAMELS offered an escape during both catastrophic droughts and the rainy seasons, which occurred from March to May and October to

December. Other animals, such as sheep and goats, added important staples like milk products to the Somali diet. The maintenance of their herds was critical, and clans frequently clashed as a result of strong competition for grazing land and water.

Early Trading Ties Known to the ancient world as the Land of PUNT, Somalia's location provided an important link to the Red Sea, MEDITERRANEAN SEA, and Indian Ocean trade. The recovery of Parthian coins from the first and second century, as well as Roman coins dating back to the third century CE, confirm the existence of widespread trading activities. TRADE also encouraged the rise of Somalian civilization, whose economic advantages once rivaled EGYPT, KUSH, and its neighbor, Ethiopia. Expeditions from Egypt to Punt began as early as ancient Egypt's First and Second Dynasties (c. 3407–2888 BCE) and initially consisted of caravans that followed overland routes through the NILE RIVER valley. These methods of transportation were abandoned by the time of the Fifth Dynasty, and King Sahure (2708–2697 BCE) made one of the first recorded attempts to reach Punt by boat. Egyptians grew dependent upon Somalia for its rare goods, including GOLD, ivory, incense trees, animal skins and other rare items. In return, Somalia received weapons, such as daggers and hatchets, and valuable pieces of jewelry.

The most notable visitor to Punt in this early period was Hatshepsut (1479–1457 BCE), whose tomb at DEIR EL-BAHRI in Thebes contained images of her journey. These scenes offer one of the few portrayals of the ancient world, with its inhabitants living in cone-shaped huts reached by ladder. A local chief, known as Perehu, and his wife, Ese, were also depicted. Centuries of trading also introduced elements of Egyptian culture into Somalia, including the worship of AMUN and the observance of an annual holiday known as the Feast of the Pharaoh.

Much later in history, the Arabs who traded in Somalia established commercial ports there, exporting cinnamon, tortoiseshell, ivory, rhinoceros horn, and palm oil. By the end of the fourth century, these ports had grown into thriving settlements, which was a contributing factor in the eventual spread of Islam in Somalia.

See also: INDIAN OCEAN TRADE (Vol. II); SOMALI (Vol. II); SOMALIA (Vol. III).

sorghum

Cereal type of grain made from a domesticated plant indigenous to Africa. Sorghum has been described as one of the most important cereal grains in Africa.

Evidence of its earliest use has been traced to the Late STONE AGE. However, more is known about its use in various regions of the Sudan during the period between approximately 6000 to 5000 BCE. Sorghum initially grew in the wild, and its cultivation has been linked to the development of microlithic, or small, sharpened blades and grinding tools. It became domesticated over centuries of planting and harvesting and is therefore linked to the settlement and growth of sedentary populations. Division of labor by age and gender also developed from annual cycles of planting.

Sudan's regional variety of sorghum, also known as *durra*, gained additional popularity further north along the NILE RIVER, and it has been widely referenced as a diet staple in EGYPT and the neighboring Kushite kingdom of MEROË.

Considered a carbohydrate, sorghum was made into porridge or served with fish, meat, or other vegetables. It was common for many families to consume this staple from a shared dish, a tradition reflecting the value of shared labor.

Sorghum plants were transplanted to other regions through trade, changing in form and texture in response to environmental conditions. Consequently, at least five different varieties flourished throughout Africa. The plant reportedly reached ETHIOPIA and regions bordering the SAHARA Desert between 3500 and 2500 BCE. In East Africa, sorghum was called *mtama*, while in West Africa it eventually became known as Guinea corn. South Africa was the last region of the continent to receive sorghum; it was probably transplanted there by migrating BANTU speakers.

By 1000 BCE, this popular African staple had been transported to India, where it was widely cultivated.

See also: AGRICULTURE (Vol. I); CROPS (Vol. II); FOOD (Vol. II).

Further reading: Elizabeth Isichei, *A History of African Societies to 1870* (New York: Cambridge University Press, 1997); Phyllis M. Martin and Patrick O'Meara, *Africa* (Bloomington: Indiana University Press, 1995); James L. Newman, *The Peopling of Africa* (New Haven, Conn.: Yale University Press, 1995).

spider

. Spiders live in many different terrains and exist in over 34,000 species. The spider is a common figure in African lore, and the ASHANTI spider god ANANSI is especially well-known.

spirit possession

The condition of being physically and mentally controlled by spiritual entities. Although widely misunderstood, for centuries spirit possession has served as an integral component of African religion. As such, it is a common feature and has existed in most societies from an ancient period. Individuals who have undergone possession have variously described it as being taken over, invaded, or displaced by an entity over which little or no control can be exerted. Some individuals in the throes of possession shake violently; some become sick and may faint. After the initial shock to the body, the person possessed serves as a medium for the spirit and often counsels those in attendance.

In Songhai, in the present-day Republic of Niger, women traditionally served as mediums. Their ability to become a medium for the spirits was reportedly acquired from relatives or friends. Once chosen to perform this task, mediums were expected to pay homage to the spirit by performing helpful acts within their society.

There are a number of ways in which the spirits are "called" into action. In Songhai society, the *godji* has long been considered a sacred instrument used for this purpose. Sometimes compared to a one-string violin in look and sound, the *godji* is made from a CALABASH gourd covered with animal skin. When played, it produces a unique vibrational sound as a result of the tautness of the string, usually horsehair, and the empty cavity of the calabash. Some have even compared the sound produced by the wooden bow to a high-pitched cry.

Other groups, such as the YORUBA and Tiv of NIGERIA have traditionally used DRUMS along with specific songs and DANCE to induce spirit possession among initiates and devotees. Sacred or ritual dance often involves complex movements, and the drum is said to create a higher awareness through its deeply rhythmic tones. The drum has traditionally offered many societies the ability to tap into an important source of mystical power.

These aspects, while highly significant, have always represented only a small portion of the concept of spirit possession. While in this state, individuals have been known to effectively heal infertility or cure bodily illness with a "laying on of hands" to specific parts of the body. Medicinal herbs, and communal treatment might also be employed to correct personal or societal imbalances. Mediums usually maintain their ability to act as a voice for the gods by tending a special shrine and performing ritual offerings consisting of food, COWRIE SHELLS, or other forms of currency, as well as sacrificial gifts of small animals.

See also: EGUNGUN (Vol. I); MASK (Vol. I); ORACLE (Vol. I); ORISHA (Vol. I); RELIGION, TRADITIONAL (Vol. I); WITCHCRAFT (Vol. I); SONGHAI (Vol. II).

Further reading: Samuel A. Floyd, Jr. *The Power of Black Music: Interpreting Its History from Africa to the United States* (New York: Oxford University Press, 1995); John S. Mbiti, *African Religions and Philosophy,* 2nd ed. (Oxford, Eng.: Heinemann Educational Publishers, 1999); Paul Stoller, "Sounds and Things: Pulsations of Power in Songhai," in *The Performance of Healing*, Carol Laderman and Marina Roseman, eds. (New York: Routledge, 1996).

step pyramid of Djoser Built around the twenty-eighth century BCE, this large structure is considered to be the first pyramid in history and the earliest stone building in ancient Egypt. Located in SAQQARA, commissioned by the pharaoh Djoser (2650–2575 BCE), and designed by the architect IMHOTEP, it represents a dramatic and innovative departure in tomb architecture from the flat-roofed, mud-brick mastabas that preceded it.

Scholars believe that when Djoser, the second king of the Third Dynasty, ordered the building of his tomb at Saqqara, he intended to have a mastaba, which is a an oblong-shaped tomb. The royal tomb is in the original building and is found 90 feet (27.4 m) under the ground, with a vertical shaft leading to it—a design typical of previous mastabas. However, the architect Imhotep departed from the tradition of using mud bricks and constructed this building entirely of stone, which, as far as historians know, had never been done before. A block of granite weighing 3 tons (2.7 metric tons) was used to close the tomb, and the face was covered in Tura limestone.

The building was enlarged in the next phase of construction, and, in a third phase, a second tier was added. The architecture of the mastaba was now changed significantly. In addition to the innovation of stone as the sole building material, the shape became square instead of rectangular and the tomb building no longer had the traditional flat top. Plans developed to add two more tiers, each one smaller in size than the one underneath it, thus creating a stepped building. Then two more steps were added to the four that already existed, creating the final, six-stepped pyramid. When the six phases of building were completed, the pyramid rose to a height of around 200 feet (61 m).

Inside this great pyramid, passageways link several chambers, some of which are tiled in blue. The walls of the Tomb Chamber bear inscriptions stating that its intended purpose was burial use. Outside, white limestone temples and other buildings stood around the pyramid. Surrounding the entire area was a wall, believed to be a reproduction of the MEMPHIS walls.

Some of the casing blocks used to support the tiers of the pyramid are still intact today, but the outer limestone casing has disappeared, as has part of the stone structure. A statue of Djoser was found in the Tomb Chamber by excavators in the 1920s, and can be seen today in the Egyptian Museum in CAIRO.

Stone Age Early period of human development characterized by the use of stone tools. Over the years, Africa has been a leading source of information about both these tools and the early humans who created them. Many archaeological excavations have been carried out on the continent, and discoveries made in present-day Kenya, South Africa, Tanzania, and ETHIOPIA have added significantly to our understanding of our earliest human ancestors. Thousands of fossilized remains have been found at these archaeological sites, some, like one in Aramis, Ethiopia, dating back more than 4.4 million years. From these discoveries, scientists have been able to establish that Africa is the most likely birthplace of humankind.

They also have been able to establish a clear-cut chronology of human development during the period we now call the Stone Age.

Early Stone Age The earliest known stone tools recovered with the *Homo* species have led archaeologists to determine that Early Stone Age began about 2.5 million BCE and was divided into two parts. The first part is known as the OLDOWAN phase. It was named for the tools found at OLDUVAI GORGE in Tanzania and is linked with both *HOMO HABILIS* and *HOMO ERECTUS*. (Archaeologists have found examples of these tools among the fossilized remains of *Homo habilis*.) These tools represent a significant advancement over the digging sticks and simple stone tools that first gave the Stone Age its name.

The tools made at Olduvai had flaked or sharpened edges and were used to cut, scrape, and chop food. (The food was most likely obtained through scavenging.) These tools probably were made by repeatedly striking one stone against another, gradually chipping away pieces until the tool was left with a sharpened edge.

Scientists use several dating methods to unlock the mysteries of the past. One of the most prominent methods is radiocarbon (carbon 14 or C) dating. Radiocarbon dating can analyze evidence dating back to 40,000 BCE. This system is based on the radioactivity present in the atmosphere of the earth. All living matter ingests trace amounts of carbon 14. When death occurs, carbon 14 is released at a rate that can be measured in fossils, charcoal, burned bone, shell, hair, and other organic materials. Using this system, archaeologists have been able to reconstruct a chronology of human history starting with the Stone Age and progressing to the AGRICULTURAL REVOLUTION and IRON AGE.

Middle Stone Age (Acheulean Period) This middle phase of the Stone Age lasted from c. 1.5 million to 40,000 BCE. This period is known for the widespread use of what has become known as the ACHEULEAN TOOLKIT, a distinctive set of hand axes and scrapers. (The name comes from the region in southern France where the tools of this type were first discovered.)

Although these and other Acheulean tools have also been unearthed in Europe and Asia, the vast majority of the items have been recovered in Africa, particularly in an area spreading from the MAHGRIB to the Cape of Good Hope.

Regardless of where they have been found, however, these tools all exhibit a remarkably similar shape and rely on a similar method of construction. This has led some archaeologists to speculate that *Homo erectus*, the human species dominant in Africa through most of the Middle Stone Age, was the first human species to use the tools. These archaeologists also believe that *Homo erectus* later crossed early land bridges and migrated to places outside Africa.

In comparison to Oldowan tools, Acheulean tools are sharper and heavier. They have chipped flakes on both sides as well as sharpened points. Some of these tools seem to have had religious or ritual functions, including the burial of the dead. But most of the tools were used, in one way or another, for preparing food. The use of these tools allowed the diet of early humans to become more diverse, and there is evidence that *Homo erectus* consumed hares, warthogs, and antelopes, as well as fish and seals caught along Africa's western and southern coasts. *Homo erectus* also mastered the use of fire during this period and began moving in groups to specific sites or camps as the seasons changed. These camps often were located in wooded landscapes, which allowed these early humans to take advantage of natural caves and rock shelters. Investigations at the most well-used of these sites have found signs of regular social activities, including cooperative food preparation, communal cooking, and protection from a dangerous environment.

About 150,000 years ago, near the end of the Middle Stone Age, the human species we now know as *HOMO SAPIENS* emerged. *Homo sapiens* used an even more varied stone toolkit, all made from a prepared "core" or model. This form of tool production produced sharper knives and scrapers, as well as the spearheads they attached to

Early Stone Age Tool Sites

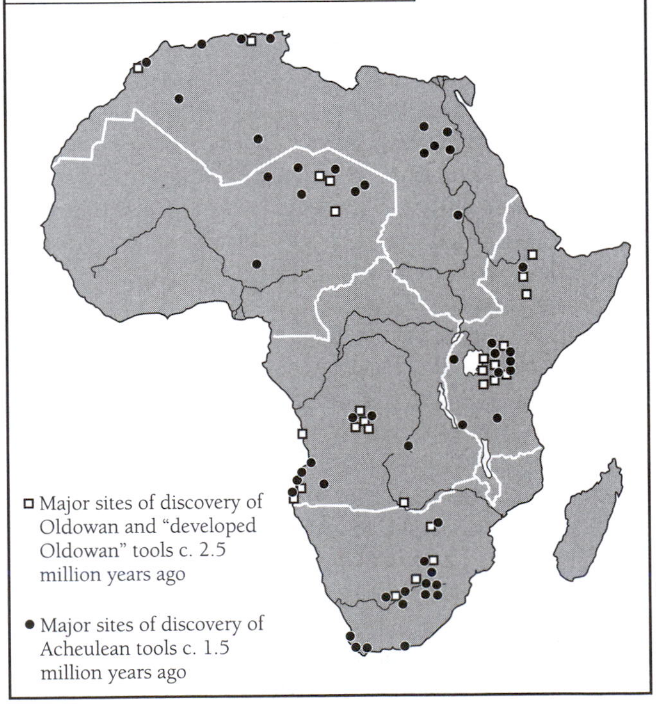

wooden shafts by some form of vegetable glue. Archaeologists speculate that during this period, *Homo sapiens* built the first houses, using such natural elements as branches, grass, and stones. In the cooler regions of northern and southern Africa, however, groups of *Homo sapiens* continued to live in rock shelters.

Late Stone Age During the Late Stone Age, which lasted from c. 40,000 to 3200 BCE, *Homo sapiens* dominated the African landscape. Although the tools they used varied from region to region, *Homo sapiens's* use of microliths ("tiny stones") marked the most advanced phase of stone tool production. Microliths, which archaeologists have found in savanna grasslands and dry woodlands, are stone flakes that have been refined into tiny points and blades, sometimes shaped into triangles or crescents.

One of the best-preserved Late Stone Age sites is found at Gwisho Springs in central Zambia. Microlith artifacts, along with the skeletal remains of approximately thirty early humans, have been found in the waterlogged soil of Kafue Valley.

Late Stone Age hunters fashioned weapons with sharp rock tools, including, in the savanna regions, the earliest known form of the bow and arrow. The sharp stone tips were coated with a form of poison that slowly killed large animals. Other tools included decorated stones with bored holes designed to fit over digging sticks; harpoon barbs made of bone; awls; needles; fishhooks; and an assortment of fine bone tools. In the woodland regions, people still used many of the Acheulean tools developed in the Middle Stone Age, including hand axes and spears. Late Stone Age hunters also set carefully concealed traps and pits to catch animals.

The widespread use of these and other tools by 10,000 BCE indicates a broad and well-defined range of human activity. It seems likely that early humans lived in kinship groups, with men hunting wild animals to provide meat, and women and children gathering wild fruit, nuts, melons, and edible insects like termites, caterpillars, and LOCUSTS. They also used digging sticks to find roots and tubers beneath the soil.

Excavations have shown that, during the Late Stone Age, humans wore body ornaments made of eggshell, bone, or stones, and animal skins were used for CLOTHING and shelter. Much about life at this time has been learned from ROCK ART, and various scenes of ancient life have been found in desert caves. These include images of animals, grain harvests, women performing ritual dances, and symbols whose meanings are not yet understood.

See also: HUMAN ORIGINS (Vol. I); NEOLITHIC AGE (Vol. I).

Further reading: Philip Curtin, Steven Feierman, Leonard Thompson and Jan Vansina, *African History: From Ancient Times to Independence* (London: Longman Group Limited, 1995); Rosalind Jefferies, "The Image of Women in African Cave Art," Ivan Van Sertima, ed. *Black Women in Antiquity* (New Brunswick, N.J.: Transaction Publishers, 1997); Samuel Kasule, *The History Atlas of Africa* (New York: Macmillan, Inc., 1998).

stratigraphy The study of sequences of sediments, soils, and rocks used by archaeologists to determine the approximate age of a region.

The archaeological study of strata, or layers of deposit, developed from the study of rock layers in geology. This type of study helps determine what human events, cultural rituals, or agricultural practices occurred over time, creating a chronology of historical events. Generally, the oldest layers make up the bottom layers and may sometimes be lighter in color. The more recent layers are closer to the top and may appear darker. This is known as the Law of Superposition. Stratigraphy has played an especially important role in many regions of Africa, where centuries of natural erosion have exposed layers of deposits. An important example of this occurred in HADAR, a site located in ETHIOPIA. Based on the analysis of the fossilized remains of a young woman and the strata that surrounded her, archaeologists have been able to determine that this woman, called Dinkenesh by the Ethiopians and LUCY by the scientific community, lived millions of years ago.

See also: ARCHAEOLOGY (Vol. I)

Sudd Vast swamp in southern Sudan, approximately 200 miles (320 km) long and 225 miles (360 km) wide. *Sudd* is an Arabic word that refers to the barrier created by floating water plants, dense PAPYRUS, vegetation, tangled reeds, and marshes. Although the swamp is fed by the tributaries of the WHITE NILE, the Sudd's floating matter forms thick stagnant islands, due largely to the lower gradient of the land.

In ancient times, the Sudd prevented the Egyptians from exploring lands south of the Nile. Later, the Roman commentator Seneca claimed that the Sudd prevented Emperor Nero's Roman army from being able to "penetrate ETHIOPIA." Infested with deadly diseases and inhabited by dangerous wildlife, including CROCODILES, HIPPOPOTAMUS, snakes, and biting insects, the Sudd has, for centuries, been the homeland of the Dinka and NUER peoples, seminomads who inhabit the grassy plains between water courses.

See also: DINKA (Vols. II, III).

Sumeria Ancient civilization located in MESOPOTAMIA, in the fertile valley formed by the Tigris and Euphrates Rivers.

Along the banks of the Tigris are ruins of such ancient cities as Nineveh, Ctesiphon, and Seleucia. The Sumerians, who some believe to have been of African descent, were the first people to inhabit Mesopotamia. Around 5000 BCE, they drained and settled the swampland areas of the Persian Gulf and then built settlements and established farms. The silt from the flooding of the Tigris made the Mesopotamian land especially fertile. Major crops of this area were wheat, barley, MILLET, rice, corn, and SORGHUM. These early settlements later became Sumeria's city-states—the first cities in human history—and included Eridu, Lagash, Nippur, and Ur. The Sumerians achieved many cultural milestones, among them early systems of writing, mathematics, law, and ASTRONOMY. Much of their influence was seen in such other cultures as the Akkadian and Israelite.

The Sumerians developed canals and IRRIGATION systems to control the flooding of the Tigris. As early as 2400 BCE, a canal was dug from the Tigris to the city-state of Lagash. Records from 3000 BCE indicate that the Sumerians also understood the problems of over-irrgation. Their response was to rotate crops, shifting from wheat to more SALT-resistant barley in order to deal with the ill effects of salinization. (Salinization, which is the buildup of salt in soil, often occurs in land that has been irrigated for long periods.)

Following the decline of Sumerian civilization around 2000 BCE, a number of civilizations, including the ASSYRIANS and the Persians, were established in the area. As a testament to the ingenuity of the Sumerians, the people who succeeded them continued many of the practices that the Sumerians had established.

Suswa Ancient volcano located in western Kenya, near Lake Laivasha. Mount Suswa is located on the floor of the Great RIFT VALLEY and consists of two concentric craters. The outer crater has a diameter of 6 miles (9.7 km), with its south and east sides eroded. The outer crater also contains numerous caves. The inner crater has a diameter of between 2 and 3 miles (3.2 and 4.8 km) and consists of a sloping island surrounded by a sort of moat. No eruptions of Mount Suswa have been recorded, although geologists believe that the volcano may have erupted at some time during the past 10,000 years.

T

Tallensi (Talis) Sedentary agriculturists who have long been situated primarily in the northeastern region of GHANA. The Tallensi appear to be one of the few peoples in Africa that have maintained an ancient way of life. As long ago as the IRON AGE, and possibly earlier, the Tallensi began to live in a highly organized CLAN structure whose members trace their descent from a single male figure. Elected clan leaders rule the group.

One of the most important political institutions that developed in Tallensi society is called *Tendana*, which means the "custodians of the earth." This organization emphasizes the life-sustaining properties of the earth. Those chosen to serve as custodians inherit the responsibility from clan members. Traditionally, they are identified by the animal skins they wear, and they participate in rituals and work at special shrines to ensure the fertility of the earth. Priests and ritual specialists among the custodians also are supposed to mediate between earth and water.

See also: NUER (Vol. I).

Further reading: Martha G. Anderson and Christine Mullen Kreamer, *Wild Spirits Strong Medicine: African Art and the Wilderness* (New York: The Center for African Art, 1989); Kwame Anthony Appiah and Henry Louis Gates, Jr., eds., *Africana: The Encyclopedia of the African and African American Experience* (New York: Basic Civitas Books, 1999): Basil Davidson, *Africa in History*, rev. ed. (New York: Touchstone Books, 1995)

Ta-Meri One of the original names for EGYPT; Ta-Meri means "beloved land" or "land of love."

The name *Egypt* comes from the Greek word *Aigyptos*, the Greek misspelling and mispronunciation of *Hikuptah*, or the temple of Ptah in MEMPHIS. The people of Egypt also called their land KEMET, meaning the "black land," a term that describes the fertile black earth in the valley of the NILE RIVER. Egyptians referred to themselves as "people of Kemet." In contrast, *Ta-Meri* was used in a general way to describe one's homeland, much in the same way that people use the English word "country."

Tanganyika, Lake Second largest of the East African lakes, located on the border between present-day Tanzania and the Democratic Republic of the Congo in the southern portion of the western RIFT VALLEY. Along with extensive mountain ranges and other lakes, Lake Tanganyika forms the boundary between West and East Africa. Tanganyika, at 440 miles (708 km) in length, is the longest freshwater lake in the world, as well as the second deepest at 4,710 feet (1,436 m). The narrow lake is only 45 miles (72 km) across at its widest. Three large rivers flow into the lake—the Malagarasi, the RUZIZI, and the Kalamabo—and its only outlet is the Lukuga River, which flows into the Lualaba.

See also: TANGANYIKA, LAKE (Vol. II).

Tanite The Twenty-first Dynasty of ancient EGYPT; seven Tanite kings reigned from 1075 to 945 BCE. During their rule, Tanite kings maintained control over the priests at Thebes, but their power in areas like Palestine and Syria weakened.

The name *Tanite* is derived from the city of Tanis, which SMENDES, the first Tanite king, established as his capital. Located on the eastern part of the NILE DELTA,

Tanis, at one time, was a commercial center of Egypt. However, the accumulation of silt in the mouth of the Nile near Tanis diverted trade to Alexandria. Tanis was also the capital of the HYKSOS kings of Egypt in the seventeeth century BCE.

After a rebellion against Rome in 174 CE, Tanis was destroyed. The ancient city now sits in ruins, its site partly occupied by the fishing village of San. Studying these ruins, archaeologists have found the remnants of several temples, statues, and a royal necropolis.

Taung Child

Taung Child Remains of an *Australopithecus africanus* child discovered at Taung, in modern-day BOTSWANA.

See also: HUMAN ORIGINS (Vol. I).

The skull of the 1- to 2-million-year-old Taung Child (*Australopithecus africanus*), uncovered in Botswana, fluoresces in black light during a 1985 research study at the National Physical Research Laboratory in Pretoria, South Africa. *© Jonathan Blair/CORBIS*

Tefnakhte (Tefnakht)

Tefnakhte (Tefnakht) (r. c. 727–712 BCE) *Ruler of Sais, in the northwestern Nile Delta region; first king of Egypt's Twenty-fourth Dynasty.*

Tefnakhte has been variously described as a delta prince, a Libyan prince, a lord or chieftain of Sais, and a prophet. As ruler of LOWER EGYPT, Tefnakhte advanced south in an ultimately unsuccessful attempt to capture UPPER EGYPT from PIANKHY, the king of NUBIA.

From his capital of Sais, in the NILE DELTA, Tefnakhte succeeded in gathering allies and claiming territory to the west and as far south as Lisht. He then turned his campaigns toward the east and conquered several towns on the eastern bank of the NILE RIVER. Looking to claim UPPER EGYPT for his own, Tefnakhte moved on and conquered the Middle Egyptian town of Hermopolis. Piankhy was stirred to action by this and quickly drove Tefnakhte's forces back to MEMPHIS.

At Memphis, according to ancient historian MANETHO, Tefnakhte organized 8,000 soldiers for battle, while Tefnakhte himself rode north on horseback in an effort to rally other Delta princes to his aid. Piankhy defeated Tefnakhte's forces at Memphis, after which Tefnakhte submitted and swore an oath to obey the king who had defeated him. Inexplicably, Piankhy returned to his home at Napata, in NUBIA, upon which Tefnakhte declared himself king of EGYPT.

Tehuti (Thoth, Hermes)

Tehuti (Thoth, Hermes) *Ancient scribe, or writer, associated with universal wisdom and truth.*

Considered the SCRIBE of the gods as well as the inventor of both WRITING and MUSIC, Tehuti was also the primary lawgiver. According to many ancient beliefs, it was Tehuti who carved sacred HIEROGLYPHICS on stelae for an extinct race of people known as the Anu (Kushites). Prominent in Egyptian mythology, he also appears in the BOOK OF THE DEAD, usually assisting OSIRIS, the judge of the dead, in the task of recording the weight of human deeds. Tehuti was also associated with the goddess ISIS, providing her with the magic she needed in order to resurrect her murdered husband, Osiris. The planet Mercury, the number seven, and the ibis were just a few of his sacred symbols.

Some ancient myths indicate that Tehuti wrote nearly 40,000 books and lived more than 300 years. This notable longevity was supposedly the result of Tehuti's encounter with the Great Dragon, the Egyptian symbol for intellect and the "Mind of the Universe." Other myths dispute this, indicating instead that there were two individuals with the same name, one living during Egypt's prehistoric era and the other during the time of IMHOTEP (c. 2700 BCE). Regardless, by the fifth century BCE, the Greeks recognized Tehuti as Hermes Mercurius Trismegistus, the "thrice great" or "master of masters."

According to legend, Tehuti's vast knowledge was recorded as the Book of THOTH and kept in a golden box.

During the early Christian period, the legends continue, one of Tehuti's initiates sought to safeguard the box by transporting it to an unnamed region, where it was never found again. Instead, forty-two fragmentary writings attributed to Tehuti have survived as the Hermetic philosophy, elements of which can be found in the Christian Bible, Chinese mythology, and the Buddhist traditions of South Asia.

Tetisheri (r. c. 1570 BCE) *Queen of ancient Egypt's Seventeenth Dynasty.*

Tetisheri paved the way for the even more powerful female rulers who succeeded her, including her descendant Hatshepsut (Eighteenth Dynasty), one of the few women pharaohs of ancient EGYPT.

Unlike women in other ancient male-dominated cultures, Egyptian women, even commoners, had legal rights, could own and inherit property, and held public office. Tetisheri was such a common Egyptian woman who married Ta'o I and became queen in Thebes. During the late Seventeenth Dynasty, the role of the queen changed into a more powerful and influential position in which queen consorts like Tetisheri probably acted as regents, or members of a governing body. Tetisheri and the queens who succeeded her, Ahhotep II and Ahmose-Nefertary, all contributed to the general understanding of women as influential and capable rulers, paving the way for Hatshepsut to become one of the most remarkable female pharaohs in the history of ancient Egypt.

Tetishiri lived to be seventy years old and was honored for her service to her country. She has been called the "mother of the NEW KINGDOM" due to her influential role and because of the importance of her son, Ta'o II, and grandsons, WADJKHEPERRE (also called Kamose; last king of the Seventeenth Dynasty) and AHMOSE I (first king of the New Kingdom). She was given an estate and a tomb, in addition to the monument that was erected for her at ABYDOS. Information about Tetisheri is known from a stele describing the words of King Amosis in which he speaks of the deceased great queen. Although two statuettes of Tetisheri are thought to have come from her tomb at Thebes, the one brought to the British Museum in 1890 has been proven to be a forgery.

Further reading: Ivan van Sertima, ed., *Black Women in Antiquity* (New Brunswick, N.J.: Transaction Publishers, 1997); Barbara Watterson, *The Egyptians* (Oxford, Eng.: Blackwell Publishers, 1998).

textile production The manufacturing of woven or knit cloth for use as CLOTHING, blankets, bandages, burial shrouds, and tents; textiles have been produced since the beginning of civilization.

One of the earliest known fabrics of human manufacture was linen, which was made from flax, a long-stemmed plant that grew along the NILE RIVER. Ancient Egyptians made linen as early as 5000 BCE. First, the flax was pulled from the ground and soaked in water. The fibers were then separated from the stems and beaten until they were soft. These fibers were next twisted into thread that was woven into linen on a loom. The ancient Egyptians used linen for everything from the robes and loincloths they wore to the bandages in which they wrapped their mummies.

Elsewhere in Africa, nomadic Bedouins used the hair of domesticated goats and sheep to weave the tents in which they lived. Strips of coarse CLOTH known as *fala'if* made from this animal hair were then sewn together into a long rectangular shape and supported by tent poles. These tents were lightweight and easily taken down.

The BERBER people of North Africa also used animal hair and wool to weave tents and carpets. These textiles were often dyed with roots and herbs and featured intricately woven symbols that were meant to scare away evil spirits.

The ASHANTI people of GHANA and the Kuba people of Congo (formerly Zaïre) were also renowned for their intricate textiles, which are woven from palm fibers. The best-known Ashanti cloth is called *kente* and is worn at various ceremonies. (See picture, page 220.)

See also: EGYPT (Vol. 1); CLOTH (Vols. II, III).

Thinis (This) Ancient town in UPPER EGYPT, south of CAIRO, long believed to be the origin or capital of the First and Second Dynasties (c. 3050–2705 BCE); however, many scholars now doubt the accuracy of this assertion.

Excavations at ABYDOS near Thinis uncovered several mastabas, or open stone tombs, that were thought to be the burial sites of the Egyptian First Dynasty rulers. The historian MANETHO (c. third century BCE) claimed that Thinis was the capitol of both the First and Second Dynasties. However, larger and more elaborate tombs of the same period have been found elsewhere, as have other important mastabas. This has led scholars to question the claims that the early dynasties originated at Thinis. It is not known whether the mastabas near Thinis were used for burials or just for memorials.

Two notable figures from Egyptian history are often associated with Thinis. One was the mythical god of hunting and war, Anhur, whose cult began in Thinis. In addition, MENES (also known as Narmer), the figure who became known for uniting the lands of UPPER EGYPT and LOWER EGYPT, was reputedly born in the town of Thinis.

Thoth Greek name for the ancient Egyptian god of wisdom, WRITING, learning, and the moon; according to legend, Thoth invented HIEROGLYPHICS and possessed magical powers; also according to legend, he was present at the reckoning of the dead.

As a SCRIBE of the AFTERLIFE, Thoth was credited with writing the BOOK OF THE DEAD. As the representative of the

This textile from the footrest of Tutankhamun (c. 1347–1337 BCE) shows conquered African and Asian warriors. Egyptian Museum, Cairo, Egypt © *Gianni Dagli Orti/CORBIS*

Thoth, the Egyptian god of wisdom, writing, learning, and the Moon, is often depicted as a human being with the head of an ibis. The Louvre Museum, Paris, France © *Gianni Dagli Orti/CORBIS*

sun god, RA, Thoth used a balance scale to measure the heart of the deceased against the weight of the feather of Truth, supposedly in order to see if the heart was light. Thoth reported on the deceased to other gods who passed judgment.

The method of picture-writing called HIEROGLYPHICS is credited to Thoth, and he is often represented carrying a pen and a scroll. Also, the Moon is said to have come into being because of Thoth's desire to rid the nighttime world of darkness. Possessing magic powers and creating the magical arts, Thoth is considered to have invented the tarot deck, which is often called the Book of Thoth.

Thoth was typically pictured as a human with the head of an ibis, a bird which is a member of the stork family, although sometimes he was depicted as a BABOON.

According to legend, Thoth created himself, as did MA'AT, the goddess of truth. Together, they were said to have eight children, including the god AMUN.

Thutmose I (King Akheperkare Thutmose I, Thutmosis I) (r. c. 1525–1512 BCE) *Third king of the ancient Egyptian Eighteenth Dynasty, who was renowned for restoring Egyptian military might.*

Thutmose legitimized his claim to the throne that his brother-in-law, AMENHOTEP I, had left him by marrying Amenhotep's sister, the princess Ahmose. Their marriage produced four children. One of the siblings, a daughter named Hatshepsut, later succeeded to the throne of Egypt, following the reign of her half-brother THUTMOSE II.

A great warrior, Thutmose I conducted several military campaigns against Egypt's old enemies, the Nubians and the HYKSOS. The king's ferocity is immortalized in the story of his triumphant return from a Nubian campaign with the body of a Nubian chieftain hanging from the prow of his ship. Thutmose was so successful in waging war against the Hyksos in Syria that he extended his empire as far as the Euphrates River. Thutmose's empire-building set a pattern that his successors copied throughout the remainder of the Eighteenth Dynasty.

Thutmose's two sons by Queen Ahmose both died before him. Thutmose II, the king's son by a lesser wife, succeeded his father to the throne.

Thutmose II (King Akheperenre Thutmose II, Thutmosis II) (r. c. 1512–c. 1504 BCE) *Fourth king of the Eighteenth Dynasty in Egypt.*

The son of THUTMOSE I and a lesser wife named Mutnofret, Thutmose II married his half-sister Hatshepsut and remained in her shadow throughout his reign. Their union produced no son to succeed him. Although Thutmose II was never in good health, he managed to oversee several successful military campaigns in both Syria and Nubia. He died at about the age of thirty, leaving the throne to THUTMOSE III, a son by a concubine named Isis.

Thutmose III (King Menkheperre Thutmose III, Thutmosis III) (r. c. 1504–c.1450 BCE) *Fifth king and great military leader of the ancient Egyptian Eighteenth Dynasty whose campaigns established Egyptian supremacy in Nubia and Asia Minor.*

The son of THUTMOSE II and a concubine, Isis, Thutmose III was not old enough to rule alone when his father died. As a result, he shared the throne with his late father's queen, Hatshepsut, ruling with her for about two years until Hatshepsut abandoned the co-regency and seized the throne for herself. She pushed Thutmose III into the background, where he remained until her death c. 1482 BCE. When he finally regained the throne, Thutmose III sought to erase the memory of Hatshepsut's reign by destroying the monuments she and her supporters had built.

While Hatshepsut reigned as pharaoh, Thutmose III apparently spent his time in the army. Ironically, his military exile ultimately served him well: As soon as he became pharaoh in his own right, Thutmose III was faced with a Mitanni revolt in Asia Minor. The struggle with the Mitanni, one of Egypt's greatest enemies, continued throughout Thutmose III's reign. He is reported to have engaged in seventeen campaigns before he conquered them. It was these military expeditions, more than any others he conducted, that established Thutmose's reputation as a great general.

Thutmose III was as enthusiastic about building as about waging war. In the last years of his reign, during a period of peace and prosperity for Egypt, he erected and transformed many splendid monuments. One of the most important of these was the Temple of KARNAK at Thebes, dedicated to the god AMUN.

Thutmose was succeeded by AMENHOTEP II, his son from his marriage to his second wife, Hatshepsut-Merytre. Well into his eighties when he died, Thutmose III was buried in a tomb in the VALLEY OF THE KINGS.

See also: RA (Vol. I).

Thutmose IV (King Menkheprure Thutmose IV, Thutmose IV) (c. 1425–1417 BCE) *Seventh king of the ancient Egyptian Eighteenth Dynasty; known for his piety and his restoration of the Great Sphinx at Giza.*

Son of AMENHOTEP II and his sister, Queen Tio, Thutmose IV married Mutemwiya, who most likely was a Mitanni princess. The reign of Thutmose IV was, for the most part, uneventful, except for two military campaigns, one in Nubia and the other in Syria. The Syrian campaign earned him the title "Conqueror of Syria."

Thutmose IV was succeeded by AMENHOTEP III, his son by Queen Mutemwiya. Buried in the VALLEY OF THE KINGS, Tuthmosis IV's mummy was found in 1898 in the tomb of AMENHOTEP II, along with those of other pharaohs.

tigil Ancient Ethiopian sport involving fists and wrestling poses.

See also: BOXING (Vol. I).

Tigray Remote region situated near the Eritrean border in the northeastern Ethiopian Highlands; also the Tigray people who live there.

At least 40,000 years ago, small communities of farmers and pastoralists dominated the mountainous landscape of Tigray. Primarily Kushitic speakers, they included the Amarar, the Hassaub, and the BEJA. By about 1000 BCE, these groups were joined by traders who crossed the RED SEA from southern Arabia. Centuries of intermarriage between these groups and others followed. The result was a culture that combined the traditions of many different groups and a writing script, known as GE'EZ, that grew out of such languages as TIGRINYA, ARABIC, and Hebrew.

Between 800–300 BCE, Da'amat and Saba flourished as well-established centers of trade and commerce at the Tigray-Eritrean border. Their rulers, known as Mukarribs, built temples with inscribed altars and stone sculptures. The Temple of Ilmuqah, considered the most ancient building in ETHIOPIA, is one of the few surviving relics attesting to the former greatness of Da'amat and Saba. Eventually, Da'amat and Saba were supplanted as the area's most prosperous trading centers by the neighboring kingdom of AKSUM.

See also: BETA ISRAEL (Vol. I); ERITREA (Vols. I, II, III); TIGRAY (VOL. II).

Further reading: James L. Newman, *The Peopling of Africa: A Geographic Interpretation* (New Haven, Conn.: Yale University Press, 1995); Roland Oliver and Brian Fagan, *African in the Iron Age* (New York: Cambridge University Press, 1994).

Tigré A primarily Muslim, Tigré-speaking people who share a common heritage with the Christian Tigrinya-speaking people, called TIGRAY, who founded the ancient kingdom of AKSUM in present-day ETHIOPIA. Both the Tigré and the Tigrinya languages are related to GE'EZ, the ancient liturgical language of Ethiopia. The two peoples and the two languages are sometimes confused by outsiders. Thus, the Muslim Tigré are sometimes called the northern Tigre in order to distinguish them from the Tigrinya speakers who live to the south. It is thought that the ancestors of the Tigré migrated into the region shortly before the first century. The nomadic pastoralist Tigré, however, were converted to Islam by Muslim traders who brought Islam to the lands bordering the Dahlak Islands and down the coast shortly after the start of the eighth century. Politically, the Tigré are organized into CLANS based on family ties.

See also: PASTORALISM (Vol. I); ISLAM (Vol. II); TIGRAY (Vol. II).

Tigrinya Semitic language from the Afro-Asiatic language group spoken in the highlands of ERITREA. Tigrinya is spoken by the Tigrinya, or TIGRAY, people, whose ancestors resulted from an intermingling of native Kushitic peoples with Semitic immigrants who came to Africa from Arabia at the beginning of the common era. The Tigrinya language developed from GE'EZ, the ancient Ethiopian written language that has been traced as far back as the kingdom of AKSUM. Unlike Ge'ez, however, Tigrinya primarily a spoken language.

See also: ETHIOPIA (Vols. I, II, III); KUSH (Vol. I).

totemism Ancient system of belief that recognizes divine spirits through symbols or objects associated with nature. For thousands of years, the people of Africa have created totems representing animals, plants, trees, rivers, and even sacred sites. More than just symbols of the divine, these totems served as companions and guides. They also served to foster cultural identity among ancestral CLANS and, thus, often played important roles in funerals, festivals, and similar events.

Totemism in Africa dates back at least to ancient EGYPT, where, prior to 3200 BCE, a number of Egyptian deities were identified with various natural phenomena. In the NILE VALLEY, for example, OSIRIS originally was represented as a god of vegetation. Similarly, devotees of Sobek, the Egyptian water god, revered the CROCODILE, and the goddess HATHOR was seen in terms of the sacred nature of cows. This totemism remained an important part of Egyptian religious and cultural life down through the Roman occupation.

trade Trade, in Africa, dates back to the earliest times, when STONE AGE HUNTER-GATHERERS simply exchanged tools, food, weapons, livestock, and other items. In many parts of Africa, however, there soon developed more elaborate systems of exchange, and, in some areas, extensive trade routes emerged. Ancient EGYPT, of course, was in the forefront of this, not only utilizing marketplaces and other means of exchange but also sending out trading expeditions to farflung regions. These, as the records of the voyages of HARKUF (c. 2290–2270 BCE) make clear, ventured far down the NILE RIVER and into what was known to the Egyptians as PUNT.

Elsewhere, along the Mediterranean coast, Phoenician and Greek sailors and merchants established settlements in various locations. The most notable of these was CARTHAGE, which was founded c. 800 BCE and which quickly developed into a regional economic and military power. By the sixth century BCE, it was, arguably, the most powerful city in the world, trading extensively in food, slaves, cloth, and metal goods. Its merchants also held monopolies in the trade in GOLD, silver, tin, and iron. Carthaginian sailors and traders led extensive expeditions along the Atlantic coasts of Spain and Portugal, France, and Morocco, venturing, it is believed, as far as Sierra Leone.

Elsewhere, in eastern Africa, Arabian hunters and traders began crossing the Red Sea to do business in ETHIOPIA sometime before 500 BCE. The settlements they founded eventually developed into towns and cities and became the trading centers of MEROË and AKSUM. Meroë served as a nexus for trade between the Roman Empire and the lands beyond, which included those along the Red Sea, the Indian Ocean, and beyond. This mercantile empire flourished for several hundred years before entering a period of decline c. 200–300 CE. Later, during the Aksumite period, this trade became even more extensive. Aksumite traders ventured, on a regular basis, as far as Egypt, Persia, Arabia, India, and Ceylon. Their exports included ivory, obsidian stone, tortoiseshell, and RHINOCEROS horn, while their imports ranged from cloth and metal goods to luxury goods such as wine, olive oil, and lacquerware. The Aksumite economic empire was backed by force, and it conquered lands as distant as southern Arabia in order to maintain its domination of the trade between the Roman Empire and the lands to the east. These militarily protected trading routes were made until Aksum declined midway through the first millennium of the common era.

Trajan's Kiosk Beautiful but unfinished building, supported by fourteen huge columns with carved tops, started by the Roman emperor Trajan, the ruler of Egypt from c. 98 CE to 117 CE.

Trajan's Kiosk was one of several buildings in a complex on Philae Island (or Pilak in ancient Egyptian) whose construction began at the time of Ptolemy II and extended 800 years to the rule of the Roman emperors. Though simple in architecture and design, the tall fourteen columns of the kiosk bear capitals of floral carving. Trajan is depicted in relief on the inside of the kiosk, where he is shown as a king, or pharaoh, making offerings to the gods. The island was often associated with the goddess Isis, who, according to legend, left her scared ship at the kiosk while on the island.

Tswana BANTU-speaking people who migrated into the area of the TSWAPONG HILLS, near present-day BOTSWANA, during the first century.

See also: TSWANA (Vol. III).

Tswapong Hills Elevated area in present-day BOTSWANA that rises 980 to 1,300 feet (300 to 400 m) above the surrounding Kalahari sand. The hills are a source of evidence about BANTU-speaking peoples who migrated into the area c. first century.

See also: HUMAN ORIGINS (Vol. I).

Tuaregs Subgroup of the BERBER people; for centuries, the nomadic Tuaregs have inhabited the SAHARA and SAHEL regions of North Africa.

The Tuareg's presence in northern Africa was noted as long ago as the fifth century BCE by the Greek historian HERODOTUS. Since then, much about these indigo-robed warriors has been shrouded in mystery. Despite pressures that have forced many of the Tuaregs to adopt a more sedentary way of life than their nomadic ancestors, many continue to follow traditions that were established thousands of years ago. They have remained fiercely independent.

Throughout most of their history, the Tuaregs' economic lifeblood depended on the Saharan TRADE and caravan routes that stretched across the desert between the MEDITERRANEAN SEA and the cities to the south. Carrying primarily luxury items—high-profit goods, including slaves, that could be easily transported by the caravans—these merchants brought items to the coast for distribution to the rest of the world. As might be expected, many Tuaregs settled into the communities through which they passed, often serving as agents for the Tuaregs who continued to operate the caravan trade.

Traditionally, the Tuaregs have maintained a feudal society. At one end of the social order were the nobles and clergy, followed by the nobles' vassals and the craftspeople. At the lower end of the social hierarchy were the *iklan*, laborers who most likely were former slaves. As a whole, the society was divided into two groups: farmers and traders. Farming was regarded as lower-class work, while trading was reserved for the upper classes. Over the centuries, however, this distinction was blurred as many sedentary farmers accumulated a great degree of wealth and as the caravan trade lost its importance.

Although the Tuaregs are considered to be Berbers, not Arabs, most are Muslims, reciting daily prayers and observing the major feasts of Islam. Beginning at about the age of twenty-five, Tuareg men begin wearing a veil, concealing all of their faces except for their eyes. In contrast to other Muslim populations, however, Tuareg women never wear veils.

See also: ISLAM (Vol. II); TUAREGS (Vols. II, III).

Tunisia North African country on the coast of the MEDITERRANEAN SEA that was home, in ancient times, to native BERBERS. Due to its proximity to Europe and the Middle East, Tunisia was dominated by a variety of people and kingdoms, including CARTHAGE, the Roman Empire, and the VANDALS.

In the distant past, the PHOENICIANS settled in the northern coastal areas of the African continent for purposes of TRADE, bringing with them new ideas and innovations about farming and city life that influenced the native Berbers. One of these ancient trading posts became Carthage, the capital and largest city of the Carthaginian Empire. Believed to have been established c. 814 BCE under the rule of Queen Dido, Carthage was located near present-day Tunis.

The powerful Carthaginian Empire came to rule most of the North African coast and a large part of Spain, as well as most of Sicily, Corsica, and Sardinia. The great empire ruled for centuries with no serious threats to its control. That changed, however, with Rome's rise to power.

Even though Rome had signed treaties with the Carthaginians, the Romans clearly were seeking opportunities to conquer their rival. The PUNIC WARS, a series of three deadly struggles fought between the Roman and the Carthaginian Empires, began about 264 BCE and ended about 146 BCE. These conflicts resulted in the destruction of the great city of Carthage and the final conquest of North Africa by the Romans.

For the next several centuries, most of Tunisia was known as the Roman province of Africa, or Africa Vetus, and Carthage became an important site of Christian learning and thought. The great Chrstian theologian St. Augustine, for example, is said to have been educated at Carthage.

As with other areas under Roman rule, Tunisa's natural resources were exploited and its land was cultivated by its overlords. Olive oil, wool, wood, and wheat were among the major goods produced in Roman Tunisia. The valley of the Majardah River was the location of an ancient Roman granary, and the area is still one of the largest producers of grain in Tunisia.

The influence of the Roman Empire began to fade by the fifth century, opening the door for the invasion of the Vandals. The Vandals, a Teutonic or Germanic people, ruled Jutland (now Denmark) and invaded lands on the Iberian Peninsula before conquering areas on the northern Mediterranean coast. After 100 years of Vandal rule, the Byzantines, under the command of General Belisarius, again claimed Tunisia for the Eastern Roman Empire, c. 533 CE.

See also: TUNISIA (Vol. III).

Turkana, Lake Large body of water in northwest Kenya and southwest ETHIOPIA; also known in modern times as Lake Rudolph.

Covering an area of about 2,500 square miles (6,475 sq km), Lake Turkana is Africa's fourth-largest lake. HUNTER-GATHERERS are believed to have first inhabited the area surrounding Lake Turkana about 8000 BCE. Five thousand years later, Kushitic peoples moved into the region, probably sharing it with the original natives. Beginning in the first millennium BCE, BANTU-speaking people migrated into the vicinity around, bringing with them both their iron smelting and more advanced agricultural techniques.

A present-day Turkana man stands at the shore of Lake Turkana, Kenya. *© Daniel Laine/CORBIS*

Turkana Boy Example of *Homo erectus* skeleton found in present-day Kenya in 1984; lived approximately 1.6 million years ago.

See also: HUMAN ORIGINS (Vol. I).

Tutankhamun (King Nebkheprure TutbeAnkh-Amen, Tutankhaten, King Tut) (r. c. 1361–1352 BCE) *Eleventh king of Egypt's eighteen Dynasty)*

Tutankhamun became pharaoh at the age of eight or nine, and the boy-king appears to have died at about the age of eighteen. He was married to Ankhesenamun, one of the six daughters of AKHENATEN and his queen, NEFERTITI. Tutankhamun and Ankhesenamun produced no male heirs.

The young royal couple began their lives in Akhenaten's new capital at AMARNA. But, after Akhenaten's death, they fell under the influence of Ay and HOREMHEB, Tutankhamun's successors, and moved to MEMPHIS. There, Tutankhamun was crowned king, and steps were taken to reestablish the old religion abandoned by Akhenaten. By changing their royal names so that they ended in *-amun* instead of *-aten*, Tutankhamun and his queen gave a clear sign of their dedication to the restoration of the traditional religion. It was during this time that Thebes once again became the religious capital of Egypt.

There is a great deal of speculation as to the cause of Tutankhamun's death. It was once commonly believed that he had succumbed to tuberculosis, and it has also been suggested that he died of a brain hemorrhage. However, based on the examination of Tutankhamun's mummy, most scholars agree that he died as a result of a blow to the head. Whether this wound was caused by an accident, a blow sustained during battle, or was the result of an assassination remains a mystery.

After Tutankhamun's death, Ankhesenamun took the unusual action of seeking the help of the HITTITE king, Suppiluliumas I. Without a son to succeed her late husband as pharaoh and continue the royal line, she asked to marry one of the Suppiluliumas's many sons. The king assented and sent one of his sons to Egypt. But the prince never reached his destination, as he was murdered just as he reached the border, possibly on orders from Horemheb.

Tutankhamun's reign was unremarkable. His most important legacy is his tomb, which British archaeologist Howard Carter discovered in 1922, practically untouched more than 3,200 years after his burial. Its contents included magnificent artifacts of GOLD and precious jewels, intricately carved furniture and weapons, luxurious CLOTHING, and, perhaps best known to the modern world, the life-like gold MASK that adorned the case of Tutankhamun's mummy. This tomb was probably not intended as Tutankhamun's final resting place. There is evidence to suggest that it was intended for his predecessor, SMENKHARE, or quite possibly his VIZIER and successor, AY.

See also: AFTERLIFE (Vol. I)

Further reading: Cyril Aldred, *Egyptian Art* (New York: Oxford University Press, 1980); John Romer, *Valley of the Kings* (New York: William Morrow, 1981).

Twa See HUNTER-GATHERERS (Vol. I); TWA (Vol. II).

U

Ubangi River The main northern tributary of the CONGO RIVER system.

The Bomu and Uele Rivers meet to become the Ubangi River, which forms part of the border between what is presently the Democratic Republic of the Congo, also known as Congo (Kinshasa), and the CENTRAL AFRICAN REPUBLIC. The Ubangi River also creates the northwestern border between The Democratic Republic of the Congo and the Republic of the Congo (Brazzaville). After a 1,400-mile (2,253-km) journey through equatorial rain forest, around river islands, and down rapids, the Ubangi enters the Congo River near Lake Tumba in what is now the Democratic Republic of Congo.

The river is navigable for roughly half its length, from present-day Bangui, the capital of the Central African Republic, to the confluence of the Ubangi and the Congo Rivers. The land along its banks is equatorial rain forest and swamp. The MBUTI were the original inhabitants of this somewhat sparsely populated, tropical land. Starting 2,000 years ago, other peoples, especially the Kongo, the Bateke, and the Sangha, began to migrate into the region to farm or fish.

See also: BAKONGO (Vol. II); KONGO KINGDOM (Vol. II).

Unas (c. 2498–2323 BCE) *Last king of ancient Egypt's Fifth Dynasty.*

Unas was the first pharaoh to inscribe the inner walls of his tomb with rituals, spells, and formulas to aid him in the AFTERLIFE. This practice continued to be used in the tombs of the Sixth Dynasty. Called Pyramid Texts, these inscriptions were later transcribed onto PAPYRUS and became known as the BOOK OF THE DEAD, which is considered to be the world's earliest preserved literature.

The pyramid of Unas is located south of the great step pyramid near MEMPHIS. Rather than signaling a new belief in helping the dead in the afterlife, the Pyramid Texts mark an evolution in the idea of writing. Scholars believe that many of the texts were old when they were first inscribed.

According to myth, the Pyramid Texts show that OSIRIS, the god of the dead, aided the deceased in the journey to the afterlife. Osiris may have been gaining in importance at this time over the sun god, RA, who was considered an important deity during the earlier part of the Fifth Dynasty. Magical or religious spells, offerings, hymns, and instructions were added to the tomb to help alleviate fears about the afterlife, to provide for a prosperous life after death, and to help a ruler find his proper place in the afterworld.

The autobiographical information found in these writings is the source of our modern knowledge of many ancient practices, beliefs, and ideas. The inscriptions in the tomb of Unas, for example, tell of trade with Middle Easterners, famine, and the transportation of granite for the construction of the temple. They also show the first battle ever to be recorded in HIEROGLYPHICS. Other inscriptions, which later were made not only in royal tombs but also in the tombs of administrators and officials, have led scholars to conclude that the power of the royalty was diminishing at the time, with more governance coming from nonroyal officials.

See also: FUNERAL CUSTOMS (Vol. I).

Upper Egypt Land along the NILE RIVER south of the NILE DELTA region; along with LOWER EGYPT, one of the two kingdoms of ancient EGYPT. Upper Egypt consisted of a long, narrow strip of fertile land (the floodplain) surrounded by desert. For about two months every summer, when rains caused the waters of the Nile to rise above its banks, the floodplain of Upper Egypt lay under water. The receding waters, however, left a fertile mud that proved ideal for growing crops.

Upper Egypt is south of Lower Egypt because it is upstream, closer to the source of the Nile (which flows northward). It extended from just south of present-day CAIRO to Lake Nasser, formed by the erection of the Aswan High Dam.

Upper Egypt was symbolized by a WHITE CROWN and chose the sedge plant as its emblem. Its chief god was SETH, who, according to Egyptian mythology, killed his brother OSIRIS, father of HORUS (the chief god of Lower Egypt).

Upper Egypt has a rich cultural heritage. The Tasian culture and the BADARIAN CULTURE, both of which flourished in the late fifth millennium BCE, were pastoral people with little or no central political organization. Settlements in Upper Egypt became more concentrated with later predynastic peoples, including the AMRATIAN CULTURE and the GERZEAN CULTURE. Outside of the Nile River valley region, NOMADS roamed the desert, probably until the late third millennium BCE.

Not until late predynastic times did the settlements of Upper Egypt unify into a single kingdom. When, around 3000 BCE, Upper Egypt defeated Lower Egypt in war, the two lands united, founding the first Egyptian dynasty. The combined resources of the two lands and the large-scale projects undertaken after the unification added greatly to the wealth of the Egyptian dynasty and its kings.

Useraf (Userkaf, Userkhaf) (c. 2465–2325 BCE)

Founder of ancient Egypt's Fifth Dynasty.

Useraf is best known for enhancing the importance of the mythological sun god, RA, and for building the first sun temple. His marriage to Queen Khentkaues may have ended strife between two branches of the Fourth Dynasty.

Useraf was responsible for significant changes in how ancient Egyptians thought about Ra. Usually depicted as a HAWK or a man bearing the head of a hawk, Ra was thought of as a creator. According to legend, Useraf was asked to be the high priest of Ra, and the term *Sa-Ra* (Son of Ra) was added to the titles of the kings.

Useraf built the first of five or six sun temples, obelisk monuments erected to honor Ra. Usuraf's obelisk, a stone pillar rising from a square base in a fashion similar to a pyramid, was thought to have been modeled after an ancient stone in Heliopolis, the city of Ra, and was thought to represent the Sun's rays. The sun temple built by Useraf at ABUSIR is one of only two remaining temples. It is in poor condition today, due to its original construction of mud brick.

Though not much is known about the origins and reign of Useraf, it is likely that he was the descendent of a Fourth Dynasty king named Redjedef (2575–2465 BCE). Scholars believe that Useraf may have married Queen Khentkaues, who was of royal descent, in order to gain prominence as a ruler. This marriage likely ended a period of disharmony between two factions of the Fourth Dynasty. Archaeological evidence suggests that Khentkaues may have ruled Egypt on her own for a time or may have been a co-regent with Useraf.

Useraf built his pyramid and mortuary temple at SAQQARA. Although it is smaller than the pyramids of the Fourth Dynasty, the splendor of his pyramid is an example of the artistic mastery of this period. Square granite columns, relief sculptures, busts, and a great red granite statue of Useraf were known to have existed in the pyramid and temple. Though the pyramid complex is now in ruins, the head of Useraf's statue is preserved in the Egyptian Museum in CAIRO.

V

Valley of the Kings The royal city of the dead, or necropolis, situated in the desert hills on the west bank of the NILE RIVER across from the ancient capital of Thebes. The Valley of the Kings came into existence at the beginning of the NEW KINGDOM (c.1750 BCE). THUTMOSE I (c. 1525–1492 BCE), the third pharaoh of Egypt's Eighteenth Dynasty, is credited with having erected the first tomb there.

Archaeologists divide the site into two sections, the East Valley and the West Valley. It is the East Valley that contains the most royal tombs, which were cut into the solid rock of the cliffs surrounding the valley's barren landscape. The interior of each tomb consisted of a series of complex passageways and rooms leading to a central burial chamber. The many decorations on the walls inside the tombs focus on the activities of the AFTERLIFE found in the texts of the BOOK OF THE DEAD. The most elaborate tomb found in the valley is that of the Nineteenth Dynasty pharaoh SETI I (ruled c. 1318 BCE).

The tombs in the Valley of the Kings represented a new approach to the construction of royal mortuary buildings. Prior to the advent of the New Kingdom, pharaohs were buried in pyramids, with attached temples in which funerary rituals were performed. In the new location at Thebes, the two buildings were separated: The mortuary temple for each ruler was built apart from his or her tomb and placed in a different part of the valley on a plain closer to the Nile.

The Valley of the Kings continued to be the traditional royal burial ground until the end of the Twentieth Dynasty (c.1069 BCE). However, by the time of the succeeding Twenty-first Dynasty, most of the tombs there had fallen prey to grave robbers who vandalized them and stole a good deal of their precious contents. The one notable exception to this plunder was the tomb of the boy-king TUTANKHAMUN, which was discovered almost intact in 1922. As a result of the widespread ravaging of the royal tombs at Thebes, pharaohs of later dynasties were forced to abandon the site, establishing their final resting places in other locations throughout Egypt.

Vandals Christian people of Germanic origin who conquered Carthage in 439 and occupied North Africa; settled most heavily in the province of Africa Proconsularis in LIBYA, or Roman North Africa

In 429, King Genseric of the Vandals led 80,000 of his people across the Straits of Gibraltar on a quest to secure land and establish a kingdom. Within ten years, the Vandals had conquered CARTHAGE, wresting power from Rome, and, by 455, they controlled the eastern zone of Roman Africa. Eventually, Vandal control extended westward into the region of Djemila-Cuicul. It is difficult, however, to determine precise boundaries for the Vandal empire, primarily because the Vandals seem to have been perpetually warring along their frontiers with the indigenous North African Moors for control of their southern and western borders.

Roman Africa was nominally Christian, but during the fifth century the church was in crisis. Roman military might had declined in Africa, and local peoples had begun plundering churches and massacring clergy. This was compounded by the arrival of the Vandals, who practiced a form of CHRISTIANITY that had been officially branded a heresy by the leadership of the church. Called Arianism, it had first been introduced to the Vandals by missionaries to the Danube River region.

Determined to establish Arianism in North Africa, Genseric embarked on a policy of political and religious persecution of Catholics. He exiled Catholic bishops and refused to allow the church to replace them. He also confiscated lands from the Catholic nobility. This policy was continued after Genseric's death in 477 by his son Huneric (r. 477–484), who shared his father's fierce determination to establish the Arian doctrine. Huneric gathered together all the Catholic bishops in his empire in 484 and imposed an ultimatum to convert to Arianism or face exile.

Ultimately, however, the Vandals were unable to impose the Arian faith on North Africa. In part this was because the Vandals were greatly outnumbered by the larger population of Romano-Africans, and, as a result, the actual administration of the Vandal territories was left to the local Catholic nobility. The failure also stemmed from the fact that Huneric's successors, Gunthamund (r. 484–496) and Thrasamund (r. 496–523), did not defend Arianism as vigorously as their predecessors.

The Catholic Church, however, did not benefit from the failure of the Vandals to impose their faith on North Africa. In fact, Catholicism fell from power, due in part to persecution by the Vandals and in part to the decline of the towns that were the centers of the church. One constant in the area, though, was the Latin LANGUAGE, which remained in use among the conquered people of North Africa in spite of the Vandal occupation. Examples of that language, in the form of the poetry of Luxorius and Dracontius, have survived into the modern era.

The Vandal domination of North Africa lasted for about 400 years. But even before then, NOMADS from the desert to the south and southeast began making inroads into Vandal territory. During the latter part of the reign of King Thrasamund, the Vandal army was badly defeated by invading nomads known as the Louata. Independent BERBER kingdoms also emerged, and by 533, the Byzantine general Belisarius finally destroyed the weakened Vandal kingdom.

While some historians insist that the Vandals had no lasting influence on North Africa, others argue that modern Berbers with blond hair and blue eyes clearly are descended from these Germanic invaders.

See aslo: BYZANTINE AFRICA (Vol. II); CHRISTIANITY (Vols. I, II); KINGDOMS AND EMPIRES (Vol. II); KINGDOMS AND EMPIRES OF THE MAGHRIB (Vol. II).

Victoria, Lake Largest lake in Africa, located in present-day Tanzania and Uganda, and bordering on Kenya. Lake Victoria, also called Victoria Nyanza, is a freshwater lake and the chief reservoir of the NILE RIVER. The lake covers 26,838 square miles (69,510 sq km), with its greatest length from north to south being 210 miles (338 km), and its greatest width across being 150 miles (241 km). Its basin area covers 92,240 square miles (238,900 sq km). The lake sits at an altitude of 3,720 feet (1,134 m) above sea level in a shallow depression that lies between the western and eastern RIFT VALLEYS; it reaches a depth of 270 feet (82 m). Victoria is fed by the Kagera and Katonga Rivers on the western side, and its only outlet is the Victoria Nile, located to the north. The lake has three different gulfs: the Kavirondo, in the north; the Speke, in the southeast; and the Emin Pasha, in the southwest. At the lake's northwestern corner is the Sese Archipelago, which is made up of sixty-two islands. The lake holds more than 200 different species of fish, which have long provided food for the surrounding populations.

See also: VICTORIA, LAKE (Vol. II).

vizier High official in the government of ancient EGYPT. The vizier was the head of Egypt's elaborate bureaucracy and reported directly to the pharaoh. He held power as the chief justice, head of the treasury, and overseer of records.

The office of vizier dates back at least as early as the Fourth Dynasty (c. 2575–2465 BCE). By the reign of Sesostris III (1836–1818 BCE), the vizier controlled the entire bureaucracy of ancient Egypt.

Below the vizier were governors of the nomes, or provinces, of ancient Egypt. These governors were appointed by the pharaoh and reported to the vizier. Later on the term *vizier* also was applied to the high government officials in Muslim states.

See also: NOMARCH (Vol. I).

vulture Scavenging bird of prey, related to HAWKS and EAGLES; found in temperate and tropical areas. Most vultures have dark feathers and bare heads. They are usually solitary animals, soaring in the sky on their broad wings. They have keen sight, which they use to locate dead or dying animals.

Northeastern Africa is home to the Egyptian vulture, which grows up to 24 inches (61 cm) long. In ancient times, Egyptians associated the vulture with a number of deities, including the goddess NEKHBET, the protector of UPPER EGYPT and its rulers. She is often depicted as a woman with a vulture's head and a white crown. Nekhbet is also the goddess of childbirth. She was worshiped in the towns of Nekhen (HIERANKOPOLIS) and al-Kab.

W

Wadjkheperre (Kamose) (r. c. 1576–1570 BCE) *Son of Sekenenre Tao (Seqenenre), brother of Ahmose I, and the last king of Egypt's Seventeenth Dynasty*.

During his brief rule, Wadjkheperre warred with both KUSH and the HYKSOS in an attempt to unify EGYPT under Theban control.

The Hyksos had at first controlled the NILE RIVER delta from their capital at Avaris but later extended their territory. Some scholars believe that Sekenenre Tao was at war with the Hyksos when he died. His son, Wadjkheperre, apparently continued this war upon his succession to the throne of southern Egypt. He also attempted to drive out the Kushites. In this latter campaign, Wadjkheperre forced the Kushites south, taking control of the Buhen fort. Wadjkheperre is also credited with regaining territory from the Hyksos, including the oasis of Baharia.

There is evidence that the Kushites and the Hyksos may have joined forces against the Thebans. Although Wadjkheperre sought to remove both enemies from Egypt, he died before he could accomplish this. Wadjkheperre's brother, AHMOSE I (c. 1570–c. 1546 BCE), succeeded him as king and reunified Egypt to begin the NEW KINGDOM.

waist beads In Africa, a type of BODY ADORNMENT worn by men and women. The wearing of waist beads, or beaded girdles, is an ancient practice in Africa, and it generally represented a sign of ethnic affiliation and social status. Waist beads also have been seen as a distinctive sign of beauty. Most likely, ancient waist beads were made of such natural objects as feathers, flowers, or stones. Later, BEADS that had been obtained by either TRADE or early forms of a craft industry were used.

Some of the earliest examples of waist beads have been found in the BADARIAN civilization of southern Egypt (c. 5000–3800 BCE), where men apparently were the primary wearers of beaded girdles. Excavations have led to the recovery of the remains of at least one individual wearing several strands of beads around his waist, some of which were made of steatite, a precious stone. These stones were also glazed with malachite, a green carbonate mineral.

Although it is not certain whether women wore waist beads in the Badarian period, by ancient Egypt's MIDDLE KINGDOM (c. 1963–1786 BCE), Egyptian women were wearing waist beads as a status symbol. Archaeological excavations have recovered a beaded girdle worn by Princess Set-Hathor, the daughter of the pharaoh Seostris II (r. 1868–1862 BCE). The princess's girdle was made of GOLD, lapis lazuli, and green feldspar and was also decorated with COWRIE SHELLS. The addition of cowrie shells on the beaded strand apparently represented a safeguard against the evil eye. Elsewhere, in a tradition that continued up until modern times, waist beads often were used to signal the marital status of women.

See also: BEADS (Vol. I); CLOTHING (Vol. I); JEWELRY (Vol. I); TRADE (Vol. II).

Further reading: Martha G. Anderson and Christine Mullen Kreamer, *Wild Spirits Strong Medicine: African Art and the Wilderness* (New York: The Center for African Art, 1989); Barbara Watterson, *The Egyptians* (Oxford, Eng.: Blackwell Publishers, 1998).

Walls of the Ruler Fortresses on the east bank of the NILE, built to guard ancient EGYPT from the threat of the LIBYANS, Asiatics, and the Setyu. The Walls of the Ruler are believed to have been built by Amenemhet I (r. 1938–1908 BCE) and his son, Sesostris I (r. 1908–1875 BCE), at the beginning of the Twelfth Dynasty (c. 1991–1759 BCE).

Amenemhet I, also known as Amonemhet I, led campaigns against the Libyans and Asiatics before taking over the rule of Egypt and establishing the Twelfth Dynasty. Some scholars believe that Amenemhet I envisioned ruling a great Egypt like that of the pharaohs of the OLD KINGDOM, but he seems also to have considered his rule as the beginning of a new era. In an effort to guard the eastern borders, he built the fortresses known as the Walls of the Ruler (also called the Wall of the Prince). Though the exact location of the Walls of the Ruler is not known, it is believed that they were built on the eastern bank of the Nile. Amenemhet's son, Sesostris I (also called Senwosre I or Senwosret I), completed construction of the fortresses.

waret Administrative department of ancient EGYPT created by Sesostris III (Senwosret III) during ancient Egypt's Twelfth Dynasty; warets served to strengthen Egypt's central government.

Sesostris III, also called Senwosret III, ruled Egypt from about 1836–1817 BCE. During this time he significantly reorganized the government of Egypt and created three or four warets, or districts, whose administrators reported to the VIZIER. In addition to the ministry of the vizier, Sesostris created the departments of war, labor, agriculture, and treasury. This reorganization of the government of Egypt marked a strengthening of the main government and a rise of the middle class. It also added the administration of Nubia (KUSH) to the central government of Egypt for the first time.

warfare Peoples or rulers go to war for many reasons. They may need more land or seek a protective barrier from a neighbor's attacks. They may want to gain wealth by collecting taxes and tribute from subject peoples, as ALEXANDER THE GREAT did when he attacked the Persian Empire in 334 BCE. They may, as ROME did when it fought the three PUNIC WARS (264–241 BCE, 218–201 BCE, and 149–146 BCE) against CARTHAGE, seek to increase their power in a region and dominate or destroy a rival.

Early Warfare No evidence for the practice of war exists until after 12,000 BCE. A few types of weapons, notably spears, stones, and clubs, are known to have been in use for many thousands of years, and it is likely that weapons used for hunting were used at times to kill other human beings in anger.

The earliest evidence of warfare was discovered in the 1960s near Wadi Halfa in the Sudan. A large burial plot, dating from c. 12,000 BCE, was found to contain fifty-nine skeletons and a variety of stone projectiles. Projectile points located in the skulls, spines, pelvises, and limb bones of the skeletons indicated violent deaths. Scholars suggest this massacre was the result of an unstable agricultural system in the NILE VALLEY, where crop output varied. Any population increase that occurred during periods of increased crop yield would cause competition during less productive periods. Therefore, this violence was most likely the result of competition for the limited resources of the area. Whether the deaths were the result of an organized military campaign or a brutal skirmish between neighbors is unknown.

Two weapons that increased the fire power of the individual warrior made their appearance in lands along the MEDITERRANEAN SEA at this time: the bow and arrow (by 10,000 BCE) and the sling (by 7000 BCE), a weapon more accurate than the early simple bow. Both held an advantage over the throwing spear in the distance they could cover and the volume of fire they could produce. Projectiles from a sling can be especially deadly when the stones used are the size of fists.

There is a difference between fighting and organized warfare. When groups of warriors fight, they often engage each other in individual combat with minimal regard for long-term strategy and tactics. Campaigns can end in a day or a few days once some goal has been met or vengeance taken. When larger groups of warriors band together, they may fight as an undisciplined hoard, swarming over and capturing or destroying whatever is in their way. True war requires a disciplined army of soldiers that can march in columns, take orders, and fight in line. It is a truism in military science that a disciplined army always has the advantage over one that lacks military training and teamwork.

When primitive societies began to transform themselves into states, armies became important organs of the state. Dating from the Predynastic Period in Egyptian history (before 3100 BCE), the Palette of the Fortresses shows fortified towns under siege. The NARMER PALETTE from the First Dynasty (2920–2770 BCE) depicts Narmer, the first pharaoh, slaying his enemies and reviewing their headless bodies under the banners of his army.

The Size of Armies Despite the ancient world's significantly smaller populations, ancient armies could sometimes be quite large. Iron age armies were the equivalent of modern armies in terms of size. The Egyptian army in the times of RAMESSES II (c. 1300 BCE) was probably 100,000 men, mostly conscripts. At the battle of KADESH in 1303 BCE, the first battle for which historians have reliable troop strength figures, an Egyptian force of 20,000 soldiers faced a HITTITE army of 17,000. The ASSYRIAN army of 800 BCE, the first in history to be entirely armed with iron weapons, numbered between 150,000 and 200,000 infantry and cavalrymen. At the battle of Cannae in Italy in 218 BCE, the Roman consuls of 216

Ramesses II (r. 1304–1237 BCE), riding a chariot, storms a Syrian fortress in this relief from the Great Temple at Abu Simbel. *© Roger Wood/CORBIS*

BCE, Lucius Aemilius Paulus and Gaius Terentius Varro, faced HANNIBAL of CARTHAGE with an army of 80,000 soldiers. The victorious Hannibal's troops killed or wounded more than 50,000 Roman legionnaires in a single day of fighting.

The Bronze Age and the Chariot The BRONZE AGE (3500–1000 BCE) saw the development of cast bronze weapons, which featured sharper cutting edges than earlier STONE AGE weapons had, and a limited introduction of body armor. At the same time, cities began to build defensive walls behind which the populace could protect themselves from marauders. Up to that time, most combat took place at a sword's, spear's, or axe's length from one's opponent. During the third millennium BCE, on the plains between ancient Egypt and its Mesopotamian neighbors, a major advance in weaponry changed the face of combat: The bow and arrow, the wheel, and the domesticated horse were combined to create the war chariot. For the first time, soldiers could advance on a position in a surprise attack, deliver a deadly javelin or arrow attack from a mobile platform, and quickly race away to regroup or engage in lethal pursuit of a terrified and broken foe. Chariot-borne warriors became the elite strike force of the Egyptian army and gave Egypt a tactical advantage over its foes.

The first chariots were four-wheeled carts with solid wooden wheels without pivoting front axles and pulled by onagers, fast-running relatives of the DONKEY. Over time, the war chariot evolved into a lightweight car with spoked wheels and metal axles and pulled by three or four horses. The Persian army of Cyrus the Great used deadly scythed chariots, with sharp blades extending from the axles, in battle with Alexander the Great in the sixth century BCE.

The breeding of HORSES with sufficient strength and stamina to carry armed riders into battle led to the decline of the chariot as a weapon of war, starting at the end of the second millennium BCE. The Assyrians were responsible for the development of cavalry in the ancient world. Riders used their legs to control the animal. Neck and belly straps helped them maintain their seat.

The stirrup, which allows riders to stay in the saddle and deliver a strong blow from lance or sword without being unseated by the movement, had not yet been invented. It would reach Europe from India by way of China during the Middle Ages and shift the balance in battle from infantry to mounted men, very often knights.

Iron Age Advances The discovery of iron had an important impact on warfare. Iron weapons were forged, not cast like bronze, so that they were less brittle and more reliable than earlier weapons made from bronze. Furthermore, unlike bronze, which required hard-to-find tin to produce, iron was widely available, which allowed armies to obtain a plentiful supply of inexpensive weapons. The Hittites were the first to make iron weapons, in c. 1300 BCE. Within 100 years, the technique had spread into Egypt and MESOPOTAMIA.

Whereas for centuries, the common people had been conscripted into the army only in time of war, the IRON AGE saw the growth of standing armies in peacetime and the resulting permanent corps of professional soldiers needed to train and lead them. Egypt was among the first to practice wartime conscription. In the iron age, conscription gave birth to the standing peacetime army.

Other Advances Perhaps the greatest advance in warfare in the ancient world was the Roman legion, which Hannibal faced in Italy and which was instrumental in the destruction of Carthage in North Africa. A legion was made up of ten 360-man units called cohorts, each of which contained up to three 120-man companies called maniples. A maniple, in turn, contained two centuries, each led by a centurion. (The 100-man century was eventually reduced to sixty men because it was judged easier to command.) The basic battle formation of the Roman legion consisted of three lines. The first two were javelin-armed heavy infantry; the third was a mixture of light and heavy infantry and cavalry. The lines were staggered to allow for great flexibility and movement. Roman generals relied on massive frontal assaults that took full advantage of the soldiers' discipline and the power of the Roman short sword, or *gladius*, to inflict severe wounds in close, hand-to-hand combat. Legions were powerful but not invincible. At Cannae in 218 BCE, Hannibal capitalized on his cavalry and encircled the Roman legions from behind, annihilating them.

Warfare in Ancient Sub-Saharan Africa Very little is known of warfare in sub-Saharan Africa prior to European expansion. Although foreign accounts and oral histories indicate that there were episodes of military strife prior to colonialism, virtually no archaeological evidence exists. In East Africa, weapons have been found in the middle Senegal valley and in Great Zimbabwe (c. 1200–1450 CE), the Iron Age empire that flourished in the southestern part of modern Zibabwe, but these could be ceremonial or hunting implements. Because communities were small and scattered, it is likely that any disagreement led to the dispersal of peoples rather than to conflict.

At the same time, a warrior tradition was part of many cultures. After growing up and gaining strength and skills, a young male underwent INITIATION RITES and became an adult and a warrior, ready to fight when the elders commanded, to protect the people and their CATTLE from predators and neighbors, and to engage in cattle raids on other villages. The MAASAI have traditionally valued the stoic endurance of pain. In earlier times it was a custom for the warrior in training, armed only with a dagger, to prove his manhood by killing a lion with his bare hands.

The newly initiated warrior was given a sword and spear. He wore a special garment and let his hair grow long, braiding it and decorating it with ochre and sheep fat. His life was strictly governed by Maasai law and custom. A warrior drank no alcoholic beverages and ate only in the company of his AGE SET. He also avoided sexual relations until ten or more years after his initiation into manhood, whereupon he was then promoted to senior warrior and allowed to marry. Throughout his term of service, until he became an elder, he served his people with honor.

Little is recorded about the strategy and tactics that these warriors used or about the duration and the ferocity of the battles they fought.

See also: CAVALRY (Vol. II); WARFARE AND WEAPONS (Vols. II, III).

Waset Also known as Thebes and Luxor. Centralized state in ancient EGYPT, established during the Twelfth and Thirteenth Dynasties (c. 1991–1668 BCE) as the First Intermediate Period closed and the Middle Kingdom began.

Waset, which means "scepter," was established by the pharaoh MENTUHOTEP II (c. 2008–c. 1957 BCE) following widespread political upheaval among the lesser kings and regional rulers (called NOMARCHS) of UPPER EGYPT and LOWER EGYPT. By the Twelfth Dynasty and the reign of Amenemhet II (c. 1929 BCE), peace and stability had been restored, and Egypt entered what historians have called "the literary age." The realms of religion and art saw major achievements. Some of the literary works, usually written on PAPYRUS by SCRIBES, served to advertise the good deeds of ruling kings or to recruit supporters to the administration. Still others, such as the classic tale *The Story of Sinuhe*, were written simply to entertain.

During this period Egypt also returned to the practice of pyramid building. Sometimes this meant creating new structures from the ruins of old tombs at GIZA, SAQQARA, and Dahshur. The white limestone pyramid built for Amenemhet II at Dashur, standing 166 feet (55 meters) high, was one example of this. A different style tomb was created for Mentuhotep II. He was buried in the cliffs at DEIR AL-BAHRI in what is known as a mastaba, usually a bench made of mud brick. His tomb was unusual in that it was surrounded by columns with a ramp at the entrance.

Waset's development came to an abrupt halt when HYKSOS invaders occupied the region from the Fifteenth through Seventeenth Dynasties (c. 1675–1565 BCE). Once Egyptian power was restored, however, Waset went on to evolve into a magnificent city of palaces and great temples. When the Greeks appropriated the city during the first few centuries of the Christian era, they renamed it Thebes. Sometime later the Arab name for the city, *L'Ouqsor*, evolved to become the Westernized version *Luxor*.

Over a period of 2,000 years, numerous temples were built in the former city of Waset. One of the largest of these complex structures was the sacred Temple of KARNAK. Few, if any, structures have been built with equal mathematical precision. It was even built on an angle that caught the first rays of the summer solstice and, like a telescope, projected them into the temple.

See also: EGYPT (VOL. I); GREECE (VOL. I); TETISHERI (VOL. I).

Further reading: Anthony T. Browder, *Nile Valley Contributions to Civilization* (Washington, D.C.: Insititute of Karmic Guidance, 1992); George Steindorff and Keith C. Seele, *When Egypt Ruled the East* (Chicago: University of Chicago Press, 1957).

Waswahili See KISWAHILI (Vols. II, III).

water buffalo Large mammal belonging to the same family as the cape buffalo and CATTLE.

Water buffalo have been domesticated as draft animals since the beginning of history. Originally an Asian animal, the water buffalo was introduced into EGYPT relatively late, around 600 BCE. Egyptian farmers used the animals for plowing and also for milk, meat, and fertilizer.

Domesticated water buffalo are gentle, hardy creatures that rarely catch disease and can live up to thirty-five years, even under harsh working conditions.

In the wild, water buffalo are fierce masters of their territory when threatened. Otherwise, they spend much of their time peacefully wallowing in mud and grazing on water plants.

Wawat Ancient name for the region known as Lower KUSH or Nubia.

Beginning under the pharaoh Amenophis (c. 91–62 BCE), Egypt launched a series of invasions against Nubia. The first of these resulted in Amenophis's conquest of Wawat, as the northern region of Kush near the second cataract of the NILE was called. The southern part of the land retained the name "Land of Kush." As a result of this invasion and the ones that followed, Nubia was to pay Egypt yearly tributes of GOLD, ivory, ebony, ostrich feathers, animal hides, grain, CATTLE, and enslaved workers.

See also: EGYPT (VOL. I); KUSH; (VOL. I); MIDDLE KINGDOM (Vol. I).

weapons The earliest known weapons date back to the STONE AGE (C. 2500,000–7000 BCE), which saw daggers, bows and arrows, spears, and the stone and sling used for conflict between people, as well as for hunting. Throughout this period, these instruments were used for both hunting and battle, and little effort seems to have been expended developing specific weapons for WARFARE. This situation continued in many parts of the ancient world even during the BRONZE AGE (C. 3500 BCE), until the mace was developed. This heavy weapon, which was of little or no use in the hunt, became the first tool designed exclusively for war.

In the early stage in the development and use of weapons, human muscle remained an essential element. In ancient times, strength was needed to wield weapons effectively, and, until the development of effective transport vehicles, it also was needed to carry everything from supplies to equipment.

The NARMER PALETTE is one of the most famous artifacts to come down from ancient EGYPT. It contains the earliest known inscription about a historical person, describing the accomplishments of King MENES, or Narmer, the legendary pharaoh who reputedly unified Upper and Lower Egypt. The palette's illustration of Menes ritually smashing an enemy's forehead with a war mace also gives a glimpse of what warfare of the time was like.

The spear was a major part of the development of ancient weapons. The first spears were made of fire-hardened wood and played an important role in both hunting and conflict between peoples. Later, during the Stone Age, stone spearheads were attached, then ones made from bronze, an alloy of tin and COPPER. The earliest spears were short—shorter, in fact, than the hunters and warriors who carried them. As the body armor of soldiers grew heavier, however, spears grew in size. By the time ALEXANDER THE GREAT conquered Egypt in the fourth century BCE, the spears carried by his soldiers had reached 18 feet (5.5 m) in length.

The bow represented another major innovation in weaponry. Early hunting bows, simple bows that appeared as early as 30,000 BCE, gave hunters the ability to surprise their prey and strike from a relatively safe distance. The first war bows did much the same, allowing archers to shoot high-velocity missiles with deadly accuracy and force. As time passed, more sophisticated bows were produced, including the reflex curved bow, which concentrated the strength of the bow in its curved center. Later bows added a layer of bone or horn to the belly of the bone, reinforcing it and giving it even greater strength. The front of the bow was then overlaid with sinew to make it even more powerful. Bows like these were so highly stressed that, when unstrung, they unbowed and reversed their curvature.

Bronze weaponry prevailed for centuries in much of the known ancient world until displaced by the superior edges and strength of iron. Not surprisingly, it was iron weaponry—as well as such new, sophisticated war machines as the catapult—that helped the Romans transform northern Africa into a Roman province.

Although the IRON AGE came to Africa at various times and in various places, the NOK CULTURE were among the first sub-Saharan people to produce and use iron. From about 400 BCE until about 200 CE, their sophisticated culture enjoyed the use of iron tools and weapons. MEROË, too, was an iron-producing culture, and during the sixth century BCE, its iron weapons played a major role in its dominance.

Iron weapons also aided the BANTU-speaking peoples as they took part, from c. 1000 BCE to 1000 CE, in what was most likely the largest-scale migration in human history. Just as these people's iron tools gave them agricultural advantages over others, likewise, their iron weapons helped them dominate the people they encountered.

See also: CAVALRY (Vol. II); WARFARE AND WEAPONS (Vols. II, III).

white crown The crown of UPPER (southern) EGYPT.

One of the royal emblems of the kings of ancient Egypt, the white crown was cone-shaped and bore the *uraeus*, or COBRA emblem, in front. The cobra represented the fiery eye of RA, the sun god, and was a symbol of protection. (The Egyptians believed that the cobra would spit fire at any enemy that approached.) When Upper and LOWER EGYPT were united, in about 3050 BCE, the white crown of Upper Egypt was joined with the RED CROWN of Lower Egypt to form a double crown that symbolized the union.

MENES (Narmer), who founded the First Dynasty (c. 3100 BCE), is the first pharaoh depicted wearing the double crown. Pharaohs are also shown wearing a royal headcloth called a *nemes*. The *nemes* was pulled tight across the forehead and had two broad flaps hanging at the sides. On the front were a cobra and a VULTURE, another symbol of protection.

See also: RED CROWN (Vol. I).

White Nile Tributary of the NILE RIVER, flowing between the vast swamp known as the SUDD and Khartoum, in SUDAN. Along with the Atbara River and the BLUE NILE, which it joins at Khartoum, the White Nile forms one of the Nile's three main tributaries.

witchcraft The use of ritual magic or sorcery to bring about a specific, usually negative, outcome. Witchcraft, still a powerful force in many African societies today, has been a common practice throughout Africa's history and has been mistakenly linked to traditional African religion. Most African societies maintain that nothing happens by chance. Therefore, from an ancient period the existence and practice of witchcraft has been associated with negative or opposing displays of power. It has been blamed for unforeseen disasters, afflictions, declining health and sudden death. Practitioners have also been known to send harmful representations of their power, such as insects, animals, bats, or snakes. Among the Kuranko of Sierra Leone, witches were believed to shift form, becoming fearful animals. Objects designed to cause harm were often found buried under the earth of failed crops, under doorways, or hidden in the houses of intended victims.

Attempts to answer the question of witchcraft's existence can be found among the YORUBA of Nigeria, who maintain the belief that humans were created with the power to select their destinies on earth and therefore have the power to choose to become witches. In contrast, the Manianga of the Congo region believe that witchcraft involves a secretive initiation process that begins at a very young age; it is, they believe, a fate assigned to children by their mothers.

Regarding witchcraft, especially in ancient times, each society formed its own recognition and language concerning magical power and those who wield it. The Manianga know this power as *kindoki*. The Ngombe—a BANTU-speaking people who have populated the northwestern regions of the Congo, Rwanda, and Burundi—call individuals with the ability to manipulate power the *bemba*. The practitioners of witchcraft may be male or female, but women are overwhelmingly identified as witches, particularly in matrilineal societies. In contrast, the use of witchcraft in other societies sometimes entails the participation of entire groups, such as the elders.

Individuals can sometimes be accused of being witches because of their acquisition of ritual knowledge, wealth, or property. The jealousy of their accusers, often the younger members of a particular society, may be linked to larger social issues involving societal control and the maintenance of order.

The task of identifying witches is traditionally accomplished through the use of a human ORACLE or traditional ritual practices. Among the Azande, witches are tortured with poisonous bark to get them to confess; other groups subject suspected witches to public beatings or apply stinging ointments or herbs. Ritual specialists, such as the Nganga, are known to employ methods of drowning. Fanti priests who form part of the Akan nation of GHANA traditionally use the sacred *asfo* drum to extract confessions. Accused individuals, forced to drink a special mixture of herbs along with water used to wash the drum, are expected either to confess their actions or die. In contrast, the Vagala, a pastoral society of present-day Burkina Faso, guard against the effects of witchcraft by drinking *tagdunna*, a protective potion. In other societies, "witch cleansing" is accomplished through the destruction of medicines and associated ritual objects.

Witchcraft involves an awareness of the duality of power. Therefore, its practitioners usually acknowledge that the same ability to cause willful destruction can also be used to combat witchcraft and promote beneficial healing. For this reason the ritual knowledge acquired by priests, priestesses, healers, initiation circles or village councils has often been cloaked in secrecy. But, despite widespread fear of witchcraft's disruptive and dangerous power and the occasional call for reform, the powerful magical arts are greatly respected and continue to exert influence in African society.

See also: DIVINATION (Vol. I); RELIGION, PREHISTORIC (Vol. I); RELIGION, TRADITIONAL (Vol. I); SPIRIT POSSESSION (Vol. I).

Further reading: Anthony Ephirim-Donkor, *African Spirituality: On Becoming Ancestors* (N.J.: Africa World Press, Inc., 1997); John R. Hinnells, ed., *Penguin Dictionary of Religions* (London: The Penguin Group, 1995); John S. Mbiti, *African Religions and Philosophy*, 2nd ed. (Oxford, Eng.: Heinemann Educational Publishers, 1999); Benjamin C. Ray, *African Religions: Symbol, Ritual, and Community*, 2nd ed. (Englewood Cliffs, N.J.: Prentice Hall, 2000);

women in ancient Africa Recent scholarship concerning women in Africa has begun to examine the multifaceted role they have played in the continent's economic, social, and cultural development. This interest is a reaction to a critical imbalance in earlier scholarship created by the absence of women in historical literature and too great a focus on royalty rather than on the day-to-day activities of average people. The large body of ORAL TRADITIONS, which include myths, origin stories, and other forms of folk wisdom, has also sparked renewed interest in the role of African women. It appears that viewing women as universal mother figures and creators or cocreators of the universe and humankind was fairly widespread. The numerous examples of female divinities include Eka-Abassi among the Ibibio of NIGERIA and the dual creator god known as Mawu, the female who represents fertility, and Lisa, her male counterpart, among the Ewe of GHANA and the Fon of Dahomey. In Egypt, the numerous shrines and temples erected to ISIS, HATHOR, and many other female deities help to confirm the Egyptians' traditional beliefs concerning agriculture, motherhood, fertility, and family.

Archaeologists in EGYPT have discovered clay female figurines dating from c. 3000 BCE; similar figurines from between 3100 and 2780 BCE have been found in the graves of royal leaders in KUSH. These figures and the rock and cave images found in present-day ALGERIA and South Africa appear to support widespread reverence for agricultural or fertility goddesses. The evidence also confirms that in some regions, religion and political leadership of women were once closely intertwined.

Women and Religion The forms of religion appear to have been tied to agricultural labor, viewed as a form of regeneration. Female reproduction may have also shaped early forms of worship and in some cases allowed women to transcend traditional roles as mother and wives. This was true of the women related to the Nubian founders of Egypt's Twenty-fifth Dynasty (c. 750–663 BCE). Wives, sisters, and daughters served as priestesses of AMUN, gaining power, land, and wealth, and forming their own dynasty. AMENIRDIS I was among the first to adapt this long-standing Egyptian tradition. Women in ancient sub-Saharan Africa commonly functioned as priests, with a variety of ritual and judicial functions; as traditional doctors, often mistakenly labeled witch doctors, providing ritual cleansings and protection from evil forces; and as mediums and diviners, playing an essential, if secondary, role in facilitating SPIRIT POSSESSION and relaying messages from the other world.

Oral and historical accounts of women include some hints about the *negbe Sande*, the powerful rites and practices associated with Mende and Gola women who preside over the SECRET SOCIETIES known today as the Sande. Erroneously described as a cult, it is an age-old institution that embodies solidarity and social power.

Food Production and Early Societies Until approximately the first millennium BCE, regional economies were largely based on HUNTER-GATHERER activities. Studies of various BANTU farmers, Kushite PASTORALISTS, and other early groups have concluded that women worked longer hours than men as a result of agricultural work that involved the tending, harvesting, and preparation of food along with child rearing and other duties that tied them to the home. Modern studies of the SAN, for example, have attempted to reconstruct what life was like in the Late STONE AGE. Although some questions have been raised as to how much the San's present-day subsistence lifestyle can be considered representative of the past, the studies generally surmise that women looked after their children's welfare, supplied the family with water and firewood, and prepared the family dwelling. They also contributed a large portion, possibly 60%, of daily subsistence in the form of wild plants. The men were primarily responsible for supplying the community with sufficient meat by hunting large game. There is ongoing debate as to whether men and women could have played an equal role in all decision-making processes.

Once various foods had been domesticated in approximately the second millennium BCE, the family became an essential unit in food production in many African societies. Women's labor and the future labor of her children shaped the various forms of BRIDEWEALTH, or bride price, provided by the prospective groom. Designed to emphasize the value of women within the economy, bridewealth might have taken the form of farming implements or CATTLE; among the IBO of southern Nigeria and the NUBA of the Sudan. The groom might be expected to cultivate the land of the prospective bride prior to marriage.

Once married, a woman was assigned many prominent food staples for exclusive cultivation, harvesting, trading, or marketing activities—sometimes through organized trade collectives. The AMHARA women of ETHIOPIA owned, cultivated, and harvested their own plants for centuries. In various regions of West Africa, the COCOYAM, a root vegetable, traditionally provided a notable source of income for women farmers.

Women in Africa also contributed to the economy through craftsmanship. In many societies, POTTERY, TEXTILE PRODUCTION, beaded JEWELRY, and numerous other crafts were considered women's work. In both EGYPT and Nubia (KUSH), there have been conflicting reports concerning the division of labor in terms of pottery making, spinning, and weaving cloth. Although weaving appears to have been carried out primarily by women, some sources indicate that men also did weaving. When they began to gain acceptance as commodities at trading markets, many of these crafts were shifted to the control of men This was true among the Kono of Sierra Leone, where women were the spinners and men were the weavers of cloth. This was also true among the Baoule of the IVORY COAST. Significantly, women of the Yoruba and Nupe peoples played an essential role in long-distance trading.

Consequently, the domestic economy—AGRICULTURE, pottery, textiles, and other forms of potential wealth produced by women—helped to build political power that was reinforced through marriage. Ancient rulers often made marriage arrangements between siblings and first cousins in order to maintain this political control with the family.

Queen Mothers and Female Regencies A number of women were reigning queens, regents, or other high-ranking officials in the ancient world. These women appear to have acquired power in at least three distinctive ways. The first was the direct outgrowth of egalitarian societies and their beliefs. One example can be seen among the Luvedu of what is now South Africa who traditionally chose a rain queen as the political and divine ruler of the kingdom. Her powers were so great that it was believed that her anger could generate drought. The TUAREGS were also considered an egalitarian society, as the tomb of Queen Hinan attests. Her skeletal remains and the GOLD and silver jewelry archaeologists recovered from her tomb, reflect the high regard Tuareg society had for her.

A second way in which women assumed power in the ancient world was through inheritance. In Napata and MEROË, queens, or KANDAKES, acquired power as the mothers or wives of kings, including Queen Shankiakhete (r. 170–160 BCE) and Queen Amanishakhete (r. 41–23 BCE). Queen Amanishakhete was in fact coruler at the height of MEROË's economic and social power, which was built from its reputation as an international trading port. The queen's elaborate tomb still remains in the northern region of Meroë, although excavations have resulted in the removal of much of her elaborate jewelry and other artifacts. Nubian queens officiated at coronation ceremonies and provided invaluable counsel. They built numerous public works and, when necessary, engaged enemies of the state in battle.

The legendary MAKEDA, queen of Sheba, was typical of many queens reigning in ETHIOPIA who inherited power through familial links. She was widely known for establishing important TRADE networks, commanding armies, and collecting vast wealth from the many regions she ruled over prior to her romantic entanglement with King Solomon. Queen Hatshepsut, who ruled Egypt c. 1501–c. 1482 BCE with THUTMOSE III (c. 1504–c. 1450), inherited her notable abilities as an independent ruler from her father. During her rule, she built numerous monuments and was noted for having authorized many expeditions to the fabled land of PUNT; however, evidence of her reign was destroyed after her death.

The rights of nonroyal women in Egypt are equally insightful. Among the numerous documents that have survived in Egypt are legal documents indicating that at various times in Egypt's history, such as the NEW KINGDOM (c. 1500–1000 BCE), men and women lived as equals under the law. Women could own property, enter into business transactions, and arrange marriage and divorce contracts. There are even records that show they sued for monetary relief in courts. Problems associated with these laws can be seen in the fact that women were almost always the defendants in monetary claims of nonpayment or the wrongful sale of property. One case involved a woman named Heria of Deir el-Medina who reportedly stole tools. Although she denied it, the tools were later found in her house with other items. The fact that she was sent outside of the court's jurisdiction to another and perhaps higher court indicates that it was considered a highly unusual circumstance. Women received the same kinds of punishment for crimes as men, including being beaten.

A third way that women gained power was by matrilineal lineage. The women of matrilineal societies were sometimes known as "king-makers." It has been suggested that some women who held power were postmenopausal. Some societies ostracized women during menstruation or immediately following childbirth because of taboos related to blood. The age connection, however, has not been conclusively proved, and evidence indicates that some titled women were young or married when they assumed power.

Societies south of the Sahara ruled by powerful female leaders included the AKAN of Ghana, whose royal line of queen mothers began as the State of the Elder Woman. Described as an *ohemma,* or female king, her divinity was linked to her ability to bring forth new life. As king she ruled over informal groups of family clans that eventually became city-states. Her symbol, a knotted cloth tied around a long staff, has also been noted among women rulers and goddesses associated with the Tuaregs and GARAMANTES.

See also: AMANITARE (Vol. I); CIRCUMCISION (Vol. I) FAMILY STRUCTURE (Vol. I); ISIS (Vol. I); TETISHERI (Vol. I); WITCHCRAFT (Vol. I); WOMEN IN MEDIEVAL AFRICA (Vol. II); WOMEN IN PRECOLONIAL AFRICA (Vol. III).

Further reading: Ralph Austin, *Africa in Economic History* (London: James Curry, 1996); Iris Berger and E. Francis White, eds., *Women in Sub-Saharan Africa* (Bloomington: Indiana University Press, 1999); Catherine Coquery-Vidrovitch, *African Women: A Modern History* (Boulder, Colo.: Westview Press, 1997); Elizabeth Isichei, *A History of African Societies to 1870* (Cambridge, Eng.: Cambridge University Press, 1997); Gay Robins, *Women in Ancient Egypt* (Cambridge, Mass: Harvard University Press, 1996); Ivan Van Sertima, ed., *Black Women in Antiquity,* (New Brunswick, N.J.: Transaction Publishers, 1997).

writing In ancient Africa, EGYPT was probably the earliest society to develop writing. Recent archaeological discoveries, including those made during the 1980s at ABYDOS, confirm that Egyptian writing began as early as the fourth millenium BCE and that it was a fully developed, highly sophisticated system by 3300 BCE. This dating challenges the long-held belief that the earliest writing system was invented by the Sumerians of ancient MESOPOTAMIA.

Not surprisingly, given the region's frequent floods and droughts, Egyptian writing began with basic forms of calendars. The need to collect and record taxes and keep accounts of commercial transactions also played a significant role in the development of writing. At first, writing was done on objects such as clay jars and vases, ivory, and even pieces of bone. Examples of these, marked with records of tax payments and with the origins of various goods, have been found dating as far back as c. 3200 BCE. Later, stone became a common medium for Egyptian writing, with the NARMER PALETTE, a stone tablet inscribed with the conquests of King Narmer (MENES), being one of the earliest examples recovered thus far.

In time, however, the Egyptians developed PAPYRUS, on which they wrote with INK using reed pens and brushes. Papyrus became so important that the Egyptians kept a carefully controlled monopoly on its production until the use of parchment became widespread some 2,000 to 2,200 years ago.

Called *medu netcher* ("the words of the gods") by the ancient Egyptians, writing was considered to be a sacred gift from TEHUTI, the god of universal wisdom and intelligence. Priests, not surprisingly, played an important role in the writing process, writing prayers, burial rituals, magic spells, and formulas on stone tablets, as well as on the walls of temples, tombs, and monuments. Since the majority of the Egyptian population could not write, the priests and SCRIBES who could do so usually held high positions within the kingdom's government and courts.

With twenty-four picture-letters and syllables, Egyptian HIEROGLYPHICS were made up of consonants rather than vowels. However, as time went on, the Egyptians developed three different scripts for writing. Of the three, the system of hieroglyphics was the oldest, dating back beyond 3000 BCE. The later HIERATIC script was a type of shorthand that priests and scribes used for writing on papyrus. The third form of Egyptian writing,

DEMOTIC, was a faster, cursive style that appeared about 600 BCE. Not as regularized as the traditional hieroglyphics, demotic varied greatly in appearance, depending on everything from geographical differences to the type of text being written (business letters, legal documents, religious texts, and so on), and even to differences in individual handwriting.

The neighboring kingdom of KUSH also developed a form of sacred writing. Known as Meroitic script, it consisted of twenty-three symbols used with colon signs separating the various words. Religious themes have been identified on the Temples at NAGA, and at GEBEL BARKAL, where inscribed stone monuments, called stelae, date back to at least the eighth century BCE. Researchers have been able to decipher and classify a number of recovered Meroitic scripts, but as many as 800 more still await translation.

Other ancient African systems of writing developed in what is now ETHIOPIA. For the most part, these can be traced to Arab settlers who crossed to Africa from the Arabian Peninsula, about the fifth or sixth century BCE, and founded the kingdom of Saba. The Sabaeans developed a script that, in time, evolved into the classic Ethiopian writing system, which has remained in use, in one form or another, until the twenty-first century.

Basically a syllabic system, the Ethiopic writing system consisted of twenty-six letters, all representing consonants, which become syllables when vowel sounds are added. Sentences were written from right to left and then back to the right.

A form of writing that developed from Ethiopic, called Lessana Ge'ez ("the language of the free"), emerged centuries before the Christian era. GE'EZ (or Geez, as it is sometimes spelled) is considered the classic script of Ethiopia, and is read left to right rather than right to left in the manner of other Semitic-based languages. Popular until the seventh century, Ge'ez was utilized for numerous Aksumite inscriptions on coins, stelae, and monuments. After the seventh century, the use of Ge'ez became less prevalent, primarily restricted to the religious writings of the Ethiopican Orthodox Church.

Ancient Ethiopic writing had twenty-six letters. Twenty-four of these were derived from the Sabaean writing system. To these were added two other letters, representing the *p* sound, which was not represented in Sabaean.

Ethiopian scribes were required to rule the pages of religious books with a reed and awl. Ink was made from natural elements and dispensed from special cow horns, one with black ink for script and another with red ink for sacred names and references. While religious works were emphasized, especially the stories of saints, writing was also used to preserve poetry, law, medicine, and rituals.

Other African societies placed greater emphasis on ORAL TRADITIONS, but, in many of these groups, SECRET SOCIETIES developed writing at an ancient, if undetermined, period. These "secret scripts"—including rituals for priests, initiation ceremonies, and other rites of passage—were created to transmit cultural knowledge to future generations. Among the groups using these secret writings were the Vai, BAMANA, Benin, BaKongo, Peul, and the Akan.

See also: GE'EZ (Vol. II).

Further reading: Brian M. Fagan, *World Prehistory: A Brief Introduction*. 3rd ed. (New York: HarperCollins, 1996); Ali A. Mazrui, *The Africans: A Triple Heritage* (London: BBC Publications, 1986; Barbara Watterson, *The Egyptians* (Oxford, Eng.: Blackwell, 1998).

X

X-Group Term used to describe the ethnic groups who are believed to have inhabited MEROË following the Aksumite invasion c. 350 CE; also called the BALLANA CULTURE. Archaeologists suggest that, after the decline of Meroë, the surviving inhabitants may have been joined by such groups as the NUBA, who migrated into the area from the Western Desert, or the Blemmyes, who apparently originated in the arid region to the east. Whether the people who made up the inhabitants of Meroë at this time were descended from one or both or from an even more complex combination is still unknown. As a result, the terms *X-Group* or *Ballana Culture* have been generally accepted.

The main evidence of the diverse culture of the X-Group has been found at Ballana, where excavations have revealed giant tumuli. These enormous, mound-shaped graves were built for royal burials and were large enough to accommodate deceased kings and the living members of their households—wives, servants, and even HORSES—that were buried with them.

These graves of X-Group kings also reveal evidence of Egyptian, Byzantine, Meroitic, and Sabean culture. Silver bracelets with colored stones, for example, have been found that are similar to those made in EGYPT and Meroë. A bust of the Egyptian goddess ISIS also has been recovered. Among the other artifacts that have been found are TRADE goods that are believed to have been imported from Alexandria, including bronze lamps, wooden chests, and a plate engraved with the image of the god TEHUTI. In these graves, such goods are mixed with pottery that is clearly of a Meroitic origin, showing the extent to which the products of various cultures intermingled at Ballana.

Archaeologists speculate that members of the X-group intermarried with Kushites, creating an ethnic and cultural blend that dominated the area from the fall of Axum to approximately 500 CE. The entire region apparently became Christianized by the sixth century.

See also: KUSH (Vol. I); NUBIA, CHRISTIAN (Vol. II).

Further reading: Basil Davidson, *Africa in History* (New York: Touchstone, 1991); Roland Oliver and Brian M. Fagan, *Africa in the Iron Age* (New York: Cambridge University Press, 1994).

Y

yam Tuberous roots grown principally in the equatorial forest regions of West Africa. Considered the foremost crop of West Africa, yams hold a special place in the region's economic and social history. There are two main varieties of yam grown in Africa. The yellow Guinea yam *(Discorea cayensis)* grows in the wild and may be toxic when it is either not fully mature or prepared improperly. The other type is the white Guinea yam *(Dioscorea rotundata)*, which is believed to have first been domesticated about 5000 BCE. Other varieties of yam in Africa evolved from various cultivating methods or were introduced from Southeast Asia during the second century CE.

In the northern region of present-day GHANA, yams were grown using early forms of hoe AGRICULTURE. Although they had little nutritional value, the yams were usually eaten with animal proteins. Yams could also be stored for long periods without spoiling. Archaeologists have discovered evidence of yam plantings in central Ghana and CAMEROON that date back more than 3,000 years. Farmers in these regions usually created numerous mounds, sometimes measuring 3 to 5 feet (0.9 to 1.5 meters) high. During January, small portions of the plant, used as seeds, were placed on either side of the mound to generate a new crop. This new generation matured in about seven months, depending on the type or quality of soil. Secondary crops such as MILLET were often planted between yam mounds. This method had many variations in western Africa. In central Nigeria, for example, the Tiv peoples planted secondary crops at the bottom of the mound.

From an economic and cultural perspective, yams have long held an important place in many African societies. Some societies created myths and proverbs that emphasized their value, while others, such as the IBO of Nigeria, held annual new yam festivals, that centered around yams and their cultivation.

See also: AGRICULTURE (Vol. I).

Further reading: John Middleton, ed. *Encyclopedia of Africa South of the Sahara* (New Haven, Conn.: Yale University Press, 1998).

Yoruba General term used to describe the language, peoples and kingdoms of Yorubaland; also known as Nago. Occupying a region stretching from the savannas west of the lower Niger to the forest regions near Africa's coast, the Yoruba can be found in BENIN as well as parts of GHANA, Niger, Nigeria, Sierra Leone, and Togo. From an ancient, if undetermined, period, the Yoruba labored as farmers, hunters, and traders and lived in small, scattered communities. The population grew as a result of long-distance trade with inhabitants of the SAHARA. By the time the IRON AGE came to the area (c. 500 BCE–1000 CE), a growing economy helped Yoruba villages expand. At the same time, cooperative work efforts led villages to join together under the authority of a central ruler or king. As a result, the region became one of the earliest models for urban life in Africa.

From ancient times, most of the Yoruba have followed a powerful and enduring religious tradition. Their creation stories trace human origins to the city of ILE-IFE, crediting the God Oduduwa as the founder of the city and Yoruba state. Although there are several versions of the tale, the basic story recalls how Oduduwa was lowered to earth by OLORUN, the god of the sky, carrying a snail shell filled with earth and a chicken to spread that earth over the waters. Oduduwa also carried a chameleon that tested the suitability of the earth for humans. Based on the chameleon's positive response, he named the place Ile-Ife, loosely translated as "a home that is wide enough." Oduduwa represented divine kingship along with his sons, who founded other major Yoruba kingdoms. Reigning Yoruba kings, known as *ooni*, claim descent from this first king.

See also: IFA (Vol. I); RELIGION, TRADITIONAL (Vol. I); YORUBA (Vol. II).

Z

Zambia Modern nation in South-central Africa. Landlocked, Zambia shares borders with the Democratic Republic of the Congo (formerly Zaïre) on the north, Botswana and Namibia on the south, Malawi and Mozambique on the east, and Tanzania on the northeast.

Archaeologists trace the origins of humanity to the Great RIFT VALLEY, which extends from the headwaters of the River Jordan in Sothwest Asia to the Lower Zambezi River in southern Zambia. Artifacts unearthed at STONE AGE sites in Zambia suggest that early humans were present between 1 and 2 million years ago. The most significant of these sites are at Kalambo Falls in the north and Victoria Falls in the south.

Examples of ROCK ART are observable in Kasama District, where some 700 of the more than 1,000 rock art sites in Zambia exist. The sites in Zambia lack the sophistication of comparable sites in ZIMBABWE and South Africa, and the seasonally humid climate of Zambia has very likely caused many rock paintings to fade and disappear. It is thought that Zambian rock art had religious or ritual uses; the eland, sacred to Late Stone Age peoples in South Africa, appears in Zambian rock art as well.

Early IRON AGE peoples settled in the region with their agriculture and domestic animals about 2,000 years ago. By 350, COPPER came into use both for currency and for adornment. The BANTU-speaking ancestors of the modern Tonga people reached the region between 800 and 1000 CE. These newcomers kept CATTLE, made pottery and metalwork, and lived in lathe and plaster houses. They totally supplanted the indigenous Stone Age peoples of Zambia, who probably resembled the SAN in appearance and lifestyle.

See also: JEWELRY (Vol. I); ZAMBIA (Vols. II, III).

zebra Striped, hoofed mammal belonging to the same animal family as the HORSE and the DONKEY.

Most zebras live in the plains or brush areas of eastern and southern Africa, although one type of zebra, the mountain zebra, inhabits the rocky hillsides of Namibia. Zebras usually live in small groups consisting of one stallion (a male zebra) and several mares (female zebras) with their foals (children). Their natural enemies are the LION and the LEOPARD.

The zebra has long fascinated the people of southern Africa. One group, the MBUTI, invented a myth to explain how the zebra got its stripes. Long ago, according to MBUTI legend, water was very scarce. A zebra approached a pool of water guarded by a BABOON, who was sitting by a fire. The baboon was unwilling to share his water and challenged the zebra to a fight. During their battle, as the zebra kicked the baboon into the mountains, he fell on the baboon's fire, leaving the zebra with dark stripes across his white fur. While the baboon stayed in the mountains, the burnt zebra ran away to the grassy plains, where it has remained since.

Zinjanthropus Name once used to describe a certain fossilized human. Recovered in 1959 by archaeologists Louis and Mary LEAKEY, *Zinjanthropus* lived approximately 1.5 million to 1.75 million years ago.

Archaeologists originally used the name *Zinjanthropus*, or "The Man of Zinj," after the Arabic name for the region in which the fossilized human was found. The current name used by archaeologists for this fossilized find, however, is *Australopithecus boisei* (*A. bosei*), which places him in the same scientific category as other australopithecines unearthed in the neighboring regions. Those regions include the Omo Valley in Tanzania, Koobi Fora in Kenya, and Taung in the South African Transvaal. The size of *A. bosei*'s skull indicates that he had a brain about one-third the size of that of modern human beings. Like other australopithecines, he was approximately 4 to 5 feet (1.3 to 1.6 m) tall, able to stand upright, and walked on two legs. *A. bosei* used chipped pebble tools, which were recovered as well.

See also: HADAR (Vol. I); *HOMO HABILIS* (Vol. I).

Glossary

agriculturalists Sociological term for "farmers."

alafin Yoruba word for "ruler" or "king."

al-Andalus Muslim Spain.

Allah Arabic for "God" or "Supreme Being."

almamy Religious leader of the Fulani in Fouta Djallon.

amoles Salt, in the form of bars to facilitate trade.

ancestor worship Name incorrectly given to the traditional African reverence for the spirits of those now dead who deserve the recognition and gratitude of the living.

animism Belief that inanimate objects have a soul or life force.

apartheid Afrikaans word that means "separateness"; a system and policy of racial segregation and political and economic discrimination against South Africa's nonwhite majority and formally made into law by the Land Act of 1950.

aphrodesiac Food or other agent thought to arouse or increase sexual desire.

askia Arabic word that means "general"; applied to the Songhai kings. Capitalized, the word refers to a dynasty of Songhai rulers.

ata Igala word for "king."

Australopithicus afarensis Species of Dinkanesh (also known as Lucy), the most famous of the hominid *Australopithicus* specimens found by archaeologists thus far.

Australopithicus africanus *Australopithecus* hominid species that branched off into *Homo habilis* and *A. robustus*.

Australopithicus anamensis Second-oldest species of the hominid *Australopithicus*.

Australopithicus ramadus Oldest of the apelike, hominid species of *Australopithicus*.

Australopithicus robustus A sturdy species of *Australopithicus* that came after *A. africanus* and appears to have been an evolutionary dead end. *Australopithecus robustus* roamed the Earth at the same time as *Homo habilis*.

babalawo Yoruba priest; literally "father of mysteries."

bakwai Hausa word for "state."

bey Provincial governor of the Ottoman Empire.

Bilad al-Sudan Arabic for "Land of the Blacks."

Bosjiemen Dutch for "men of the forest"; the base of the English word *Bushmen*.

bride price The payment made by a groom and his family to compensate the bride's father for the loss of her services because of marriage.

burba jolof Wolof phrase for "king of the Wolof."

caliph Arabic word for "successor"; used as a title for the Muslim political and spiritual leaders who are the successors of the prophet Muhammad.

caliphate Political and religious state that arose after the death of the prophet Muhammad and, in the ninth century, extended from Southwest Asia through North Africa and into Spain.

caravel A small, maneuverable ship used by the Portuguese during the Age of Discovery.

caste A division of society based on wealth, privilege, rank, or occupation.

circumcision The cutting of the clitoris (also called clitorectomy or clitoridectomy) or the prepuce of the penis; a rite of passage in many African societies.

cire perdu French for "lost wax," a technique used to cast metals.

citemene Technique used for burning, clearing, and cultivating land.

clan A group that traces it's descent from a common ancestor.

conquistadores Spanish for "conquerors"; term used to describe the Spanish leaders of the conquest of the Americas during the 1500s.

degredados Portuguese criminals who were sent to Africa by the Portuguese king to perform hazardous duties related to exploration and colonization.

dhow Arabic word for a wooden sailing vessel with a triangular sail that was commonly used to transport trade goods.

dia Songhai word for "king."

divination The interpretation of supernatural signs, usually done by a medicine man or priest.

djembe African drum, often called "the healing drum" because of its use in healing ceremonies.

emir An Islamic ruler or commander.

endogamy Marriage within one's ethnic group, as required by custom or law.

ensete Another name for the "false banana" plant (genus *Ensete*), common in Africa.

ergs Rock-strewn plateaus and sand dunes of the Sahara Desert.

ethnolinguistic Word used to describe a group whose individuals share racial characteristics and a common language.

eunuch A man who has been castrated (had his testicles removed), generally so that he might be trusted to watch over a ruler's wife or wives.

fama Bambara word for "king."

Freeburghers Employees of the Dutch East India Company in South Africa granted the right to farm for profit; later, any Africans of Dutch descent.

fufu A gelatinous food made from cassava that is common in West Africa.

Garamantes Greek name for the Fezzan region.

ghana Soninke word for "king."

griot Storyteller, common in West African cultures, who preserves and relates the oral history of his people, often with musical accompaniment.

hadith Arabic for "sayings"; the name of a book of Muslim wisdom, based on oral traditions.

hajj In Islam, a pilgrimage to Mecca.

hajjiyy "Pilgrim" in Arabic.

hegira Arabic for "flight" or "exodus"; generally used to describe the move of the Muslim prophet Muhammad from Mecca to Medina.

hominid Biological term used to describe the various branches of the Hominidae, the family from which modern humans descend according to evolutionary theory.

Homo erectus Name given to an early hominid species. (*Erectus* is Latin for "upright.")

Homo habilis Name given to one of the early hominid species. (*Habilis* is Latin for "handy.")

Homo sapiens Name given to the most recent species of hominid: human beings. (*Sapiens* is Latin for "wise.")

imam A spiritual and political leader of a Muslim state.

imamate The region or state ruled by an imam.

Janissary From the Turkish for "new soldier," a member of an elite Ottoman military corps.

jebel "Mountain" in Arabic.

jihad Islamic "holy war"; also the daily struggle of Muslims to reform society along Islamic laws.

kabaka The word for "king" in Babito and Buganda cultures.

kahina "Priestess" in Arabic.

kels Tuareg political clan structures.

kemet Egyptian for "black earth."

kintu Mande for "first man."

kora Small percussion instrument played by some griots.

Koran Arabic for "recitation," and the name of the book of Muslim sacred writings.

kraal Enclosure for cattle or a group of houses surrounding such an enclosure.

lineage A group whose individuals trace their descent from a common ancestor; usually a subgroup of a larger clan.

Luso-African Word that describes the combined Portuguese and African cultures, especially the offspring of Portuguese settlers and indigenous African women. (The Latin name for the area of the Iberian Peninsula occupied by modern Portugal was *Lusitania*.)

mahdi Arabic word for "enlightened one," or "righteous leader"; specifically, the Muslim savior who, in Islamic belief, is to arrive shortly before the end of time.

mai Sefuwa for "king."

mamluk Arabic for "one who is owned"; capitalized: member of an elite military unit made up of captives enslaved and used by Islamic rulers to serve in Middle Eastern and North African armies.

manikongo Kongo word for "king."

mansa Mande term for "king" or "emperor."

marabout A mystical Muslim spiritual leader.

massif A mountainous geological feature.

mastaba Arabic for an inscribed stone tomb.

matrilineal Relating to descent on the maternal, or mother's, side.

medina Arabic word for the old section of a city.

megaliths Archaeological term meaning "large rocks"; used to describe stelae and such features as cairns and tumuli that mark important places or events for many ancient cultures.

mestizo Adjective meaning "of mixed blood."

mfecane Bantu for "the crushing"; used to refer specifically to the forced migration of South African people during the Zulu campaigns of territorial expansion in the early nineteenth century.

microliths Archaeological term meaning "small rocks"; used to describe sharpened stone blade tools of Stone Age cultures.

Monophysite Related to the Christian tradition that holds that Jesus Christ had only one (divine) nature.

Moor An Arab or Berber conqueror of al-Andalus (Muslim Spain).

mugabe Bantu word for "king," often the title of the kings of Ugandan societies.

mulatto The offspring of a Negroid (black) person and a Caucasoid (white) person.

mwami Head of the Tutsi political structure, believed to be of divine lineage.

negusa negast "King of kings" in Ethiopic; traditional title given to the ruler of Ethiopia.

Nilotic Relating to peoples of the Nile, or Nile River basin, used especially to describe the languages spoken by these peoples.

Nsibidi Secret script of the Ekoi people of Nigeria

nyim Bantu word for "king" in Bakuba

oba Yoruba king or chieftain.

olu The Itsekiri word for "king."

omukama Bunyoro for "king."

pasha A high-ranking official in the Ottoman Empire.

pashalik Territory or province of the Ottoman Empire governed by a pasha.

pastoralists Sociological term for "herders."

patriarch Male head of a family, organization, or society.

patrilineal Relating to descent through the paternal, or father's, side.

polygyny The practice of having more than one wife or female mate at one time.

prazeros Portuguese settlers in Africa who held *prazos*.

prazos Similar to feudal estates, parcels of land in Africa that were leased to Portuguese settlers by the Portuguese king.

primogeniture A hereditary system common in Africa by which the eldest child, or more commonly, the eldest son, receives all of a family's inheritance.

pygmy Greek for "fist," a unit of measurement; used to describe the short-statured Mbuti people.

qadi Arabic for "judge."

ras A title meaning "regional ruler" in Ethiopia.

ribat Arabic for "monastery" or "retreat."

rondavel Small, round homes built by many Bantu people.

salaam Arabic for "peace."

sarki Hausa word for "king."

scarification Symbolic markings made by pricking, scraping, or cutting the skin.

secret society Formal organizations united by an oath of secrecy and constituted for political or religious purposes.

sharia Muslim law, which governs the civil and religious behavior of believers.

sharif In Islamic culture, one of noble ancestry.

sheikh (shaykh, sheik) Arabic word for patrilineal clan leaders.

sirocco Name given to a certain type of strong wind in the Sahara Desert.

souk Arabic word for "market."

stelae Large stone objects, usually phallus-shaped, whose markings generally contain information important to those who produced them.

stratified Arranged into sharply defined classes.

sultan The king or sovereign of a Muslim state.

sultanate The lands or territory ruled by a sultan.

sunna Arabic word for "the words and deeds of Muhammad."

syncretism The combination of different religious beliefs or practices.

tafsir Arabic for "interpretation," especially as regards the Koran.

taqwa In Islam, the internal ability to determine right from wrong.

taro Another name for the cocoyam, an edible tuber common throughout Africa.

tauf Puddled mud that served as the foundation for some homes in sub-Saharan Africa.

vizier A high-ranking officer of a Muslim state.

Suggested Readings

Abir, Mordechai. *Ethiopia: The Era of the Princes: The Challenge of Islam and the Re-unification of the Christian Empire 1769–1855*. London and Harlow: Longmans, Green and Co., 1968.

Aldred, Cyril. *Egyptian Art*. New York: William Morrow, 1981.

Alpern, Stanley B. *Amazons of Black Sparta: The Women Warriors of Dahomey*. New York: New York University Press, 1999.

Anderson, Martha G., and Mullen Kreamer, Christine. *Wild Spirits, Strong Medicine: African Art and the Wilderness*. New York: Basic Civitas Books, 1999.

Andrews, Carol, ed. *The Ancient Egyptian Book of the Dead*. University of Texas Press: Austin, 1990.

Austen, Ralph A. *Africa in Economic History*. London: James Currey, 1996.

Awolalu, Omosade. *Yoruba Beliefs and Sacrificial Rites*. New York: Longman, 1979.

Ball, David. *Empires of Sand*. New York: Bantam Doubleday Dell, 1999.

Bascomb, William R., and Herskovits, Melville J. *Continuity and Change in African Cultures*. Chicago: University of Chicago Press, 1975.

Bates, Daniel G. *Cultural Anthropology*. New York: Simon & Schuster, 1996.

Baur, John. *2000 Years of Christianity in Africa: An African History, 62–1992*. Nairobi, Kenya: Paulines, 1994.

Berens, Penny, Malherbe, Candy, and Smith, Andy. *The Cape Herders: A History of the Khoikhoi of Southern Africa*. Emile Boonzaier, ed. Athens: Ohio University Press, 1998.

Berger, Iris and White, E. Francis, eds. *Women in Sub-Saharan Africa*. Bloomington: Indiana University Press, 1999.

Beyan, Amos J., Burrowes, Carl Patrick, and Dunn, D. Elwood. *Historical Dictionary of Liberia*. Lanham, Md.: Scarecrow Press, 2000.

Bovill, Edward William. *The Golden Trade of the Moors: West African Kingdoms in the 14th Century*. London: Oxford University Press, 1958.

Brett, Michael, and Fentress, Elizabeth. *The Berbers (The People of Africa)*. Malden, Mass.: Blackwell Publishing, 1997.

Brooks, Miguel F., trans. and ed. *Kebra Nagast* [The Glory of Kings]. Lawrenceville, N.J.: Red Sea Press, 1998.

Browder, Anthony T. *Nile Valley Contributions to Civilization*. Washington, D.C.: Institute of Karmic Guidance, 1992.

Budge, E. A. Wallis. *The Gods of the Egyptians: Studies in Egyptian Mythology*. New York: Dover Publications, 1969.

Burr, Sandra and Potkay, Adam, eds. *Black Atlantic Writers of the Eighteenth Century: Living the New Exodus in England and the Americas: Selections from the Writings of Ukawsaw Gronniosaw, John Marrant, Quobna Ottobah Cuguano, and Olaudah Equiano*. Hampshire, Eng.: Palgrave, 1995.

Butt-Thompson, F. W. *West African Secret Societies*. London: H. F. & G. Witherby, 1929.

Buxton, David. *The Abysinnians*. New York: Praeger Publishers, 1970.

Chauveau, Michel. *Egypt in the Age of Cleopatra*. Ithaca, N.Y.: Cornell University Press, 2000.

Clarke, Peter B. *West Africa and Christianity*. London: E. Arnold, 1986.

Clifford, Mary Louise. *From Slavery to Freetown; Black Loyalists After the American Revolution*. Jefferson, N.C.: McFarland & Company, 1999.

Coquery-Vidrovitch, Catherine. *African Women: A Modern History*. Boulder, Colo.: Westview Press, 1997.

Cugoano, Ottobah. *Thoughts and Sentiments on the Evil of Slavery and Other Writings*. Vincent Caretta, ed. New York: Penguin, 1999.

Curtin, Philip D. *African History*. Reading, Mass.: Addison-Wesley, 1995.

Davidson, Basil. *Africa in History*. New York: Touchstone, 1991.

_____. *African Civilization Revisited*. Trenton, New Jersey: Africa World Press, 1998.

Decorse, Christopher R. *An Archaeology of Elmina: Africans and Europeans on the Gold Coast, 1400–1900*. Washington, D.C.: Smithsonian Institution Press, 2001.

Diagram Group, The. *Encyclopedia of African Peoples*. New York: Facts On File, 2000.

Duffy, James. *Portuguese Africa*. Cambridge, Mass.:

Harvard University Press, 1959.
Eades, J. S. *The Yoruba Today*. New York: Cambridge University Press, 1980.
Elleh, Nnamdi. *African Architecture: Evolution and Transformation*. New York: McGraw-Hill, 1996.
Ephirim-Donkor, Anthony. *African Spirituality*. Trenton, N.J.: Africa World Press, 1998.
Equiano, Olaudah. *The Interesting Narrative of the Life of Olaudah Equiano, or Gustavus Vassa the African, Written by Himself*. Werner Sollors, ed. New York: Norton, 2000.
Esposito, John L., ed. *The Oxford History of Islam*. New York, Oxford University Press, 2000.
Fagan, Brian M. *World Prehistory: A Brief Introduction*. 3d ed. New York: HarperCollins, 1996.
Fage, J. D. *A History of Africa*. 3d ed. London: Routledge, 1995.
Fisher, Robert B. *West African Religious Traditions*. Maryknoll, New York: Orbis Books, 1998.
Floyd, Samuel A., Jr. *The Power of Black Music*. New York: Oxford University Press, 1995.
Forester, C. S. *The Barbary Pirates*. Mattituck, New York: Amereon House, 1975).
Frobenius, Leo, and Fox, Douglas C. *African Genesis: Folk Tales and Myths of Africa*. New York: Dover Publications, 1999.
Gailey, Harry A., Jr. *A History of the Gambia*. London: Routledge & Kegan Paul, 1964.
_____. *History of Africa from Earliest Times to 1800*. New York: Holt, Rinehart and Winston, 1970.
Gamble, David P. *The Gambia*. Oxford: Clio Press, 1988.
Gardinier, David E. *Historical Dictionary of Gabon*. Lanham, Md.: Scarecrow Press, 1994.
Garrard, Timothy F. *Akan Weights and the Gold Trade*. London: Longmans, 1980.
Gronniosaw, James Albert Ukawsaw. *A Narrative of the Most Remarkable Particulars in the life of James Albert Ukawsaw Gronniosaw, and African Prince, Written By Himself*. Bath, Eng., 1774.
Grove, A. T. *The Changing Geography of Africa*. New York: Oxford University Press, 1993.
Hackett, Rosalind J. *Art and Religion in Africa*. London: Cassell, 1996.
Hair, P. E. H., Jones, Adam, and Law, Robin, eds. *Barbot on Guinea: The Writings of Jean Barbot on West Africa 1678–1712*. London: The Hakluyt Society, 1992.
Handloff, Robert E., ed. *Côte d'Ivoire: A Country Study*. Washington D.C.: Library of Congress, 1991.
Harrison, Babs Suzanne, Rada, Staefan Eduard, et al. *The Lion in the Moon: Two Against the Sahara*. New York: Rainbow Books, 1994.
Hatch, John. *Tanzania: A Profile*. New York: Praeger, 1972).
Hilton, Anne. *The Kingdom of Kongo*. Oxford: Oxford Studies in African Affairs, 1985.
Hinnells, John R., ed. *The Penguin Dictionary of Religions*. London: The Penguin Group, 1995.
Hiskett, Mervyn. *The Course of Islam in Africa*. Edinburgh: Edinburgh University Press, 1994.
_____ *The Sword of Truth: The Life and Times of the Shehu Usuman dan Fodio*. New York: Oxford University Press, 1973.
Hrbek, I., ed. *Africa from the Seventh Century to the Eleventh Century*. Vol. 3, *General History of Africa*. Abridged ed. Paris: UNESCO, 1992.
Hull, Richard W. *African Cities and Towns before the European Conquest*. New York: Norton, 1976.
Idowu, E. Bolaji. *African Traditional Religions: A Definition*. New York: Orbis Books, 1973.
Ifeka, Caroline, and Stride, G. T. *Peoples and Empires of West Africa*. New York: Africana Publishing Company, 1971.
Isichei, Elizabeth A. *A History of African Societies to 1870*. New York: Cambridge University Press, 1997.
_____. *A History of Christianity in Africa: From Antiquity to the Present*. Lawrenceville, N.J.: Africa World Press,1995.
_____. *A History of Nigeria*. London: Longmans, 1983.
Doresse, Jean. *Ethiopia*. New York: Frederick Ungar Publishing, 1959.
Johnson, Douglas H. *Nuer Prophets*. New York: Oxford University Press, 1994.
Kallen, Stuart. *The Lost Kingdoms of Africa: Black Africa Before 1600*. Edina, Minn.: Abdo & Daughters, 1990.
Kasule, Samuel. *The History Atlas of Africa*. New York: Macmillan, 1998.
Kimambo, I. N., and Temu, A. J. *A History of Tanzania*. Nairobi: East African Publishing House, 1969.
Ki-Zerbo, J. *Methodology and African Prehistory*. Vol. 1, *General History of Africa*. Abridged ed. Paris: UNESCO, 1990.
Ki-Zerbo, J., and Niane, D. T., eds. *Africa from the 12th to the 16th Century*. Vol 4, *General History of Africa*. Paris: UNESCO, 1997.
Kopytoff, Igor and Miers, Suzanne, eds. *Slavery in Africa: Historical and Anthropological Perspectives*. Madison: University of Wisconsin Press, 1977.
Kuper, Hilda and Kuper, Leo, eds. *African Law: Adaptation and Development*. Berkeley: University of California Press, 1965.
Kurtz, Laura S. *Historical Dictionary of Tanzania*. Lanham, Md.: Scarecrow Press, 1978.
Kusimba, Chapurukha M. *The Rise and Fall of the Swahili States*. Walnut Creek, Calif.: Altamira Press, 1999.
Laderman, Carol, and Roseman, Marina, eds. *The Performance of Healing*. New York: Routledge, 1996.
Law, Robin. *The Oyo Empire 1600–1836 A West African Imperialism in the Era of the Atlantic Slave Trade*. Oxford: Clarendon Press, 1977.
Levine, Donald N. *Wax and Gold: Tradition and Innovation*

in Ethiopian Culture. Chicago: University of Chicago Press, 1965).

Levtzion, Nehemia. *Ancient Ghana and Mali.* New York: Holmes and Meier Publishing, 1973.

Levtzion, Nehemia and Randall L. Pouwels, eds., *The History of Islam in Africa.* Athens: Ohio University Press, 2000.

Loth, Heinrich. *Women in Ancient Africa.* Trans., Sheila Marnie. Westport, Conn.: Lawrence Hill, 1987.

Mansour, H. Mansour. *The Maliki School of Law: Spread and Domination in North and West Africa 8th to 14th Centuries, C.E.* Bethesda, Md.: Austin and Winfield Publishers, 1994.

Marcus, Harold G. *A History of Ethiopia.* Berkeley: University of California Press, 1994.

Mazrui, Ali A. *The Africans: A Triple Heritage.* London: BBC Publications, 1986.

Mbiti, John. *African Religions and Philosophy.* 2d ed. Oxford: Heinemann Educational Publishers, 1990.

McCarthy, Justin. *The Ottoman Turks: An Introductory History to 1923.* New York: Longman, 1997.

McIntosh, Susan Keech. *Excavations at Jenne-Jeno, Hambarkatolo, and Kanianga: The 1981 Season.* Berkeley: University of California Press, 1995.

Meyer, Laurie. *Art and Craft in Africa.* Paris: Terrail, 1995.

Middleton, John. *The World of the Swahili.* New Haven, Conn.: Yale University Press, 1992.

_____, ed. *Encyclopedia of Africa South of the Sahara.* New Haven, Conn.: Yale University Press, 1998.

Miers, Suzanne, and Kopytoff, Igor, eds. *Slavery in Africa: Historical and Anthropological Perspectives.* Madison: University of Wisconsin Press, 1977.

Mokhtar, G., ed. *Ancient Civilizations of Africa.* Vol. 2, *General History of Africa.* Paris: UNESCO, 1990.

Morell, Virginia. *Ancestral Passions: The Leakey Family and the Quest for Humankind's Beginnings.* New York: Touchstone Books, 1996.

Murray, Jocelyn, ed. *Cultural Atlas of Africa.* New York: Checkmark Books, 1998.

Newman, James L. *The Peopling of Africa: A Geographic Interpretation.* New Haven, Conn.: Yale University Press, 1995.

Noote, Mary H. *Secrecy: African Art that Conceals and Reveals.* New York: Museum for African Art, 1993.

Nurse, Derek, and Heine, Bernd. *African Languages: An Introduction.* New York: Cambridge University Press, 2000.

Ofcansky, Thomas P. *Uganda: Tarnished Pearl of Africa.* New York: Westview Books, 1996).

Ojo, G. J. Afolabi. *Yoruba Culture: A Geographical Analysis.* London: University of London Press, 1966.

Oliver, Roland, and Fagan, Brian. *Africa in the Iron Age.* New York: Cambridge University Press, 1994.

Page, Willie F. *The Dutch Triangle: The Netherlands and the Atlantic Slave Trade, 1621–1664.* New York: Garland Publishing, 1997.

Pankhurst, Richard. *History of Ethiopian Towns from the Middle Ages to the Early Nineteenth Century.* Philadelphia: Coronet Books, 1985.

_____. *The Ethiopian Borderlands.* Lawrenceville, N. J.: The Red Sea Press; 1997.

Park, Mungo. *Travels in the Interior Districts of Africa.* Kate Ferguson Marsters, ed. Durham, N. C.: Duke University Press, 2000.

Parry, J. H. *The Age of Reconnaisance.* Berkeley: University of California Press, 1982.

Pazzanita, Anthony G. and Hodges, Tony. *Historical Dictionary of Western Sahara.* New York: Scarecrow Press, 1994.

Pearson, Michael N. *Port Cities and Intruders: The Swahili Coast, India, and Portugal in the Early Modern Era.* Baltimore, Md.: Johns Hopkins University Press, 1999.

Peters, F. E. *The Hajj.* Princeton, N. J.: Princeton University Press, 1994.

Quarcoopome, T.N.O. *West African Traditional Religion.* Ibadan: African Universities Press, 1987.

Quataert, Donald *The Ottoman Empire, 1700–1922.* Cambridge, Eng.: Cambridge University Press, 2000.

Ray, Benjamin C. *African Religions: Symbol, Ritual, and Community*, 2d ed. Upper Saddle River, N.J.: Prentice Hall, 2000.

Robins, Gay. *Women In Ancient Egypt.* Cambridge, Mass.: Harvard University Press, 1993.

Scarr, Deryck. *Slaving and Slavery in the Indian Ocean.* Hampshire, Eng.: Palgrave, 1998).

Schoffeleers, J. Matthew. *River of Blood: The Genesis of a Martyr Cult in Southern Malawi, c. A.D. 1600.* Madison: University of Wisconsin Press, 1992.

Schraeder, Peter J. *African Politics and Society: A Mosaic in Transformation.* New York: St. Martin's Press, 1999.

Seeskin, Kenneth. *Searching for a Distant God: the Legacy of Maimonides.* New York: Oxford University Press, 2000.

Sheehan, Patricia. *Cultures of the World: Côte d'Ivoire.* Malaysia: Times Media Private Limited, 2000.

Sherman, Richard. *Eritrea: The Unfinished Revolution.* New York: Praeger Publishers, 1980.

Shillington, Kevin. *History of Africa.* New York: St. Martins Press, 1995.

Shorter, Aylward. *Chiefship in Western Tanzania.* Oxford: Clarendon Press, 1972.

Smith, Anthony. *The Great Rift: Africa's Changing Valley.* London: BBC Books, 1988.

Snowden, Frank M., Jr. *Blacks in Antiquity.* Cambridge, Mass.: Belknap, 1970.

St. John, Ronald B. *Historical Dictionary of Libya.* Lanham, Md.: Scarecrow Press, 1998.

Steindorff, George and Seele, Keith C. *When Egypt Ruled the East.* Rev. ed. Chicago: University of Chicago

Press, 1957.
Sugar, H. *Côte d'Ivoire*. Santa Barbara, Calif.: ABC Clio, 1996.
Swantz, Lloyd W. *The Zaramo of Tanzania*. Dar es Salaam: Nordic Tanganyika Project, 1965.
Thogbani, Akbarall. *Mansa Musa: The Golden King of Mali*. Dubuque, Iowa: Kendall/Hunt Publishing, 1998.
Thomas-Emeagwali, Gloria, ed. *Science and Technology in African History with Case Studies from Nigeria, Sierra Leone, Zimbabwe and Zambia*. Lewiston, N.Y.: The Edwin Mellen Press, 1992.
Thompson, Robert Farris. *Flash of the Spirit: African and Afro-American Art and Philosophy*. New York: Random House, 1984.
Van Sertima, Ivan. *They Came Before Columbus: The African Presence in Ancient America*. New York: Random House, 1976.
_____, ed. *Blacks in Science: Ancient and Modern*. New Brunswick, N.J.: Transaction Publishers, 1983.
_____, ed. *Black Women in Antiquity*. New Brunswick, N.J.: Transaction Publishers, 1997.
Vansina, Jan. *Art History in Africa: An Introduction to Method*. New York: Longman, 1984.
Watterson, Barbara. *The Egyptians*. Oxford: Blackwell Publishers, 1998.
Wheatly, Phillis. *Complete Writings*. Vincent Carretta, ed. New York: Penguin, 2001.
Wrigley, Christopher. *Kingship and State: The Buganda Dynasty*. New York: Cambridge University Press, 1996.
Wyatt, Thomas, ed. *The Koran*. Dawood, N.J., trans. New York: Penguin, 1990.
Zaslavsky, Claudia. *Africa Counts: Number and Pattern in African Cultures*, 3d ed. Chicago: Lawrence Hill Books, 1999.

Index

Italic page numbers indicate main entries. Page numbers followed by the letter *f* refer to illustrations; the letter *m* indicates a map; and the letter *t* indicates a table.

B

I

L

P

Q

R

S

T

U

V

W

X

Y

Z